THE RISE AND FALL
OF THE
CONFEDERATE
GOVERNMENT

★ VOLUME I ★

JEFFERSON DAVIS, AGED 32

THE RISE AND FALL OF THE CONFEDERATE GOVERNMENT

★ VOLUME I ★

JEFFERSON DAVIS

NEW FOREWORD BY
JAMES M. McPHERSON

A DA CAPO PAPERBACK

Library of Congress Cataloging in Publication Data

Davis, Jefferson, 1808-1889.
   The rise and fall of the Confederate government / by Jefferson Davis;
new foreword by James M. McPherson.
      p.   cm. — (A Da Capo paperback)
   Reprint. Originally published: Richmond, Va.: Garrett and Massie,
1938.
   ISBN 0-306-80418-2 (Volume I)
   1. Confederate States of America—History. 2. Confederate States of
America—Politics and government. 3. Davis, Jefferson, 1808-1889. 4.
United States—History—Civil War, 1861-1865—Personal narratives,
Confederate. I. Title.
E487.D263   1990   90-3752
973.7'13—dc20   CIP

This Da Capo Press paperback edition of *The Rise and Fall of the
Confederate Government* is an unabridged republication of
Jefferson Davis's memoir, which was originally published in 1881.

Foreword copyright © 1990 by James M. McPherson

Published by Da Capo Press, Inc.
A Subsidiary of Plenum Publishing Corporation
233 Spring Street, New York, New York 10013

Manufactured in the United States of America

TO

THE WOMEN OF THE CONFEDERACY

WHOSE PIOUS MINISTRATIONS TO OUR WOUNDED SOLDIERS
SOOTHED THE LAST HOURS OF THOSE
WHO DIED FAR FROM THE OBJECTS OF THEIR TENDEREST LOVE

WHOSE DOMESTIC LABORS
CONTRIBUTED MUCH TO SUPPLY THE WANTS OF OUR DEFENDERS IN THE FIELD

WHOSE ZEALOUS FAITH IN OUR CAUSE
SHONE A GUIDING STAR UNDIMMED BY THE DARKEST CLOUDS OF WAR

WHOSE FORTITUDE
SUSTAINED THEM UNDER ALL THE PRIVATIONS TO WHICH THEY WERE SUBJECTED

WHOSE ANNUAL TRIBUTE
EXPRESS THEIR ENDURING GRIEF, LOVE, AND REVERENCE
FOR OUR SACRED DEAD

AND

WHOSE PATRIOTISM
WILL TEACH THEIR CHILDREN
TO EMULATE THE DEEDS OF OUR REVOLUTIONARY SIRES
THESE PAGES ARE DEDICATED

BY THEIR COUNTRYMAN

JEFFERSON DAVIS

FOREWORD

HISTORY has not been kind to Jefferson Davis. As head of a rebellion to preserve slavery, he led his people to a disastrous defeat that destroyed their society and left the South in poverty for generations. Most Americans considered the cause he conducted to be evil and treasonous; many of his Confederate compatriots considered his leadership incompetent. A Richmond journalist described Davis in 1862 as "cold, haughty, peevish, narrow-minded, pig-headed, *malignant*." The powerful Georgia politician Robert Toombs denounced Davis as a "false and hypocritical wretch," while a South Carolinian in the Confederate Congress lamented that the President's "incredible incompetency" had "brought us to the brink of ruin." Even his Vice President, Alexander Stephens, privately criticized Davis as "weak and vacillating, timid, petulant, peevish, obstinate."

These were hardly objective appraisals; some of them were self-serving attacks by political opponents; others were obviously intended to set up Davis as a scapegoat for Confederate failures. The capture of Davis by Union cavalry in May 1865, and his imprisonment for two years awaiting a trial for treason that never came, made him a martyr to Yankee vengeance in the eyes of many ex-Confederates, and restored part of his tarnished reputation in the South. Recognizing the difficulty of the task he had faced as Confederate President, some historians concluded that he did about as well as could have been expected. Others, however, have reaffirmed the uncomplimentary judgments of Davis's contemporary critics, in less captious language. Davis was "narrow and legalistic in his thinking . . . notoriously inept at getting along with people," wrote the dean of Southern Civil War historians Bell Irvin Wiley. "Compounding his short temper was an unattractive streak of self-righteousness," according to biographer Paul Escott. Davis "seemed to think in abstractions and to speak in platitudes," declared historian David M. Potter. "It hardly seems unrealistic to assume that if the Union and Confederacy had exchanged presidents with one another, the Confederacy might have won its independence."

This probably overstates the case against Davis. Nevertheless, as the passage suggests, the Confederate President suffers in the comparison to Abraham Lincoln. Only a few diehard neo-Confederate historians would dissent from the following statements: Lincoln was more eloquent than Davis in expressing war aims, more successful in com-

i

municating with the people, more skillful as a political leader in keeping factions working together for the war effort, better able to endure criticism and to work with his critics to achieve a common goal. Lincoln was flexible, pragmatic, with a sense of humor to smooth relationships and help him survive the stress of his job; Davis was austere, rigid, humorless, with the type of personality that readily made enemies. Lincoln picked good administrative subordinates and knew how to delegate authority to them; Davis went through five secretaries of war in four years; he spent a great deal of time and energy on petty administrative details that he should have left to subordinates. Lincoln had a strong physical constitution; Davis suffered from dyspepsia and a neuralgia that frequently prostrated him, left him blind in one eye, and exacerbated his waspish temper. A disputatious man, Davis sometimes seemed to prefer winning an argument to winning the war; Lincoln was happy to lose an argument if it would help win the war. Davis's well-known feuds with two of the South's premier generals, Pierre G. T. Beauregard and Joseph E. Johnston, undoubtedly hurt the Confederacy's war effort, as did his stubborn fealty to General Braxton Bragg and Commissary-General Lucius B. Northrop after they had lost the confidence of the Confederate people.

A graduate of West Point (1828) and a hero of the Battle of Buena Vista in the Mexican War as colonel of a Mississippi regiment, Davis had been a successful cotton planter, an influential Senator from Mississippi, and an outstanding Secretary of War (1853-1857) before the Civil War. He was an obvious choice for Confederate President in 1861, and perhaps the best choice the fledgling nation could have made. He took office with the almost universal support and good will of the Confederate populace. The excruciating pressures of war and defeat revealed his deficiencies as commander-in-chief and eroded that good will. Davis's thin-skinned pride and oversized sense of honor were wounded by Northern vilification of his "treason" and by Southern criticisms of his leadership, especially those that began to appear in the 1870s in memoirs like those of Joseph E. Johnston. Writing *The Rise and Fall of the Confederate Government* (originally published in 1881) proved a catharsis for his insulted pride and outraged honor. Davis joined the war of memoirs with a fierce sense of joy which seemed to demonstrate that, for him at least, the pen was indeed mightier than the sword.

The defensive, self-righteous tone of these volumes is characteristic of Confederate memoirs. As leaders of a discredited, defeated cause, many

Confederate statesmen and generals who survived the war eventually took up the pen to prove that not they but someone else made the mistakes that led to disaster and defeat. What is unusual, perhaps, about Davis's 1279-page justification of the Lost Cause is his unrelenting insistence that *neither he nor the Cause was ever wrong in any particular.* Davis was the quintessential unreconstructed rebel. Defeat did not prove the South wrong; it merely confirmed the overweening and vicious power of the United States. Southern states had a constitutional right to secede; the Lincoln administration had no constitutional right to stop them. The Confederacy did not start the war by firing on the American flag and American soldiers at Fort Sumter; the Lincoln administration started it by refusing to withdraw its troops from a fort that had been, to be sure, built and paid for by the federal government but (in Davis's view) was rightfully claimed by South Carolina. In a sentence whose logic was perfectly clear to Davis if not to most readers north of the Mason-Dixon line, he wrote that "He who makes the assault is not necessarily he that strikes the first blow or fires the first gun." Therefore, wrote Davis in a prefatory passage that set the tone for the twelve hundred pages to follow, the North was entirely responsible "for the deplorable fact of the war, for the cruel manner in which it was waged, for the sad physical and yet sadder moral results it produced."

Among those sad results, from Davis's viewpoint, was the abolition of slavery. This benign institution had transformed "unprofitable savages" into "millions of efficient Christian laborers" and trained them "in the gentle arts of peace and order and civilization," wrote Davis in 1881. Its abolition was brought about by "pseudo-philanthropists and fanatics" who were harmless when standing alone but became dangerous when joined by "political demagogues" (Republicans) who "seized upon [the slavery issue] as a means to acquire power." Once they achieved it, and with the war as an excuse, they carried out their "usurpation of power for the destruction of the right of citizens to hold property in slaves." Thus "at a single dash of the pen" (Lincoln's Emancipation Proclamation) "our property was to be annihilated, the whole social fabric of the Southern states disrupted, all branches of industry disarranged, good order destroyed, and a flood of evils many times greater than the loss of property inflicted upon the people of the South."

Compounding this "tyranny" was the Northern decision to arm black men (mostly former slaves) as soldiers "for a servile war which in its nature, as exemplified in other lands, far exceeds the horrors and merciless atrocities of savages." Never mind that the 180,000 black Union soldiers committed no such atrocities. Nor that white Confederate soldiers on several occasions murdered unarmed black soldiers after they had surrendered, most notoriously at Fort Pillow on the Mississippi River. These events do not find their way into Davis's account. He also appears to have forgotten, when discussing the "atrocity" of Union black soldiers, that four hundred pages earlier he had described his own role in obtaining passage of a bill to arm black soldiers to fight for the Confederacy.

Davis elaborates an argument that emerged in the South after the war and became neo-Confederate orthodoxy for a century or more: the South did not secede to protect slavery, but to vindicate state sovereignty. This is the virgin-birth theory of secession: the Confederacy was not conceived by any worldly cause, but by divine principle. "The existence of African servitude," insisted Davis in 1881, "was in no wise the cause of the conflict, but only an incident." He had not spoken this way in 1861. Then he had justified secession as an act of self-defense against the Black Republicans whose policy of excluding slavery from the territories would make "property in slaves so insecure as to be comparatively worthless . . . thereby annihilating in effect property worth thousands of millions of dollars." But after 1865 it became unfashionable in the South to admit having fought to keep four million people in slavery. So while Davis could unblushingly denounce the abolition of slavery as an act of "tyranny . . . against liberty and justice," he could also insist *ad infinitum* that Confederate states fought solely "for the defense of an inherent, unalienable right . . . to withdraw from a Union into which they had, as sovereign communities, voluntarily entered."

The reader of these pages will soon be convinced that Jefferson Davis missed his calling. He should have been a lawyer. His approach to most issues, and especially to that of secession, was relentlessly legalistic. Much of the argument in these volumes is a painstaking brief for the "compact theory" of the Union. This theory held that the United States Constitution was a compact, or contract, among sovereign states which in 1789 had authorized a federal government to act as their agent in the exercise of certain functions of sovereignty. But the states had never transferred the sovereignty itself. Having delegated these functions by the ratifying act of a convention, a state could withdraw from the compact and reassert its full sovereignty by the act of another convention. This was precisely what the seceding states did in 1861.

In Volume I of *Rise and Fall,* Davis devotes fifteen chapters to this matter. These chapters provide perhaps the most thorough exegesis of the compact theory. But Davis was clearly obsessed by a concern that the reader might miss the point. So he returns to it again and again every second or third chapter through much of the remainder of the book. He seems unembarrassed by the inconsistency of the theory with the actions of his own Confederate administration, which under wartime pressures created a more centralized and powerful government than Abraham Lincoln had ever dreamed of before 1861. Wartime state governors like Joseph Brown of Georgia who invoked Davis's cherished principle of state sovereignty to oppose such measures as conscription, impressment of slaves and food, and certain Confederate taxes, became in Davis's eyes malignant obstructionists.

It should be noted, though, that Davis is more temperate and subtle in his treatment of Southern adversaries and critics than they were of him. All the same, he makes it clear that he was always right and they were always wrong. Most contemporaries as well as subsequent historians questioned Davis's judgment in keeping Commissary-General Lucius Northrop and Army of Tennessee commander Braxton Bragg at their posts after they had demonstrated their incapacity and unpopularity. Nearly twenty years later, Davis still praised Northrop as "a man of rare capacity and character" who performed his "difficult task" with "success." Davis described Bragg's generalship on one important occasion as "a brilliant piece of strategy"; on another it reflected his "large-hearted and comprehensive view" of military questions. Critics of these men, Davis hints at one point, are either "wilfully blind, or maliciously intent on the circulation of falsehood." In contrast to this strong language, Davis pulls his punches in references to Joseph Johnston and Pierre G. T. Beauregard. But the careful reader will discern that he considered Beauregard responsible for turning Confederate victory into retreat at Shiloh, and Johnston responsible for the loss of Vicksburg and of Atlanta.

Nevertheless, it is the Yankees rather than fellow Southerners who are the real targets of Davis's anger. Their "war of subjugation" against helpless Southern people, their "lust for empire . . . power, plunder, and extended rule" parade through these pages. Such sentiments caused *Rise and Fall* to be dismissed in the North as the ravings of an unrepentant traitor. Since Davis's release from prison in 1867, most Northerners had been content to ignore him. Many Southerners, to Davis's chagrin, also paid little attention to the book when it appeared in 1881. They wished to get on with their lives and build up the New South rather than to recall the grievances and glory of the Old South. Not until the romance and mythology of the Lost Cause began its extraordinary domination of Southern culture in the decades after Davis's death in 1889 did his book—despite its great length, sprawling, repetitious structure, and legalistic style—gain an important place in Southern libraries. The United Daughters of the Confederacy reprinted it in 1938—when, not coincidentally, *Gone With the Wind* had become a runaway best seller and was about to become a movie.

These volumes are worth reading today, not only as an exposition of Confederate history and theory by their foremost advocate, but also as an explication of the Lost Cause mentality, which continues to share Jefferson Davis's conviction that while the Civil War's outcome proved secession "to be impracticable . . . this did not prove it to be wrong. . . . the war was, on the part of the United States government, one of aggression and usurpation, and, on the part of the South, was for the defense of an inherent, unalienable right." The Civil War, and the issues of federalism and race relations that caused it, are still very much with us today. Jefferson Davis's views on these issues are no longer widely accepted. But they are crucial to understanding the South in the nineteenth century and the Confederacy from 1861-1865. For this reason, his two volumes are *must* reading for every student of the Civil War.

—JAMES M. MCPHERSON
Princeton, New Jersey
May, 1990

PREFACE

THE object of this work has been from historical data to show that the Southern States had rightfully the power to withdraw from a Union into which they had, as sovereign communities, voluntarily entered; that the denial of that right was a violation of the letter and spirit of the compact between the States; and that the war waged by the Federal Government against the seceding States was in disregard of the limitations of the Constitution, and destructive of the principles of the Declaration of Independence.

The author, from his official position, may claim to have known much of the motives and acts of his countrymen immediately before and during the war of 1861-'65, and he has sought to furnish material for the future historian, who, when the passions and prejudices of the day shall have given place to reason and sober thought, may, better than a contemporary, investigate the causes, conduct, and results of the war.

The incentive to undertake the work now offered to the public was the desire to correct misapprehensions created by industriously circulated misrepresentations as to the acts and purposes of the people and the General Government of the Confederate States. By the reiteration of such unappropriate terms as "rebellion" and "treason," and the asseveration that the South was levying war against the United States, those ignorant of the nature of the Union, and of the reserved powers of the States, have been led to believe that the Confederate States were in the condition of revolted provinces, and that the United States were forced to resort to arms for the preservation of their existence. To those who knew that the Union was formed for specific enumerated purposes, and that the States had never surrendered their sovereignty, it was a palpable absurdity to apply to them, or to their citizens when obeying their mandates, the terms "rebellion" and "treason"; and, further, it is shown in the following pages that the Confederate States, so far from making war or seeking to destroy the United States, as soon as they had an official organ, strove earnestly, by peaceful recognition, to equitably adjust all questions growing out of the separation from their late associates.

Another great perversion of truth has been the arraignment of the men who participated in the formation of the Confederacy and who bore arms in its defense, as the instigators of a controversy leading to disunion. Sectional issues appear conspicuously in the debates of the Convention which framed the Federal Constitution, and its many compromises were designed to secure an equilibrium between the sections, and to preserve the interests as well as the liberties of the several States. African servitude at that time was not confined to a section, but was numerically greater in the South than in the North, with a tendency to its continuance in the former and cessation in the latter. It therefore thus early presents itself as a disturbing element, and the provisions of the Constitution, which were known to be necessary for its adoption, bound all the States to recognize and protect that species of property. When at a subsequent period there arose in the Northern States an antislavery agitation, it was a harmless and scarcely noticed movement until political demagogues seized upon it as a means to acquire power. Had it been left to pseudo-philanthropists and fanatics, most zealous where least informed, it never could have shaken the foundations of the Union and have incited one section to carry fire and sword into the other. That the agitation was political in its character, and was clearly developed as early as 1803, it is believed has been established in these pages. To preserve a sectional equilibrium and to maintain the equality of the States was the effort on one side, to acquire empire was the manifest purpose on the other. This struggle began before the men of the Confederacy were born; how it arose and how it progressed it has been attempted briefly to show. Its last stage was on the question of territorial governments; and, if in this work it has not been demonstrated that the position of the South was justified by the Constitution and the equal rights of the people of all the States, it must be because the author has failed to present the subject with a sufficient degree of force and clearness.

In describing the events of the war, space has not permitted, and the loss of both books and papers has prevented, the notice of very many entitled to consideration, as well for the humanity as the gallantry of our men in the unequal combats they fought. These numerous omissions, it is satisfactory to know, the official reports made at the time and the subsequent contributions which have been and are being published by the actors, will supply more fully and graphically than could have been done in this work.

Usurpations of the Federal Government have been presented, not in a spirit of hostility, but as a warning to the people against the dangers by which their liberties are beset. When the war ceased, the pretext on which it had been waged could no longer be alleged. The emancipation proclamation of Mr. Lincoln, which, when it was issued, he humorously admitted to be a nullity, had acquired validity by the action of the highest authority known to our institutions—the people assembled in their several State Conventions. The soldiers of the Confederacy had laid

down their arms, had in good faith pledged themselves to abstain from
further hostile operations, and had peacefully dispersed to their homes;
there could not, then, have been further dread of them by the Government of the United States. The plea of necessity could, therefore, no
longer exist for hostile demonstration against the people and States of
the deceased Confederacy. Did vengeance, which stops at the grave,
subside? Did real peace and the restoration of the States to their former
rights and positions follow, as was promised on the restoration of the
Union? Let the recital of the invasion of the reserved powers of the
States, or the people, and the perversion of the republican form of government guaranteed to each State by the Constitution, answer the question. For the deplorable fact of the war, for the cruel manner in which
it was waged, for the sad physical and yet sadder moral results it produced, the reader of these pages, I hope, will admit that the South, in
the forum of conscience, stands fully acquitted.

Much of the past is irremediable; the best hope for a restoration in
the future to the pristine purity and fraternity of the Union, rests on the
opinions and character of the men who are to succeed this generation:
that they may be suited to that blessed work, one, whose public course is
ended, invokes them to draw their creed from the fountains of our political history, rather than from the lower stream, polluted as it has been
by self-seeking place-hunters and by sectional strife.

THE AUTHOR.

CONTENTS

CONTENTS

PART II: THE CONSTITUTION

CONTENTS

CONTENTS

PART III: SECESSION AND CONFEDERATION

CONTENTS

PART IV: THE WAR

CONTENTS

CONTENTS

CONTENTS

APPENDIXES

APPENDIXES

ILLUSTRATIONS

INTRODUCTION

A DUTY to my countrymen; to the memory of those who died in defense of a cause consecrated by inheritance, as well as sustained by conviction; and to those who, perhaps less fortunate, staked all, and lost all save life and honor, in its behalf, has impelled me to attempt vindication of their cause and conduct. For this purpose I have decided to present an historical sketch of the events which preceded and attended the struggle of the Southern states to maintain their existence and their rights as sovereign communities—the creators, not the creatures, of the general government.

The social problem of maintaining the just relation between constitution, government, and people has been found so difficult that human history is a record of unsuccessful efforts to establish it. A government, to afford the needful protection and exercise proper care for the welfare of a people, must have homogeneity in its constituents. It is this necessity which has divided the human race into separate nations, and finally has defeated the grandest efforts which conquerors have made to give unlimited extent to their domain. When our fathers dissolved their connection with Great Britain, by declaring themselves free and independent states, they constituted thirteen separate communities, and were careful to assert and preserve, each for itself, its sovereignty and jurisdiction.

At a time when the minds of men are straying far from the lessons our fathers taught, it seems proper and well to recur to the original principles on which the system of government they devised was founded. The eternal truths which they announced, the rights which they declared "unalienable," are the foundation-stones on which rests the vindication of the Confederate cause.

He must have been a careless reader of our political history who has not observed that, whether under the style of "United Colonies" or "United States," which was adopted after the *Declaration of Independence,* whether under the articles of confederation or the compact of union, there everywhere appears the distinct assertion of state sovereignty, and nowhere the slightest suggestion of any purpose on the part of the states to consolidate themselves into one body. Will any candid, well-informed man assert that, at any time between 1776 and 1790, a proposition to surrender the sovereignty of the states and merge them in a central government would have had the least possible chance of adoption? Can any historical fact be more demonstrable than that the States did, both in the confederation and in the union, retain their sovereignty and independence as distinct communities, voluntarily consenting to federation, but never becoming the fractional parts of a nation? That such opinions should find adherents in our day may be attributable to the natural law of aggregation; surely not to a conscientious regard for the terms of the compact for union by the states.

In all free governments the constitution or organic law is supreme over the government, and in our federal union this was most distinctly marked by limitations and prohibitions against all which was beyond the expressed grants of power to the general government. In the foreground, therefore, I take the position that those who resisted violations of the compact were the true friends, and those who maintained the usurpation of undelegated powers were the real enemies of the constitutional union.

PART I.

CHAPTER I: *African Servitude—A Retrospect—Early Legislation with Regard to the Slave Trade—The Southern States Foremost in Prohibiting It—A Common Error Corrected—The Ethical Question Never at Issue in Sectional Controversies—The Acquisition of Louisiana—The Missouri Compromise—The Balance of Power—Note—The Indiana Case.*

INASMUCH as questions growing out of the institution of negro servitude, or connected with it, will occupy a conspicuous place in what is to follow, it is important that the reader should have, at the very outset, a right understanding of the true nature and character of those questions. No subject has been more generally misunderstood or more persistently misrepresented. The institution itself has ceased to exist in the United States; the generation, comprising all who took part in the controversies to which it gave rise, or for which it afforded a pretext, is passing away; the misconceptions which have prevailed in our own country, and still more among foreigners remote from the field of contention, are likely to be perpetuated in the mind of posterity, unless corrected before they become crystallized by tacit acquiescence.

It is well known that at the time of the adoption of the federal Constitution African servitude existed in all the states that were parties to that compact, unless with the single exception of Massachusetts, in which it had, perhaps, very recently ceased to exist. The slaves, however, were numerous in the Southern, and very few in the Northern, states. This diversity was occasioned by differences of climate, soil, and industrial interests—not in any degree by moral considerations, which at that period were not recognized as an element in the question. It was simply because negro labor was more profitable in the South than in the North that the importation of negro slaves had been, and continued to be, chiefly directed to the Southern ports.[1] For the same reason slavery was abolished by the states of the Northern section (though it existed in several of them for more than fifty years after the adoption of the Constitution), while the importation of slaves into the South continued to be carried on by Northern merchants and Northern ships, without inter-

---

[1] It will be remembered that, during her colonial condition, Virginia made strenuous efforts to prevent the importation of Africans, and was overruled by the Crown; also that Georgia, under Oglethorpe, did prohibit the introduction of African slaves until 1752, when the proprietors surrendered the charter, and the colony became a part of the royal government, and enjoyed the same privileges as the other colonies.

ference in the traffic from any quarter, until it was prohibited by the spontaneous action of the Southern states themselves. The Constitution expressly forbade any interference by Congress with the slave trade—or, to use its own language, with the "migration or importation of such persons" as any of the states should think proper to admit—"prior to the year 1808." During the intervening period of more than twenty years, the matter was exclusively under the control of the respective states. Nevertheless, every Southern state, without exception, either had already enacted, or proceeded to enact, laws forbidding the importation of slaves.[2] Virginia was the first of all the states, North or South, to prohibit it, and Georgia was the first to incorporate such a prohibition in her organic constitution.

Two petitions for the abolition of slavery and the slave trade were presented February 11 and 12, 1790, to the very first Congress convened under the Constitution.[3] After full discussion in the House of Representatives, it was determined, with regard to the first-mentioned subject, "that Congress have no authority to interfere in the emancipation of slaves, or in the treatment of them within any of the states"; and, with regard to the other, that no authority existed to prohibit the migration or importation of such persons as the states might think proper to admit, "prior to the year 1808." So distinct and final was this statement of the limitations of the authority of Congress considered to be that, when a similar petition was presented two or three years afterward, the clerk of the House was instructed to return it to the petitioner.[4]

In 1807 Congress, availing itself of the very earliest moment at which the constitutional restriction ceased to be operative, passed an act pro-

---

[2]South Carolina subsequently (in 1803) repealed her law forbidding the importation of slaves. The reason assigned for this action was the impossibility of enforcing the law without the aid of the federal government, to which entire control of the revenues, revenue police, and naval forces of the country had been surrendered by the states. "The geographical situation of our country," said Mr. Lowndes of South Carolina in the House of Representatives on February 14, 1804, "is not unknown. With navigable rivers running into the heart of it, it was impossible, with our means, to prevent our Eastern brethren . . . . engaged in this trade, from introducing them [the negroes] into the country. The law was completely evaded. . . . Under these circumstances, sir, it appears to me to have been the duty of the legislature to repeal the law, and remove from the eyes of the people the spectacle of its authority being daily violated." The effect of the repeal was to permit the importation of negroes into South Carolina during the interval from 1803 to 1808. It is probable that an extensive *contrabrand* trade was carried on by the New England slavers with other ports, on account of the lack of means to enforce the laws of the Southern states forbidding it.

[3]One from the Society of Friends assembled at Philadelphia and New York, the other from the Pennsylvania society of various religious denominations combined for the abolition of slavery.
For report of the debate, see Benton's *Abridgment,* Vol. I, pp. 201-207 *et seq.*

[4]See Benton's *Abridgment,* Vol. I, p. 397.

hibiting the importation of slaves into any part of the United States from and after the first day of January, 1808. This act was passed with great unanimity. In the House of Representatives there were one hundred thirteen (113) yeas to five (5) nays; it is a significant fact, as showing the absence of any sectional division of sentiment at that period, that the five dissentients were divided as equally as possible between the two sections, two of them being from Northern and three from Southern states.[5]

The slave trade had thus been finally abolished some months before the birth of the author of these pages, and has never since had legal existence in any of the United States. The question of the maintenance or extinction of the system of negro servitude already existing in any state was one exclusively belonging to such state. It is obvious, therefore, that no subsequent question legitimately arising in federal legislation could properly have any reference to the merits or the policy of the institution itself. A few zealots in the North afterward created much agitation by demands for the abolition of slavery within the states by federal intervention, and by their activity and perseverance finally became a recognized party which, holding the balance of power between the two contending organizations in that section, gradually obtained the control of one, and to no small degree corrupted the other. The dominant idea, however, at least of the absorbed party, was sectional aggrandizement, looking to absolute control, and theirs is the responsibility for the war that resulted.

No moral nor sentimental considerations were really involved in either the earlier or later controversies which so long agitated and finally ruptured the Union. They were simply struggles between different sections, with diverse institutions and interests.

It is absolutely requisite, in order to a right understanding of the history of the country, to bear these truths clearly in mind. The phraseology of the period referred to will otherwise be essentially deceptive. The antithetical employment of such terms as *freedom* and *slavery,* or "anti-slavery" and "pro-slavery," with reference to the principles and purposes of contending parties or rival sections, has had immense influence in misleading the opinions and sympathies of the world. The idea of freedom is captivating, that of slavery repellent to the moral sense of mankind in general. It is easy, therefore, to understand the effect of applying the one set of terms to one party, the other to another, in a contest which

[5]One was from New Hampshire, one from Vermont, two from Virginia, and one from South Carolina.—Benton's *Abridgment,* Vol. III, p. 519.
No division on the final vote in the Senate.

had no just application whatever to the essential merits of freedom or slavery. Southern statesmen may perhaps have been too indifferent to this consideration—overlooking in their ardent pursuit of principles, the effects of phrases. This is especially true with regard to that familiar but most fallacious expression, "the extension of slavery." To the reader unfamiliar with the subject, or viewing it only on the surface, it would perhaps never occur that, as used in the great controversies respecting the territories of the United States, it does not, never did, and never could, imply the addition of a single slave to the number already existing. The question was merely whether the slaveholder should be permitted to go, with his slaves, into territory (the common property of all) into which the non-slaveholder could go with *his* property of any sort. There was no proposal nor desire on the part of the Southern states to reopen the slave trade, which they had been foremost in suppressing, or to add to the number of slaves. It was a question of the distribution, or dispersion, of the slaves, rather than of the "extension of slavery." Removal is not extension. Indeed, if emancipation was the end to be desired, the dispersion of the negroes over a wider area among additional territories, eventually to become states, and in climates unfavorable to slave labor, instead of hindering, would have promoted this object by diminishing the difficulties in the way of ultimate emancipation.

The distinction here defined between the distribution, or dispersion, of slaves and the extension of slavery—two things altogether different, although so generally confounded—was early and clearly drawn under circumstances and in a connection which justify a fuller notice.

Virginia, it is well known, in the year 1784, ceded to the United States—then united only by the original Articles of Confederation—her vast possessions northwest of the Ohio, from which the great states of Ohio, Indiana, Michigan, Illinois, Wisconsin, and part of Minnesota, have since been formed. In 1787—before the adoption of the federal Constitution—the celebrated "ordinance" for the government of this Northwestern Territory was adopted by the Congress, with the full consent, and indeed at the express instance, of Virginia. This ordinance included six definite "Articles of compact between the original States and the people and States in the said Territory," which were to "for ever remain unalterable unless by common consent." The sixth of these articles ordains that "there shall be neither slavery nor involuntary servitude in the said Territory, otherwise than in the punishment of crimes whereof the party shall have been duly convicted."

In December, 1805, a petition of the Legislative Council and House of Representatives of the Indiana territory—then comprising all the area now occupied by the states of Indiana, Illinois, Michigan, and Wisconsin —was presented to Congress. It appears from the proceedings of the House of Representatives that several petitions of the same purport from inhabitants of the territory, accompanied by a letter from William Henry Harrison, the governor (afterward President of the United States), had been under consideration nearly two years earlier. The prayer of these petitions was for a *suspension* of the sixth article of the ordinance, so as to permit the introduction of slaves into the territory. The whole subject was referred to a select committee of seven members, consisting of representatives from Virginia, Ohio, Pennsylvania, South Carolina, Kentucky, and New York, and the delegate from the Indiana territory.

On the 14th of the ensuing February (1806), this committee made a report favorable to the prayer of the petitioners, and recommending a suspension of the prohibitory article for ten years. In their report the committee, after stating their opinion that a qualified suspension of the article in question would be beneficial to the people of the Indiana territory, proceeded to say:

The suspension of this article is an object almost universally desired in that Territory. It appears to your committee to be a question entirely different from that between slavery and freedom, inasmuch as it would merely occasion the removal of persons, already slaves, from one part of the country to another. The good effects of this suspension, in the present instance, would be to accelerate the population of that Territory, hitherto retarded by the operation of that article of compact; as slaveholders emigrating into the Western country might then indulge any preference which they might feel for a settlement in the Indiana Territory, instead of seeking, as they are now compelled to do, settlements in other States or countries permitting the introduction of slaves. The condition of the slaves themselves would be much ameliorated by it, as it is evident, from experience, that the more they are separated and diffused the more care and attention are bestowed on them by their masters, each proprietor having it in his power to increase their comforts and conveniences in proportion to the smallness of their numbers.

These were the dispassionate utterances of representatives of every part of the Union—men contemporary with the origin of the Constitution, speaking before any sectional division had arisen in connection with the subject. It is remarkable that the very same opinions which they express and arguments which they adduce had, fifty years afterward, come to be denounced and repudiated by one-half of the Union as partisan and sectional when propounded by the other half.

No final action seems to have been taken on the subject before the adjournment of Congress, but it was brought forward at the next session in a more imposing form. On January 20, 1807, the Speaker laid before the House of Representatives a letter from Governor Harrison, enclosing certain resolutions formally and *unanimously* adopted by the Legislative Council and House of Representatives of the Indiana territory, in favor of the suspension of the sixth article of the ordinance and the introduction of slaves into the territory, which they said would "meet the approbation of at least nine tenths of the good citizens of the same." Among the resolutions were the following:

Resolved unanimously, That the abstract question of liberty and slavery is not considered as involved in a suspension of the said article, inasmuch as the number of slaves in the United States *would not be augmented* by this measure.

Resolved unanimously, That the suspension of the said article would be equally advantageous to the Territory, to the States from whence the negroes would be brought, and to the negroes themselves. . . .

The States which are overburdened with negroes would be benefited by their citizens having an opportunity of disposing of the negroes which they can not comfortably support, or of removing with them to a country abounding with all the necessaries of life; and the negro himself would exchange a scanty pittance of the coarsest food for a plentiful and nourishing diet, and a situation which admits not the most distant prospect of emancipation for one which presents no considerable obstacle to his wishes.

These resolutions were submitted to a committee drawn, like the former, from different sections of the country, which again reported favorably, reiterating in substance the reasons given by the former committee. Their report was sustained by the House, and a resolution to suspend the prohibitory article was adopted. The proposition failed, however, in the Senate, and there the matter seems to have been dropped. The proceedings constitute a significant and instructive episode in the political history of the country.

The allusion which has been made to the Ordinance of 1787 renders it proper to notice, very briefly, the argument put forward during the discussion of the Missouri question, and often repeated since, that the ordinance afforded a precedent in support of the claim of a power in Congress to determine the question of the admission of slaves into the territories, and in justification of the prohibitory clause applied in 1820 to a portion of the Louisiana Territory.

The difference between the Congress of the Confederation and that of the federal Constitution is so broad that the action of the former can, in no just sense, be taken as a precedent for the latter. The Congress of the Confederation represented the states in their sovereignty, each delegation having one vote, so that all the states were of equal weight in the decision of any question. It had legislative, executive, and in some degree judicial powers, thus combining all departments of government in itself. During its recess a committee known as the Committee of the States exercised the powers of the Congress, which was in spirit, if not in fact, an assemblage of the states.

On the other hand, the Congress of the Constitution is only the legislative department of the general government, with powers strictly defined and expressly limited to those delegated by the states. It is further held in check by an executive and a judiciary, and consists of two branches, each having peculiar and specified functions.

If, then, it be admitted—which is at least very questionable—that the Congress of the Confederation had rightfully the power to exclude slave property from the territory northwest of the Ohio River, that power must have been derived from its character as an assemblage of the sovereign states; not from the Articles of Confederation, in which no indication of the grant of authority to exercise such a function can be found. The Congress of the Constitution is expressly prohibited from the assumption of any power not distinctly and specifically delegated to it as the legislative branch of an organized government. What was questionable in the former case, therefore, becomes clearly inadmissible in the latter.

But there is yet another material distinction to be observed. The states, owners of what was called the Northwestern Territory, were component members of the Congress which adopted the ordinance for its government, and gave thereto their full and free consent. The ordinance may, therefore, be regarded as virtually a treaty between the states which ceded and those which received that extensive domain. In the other case, Missouri and the whole region affected by the Missouri Compromise were parts of the territory acquired from France under the name of Louisiana; as it requires two parties to make or amend a treaty, France and the government of the United States should have coöperated in any amendment of the treaty by which Louisiana had been acquired, and which guaranteed to the inhabitants of the ceded territory "all the rights, advantages, and immunities of citizens of the United States," and "the free enjoyment of their liberty, property, and religion they profess."[6]

For all the reasons thus stated, it seems to me conclusive that the action of the Congress of the Confederation in 1787 could not constitute a precedent to justify the action of the Congress of the United States in

---

[6] *State Papers*, Vol. II, "Foreign Relations," p. 507.

1820, and that the prohibitory clause of the Missouri Compromise was without constitutional authority, in violation of the rights of a part of the joint owners of the territory, and in disregard of the obligations of the treaty with France.

The basis of sectional controversy was the question of the balance of political power. In its earlier manifestations this was undisguised. The purchase of the Louisiana Territory from France in 1803, and the subsequent admission of a portion of that territory into the Union as a state, afforded one of the earliest occasions for the manifestation of sectional jealousy, and gave rise to the first threats or warnings (which proceeded from New England) of a dissolution of the Union. Yet, although negro slavery existed in Louisiana, no pretext was made of that as an objection to the acquisition. The ground of opposition is frankly stated in a letter of that period from one Massachusetts statesman to another—"that the influence of *our* part of the Union must be diminished by the acquisition of more weight at the other extremity."[7]

Some years afterward (in 1819-'20) occurred the memorable contest with regard to the admission into the Union of Missouri, the second state carved out of the Louisiana Territory. The controversy arose out of a proposition to attach to the admission of the new state a proviso prohibiting slavery or involuntary servitude therein. The vehement discussion that ensued was continued into the first session of a different Congress from that in which it originated, and agitated the whole country during the interval between the two. It was the first question that ever seriously threatened the stability of the Union, and the first in which the sentiment of opposition to slavery in the abstract was introduced as an adjunct of sectional controversy. It was clearly shown in debate that such considerations were altogether irrelevant; that the number of existing slaves would not be affected by their removal from the older states to Missouri; and moreover, that the proposed restriction would be contrary to the spirit, if not to the letter, of the Constitution.[8] Notwithstanding all this the restriction was adopted, by a vote almost strictly sectional, in the House of Representatives. It failed in the Senate through the firm resistance of the Southern, aided by a few patriotic and

---

[7] Cabot to Pickering, who was then Senator from Massachusetts. (See *Life and Letters of George Cabot*, by H. C. Lodge, p. 334.)

[8] The true issue was well stated by the Hon. Samuel A. Foot, a representative from Connecticut, in an incidental reference to it in debate on another subject, a few weeks after the final settlement of the Missouri case. He said: "The Missouri question did not involve the question of freedom or slavery, but merely *whether slaves now in the country might be permitted to reside in the proposed new State; and whether Congress or Missouri possessed the power to decide.*"

conservative Northern, members of that body. The admission of the new state without any restriction was finally accomplished by the addition to the bill of a section forever prohibiting slavery in all that portion of the Louisiana Territory lying north of thirty-six degrees and thirty minutes, north latitude, except Missouri—by implication leaving the portion south of that line open to settlement either with or without slaves.

This provision, as an offset to the admission of the new state without restriction, constituted the celebrated Missouri Compromise. It was reluctantly accepted by a small majority of the Southern members. Nearly half of them voted against it, under the conviction that it was unauthorized by the Constitution, and that Missouri was entitled to determine the question for herself, as a matter of right, not of bargain or concession. Among those who thus thought and voted were some of the wisest statesmen and purest patriots of that period.[9]

This brief retrospect may have sufficed to show that the question of the right or wrong of the institution of slavery was in no wise involved in the earlier sectional controversies. Nor was it otherwise in those of a later period, in which it was the lot of the author of these memoirs to bear a part. They were essentially struggles for sectional equality or ascendancy—for the maintenance or the destruction of that balance of power or equipoise between North and South, which was early recognized as a cardinal principle in our federal system. It does not follow that both parties to this contest were wholly right or wholly wrong in their claims. The determination of the question of right or wrong must be left to the candid inquirer after examination of the evidence. The object of these preliminary investigations has been to clear the subject of the obscurity produced by irrelevant issues and the glamour of ethical illusions.

---

[9]The votes on the proposed *restriction*, which eventually failed of adoption, and on the *compromise*, which was finally adopted, are often confounded. The advocacy of the former measure was exclusively sectional, no Southern member voting for it in either house. On the adoption of the compromise line of thirty-six degrees and thirty minutes, the vote in the Senate was 34 yeas to 10 nays. The Senate consisted of forty-four members from twenty-two states, equally divided between the two sections—Delaware being classed as a Southern state. Among the yeas were all the Northern votes, except two from Indiana—being 20—and 14 Southern. The nays consisted of 2 from the North, and 8 from the South.

In the House of Representatives, the vote was 134 yeas to 42 nays. Of the yeas, 95 were Northern, 39 Southern; of the nays, 5 Northern, and 37 Southern.

Among the nays in the Senate were Messrs. James Barbour and James Pleasants of Virginia, Nathaniel Macon of North Carolina, John Gaillard and William Smith of South Carolina. In the House Philip P. Barbour, John Randolph, John Tyler, and William S. Archer of Virginia, Charles Pinckney of South Carolina (one of the authors of the Constitution), Thomas W. Cobb of Georgia, and others of more or less note.

(See speech of the Hon. D. L. Yulee of Florida in the United States Senate, on the admission of California, August 6, 1850, for a careful and correct account of the compromise. That given in the second chapter of Benton's *Thirty Years' View* is singularly inaccurate; that of Horace Greeley, in his *American Conflict*, still more so.)

CHAPTER II: *The Session of 1849-'50—The Compromise Measures—Virtual Abrogation of the Missouri Compromise—The Admission of California—The Fugitive Slave Law—Death of Calhoun—Anecdote of Clay.*

THE first session of the Thirty-first Congress (1849-'50) was a memorable one. The recent acquisition from Mexico of New Mexico and California required legislation by Congress. In the Senate the bills reported by the Committee on Territories were referred to a select committee of which Clay, the distinguished Senator from Kentucky, was chairman. From this committee emanated the bills which, taken together, are known as the compromise measures of 1850.

With some others, I advocated the division of the newly acquired territory by an extension to the Pacific Ocean of the Missouri Compromise line of thirty-six degrees and thirty minutes north latitude. This was not because of any inherent merit or fitness in that line, but because it had been accepted by the country as a settlement of the sectional question which, thirty years before, had threatened a rupture of the Union, and it had acquired in the public mind a prescriptive respect which it seemed unwise to disregard. A majority, however, decided otherwise, and the line of political conciliation was then obliterated, as far as it lay in the power of Congress to do so. An analysis of the vote will show that this result was effected almost exclusively by the representatives of the North, and that the South was not responsible for an action which proved to be the opening of Pandora's box.[1]

However objectionable it may have been in 1820 to adopt that political line as expressing a geographical definition of different sectional interests, and however it may be condemned as the assumption by Congress of a function not delegated to it, it is to be remembered that the act had received such recognition and quasi-ratification by the people of the states as to give it a value which it did not originally possess. Pacification had been the fruit borne by the tree, and it should not have been recklessly hewed down and cast into the fire. The frequent assertion then made was that all discrimination was unjust, and that the popular will should be left untrammeled in the formation of new states. This theory

[1]The vote in the Senate on the proposition to continue the line of the Missouri Compromise through the newly acquired territory to the Pacific was twenty-four yeas to thirty-two nays. Reckoning Delaware and Missouri as Southern states, the vote of the two sections was exactly equal. The yeas were *all* cast by Southern Senators; the nays were all Northern except two from Delaware, one from Missouri, and one from Kentucky.

J. C. CALHOUN

was good enough in itself, and as an abstract proposition could not be gainsaid; its practical operation, however, has but poorly sustained the expectations of its advocates, as will be seen when we come to consider the events that occurred a few years later in Kansas and elsewhere. Retrospectively viewed under the mellowing light of time, and with the calm consideration we can usually give to the irremediable past, the compromise legislation of 1850 bears the impress of that sectional spirit so widely at variance with the general purposes of the Union, and so destructive of the harmony and mutual benefit which the Constitution was intended to secure.

The refusal to divide the territory acquired from Mexico by an extension of the line of the Missouri Compromise to the Pacific was a consequence of the purpose to admit California as a state of the Union before it had acquired the requisite population, and while it was mainly under the control of a military organization sent from New York during the war with Mexico and disbanded in California upon the restoration of peace. The inconsistency of the argument against the extension of the line was exhibited in the division of the territory of Texas by that parallel, and payment to the state of money to secure her consent to the partition of her domain. In the case of Texas, the North had everything to gain and nothing to lose by the application of the practice of geographical compromise on an arbitrary line. In the case of California, the conditions were reversed; the South might have been the gainer and the North the loser by a recognition of the same rule.

The compensation which it was alleged that the South received was a more effective law for the rendition of fugitives from service or labor. But it is to be remarked that this law provided for the execution by the general government of obligations which had been imposed by the federal compact upon the several states of the Union. The benefit to be derived from a fulfillment of that law would be small in comparison with the evil to result from the plausible pretext that the states had thus been relieved from a duty which they had assumed in the adoption of the compact of union. Whatever tended to lead the people of any of the states to feel that they could be relieved from their constitutional obligations by transferring them to the general government, or that they might thus or otherwise evade or resist them, could not fail to be like the tares which the enemy sowed amid the wheat. The union of states, formed to secure the permanent welfare of posterity and to promote harmony among the constituent states, could not, without changing its character, survive such alienation as rendered its parts hostile to the security, prosperity, and happiness of one another.

It was reasonably argued that, as the legislatures of fourteen of the states had enacted what were termed "personal liberty laws," which forbade the coöperation of state officials in the rendition of fugitives from service and labor, it became necessary that the general government should provide the requisite machinery for the execution of the law. The result proved what might have been anticipated—that those communities which had repudiated their constitutional obligations, which had nullified a previous law of Congress for the execution of a provision of the Constitution, and had murdered men who came peacefully to recover their property, would evade or obstruct, so as to render practically worthless, *any* law that could be enacted for that purpose. In the exceptional cases in which it might be executed, the event would be attended with such conflict between the state and federal authorities as to produce consequent evils greater than those it was intended to correct.

It was during the progress of these memorable controversies that the South lost its most trusted leader, and the Senate its greatest and purest statesman. He was taken from us—

> Like a summer-dried fountain,
> When our need was the sorest—

when his intellectual power, his administrative talent, his love of peace, and his devotion to the Constitution might have averted collision; failing in that, he might have been to the South the Palinurus to steer the bark in safety over the perilous sea. Truly did Webster—his personal friend, although his greatest political rival—say of him in his obituary address, "There was nothing groveling, or low, or meanly selfish, that came near the head or the heart of Mr. Calhoun." His prophetic warnings speak from the grave with the wisdom of inspiration. Would that they could have been appreciated by his countrymen while he yet lived!

✸ ✸ ✸ ✸

While the compromise measures of 1850 were pending, and the excitement concerning them was at its highest, I one day overtook Clay of Kentucky and Berrien of Georgia in the Capitol grounds. They were in earnest conversation. It was the 7th of March—the day on which Webster had delivered his great speech. Clay, addressing me in the friendly manner which he had always employed since I was a schoolboy in Lexington, asked me what I thought of the speech. I liked it better than he did. He then suggested that I should "join the compromise men," saying that it was a measure which he thought would probably give peace to the country for thirty years—the period that had elapsed since the adoption of the compromise of 1820. Then, turning to Berrien, he said, "You and I will be under ground before that time, but our young friend here may have trouble to meet." I somewhat impatiently declared my unwillingness to transfer to posterity a trial which they would be relatively less able to meet than we were, and passed on my way.

CHAPTER III: *Reëlection to the Senate—Political Controversies in Mississippi—Action of the Democratic State Convention— Defeat of the State-Rights Party—Withdrawal of General Quitman and Nomination of the Author as Candidate for the Office of Governor—The Canvass and its Result—Retirement to Private Life.*

I HAD been reëlected by the legislature of Mississippi as my own successor, and entered upon a new term of service in the Senate on March 4, 1851.

On my return to Mississippi in 1851, the subject chiefly agitating the public mind was that of the "compromise" measures of the previous year. Consequent upon these was a proposition for a convention of delegates, from the people of the Southern states respectively, to consider what steps ought to be taken for their future peace and safety, and the preservation of their constitutional rights. There was diversity of opinion with regard to the merits of the measures referred to, but the disagreement no longer followed the usual lines of party division. They who saw in those measures the forerunner of disaster to the South had no settled policy beyond a convention, the object of which should be to devise new and more effectual guarantees against the perils of usurpation. They were unjustly charged with a desire to destroy the Union—a feeling entertained by few, very few, if by any, in Mississippi, and avowed by none.

There were many, however, who held that the principles of the *Declaration of Independence,* and the purposes for which the Union was formed, were of higher value than the mere Union itself. Independence existed before the compact of union between the states; and if that compact should be broken in part and therefore destroyed in whole, it was hoped that the liberties of the people in the states might still be preserved. Those who were most devoted to the Union of the Constitution might, consequently, be expected to resist most sternly any usurpation of undelegated power, the effect of which would be to warp the federal government from its proper character, and, by sapping the foundation, to destroy the union of the states.

My recent reëlection to the United States Senate had conferred upon me for six years longer the office which I preferred to all others. I could not, therefore, be suspected of desiring a nomination for any other office from the Democratic Convention, the meeting of which was then draw-

BRIARFIELD, EARLY RESIDENCE OF MR. DAVIS

ing near. Having, as a Senator of the state, freely participated in debate on the measures which were now exciting so much interest in the public mind, it was very proper that I should visit the people in different parts of the state and render an account of my stewardship.

My devotion to the Union of our fathers had been so often and so publicly declared; I had, on the floor of the Senate, so defiantly challenged any question of my fidelity to it; my services, civil and military, had now extended through so long a period, and were so generally known—that I felt quite assured that no whisperings of envy or ill will could lead the people of Mississippi to believe that I had dishonored their trust by using the power they had conferred on me to destroy the government to which I was accredited. Then, as afterward, I regarded the separation of the states as a great, though not the greatest, evil.

I returned from my tour among the people at the time appointed for the meeting of the nominating convention of the Democratic (or State-Rights) party. During the previous year the governor, General John A. Quitman, had been compelled to resign his office to answer an indictment against him for complicity with the "filibustering" expeditions against Cuba. The charges were not sustained; many of the Democratic party of Mississippi, myself included, recognized a consequent obligation to renominate him for the office of which he had been deprived. When, however, the delegates met in party convention, the committee appointed to select candidates, on comparison of opinions, concluded that, in view of the effort to fix upon the party the imputation of a purpose of disunion, some of the antecedents of General Quitman might endanger success. A proposition was therefore made, in the committee on nominations, that I should be invited to become a candidate, and that, if General Quitman would withdraw, my acceptance of the nomination and the resignation of my place in the United States Senate, which it was known would result, was to be followed by the appointment by the governor of General Quitman to the vacated place in the Senate. I offered no objection to this arrangement, but left it to General Quitman to decide. He claimed the nomination for the governorship, or nothing, and was so nominated.

To promote the success of the Democratic nominees, I engaged actively in the canvass, and continued in the field until stricken down by disease. This occurred just before the election of delegates to a state convention, for which provision had been made by the legislature, and the canvass for which, conducted in the main upon party lines, was in progress simultaneously with that for the ordinary state officers. The

Democratic majority in the state when the canvass began was estimated at eight thousand. At this election, in September, for delegates to the state convention, we were beaten by about seven thousand five hundred votes. Seeing in this result the foreshadowing of almost inevitable defeat, General Quitman withdrew from the canvass as a candidate, and the Executive Committee of the party (empowered to fill vacancies) called on me to take his place. My health did not permit me to leave home at that time, and only about six weeks remained before the election was to take place; being assured, however, that I was not expected to take any active part, and that the party asked only the use of my name, I consented to be announced, and immediately resigned from the United States Senate. Nevertheless, I soon afterward took the field in person, and worked earnestly until the day of election. I was defeated, but the majority of more than seven thousand votes, that had been cast a short time before against the party with which I was associated, was reduced to less than one thousand.[1]

In this canvass, both before and after I became a candidate, no argument or appeal of mine was directed against the perpetuation of the Union. Believing, however, that the signs of the time portended danger to the South from the usurpation by the general government of undelegated powers, I counseled that Mississippi should enter into the proposed meeting of the people of the Southern states, to consider what

---

[1] The following letter, written in 1853 to the Hon. William J. Brown of Indiana, formerly a member of Congress from that state, and subsequently published, relates to the events of this period, and affords nearly contemporaneous evidence in confirmation of the statements of the text:

WASHINGTON, D. C., May 7, 1853.

"MY DEAR SIR: I received the 'Sentinel' containing your defense of me against the false accusation of disunionism, and, before I had returned to you the thanks to which you are entitled, I received this day the St. Joseph 'Valley Register,' marked by you, to call my attention to an article in answer to your defense, which was just in all things, save your too complimentary terms.

"I wish I had the letter quoted from, that you might publish the whole of that which is garbled to answer a purpose. In a part of the letter not published, I put such a damper on the attempt to fix on me the desire to break up our Union, and presented other points in a form so little acceptable to the unfriendly inquirers, that the publication of the letter had to be drawn out of them.

"At the risk of being wearisome, but encouraged by your marked friendship, I will give you a statement in the case. The meeting of October, 1849, was a convention of delegates equally representing the Whig and Democratic parties in Mississippi. The resolutions were decisive as to equality of right in the South with the North to the Territories acquired from Mexico, and proposed a convention of the Southern States. I was not a member, but on invitation addressed the Convention. The succeeding Legislature instructed me, as a Senator, to assert this equality, and, under the existing circumstances, to resist by all constitutional means the admission of California as a State. At a called session of the Legislature in 1850, a self-constituted committee called on me, by letter, for my views. They were men who had enacted or approved the resolutions of the Convention of 1849, and instructed me, as members of the Legislature, in regular session, in the early part of the year 1850. To them I re-

could and should be done to insure our future safety, frankly stating my conviction that, unless such action were taken then, sectional rivalry would engender greater evils in the future, and that, if the controversy was postponed, "the last opportunity for a peaceful solution would be lost, then the issue would have to be settled by blood."

---

plied that I adhered to the policy they had indicated and instructed me in their official character to pursue.

"I pointed out the mode in which their policy could, in my opinion, be executed without bloodshed or disastrous convulsion, but in terms of bitter scorn alluded to such as would insult me with a desire to destroy the Union, for which my whole life proved me to be a devotee.

"Pardon the egotism, in consideration of the occasion, when I say to you that my father and my uncles fought through the Revolution of 1776, giving their youth, their blood, and their little patrimony to the constitutional freedom which I claim as my inheritance. Three of my brothers fought in the war of 1812. Two of them were comrades of the Hero of the Hermitage, and received his commendation for gallantry at New Orleans. At sixteen years of age I was given to the service of my country; for twelve years of my life I have borne its arms and served it zealously, if not well. As I feel the infirmities, which suffering more than age has brought upon me, it would be a bitter reflection, indeed, if I was forced to conclude that my countrymen would hold all this light when weighed against the empty panegyric which a time-serving politician can bestow upon the Union, for which he never made a sacrifice.

"In the Senate I announced that, if any respectable man would call me a disunionist, I would answer him in monosyllables. . . . But I have often asserted the right, for which the battles of the revolution were fought—the right of a people to change their government whenever it was found to be oppressive, and subversive of the objects for which governments are instituted—and have contended for the independence and sovereignty of the States, a part of the creed of which Jefferson was the apostle, Madison the expounder, and Jackson the consistent defender.

"I have written freely, and more than I designed. Accept my thanks for your friendly advocacy. Present me in terms of kind remembrance to your family, and believe me, very sincerely yours,   JEFFERSON DAVIS.

"NOTE.—No party in Mississippi ever advocated disunion. They differed as to the mode of securing their rights in the Union, and on the power of a State to secede—neither advocating the exercise of the power.   J. D."

CHAPTER IV: *The Author Enters the Cabinet—Administration of the War Department—Surveys for a Pacific Railway—Extension of the Capitol—New Regiments Organized—Colonel Samuel Cooper, Adjutant General—A Bit of Civil Service Reform—Reëlection to the Senate—Continuity of the Pierce Cabinet—Character of Franklin Pierce.*

HAPPY in the peaceful pursuits of a planter, busily engaged in cares for servants, in the improvement of my land, in building, in rearing livestock, and the like occupations, the time passed pleasantly away until my retirement was interrupted by an invitation to take a place in the cabinet of Pierce, who had been elected to the presidency of the United States in November, 1852. Although warmly attached to Pierce personally, and entertaining the highest estimate of his character and political principles, private and personal reasons led me to decline the offer. This was followed by an invitation to attend the ceremony of his inauguration, which took place on March 4, 1853. While in Washington on this visit, I was induced by public considerations to reconsider my determination and accept the office of Secretary of War. The public records of that period will best show how the duties of that office were performed.

While in the Senate, I had advocated the construction of a railway to connect the valley of the Mississippi with the Pacific coast; when an appropriation was made to determine the most eligible route for that purpose, the Secretary of War was charged with its application. We had then but little of that minute and accurate knowledge of the interior of the continent which was requisite for a determination of the problem. Several different parties were therefore organized to examine the various routes supposed to be practicable within the northern and southern limits of the United States. The arguments which I had used as a Senator were "the military necessity for such means of transportation, and the need of safe and rapid communication with the Pacific slope, to secure its continuance as a part of the Union."

In the organization and equipment of these parties, and in the selection of their officers, care was taken to provide for securing full and accurate information upon every point involved in the determination of the route. The only discrimination made was in the more prompt and thorough equipment of the parties for the extreme northern line, and this was only because that was supposed to be the most difficult of execution of all the surveys.

In like manner, my advocacy while in the Senate of an extension of the Capitol, by the construction of a new Senate Chamber and Hall of Representatives, may have caused the appropriation for that object to be put under my charge as Secretary of War.

During my administration of the War Department, material changes were made in the models of arms. Iron gun carriages were introduced, and experiments were made which led to the casting of heavy guns hollow, instead of boring them after casting. Inquiries were made with regard to gunpowder which subsequently led to the use of a coarser grain for artillery.

During the same period the army was increased by the addition of two regiments of infantry and two of cavalry. The officers of these regiments were chosen partly by selection from those already in service in the regular army and partly by appointment from civil life. In making the selections from the army I was continually indebted to the assistance of that pure-minded and accurately informed officer, Colonel Samuel Cooper, the Adjutant General, of whom it may be proper here to say that, although his life had been spent in the army, and he, of course, had the likes and dislikes inseparable from men who are brought into close contact and occasional rivalry, I never found in his official recommendations any indication of partiality or prejudice toward any one.

When the first list was made out, to be submitted to the President, a difficulty was found to exist which had not occurred either to Colonel Cooper or myself. This was that the officers selected purely on their military record did not constitute a roster conforming to that distribution among the different states, which, for political considerations, it was thought desirable to observe—that is to say, the number of such officers of Southern birth was found to be disproportionately great. Under instructions from the President, the list was therefore revised and modified in accordance with this new element of geographical distribution. This, as I am happy to remember, was the only occasion in which the current of my official action while Secretary of War was disturbed in any way by sectional or political considerations.

Under former administrations of the War Office it had not been customary to make removals or appointments upon political grounds, except in the case of clerkships. To this usage I not only adhered, but extended it to include the clerkships also. The chief clerk, who had been removed by my predecessor, had peculiar qualifications for the place;

although known to me only officially, he was restored to the position. It will probably be conceded by all who are well informed on the subject that his restoration was a benefit to the public service[1]

Having been again elected by the legislature of Mississippi as Senator to the United States, I passed from the cabinet of Pierce, on the last day of his term (March 4, 1857) to take my seat in the Senate.

The administration of Franklin Pierce presents the only instance in our history of the continuance of a cabinet for four years without a single change in its personnel. When it is remembered that there was much dissimilarity if not incongruity of character among the members of that cabinet, some idea may be formed of the power over men possessed and exercised by Pierce. Chivalrous, generous, amiable, true to his friends, and to his faith, frank and bold in the declaration of his opinions, he never deceived any one. And if treachery had ever come near him, it would have stood abashed in the presence of his truth, his manliness, and his confiding simplicity.

---

[1] Soon after my entrance upon duty as Secretary of War, General Jesup, the Quartermaster General, presented to me a list of names from which to make selection of a clerk for his department. Observing that he had attached certain figures to these names, I asked whether the figures were intended to indicate the relative qualifications, or preference in his estimation, of the several applicants; and, upon his answer in the affirmative, without further question, authorized him to appoint "No. 1" of his list. A day or two afterward, certain Democratic members of Congress called on me and politely inquired whether it was true that I had appointed a Whig to a position in the War Office. "Certainly not," I answered. "We thought you were not aware of it," they said, and proceeded to inform me that Mr. ——, the recent appointee to the clerkship just mentioned, was a Whig. After listening patiently to this statement, I answered that it was they who were deceived, not I. I had appointed a clerk. He had been appointed neither as a Whig nor as a Democrat, but merely as the fittest candidate for the place in the estimation of the chief of the bureau to which it belonged. I further gave them to understand that the same principle of selecion would be followed in similar cases, so far as my authority extended. After some further discussion of the question, the visitors withdrew, dissatisfied with the result of the interview.

The Quartermaster General, on hearing of this conversation, hastened to inform me that it was all a mistake—that the appointee to the office had been confounded with his father, who was a well-known Whig, but that he (the son) was a Democrat. I assured the General that this was altogether immaterial, adding that it was "a very pretty quarrel" as it stood, and that I had no desire to effect a settlement of it on any inferior issue. Thenceforth, however, I was but little troubled with any pressure for political appointments in the department.

The reader desirous for further information relative to the administration of the War Department during this period may find it in the various official reports and estimates of works of defense prosecuted or recommended, arsenals of construction and depots of arms maintained or suggested, and foundries employed, during the presidency of Pierce, 1853-'57.

CHAPTER V: *The Territorial Question—An Incident at the White House—The Kansas and Nebraska Bill—The Missouri Compromise Abrogated in 1850, not in 1854—Origin of "Squatter Sovereignty"—Sectional Rivalry and its Consequences—The Emigrant Aid Societies—"The Bible and Sharpe's Rifles"—False Pretensions as to Principle—The Strife in Kansas—A Retrospect—The Original Equilibrium of Power and its Overthrow—Usurpations of the Federal Government—The Protective Tariff—Origin and Progress of Abolitionism—Who Were the Friends of the Union?—An Illustration of Political Morality.*

THE organization of the territory of Kansas was the first question that gave rise to exciting debate after my return to the Senate. The celebrated Kansas-Nebraska bill had become a law during the administration of Pierce. As this occupies a large space in the political history of the period, it is proper to state some facts connected with it which were not public, but were known to me and to others yet living.

The declaration, often repeated in 1850, that climate and the will of the people concerned should determine their institutions when they should form a constitution, and as a state be admitted into the Union, and that no legislation by Congress should be permitted to interfere with the free exercise of that will when so expressed, was but the announcement of the fact so firmly established in the Constitution, that sovereignty resided alone in the states, and that Congress had only delegated powers. It has been sometimes contended that because the Congress of the Confederation, by the Ordinance of 1787, prohibited involuntary servitude in all the Northwestern Territory, the framers of the Constitution must have recognized such power to exist in the Congress of the United States. Hence the deduction that the prohibitory clause of what is known as the Missouri Compromise was justified by the precedent of the Ordinance of 1787. To make the action of the Congress of the Confederation a precedent for the Congress of the United States is to overlook the great distinction between the two.

The Congress of the Confederation represented the states in their sovereignty; as such representatives, it had legislative, executive, and, in some degree, judicial power confided to it. Virtually, it was an assemblage of the states. In certain cases a majority of nine states were required to decide a question, but there is no express limitation, or restriction, such as is to be found in the ninth and tenth amendments to the Constitution of the United States. The general government of the Union is composed of three departments, of which the Congress is the legislative branch, and which is checked by the revisory power of the judiciary, and the veto of the executive, and, above all, is expressly limited in legislation to powers expressly delegated by the states. If, then, it be admitted, which is certainly questionable, that the Congress of the Confederation had power to exclude slave property northwest of the Ohio River, that power must have been derived from its character as representing the states in their sovereignty, for no indication of such a power is to be found in the Articles of Confederation.

If it be assumed that the absence of a prohibition was equivalent to the admission of the power in the Congress of the Confederation, the assumption would avail nothing in the Congress under the Constitution, where power is expressly limited to what has been delegated. More briefly, it may be stated that the Congress of the Confederation could, like the legislature of a state, do what had not been prohibited; but the Congress of the United States could only do what had been expressly permitted. It is submitted whether this last position is not conclusive against the possession of power by the United States Congress to legislate slavery into or exclude it from territories belonging to the United States.

This subject, which had for more than a quarter of a century been one of angry discussion and sectional strife, was revived, and found occasion for renewed discussion in the organization of territorial governments for Kansas and Nebraska. The Committees on Territories of the two houses agreed to report a bill in accordance with that recognized principle, provided they could first be assured that it would receive favorable consideration from the President. This agreement was made on Saturday, and the ensuing Monday was the day (and the only day for two weeks) on which, according to the order of business established by the rules of the House of Representatives, the bill could be introduced by the committee of that house.

On Sunday morning, January 22, 1854, gentlemen of each committee called at my house; Douglas, chairman of the Senate committee, fully explained the proposed bill, and stated their purpose to be, through my aid, to obtain an interview on that day with the President, to ascertain whether the bill would meet his approbation. The President was known to be rigidly opposed to the reception of visits on Sunday for the discussion of any political subject, but in this case it was urged as necessary, in order to enable the committee to make their report the next day. I went with them to the executive mansion, and, leaving them in the reception room, sought the President in his private apartments and explained to him the occasion of the visit. He thereupon met the gentlemen, patiently listened to the reading of the bill and their explanations of it, decided that it rested upon sound constitutional principles, and recognized in it only a return to that rule which had been infringed by the compromise of 1820, and the restoration of which had been foreshadowed by the legislation of 1850. This bill was not, therefore, as has been improperly asserted, a measure inspired by Mr. Pierce or any of his cabinet. Nor was it the first step taken toward the repeal of the conditions or obligations expressed or implied by the establishment, in 1820, of the politico-sectional line of thirty-six degrees and thirty minutes. That compact had been virtually abrogated, in 1850, by the refusal of the representatives of the North to apply it to the territory then recently acquired from Mexico. In May, 1854, the Kansas-Nebraska bill was passed; its purpose was declared in the bill itself to be to carry into practical operation the "propositions and principles established by the compromise measures of 1850." The Missouri Compromise, therefore, was not repealed by that bill—its virtual repeal by the legislation of 1850 was recognized as an existing fact, and it was declared to be "inoperative and void."

It was added that the "true intent and meaning" of the act was "not to legislate slavery into any Territory or State, nor to exclude it therefrom, but to leave the people thereof perfectly free to form and regulate their domestic institutions in their own way, subject only to the Constitution of the United States."

From the terms of this bill, as well as from the arguments that were used in its behalf, it is evident that its purpose was to leave the territories equally open to the people of all the states, with every species of property recognized by any of them; to permit climate and soil to determine the current of immigration, and to secure to the people themselves the right to form their own institutions according to their own will, as soon as they should acquire the right of self-government; that is to say, as soon as their numbers should entitle them to organize themselves into a state, prepared to take its place as an equal, sovereign member of the federal Union. The claim, afterward advanced by Douglas and others, that this declaration was intended to assert the right of the first settlers of a territory, in its inchoate, rudimental, dependent, and transi-

tional condition, to determine the character of its institutions, constituted the doctrine popularly known as "squatter sovereignty." Its assertion led to the dissensions which ultimately resulted in a rupture of the
Democratic party.

Sectional rivalry, the deadly foe of the "domestic tranquillity" and the
"general welfare," which the compact of union was formed to insure,
now interfered, with gigantic efforts to prevent that free migration
which had been promised, and to hinder the decision by climate and the
interests of the inhabitants of the institutions to be established by these
embryo states. Societies were formed in the North to supply money and
send emigrants into the new territories; a famous preacher, addressing
a body of those emigrants, charged them to carry with them to Kansas
"the Bible and Sharpe's rifles." The latter were of course to be leveled
against the bosoms of their Southern brethren who might migrate to the
same territory, but the use to be made of the Bible in the same fraternal
enterprise was left unexplained by the reverend gentleman.

The war-cry employed to train the Northern mind for the deeds contemplated by the agitators was "No extension of slavery!" Was this
sentiment real or feigned? The number of slaves (as has already been
clearly shown) would not have been increased by their transportation
to new territory. It could not be augmented by further importation, for
the law of the land made that piracy. Southern men were the leading
authors of that enactment, and the public opinion of their descendants,
stronger than the law, fully sustained it. The climate of Kansas and Nebraska was altogether unsuited to the negro, and the soil was not adapted
to those productions for which negro labor could be profitably employed.
If, then, any negroes held to service or labor, as provided in the compact
of union, had been transported to those territories, they would have been
such as were bound by personal attachment mutually existing between
master and servant, which would have rendered it impossible for the
former to consider the latter as property convertible into money. As
white laborers, adapted to the climate and its products, flowed into the
country, negro labor would have inevitably become a tax to those who
held it, and their emancipation would have followed that condition, as
it has in all the Northern states, old or new—Wisconsin furnishing the
last example.[1] It may, therefore, be reasonably concluded that the war-

---

[1] Extracts from a speech of Davis of Mississippi in the Senate of the United States,
May 17, 1860: "There is a relation belonging to this species of property, unlike that of the
apprentice or the hired man, which awakens whatever there is of kindness or of nobility of
soul in the heart of him who owns it; this can only be alienated, obscured, or destroyed, by
collecting this species of property into such masses that the owner is not personally ac-

cry was employed by the artful to inflame the minds of the less informed and less discerning, that it was adopted in utter disregard of the means by which negro emancipation might have been peaceably accomplished in the Territories, and with the sole object of obtaining sectional control and personal promotion by means of popular agitation.

The success attending this artifice was remarkable. To such an extent was it made available that Northern indignation was aroused on the absurd accusation that the South had destroyed "that sacred instrument, the compromise of 1820." The internecine war which raged in Kansas for several years was substituted for the promised peace under the operation of the natural laws regulating migration to new countries. For the fratricide which dyed the virgin soil of Kansas with the blood of those who should have stood shoulder to shoulder in subduing the wilderness; for the frauds which corrupted the ballot-box and made the name of election a misnomer—let the authors of "squatters sovereignty" and the fomenters of sectional hatred answer to the posterity for whose peace and happiness the fathers formed the federal compact.

In these scenes of strife were trained the incendiaries who afterward invaded Virginia under the leadership of John Brown; at this time germinated the sentiments which led men of high position to sustain, with their influence and their money, this murderous incursion into the South.[2]

Now was seen the lightning of that storm, the distant muttering of which had been heard so long, and against which the wise and the patriotic had given solemn warning, regarding it as the sign which portended a dissolution of the Union.

Diversity of interests and of opinions among the states of the Confederation had in the beginning presented great difficulties in the way of the formation of a more perfect union. The compact was the result of compromise between the states, at that time generally distinguished as navigating and agricultural, afterward as Northern and Southern. When the first census was taken, in 1790, there was but little numerical difference in the population of these two sections, and (including states

---

quainted with the individuals who compose it. In the relation, however, which can exist in the Northwestern Territories, the mere domestic connection of one, two, or at most half a dozen servants in a family, associating with the children as they grow up, attending upon age as it declines, there can be nothing against which either philanthropy or humanity can make an appeal. Not even the emancipationist could raise his voice; for this is the highroad and the open gate to the condition in which the masters would, from interest, in a few years, desire the emancipation of every one who may thus be taken to the northwestern frontier."

[2] See "Report of Senate Committee of Inquiry into the John Brown Raid."

about to be admitted) there was also an exact equality in the number of states. Each section had, therefore, the power of self-protection, and might feel secure against any danger of federal aggression. If the disturbance of that equilibrium had been the consequence of natural causes, and the government of the whole had continued to be administered strictly for the general welfare, there would have been no ground for complaint of the result.

Under the old Confederation the Southern states had a large excess of territory. The acquisition of Louisiana, of Florida, and of Texas, afterward greatly increased this excess. The generosity and patriotism of Virginia led her, before the adoption of the Constitution, to cede the Northwest Territory to the United States. The Missouri Compromise surrendered to the North all the newly acquired region not included in the state of Missouri, and north of the parallel of thirty-six degrees and a half. The northern part of Texas was in like manner given up by the compromise of 1850; and the North, having obtained, by those successive cessions, a majority in both houses of Congress, took to itself all the territory acquired from Mexico. Thus, by the action of the general government, the means were provided permanently to destroy the original equilibrium between the sections.

Nor was this the only injury to which the South was subjected. Under the power of Congress to levy duties on imports, tariff laws were enacted, not merely "to pay the debts and provide for the common defense and general welfare of the United States," as authorized by the Constitution, but, positively and primarily, for the protection against foreign competition of domestic manufactures. The effect of this was to impose the main burden of taxation upon the Southern people, who were consumers and not manufacturers, not only by the enhanced price of imports, but indirectly by the consequent depreciation in the value of exports, which were chiefly the products of Southern states. The imposition of this grievance was unaccompanied by the consolation of knowing that the tax thus borne was to be paid into the public treasury, for the increase of price accrued mainly to the benefit of the manufacturer. Nor was this all: a reference to the annual appropriations will show that the disbursements made were as unequal as the burdens borne—the inequality in both operating in the same direction.

These causes all combined to direct immigration to the Northern section; and with the increase of its preponderance appeared more and more distinctly a tendency in the federal government to pervert functions delegated to it, and to use them with sectional discrimination against the minority.

The resistance to the admission of Missouri as a state in 1820 was evidently not owing to any moral or constitutional considerations, but merely to political motives; the compensation exacted for granting what was simply a right was the exclusion of the South from equality in the enjoyment of territory which justly belonged equally to both, and which was what the enemies of the South stigmatized as "slave territory," when acquired.

The sectional policy then indicated brought to its support the passions that spring from man's higher nature, but which, like all passions, if misdirected and perverted, become hurtful and, it may be, destructive. The year 1835 was marked by the public agitation for the abolition of that African servitude which existed in the South, which antedated the Union, and had existed in every one of the states that formed the Confederation. By a great misconception of the powers belonging to the general government, and the responsibilities of citizens of the Northern states, many of those citizens were, little by little, brought to the conclusion that slavery was a sin for which *they* were answerable, and that it was the duty of the federal government to abate it. Though, at the date above referred to, numerically so weak, when compared with either of the political parties at the North, as to excite no apprehension of their power for evil, the public demonstrations of the Abolitionists were violently rebuked generally at the North. The party was contemned on account of the character of its leaders, and the more odious because chief among them was an Englishman, one Thompson, who was supposed to be an emissary, whose mission was to prepare the way for a dissolution of the Union. Let us hope that it was reverence for the obligations of the Constitution as the soul of the Union that suggested lurking danger, and rendered the supposed emissary for its destruction so odious that he was driven from a Massachusetts hall where he attempted to lecture. But bodies in motion will overcome bodies at rest, and the unreflecting too often are led by captivating names far from the principles they revere.

Thus, by the activity of the propagandists of abolitionism, and the misuse of the sacred word Liberty, they recruited from the ardent worshipers of that goddess such numbers as gave them in many Northern states the balance of power between the two great political forces that stood arrayed against each other; then and there they came to be courted by both of the great parties, especially by the Whigs, who had become the weaker party of the two. Fanaticism, to which is usually accorded sincerity as an extenuation of its mischievous tenets, affords the best excuse to be offered for the original abolitionists, but that cannot be conceded to the political associates who joined them for the purpose of acquiring power; with them it was but hypocritical cant, intended to deceive. Hence arose the declaration of the existence of an "irrepressible conflict," because of the domestic institutions of sovereign, self-governing states—institutions over which neither the federal government nor the people outside of the limits of such states had any control, and for which they could have no moral or legal responsibility.

Those who are to come after us, and who will look without prejudice or excitement at the record of events which have occurred in our day, will not fail to wonder how men professing and proclaiming such a belief should have so far imposed upon the credulity of the world as to be able to arrogate to themselves the claim of being the special friends of a Union contracted in order to insure "domestic tranquillity" among the people of the states united; that *they* were the advocates of peace, of law, and of order, who, when taking an oath to support and maintain the Constitution, did so with a mental reservation to violate one of the provisions of that Constitution—one of the conditions of the compact—without which the Union could never have been formed. The tone of political morality which could make this possible was well indicated by the toleration accorded in the Senate to the flippant, inconsequential excuse for it given by one of its most eminent exemplars—"Is thy servant a dog, that he should do this thing?"—meaning thereby, not that it would be the part of a dog to *violate* his oath, but to *keep* it in the matter referred to.[3]

---

[3] See Appendix D.

CHAPTER VI:

Agitation Continued—Political Parties: Their Origin, Changes, and Modifications—Some Account of the "Popular Sovereignty," or "Non-Intervention," Theory—Rupture of the Democratic Party—The John Brown Raid—Resolutions Introduced by the Author into the Senate on the Relations of the States, the Federal Government, and the Territories: Their Discussion and Adoption.

THE strife in Kansas and the agitation of the territorial question in Congress and throughout the country continued during nearly the whole of Buchanan's administration, finally culminating in a disruption of the Union. Meantime the changes or modifications which had occurred or were occurring in the great political parties were such as may require a word of explanation to the reader not already familiar with their history.

The names adopted by political parties in the United States have not always been strictly significant of their principles. The old Federal party inclined to nationalism or consolidation, rather than federalization of the states. On the other hand, the party originally known as Republican, and afterward as Democratic, can scarcely claim to have been distinctively or exclusively such in the primary sense of these terms, inasmuch as no party has ever avowed opposition to the general principles of government by the people. The fundamental idea of the Democratic party was that of the sovereignty of the states and the federal, or confederate, character of the Union. Other elements have entered into its organization at different periods, but this has been the vital, cardinal, and abiding principle on which its existence has been perpetuated. The Whig, which succeeded the old Federal party, though by no means identical with it, was in the main favorable to a strong central government, therein antagonizing the transatlantic traditions connected with its name. The "Know-Nothing," or "American" party, which sprang into existence on the decadence of the Whig organization, based upon opposition to the alleged overgrowth of the political influence of naturalized foreigners and of the Roman Catholic Church, had but a brief duration, and after the presidential election of 1856 declined as rapidly as it had risen.

At the period to which this narrative has advanced, the "Free-Soil," which had now assumed the title of "Republican" party, had grown to a magnitude which threatened speedily to obtain entire control of the government. Based, as has been shown, upon sectional rivalry and opposition to the growth of the Southern equally with the Northern states of the Union, it had absorbed within itself not only the abolitionists, who were avowedly agitating for the destruction of the system of negro servitude, but other diverse and heterogeneous elements of opposition to the Democratic party. In the presidential election of 1856, their candidates (Fremont and Dayton) had received 114 of a total of 296 electoral votes, representing a popular vote of 1,341,264 in a total of 4,053,967. The elections of the ensuing year (1857) exhibited a diminution of the so-called Republican strength, and the Thirty-fifth Congress, which convened in December of that year, was decidedly Democratic in both branches. In the course of the next two years, however, the Kansas agitation and another cause, to be presently noticed, had so swollen the ranks of the so-called Republicans that, in the House of Representatives of the Thirty-sixth Congress, which met in December, 1859, neither party had a decided majority, the balance of power being held by a few members still adhering to the virtually extinct Whig and American (or Know-Nothing) organizations, and a still smaller number whose position was doubtful or irregular. More than eight weeks were spent in the election of a Speaker, and a so-called Republican (Pennington of New Jersey) was finally elected by a majority of one vote. The Senate continued to be decidedly Democratic, though with an increase of the so-called Republican minority.

The cause above alluded to, as contributing to the rapid growth of the Republican party after the elections of the year 1857, was the dissension among the Democrats, occasioned by the introduction of the doctrine called by its inventors and advocates "popular sovereignty," or "non-intervention," but more generally and more accurately known as "squatter sovereignty." Its character has already been concisely stated in the preceding chapter. Its origin is generally attributed to General Cass, who is supposed to have suggested it in some general expressions of his celebrated Nicholson letter, written in December, 1847. On May 16 and 17, 1860, it became necessary for me, in a debate in the Senate, to review that letter of Cass. From my remarks then made, the following extract is taken:

The Senator [Douglas] might have remembered, if he had chosen to recollect so unimportant a thing, that I once had to explain to him, ten years ago, the fact that I repudiated the doctrine of that letter at the time it was published, and that the Democracy of Mississippi had well-nigh crucified me for the construction which I placed upon it. There were men mean enough to suspect that the construction I gave to the Nicholson letter was prompted by the confidence and affection I felt for General Taylor. At a subsequent period, however, Mr. Cass thoroughly reviewed it. He uttered (for him) very harsh language against all who had doubted the true construction of his letter, and he construed it just as I had done during the canvass of 1848. It remains only to add that I supported Mr. Cass, not because of the doctrine of the Nicholson letter, but in despite of it; because I believed a Democratic President, with a Democratic Cabinet and Democratic counselors in the two houses of Congress, and he as honest a man as I believed Mr. Cass to be, would be a safer reliance than his opponent, who personally possessed my confidence as much as any man living, but who was of, and must draw his advisers from, a party the tenets of which I believed to be opposed to the interests of the country, as they were to all my political convictions.

I little thought at that time that my advocacy of Mr. Cass upon such grounds as these, or his support by the State of which I am a citizen, would at any future day be quoted as an endorsement of the opinions contained in the Nicholson letter, as those opinions were afterward defined. But it is not only upon this letter, but equally upon the resolutions of the Convention as constructive of that letter, that the Senator rested his argument. [I will here say to the Senator that, if at any time I do him the least injustice, speaking as I do from such notes as I could take while he progressed, I will thank him to correct me.]

But this letter entered into the canvass; there was a doubt about its construction: there were men who asserted that they had positive authority for saying that it meant that the people of a Territory could only exclude slavery when the Territory should form a Constitution and be admitted as a State. This doubt continued to hang over the construction, and it was that doubt alone which secured Mr. Cass the vote of Mississippi. If the true construction had been certainly known, he would have had no chance to get it.

Whatever meaning that generally discreet and conservative statesman, Cass, may have intended to convey, it is not at all probable that he foresaw the extent to which the suggestions would be carried and the consequences that would result from it.

In the organization of a government for California in 1850, the theory was more distinctly advanced, but it was not until after the passage of the Kansas-Nebraska bill, in 1854, that it was fully developed under the plastic and constructive genius of the Hon. Stephen A. Douglas of Illinois. The leading part which that distinguished Senator had borne in the authorship and advocacy of the Kansas-Nebraska bill, which affirmed the right of the people of the territories "to form and regulate their domestic institutions in their own way, subject only to the Constitution of the United States," had aroused against him a violent storm of denunciation in the state which he represented and in other Northern states. He met it very manfully in some respects, and defended his action resolutely, but in so doing was led to make such concessions of principle and to attach such an interpretation to the bill as would have rendered it practically nugatory—a thing to keep the promise of peace to the ear and break it to the hope.

The Constitution expressly confers upon Congress the power to admit new states into the Union, and also to "dispose of and make all needful rules and regulations respecting the territory or other property belonging to the United States." Under these grants of power, the uniform practice of the government had been for Congress to lay off and divide the common territory by convenient boundaries for the formation of future states; to provide executive, legislative, and judicial departments of government for such territories during their temporary and provisional period of pupilage; to delegate to these governments such authority as might be expedient—subject always to the supervision and controlling government of the Congress; and finally, at the proper time, and on the attainment by the territory of sufficient strength and population for self-government, to receive it into the Union on a footing of entire equality with the original states—sovereign and self-governing. All this is no more inconsistent with the true principles of "popular sovereignty," properly understood, than the temporary subjection of a minor to parental control is inconsistent with the doctrines of the *Declaration of Independence,* or the exceptional discipline of a man-of-war or a military post with the principles of republican freedom.

The usual process of transition from a territorial condition to that of a state was, in the first place, by an act of Congress authorizing the inhabitants to elect representatives for a convention to form a state constitution, which was then submitted to Congress for approval and ratification. On such ratification the supervisory control of Congress was withdrawn and the new state authorized to assume its sovereignty, and the inhabitants of the territory became citizens of a state. In the cases of Tennessee in 1796, and Arkansas and Michigan in 1836, the failure of the inhabitants to obtain an "enabling act" of Congress before organizing themselves very nearly caused the rejection of their applications for admission as states, though they were eventually granted on the ground that the subsequent approval and consent of Congress could heal the prior irregularity. The entire control of Congress over the whole subject of territorial government had never been questioned in earlier times. Necessarily conjoined with the power of this protectorate was, of course, the duty of exercising it for the safety of the persons and property of all citizens of the United States permanently or temporarily resident in any part of the domain belonging to the states in common.

Logically carried out, the new theory of "popular sovereignty" would apply to the first adventurous pioneers settling in the wilderness before the organization of any territorial government by Congress, as well as afterward. If "sovereignty" is inherent in a thousand or five thousand persons, there can be no valid ground for denying its existence in a dozen, as soon as they pass beyond the limits of the state governments. The advocates of this novel doctrine, however, if rightly understood, generally disavowed any claim to its application prior to the organization of a territorial government.

The territory legislatures, to which Congress delegated a portion of its power and duty to "make all needful rules and regulations respecting the Territory," were the mere agents of Congress, exercising an authority subject to Congressional supervision and control—an authority conferred only for the sake of convenience, and liable at any time to be revoked and annulled. Yet it is proposed to recognize in these provisional, subordinate, and temporary legislative bodies a power not possessed by Congress itself. This is to claim that the creature is endowed with an authority not possessed by the creator, or that the stream has risen to an elevation above that of its source.

Furthermore, in contending for a power in the territorial legislatures permanently to determine the fundamental, social, and political institutions of the territory, and thereby virtually to prescribe those of the future state, the advocates of "popular sovereignty" were investing those dependent and subsidiary bodies with powers far above any exercised by the legislatures of the fully organized and sovereign states. The authority of the state legislatures is limited, both by the federal Constitution and by the respective state Constitutions from which it is derived. This latter limitation did not and could not exist in the territories.

Strange as it may seem, a theory founded on fallacies so flimsy and leading to conclusions so parodoxical was advanced by eminent and experienced politicians, and accepted by many persons, both in the North and in the South—not so much, perhaps, from intelligent conviction as under the delusive hope that it would afford a satisfactory settlement of the "irrepressible conflict" which had been declared. The terms "popular sovereignty" and "non-intervention" were plausible, specious, and captivating to the public ear. Too many lost sight of the elementary truth that political sovereignty does not reside in unorganized or partially organized masses of individuals, but in the people of regularly and permanently constituted states. As to the "non-intervention" proposed, it meant merely the abnegation by Congress of its duty to protect the inhabitants of the territories subject to its control. The raid into Virginia under John Brown—already notorious as a fanatical partisan leader in the Kansas troubles—occurred in October, 1859, a few weeks before the meeting of the Thirty-sixth Congress. Insignificant in itself and in its immediate results, it afforded a startling revelation of the extent to which sectional hatred and political fanaticism had blinded the conscience of a class of persons in certain states of the Union, forming a party steadily growing stronger in numbers, as well as in activity. Sympathy with its purposes or methods was earnestly disclaimed by the representatives of all parties in Congress; it was charged, on the other hand, that it was only the natural outgrowth of doctrines and sentiments which for some years had been freely avowed on the floors of both houses. A committee of the Senate made a long and laborious investigation of the facts, with no very important or satisfactory results. In their final report, June 15, 1860, accompanying the evidence obtained and submitted, this Committee said:

It [the incursion] was simply the act of lawless ruffians, under the sanction of no public or political authority, distinguishable only from ordinary felonies by the ulterior ends in contemplation by them, and by the fact that the money to maintain the expedition, and the large armament they brought with them, had been contributed and furnished by the citizens of other States of the Union under circumstances that must continue to jeopard the safety and peace of the Southern States, and against which Congress has no power to legislate.

If the several States [adds the Committee], whether from motives of policy or a desire to preserve the peace of the Union, if not from fraternal feeling, do not hold it incumbent on them, after the experience of the country, to guard in future by appropriate legislation against occurrences similar to the one here inquired into, the Committee can find no guarantee elsewhere for the security of peace between the States of the Union.

On February 2, 1860, the author submitted in the Senate of the United States a series of resolutions, afterward slightly modified to read as follows:

1. *Resolved,* That, in the adoption of the Federal Constitution, the States, adopting the same, acted severally as free and independent sovereignties, delegating a portion of their powers to be exercised by the Federal Government for the increased security of each against dangers, *domestic* as well as foreign; and that any intermeddling by any one or more States, or by a combination of their citizens, with the domestic institutions of the others, on any pretext whatever, political, moral, or religious, with the view to their disturbance or subversion, is in violation of the Constitution, insulting to the States so interfered with, endangers their domestic peace and tranquillity—objects for which the Constitution was formed—and, by necessary consequence, tends to weaken and destroy the Union itself.

2. *Resolved*, That negro slavery, as it exists in fifteen States of this Union, composes an important portion of their domestic institutions, inherited from our ancestors, and existing at the adoption of the Constitution, by which it is recognized as constituting an important element in the apportionment of powers among the States, and that no change of opinion or feeling on the part of the non-slaveholding States of the Union in relation to this institution can justify them or their citizens in open covert attacks thereon, with a view to its overthrow; and that all such attacks are in manifest violation of the mutual and solemn pledge to protect and defend each other, given by the States respectively, on entering into the constitutional compact which formed the Union, and are a manifest breach of faith and a violation of the most solemn obligations.

3. *Resolved*, That the Union of these States rests on the equality of rights and privileges among its members, and that it is especially the duty of the Senate, which represents the States in their sovereign capacity, to resist all attempts to discriminate either in relation to persons or property in the Territories, which are the common possessions of the United States, so as to give advantages to the citizens of one State which are not equally assured to those of every other State.

4. *Resolved*, That neither Congress nor a Territorial Legislature, whether by direct legislation or legislation of an indirect and unfriendly character, possesses power to annul or impair the constitutional right of any citizen of the United States to take his slave property into the common Territories, and there hold and enjoy the same while the territorial condition remains.

5. *Resolved*, That if experience should at any time prove that the judiciary and executive authority do not possess means to insure adequate protection to constitutional rights in a Territory, and if the Territorial government shall fail or refuse to provide the necessary remedies for that purpose, it will be the duty of Congress to supply such deficiency.[1]

6. *Resolved*, That the inhabitants of a Territory of the United States, when they rightfully form a Constitution to be admitted as a State into the Union, may then, for the first time, like the people of a State when forming a new Constitution, decide for themselves whether slavery, as a domestic institution, shall be maintained or prohibited within their jurisdiction; and they shall be received into the Union with or without slavery, as their Constitution may prescribe at the time of their admission.

7. *Resolved*, That the provision of the Constitution for the rendition of fugitives from service or labor, "without the adoption of which the Union could not have been formed," and that the laws of 1793 and 1850, which were enacted to secure its execution, and the main features of which, being similar, bear the impress of nearly seventy years of sanction by the highest judicial authority, should be honestly and faithfully observed and maintained by all who enjoy the benefits of our compact of union; and that all acts of individuals or of State Legislatures to defeat the purpose or nullify the requirements of that provision, and the laws made in pursuance of it, are hostile in character, subversive of the Constitution, and revolutionary in their effect.[2]

---

[1] The words, "within the limits of its constitutional powers," were subsequently added to this resolution, on the suggestion of Toombs of Georgia, with the approval of the mover.

[2] The speech of the author, delivered on the 7th of May ensuing, in exposition of these resolutions, will be found in Appendix F.

After a protracted and earnest debate, these resolutions were adopted *seriatim* on May 24 and 25 by a decided majority of the Senate (varying from thirty-three to thirty-six yeas against from two to twenty-one nays), the Democrats, both Northern and Southern, sustaining them unitedly, with the exception of one adverse vote (that of Pugh of Ohio) on the fourth and sixth resolutions. The Republicans all voted against them or refrained from voting at all, except that Teneyck of New Jersey voted for the fifth and seventh of the series. Douglas, the leader if not the author of "popular sovereignty," was absent on account of illness, and there were a few other absentees.

The conclusion of a speech in reply to Douglas, a few days before the vote was taken on these resolutions, is introduced here as the best evidence of the position of the author at that period of excitement and agitation:

CONCLUSION OF REPLY TO MR. DOUGLAS, MAY 17, 1860.

MR. PRESIDENT: I briefly and reluctantly referred, because the subject had been introduced, to the attitude of Mississippi on a former occasion. I will now as briefly say that in 1851, and in 1860, Mississippi was, and is, ready to make every concession which it becomes her to make to the welfare and the safety of the Union. If, on a former occasion, she hoped too much from fraternity, the responsibility for her disappointment rests upon those who failed to fulfill her expectations. She still clings to the Government as our fathers formed it. She is ready to-day and to-morrow, as in her past and though brief yet brilliant history, to maintain that Government in all its power, and to vindicate its honor with all the means she possesses. I say brilliant history; for it was in the very morning of her existence that her sons, on the plains of New Orleans, were announced, in general orders, to have been the admiration of one army and the wonder of the other. That we had a division in relation to the measures enacted in 1850, is true; that the Southern rights men became the minority in the election which resulted, is true; but no figure of speech could warrant the Senator in speaking of them as subdued—as coming to him or anybody else for quarter. I deemed it offensive when it was uttered, and the scorn with which I repelled it at the instant, time has only softened to contempt. Our flag was never borne from the field. We had carried it in the face of defeat, with a knowledge that defeat awaited it; but scarcely had the smoke of the battle passed away which proclaimed another victor, before the general voice admitted that the field again was ours. I have not seen a sagacious, reflecting man, who was cognizant of the events as they transpired at the time, who does not say that, within two weeks after the election, our party was in a majority; and the next election which occurred showed that we possessed the State beyond controversy. How we have wielded that power it is not for me to say. I trust others may see forbearance in our conduct—that, with a determination to insist upon our constitutional rights, then and now, there is an unwavering desire to maintain the Government, and to uphold the Democratic party.

We believe now, as we have asserted on former occasions, that the best hope for the perpetuity of our institutions depends upon the coöperation, the harmony, the zealous action, of the Democratic party. We cling to that party from conviction that its principles and its aims are those of truth and the country, as we cling to the Union for the fulfillment of the purposes for which it was formed. Whenever we shall be taught that the Democratic party is recreant to its principles; whenever we shall learn that it can not be relied upon to maintain the great measures which constitute its vitality—I for one shall be ready to leave it. And so, when we declare our tenacious adherence to the Union, it is the Union of the Constitution. If the compact between the States is to be trampled into the dust; if anarchy is to be substituted for the usurpation and consolidation which threatened the Government at an earlier period; if the Union is to become powerless for the purposes for which it was established, and we are vainly to appeal to it for protection— then, sir, conscious of the rectitude of our course, the justice of our cause, self-reliant, yet humbly, confiding trusting in the arm that guided and protected our fathers, we look beyond the confines of the Union for the maintenance of our rights. An habitual reverence and cherished affection for the Government will bind us to it longer than our interests would suggest or require; but he is a poor student of the world's history who does not understand that communities at last must yield to the dictates of their interests. That the affection, the mutual desire for the mutual good, which existed among our fathers, may be weakened in succeeding generations by the denial of right, and hostile demonstration, until the equality guaranteed but not secured within the Union may be sought for without it, must be evident to even a careless observer of our race. It is time to be up and doing. There is yet time to remove the causes of dissension and alienation which are now distracting, and have for years past divided, the country.

If the Senator correctly described me as having at a former period, against my own preferences and opinions, acquiesced in the decision of my party; if, when I had youth, when physical vigor gave promise of many days, and the future was painted in the colors of hope, I could thus surrender my own convictions, my own prejudices, and coöperate with my political friends according to their views of the best method of promoting the public good—now, when the years of my future can not be many, and experience has sobered the hopeful tints of youth's gilding; when, approaching the evening of life, the shadows are reversed, and the mind turns retrospectively, it is not to be supposed that I would abandon lightly, or idly put on trial, the party to which I have steadily adhered. It is rather to be assumed that conservatism, which belongs to the timidity or caution of increasing years, would lead me to cling to, to be supported by, rather than to cast off, the organization with which I have been so long connected. If I am driven to consider the necessity of separating myself from those old and dear relations, of discarding the accustomed support, under circumstances such as I have described, might not my friends who differ from me pause and inquire whether there is not something involved in it which calls for their careful revision?

I desire no divided flag for the Democratic party.

Our principles are national; they belong to every State of the Union; and, though elections may be lost by their assertion, they constitute the only foundation on which we can maintain power, on which we can again rise to the dignity the Democracy once possessed. Does not the Senator from Illinois see in the sectional character of the vote he received,[3] that his opinions are not acceptable to every portion of the country? Is not the fact that the resolutions adopted by seventeen States, on which the greatest reliance must be placed for Democratic support, are in opposition to the dogma to which he still clings, a warning that, if he persists and succeeds in forcing his theory upon the Democratic party, its days are numbered? We ask only for the Constitution. We ask of the Democracy only from time to time to declare, as current exigencies may indicate, what the Constitution was intended to secure and provide. Our flag bears no new device. Upon its folds our principles are written in living light; all proclaiming the constitutional Union, justice, equality, and fraternity of our ocean-bound domain, for a limitless future.

---

[3] In the Democratic Convention, which had been recently held in Charleston. See the ensuing chapter.

CHAPTER VII: *A Retrospect—Growth of Sectional Rivalry— The Generosity of Virginia—Unequal Accessions of Territory —The Tariff and its Effects—The Republican Convention of 1860, its Resolutions and its Nominations—The Democratic Convention at Charleston, its Divisions and Disruption—The Nominations at Baltimore—The "Constitutional-Union" Party and its Nominees—An Effort in Behalf of Agreement Declined by Douglas—The Election of Lincoln and Hamlin—Proceedings in the South—Evidences of Calmness and Deliberation— Buchanan's Conservatism and the Weakness of his Position —Republican Taunts—The "New York Tribune," etc.*

WHEN, at the close of the war of the Revolution, each of the thirteen colonies that had been engaged in that contest was severally acknowledged by the mother country, Great Britain, to be a free and independent state, the confederation of those states embraced an area so extensive, with climate and products so various, that rivalries and conflicts of interest soon began to be manifested. It required all the power of wisdom and patriotism, animated by the affection engendered by common sufferings and dangers, to keep these rivalries under restraint, and to effect those compromises which it was fondly hoped would insure the harmony and mutual good offices of each for the benefit of all. It was in this spirit of patriotism and confidence in the continuance of such abiding good will as would for all time preclude hostile aggression, that Virginia ceded, for the use of the confederated states, all that vast extent of territory lying north of the Ohio River, out of which have since been formed five states and part of a sixth. The addition of these states has accrued entirely to the preponderance of the Northern section over that from which the donation proceeded, and to the disturbance of that equilibrium which existed at the close of the war of the Revolution.

It may not be out of place here to refer to the fact that the grievances which led to that war were directly inflicted upon the Northern colonies. Those of the South had no material cause of complaint; actuated by sympathy for their Northern brethren, however, and a devotion to the principles of civil liberty and community independence, which they had inherited from their Anglo-Saxon ancestry, and which were set forth in the *Declaration of Independence,* they made common cause with their neighbors, and may, at least, claim to have done their full share in the war that ensued.

[41]

By the exclusion of the South, in 1820, from all that part of the Louisiana purchase lying north of the parallel of thirty-six degrees thirty minutes, and not included in the state of Missouri; by the extension of that line of exclusion to embrace the territory acquired from Texas; and by the appropriation of all the territory obtained from Mexico under the treaty of Guadalupe Hidalgo, both north and south of that line, it may be stated with approximate accuracy that the North had monopolized to herself more than three-fourths of all that had been added to the domain of the United States since the *Declaration of Independence.* This inequality, which began, as has been shown, in the more generous than wise confidence of the South, was employed to obtain for the North the lion's share of what was afterward added at the cost of the public treasure and the blood of patriots. I do not care to estimate the relative proportion contributed by each of the two sections.

Nor was this the only cause that operated to disappoint the reasonable hopes and to blight the fair prospects under which the original compact was formed. The effects of discriminating duties upon imports have been referred to in a former chapter—favoring the manufacturing region, which was the North; burdening the exporting region, which was the South; and so imposing upon the latter a double tax; one, by the increased price of articles of consumption, which, so far as they were of home production, went into the pockets of the manufacturer; the other, by the diminished value of articles of export, which was so much withheld from the pockets of the agriculturist. In like manner the power of the majority section was employed to appropriate to itself an unequal share of the public disbursements. These combined causes—the possession of more territory, more money, and a wider field for the employment of special labor—all served to attract immigration; with increasing population, the greed grew by what it fed on.

This became distinctly manifest when the so-called Republican convention assembled in Chicago on May 16, 1860, to nominate a candidate for the presidency. It was a purely sectional body. There were a few delegates present, representing an insignificant minority in the "border states," Delaware, Maryland, Virginia, Kentucky, and Missouri; but not one from any state south of the celebrated political line of thirty-six degrees thirty minutes. It had been the invariable usage with nominating conventions of all parties to select candidates for the presidency and vice presidency, one from the North and the other from the South, but this assemblage nominated Lincoln of Illinois for the first office, and for the second, Hamlin of Maine—both Northerners. Lincoln, its nominee for the presidency, had publicly announced that the Union "could not permanently endure, half slave and half free." The resolutions adopted contained some carefully worded declarations, well adapted to deceive the credulous who were opposed to hostile aggressions upon the rights of the states. In order to accomplish this purpose, they were compelled to create a fictitious issue, in denouncing what they described as "the new dogma that the Constitution, of its own force, carries slavery into any or all of the Territories of the United States"—a "dogma" which had never been held or declared by anybody, and which had no existence outside of their own assertion. There was enough in connection with the nomination to assure the most fanatical foes of the Constitution that their ideas would be the rule and guide of the party.

Meantime, the Democratic party had held a convention, composed as usual of delegates from all the states. They met in Charleston, South Carolina, on April 23d, but an unfortunate disagreement with regard to the declaration of principles to be set forth rendered a nomination impracticable. Both divisions of the convention adjourned, and met again in Baltimore in June. Then, having finally failed to come to an agreement, they separated and made their respective nominations apart. Douglas of Illinois was nominated by the friends of the doctrine of "popular sovereignty," with Fitzpatrick of Alabama for the vice presidency. Both these gentlemen at that time were Senators from their respective states. Fitzpatrick promptly declined the nomination, and his place was filled with the name of Herschel V. Johnson, a distinguished citizen of Georgia.

The convention representing the conservative, or state-rights, wing of the Democratic party (the president of which was the Hon. Caleb Cushing of Massachusetts) on the first ballot unanimously made choice of John C. Breckinridge of Kentucky, then Vice-President of the United States, for the first office, and with like unanimity selected General Joseph Lane, then a Senator from Oregon, for the second. The resolutions of each of these two conventions denounced the action and policy of the Abolition party, as subversive of the Constitution, and revolutionary in their tendency.

Another convention was held in Baltimore about the same period[1] by those who still adhered to the old Whig party, reënforced by the remains of the "American" organization, and perhaps some others. This convention also consisted of delegates from all the states and, repudiating all geographical and sectional issues, and declaring it to be "both the

---

[1] May 19, 1860.

part of patriotism and of duty to recognize no political principle other than the Constitution of the country, the Union of the States, and the enforcement of the laws," pledged itself and its supporters "to maintain, protect, and defend, separately and unitedly, those great principles of public liberty and national safety against all enemies at home and abroad." Its nominees were John Bell of Tennessee and Edward Everett of Massachusetts, both of whom had long been distinguished members of the Whig party.

The people of the United States now had four rival tickets presented to them by as many contending parties, whose respective position and principles on the great and absorbing question at issue may be briefly recapitulated as follows:

1. The "Constitutional-Union" party, as it was now termed, led by Bell and Everett, which ignored the territorial controversy altogether, and contented itself, as above stated, with a simple declaration of adherence to "the Constitution, the Union, and the enforcement of the laws."

2. The party of "popular sovereignty," headed by Douglas and Johnson, who affirmed the right of the people of the territories, in their territorial condition, to determine their own organic institutions, independently of the control of Congress; denying the power or duty of Congress to protect the persons or property of individuals or minorities in such territories against the action of majorities.

3. The State-Rights party, supporting Breckinridge and Lane, who held that the territories were open to citizens of all the states, with their property, without any inequality or discrimination, and that it was the duty of the general government to protect both persons and property from aggression in the territories subject to its control. At the same time they admitted and asserted the right of the people of a territory, on emerging from their territorial condition to that of a state, to determine what should then be their domestic institutions, as well as all other questions of personal or proprietary right, without interference by Congress, and subject only to the limitations and restrictions prescribed by the Constitution of the United States.

4. The so-called Republicans, presenting the names of Lincoln and Hamlin, who held, in the language of one of their leaders,[2] that "slavery can exist only by virtue of municipal law"; and there was "no law for it in the Territories, and no power to enact one"; and that Congress was "bound to prohibit it in or exclude it from any and every Federal Terri-

---

[2]Horace Greeley, *The American Conflict,* Vol. I, p. 322.

tory." In other words, they asserted the right and duty of Congress to exclude the citizens of half the states of the Union from the territory belonging in common to all, unless on condition of the sacrifice or abandonment of their property recognized by the Constitution—indeed, of the only species of their property distinctly and specifically recognized as such by that instrument.

On the vital question underlying the whole controversy—that is, whether the federal government should be a government of the whole for the benefit of all its equal members, or (if it should continue to exist at all) a sectional government for the benefit of a part—the first three of the parties above described were in substantial accord as against the fourth. If they could or would have acted unitedly, they could certainly have carried the election, and averted the catastrophe which followed. Nor were efforts wanting to effect such a union.

Bell, the Whig candidate, was a highly respectable and experienced statesman, who had filled many important offices, both state and federal. He was not ambitious to the extent of coveting the presidency, and he was profoundly impressed by the danger which threatened the country. Breckinridge had not anticipated, and it may safely be said did not eagerly desire, the nomination. He was young enough to wait, and patriotic enough to be willing to do so, if the weal of the country required it. Thus much I may confidently assert of both those gentlemen, for each of them authorized me to say that he was willing to withdraw, if an arrangement could be effected by which the divided forces of the friends of the Constitution could be concentrated upon some one more generally acceptable than either of the three who had been presented to the country. When I made this announcement to Douglas—with whom my relations had always been such as to authorize the assurance that he could not consider it as made in an unfriendly spirit—he replied that the scheme proposed was impracticable, because his friends, mainly Northern Democrats, if he were withdrawn, would join in the support of Lincoln, rather than of any one that should supplant him (Douglas) ; that he was in the hands of his friends, and was sure they would not accept the proposition.

It needed but little knowledge of the status of parties in the several states to foresee a probable defeat if the conservatives were to continue divided into three parts, and the aggressives were to be held in solid column. But angry passions, which are always bad counselors, had been aroused, and hopes were still cherished, which proved to be illusory.

The result was the election, by a minority, of a President whose avowed principles were necessarily fatal to the harmony of the Union.

Of 303 electoral votes, Lincoln received 180, but of the popular suffrage of 4,676,853 votes, which the electors represented, he obtained only 1,866,352—something over a third of the votes. This discrepancy was owing to the system of voting by "general ticket"—that is, casting the state votes as a unit, whether unanimous or nearly equally divided. Thus, in New York, the total popular vote was 675,156, of which 362,646 were cast for the so-called Republican (or Lincoln) electors, and 312,510 against them. New York was entitled to 35 electoral votes. Divided on the basis of the popular vote, 19 of these would have been cast for Lincoln, and 16 against him. But under the "general ticket" system the entire 35 votes were cast for the Republican candidates, thus giving them not only the full strength of the majority in their favor, but that of the great minority against them superadded. So of other Northern states, in which the small majorities on one side operated with the weight of entire unanimity, while the virtual unanimity in the Southern states, on the other side, counted nothing more than a mere majority would have done.

The manifestations which followed this result in the Southern states did not proceed, as has been unjustly charged, from chagrin at their defeat in the election, or from any personal hostility to the President-elect, but from the fact that they recognized in him the representative of a party professing principles destructive to "their peace, their prosperity, and their domestic tranquillity." The long-suppressed fire burst into frequent flame, but it was still controlled by that love of the Union which the South had illustrated in every battlefield, from Boston to New Orleans. Still it was hoped against hope that some adjustment might be made to avert the calamities of a practical application of the theory of an "irrepressible conflict." Few, if any, then doubted the right of a state to withdraw its grants delegated to the federal government, or in other words to secede from the Union; in the South, however, this was generally regarded as the remedy of last resort, to be applied only when ruin or dishonor was the alternative. No rash or revolutionary action was taken by the Southern states, but the measures adopted were considerate, and executed advisedly and deliberately. The presidential election occurred (as far as the popular vote, which determined the result, was concerned) in November, 1860. Most of the state legislatures convened soon afterward in regular session. In some cases special sessions were convoked for the purpose of calling state conventions—the recognized representatives of the sovereign will of the people—to be elected expressly for the purpose of taking such action as should be considered needful and proper under the existing circumstances.

These conventions, as it was always held and understood, possessed all the power of the people assembled in mass; therefore it was conceded that they, and they only, could take action for the withdrawal of a state from the Union. The consent of the respective states to the formation of the Union had been given through such conventions, and it was only by the same authority that it could properly be revoked. The time required for this deliberate and formal process precludes the idea of hasty or passionate action, and none who admit the primary power of the people to govern themselves can consistently deny its validity and binding obligation upon every citizen of the several states. Not only was there ample time for calm consideration among the people of the South, but for due reflection by the general government and the people of the Northern states.

President Buchanan was in the last year of his administration. His freedom from sectional asperity, his long life in the public service, and his peace-loving and conciliatory character, were all guarantees against his precipitating a conflict between the federal government and any of the states; the feeble power that he possessed in the closing months of his term to mold the policy of the future was, however, painfully evident. Like all who had intelligently and impartially studied the history of the formation of the Constitution, he held that the federal government had no rightful power to coerce a state. Like the sages and patriots who had preceded him in the high office that he filled, he believed that "our Union rests upon public opinion, and can never be cemented by the blood of its citizens shed in civil war. If it cannot live in the affections of the people, it must one day perish. Congress may possess many means of preserving it by conciliation, but the sword was not placed in their hand to preserve it by force."[3]

Ten years before, Calhoun, addressing the Senate with all the earnestness of his nature, and with that sincere desire to avert the danger of disunion which those who knew him best never doubted, had asked the emphatic question, "How can the Union be saved?" He answered his question thus:

There is but one way by which it can be [saved] with any certainty; and that is by a full and final settlement, on the principles of justice, of all the questions at issue between the sections. The South asks for justice—simple justice—and less

[3]Message of December 3, 1860.

she ought not to take. She has no compromise to offer but the Constitution, and no concession or surrender to make. . . .

Can this be done? Yes, easily! Not by the weaker party; for it can of itself do nothing—not even protect itself—but by the stronger. . . . But will the North agree to do this? It is for her to answer this question. But, I will say, she can not refuse if she has half the love of the Union which she professes to have, nor without exposing herself to the charge that her love of power and aggrandizement is far greater than her love of the Union.

During the ten years that intervened between the date of this speech and the message of Buchanan cited above, the progress of sectional discard and the tendency of the stronger section to unconstitutional aggression had been fearfully rapid. With very rare exceptions, there were none in 1850 who claimed the right of the federal government to apply coercion to a state. In 1860 men had grown to be familiar with threats of driving the South into submission to any act that the government, in the hands of a Northern majority, might see fit to perform. During the canvass of that year, demonstrations had been made by quasi-military organizations in various parts of the North, which looked unmistakably to purposes widely different from those enunciated in the preamble to the Constitution, and to the employment of means not authorized by the powers which the states had delegated to the federal government.

Well-informed men still remembered that, in the convention which framed the Constitution, a proposition was made to authorize the employment of force against a delinquent state, on which Madison remarked that "the use of force against a state would look more like a declaration of war than an infliction of punishment, and would probably be considered by the party attacked as a dissolution of all previous compacts by which it might have been bound." The convention expressly refused to confer the power proposed, and the clause was lost. While, therefore, in 1860, many violent men, appealing to passion and the lust of power, were inciting the multitude, and preparing Northern opinion to support a war waged against the Southern states in the event of their secession, there were others who took a different view of the case. Notable among such was the *New York Tribune,* which had been the organ of the abolitionists, and which now declared that, "if the cotton States wished to withdraw from the Union, they should be allowed to do so"; that "any attempt to compel them to remain, by force, would be contrary to the principles of the *Declaration of Independence* and to the fundamental ideas upon which human liberty is based"; and that, "if the *Declaration of Independence* justified the secession from the

British Empire of three millions of subjects in 1776, it was not seen why it would not justify the secession of five millions of Southerners from the Union in 1861." Again, it was said by the same journal that "sooner than compromise with the South and abandon the Chicago platform," they would "let the Union slide." Taunting expressions were freely used—as, for example, "If the Southern people wish to leave the Union we will do our best to forward their views."

All this, it must be admitted, was quite consistent with the oft-repeated declaration that the Constitution was a "covenant with hell," which stood as the caption of a leading abolitionist paper of Boston. That signs of coming danger so visible, evidences of hostility so unmistakable, disregard of constitutional obligations so wanton, taunts and jeers so bitter and insulting, should serve to increase excitement in the South, was a consequence flowing as much from reason and patriotism as from sentiment. He must have been ignorant of human nature who did not expect such a tree to bear fruits of discord and division.

CHAPTER VIII: *Conference with the Governor of Mississippi —The Author Censured as "Too Slow"—Summons to Washington—Interview with the President—His Message— Movements in Congress—The Triumphant Majority—The Crittenden Proposition—Speech of the Author on Green's Resolution—The Committee of Thirteen—Failure to Agree—The "Republicans" Responsible for the Failure—Proceedings in the House of Representatives—Futility of Efforts for an Adjustment—The Old Year Closes in Clouds.*

IN NOVEMBER, 1860, after the result of the presidential election was known, the governor of Mississippi, having issued his proclamation convoking a special session of the legislature to consider the propriety of calling a convention, invited the Senators and Representatives of the state in Congress, to meet him for consultation as to the character of the message he should send to the legislature when assembled.

While holding, in common with my political associates, that the right of a state to secede was unquestionable, I differed from most of them as to the probability of our being permitted peaceably to exercise the right. The knowledge acquired by the administration of the War Department for four years, and by the chairmanship of the Military Committee of the Senate at two different periods, still longer in combined duration, had shown me the entire lack of preparation for war in the South. The foundries and armories were in the Northern states, and there were stored all the new and improved weapons of war. In the arsenals of the Southern states were to be found only arms of the old and rejected models. The South had no manufactories of powder, and no navy to protect our harbors, no merchant ships for foreign commerce. It was evident to me, therefore, that, if we should be involved in war, the odds against us would be far greater than what was due merely to our inferiority in population. Believing that secession would be the precursor of war between the states, I was consequently slower and more reluctant than others, who entertained a different opinion, to resort to that remedy.

While engaged in the consultation with the governor just referred to, a telegraphic message was handed to me from two members of Buchanan's cabinet, urging me to proceed "immediately" to Washington. This dispatch was laid before the governor and the members of Congress from the state who were in conference with him, and it was decided that

I should comply with the summons. I was afterward informed that my associates considered me "too slow," and they were probably correct in the belief that I was behind the general opinion of the people of the state as to the propriety of prompt secession.[1]

On arrival at Washington I found, as had been anticipated, that my presence there was desired on account of the influence which it was supposed I might exercise with the President (Buchanan) in relation to his forthcoming message to Congress. On paying my respects to the President, he told me that he had finished the rough draft of his message, but that it was still open to revision and amendment, and that he would like to read it to me. He did so, and very kindly accepted all the modifications which I suggested. The message was, however, afterward somewhat changed, and with great deference to the wisdom and statesmanship of its author, I must say that, in my judgment, the last alterations were unfortunate—so much so that, when it was read in the Senate, I was reluctantly constrained to criticise it. Compared, however, with documents of the same class which have since been addressed to the Congress of the United States, the reader of presidential messages must regret that it was not accepted by Buchanan's successors as a model, and that his views of the Constitution had not been adopted as a guide in the subsequent action of the federal government.

The popular movement in the South was tending steadily and rapidly toward the secession of those known as "planting states"; yet, when Congress assembled on December 3, 1860, the representatives of the people of all those states took their seats in the House, and they were all represented in the Senate, except South Carolina, whose Senators had tendered their resignation to the government immediately on the an-

---

[1] The following extract from a letter of the Hon. O. R. Singleton, then a Representative of Mississippi in the United States Congress, in regard to the subject treated, is herewih annexed: "CANTON, MISSISSIPPI, July 14, 1877.

*　　*　　*　　*

"In 1860, about the time the ordinance of secession was passed by the South Carolina Convention, and while Mississippi, Alabama, and other Southern States were making active preparations to follow her example, a conference of the Mississippi delegation in Congress, Senators and Representatives, was asked for by Governor J. J. Pettus, for consultation as to the course Mississippi ought to take in the premises.

"The meeting took place in the fall of 1860, at Jackson, the capital, the whole delegation being present, with perhaps the exception of one Representative.

"The main question for consideration was: 'Shall Mississippi, as soon as her Convention can meet, pass an ordinance of secession, thus placing herself by the side of South Carolina, regardless of the action of other States; or shall she endeavor to hold South Carolina in check, and delay action herself, until other States can get ready, through their conventions, to unite with them, and then, on a given day and at a given hour, by concert of action, all the States willing to do so, secede in a body?'

"Upon the one side, it was argued that South Carolina could not be induced to delay

nouncement of the result of the presidential election. Hopes were still cherished that the Northern leaders would appreciate the impending peril, would cease to treat the warnings, so often given, as idle threats, would refrain from the bravado, so often and so unwisely indulged, of ability "to whip the South" in thirty, sixty, or ninety days, and would address themselves to the more manly purpose of devising means to allay the indignation, and quiet the apprehensions, whether well founded or not, of their Southern brethren. But the debates of that session manifest, on the contrary, the arrogance of a triumphant party, and the determination to reap to the uttermost the full harvest of a party victory.

Crittenden of Kentucky, the oldest and one of the most honored members of the Senate,[2] introduced into that body a joint resolution proposing certain amendments to the Constitution—among them the restoration and incorporation into the Constitution of the geographical line of the Missouri Compromise, with other provisions, which it was hoped might be accepted as the basis for an adjustment of the difficulties rapidly hurrying the Union to disruption. But the earnest appeals of that venerable statesman were unheeded by Senators of the so-called Republican party. Action upon his proposition was postponed from time to time, on

---

action a single moment beyond the meeting of her Convention, and that our fate should be hers, and to delay action would be to have her crushed by the Federal Government; whereas, by the earliest action possible, we might be able to avert this calamity. On the other side, it was contended that delay might bring the Federal Government to consider the emergency of the case, and perhaps a compromise could be effected; but, if not, then the proposed concert of action would at least give dignity to the movement, and present an undivided Southern front.

"The debate lasted many hours, and Mr. Davis, with perhaps one other gentleman in that conference, opposed immediate and separate State action, declaring himself opposed to secession as long as the hope of a peaceable remedy remained. He did not believe we ought to precipitate the issue, as he felt certain from his knowledge of the people, North and South, that, once there was a clash of arms, the contest would be one of the most sanguinary the world had ever witnessed.

"A majority of the meeting decided that no delay should be interposed to separate State action, Mr. Davis being on the other side; but, after the vote was taken and the question decided, Mr. Davis declared he would stand by whatever action the Convention representing the sovereignty of the State of Mississippi might think proper to take.

"After the conference was ended, several of its members were dissatisfied with the course of Mr. Davis, believing that he was entirely opposed to secession, and was seeking to delay action upon the part of Mississippi, with the hope that it might be entirely averted.

"In some unimportant respects my memory may be at fault, and possibly some of the inferences drawn may be incorrect; but every material statement made, I am sure, is true, and if need be, can be, easily substantiated by other persons.

"Very respectfully, your obedient servant,"

(Signed)   "O. R. SINGLETON."

[2] Crittenden had been a life-long Whig. His first entrance into the Senate was in 1817, and he was a member of that body at various periods during the ensuing forty-four years. He was Attorney General in the Whig cabinets of both General Harrison and Fillmore, and supported the Bell and Everett ticket in 1860.

one pretext or another, until the last day of the session—when seven states had already withdrawn from the Union and established a confederation of their own—and it was then defeated by a majority of one vote.[8]

Meantime, among other propositions made in the Senate were two introduced early in the session, which it may be proper specially to mention. One of these was a resolution offered by Powell of Kentucky, which, after some modification by amendment, when finally acted upon, had taken the following form:

Resolved, That so much of the Presdent's message as relates to the present agitated and distracted condition of the country, and the grievances between the slaveholding and the non-slaveholding States, be referred to a special committee of thirteen members, and that said committee be instructed to inquire into the present condition of the country, and report by bill or otherwise.

The other was a resolution offered by Green of Missouri, to the following effect:

Resolved, That the Committee on the Judiciary be instructed to inquire into the propriety of providing by law for establishing an armed police force at all necessary points along the line separating the slaveholding States from the non-slaveholding States, for the purpose of maintaining the general peace between those States, of preventing the invasion of one State by citizens of another, and also for the efficient execution of the fugitive-slave laws.

In the discussion of these two resolutions I find, in the proceedings of the Senate on December 10th, as reported in the *Congressional Globe,* some remarks of my own, the reproduction of which will serve to exhibit my position at that period—a position which has since been often misrepresented:

Mr. President, if the political firmament seemed to me dark before, there has been little in the discussion this morning to cheer or illumine it. When the proposition of the Senator from Kentucky was presented—not very hopeful of a good result—I was yet willing to wait and see what developments it might produce. This morning, for the first time, it has been considered; and what of encouragement have we received? One Senator proposes, as a cure for the public evil impending over us, to invest the Federal Government with such physical power as properly belongs to monarchy alone; another announces that his constituents cling to the Federal Government, if its legislative favors and its Treasury secure works of improvement and the facilities which they desire; while another rises to point out that the evils of the land are of a party character. Sir, we have fallen upon evil times indeed, if the great convulsion which now shakes the body-politic

---

[8] The vote was nineteen yeas to twenty nays; total, thirty-nine. As the consent of two-thirds of each house is necessary to propose an amendment for action by the states, twenty-six of the votes cast in the Senate would have been necessary to sustain the proposition. It actually failed, therefore, by seven votes, instead of one.

to its center is to be dealt with by such nostrums as these. Men must look more deeply, must rise to a higher altitude; like patriots they must confront the danger face to face, if they hope to relieve the evils which now disturb the peace of the land, and threaten the destruction of our political existence.

First of all, we must inquire what is the cause of the evils which beset us? The diagnosis of the disease must be stated before we are prepared to prescribe. Is it the fault of our legislation here? If so, then it devolves upon us to correct it, and we have the power. Is it the defect of the Federal organization, of the fundamental law of our Union? I hold that it is not. Our fathers, learning wisdom from the experiments of Rome and of Greece—the one a consolidated republic, and the other strictly a confederacy—and taught by the lessons of our own experiment under the Confederation, came together to form a Constitution for "a more perfect union," and, in my judgment, made the best government which has ever been instituted by man. It only requires that it should be carried out in the spirit in which it was made, that the circumstances under which it was made should continue, and no evil can arise under this Government for which it has not an appropriate remedy. Then it is outside of the Government—elsewhere than to its Constitution or to its administration—that we are to look. Men must not creep in the dust of partisan strife and seek to make points against opponents as the means of evading or meeting the issues before us. The fault is not in the form of the Government, nor does the evil spring from the manner in which it has been administered. Where, then, is it? It is that our fathers formed a Government for a Union of friendly States; and though under it the people have been prosperous beyond comparison with any other whose career is recorded in the history of man, still that Union of friendly States has changed its character, and sectional hostility has been substituted for the fraternity in which the Government was founded.

I do not intend here to enter into a statement of grievances; I do not intend here to renew that war of crimination which for years past has disturbed the country, and in which I have taken a part perhaps more zealous than useful; but I call upon all men who have in their hearts a love of the Union, and whose service is not merely that of the lip, to look the question calmly but fully in the face, that they may see the true cause of our danger, which, from my examination, I believe to be that a sectional hostility has been substituted for a general fraternity, and thus the Government rendered powerless for the ends for which it was instituted. The hearts of a portion of the people have been perverted by that hostility, so that the powers delegated by the compact of union are regarded not as means to secure the welfare of all, but as instruments for the destruction of a part—the minority section. How, then have we to provide a remedy? By strengthening this Government? By instituting physical force to overawe the States, to coerce the people living under them as members of sovereign communities to pass under the yoke of the Federal Government? No, sir; I would have this Union severed into thirty-three fragments sooner than have that great evil befall constitutional liberty and representative government. Our Government is an agency of delegated and strictly limited powers. Its founders did not look to its preservation by force; but the chain they wove to bind these States together was one of love and mutual good offices. They had broken the fetters of despotic power; they had separated themselves from the mother-country upon the question of community independence; and their sons will be degenerate indeed if, clinging to the mere name and forms of free government, they forge and rivet upon their posterity the fetters which their ancestors broke. . . .

The remedy for these evils is to be found in the patriotism and the affection of the people, if it exists; and, if it does not exist, it is far better, instead of attempting to preserve a forced and therefore fruitless Union, that we should peacefully part and each pursue his separate course. It is not to this side of the Chamber that we should look for propositions; it is not here that we can ask for remedies. Complaints, with much amplitude of specification, have gone forth from the members on this side of the Chamber heretofore. It is not to be expected that they will be renewed, for the people have taken the subject into their own hands. States, in their sovereign capacity, have now resolved to judge of the infractions of the Federal compact, and of the mode and measure of redress. All we can usefully or properly do is to send to the people, thus preparing to act for themselves, evidence of error, if error there be; to transmit to them the proofs of kind feeling, if it actuates the Northern section, where they now believe there is only hostility. If we are mistaken as to your feelings and purposes, give a substantial proof, that here may begin that circle which hence may spread out and cover the whole land with proofs of fraternity, of a reaction in public sentiment, and the assurance of a future career in conformity with the principles and purposes of the Constitution. All else is idle. I would not give the parchment on which the bill would be written that is to secure our constitutional rights within the limits of a State, where the people are all opposed to the execution of that law. It is a truism in free governments that laws rest upon public opinions, and fall powerless before its determined opposition.

The time has passed, sir, when appeals might profitably be made to sentiment. The time has come when men must of necessity reason, assemble facts, and deal with current events. I may be permitted in this to correct an error into which one of my friends fell this morning, when he impressed on us the great value of our Union as measured by the amount of time and money and blood which were spent to form this Union. It cost very little time, very little money, and no blood. It was one of the most peaceful transactions that mark the pages of human history. Our fathers fought the war of the Revolution to maintain the rights asserted in their *Declaration of Independence*.

MR. POWELL: The Senator from Mississippi will allow me to say that I spoke of the Government, not of the Union. I said time and money and blood had been required to form the Government.

MR. DAVIS: The Government is the machinery established by the Constitution; it is the agency created by the States when they formed the Union. Our fathers, I was proceeding to say, having fought the war of the Revolution, and achieved their independence—each State for itself, each State standing out an integral part, each State separately recognized by the parent Government of Great Britain—these States as independent sovereignties entered into confederate alliance. After having tried the Confederation and found it to be a failure, they, of their own accord, came peacefully together, and in a brief period made a Constitution, which was referred to each State and voluntarily ratified by each State that entered the Union; little time, little money, and no blood being expended to form this Government, the machine for making the Union useful and beneficial. Blood, much and precious, was expended to vindicate and to establish community independence, and the great American idea that all governments rest on the consent of the governed, and that the people may at their will alter or abolish their government, however or by whomsoever instituted.

But our existing Government is not the less sacred to me because it was not sealed with blood. I honor it the more because it was the free-will offering of men who chose to live together. It rooted in fraternity, and fraternity supported its trunk and all its branches. Every bud and leaflet depends entirely on the nurture it receives from fraternity as the root of the tree. When that is destroyed, the trunk decays, and the branches wither, and the leaves fall; and the shade it was designed to give has passed away for ever. I cling not merely to the name and form, but to the spirit and purpose of the Union which our fathers made. It was for domestic tranquillity; not to organize within one State lawless bands to commit raids upon another. It was to provide for the common defense; not to disband armies and navies, lest they should serve the protection of one section of the country better than another. It was to bring the forces of all the States together to achieve a common object, upholding each the other in amity, and united to repel exterior force. All the custom-house obstructions existing between the States were destroyed; the power to regulate commerce transferred to the General Government. Every barrier to the freest intercourse was swept away. Under the Confederation it had been secured as a right to each citizen to have free transit over all the other States; and under the Union it was designed to make this more perfect. Is it enjoyed? Is it not denied? Do we not have mere speculative questions of what is property raised in defiance of the clear intent of the Constitution, offending as well against its letter as against its whole spirit? This must be reformed, or the Government our fathers instituted is destroyed. I say, then, shall we cling to the mere forms or idolize the name of Union, when its blessings are lost, after its spirit has fled? Who would keep a flower, which had lost its beauty and its fragrance, and in their stead had formed a seed-vessel containing the deadliest poison? Or, to drop the figure, who would consent to remain in alliance with States which used the power thus acquired to invade his tranquility, to impair his defense, to destroy his peace and security? Any community would be stronger standing in an isolated position, and using its revenues to maintain its own physical force, than if allied with those who would thus war upon its prosperity and domestic peace; and reason, pride, self-interest, and the apprehension of secret, constant danger would impel to separation.

I do not comprehend the policy of a Southern Senator who would seek to change the whole form of our Government, and substitute Federal force for State obligation and authority. Do we want a new Government that is to overthrow the old? Do we wish to erect a central Colossus, wielding at discretion the military arm, and exercising military force over the people and the States? This is not the Union to which we were invited; and so carefully was this guarded that, when our fathers provided for using force to put down insurrection, they required that the fact of the insurrection should be communicated by the authorities of the State before the President could interpose. When it was proposed to give to Congress power to execute the laws against a delinquent State, it was refused on the ground that that would be making war on the States; and, though I know the good purpose of my honorable friend from Missouri is only to give protection to constitutional rights, I fear his proposition is to rear a monster, which will break the feeble chain provided, and destroy rights it was intended to guard. That military Government which he is about to institute, by passing into hostile hands, becomes a weapon for his destruction, not for his protection. All dangers which we may be called upon to confront as independent communities are light, in my estimation, compared with that which would hang over us if this Federal Government had such physical force; if its character was changed from a representative agent of States to a central Government, with a military power to be used at discretion against the States. To-day it may be the idea that it will be used against some State which nullifies the Constitution and the laws; some State which passes laws to obstruct or repeal the laws of the United States; some State which, in derogation of our rights of transit under the Constitution, passes laws to punish a citizen found there with property recognized by the Constitution of the United States, but prohibited by the laws of that State.

But how long might it be before that same military force would be turned against the minority section which had sought its protection; and that minority thus become mere subjugated provinces under the great military government that it had thus contributed to establish? The minority, incapable of aggression, is, of necessity, always on the defensive, and often the victim of the desertion of its followers and the faithlessness of its allies. It therefore must maintain, not destroy, barriers.

I do not know that I fully appreciate the purpose of my friend from Missouri; whether, when he spoke of establishing military posts along the borders of the States, and arming the Federal Government with adequate physical power to enforce constitutional rights (I suppose he meant obligations), he meant to confer upon this Federal Government a power which it does not now possess to coerce a State. If he did, then, in the language of Mr. Madison, he is providing, not for a union of States, but for the destruction of States; he is providing, under the name of Union, to carry on a war against States; and I care not whether it be against Massachusetts or Missouri, it is equally objectionable to me; and I will resist it alike in the one case and in the other, as subversive of the great principle on which our Government rests; as a heresy to be confronted at its first presentation, and put down there, lest it grow into proportions which will render us powerless before it.

The theory of our Constitution, Mr. President, is one of peace, of equality of sovereign States. It was made by States and made for States; and for greater assurance they passed an amendment, doing that which was necessarily implied by the nature of the instrument, as it was a mere instrument of grants. But, in the abundance of caution, they declared that everything which had not been delegated was reserved to the States, or to the people—that is, to the State governments as instituted by the people of each State, or to the people in their sovereign capacity.

I need not, then, go on to argue from the history and nature of our Government that no power of coercion exists in it. It is enough for me to demand the clause of the Constituton which confers the power. If it is not there, the Government does not possess it. That is the plain construction of the Constitution—made plainer, if possible, by its amendment.

This Union is dear to me as a Union of fraternal States. It would lose its value if I had to regard it as a Union held together by physical force. I would be happy to know that every State now felt that fraternity which made this Union possible; and, if that evidence could go out, if evidence satisfactory to the people of the South could be given that that feeling existed in the hearts of the Northern people, you might burn your statute-books and we would cling to the Union still. But it is because of their conviction that hostility, and not fraternity, now exists in the hearts of the people, that they are looking to their reserved rights and to their independent powers for their own protection. If there be any good, then, which we can do, it is by sending evidence to them of that which I fear does not exist— the purpose of your constituents to fulfill in the spirit of justice and fraternity all their constitutional obligations. If you can submit to them that evidence, I feel confident that, with the assurance that aggression is henceforth to cease, will terminate all the measures for defense. Upon you of the majority section it depends to restore peace and perpetuate the Union of equal States; upon us of the minority section rests the duty to maintain our equality and community rights; and the means in one case or the other must be such as each can control.

The resolution of Powell was eventually adopted on the 18th of December, and on the 20th the Committee was appointed, consisting of Powell and Crittenden of Kentucky, Hunter of Virginia, Toombs of Georgia, Davis of Mississippi, Douglas of Illinois, Bigler of Pennsylvania, Rice of Minnesota, Collamer of Vermont, Seward of New York, Wade of Ohio, Doolittle of Wisconsin, and Grimes of Iowa. The first five of the list, as here enumerated, were Southern men; the next three were Northern Democrats, or Conservatives; the last five, Northern Republicans, so called.

The supposition was that any measure agreed upon by the representatives of the three principal divisions of public opinion would be approved by the Senate and afterward ratified by the House of Representatives. The Committee therefore determined that a majority of each of its three divisions should be required in order to adopt any proposition presented. The Southern members declared their readiness to accept any terms that would secure the honor of the Southern states and guarantee their future safety. The Northern Democrats and Crittenden generally coöperated with the State-Rights Democrats of the South; but the so-called Republican Senators of the North rejected every proposition which it was hoped might satisfy the Southern people, and check the progress of the secession movement. After fruitless efforts, continued for some ten days, the committee determined to report the journal of their proceedings, and announce their inability to attain any satisfactory conclusion. This report was made on December 31—the last day of that memorable and fateful year, 1860.

Subsequently, on the floor of the Senate, Douglas, who had been a member of the committee, called upon the opposite side to state what they were willing to do. He referred to the fact that they had rejected every proposition that promised pacification; stated that Toombs of Georgia and Davis of Mississippi, as members of the committee, had, been willing to renew the Missouri Compromise, as a measure of conciliation, but had met no responsive willingness on the part of their associates of the opposition; he pressed the point that, as they had rejected every overture made by the friends of peace, it was now incumbent upon them to make a positive and affirmative declaration of their purpose.

Seward of New York, as we have seen, was a member of that committee—the man who, in 1858, had announced the "irrepressible conflict," and who, in the same year, speaking of and for abolitionism, had said: "It has driven you back in California and in Kansas; it will invade your soil." He was to be the Secretary of State in the incoming administration, and was very generally regarded as the "power behind the throne," greater than the throne itself. He was present in the Senate, but made no response to Douglas's demand for a declaration of policy.

Meantime the efforts for an adjustment made in the House of Representatives had been equally fruitless. Conspicuous among these efforts had been the appointment of a committee of thirty-three members—one from each state of the Union—charged with a duty similar to that imposed upon the Committee of Thirteen in the Senate, but they had been alike unsuccessful in coming to any agreement. It is true that, a few days afterward, they submitted a majority and two minority reports, and that the report of the majority was ultimately adopted by the House; even if this action had been unanimous, and had been taken in due time, it would have been practically futile on account of its absolute failure to provide or suggest any solution of the territorial question, which was the vital point in controversy.

No wonder, then, that under the shadow of the failure of every effort in Congress to find any common ground on which the sections could be restored to amity, the close of the year should have been darkened by a cloud in the firmament, which had lost even the silver lining so long seen, or thought to be seen, by the hopeful.

CHAPTER IX: *Preparation for Withdrawal from the Union— Northern Precedents—New England Secessionists—Cabot, Pickering, Quincy, etc.—On the Acquisition of Louisiana— The Hartford Convention—The Massachusetts Legislature on the Annexation of Texas, etc.*

THE convention of South Carolina had already (on December 20, 1860) unanimously adopted an ordinance revoking her delegated powers and withdrawing from the Union. Her representatives, on the following day, retired from their seats in Congress. The people of the other planting states had been only waiting in the lingering hope that some action might be taken by Congress to avert the necessity for action similar to that of South Carolina. In view of the failure of all overtures for conciliation during the first month of the session, they were now making their final preparations for secession. This was generally admitted to be an unquestionable right appertaining to their sovereignty as states, and the only peaceable remedy that remained for the evils already felt and the dangers apprehended.

In the prior history of the country, repeated instances are found of the assertion of this right, and of a purpose entertained at various times to put it in execution. Notably is this true of Massachusetts and other New England states. The acquisition of Louisiana in 1803 had created much dissatisfaction in those states for the reason, expressed by an eminent citizen of Massachusetts,[1] that "the influence of our [the Northeastern] part of the Union must be diminished by the acquisition of more weight at the other extremity." The project of a separation was freely discussed, with no intimation, in the records of the period, of any idea among its advocates that it could be regarded as treasonable or revolutionary.

Colonel Timothy Pickering, who had been an officer of the war of the Revolution, afterward successively Postmaster General, Secretary of War, and Secretary of State, in the cabinet of General Washington, and still later, long a representative of the state of Massachusetts in the Senate of the United States, was one of the leading secessionists of his day. Writing from Washington to a friend, on December 24, 1803, he says:

I will not yet despair. I will rather anticipate *a new confederacy,* exempt from

---

[1] George Cabot, who had been United States Senator from Massachusetts for several years during the administration of Washington. See *Life of Cabot,* by Lodge, p. 334.

the corrupt and corrupting influence and oppression of the aristocratic democrats of the South. There will be (and our children, at farthest, will see it) a separation. The white and black population will mark the boundary.[2]

In another letter, written a few weeks afterward (January 29, 1804), speaking of what he regarded as wrongs and abuses perpetrated by the then existing administration, he thus expresses his views of the remedy to be applied:

The principles of our Revolution point to the remedy—*a separation*. That this can be accomplished, and without spilling one drop of blood, I have little doubt. . . .

I do not believe in the practicability of a long-continued Union. A *Northern Confederacy* would unite congenial characters and present a fairer prospect of public happiness; while the Southern States, having a similarity of habits, might be left to "manage their own affairs in their own way." If a separation were to take place, our mutual wants would render a friendly and commercial intercourse inevitable. The Southern States would require the naval protection of the *Northern Union,* and the products of the former would be important to the navigation and commerce of the latter. . . .

It [the separation] must begin in Massachusetts. The proposition would be welcomed in Connecticut; and could we doubt of New Hampshire? But New York must be associated; and how is her concurrence to be obtained? She must be made the center of the Confederacy. Vermont and New Jersey would follow of course, and Rhode Island of necessity.[3]

Substituting South Carolina for Massachusetts; Virginia for New York; Georgia, Mississippi, and Alabama, for New Hampshire, Vermont, and Rhode Island; Kentucky for New Jersey, etc., we find the suggestions of 1860-'61 only a reproduction of those thus outlined nearly sixty years earlier.

Pickering seems to have had a correct and intelligent perception of the altogether pacific character of the secession which he proposed, and of the mutual advantages likely to accrue to both sections from a peaceable separation. Writing in February, 1804, he explicitly disavows the idea of hostile feeling or action toward the South, expressing himself as follows:

While thus contemplating the only means of maintaining our ancient institutions in morals and religion, and our equal rights, we wish no ill to the Southern States and those naturally connected with them. The public debts might be equitably apportioned between the new confederacies, and a separation somewhere about the line above suggested would divide the different characters of the existing Union. The manners of the Eastern portion of the States would be sufficiently congenial to form a Union, and their interests are alike intimately connected with

---

[2] See *Life of Cabot,* p. 491; letter of Pickering to Higginson.
[3] Pickering to Cabot, *Life of Cabot,* pp. 338-340.

agriculture and commerce. A friendly and commercial intercourse would be maintained with the States in the Southern Confederacy as at present. Thus all the advantages which have been for a few years depending on the general Union would be continued to its respective portions, without the jealousies and enmities which now afflict both, and which peculiarly embitter the condition of that of the North. It is not unusual for two friends, when disagreeing about the mode of conducting a common concern, to separate and manage, each in his own way, his separate interest, and thereby preserve a useful friendship, which without such separation would infallibly be destroyed.[4]

Such were the views of an undoubted patriot who had participated in the formation of the Union, and who had long been confidentially associated with Washington in the administration of its government, looking at the subject from a Northern standpoint, within fifteen years after the organization of that government under the Constitution. Whether his reasons for advocating a dissolution of the Union were valid and sufficient, or not, is another question which it is not necessary to discuss. His authority is cited only as showing the opinion prevailing in the North at that day with regard to the right of secession from the Union, if deemed advisable by the ultimate and irreversible judgment of the people of a sovereign state.

In 1811, on the bill for the admission of Louisiana as a state of the Union, the Hon. Josiah Quincy, a member of Congress from Massachusetts, said:

If this bill passes, it is my deliberate opinion that it is virtually a dissolution of this Union; that it will free the States from their moral obligation; and as it will be the right of all, so it will be the duty of some, definitely to prepare for a separation—amicably if they can, violently if they must.

Poindexter, delegate from what was then the Mississippi territory, took exception to these expressions of Quincy, and called him to order. The Speaker (Varnum of Massachusetts) sustained Poindexter, and decided that the suggestion of a dissolution of the Union was out of order. An appeal was taken from this decision, and it was reversed. Quincy proceeded to vindicate the propriety of his position in a speech of some length, in the course of which he said:

Is there a principle of public law better settled or more conformable to the plainest suggestions of reason than that the violation of a contract by one of the parties may be considered as exempting the other from its obligations? Suppose, in private life, thirteen form a partnership, and ten of them undertake to admit a new partner without the concurrence of the other three; would it not be at their option to abandon the partnership after so palpable an infringement of their rights? How much more in the political partnership, where the admission of new

---

[4] Letter to Theodore Lyman, *Life of Cabot*, pp. 445, 446.

associates, without previous authority, is so pregnant with obvious dangers and evils!

It is to be remembered that these men—Cabot, Pickering, Quincy, and others—whose opinions and expressions have been cited, were not Democrats, misled by extreme theories of state rights, but leaders and expositors of the highest type of "Federalism, and of a strong central Government." This fact gives their support of the right of secession the greater significance.

The celebrated Hartford convention assembled in December, 1814. It consisted of delegates chosen by the legislatures of Massachusetts, Rhode Island, and Connecticut, with an irregular or imperfect representation from the other two New England states, New Hampshire and Vermont,[5] convened for the purpose of considering the grievances complained of by those states in connection with the war with Great Britain. They sat with closed doors, and the character of their deliberations and discussions has not been authentically disclosed. It was generally understood, however, that the chief subject of their considerations was the question of the withdrawal of the states they represented from the Union. The decision, as announced in their published report, was adverse to the expediency of such a measure at that time, and under the then existing conditions; they proceeded, however, to indicate the circumstances in which a dissolution of the Union might become expedient, and the mode in which it should be effected; and their theoretical plan of separation corresponds very nearly with that actually adopted by the Southern states nearly fifty years afterward. They say:

If the Union be destined to dissolution by reason of the multiplied abuse of bad administration, it should, if possible, be the work of peaceable times and deliberate consent. Some *new form of confederacy* should be substituted among those States which shall intend to maintain a federal relation to each other. Events may prove that the causes of our calamities are deep and permanent. They may be found to proceed, not merely from the blindness of prejudice, pride of opinion, violence of party spirit, or the confusion of the times; but they may be traced to implacable combinations of individuals or of States to monopolize power and office, and to trample without remorse upon the rights and interests of commercial sections of the Union. Whenever it shall appear that the causes are radical and permanent, a separation by equitable arrangement will be preferable to an alliance by constraint among nominal friends, but real enemies.

The omission of the single word "commercial," which does not affect the principle involved, is the only modification necessary to adapt this extract exactly to the condition of the Southern states in 1860-'61.

---

[5] Maine was not then a state.

The obloquy which has attached to the members of the Hartford convention has resulted partly from a want of exact knowledge of their proceedings, partly from the secrecy by which they were veiled, but mainly because it was a recognized effort to paralyze the arm of the federal government while engaged in a war arising from outrages committed upon American seamen on the decks of American ships. The indignation felt was no doubt aggravated by the fact that those ships belonged in a great extent to the people who were now plotting against the war measures of the government, and indirectly, if not directly, giving aid and comfort to the public enemy. Time, which has mollified passion and revealed many things not then known, has largely modified the first judgment passed on the proceedings and purposes of the Hartford convention; but for the circumstances of existing war which surrounded it, they might have been viewed as political opinions merely, and have received justification instead of censure.

Again in 1844-'45 the measures taken for the annexation of Texas evoked remonstrances, accompanied by threats of a dissolution of the Union from the Northeastern states. The legislature of Massachusetts in 1844 adopted a resolution declaring, in behalf of that state, that "the Commonwealth of Massachusetts, faithful to the compact between the people of the United States, according to the plain meaning and intent in which it was understood by them, is sincerely anxious for its preservation; but that it is determined, as it doubts not the other States are, *to submit to undelegated powers in no body of men on earth"*; and that "the project of the annexation of Texas unless arrested on the threshold, *may tend to drive these States into a dissolution of the Union."*

Early in the next year (February 11, 1845) the same legislature adopted and communicated to Congress a series of resolutions on the same subject, in one of which it was declared that, "as the powers of legislation granted in the Constitution of the United States to Congress do not embrace a case of the admission of a foreign state or foreign territory, by legislation, into the Union, such an act of admission would have *no binding force whatever on the people of Massachusetts"*— language which must have meant that the admission of Texas would be a justifiable ground for secession, unless it was intended to announce the purpose of nullification. It is evident, therefore, that the people of the South, in the crisis which confronted them in 1860, had no lack either of precept or of precedent for their instruction and guidance in the teaching and the example of our brethren of the North and East. The only practical difference was, that the North threatened and the South acted.

CHAPTER X: *False Statements of the Grounds for Separation—Slavery not the Cause, but an Incident—The Southern People not "Propagandists" of Slavery—Early Accord Among the States With Regard to African Servitude—Statement of the Supreme Court—Guarantees of the Constitution—Disregard of Oaths—Fugitives From Service and the "Personal Liberty Laws"—Equality in the Territories the Paramount Question—The Dred Scott Case—Disregard of the Decision of the Supreme Court—Culmination of Wrongs—Despair of their Redress—Triumph of Sectionalism.*

AT THE period to which this review of events has advanced, one state had already withdrawn from the Union. Seven or eight others were preparing to follow her example, and others yet were anxiously and doubtfully contemplating the probably impending necessity of taking the same action. The efforts of Southern men in Congress, aided by the cooperation of the Northern friends of the Constitution, had failed, by the stubborn refusal of a haughty majority, controlled by "radical purposes, to yield anything to the spirit of peace and conciliation. This period, coinciding, as it happens, with the close of a calendar year, affords a convenient point to pause for a brief recapitulation of the causes which had led the Southern states into the attitude they then held, and for a more full exposition of the constitutional questions involved.

The reader of many of the treatises on these events, which have been put forth as historical, if dependent upon such alone for information, might naturally enough be led to the conclusion that the controversies which arose between the states, and the war in which they culminated, were caused by efforts on the one side to extend and perpetuate human slavery, and on the other to resist it and establish human liberty. The Southern states and Southern people have been sedulously represented as "propagandists" of slavery, and the Northern as the defenders and champions of universal freedom, and this view has been so arrogantly assumed, so dogmatically asserted, and so persistently reiterated, that its authors have, in many cases, perhaps, succeeded in bringing themselves to believe it, as well as in impressing it widely upon the world.

The attentive reader of the preceding chapters—especially if he has compared their statements with contemporaneous records and other original sources of information—will already have found evidence enough to enable him to discern the falsehood of these representations, and to perceive that, to whatever extent the question of slavery may have served as an *occasion*, it was far from being the *cause* of the conflict.

I have not attempted, and shall not permit myself to be drawn into any discussion of the merits or demerits of slavery as an ethical or even as a political question. It would be foreign to my purpose, irrelevant to my subject, and would only serve—as it has invariably served in the hands of its agitators— to "darken counsel" and divert attention from the genuine issues involved.

As a mere historical fact, we have seen that African servitude among us—confessedly the mildest and most humane of all institutions to which the name "slavery" has ever been applied—existed in all the original states, and that it was recognized and protected in the fourth article of the Constitution. Subsequently, for climatic, industrial, and economical—not moral or sentimental—reasons, it was abolished in the Northern, while it continued to exist in the Southern states. Men differed in their views as to the abstract question of its right or wrong, but for two generations after the Revolution there was no geographical line of demarkation for such differences. The African slave trade was carried on almost exclusively by New England merchants and Northern ships. Jefferson—a Southern man, the founder of the Democratic party, and the vindicator of state rights—was in theory a consistent enemy to every form of slavery. The Southern states took the lead in prohibiting the slave trade, and, as we have seen, one of them (Georgia) was the first state to incorporate such a prohibition in her organic Constitution. Eleven years after the agitation on the Missouri question, when the subject first took a sectional shape, the abolition of slavery was proposed and earnestly debated in the Virginia legislature, and its advocates were so near the accomplishment of their purpose, that a declaration in its favor was defeated by only a small majority, and that on the ground of expediency. At a still later period, abolitionist lecturers and teachers were mobbed, assaulted, and threatened with tar and feathers in New York, Pennsylvania, Massachusetts, New Hampshire, Connecticut, and other states. One of them (Lovejoy) was actually killed by a mob in Illinois as late as 1837.

These facts prove incontestably that the sectional hostility which exhibited itself in 1820, on the application of Missouri for admission into the Union, which again broke out on the proposition for the annexation of Texas in 1844, and which reappeared after the Mexican war, never again to be suppressed until its fell results had been fully accomplished, was not the consequence of any difference on the abstract question of slavery. It was the offspring of sectional rivalry and political ambition. It would have manifested itself just as certainly if slavery had existed in all the states, or if there had not been a negro in America. No such pretension was made in 1803 or 1811, when the Louisiana purchase, and afterward the admission into the Union of the state of that name, elicited threats of disunion from the representatives of New England. The complaint was not of slavery, but of "the acquisition of more weight at the other extremity" of the Union. It was not slavery that threatened a rupture in 1832, but the unjust and unequal operation of a protective tariff.

It happened, however, on all these occasions, that the line of demarkation of sectional interests coincided exactly or very nearly with that dividing the states in which negro servitude existed from those in which it had been abolished. It corresponded with the prediction of Mr. Pickering, in 1803, that, in the separation certainly to come, "the white and black population would mark the boundary"—a prediction made without any reference to slavery as a source of dissension.

Of course the diversity of institutions contributed, in some minor degree, to the conflict of interests. There is an action and reaction of cause and consequence which limits and modifies any general statement of a political truth. I am stating general principles—not defining modifications and exceptions with the precision of a mathematical proposition or a bill in chancery. The truth remains intact and incontrovertible, that the existence of African servitude was in no wise the cause of the conflict, but only an incident. In the later controversies that arose, however, its effect in operating as a lever upon the passions, prejudices, or sympathies of mankind was so potent that it has been spread like a thick cloud over the whole horizon of historic truth.

As for the institution of negro servitude, it was a matter entirely subject to the control of the states. No power was ever given to the general government to interfere with it, but an obligation was imposed to protect it. Its existence and validity were distinctly recognized by the Constitution in at least three places:

First, in that part of the second section of the first article which prescribes that "representatives and direct taxes shall be apportioned among the several States which may be included within this Union, according to their respective members, which shall be determined by adding to the whole number of free persons, including those bound to service for a term of years, and, excluding Indians not taxed, three fifths of all other persons." "Other persons" than "free persons" and those "bound to service for a term of years" must, of course, have meant those permanently bound to service.

Secondly, it was recognized by the ninth section of the same article, which provided that "the migration or importation of such persons as any of the States now existing shall think proper to admit shall not be prohibited by Congress prior to the year one thousand eight hundred and eight." This was a provision inserted for the protection of the interests of the slave-trading New England states, forbidding any prohibition of the trade by Congress for twenty years, and thus virtually giving sanction to the legitimacy of the demand which that trade was prosecuted to supply, and which was its only object.

Again, and in the third place, it was specially recognized, and an obligation imposed upon every state, not only to refrain from interfering with it in any other state, but in certain cases to aid in its enforcement, by that clause, or paragraph, of the second section of the fourth article which provides as follows:

No person held to service or labor in one State, under the laws thereof, escaping into another, shall, in consequence of any law or regulation therein, be discharged from such service or labor, but shall be delivered up on claim of the party to whom such service or labor may be due.

The President and Vice-President of the United States, every Senator and Representative in Congress, the members of every state legislature, and "all executive and judicial officers, both of the United States and of the several States," were required to take an oath (or affirmation) to support the Constitution containing these provisions. It is easy to understand how those who considered them in conflict with the "higher law" of religion or morality might refuse to take such an oath or hold such an office—as the members of some religious sects refuse to take any oath at all or to bear arms in the service of their country—but it is impossible to reconcile with the obligations of honor or honesty the conduct of those who, having taken such an oath, made use of the powers and opportunities of the offices held under its sanctions to nullify its obligations and neutralize its guarantees. The halls of Congress afforded the vantage ground from which assaults were made upon these guarantees. The legislatures of various Northern states enacted laws to hinder the execution of the provisions made for the rendition of fugitives from service; state officials lent their aid to the work of thwarting them; city mobs assailed the officers engaged in the duty of enforcing them.

With regard to the provision of the Constitution above quoted, for the restoration of fugitives from service or labor, my own view was, and is, that it was not a proper subject for legislation by the federal Congress, but that its enforcement should have been left to the respective states, which, as parties to the compact of union, should have been held accountable for its fulfillment. Such was actually the case in the early and better days of the republic. No fugitive slave law existed, or was required, for two years after the organization of the federal government, and when one was then passed, it was merely as an incidental appendage to an act regulating the mode of rendition of fugitives from justice—not from service or labor.[1]

In 1850 a more elaborate law was enacted as part of the celebrated compromise of that year. But the very fact that the federal government had taken the matter into its own hands, and provided for its execution by its own officers, afforded a sort of pretext to those states which had now become hostile to this provision of the Constitution, not only to stand aloof, but in some cases to adopt measures (generally known as "personal liberty laws") directly in conflict with the execution of the provisions of the Constitution.

The preamble to the Constitution declared the object of its founders to be "to form a more perfect union, establish justice, insure domestic tranquillity, provide for the common defense, promote the general welfare, and secure the blessings of liberty to ourselves and our posterity." Now, however (in 1860), the people of a portion of the states had assumed an attitude of avowed hostility, not only to the provisions of the Constitution itself, but to the "domestic tranquillity" of the people of other states. Long before the formation of the Constitution, one of the charges preferred in the *Declaration of Independence* against the government of Great Britain, as justifying the separation of the colonies from that country, was that of having "excited domestic insurrections

---

[1] "There was but little necessity in those times, nor long after, for an act of Congress to authorize the recovery of fugitive slaves. The laws of the free States and, still more, the force of public opinion were the owners' best safeguards. Public opinion was against the abduction of slaves; and, if any one was seduced from his owner, it was done furtively and secretly, without show or force, and as any other moral offense would be committed. State laws favored the owner, and to a greater extent than the act of Congress did or could. In Pennsylvania there was an act (it was passed in 1780, and only repealed in 1847) discriminating between the traveler and sojourner and the permanent resident, allowing the former to remain six months in the State before his slaves would become subject to the emancipation laws; and in the case of a Federal officer, allowing as much more time as his duties required him to remain. New York had the same act, only varying in time, which was nine months. While these two acts were in force, and supported by public opinion, the traveler and sojourner was safe with his slaves in those States, and the same in the other free States. There was no trouble about fugitive slaves in those times."—Note to Benton's *Abridgment of Debates*, Vol. I, p. 417.

among us." Now, the mails were burdened with incendiary publications, secret emissaries had been sent, and in one case an armed invasion of one of the states had taken place for the very purpose of exciting "domestic insurrection."

It was not the passage of the "personal liberty laws," it was not the circulation of incendiary documents, it was not the raid of John Brown, it was not the operation of unjust and unequal tariff laws, nor all combined, that constituted the intolerable grievance, but it was the systematic and persistent struggle to deprive the Southern states of equality in the Union—generally to discriminate in legislation against the interests of their people; culminating in their exclusion from the territories, the common property of the states, as well as by the infraction of their compact to promote domestic tranquillity.

The question with regard to the territories has been discussed in the foregoing chapters, and the argument need not be repeated. There was, however, one feature of it which has not been specially noticed, although it occupied a large share of public attention at the time, and constituted an important element in the case. This was the action of the federal judiciary thereon, and the manner in which it was received.

In 1854 a case (the well-known Dred Scott case) came before the Supreme Court of the United States, involving the whole question of the status of the African race and the rights of citizens of the Southern states to migrate to the territories, temporarily or permanently, with their slave property, on a footing of equality with the citizens of other states with their property of any sort. This question, as we have seen, had already been the subject of long and energetic discussion, without any satisfactory conclusion. All parties, however, had united in declaring that a decision by the Supreme Court of the United States—the highest judicial tribunal in the land—would be accepted as final. After long and patient consideration of the case, in 1857, the decision of the Court was pronounced in an elaborate and exhaustive opinion, delivered by Chief Justice Taney—a man eminent as a lawyer, great as a statesman, and stainless in his moral reputation—seven of the nine judges who composed the Court concurring in it. The salient points established by this decision were:

1. That persons of the African race were not, and could not be, acknowledged as "part of the people," or citizens, under the Constitution of the United States;

2. That Congress had no right to exclude citizens of the South from taking their negro servants, as any other property, into any part of the

common territory, and that they were entitled to claim its protection therein;

3. Finally, as a consequence of the principle just above stated, that the Missouri Compromise of 1820 insofar as it prohibited the existence of African servitude north of a designated line, was unconstitutional and void.[2] (It will be remembered that it had already been declared "inoperative and void" by the Kansas-Nebraska bill of 1854.)

Instead of accepting the decision of this then august tribunal—the ultimate authority in the interpretation of constitutional questions—as conclusive of a controversy that had so long disturbed the peace and was threatening the perpetuity of the Union, it was flouted, denounced, and utterly disregarded by the Northern agitators, and served only to stimulate the intensity of their sectional hostility.

What resource for justice—what assurance of tranquillity—what guarantee of safety—now remained for the South? Still forbearing, still hoping, still striving for peace and union, we waited until a sectional President, nominated by a sectional convention, elected by a sectional vote—and that the vote of a minority of the people—was about to be inducted into office, under the warning of his own distinct announcement that the Union could not permanently endure "half slave and half free," meaning thereby that it could not continue to exist in the condition in which it was formed and its Constitution adopted. The leader of his party, who was to be the chief of his cabinet, was the man who had first proclaimed an "irrepressible conflict" between the North and the

---

[2] The Supreme Court of the United States in stating (through Chief Justice Taney) their decision in the Dred Scott case, in 1857 say: "In that portion of the United States where the labor of the negro race was found to be unsuited to the climate and unprofitable to the master, but few slaves were held at the time of the *Declaration of Independence;* and, when the Constitution was adopted, it had entirely worn out in one of them, and measures had been taken for its gradual abolition in several others. But this change had not been produced by any change of opinion in relation to this race, but because it was discovered from experience that slave-labor was unsuited to the climate and productions of these States; for some of these States, when it had ceased, or nearly ceased, to exist, were actively engaged in the slave-trade; procuring cargoes on the coast of Africa, and transporting them for sale to those parts of the Union where their labor was found to be profitable and suited to the climate and productions. And this traffic was openly carried on, and fortunes accumulated by it, without reproach from the people of the States where they resided."

This statement, it must be remembered, does not proceed from any partisan source, but is extracted from a judicial opinion pronounced by the highest court in the country. In illustration of the truthfulness of the latter part of it may be mentioned the fact that a citizen of Rhode Island (James D'Wolf), long and largely concerned in the slave trade, was sent from that state to the Senate of the United States as late as the year 1821. In 1825 he resigned his seat in the Senate and removed to Havana, where he lived for many years, actively engaged in the same pursuit, as president of a slave-trading company. The story is told of him that, on being informed that the trade was to be declared piracy, he smiled and said, "So much the better for *us*—the Yankees will be the only people not scared off by such a declaration."

South, and who had declared that abolitionism, having triumphed in the territories, would proceed to the invasion of the states. Even then the Southern people did not finally despair until the temper of the triumphant party had been tested in Congress and found adverse to any terms of reconciliation consistent with the honor and safety of all parties.

No alternative remained except to seek the security out of the Union which they had vainly tried to obtain within it. The hope of our people may be stated in a sentence. It was to escape from injury and strife in the Union, to find prosperity and peace out of it. The mode and principles of their action will next be presented.

PART II: THE CONSTITUTION.

CHAPTER I: *The Original Confederation—"Articles of Confederation and Perpetual Union"—Their Inadequacy Ascertained—Commercial Difficulties—The Conference at Annapolis—Recommendation of a General Convention—Resolution of Congress—Action of the Several States—Conclusions Drawn Therefrom.*

WHEN certain American colonies of Great Britain, each acting for itself, although in concert with the others, determined to dissolve their political connection with the mother country, they sent their representatives to a general Congress of those colonies, and through them made a declaration that the colonies were, and of right ought to be, "free and independent States." As such they contracted an alliance for their "common defense," successfully resisted the effort to reduce them to submission, and secured the recognition by Great Britain of their separate independence, each state being distinctly recognized under its own name—not as one of a group or nation. That this was not merely a foreign view is evident from the second of the Articles of Confederation between the states, adopted subsequently to the *Declaration of Independence,* which is in these words, "Each State retains its sovereignty, freedom, and independence, and every power, jurisdiction, and right, which is not by this Confederation expressly delegated to the United States in Congress assembled."

These "Articles of Confederation and Perpetual Union between the States," as they were styled in their title, were adopted by eleven of the original states in 1778, and by the other two in the course of the three years next ensuing, and continued in force until 1789. During this period the general government was vested in the Congress alone, in which each state, through its representatives, had an equal vote in the determination of all questions whatever. The Congress exercised all the executive as well as legislative powers delegated by the states. When not in session the general management of affairs was intrusted to a "Committee of States," consisting of one delegate from each state. Provision was made for the creation, by the Congress, of courts having a certain specified jurisdiction in admiralty and maritime cases, and for the settlement of controversies between two or more states in a mode specifically prescribed.

The government thus constituted was found inadequate for some necessary purposes, and it became requisite to reorganize it. The first idea of such reorganization arose from the necessity of regulating the commercial intercourse of the states with one another and with foreign countries, and also of making some provision for payment of the debt contracted during the war for independence. These exigencies led to a proposition for a meeting of commissioners from the various states to consider the subject. Such a meeting was held at Annapolis in September, 1786; as only five states (New York, New Jersey, Delaware, Pennsylvania, and Virginia) were represented, the commissioners declined to take any action further than to recommend another convention, with a wider scope for consideration. As they expressed it, it was their "unanimous conviction that it may essentially tend to advance the interests of the Union, if the states, by whom they have been respectively delegated, would themselves concur, and use their endeavors to procure the concurrence of the other states, in the appointment of commissioners, to meet at Philadelphia on the second Monday in May next, to take into consideration the situation of the United States, to devise such further provisions as shall appear to them necessary to render the Constitution of the Federal Government adequate to the exigencies of the Union, and to report such an act for that purpose to the United States in Congress assembled, as, when agreed to by them, and afterward confirmed by the Legislatures of every State, will effectually provide for the same."

It is scarcely necessary to remind the well-informed reader that the terms, "Constitution of the Federal Government," employed above, and "Federal Constitution," as used in other proceedings of that period, do not mean the instrument to which we now apply them, and which was not then in existence. They were applied to the system of government formulated in the Articles of Confederation. This is in strict accord with the definition of the word constitution, given by an eminent lexicographer:[1] "The body of fundamental laws, as contained in written documents or prescriptive usage, which constitute the form of government for a nation, state, community, association, or society."[2] Thus we speak of the British Constitution, which is an unwritten system of "prescriptive usage"; of the constitution of Massachusetts or of Mississippi, which is the fundamental or organic law of a particular state embodied in a written instrument; and of the federal Constitution of the United States, which is the fundamental law of an association of states, at first

---

[1] Dr. Worcester.
[2] This definition is very good as far as it goes, but "the form of government" is a phrase which falls short of expressing all that should be comprehended. Perhaps it would be more accurate to say, "which constitute the form, *define the powers, and prescribe the functions* of government," etc. The words in italics would make the definition more complete.

as embraced in the Articles of Confederation, and afterward as revised, amended, enlarged, and embodied in the instrument framed in 1787, and subsequently adopted by the various states. The manner in which this revision was effected was as follows. Acting on the suggestion of the Annapolis Convention, the Congress, on the 21st of the ensuing February (1787), adopted the following resolution:

Resolved, That, in the opinion of Congress, it is expedient that, on the second Monday in May next, a convention of delegates, who shall have been appointed by the several States, be held at Philadelphia, for the sole and express purpose of revising the Articles of Confederation, and reporting to Congress and the several Legislatures such alterations and provisions therein as shall, when agreed to in Congress and confirmed by the States, render the Federal Constitution adequate to the exigencies of Government and the preservation of the Union.

The language of this resolution, substantially according with that of the recommendation made by the commissioners at Annapolis a few months before, very clearly defines the objects of the proposed convention and the powers which it was thought advisable that the states should confer upon their delegates. These were "solely and expressly," as follows:

1. To revise the Articles of Confederation with reference to the "situation of the United States";

2. To devise such alterations and provisions therein as should seem to them requisite in order to render "the Federal Constitution," or "Constitution of the Federal Government," adequate to "the exigencies of the Union," or "the exigencies of the Government and the preservation of the Union";

3. To report the result of their deliberations—that is, the "alterations and provisions" which they should agree to recommend—to Congress and the Legislatures of the several States.

Of course, their action could be only advisory until ratified by the states. The "Articles of Confederation and Perpetual Union," under which the states were already united, provided that no alteration should be made in any of them, "unless such alteration be agreed to in a Congress of the United States, and afterward confirmed by the Legislatures of every State."

The legislatures of the various states, with the exception of Rhode Island, adopted and proceeded to act upon these suggestions by the appointment of delegates—some of them immediately upon the recommendation of the Annapolis Commissioners in advance of that of the Congress, and the others in the course of a few months after the resolution adopted by Congress. The instructions given to these delegates in all cases conformed to the recommendations which have been quoted, and in one case imposed an additional restriction or limitation. As this is a matter of much importance, in order to have a right understanding of what follows, it may be advisable to cite in detail the action of the several states, italicizing such passages as are specially significant of the duties and powers of the delegates to the convention.

The General Assembly of Virginia, after reciting the recommendation made at Annapolis, enacted: "That seven commissioners be appointed by joint ballot of both Houses of Assembly, who, or any three of them, are hereby authorized, as deputies from this Commonwealth, to meet such deputies as may be appointed and authorized by other States, to assemble in convention at Philadelphia, as above recommended, and to join with them in devising and discussing *all such alterations and further provisions as may be necessary to render the Federal Constitution adequate to the exigencies of the Union, and in reporting such an act for that purpose to the United States in Congress, as, when agreed to by them, and duly confirmed by the several States,* will effectually provide for the same."

The Council and Assembly of New Jersey issued commissions to their delegates "to meet such commissioners as have been, or may be, appointed *by the other States of the Union,* at the city of Philadelphia, in the Commonwealth of Pennsylvania, on the second Monday in May next, *for the purpose of taking into consideration the state of the Union as to trade and other important objects, and of devising such other provisions as shall appear to be necessary to render the Constitution of the Federal Government adequate to the exigencies thereof.*"

The act of the General Assembly of Pennsylvania constituted and appointed certain deputies, designated by name, "with powers to meet such deputies as may be *appointed and authorized by the other States. . . .* and to join with them in devising, deliberating on, and discussing *all such alterations and further provisions* as may be necessary *to render the Federal Constitution fully adequate to the exigencies of the Union,* and in reporting such act or acts for that purpose, to the United States in Congress assembled, as, *when agreed to by them and duly confirmed by the several States,* will effectually provide for the same."

The General Assembly of North Carolina enacted that commissioners should be appointed by joint ballot of both houses, "to meet and confer with such deputies as may be *appointed by the other States* for similar purposes, and with them to discuss and decide upon the most *effectual means to remove the defects of our Federal Union, and to procure the enlarged purposes which it was intended to effect; and that they report such an act to the General Assembly of this State, as, when agreed to by them,* will effectually provide for the same." (In the case of this state alone nothing is said of a report to Congress. Neither North Carolina nor any other state, however, fails to make mention of the necessity of a submission of any action taken to the several states for ratification.)

The commissions issued to the representatives of South Carolina by the governor refer to an act of the legislature of that state authorizing their appointment "to meet such deputies or commissioners as may be *appointed and authorized by other of the United States,*" at the time and place designated, and to join with them "in devising and discussing *all such alterations, clauses, articles, and provisions,* as may be thought necessary *to render the Federal Constitution entirely adequate* to the actual situation and future good government of the *Confederate States,*" and to "join in reporting such an act to the United States in Congress assembled, as, *when approved and agreed to by them, and duly ratified and confirmed by the several States,* will effectually provide for the exigencies of the Union." In these commissions the expression, "alterations, clauses, articles, and provisions," clearly indicates the character of the duties which the deputies were expected to discharge.

The General Assembly of Georgia "ordained" the appointment of certain commissioners, specified by name, who were "authorized, as deputies from this State, to meet such deputies as may be *appointed and authorized by other States,* to assemble in convention at Philadelphia, and to join with them in devising and discussing *all such alterations and further provisions* as may be necessary *to render the Federal Constitution adequate to the exigencies of the Union,* and in reporting such an act for that purpose to the United States in Congress assembled, as, *when agreed to by them, and duly confirmed by the several States,* will effectually provide for the same."

The authority conferred upon their delegates by the Assembly of New York and the General Court of Massachusetts was in each case expressed in the exact words of the advisory resolution of Congress: they were instructed to meet the delegates of the other States "for the sole and express purpose of *revising the Articles of Confederation,* and reporting to Congress and to the several Legislatures *such alterations and provisions therein* as shall, when agreed to in Congress, and confirmed by the several States, *render the Federal Constitution adequate to the exigencies of the Union.*"

The General Assembly of Connecticut designated the delegates of that state by name, and empowered them, in conference with the delegates of other states, "to discuss upon such alterations and provisions, agreeable to the general principles of republican government, as they shall think proper to render the Federal Constitution adequate to the exigencies of the Government and the preservation of the Union," and *"to report such alterations and provisions as may be agreed to by a majority of the United States in convention,* to the Congress of the United States and to the General Assembly of this State."

The General Court of New Hampshire authorized and empowered the deputies of that state, *in conference with those of other states,* "to discuss and decide upon the most effectual means *to remedy the defects of our Federal Union, and to procure and secure the enlarged purposes which it was intended to effect"*—language almost identical with that of North Carolina, but, like the other states in general, instructed them to report the result of their deliberations to Congress for the action of that body, and subsequent confirmation "by the several States."

The delegates from Maryland were appointed by the General Assembly of that state, and instructed "to meet such deputies as may be appointed and authorized *by any other of the United States,* to assemble in convention at Philadelphia, *for the purpose of revising the Federal system,* and to join with them in considering such alterations and further provisions," etc.—the remainder of their instructions being in the same words as those given to the Georgia delegates.

The instructions given to the deputies of Delaware were substantially in accord with the others—being almost literally identical with those of Pennsylvania—but the following proviso was added: "So, always, and provided, that such alterations or further provisions, or any of them, do not extend to that part of the fifth article of the Confederation of the said States, finally ratified on the first day of March, in the year 1781, which declares that, *'in determining questions in the United States in Congress assembled, each State shall have one vote.'* "

Rhode Island, as has already been mentioned, sent no delegates.

From an examination and comparison of the enactments and instructions above quoted, we may derive certain conclusions, so obvious that they need only to be stated:

1. In the first place, it is clear that the delegates to the convention of 1787 represented, not *the people of the United States* in mass, as has been most absurdly contended by some political writers, but *the people* of the several states, *as states*—just as in the Congress of that period—Delaware, with her sixty thousand inhabitants, having entire equality with Pennsylvania, which had more than four hundred thousand, or Virginia, with her seven hundred and fifty thousand.

2. The object for which they were appointed was not to organize a *new* government, but "solely and expressly" to amend the "Federal Constitution" already existing; in other words, "to revise the Articles of Confederation," and to suggest such "alterations" or additional "provisions" as should be deemed necessary to render them "adequate to the exigencies of the Union."

3. It is evident that the term "Federal Constitution," or its equivalent, "Constitution of the Federal Government," was as freely and familiarly applied to the system of government established by the Articles of Confederation—undeniably a league or compact between states expressly retaining their sovereignty and independence—as to that amended system which was substituted for it by the Constitution that superseded those articles.

4. The functions of the delegates to the Convention were, of course, only to devise, deliberate, and discuss. No validity could attach to any action taken, unless and until it should be afterward ratified by the several states. It is evident, also, that what was contemplated was the process provided in the Articles of Confederation for their own amendment —first, a recommendation by the Congress; and, afterward, ratification "by the Legislatures of every State," before the amendment should be obligatory upon any. The departure from this condition, which actually occurred, will presently be noticed.

CHAPTER II: *The Convention of 1787—Diversity of Opinion— Luther Martin's Account of the Three Parties—The Question of Representation—Compromise Effected—Randolph's Resolutions—The Word "National" Condemned—Plan of Government Framed—Difficulty with Regard to Ratification, and its Solution—Provision for Secession from the Union—Views of Gerry and Madison—False Interpretations—Close of the Convention.*

WHEN the convention met in Philadelphia in May, 1787, it soon became evident that the work before it would take a wider range and involve more radical changes in the "Federal Constitution" than had at first been contemplated. Under the Articles of Confederation the general government was obliged to rely upon the governments of the several states for the execution of its enactments. Except its own officers and employees, and in time of war the federal army and navy, it could exercise no control upon individual citizens. With regard to the states, no compulsory or coercive measures could be employed to enforce its authority, in case of opposition or indifference to its exercise. This last was a feature of the confederation which it was not desirable nor possible to change, and no objection was made to it; it was generally admitted, however, that some machinery should be devised to enable the general government to exercise its legitimate functions by means of a mandatory authority operating directly upon the individual citizens within the limits of its constitutional powers. The necessity for such provision was undisputed.

Beyond the common ground of a recognition of this necessity, there was a wide diversity of opinion among the members of the Convention. Luther Martin, a delegate from Maryland, in an account of its proceedings afterward given to the legislature of that state, classifies these differences as constituting three parties in the convention, which he describes as follows:

One party, whose object and wish it was to abolish and annihilate all State governments, and to bring forward one General Government over this extensive continent of a monarchical nature, under certain restrictions and limitations. Those who openly avowed this sentiment were, it is true, but few; yet it is equally true that there was a considerable number, who did not openly avow it, who were, by myself and many others of the Convention, considered as being in reality favorers of that sentiment. . . .

The second party was not for the abolition of the State governments nor for the introduction of a monarchical government under any form; but they wished to establish such a system as could give their own States undue power and influence in the government over the other States.

A third party was what I considered truly federal and republican. This party was nearly equal in number with the other two, and was composed of the delegates from Connecticut, New York, New Jersey, Delaware, and in part from Maryland; also of some individuals from other representations. This party were for proceeding upon terms of federal equality: they were for taking our present federal system as the basis of their proceedings, and, as far as experience had shown that other powers were necessary to the Federal Government, to give those powers. They considered this the object for which they were sent by their States, and what their States expected from them.

In his account of the second party above described Martin refers to those representatives of the larger states who wished to establish a numerical basis of representation in the Congress, instead of the equal representation of the states (whether large or small) which existed under the Articles of Confederation. There was naturally much dissatisfaction on the part of the greater states—Virginia, Pennsylvania, North Carolina, and Massachusetts—whose population at that period exceeded that of all the others combined, but which, in the Congress, constituted less than one third of the voting strength. On the other hand, the smaller states were tenacious of their equality in the Union. Of the very smallest, one, as we have seen, had sent no representatives to the convention, and the other had instructed her delegates, unconditionally, to insist upon the maintenance of absolute equality in the Congress. This difference gave more trouble than any other question that came before the convention, and for some time threatened to prove irreconcilable and to hinder any final agreement. It was ultimately settled by a compromise. Provision was made for the representation of the people of the states in one branch of the federal legislature (the House of Representatives) in proportion to their numbers; in the other branch (the Senate), for the equal representation of the states as such. The perpetuity of this equality was furthermore guaranteed by a stipulation that no state should ever be deprived of its equal suffrage in the Senate without its own consent.[1] This compromise required no sacrifice of principle on either side, and no provision of the Constitution has in practice proved more entirely satisfactory.

It is not necessary, and would be beyond the scope of this work, to undertake to give a history of the proceedings of the convention of 1787. That may be obtained from other sources. All that is requisite for the

---

[1] Constitution, Article V.

present purpose is to notice a few particulars of special significance or relevancy to the subject of inquiry.

Early in the session of the convention a series of resolutions was introduced by Edmund Randolph of Virginia, embodying a proposed plan of government, which were considered in committee of the whole House, and formed the basis of a protracted discussion. The first of these resolutions, as amended before a vote was taken, was in these words:

Resolved, That it is the opinion of this committee that a national Government ought to be established, consisting of a supreme legislative, executive, and judiciary.

This was followed by other resolutions—twenty-three in all, as adopted and reported by the committee—in which the word "national" occurred twenty-six times.

The day after the report of the committee was made, Ellsworth of Connecticut moved to strike out the words "national Government" in the resolution above quoted, and to insert the words "Government of the United States," which he said was the proper title. "He wished also the plan to go forth as an amendment of the Articles of Confederation."[2] That is to say, he wished to avoid even the appearance of undertaking to form a new government, instead of reforming the old one, which was the proper object of the convention. This motion was agreed to without opposition, and, as a consequence, the word "national" was stricken out wherever it occurred, and nowhere makes its appearance in the Constitution finally adopted. The prompt rejection, after introduction, of this word "national," is obviously much more expressive of the intent and purpose of the authors of the Constitution than its mere absence from the Constitution would have been. It is a clear indication that they did not mean to give any countenance to the idea which, "scotched, not killed," has again reared its mischievous crest in these latter days—that the government which they organized was a consolidated nationality, instead of a confederacy of sovereign members.

Continuing their great work of revision and reorganization, the convention proceeded to construct the framework of a government for the confederacy, strictly confined to certain specified and limited powers, but complete in all its parts, legislative, executive, and judicial, and provided

---

[2] See Elliott's *Debates,* Vol. V, p. 214. This reference is taken from *The Republic of Republics,* Part III, Chapter VII, p. 217. This learned, exhaustive, and admirable work, which contains a wealth of historical and political learning, will be freely used, by kind consent of the author, without the obligation of a repetition of special acknowledgment in every case. A like liberty will be taken with the late Dr. Bledsoe's masterly treatise on the right of secession, published in 1866, under the title, "Is Davis a Traitor? or, Was Secession a Constitutional Right?"

with the means for discharging all its functions without interfering with the "sovereignty, freedom, and independence" of the constituent states. All this might have been done without going beyond the limits of their commission "to revise the Articles of Confederation," and to consider and report such "alterations and provisions" as might seem necessary to "render the Federal Constitution adequate to the exigencies of government and the preservation of the Union." A serious difficulty, however, was foreseen. The thirteenth and last of the aforesaid articles had this provision, which has already been referred to: "The Articles of this Confederation *shall be inviolably observed by every State, and the union shall be perpetuated; nor shall any alteration, at any time hereafter, be made in any of them,* unless such alteration be agreed to in a Congress of the United States, and be afterward confirmed by the Legislatures of *every State.*"

It is obvious, from an examination of the records, as has already been shown, that the original idea in calling a convention was that their recommendations should take the course prescribed by this article—first, a report to the Congress, and then, if approved by that body, a submission to the various legislatures for final action. There was no reason to apprehend the nonconcurrence of Congress, in which a mere majority would determine the question; but the consent of the legislatures of "every State" was requisite in order to final ratification, and there was serious reason to fear that this consent could not be obtained. Rhode Island, as we have seen, had declined to send any representatives to the convention; of the three delegates from New York, two had withdrawn; other indications of dissatisfaction had appeared. In case of the failure of a single legislature to ratify, the labors of the convention would go for naught, under a strict adherence to the letter of the article above cited. The danger of a total frustration of their efforts was imminent.

In this emergency the convention took the responsibility of transcending the limits of their instructions, and recommending a procedure which was in direct contravention of the letter of the Articles of Confederation. This was the introduction of a provision into the new Constitution, that the ratification of nine States should be sufficient for its establishment among themselves. In order to validate this provision, it was necessary to refer it to authority higher than that of Congress and the state legislatures—that is, to the *people* of the states, assembled by their representatives in convention. Hence it was provided, by the seventh and last article of the new Constitution, that "the ratification of the *Conventions* of nine States" should suffice for its establishment "between the States so ratifying the same."

There was another reason, of a more general and perhaps more controlling character, for this reference to conventions for ratification, even if entire unanimity of the state legislatures could have been expected. Under the American theory of republican government, conventions of the people, duly elected and accredited as such, are invested with the plenary power inherent in the people of an organized and independent community, assembled in mass. In other words, they represent and exercise what is properly the sovereignty of the people. State legislatures, with restricted powers, do not possess or represent sovereignty. Still less does the Congress of a union or confederacy of states, which is by two degrees removed from the seat of sovereignty. We sometimes read or hear of "delegated sovereignty," "divided sovereignty," with other loose expressions of the same sort; no such thing as a division or delegation of sovereignty is possible.

In order, therefore, to supersede the restraining article above cited and to give the highest validity to the compact for the delegation of important powers and functions of government to a common agent, an authority above that of the state legislatures was necessary. Mr. Madison, in the *Federalist*,[3] says: "It has been heretofore noted among the defects of the Confederation, that in many of the States it had received no higher sanction than a mere legislative ratification." This objection would of course have applied with greater force to the proposed Constitution, which provided for additional grants of power from the states, and the conferring of larger and more varied powers upon a general government, which was to act upon individuals instead of states, if the question of its confirmation had been submitted merely to the several state legislatures. Hence the obvious propriety of referring it to the respective *people* of the states in their sovereign capacity, as provided in the final article of the Constitution.

In this article provision was deliberately made for the secession (if necessary) of a part of the states from a union which, when formed, had been declared "perpetual," and its terms and articles to be "inviolably observed by every State."

Opposition was made to the provision on this very ground—that it was virtually a dissolution of the Union, and that it would furnish a precedent for future secessions. Gerry, a distinguished member from Massachusetts—afterward Vice-President of the United States—said, "If nine out of thirteen (States) can dissolve the compact, six out of nine will be just as able to dissolve the future one hereafter."

---

[3] No. XLIII.

Madison, who was one of the leading members of the convention, advocating afterward in the *Federalist* the adoption of the new Constitution, asks the question, "On what principle the Confederation, which stands in the solemn form of a compact among the States, can be superseded without the unanimous consent of the parties to it?" He answers this question "by recurring to the absolute necessity of the case; to the great principle of self-preservation; to the transcendent law of nature and of nature's God, which declares that the safety and happiness of society are the objects at which all political institutions aim, and to which all such institutions must be sacrifiecd." He proceeds, however, to give other grounds of justification:

It is an established doctrine on the subject of treaties, that all the articles are mutually conditions of each other; that a breach of any one article is a breach of the whole treaty; and that a breach committed by either of the parties absolves the others, and authorizes them, if they please, to pronounce the compact violated and void. Should it unhappily be necessary to appeal to these delicate truths for a justification for dispensing with the consent of particular States to a dissolution of the Federal pact, will not the complaining parties find it a difficult task to answer the multiplied and important infractions with which they may be confronted? *The time has been when it was incumbent on us all to veil the ideas which this paragraph exhibits.* The scene is now changed, and with it the part which the same motives dictate.

Madison's idea of the propriety of *veiling* any statement of the right of secession until the occasion arises for its exercise, whether right or wrong in itself, is eminently suggestive as explanatory of the caution exhibited by other statesmen of that period, as well as himself, with regard to that "delicate truth."

The only possible alternative to the view here taken of the seventh article of the Constitution, as a provision for the secession of any nine states, which might think proper to avail themselves of it, from union with such as should refuse to do so, and the formation of an amended or "more perfect union" with one another, is to regard it as a provision for the continuance of the old Union, or Confederation, under altered conditions, by the majority which should accede to them, with a recognition of the right of the recusant minority to withdraw, secede, or stand aloof. The idea of compelling any state or states to enter into or to continue in union with the others by *coercion,* is as absolutely excluded under the one supposition as under the other—with reference to one state or a minority of states, as well as with regard to a majority. The article declares that "the ratification of the Conventions of nine States shall be sufficient for the establishment of this Constitution"—not between all, but—*"between the States so ratifying the same."* It is submitted whether a fuller justification of this right of the nine states to form a new government is not found in the fact of the sovereignty in each of them, making them "a law unto themselves," and therefore the final judge of what the necessities of each community demand.

Here—although, perhaps, in advance of its proper place in the argument—the attention of the reader may be directed to the refutation, afforded by this article of the Constitution, of that astonishing fiction which has been put forward by some distinguished writers of later date, that the Constitution was established by the people of the United States "in the aggregate." If such had been the case, the will of a majority, duly ascertained and expressed, would have been binding upon the minority. No such idea existed in its formation. It was not even established by the *states in the aggregate,* nor was it proposed that it should be. It was submitted for the acceptance of each separately, the time and place at their own option, so that the dates of ratification did extend from December 7, 1787, to May 29, 1790. The long period required for these ratifications makes manifest the absurdity of the assertion, that it was a decision by the votes of one people, or one community, in which a majority of the votes cast determined the result.

We have seen that the delegates to the convention of 1787 were chosen by the several states, *as states*—it is hardly necessary to add that they voted in the convention, as in the federal Congress, by states—each state casting one vote. We have seen, also, that they were sent for the "sole and express purpose" of revising the Articles of Confederation and devising means for rendering the federal Constitution "adequate to the exigencies of government and the preservation of the Union"; that the terms "Union," "United States," "Federal Constitution," and "Constitution of the Federal Government," were applied to the old confederation in precisely the same sense in which they are used under the new; that the proposition to constitute a "national" government was distinctly rejected by the convention; that the right of any state, or states, to withdraw from union with the others was practically exemplified, and that the idea of coercion of a state, or compulsory measures, was distinctly excluded under any construction that can be put upon the action of the convention.

To the original copy of the Constitution, as set forth by its framers for the consideration and final action of the people of the states, were attached the following words:

Done in Convention, by the unanimous consent of the States present, the seventeenth day of September, in the year of our Lord one thousand seven hundred and eighty-seven, and of the Independence of the United States of America, the twelfth. In witness whereof, we have hereunto subscribed our names.

[Followed by the signatures of "George Washington, President, and deputy from Virginia," and the other delegates who signed it.]

This attachment to the instrument—a mere attestation of its authenticity, and of the fact that it had the unanimous consent *of all the states* then present by their deputies—not *of all the deputies,* for some of them refused to sign it—has been strangely construed by some commentators as if it were a part of the Constitution, and implied that it was "done," in the sense of completion of the work.[4]

But the work was not done when the convention closed its labors and adjourned. It was scarcely begun. There was no validity or binding force whatever in what had been already "done." It was still to be submitted to the states for approval or rejection. Even if a majority of eight out of thirteen states had ratified it, the refusal of the ninth would have rendered it null and void. Madison, who was one of the most distinguished of its authors and signers, writing after it was completed and signed, but before it was ratified, said: "It is time now to recollect that the powers [of the Convention] were merely advisory and recommendatory; that they were so meant by the States, and so understood by the Convention; and that the later have accordingly planned and proposed a Constitution, which is to be of no more consequence than the paper on which it is written, unless it be stamped with the approbation of those to whom it is addressed."[5]

The mode and terms in which this approval was expressed will be considered in the next chapter.

---

[4] See *Republic of Republics,* Part II, Chapters XIII and XIV.
[5] *Federalist,* No. XL.

CHAPTER III: *Ratification of the Constitution by the States—Organization of the New Government—Accession of North Carolina and Rhode Island—Correspondence between General Washington and the Governor of Rhode Island.*

THE amended system of union, or confederation (the terms are employed indiscriminately and interchangeably by the statesmen of that period), devised by the convention of 1787, and embodied, as we have seen, in the Constitution which they framed and have set forth, was now to be considered and acted on by the people of the several states. This they did in the highest and most majestic form in which the sanction of organized communities could be given or withheld—not through ambassadors, or legislatures, or deputies with limited powers, but through conventions of delegates chosen expressly for the purpose and clothed with the plenary authority of sovereign people. The action of these conventions was deliberate, cautious, and careful. There was much debate, and no little opposition to be conciliated. Eleven states, however, ratified and adopted the new Constitution within the twelve months immediately following its submission to them. Two of them positively rejected it, and although they afterward acceded to it, remained outside of the Union in the exercise of their sovereign right, which nobody then denied—North Carolina for nine months, Rhode Island for nearly fifteen, after the new government was organized and went into operation. In several of the other states the ratification was effected only by small majorities.

The terms in which this action was expressed by the several states and the declarations with which it was accompanied by some of them are worthy of attention.

Delaware was the first to act. Her convention met on December 3, 1787, and ratified the Constitution on the 7th. The readiness of this least in population and next to the least in territorial extent of all the states, to accept that instrument, is a very significant fact when we remember the jealous care with which she had guarded against any infringement of her sovereign statehood. Delaware alone had given special instructions to her deputies in the convention not to consent to any sacrifice of the principle of equal representation in Congress. The promptness and unanimity of her people in adopting the new Constitution prove very clearly, not only that they were satisfied with the preservation of that principle in the federal Senate, but that they did not understand the

Constitution, in any of its features, as compromising the "sovereignty, freedom, and independence" which she had so especialy cherished. The ratification of their convention is expressed in these words:

We, the deputies of *the people of the Delaware State,* in convention met, having taken into our serious consideration the Federal Constitution proposed and agreed upon by the deputies of the United States at a General Convention held at the city of Philadelphia on the 17th day of September, A. D. 1787, have *approved of, assented to, and ratified and confirmed,* and by these presents do, in virtue of the powers and authority to us given for that purpose, for and in behalf of ourselves and our constituents, fully, freely, and entirely, *approve of, assent to, ratify, and confirm* the said Constitution.

Done in convention at Dover, December 7, 1787.

This, and twelve other like acts, gave to the Constitution "all the life and validity it ever had, or could have, as to the thirteen united or associated States."

Pennsylvania acted next (December 12, 1787), the ratification not being finally accomplished without strong opposition, on grounds which will be referred to hereafter. In announcing its decision, the convention of this state began as follows:

In the name of *the people of Pennsylvania.* Be it known unto all men that we, *the delegates of the people of the Commonwealth of Pennsylvania,* in General Convention assembled," etc., etc., concluding with these words: "By these presents, do, *in the name and by the authority of the same people,* and for ourselves, assent to and ratify the foregoing Constitution for the United States of America.

In New Jersey the ratification, which took place on December 18, was unanimous. This is no less significant and instructive than the unanimity of Delaware, from the fact that the New Jersey delegation, in the convention that framed the Constitution, had taken the lead in behalf of the federal, or state rights, idea, in opposition to that of nationalism or consolidation. William Patterson, a distinguished citizen (afterward governor) of New Jersey, had introduced into that convention what was known as "the Jersey plan," embodying these state-rights principles, as distinguished from the various "national" plans presented. In defending them, he had said, after calling for the reading of the credentials of delegates:

Can we, on this ground, form a national Government? I fancy not. Our commissions give a complexion to the business; and can we suppose that, when we exceed the bounds of our duty, the people will approve our proceedings?

We are met here as the deputies of *thirteen independent, sovereign States, for federal purposes. Can we consolidate their sovereignty and form one nation,* and annihilate the sovereignties of our States, who have sent us here for other purposes?

Again, on a subsequent day, after stating that he was not there to pursue his own sentiments of government, but of those who had sent him, he had asked:

Can we, *as representatives of independent States,* annihilate the essential powers of independency? Are not the votes of this Convention taken on every question under the idea of independency?

The fact that this state, which, through her representatives, had taken so conspicuous a part in the maintenance of the principle of state sovereignty, ratified the Constitution with such readiness and unanimity, is conclusive proof that, in her opinion, that principle was not compromised thereby. The conclusion of her ordinance of ratification is in these words:

Now be it known that we, the delegates of *the State of New Jersey,* chosen by the people thereof for the purpose aforesaid, having maturely deliberated on and considered the aforesaid proposed Constitution, do hereby, for and on behalf of the *people of the said State of New Jersey,* agree to, ratify, and confirm the same, and every part thereof.

Done in convention, by the unanimous consent of the members present, this 18th day of December, A. D. 1787.

Georgia next, and also unanimously, on January 2, 1788, declared, through *"the delegates of the State of Georgia,* in convention met, pursuant to the provisions of the [act of the] Legislature aforesaid, . . . in virtue of the powers and authority given us [them] by *the people of the said State,* for that purpose,"* that they did "fully and entirely assent to, ratify, and adopt the said Constitution."

Connecticut (on the 9th of January) declares her assent with equal distinction of assertion as to the source of the authority: "In the name of *the people of the State of Connecticut,* we, the delegates of *the people of the said State,* in General Convention assembled, pursuant to an act of the Legislature in October last . . . . do assent to, ratify, and adopt the Constitution reported by the Convention of delegates in Philadelphia."

In Massachusetts there was a sharp contest. The people of that state were then—as for a long time afterward—exceedingly tenacious of their state independence and sovereignty. The proposed Constitution was subjected to a close, critical, and rigorous examination with reference to its bearing upon this very point. The convention was a large one, and some of its leading members were very distrustful of the instrument under their consideration. It was ultimately adopted by a very close vote (187 to 168), and then only as accompanied by certain proposed amendments, the object of which was to guard more expressly against any sacrifice or compromise of state sovereignty, and under an assurance, given by the advocates of the Constitution, of the certainty that those amendments would be adopted. The most strenuously urged of these was that ultimately adopted (in substance) as the tenth amendment to the Constitution, which was intended to take the place of the second Article of Confederation, as an emphatic assertion of the continued freedom, sovereignty, and independence of the states. This will be considered more particularly hereafter.

In terms substantially identical with those employed by the other states, Massachusetts thus announced her ratification:

In convention of the delegates of *the people of the Commonwealth of Massachusetts,* 1788. The Convention having impartially discussed and fully considered the Constitution for the United States of America, reported [etc.], . . . do, in the name and in behalf of *the people of the Commonwealth of Massachusetts,* assent to and ratify the said Constitution for the United States of America.

This was accomplished on February 7, 1788.

Maryland followed on April 28, and South Carolina on May 23, in equivalent expressions, the ratification of the former being made by "the delegates of *the people of Maryland,*" speaking, as they declared, for ourselves, and in the name and on the behalf of *the people of this State;* that of the latter, "in convention of *the people of the State of South Carolina,* by their representatives, . . . in the name and behalf of *the people of this State.*" But South Carolina, like Massachusetts, demanded certain amendments, and for greater assurance accompanied her ordinance of ratification with the following distinct assertion of the principle afterward embodied in the tenth amendment:

This Convention doth also declare that *no section or paragraph* of the said Constitution warrants a *construction that the States do not retain every power not expressly relinquished by them* and vested in the General Government of the Union.

"The delegates of *the people of the State of New Hampshire,*" in convention on June 21, "in the name and behalf of *the people of the State of New Hampshire,*" declared their approval and adoption of the Constitution. In this state, also, the opposition was formidable (the final vote being 57 to 46), and, as in South Carolina, it was "explicitly declared that all powers not expressly and particularly delegated by the aforesaid Constitution are reserved to the several States, to be by them exercised."

The debates in the Virginia convention were long and animated. Some of the most eminent and most gifted men of that period took part in them, and they have ever since been referred to for the exposition which they afford of the interpretation of the Constitution by its authors and their contemporaries. Among the members were Madison, Mason, and Randolph, who had also been members of the convention at Philadelphia. Madison was one of the most earnest advocates of the new Constitution, while Mason was as warmly opposed to its adoption; so also was Patrick Henry, the celebrated orator. It was assailed with great vehemence at every vulnerable or doubtful point, and was finally ratified June 26, 1788, by a vote of 89 to 79—a majority of only ten.

This ratification was expressed in the same terms employed by other states, by "the delegates of *the people of Virginia,* . . . in the name and in behalf of *the people of Virginia."* In so doing, however, like Massachusetts, New Hampshire, and South Carolina, Virginia demanded certain amendments as a more explicit guarantee against consolidation, and accompanied the demand with the following declaration:

That the powers granted under the Constitution, being derived from the people of the United States, may be resumed by them, whenever the same shall be perverted to their injury or oppression, and that every power not granted thereby remains with them and at their will, etc.

Whether, in speaking of a possible *resumption* of powers by "the people of the United States," the convention had in mind the action of such a people *in the aggregate*—a political community which did not exist, and of which they could hardly have entertained even an ideal conception—or of the people of Virginia, for whom they were speaking, and of the other United States then taking similar action—is a question which scarcely admits of argument, but which will be more fully considered in the proper place.

New York, the eleventh state to signify her assent, did so on July 26, 1788, after an arduous and protracted discussion, and then by a majority of but three votes—30 to 27. Even this small majority was secured only by the recommendation of certain material amendments, the adoption of which by the other states it was at first proposed to make a condition precedent to the validity of the ratification. This idea was abandoned after a correspondence between Hamilton and Madison, and, instead of conditional ratification, New York provided for the resumption of her grants; the amendments were put forth with a circular letter to the other states, in which it was declared that "nothing but the fullest confidence of obtaining a revision" of the objectionable features of the Constitution, "and an invincible reluctance to separating from our sister States, could have prevailed upon a sufficient number to ratify it without stipulating for previous amendments."

The ratification was expressed in the usual terms, as made *"by the delegates of the people of the State of New York,* . . . in the name and in behalf of the people" of the said state. Accompanying it was a declaration of the principles in which the assent of New York was conceded, one paragraph of which runs as follows:

That the powers of government may be *reassumed* by the people, whensoever it shall become necessary to their happiness; that every power, jurisdiction, and right, which is not, by the said Constitution, clearly delegated to the Congress of the United States, or the departments of the Government thereof, remains to the people of the several *States,* or to their respective State governments, to whom they may have granted the same; and that those clauses in the said Constitution which declare that Congress shall not have or exercise certain powers, do not imply that Congress is entitled to any powers not given by the said Constitution, but such clauses are to be construed either as exceptions to certain specified powers or as inserted for greater caution.

The acceptance of these eleven states having been signified to the Congress, provision was made for putting the new Constitution in operation. This was effected on March 4, 1789, when the government was organized, with George Washington as President, and John Adams, Vice-President; the Senators and Representatives elected by the states which had acceded to the Constitution organizing themselves as a Congress.

Meantime two states were standing, as we have seen, unquestioned and unmolested, in an attitude of absolute independence. The convention of North Carolina, on August 2, 1788, had rejected the proposed Constitution, or, more properly speaking, had withheld her ratification until action could be taken upon the subject matter of the following resolution adopted by her convention:

Resolved, That a declaration of rights, asserting and securing from encroachment the great principles of civil and religious liberty, and the unalienable rights of the people, together with amendments to the most ambiguous and exceptionable parts of the said Constitution of government, ought to be laid before Congress and the Convention of the States that shall or may be called for the purpose of amending the said Constitution, for their consideration, previous to the ratification of the Constitution aforesaid on the part of the State of North Carolina.

More than a year afterward, when the newly organized government had been in operation for nearly nine months, and when—although no convention of the states had been called to revise the Constitution— North Carolina had good reason to feel assured that the most important provisions of her proposed amendments and "declaration of rights" would be adopted, she acceded to the amendment compact. On November 21, 1789, her convention agreed, "in behalf of the freemen, citizens, and inhabitants of *the State of North Carolina*," to "adopt and ratify" the Constitution.

In Rhode Island the proposed Constitution was at first submitted to a direct vote of the people, who rejected it by an overwhelming majority. Subsequently—that is, on May 29, 1790, when the reorganized government had been in operation for nearly fifteen months, and when it had become reasonably certain that the amendments thought necessary would be adopted—a convention of the people of Rhode Island acceded to the new Union, and ratified the Constitution, though even then by a majority of only two votes in sixty-six—34 to 32. The ratification was expressed in substantially the same language as that which has now been so repeatedly cited:

We, the delegates of the people of the State of Rhode Island and Providence Plantations, duly elected and met in convention, . . . in the name and behalf of *the people of Rhode Island and Providence Plantations,* do, by these presents, assent to and ratify the said Constitution.

It is particularly to be noted that, during the intervals between the organization of the federal government under the new Constitution and the ratification of that Constitution by North Carolina and Rhode Island respectively, those states were absolutely independent and unconnected with any other political community, unless they be considered as still representing the "United States of America," which by the Articles of Confederation had been declared a "perpetual union." The other states had seceded from the former union—not in a body, but separately, each for itself—and had formed a new association, leaving these two states in the attitude of foreign though friendly powers. There was no claim of any right to control their action, as if they had been mere geographical or political divisions of one great consolidated community or "nation." Their accession to the Union was desired, but their freedom of choice in the matter was never questioned. And then it is to be noted, on *their* part, that, like the house of Judah, they refrained from any attempt to force the seceding sisters to return.

As illustrative of the relations existing during this period between the United States and Rhode Island, it may not be uninstructive to refer to a letter sent by the government of the latter to the President and Congress, and transmitted by the President to the Senate, with the following note:

UNITED STATES, September 26, 1789.

GENTLEMEN OF THE SENATE: Having yesterday received a letter written in this month by the Governor of Rhode Island, at the request and in behalf of the General Assembly of that State, addressed to the President, the Senate, and the

House of Representatives of the eleven United States of America in Congress assembled, I take the earliest opportunity of laying a copy of it before you.

(Signed)   GEORGE WASHINGTON.

Some extracts from the communication[1] referred to are annexed:

STATE OF RHODE ISLAND AND PROVIDENCE PLANTATIONS,
In General Assembly, September Session, 1789.

To the President, the Senate, and the House of Representatives of the eleven
. .United States of America in Congress assembled:

The critical situation in which the people of this State are placed engages us to make these assurances, on their behalf, of their attachment and friendship to their sister States, and of their disposition to cultivate mutual harmony and friendly intercourse. They know themselves to be a handful, comparatively viewed, and, although they now stand as it were alone, they have not separated themselves or departed from the principles of that Confederation, which was formed by the sister States in their struggle for freedom and in the hour of danger. . . .

Our not having acceded to or adopted the new system of government formed and adopted by most of our sister States, we doubt not, has given uneasiness to them. That we have not seen our way clear to it, consistently with our idea of the principles upon which we all embarked together, has also given pain to us. We have not doubted that we might thereby avoid present difficulties, but we have apprehended future mischief. . . .

Can it be thought strange that, with these impressions, they [the people of this State] should wait to see the proposed system organized and in operation?—to see what further checks and securities would be agreed to and established by way of amendments, before they could adopt it as a Constitution of government for themselves and their posterity? . . .

We are induced to hope that we shall not be altogether considered as foreigners having no particular affinity or connection with the United States; but that trade and commerce, upon which the prosperity of this State much depends, will be preserved as free and open between this State and the United States, as our different situations at present can possibly admit. . . .

We feel ourselves attached by the strongest ties of friendship, kindred, and interest, to our sister States; and we can not, without the greatest reluctance, look to any other quarter for those advantages of commercial intercourse which we conceive to be more natural and reciprocal between them and us.

I am, at the request and in behalf of the General Assembly, your most obedient, humble servant.

(Signed)   JOHN COLLINS, *Governor.*

His Excellency, the President of the United States.

---

[1] American State Papers, Volume I, miscellaneous.

CHAPTER IV: *The Constitution not Adopted by one People "in the Aggregate"—A Great Fallacy Exposed—Mistake of Judge Story—Colonial Relations—The United Colonies of New England—Other Associations—Independence of Communities Traced from Germany to Great Britain, and from Great Britain to America—Everett's "Provincial People" —Origin and Continuance of the Title "United States"—No Such Political Community as the "People of the United States."*

THE historical retrospect of the last three chapters and the extracts from the records of a generation now departed have been presented as necessary to a right understanding of the nature and principles of the compact of 1787, on which depended the questions at issue in the secession of 1861 and the contest that ensued between the states.

We have seen that the united colonies, when they declared their independence, formed a league or alliance with one another as "United States." This title antedated the adoption of the Articles of Confederation. It was assumed immediately after the *Declaration of Independence,* and was continued under the Articles of Confederation, the first of which declared that "the style of this confederacy shall be 'The United States of America' "; this style was retained—without question—in the formation of the present Constitution. The name was not adopted as antithetical to, or distinctive from "confederate," as some seem to have imagined. If it has any significance now, it must have had the same under the Articles of Confederation, or even before they were adopted.

It has been fully shown that the states which thus became and continued to be "united," whatever form their union assumed, acted and continued to act as distinct and sovereign political communities. The monstrous fiction that they acted as one people "in their aggregate capacity" has not an atom of fact to serve as a basis.

To go back to the very beginning, the British colonies never constituted one people. Judge Story, in his "Commentaries" on the Constitution, seems to imply the contrary, though he shrinks from a direct assertion of it, and clouds the subject by a confusion of terms. He says: "Now, it is apparent that none of the colonies before the Revolution were, in the most large and general sense, independent or sovereign communities. They were all originally settled under and subjected to the British Crown." And then he proceeds to show that they were, in their colonial condition, not sovereign—a proposition which nobody disputed. As colonies, they had no claim, and made no pretension, to sovereignty. They were subject to the British Crown, unless, like the Plymouth colony, "a law unto themselves," but they were independent of each other—the only point which has any bearing upon their subsequent relations. There was no other bond between them than that of their common allegiance to the government of the mother country. As an illustration of this may be cited the historical fact that when John Stark, of Bennington memory, was before the Revolution engaged in a hunting expedition in the Indian country, he was captured by the savages and brought to Albany, in the colony of New York, for a ransom; inasmuch as he belonged to New Hampshire, however, the government of New York took no action for his release. There was not even enough community of feeling to induce individual citizens to provide money for the purpose.

There were, however, local and partial confederacies among the New England colonies, long before the *Declaration of Independence*. As early as the year 1643 a Congress had been organized of delegates from Massachusetts, Plymouth, New Haven, and Connecticut, under the style of "The United Colonies of New England." The objects of this confederacy, according to Bancroft, were "protection against the encroachments of the Dutch and French, security against the tribes of savages, the liberties of the gospel in purity and in peace."[1] The general affairs of the company were entrusted to commissions, two from each colony; the same historian tells us that "to each its respective local jurisdiction was carefully reserved," and he refers to this as evidence that the germ-principle of state rights was even then in existence. "Thus remarkable for unmixed simplicity" (he proceeds) "was the form of the first confederated government in America. . . . There was no president, except as a moderator of its meetings, and the larger state [*sic*], Massachusetts, superior to all the rest in territory, wealth, and population, had no greater number of votes than New Haven. But the commissioners were in reality little more than a deliberative body; they possessed no executive power, and, while they could decree a war and a levy of troops, it remained for the States to carry their votes into effect."[2]

This confederacy continued in existence for nearly fifty years. Between that period and the year 1774, when the first Continental Congress met in Philadelphia, several other temporary and provisional associations of

[1] Bancroft's *History of the United States*, Vol. I, Chapter IX.
[2] *Ibid.*

colonies had been formed, and the people had been taught the advantages of union for a common purpose; they had never abandoned or compromised the great principle of community independence, however. That form of self-government, generated in the German forests before the days of the Cæsars, had given to that rude people a self-reliance and patriotism which first checked the flight of the Roman eagles, which elsewhere had been the emblem of their dominion over the known world. This principle—the great preserver of all communal freedom and of mutual harmony—was transplanted by the Saxons into England, and there sustained those personal rights which, after the fall of the Heptarchy, were almost obliterated by the encroachments of Norman despotism; having the strength and perpetuity of truth and right, they were reasserted by the mailed hands of the barons at Runnymede for their own benefit and that of their posterity. Englishmen, the early settlers, brought this idea to the wilds of America, and it found expression in many forms among the infant colonies.

Edward Everett, in his Fourth-of-July address delivered in New York in 1861, following the lead of Judge Story, and with even less caution, boldly declares that, "before their independence of England was asserted, they [the colonies] constituted *a provincial people.*" To sustain this position—utterly contrary to all history as it is—he is unable to adduce any valid American authority, but relies almost exclusively upon loose expressions employed in debate in the British Parliament about the period of the American Revolution—such as "that people," "that loyal and respectable people," "this enlightened and spirited people," etc. The speakers who made use of this colloquial phraseology concerning the inhabitants of a distant continent, in the freedom of extemporaneous debate, were not framing their ideas with the exactitude of a didactic treatise, and could little have foreseen the extraordinary use to be made of their expressions nearly a century afterward, in sustaining a theory contradictory to history as well as to common sense. It is as if the familiar expressions often employed in our own time, such as "the people of Africa," or "the people of South America," should be cited, by some ingenious theorist of a future generation, as evidence that the subjects of the Khedive and those of the King of Dahomey were but "one people," or that the Peruvians and the Patagonians belonged to the same political community.

Everett, it is true, quotes two expressions of the Continental Congress to sustain his remarkable proposition that the colonies were "a people." One of these is found in a letter addressed by the Congress to General

Gage in October, 1774, remonstrating against the erection of fortifications in Boston, in which they say, "We entreat your Excellency to consider what a tendency this conduct must have to irritate and force *a free people,* hitherto well disposed to peaceable measures, into hostilities." From this expression Everett argues that the Congress considered themselves the representatives of "a people." But, by reference to the proceedings of the Congress, he might readily have ascertained that the letter to General Gage was written in behalf of *"the town of Boston and Providence of Massachusetts Bay,"* the people of which were "considered by all America as suffering in the common causes for their noble and spirited opposition to oppressive acts of Parliament." The avowed object was "to entreat his Excellency, from the assurance we have of the peaceable disposition of *the inhabitants of the town of Boston and of the Providence of Massachusetts Bay,* to discontinue his fortifications."[3] These were the "people" referred to by the Congress; the children of the Pilgrims, who occupied at that period the town of Boston and the province of Massachusetts Bay, would have been not a little astonished to be reckoned as "one people," in any other respect than that of the "common cause," with the Roman Catholics of Maryland, the Episcopalians of Virginia, the Quakers of Pennsylvania, or the Baptists of Rhode Island.

The other citation of Everett is from the first sentence of the *Declaration of Independence:* "When in the course of human events it becomes necessary for *one people* to dissolve the political bands which have connected them with another," etc., etc. This, he says, characterizes "the good people" of the colonies as "one people."

Plainly, it does no such thing. The misconception is so palpable as scarcely to admit of serious answer. The *Declaration of Independence* opens with a general proposition. "One people" is equivalent to saying *"any* people." The use of the correlatives "one" and "another" was the simple and natural way of stating this general proposition. "One people" applies, and was obviously intended to apply, to all cases of the same category—to that of New Hampshire, or Delaware, or South Carolina, or of any other people existing or to exist, and whether acting separately or in concert. It applies to any case, and all cases, of dissolution of political bands, as well as to the case of the British colonies. It does not, either directly or by implication, assert their unification, and has no bearing whatever upon the question.

When the colonies united in sending representatives to a Congress in Philadelphia, there was no purpose—no suggestion of a purpose—

---

[3] *American Archives,* Fourth Series, Vol. I, p. 908.

to merge their separate individuality in one consolidated mass. No such idea existed, or with their known opinions could have existed. They did not assume to become a united colony or province, but styled themselves "united colonies"—colonies united for purposes of mutual counsel and defense, as the New England colonies had been united more than a hundred years before. It was as *"United States"*—not as a state, or united people—that these colonies—still distinct and politically independent of each other—asserted and achieved their independence of the mother country. As "United States" they adopted the Articles of Confederation, in which the separate sovereignty, freedom, and independence of each was distinctly asserted. They were "united States" when Great Britain acknowledged the absolute freedom and independence of each, distinctly and separately recognized by name. France and Spain were parties to the same treaty, and the French and Spanish idioms still express and perpetuate, more exactly than the English, the true idea intended to be embodied in the title—*les États-Unis,* or *los Estados Unidos*—the *States united.*

It was without any change of title—still as "United States"—without any sacrifice of individuality—without any compromise of sovereignty—that the same parties entered into a new and amended compact with one another under the present Constitution. Larger and more varied powers were conferred upon the common government for the purpose of insuring "a more perfect union"—not for that of destroying or impairing the integrity of the contracting members.

The point which now specially concerns the argument is the historical fact that, in all these changes of circumstances and of government, there has never been one single instance of action by the "people of the United States in the aggregate," or as one body. Before the era of independence, whatever was done by the people of the colonies was done by the people of each colony separately and independently of each other, although in union by their delegates for certain specified purposes. Since the assertion of their independence, the people of the United States have never acted otherwise than as the people of each state, severally and separately. The Articles of Confederation were established and ratified by the several states, either through conventions of their people or through the state legislatures. The Constitution which susperseded those articles was framed, as we have seen, by delegates chosen and empowered by the several states, and was ratified by conventions of the people of the same states—all acting in entire independence of one another. This ratification alone gave it force and validity. Without the approval and ratification of the people of the states, it would have been, as Madison expressed it, "of no more consequence than the paper on which it was written." It was never submitted to "the people of the United States in the aggregate," or *as a people*. Indeed, no such political community as the people of the United States in the aggregate exists at this day or ever did exist. Senators in Congress confessedly represent the states as equal units. The House of Representatives is not a body of representatives of "the people of the United States," as often erroneously asserted; but the Constitution, in the second section of its first article, expressly declares that it "shall be composed of members chosen by *the people of the several States*."

Nor is it true that the President and Vice-President are elected, as it is sometimes vaguely stated, by vote of the "whole people" of the Union. Their election is even more unlike what such a vote would be than that of the representatives, who in numbers at least represent the strength of their respective states. In the election of President and Vice-President the Constitution (Article II) prescribes that *"each State* shall appoint, in such manner as the Legislature thereof may direct, a number of electors" for the purpose of choosing a President and Vice-President. The number of these electors is based partly upon the equal sovereignty, partly upon the unequal population of the respective states.

It is, then, absolutely true that there has never been any such thing as a vote of "the people of the United States in the aggregate"; no such people is recognized by the Constitution; no such political community has ever existed. It is equally true that no officer or department of the general government formed by the Constitution derives authority from a majority of the whole people of the United States, or has ever been chosen by such majority. As little as any others is the United States government a government of a majority of the mass.

CHAPTER V: *The Preamble to the Constitution—"We, the people of the United States, in order to form a more perfect union, establish justice, insure domestic tranquillity, provide for the common defense, promote the general welfare, and secure the blessings of liberty to ourselves and our posterity, do ordain and establish this Constitution for the United States of America."*

THE phraseology of this preamble has been generally regarded as the stronghold of the advocates of consolidation. It has been interpreted as meaning that "we, the people of the United States," as a collective body, or as a "nation," in our aggregate capacity, had "ordained and established" the Constitution *over* the states.

This interpretation constituted, in the beginning, the most serious difficulty in the way of ratification of the Constitution. It was probably this to which that sturdy patriot, Samuel Adams of Massachusetts, alluded, when he wrote to Richard Henry Lee, "I stumble at the threshold." Patrick Henry, in the Virginia convention, on the third day of the session, and in the very opening of the debate, attacked it vehemently. He said, speaking of the system of government set forth in the proposed Constitution:

That this is a consolidated government is demonstrably clear; and the danger of such a government is, to my mind, very striking. I have the highest veneration for those gentlemen [its authors]; but, sir, give me leave to demand, What right had they to say, *We, the people?* My political curiosity, exclusive of my anxious solicitude for the public welfare, leads me to ask, Who authorized them to speak the language of *"We, the people,"* instead of *We, the States?* States are the characteristics and the soul of a confederation. If the States be not the agents of this compact, it must be one great consolidated national government of the people of all the States.[1]

Again, on the next day, with reference to the same subject, he said: "When I asked that question, I thought the meaning of my interrogation was obvious. The fate of this question and of America may depend on this. Have they said, We, the States? Have they made a proposal of a compact between States? If they had, this would be a confederation: it is otherwise most clearly a consolidated government. The question turns, sir, on that poor little thing—the expression, 'We, the people,' instead of the States of America."[2]

[1] Elliott's *Debates* (Washington edition, 1836), Vol. III, p. 54.
[2] *Ibid.*, p. 72.

The same difficulty arose in other minds and in other conventions.

The scruples of Adams were removed by the explanations of others, and by the assurance of the adoption of the amendments thought necessary—especially of that declaratory safeguard afterward embodied in the tenth amendment—to be referred to hereafter.

Henry's objection was thus answered by Madison:

Who are parties to it [the Constitution]? The people—but *not the people as composing one great body;* but the people as composing *thirteen sovereignties:* were it, as the gentleman [Mr. Henry] asserts, a consolidated government, the assent of a majority of the people would be sufficient for its establishment, and as a majority have adopted it already, the remaining States would be bound by the act of the majority, even if they unanimously reprobated it: were it such a government as is suggested, it would be now binding on the people of this State, without having had the privilege of deliberating upon it; but, sir, no State is bound by it, as it is, without its own consent. Should all the States adopt it, it will be then a government established by the thirteen States of America, not through the intervention of the Legislatures, but by the people at large. In this particular respect the distinction between the existing and proposed governments is very material. The existing system has been derived from the dependent, derivative authority of the Legislatures of the States, whereas this is derived from the superior power of the people.[3]

It must be remembered that this was spoken by one of the leading members of the convention which formed the Constitution, within a few months after that instrument was drawn up. Madison's hearers could readily appreciate his clear answers to the objection made. The "people" intended were those of the respective states—the only organized communities of people exercising sovereign powers of government; the idea intended was the ratification and "establishment" of the Constitution by direct act of the people in their conventions, instead of by act of their legislatures, as in the adoption of the Articles of Confederation. The explanation seems to have been as satisfactory as it was simple and intelligible. Henry, although he fought to the last against the ratification of the Constitution, did not again bring forward this objection, for the reason, no doubt, that it had been fully answered. Indeed, we hear no more of the interpretation which suggested it, from that period, for nearly half a century, when it was revived, and has since been employed, to sustain that theory of a "great consolidated national government" which Madison so distinctly repudiated.

But *we* have access to sources of information, not then available, which make the intent and meaning of the Constitution still plainer. When Henry made his objection, and Madison answered it, the journal

---

[3] Elliott's *Debates* (Washington edition, 1836), Vol. III, pp. 114, 115.

of the Philadelphia Convention had not been published. That body had sat with closed doors, and among its rules had been the following:

That no copy be taken of any entry on the journal during the sitting of the House, without the leave of the House.

That members only be permitted to inspect the journal.

That nothing spoken in the House be printed, or otherwise published or communicated, without leave.[4]

We can understand, by reference to these rules, how Madison should have felt precluded from making allusion to anything that had occurred during the proceedings of the convention. But the secrecy then covering those proceedings has long since been removed. The manuscript journal, which was entrusted to the keeping of General Washington, president of the convention, was deposited by him, nine years afterward, among the archives of the State Department. It has since been published, and we can trace for ourselves the origin, and ascertain the exact significance, of that expression, "We, the people," on which Patrick Henry thought the fate of America might depend, and which has been so grossly perverted in later years from its true intent.

The original language of the preamble, reported to the convention by a committee of five appointed to prepare the Constitution, as we find it in the proceedings of August 6, 1787, was as follows:

We, the people of the States of New Hampshire, Massachusetts, Rhode Island and Providence Plantations, Connecticut, New York, New Jersey, Pennsylvania, Delaware, Maryland, Virginia, North Carolina, South Carolina, and Georgia, do ordain, declare, and establish, the following Constitution for the government of ourselves and our posterity.

There can be no question here what was meant: it was "the people of the States," designated by name, that were to "ordain, declare, and establish" the compact of union for themselves and their posterity. There is no ambiguity nor uncertainty in the language, nor was there any difference in the convention as to the use of it. The preamble, as perfected, was submitted to vote on the next day, and, as the journal informs us, "it passed *unanimously* in the affirmative."

There was no subsequent change of opinion on the subject. The reason for the modification afterward made in the language is obvious. It was found that unanimous ratification of all the states could not be expected, and it was determined, as we have already seen, that the consent of nine states should suffice for the establishment of the new compact "between the States so ratifying the same." Any nine would be

---

[4] Journal of the Federal Convention, May 29, 1787, 1 Elliott's *Debates*.

sufficient to put the proposed government in operation as to them, thus leaving the remainder of the thirteen to pursue such course as might be to each preferable. When this conclusion was reached, it became manifestly impracticable to designate beforehand the consenting states by name. Hence, in the final revision, the specific enumeration of the thirteen states was omitted, and the equivalent phrase "people of the United States" inserted in its place—plainly meaning the people of such states as should agree to unite on the terms proposed. The imposing fabric of political delusion, which has been erected on the basis of this simple transaction, disappears before the light of historical record.

Could the authors of the Constitution have foreseen the perversion to be made of their obvious meaning, it might have been prevented by an easy periphrasis—such as, "We, the people of the States hereby united," or something to the same effect. The word "people" in 1787, as in 1880, was, as it is, a collective noun, employed indiscriminately, either as a unit in such expressions as "this people," "a free people," etc., or in a distributive sense, as applied to the citizens or inhabitants of one state or country or a number of states or countries. When the convention of the colony of Virginia, in 1774, instructed their delegates to the Congress that was to meet in Philadelphia, "to obtain a redress of those grievances, without which *the people of America* can neither be safe, free, nor happy," it was certainly not intended to convey the idea that the people of the American continent, or even of the British colonies in America, constituted one political community. Nor did Edmund Burke have any such meaning when he said, in his celebrated speech in Parliament in 1775, "The people of the colonies are descendants of Englishmen."

We need go no further than to the familiar language of King James's translation of the Bible for multiplied illustrations of this indiscriminate use of the term, both in its collective and distributive senses. For example, King Solomon prays at the dedication of the temple:

That thine eyes may be open unto the supplication . . . . of *thy people* Israel, to hearken unto them in all that they call for unto thee. For thou didst separate them from among *all the people* of the earth, to be thine inheritance.[5]

Here we have both the singular and plural senses of the same word— *one people,* Israel, and *all the people of the earth*—in two consecutive sentences. In "the people of the earth," the word *people* is used precisely as it is in the expression "the people of the United States" in the preamble to the Constitution, and has exactly the same force and effect. If in the latter case it implies that the people of Massachusetts and those

---

[5]I Kings VIII, 52, 53.

of Virginia were mere fractional parts of one political community, it must in the former imply a like unity among the Philistines, the Egyptians, the Assyrians, Babylonians, and Persians, and all other "people of the earth," except the Israelites. Scores of examples of the same sort might be cited if it were necessary.[6]

In the *Declaration of Independence* we find precisely analogous instances of the employment of the singular form for both singular and plural senses—"one people," "a free people," in the former, and "the good people of these colonies" in the latter. Judge Story, in the excess of his zeal in behalf of a theory of consolidation, bases upon this last expression the conclusion that the assertion of independence was the act of *"the whole people* of the united colonies" as a unit; overlooking or suppressing the fact that, in the very same sentence, the colonies declare themselves "free and independent *States"*—not a free and independent *state*—repeating the words "independent States" three times.

If, however, the *Declaration of Independence* constituted one *"whole people"* of the colonies, then that geographical section of it formerly known as the colony of Maryland was in a state of revolt or "rebellion" against the others, as well as against Great Britain, from 1778 to 1781, during which period Maryland refused to ratify or be bound by the Articles of Confederation, which, according to this theory, was binding upon her, as a majority of the "whole people" had adopted it. *A fortiori,* North Carolina and Rhode Island were in a state of rebellion in 1789-'90, while they declined to ratify and recognize the Constitution adopted by the other eleven fractions of this united people. Yet no hint of any such pretension—of any claim of authority over them by the majority—of any assertion of "the supremacy of the Union"—is to be found in any of the records of that period.

It might have been unnecessary to bestow so much time and attention in exposing the absurdity of the deductions from a theory so false, but for the fact that it has been specious enough to secure the countenance of men of such distinction as Webster, Story, and Everett, and that it has been made the plea to justify a bloody war against that principle of state sovereignty and independence, which was regarded by the fathers of the Union as the corner stone of the structure and the basis of the hope for its perpetuity.

---

[6] For a very striking illustration, see Deuteronomy, VII, 6, 7.

CHAPTER VI: *The Preamble to the Constitution—Subject Continued— Growth of the Federal Government and Accretions of Power—Revival of Old Errors—Mistakes and Misstatements—Webster, Story, and Everett—Who "Ordained and Established" the Constitution?*

In the progressive growth of the government of the United States in power, splendor, patronage, and consideration abroad, men have been led to exalt the place of the government above that of the states which created it. Those who would understand the true principles of the Constitution cannot afford to lose sight of the essential plurality of idea invariably implied in the term "United States," wherever it is used in that instrument. No such unit as the United States is ever mentioned therein. We read that "no title of nobility shall be granted by the United States, and no person holding any office of profit or trust under *them* shall, without the consent of Congress, accept," etc.[1] "The President . . . shall not receive, within that period, any other emolument from the United States, or any of *them.*"[2] "The laws of the United States, and treaties made or which shall be made under *their* authority," etc.[3] "Treason against the United States shall consist only in levying war against *them,* or in adhering to *their* enemies."[4] The federal character of the Union is expressed by this very phaseology, which recognizes the distinct integrity of its members, not as fractional parts of one great unit, but as component units of an association. So clear was this to contemporaries that it needed only to be pointed out to satisfy their scruples. We have seen how effectual was the answer of Madison to the objections raised by Patrick Henry. Tench Coxe of Pennsylvania, one of the ablest political writers of his generation, in answering a similar objection, said: "If the Federal Convention had meant to exclude the idea of 'union'— that is, of several and separate sovereignties joining in a confederacy— they would have said, 'We, the people of America'; for union necessarily involves the idea of competent States, which complete consolidation excludes."[5]

More than forty years afterward, when the gradual accretions to the power, prestige, and influence of the central government had grown to

---
[1] Article I, section 9, clause 8.
[2] Article II, section 1, clause 6.
[3] Article III, section 2.
[4] Article III, section 3.
[5] "American Museum," February, 1788.

such extent as to begin to hide from view the purposes for which it was founded, those very objections which in the beginning had been answered, abandoned, and thrown aside, were brought to light again, and presented to the country as expositions of the true meaning of the Constitution. Webster, one of the first to revive some of those early misconceptions so long ago refuted as to be almost forgotten, and to breathe into them such renewed vitality as his commanding genius could impart, in the course of his well-known debate in the Senate with Hayne in 1830, said:

It can not be shown that the Constitution is a compact between State governments. The Constitution itself, in its very front, refutes that proposition: it declares that it is ordained and established by the people of the United States. So far from saying that it is established by the governments of the several States, it does not even say that it is established by the people of the several States; but it pronounces that it is established by the people of the United States in the aggregate.[6]

Judge Story about the same time began to advance the same theory, but more guardedly and with less rashness of statement. It was not until thirty years after that it attained its full development in the annunciations of sectionists rather than statesmen. Two such may suffice as specimens:

Edward Everett, in his address delivered on July 4, 1861, and already referred to, says of the Constitution:

That instrument does not purport to be a "compact," but a constitution of government. It appears, in its first sentence, not to have been entered into by the States, but to have been ordained and established by the people of the United States for themselves and their "posterity." The States are not named in it; nearly all the characteristic powers of sovereignty are expressly granted to the General Government and expressly prohibited to the States.[7]

Mr. Everett afterward repeats the assertion that "the States are not named in it."[8]

But a yet more extraordinary statement of the "one people" theory is found in a letter addressed to the London *Times,* in the same year, 1861, on the "Causes of the Civil War," by John Lothrop Motley, afterward Minister to the Court of St. James. In this letter Motley says of the Constitution of the United States:

It was not a compact. Who ever heard of a compact to which there were no parties? or who ever heard of a compact made by a single party with himself? Yet the name of no State is mentioned in the whole document; the States them-

---

[6] Benton's *Abridgment,* Vol. X, p. 448.
[7] See address by Edward Everett at the Academy of Music, New York, July 4, 1861.
[8] *Ibid.*

selves are only mentioned to receive commands or prohibitions; and the "people of the United States" is the single party by whom alone the instrument is executed. The Constitution was not drawn up by the States, it was not promulgated in the name of the States, it was not ratified by the States. The States never acceded to it, and possess no power to secede from it. It was "ordained and established" over the States by a power superior to the States; by the people of the whole land in their aggregate capacity . . . .

It would be very hard to condense a more amazing amount of audacious and reckless falsehood in the same space. In all Motley's array of bold assertions, there is not one single truth—unless it be, perhaps, that "the Constitution was not drawn up by the States." Yet it was drawn up by their delegates, and it is of such material as this, derived from writers whose reputation gives a semblance of authenticity to their statements, that history is constructed and transmitted.

One of the most remarkable—though, perhaps, the least important—of these misstatements is that which is also twice repeated by Everett —that the name of no state is mentioned in the whole document, or, as he puts it "the States are not named in it." Very little careful examination would have sufficed to find, in the second section of the very first article of the Constitution, the names of every one of the thirteen then existent states distinctly mentioned, with the number of representatives to which each would be entitled, in case of acceding to the Constitution, until a census of their population could be taken. The mention there made of the states by name is of no special significance; it has no bearing upon any question of principle; the denial of it is a purely gratuitous illustration of the recklessness of those from whom it proceeds, and the low estimate put on the intelligence of those addressed. It serves, however, to show how much credence is to be given to their authority as interpreters and expounders.

The reason why the names of the ratifying states were not mentioned has already been given: it was simply because it was not known which states would ratify. But, as regards mention of "the several States," "each State," "any State," "particular States," and the like, the Constitution is full of it. I am informed, by one who has taken the pains to examine carefully that document with reference to this very point, that —without including any mention of "the United States" or of "foreign states," and excluding also the amendments—the Constitution, in its original draft, makes mention of the states, as states, no less than seventy times; and of these seventy times, only three times in the way of prohibition of the exercise of a power. In fact, it is full of statehood. Leave out all mention of the states—I make no mere verbal point or quibble, but mean the states in their separate, several, distinct capacity—and what would remain would be of less account than the play of the Prince of Denmark with the part of *Hamlet* omitted.

But, leaving out of consideration for the moment all minor questions, the vital and essential point of inquiry now is, by what authority the Constitution was "ordained and established." Webster says it was done "by the people of the United States in the aggregate"; Everett repeats substantially the same thing; Motley, taking a step further, says that "it was 'ordained and established' by *a power superior to the States*—by the people of the whole land in their aggregate capacity."

The advocates of this mischievous dogma assume the existence of an unauthorized, undefined power of a "whole people," or "people of the whole land," operating through the agency of the Philadelphia convention, to impose its decrees upon the states. They forget, in the first place, that this convention was composed of delegates, not of any one people, but of distinct states; in the second place, that their action had no force or validity whatever—in the words of Madison, that it was of no more consequence than the paper on which it was written—until approved and ratified by a sufficient number of states. The meaning of the preamble, "We, the people of the United States . . . do ordain and establish this Constitution," is ascertained, fixed, and defined by the final article: "The ratification of the conventions of nine States shall be sufficient for the establishment of this Constitution between the States so ratifying the same." If it was already established, what need was there of further establishment? It was not ordained or established at all, until ratified by the requisite number of states. The announcement in the preamble of course had reference to that expected ratification, without which the preamble would have been as void as the body of the instrument. The assertion that "it was not ratified by the States" is so plainly and positively contrary to well-known fact—so inconsistent with the language of the Constitution itself—that it is hard to imagine what was intended by it, unless it was to take advantage of the presumed ignorance of the subject among the readers of an English journal, to impose upon them a preposterous fiction. It was state ratification alone—the ratification of the people of each state, independently of all other people—that gave force, vitality, and validity to the Constitution.

Judge Story, referring to the fact that the voters assembled in the several states, asks where else they could have assembled—a pertinent question on our theory, but the idea he evidently intended to convey was that the voting of "the people" by states was a mere matter of geographical necessity, or local convenience; just as the people of a state vote by counties, the people of a county by towns, "beats," or "precincts," and the people of a city by wards. It is hardly necessary to say that, in all organized republican communities, majorities govern. When we speak of the will of the people of a community, we mean the will of a majority, which, when constitutionally expressed, is binding on any minority of the same community.

If, then, we can conceive, and admit for a moment, the possibility that, when the Constitution was under consideration, the people of the United States were politically "one people"—a collective unit—two deductions are clearly inevitable: in the first place, each geographical division of this great community would have been entitled to vote according to its relative population; in the second, the expressed will of the legal majority would have been binding upon the whole. A denial of the first proposition would be a denial of common justice and equal rights; a denial of the second would be to destroy all government and establish mere anarchy.

Now, neither of these principles was practiced or proposed or even imagined in the case of the action of the people of the United States (if they were one political community) upon the proposed Constitution. On the contrary, seventy thousand people in the state of Delaware had precisely the same weight—one vote—in its ratification, as seven hundred thousand (and more) in Virginia, or four hundred thousand in Pennsylvania. Would not this have been an intolerable grievance and wrong—would no protest have been uttered against it—if these had been fractional parts of one community of people?

Again, while the will of the consenting majority within any state was binding on the opposing minority in the same, no majority, or majorities, of states or people had any control whatever upon the people of another state. The Constitution was established, not *"over* the States," as asserted by Motley, but *"between* the States," and only "between *the States so ratifying* the same." Little Rhode Island, with her seventy thousand inhabitants, was not a mere fractional part of "the people of the whole land," during the period for which she held aloof, but was as free, independent, and unmolested, as any other sovereign power, notwithstanding the majority of more than three millions of "the whole people" on the other side of the question.

Before the ratification of the Constitution—when there was some excuse for an imperfect understanding or misconception of the terms proposed—Madison thus answered, in advance, the objections made on the ground of this misconception, and demonstrated its fallacy. He wrote:

That it will be a federal and not a national act, as these terms are understood by objectors—the act of the people, as forming so many independent States, not as forming one aggregate nation—is obvious from this single consideration, that it is to result neither from the decision of a *majority* of the people of the Union nor from that of a *majority* of *the States.* It must result from the *unanimous* assent of the several *States that are parties to it,* differing no otherwise from their ordinary assent than in its being expressed, not by the legislative authority, but by that of the people themselves. Were the people regarded in this transaction as forming one nation, the will of the majority of the whole people of the United States would bind the minority, in the same manner as the majority in each State must bind the minority; and the will of the majority must be determined either by a comparison of the individual votes or by considering the will of the majority of the States as evidence of the will of a majority of the people of the United States. Neither of these has been adopted. Each State, in ratifying the Constitution, is considered as a sovereign body, independent of all others, and only to be bound by its own voluntary act.[9]

It is a tedious task to have to expose the misstatements, both of fact and of principle, which have occupied so much attention, but it is rendered necessary by the extent to which they have been imposed upon the acceptance of the public, through reckless assertion and confident and incessant repetition.

" 'I remember,' says Mr. Webster, 'to have heard Chief-Justice Marshall ask counsel, who was insisting upon the authority of an act of legislation, *if he thought an act of legislation could create or destroy a fact, or change the truth of history?* "Would it alter the fact," said he, "if a Legislature should solemnly enact that Mr. Hume never wrote the History of England?" 'A Legislature may alter the law'. continues Mr. Webster, 'but no power can reverse a fact. Hence, if the Convention of 1787 had expressly declared that the Constitution was [to be] ordained by 'the people of the United States *in the aggregate,*' or by the people of America as one nation, this would not have destroyed the fact that it was ratified by each State for itself, and that each State was bound only by 'its own voluntary act.' " (Bledsoe.)

But the convention, as we have seen, said no such thing. No such community as "the people of the United States in the aggregate" is known to it, or ever acted on it. It was ordained, established, and ratified by the people of the several states; no theories or assertions of a later generation can change or conceal this fixed fact, as it stands revealed in the light of contemporaneous records.

---

[9] *Federalist,* No. **XXXIX.**

CHAPTER VII: *Verbal Cavils and Criticisms—"Compact,"* *"Confederacy," "Accession," etc.—The "New Vocabulary"—* *The Federal Constitution a Compact, and the States Acceded* *to it—Evidence of the Constitution Itself and of Contemporary* *Records.*

I HAVE habitually spoken of the federal Constitution as a compact, and of the parties to it as sovereign states. These terms should not, and in earlier times would not, have required explanation or vindication. But they have been called in question by the modern school of consolidation. These gentlemen admit that the government under the Articles of Confederation was a compact. Webster, in his rejoinder to Hayne on January 27, 1830, said:

When the gentleman says the Constitution is a compact between the States, he uses language exactly applicable to the old Confederation. He speaks as if he were in Congress before 1789. He describes fully that old state of things then existing. The Confederation was, in strictness, a compact; the States, as States, were parties to it. We had no other General Government. But that was found insufficient and inadequate to the public exigencies. The people were not satisfied with it, and undertook to establish a better. They undertook to form a General Government, which should stand on a new basis—not a confederacy, not a league, not a compact between States, but a Constitution.[1]

Again, in his discussion with Calhoun, three years afterward, he vehemently reiterates the same denial. Of the Constitution he says: "Does it call itself a compact? Certainly not. It uses the word 'compact' but once, and that when it declares that the States shall enter into no compact.[2] Does it call itself a league, a confederacy, a subsisting treaty between the States? Certainly not. There is not a particle of such language in all its pages."[3]

The artist who wrote under his picture the legend, "This is a horse," made effectual provision against any such cavil as that preferred by Webster and his followers, that the Constitution is not a compact, because it is not "so nominated in the bond." As well as I can recollect, there is no passage in the *Iliad* or the *Æneid* in which either of those great works "calls itself," or is called by its author, an epic poem, yet this would scarcely be accepted as evidence that they are not epic poems. In an examination of Webster's remarks, I do not find that he announces

[1] Gales and Seaton's *Register of Congressional Debates,* Vol. VI, Part I, p. 93.
[2] The words "with another State or with a foreign power" should have been added to make this statement accurate.
[3] *Congressional Debates,* Vol. IX, Part I, p. 563.

them to be either a speech or an argument; yet their claim to both these titles will hardly be disputed—notwithstanding the verbal criticism on the Constitution just quoted.

The distinction attempted to be drawn between the language proper to a confederation and that belonging to a constitution, as indicating two different ideas, will not bear the test of examination and application to the case of the United States. It has been fully shown, in previous chapters, that the terms "Union," "Federal Union," "Federal Constitution," "Constitution of the Federal Government," and the like, were used—not merely in colloquial, informal speech, but in public proceedings and official documents—with reference to the Articles of Confederation, as freely as they have since been employed under the present Constitution. The former Union was—as Webster expressly admits—as nobody denies—a compact between states, yet it nowhere "calls itself" "a compact"; the word does not occur in it even the one time that it occurs in the present Constitution, although the contracting states are in both prohibited from entering into any "treaty, confederation, or alliance" with one another, or with any foreign power, without the consent of Congress; and the contracting or constituent parties are termed "United States" in the one just as in the other.

Webster is particularly unfortunate in his criticisms upon what he terms the "new vocabulary," in which the Constitution is styled a compact, and the states which ratified it are spoken of as having "acceded" to it. In the same speech, last quoted, he says:

This word "accede," not found either in the Constitution itself or in the ratification of it by any one of the States, has been chosen for use here, doubtless not without a well-considered purpose. The natural converse of accession is secession; and therefore, when it is stated that the people of the States acceded to the Union, it may be more plausibly argued that they may secede from it. If, in adopting the Constitution, nothing was done but acceding to a compact, nothing would seem necessary, in order to break it up, but to secede from the same compact. But the term is wholly out of place. Accession, as a word applied to political associations, implies coming into a league, treaty, or confederacy, by one hitherto a stranger to it; and secession implies departing from such league or confederacy. The people of the United States have used no such form of expression in establishing the present Government.[4]

Repeating and reiterating in many forms what is substantially the same indea, and attributing the use of the terms which he attacks to an ulterior purpose, Webster says:

This is the reason, sir, which makes it necessary to abandon the use of con-

---

[4] *Congressional Debates,* Vol. IX, Part I, p. 556.

stitutional language for a new vocabulary, and to substitute, in the place of plain, historical facts, a series of assumptions. This is the reason why it is necessary to give new names to things; to speak of the Constitution, not as a constitution, but as a compact; and of the ratifications by the people, not as ratifications, but as acts of accession.[5]

In these and similar passages, Webster virtually concedes that, if the Constitution *were* a compact, if the Union *were* a confederacy, if the states *had,* as states, severally acceded to it—all which propositions he denies—then the sovereignty of the states and their right to secede from the Union would be deducible.

Now it happens that these very terms—"compact," "confederacy," "accede," and the like—were the terms in familiar use by the authors of the Constitution and their associates with reference to that instrument and its ratification. Other writers, who have examined the subject since the late war gave it an interest which it had never commanded before, have collected such an array of evidence in this behalf that it is necessary only to cite a few examples.

The following language of Gerry of Massachusetts in the convention of 1787, has already been referred to: "If nine out of thirteen States can dissolve *the compact,* six out of nine will be just as able to dissolve *the new one* hereafter."

Gouverneur Morris, one of the most pronounced advocates of a strong central government in the convention, said: "He came here to form *a compact* for the good of Americans. He was ready to do so with all the States. He hoped and believed they all would enter into such a *compact.* If they would not, he would be ready to join with any States that would. But, as the *compact* was to be voluntary, it is in vain for the Eastern States to insist on what the Southern States will never agree to."[6]

Madison, while inclining to a strong government, said: "In the case of a union of people under one Constitution, the nature of *the pact* has always been understood," etc.[7]

Hamilton, in the *Federalist,* repeatedly speaks of the new government as a *"confederate republic"* and a *"confederacy,"* and calls the Constitution a "compact."[8]

General Washington—who was not only the first President under the new Constitution, but who had presided over the convention that drew it up—in letters written soon after the adjournment of that body to

[5] *Ibid.,* pp. 557, 558.
[6] *Madison Papers,* pp. 1081, 1082.
[7] *Ibid.,* p. 1184.
[8] See especially Nos. IX and LXXXV.

friends in various states, referred to the Constitution as a *compact* or treaty, and repeatedly uses the terms "accede" and "accession," and once the term "secession." He asks what the opponents of the Constitution in Virginia would do, "if nine other States should *accede* to the Constitution."

Luther Martin of Maryland informs us that, in a committee of the general convention of 1787, protesting against the proposed violation of the principles of the "perpetual union" already formed under the Articles of Confederation, he made use of such language as this:

Will you tell us we ought to trust you because you now enter into a solemn *compact* with us? This you have done before, and now treat with the utmost contempt. Will you now make an appeal to the Supreme Being, and call on Him to guarantee your observance of this *compact?* The same you have formerly done for your observance of the Articles of Confederation, which you are now violating in the most wanton manner.[9]

It is needless to multiply the proofs that abound in the writings of the "fathers" to show that Webster's "new vocabulary" was the very language they familiarly used. Let two more examples suffice, from authority higher than that of any individual speaker or writer, however eminent—from authority second only, if at all inferior, to that of the text of the Constitution itself—that is, from the acts or ordinances of ratification by the states. They certainly ought to have been conclusive, and should not have been unknown to Webster, for they are the language of Massachusetts, the state which he represented in the Senate, and of New Hampshire, the state of his nativity.

The ratification of Massachusetts is expressed in the following terms:

COMMONWEALTH OF MASSACHUSETTS

The Convention, having impartially discussed and fully considered a Constitution for the United States of America, reported to Congress by the convention of delegates from the United States of America, and submitted to us by a resolution of the General Court of the said Commonwealth, passed the 25th day of October last past, and acknowledging with grateful hearts the goodness of the Supreme Ruler of the universe, in affording the people of the United States, in the course of his Providence, an opportunity, deliberately and peaceably, without fraud or surprise, of entering into an explicit and solemn COMPACT with each other, by assenting to and ratifying a new Constitution, in order to form a more perfect Union, establish justice, insure domestic tranquillity, provide for the common defense, promote the general welfare, and secure the blessings of liberty to themselves and their posterity—do, in the name and in behalf of the people of the Commonwealth of Massachusetts, assent to and ratify the said Constitution for the United States of America.

---

[9] Luther Martin's "Genuine Information," in Wilbur Curtiss's *Secret proceedings and Debates of the Convention*, p. 29.

The ratification of New Hampshire is expressed in precisely the same words, save only the difference of date of the resolution of the legislature (or "General Court") referred to, and also the use of the word "state" instead of "commonwealth." Both distinctly accept it as a *compact* of the states "with each other"—which Webster, a son of New Hampshire and a Senator from Massachusetts, declared it was not; not only so, but he repudiated the very "vocabulary" from which the words expressing the doctrine were taken.

It would not need, however, this abounding wealth of contemporaneous exposition—it does not require the employment of any particular words in the Constitution—to prove that it was drawn up as a compact between sovereign states entering into a confederacy with each other, and that they ratified and acceded to it separately, severally, and independently. The very structure of the whole instrument and the facts attending its preparation and ratification would suffice. The language of the final article would have been quite enough: "The ratification of the conventions of nine States shall be sufficient for the establishment of this Constitution between the States so ratifying the same." This is not the "language" of a superior imposing a mandate upon subordinates. The consent of the contracting parties is necessary to its validity, and then it becomes not the acceptance and recognition of an authority *over* them—as Motley represents—but of a compact *between* them. The simple word "between" is incompatible with any other idea than that of a compact by independent parties.

If it were possible that any doubt could still exist, there is one provision in the Constitution which stamps its character as a compact too plainly for cavil or question. The Constitution, which had already provided for the representation of the states in both houses of Congress, thereby bringing the matter of representation within the power of amendment, in its fifth article contains a stipulation that "no State, without its [own] consent, shall be deprived of its equal suffrage in the Senate." If this is not a compact between the states, the smaller states have no guarantee for the preservation of their equality of representation in the United States Senate. If the obligation of a contract does not secure it, the guarantee itself is liable to amendment, and may be swept away at the will of three-fourths of the states, without wrong to any party—for, according to this theory, there is no party of the second part.

CHAPTER VIII: *Sovereignty—Variety of Definitions—No Real Reason for Confusion as to Term—The State the Only Independent Corporate Unit—Their Sovereignty Never Surrendered nor Transferred, but Only Delegated—Use of the Term by Members of the Constitutional Convention.*

"THE term 'sovereign' or 'sovereignty,' " says Judge Story, "is used in different senses, which often leads to a confusion of ideas, and sometimes to very mischievous and unfounded conclusions." Without any disrespect for Judge Story, or any disparagement of his great learning and ability, it may safely be added that he and his disciples have contributed not a little to the increase of this confusion of ideas and the spread of these mischievous and unfounded conclusions. There is no good reason whatever why it should be used in different sense, or why there should be any confusion of ideas as to its meaning. Of all the terms employed in political science, it is one of the most definite and intelligible. The definition of it given by that accurate and lucid publicist, Burlamaqui, is simple and satisfactory—that "sovereignty is a right of commanding in the last resort in civil society."[1] The original seat of this sovereignty he also declares to be in the people. "But," he adds, "when once the people have transferred their right to a sovereign [i. e., a monarch], they can not, without contradiction, be supposed to continue still masters of it."[2] This is in strict accord with the theory of American republicanism, the peculiarity of which is that the people never do transfer their right of sovereignty, either in whole or in part. They only delegate to their governments the exercise of such of its functions as may be necessary, subject always to their own control, and to reassumption whenever such government fails to fulfill the purposes for which it was instituted.

I think, it has already been demonstrated that, in this country, the only political community—the only independent corporate unit—through which the people can exercise their sovereignty, is the state. Minor communities—as those of counties, cities, and towns—are merely fractional subdivisions of the state; and these do not affect the evidence that there was not such a political community as the "people of the United States in the aggregate."

That the states were severally sovereign and independent when they were united under the Articles of Confederation, is distinctly asserted in those articles, and is admitted even by the extreme partisans of consoli-

[1] *Principles du Droit Politique,* Chapt. V, section 1; also, Chapt. VII, section 1.
[2] *Ibid.,* Chapt. VII, section 12.

dation. Of right, they are still sovereign, unless they have surrendered or been divested of their sovereignty; those who deny the proposition have been vainly called upon to point out the process by which they have divested themselves, or have been divested of it, otherwise than by usurpation.

Since Webster spoke and Story wrote upon the subject, however, the sovereignty of the states has been vehemently denied, or explained away as only a partial, imperfect, mutilated sovereignty. Paradoxical theories of "divided sovereignty" and "delegated sovereignty" have arisen, to create that "confusion of ideas" and engender those mischievous and unfounded conclusions," of which Judge Story speaks. Confounding the sovereign authority of the people with the delegated powers conferred by them upon their governments, we hear of a goverment of the United States "sovereign within its sphere," and of State governments "sovereign in their sphere"; of the surrender by the states of part of their sovereignty to the United States, and the like. Now, if there be any one great principle pervading the federal Constitution, the state constitutions, the writings of the fathers, the whole American system, as clearly as the sunlight pervades the solar system, it is that no government is sovereign—that all governments derive their powers from the people, and exercise them in subjection to the will of the people—not a will expressed in any irregular, lawless, tumultuary manner, but the will of the organized political community, expressed through authorized and legitimate channels. The founders of the American republics never conferred, nor intended to confer, sovereignty upon either their state or federal governments.

If, then, the people of the states, in forming a federal union, surrendered—or, to use Burlamaqui's term, transferred—or if they meant to surrender or transfer—part of their sovereignty, to whom was the transfer made? Not to "the people of the United States in the aggregate"; there was no such people in existence, and they did not create or constitute such a people by merger of themselves. Not to the federal government; they disclaimed, as a fundamental principle, the sovereignty of any government. There was no such surrender, no such transfer, in whole or in part, expressed or implied. They retained, and intended to retain, their sovereignty in its integrity—undivided and indivisible.

"But, indeed," says Motley, "the words 'sovereign' and 'sovereignty' are purely inapplicable to the American system. In the *Declaration of Independence* the provinces declare themselves 'free and independent States,' but the men of those days knew that the word 'sovereign' was a term of fedual origin. When their connection with a time-honored feudal monarchy was abruptly severed, the word 'sovereign' had no meaning for us."[3]

If this be true, "the men of those days" had a very extraordinary way of expressing their conviction that the word "had no meaning for us." We have seen that, in the very front of their Articles of Confederation, they set forth the conspicuous declaration that each state retained "its *sovereignty,* freedom, and independence."

Massachusetts—the state, I believe, of Motley's nativity and citizenship—in her original constitution, drawn up by "men of those days," made this declaration:

The people inhabiting the territory formerly called the Province of Massachusetts Bay do hereby solemnly and mutually agree with each other to form themselves into a free, *sovereign,* and independent body politic, or State, by the name of *The Commonwealth of Massachusetts.*

New Hampshire, in her constitution, as revised in 1792, had identically the same declaration, except as regards the name of the state and the word "state" instead of "commonwealth."

Madison, one of the most distinguished of the men of that day and of the advocates of the Constitution, in a speech already once referred to, in the Virginia convention of 1788, explained that "We, the people," who were to establish the Constitution, were the people of "thirteen *sovereignties.*"[4]

In the *Federalist* he repeatedly employs the term—as, for example, when he says: "Do they [the fundamental principles of the Confederation] require that, in the establishment of the Constitution, the States should be regarded as distinct and independent *sovereigns?* They *are* so regarded by the Constitution proposed."[5]

Alexander Hamilton—another contemporary authority, no less illustrious—says, in the *Federalist:*

It is inherent in the nature of *sovereignty,* not to be amenable to the suit of an individual without its consent. This is the general sense and the general practice of mankind; and the exemption, as one of the attributes of *sovereignty,* is now enjoyed by the government of *every State* in the Union.[6]

In the same paragraph he uses these terms, "sovereign" and "sovereignty," repeatedly—always with reference to the states, respectively and severally.

Benjamin Franklin advocated equality of suffrage in the Senate as a means of securing "the *sovereignties* of the individual States."[7] James

[3] *Rebellion Record,* Vol. I, Documents, p. 211.
[4] Elliott's *Debates,* Vol. III, p. 114, edition of 1836.
[5] *Federalist,* No. XL.
[6] *Ibid.,* No. LXXXI.
[7] See Elliott's *Debates,* Vol. V, p. 266.

Wilson of Pennsylvania said sovereignty "is in the people before they make a Constitution, and remains in them," and described the people as being "thirteen independent sovereignties."[8] Gouverneur Morris, who was, as well as Wilson, one of the warmest advocates in the convention of a strong central government, spoke of the Constitution as "a *compact*," and of the parties to it as "each enjoying *sovereign* power."[9] Roger Sherman of Connecticut declared that the government "was instituted by a number of *sovereign States*."[10] Oliver Ellsworth of the same state spoke of the states as "sovereign bodies."[11] These were all eminent members of the convention which formed the Constitution.

There was scarcely a statesman of that period who did not leave on record expressions of the same sort. But why multiply citations? It is very evident that the "men of those days" entertained very different views of sovereignty from those set forth by the "new lights" of our day. Far from considering it a term of feudal origin, "purely inapplicable to the American system," they seem to have regarded it as a very vital principle in that system, and of necessity belonging to the several states—and I do not find a single instance in which they applied it to any political organization, except the states.

Their ideas were in entire accord with those of Vattel, who, in his chapter "Of Nations or Sovereign States," writes, "Every *nation* that governs itself, under what form soever, without any dependence on foreign power, is a *sovereign state*."[12]

In another part of the same chapter he gives a lucid statement of the nature of a confederate republic, such as ours was designed to be. He says:

Several sovereign and independent states may unite themselves together by a perpetual confederacy, without each in particular ceasing to be *a perfect state*. They will form together a federal republic: the deliberations in common will offer no violence to *the sovereignty of each member*, though they may, in certain respects, put some restraint on the exercise of it, in virtue of voluntary engagements. A person does not cease to be free and independent, when he is obliged to fulfill the engagements into which he has very willingly entered.[13]

What this celebrated author means here by a person, is explained by a subsequent passage: "The law of nations is the law of sovereigns; states free and independent are moral persons."[14]

[8] *Ibid.*, Vol. II, p. 443.
[9] See *Life of Gouverneur Morris*, Vol. III, p. 193.
[10] See *Writings of John Adams*, Vol. VII, letter of Roger Sherman.
[11] See Elliott's *Debates*, Vol. II, p. 197.
[12] *Law of Nations*, Book I, Chapt. I, section 4.
[13] *Ibid.*, section 10.
[14] *Ibid.*, section 12.

CHAPTER IX: *The Same Subject Continued—The Tenth Amendment—Fallacies Exposed—"Constitution," "Government," and "People" Distinguished from Each Other—Theories Refuted by Facts—Characteristics of Sovereignty—Sovereignty Identified—Never Thrown Away.*

IF any lingering doubt could have existed as to the reservation of their entire sovereignty by the people of the respective states when they organized the federal Union, it would have been removed by the adoption of the tenth amendment to the Constitution, which was not only one of the amendments proposed by various states when ratifying that instrument, but the particular one in which they substantially agreed, and upon which they most urgently insisted. Indeed, it is quite certain that the Constitution would never have received the assent and ratification of Massachusetts, New Hampshire, New York, North Carolina, and perhaps other states, but for a well-grounded assurance that the substance of this amendment would be adopted as soon as the requisite formalities could be complied with. That amendment is in these words:

The powers not delegated to the United States by the Constitution nor prohibited by it to the States are reserved to the States respectively, or to the people.

The full meaning of this article may not be as clear to us as it was to the men of that period, on account of the confusion of ideas by which the term "people"—plain enough to them—has since been obscured, and also the ambiguity attendant upon the use of the little conjunction *or,* which has been said to be the most equivocal word in our language, and for that reason has been excluded from indictments in the English courts. The true intent and meaning of the provision, however, may be ascertained from an examination and comparison of the terms in which it was expressed by the various states which proposed it, and whose ideas it was intended to embody.

Massachusetts and New Hampshire, in their ordinances of ratification, expressing the opinion "that certain amendments and alterations in the said Constitution would remove the fears and quiet the apprehensions of many of the good people of this Commonwealth [State (New Hampshire)], and more effectually guard against an undue administration of the Federal Government," each recommended several such amendments, putting this at the head in the following form:

That it be explicitly declared that all powers not expressly delegated by the aforesaid Constitution *are reserved to the several States,* to be by them exercised.

Of course, those stanch republican communities meant *the people of the states*—not their *governments,* as something distinct from their people.

New York expressed herself as follows:

That the powers of government may be reassumed by the people whenever it shall become necessary to their happiness; that every power, jurisdiction, and right, which is not by the said Constitution clearly delegated to the Congress of the United States, or the departments of the Government thereof, remains to *the people of the several States, or to their respective State governments, to whom they may have granted the same;* and that those clauses in the said Constitution, which declare that Congress shall not have or exercise certain powers, do not imply that Congress is entitled to any powers not given by the said Constitution; but such clauses are to be construed either as exceptions to certain specified powers or as inserted merely for greater caution.

South Carolina expressed the idea thus:

This Convention doth also declare that no section or paragraph of the said Constitution warrants a construction that *the States do not retain* every power not expressly relinquished by them and vested in the General Government of the Union.

North Carolina proposed it in these terms:

Each State in the Union shall respectively retain every power, jurisdiction, and right, which is not by this Constitution delegated to the Congress of the United States or to the departments of the General Government.

Rhode Island gave in her long-withheld assent to the Constitution, "in full confidence" that certain proposed amendments would be adopted, the first of which was expressed in these words:

That Congress shall guarantee *to each State* its SOVEREIGNTY, *freedom, and independence,* and every power, jurisdiction, and right, which is not by this Constitution expressly delegated to the United States.

This was in May, 1790, when nearly three years had been given to discussion and explanation of the new government by its founders and others, when it had been in actual operation for more than a year, and when there was every advantage for a clear understanding of its nature and principles. Under such circumstances, and in the "full confidence" that this language expressed its meaning and intent, the people of Rhode Island signfied their "accession" to the "Confederate Republic" of the states already united.

No objection was made from any quarter to the principle asserted in these various forms, or to the amendment in which it was finally expressed, although many thought it unnecessary, as being merely declaratory of what would have been sufficiently obvious without it—that the functions of the government of the United States were strictly limited to the exercise of such powers as were expressly delegated, and that the people of the several states retained all others.

Is it compatible with reason to suppose that people so chary of the delegation of specific powers or functions could have meant to surrender or transfer the very basis and origin of all power—their inherent sovereignty—and this, not by express grant, but by implication?

Everett, following, whether consciously or not, in the line of Webster's ill-considered objection to the term "compact," takes exception to the sovereignty of the states on the ground that "the *word* 'sovereignty' does not occur" in the Constitution. He admits that the states were sovereign under the Articles of Confederation. How could they relinquish or be deprived of their sovereignty without even a mention of it—when the tenth amendment confronts us with the declaration that *nothing* was surrendered by implication—that everything was reserved unless expressly delegated to the United States or prohibited to the states? Here is an attribute which they certainly possessed—which nobody denies, or can deny, that they *did* possess—and of which Everett says no mention is made in the Constitution. In what conceivable way, then, was it lost or alienated?

Much has been said of the "prohibition" of the exercise by the states of certain functions of sovereignty, such as making treaties, declaring war, coining money, etc. This is only a part of the general compact, by which the contracting parties covenant, one with another, to abstain from the separate exercise of certain powers, which they agree to entrust to the management and control of the union or general agency of the parties associated. It is not a prohibition imposed upon them from without, or from above, by any external or superior power, but is self-imposed by their free consent. The case is strictly analogous to that of individuals forming a mercantile or manufacturing copartnership, who voluntarily agree to refrain, as individuals, from engaging in other pursuits or speculations, from lending their individual credit, or from the exercise of any other right of a citizen, which they may think proper to subject to the consent, or entrust to the management of the firm.

The prohibitory clauses of the Constitution referred to are not at all a denial of the full sovereignty of the states, but are merely an agreement among them to exercise certain powers of sovereignty in concert, and not separately and apart.

There is one other provision of the Constitution, which is generally adduced by the friends of centralism as antagonistic to state sovereignty This is found in the second clause of the sixth article, as follows:

This Constitution, and the laws of the United States which shall be made in pursuance thereof, and all treaties made, or which shall be made, under the authority of the United States, shall be the supreme law of the land; and the judges in every State shall be bound thereby, anything in the Constitution or laws of any State to the contrary notwithstanding.

This enunciation of a principle, which, even if it had not been expressly declared, would have been a necessary deduction from the acceptance of the Constitution itself, has been magnified and perverted into a meaning and purpose entirely foreign to that which plain interpretation is sufficient to discern. Motley thus dilates on the subject:

Could language be more imperial? Could the claim to State "sovereignty" be more completely disposed of at a word? How can that be sovereign, acknowledging no superior, supreme, which has voluntarily accepted a supreme law from something which it acknowledges as superior?[1]

The mistake which Motley—like other writers of the same school—makes is one which is disposed of by a very simple correction. The states, which ordained and established the Constitution, accepted nothing besides what they themselves prescribe. They acknowledged no superior. The supremacy was both in degree and extent only that which was delegated by the states to their common agent.

There are some other considerations which may conduce to a clearer understanding of this supremacy of the Constitution and the laws made in pursuance thereof:

1. In the first place, it must be remembered that, when the federal Constitution was formed, each then existing state already had its own constitution and code of statute laws. It was, no doubt, primarily with reference to these that the provision was inserted, and not in the expectation of future conflicts or discrepancies. It is in this light alone that Madison considers it in explaining and vindicating it in the *Federalist*.[2]

2. Again, it is to be observed that the supremacy accorded to the general laws of the United States is expressly limited to those enacted in conformity with the Constitution, or, to use the exact language, "made in pursuance thereof." Hamilton, in another chapter of the *Federalist*, calls particular attention to this, saying (and the italics are all his own) "that the laws of the Confederacy, as to the *enumerated* and *legitimate* objects of its jurisdiction, will become the supreme law of the land," and that the state functionaries will coöperate in their observance and

---

[1] *Rebellion Record*, Vol. I, Documents, p. 213.
[2] *Federalist*, No. XLIV.

enforcement with the general government, *"as far as its just and constitutional authority extends."*[3]

3. In the third place, it is not the *government* of the United States that is declared to be supreme, but the *Constitution* and the laws and treaties made in accordance with it. The proposition was made in the convention to organize a government consisting of "supreme legislative, executive, and judicial powers," but it was not adopted. Its deliberate rejection is much more significant and conclusive than if it had never been proposed. Correction of so gross an error as that of confounding the government with the Constitution ought to be superfluous, but so crude and confused are the ideas which have been propagated on the subject, that no misconception seems to be too absurd to be possible. Thus, it has not been uncommon of late years to hear, even in the highest places, the oath to support the Constitution, which is taken by both state and federal officers, spoken of as an oath *"to support the government"*—an obligation never imposed upon anyone in this country, and which the men who made the Constitution, with their recent reminiscences of the Revolution, the battles of which they had fought with halters around their necks, would have been the last to prescribe. Could any assertion be less credible than that they proceeded to institute another supreme government which it would be treason to resist?

This confusion of ideas pervades the treatment of the whole subject of sovereignty. Webster has said, and very justly so far as these United States are concerned: "The sovereignty of government is an idea belonging to the other side of the Atlantic. No such thing is known in North America. Our governments are all limited. In Europe sovereignty is of feudal origin, and imports no more than the state of the sovereign. It comprises his rights, duties, exemptions, prerogatives, and powers. But with us all power is with the people. They alone are sovereign, and they erect what governments they please, and confer on them such powers as they please. None of these governments are sovereign, in the European sense of the word, all being restrained by written constitutons.[4]

But the same intellect, which can so clearly discern and so lucidly define the general proposition, seems to be covered by a cloud of thick darkness when it comes to apply it to the particular case in issue. Thus, a little afterward, we have the following:

There is no language in the whole Constitution applicable to a confederation of States. If the States be parties, as States, what are their rights, and what their

---

[3] *Federalist,* No. XXVII.
[4] *Congressional Debates,* Vol. IX, Part I, p. 565.

respective covenants and stipulations? and where are their rights, covenants, and stipulations expressed? In the Articles of Confederation they did make promises, and did enter into engagements, and did plight the faith of each State for their fulfillment; but in the Constitution there is nothing of that kind. The reason is that, in the Constitution, it is the people who speak and not the States. The people ordain the Constitution, and therein address themselves to the States and to the Legislatures of the States in the language of injunction and prohibition.[5]

It is surprising that such inconsistent ideas should proceed from a source so eminent. Its author falls into the very error which he had just before so distinctly pointed out, in confounding the people of the states with their governments. In the vehemence of his hostility to state sovereignty, he seems—as all of his disciples seem—unable even to comprehend that it means the sovereignty, not of state governments, but of people who make them. With minds preoccupied by the unreal idea of one great people of a consolidated nation, these gentlemen are blinded to the plain and primary truth that the only way in which the people ordained the Constitution was as the people of *States.* When Webster says that "in the Constitution it is the people who speak, and not the States," he says what is untenable. The states *are* the people. The people do not speak, never have spoken, and never can speak, in their sovereign capacity (without a subversion of our whole system), otherwise than as the people of states.

There are but two modes of expressing their sovereign will known to the people of this country. One is by direct vote—the mode adopted by Rhode Island in 1788, when she rejected the Constitution. The other is the method, more generally pursued, of acting by means of conventions of delegates elected expressly as representatives of the sovereignty of the people. Now, it is not a matter of opinion or theory of speculation, but a plain, undeniable, historical fact, that there never has been any act or expression of sovereignty in either of these modes by that imaginary community, "the people of the United States in the aggregate." Usurpations of power by the government of the United States, there may have been, and may be again, but there has never been either a sovereign convention or a direct vote of the "whole people" of the United States to demonstrate its existence as a corporate unit. Every exercise of sovereignty by any of the people of this country that has actually taken place has been by the people of states *as states.* In the face of this fact, is it not the merest self-stultification to admit the sovereignty of the people and deny it to the states, in which alone they have community existence?

This subject is one of such vital importance to a right understanding

---

[5] *Ibid.,* p. 566.

of the events which this work is designed to record and explain that it can not be dismissed without an effort in the way of recapitulation and conclusion, to make it clear beyond the possibility of misconception.

According to the American theory, every individual is endowed with certain unalienable rights, among which are "life, liberty, and the pursuit of happiness." He is entitled to all the freedom, in these and in other respects, that is consistent with the safety and the rights of others and the weal of the community, but political sovereignty, which is the source and origin of all the powers of government—legislative, executive, and judicial—belongs to, and inheres in, the people of an organized political community. It is an attribute of the whole people of such a community. It includes the power and necessarily the duty of protecting the rights and redressing the wrongs of individuals, of punishing crimes, enforcing contracts, prescribing rules for the transfer of property and the succession of estates, making treaties with foreign powers, leving taxes, etc. The enumeration of particulars might be extended, but these will suffice as illustrations.

These powers are of course exercised through the agency of governments, but the governments are *only* agents of the sovereign—responsible to it, and subject to its control. This sovereign—the people, in the aggregate, of each political community—delegates to the government the exercise of such powers, or functions, as it thinks proper, but in an American republic never transfers or surrenders sovereignty. That remains, unalienated and unimpaired. It is by virtue of this sovereignty alone that the Government, its authorized agent, commands the obedience of the individual citizen, to the extent of its derivative, dependent, and delegated authority. The *allegiance* of the citizen is due to the sovereign alone.

Thus far, I think, all will agree. No American statesman or publist would venture to dispute it. Notwithstanding the inconsiderate or ill-considered expressions thrown out by some persons about the unity of the American people from the beginning, no respectable authority has ever had the hardihood to deny that, before the adoption of the federal Constitution, the only sovereign political community was the people of the state—the people of *each state.* The ordinary exercise of what are generally termed the powers of sovereignty was by and through their respective governments; when they formed a confederation, a portion of those powers was entrusted to the general government, or agency. Under the confederation, the Congress of the United States represented the collective power of the states; still, the people of each state alone possessed sovereignty, and consequently were entitled to the allegiance of the citizen.

When the Articles of Confederation were amended, when the new Constitution was substituted in their place and the general government reorganized, its structure was changed, additional powers were conferred upon it, and thereby subtracted from the powers theretofore exercised by the state governments; the seat of sovereignty—the source of all those delegated and dependent powers—was not disturbed. There was a new government or an amended government—it is entirely immaterial in which of these lights we consider it—but no new *people* was created or constituted. The people, in whom alone sovereignty inheres, remained just as they had been before. The only change was in the form, structure, and relations of their governmental agencies.

No doubt the states—the people of the states—if they had been so disposed, might have merged themselves into one great consolidated state, retaining their geographical boundaries merely as matters of convenience. But such a merger must have been distinctly and formally stated, not left to deduction or implication.

Men do not alienate even an estate, without positive and express terms and stipulations. But in this case not only was there no express transfer—no formal surrender—of the preëxisting sovereignty, but it was expressly provided that nothing should be understood as even delegated—that everything was reserved, unless granted in express terms. The monstrous conception of the creation of a new people, invested with the whole or a great part of the sovereignty which had previously belonged to the people of each state, has not a syllable to sustain it in the Constitution, but is built up entirely upon the palpable misconstruction of a single expression in the preamble.

In denying that there is any such collective unit as the people of the United States in the aggregate, of course I am not to be understood as denying that there is such a political organization as the United States, or that there exists, with large and distinct powers, a government of the United States; but it is claimed that the Union, as its name implies, is constituted of states. As a British author,[6] referring to the old Teutonic system, has expressed the same idea, the states are the integers, the United States the multiple which results from them. The government of the United States derives its existence from the same source, and exercises its functions by the will of the same sovereignty that creates and confers authority upon the state governments. The people of each state

---

[6] Sir Francis Palgrave, quoted by Calhoun, *Congressional Debates,* Vol. IX, Part I, p. 541.

are, in either case, the source. The only difference is that, in the creation of the state governments, each sovereign acted alone; in that of the federal government, they acted in coöperation with the others. Neither the whole nor any part of their sovereignty has been surrendered to either government.

To whom, in fine, could the states have surrendered their sovereignty? Not to the mass of the people inhabiting the territory possessed by all the states, for there was no such community in existence, and they took no measures for the organization of such a community. If they had intended to do so, the very style, "United States," would have been a palpable misnomer, nor would treason have been defined as levying war against them. Could it have been transferred to the government of the Union? Clearly not, in accordance with the ideas and principles of those who made the *Declaration of Independence,* adopted the Articles of Confederation, and established the Constitution of the United States; in each and all of these the corner stone is the inherent and inalienable sovereignty of the people. To have transferred sovereignty from the people to a government would have been to have fought the battles of the Revolution in vain—not for the freedom and independence of the states, but for a mere change of masters. Such a thought or purpose could not have been in the heads or hearts of those who molded the Union, and could have found lodgment only when the ebbing tide of patriotism and fraternity had swept away the landmarks which they erected who sought by the compact of union to secure and perpetuate the liberties then possessed. The men who had won at great cost the independence of their respective states were deeply impressed with the value of union, but they could never have consented, like "the base Judean," to fling away the priceless pearl of state sovereignty for any possible alliance.

CHAPTER X: *A Recapitulation—Remarkable Propositions of Gouverneur Morris in the Convention of 1787, and Their Fate —Further Testimony—Hamilton, Madison, Washington, Marshall, etc.—Later Theories—Webster: His Views at Various Periods—Speech at Capon Springs—State Rights not a Sectional Theory.*

LOOKING back for a moment at the ground over which we have gone, I think it may be fairly asserted that the following propositions have been clearly and fully established:

1. That the states of which the American union was formed, from the moment when they emerged from their colonial or provincial condition, became severally sovereign, free, and independent states—not one state, or nation.

2. That the union formed under the Articles of Confederation was a compact between the states, in which these attributes of "sovereignty, freedom, and independence" were expressly asserted and guaranteed.

3. That, in forming the "more perfect union" of the Constitution, afterward adopted, the same contracting powers formed an *amended compact,* without any surrender of these attributes of sovereignty, freedom, and independence, either expressed or implied: on the contrary, that by the tenth amendment to the Constitution, limiting the power of the government to its express grants, they distinctly guarded against the presumption of a surrender of anything by implication.

4. That political sovereignty resides neither in individual citizens, nor in unorganized masses, nor in fractional subdivisions of a community, but in the people of an organized political body.

5. That no "republican form of government," in the sense in which that expression is used in the Constitution, and was generally understood by the founders of the Union—whether it be the government of a state or of a confederation of states—is possessed of any sovereignty whatever, but merely exercises certain powers delegated by the sovereign authority of the people, and subject to recall and reassumption by the same authority that conferred them.

6. That the "people" who organized the first confederation, the people who dissolved it, the people who ordained and established the Constitution which succeeded it, the only people, in fine, known or referred to in the phraseology of that period—whether the term was used collectively or distributively—were the people of the respective states,

each acting separately and with absolute independence of the others.

7. That, in forming and adopting the Constitution, the states, or the people of the states—terms which, when used with reference to acts performed in a sovereign capacity, are precisely equivalent to each other —formed a new *government,* but no new *people;* that, consequently, no new sovereignty was created—for sovereignty in an American republic can belong only to a people, never to a government—and that the federal government is entitled to exercise only the powers delegated to it by the people of the respective states.

8. That the term "people," in the preamble to the Constitution and in the tenth amendment, is used distributively; that the only "people of the United States" known to the Constitution are the people of each state in the Union; that no such political community or corporate unit as one people of the United States then existed, has ever been organized, or yet exists; that no political action by the people of the United States in the aggregate has ever taken place, or ever can take place, under the Constitution.

The fictitious idea of *one* people of the United States, contradicted in the last paragraph, has been so impressed upon the popular mind by false teaching, by careless and vicious phraseology, and by the ever-present spectacle of a great government, with its army and navy, its customhouses and post offices, its multitude of officeholders, and the splendid prizes which it offers to political ambition, that the tearing away of these illusions and presentation of the original fabric, which they have overgrown and hidden from view, have no doubt been unwelcome, distasteful, and even repellent to some of my readers. The artificial splendor which makes the deception attractive is even employed as an argument to prove its reality.

The glitter of the powers delegated to the agent serves to obscure the perception of the sovereign power of the principal by whom they are conferred, as, by the unpracticed eye, the showy costume and conspicuous functions of the drum major are mistaken for emblems of chieftaincy— while the misuse or ambiguous use of the term "union" and its congeners contributes to increase the confusion.

So much the more need for insisting upon the elementary truths which have been obscured by these specious sophistries. The reader really desirous of ascertaining truth is, therefore, again cautioned against confounding two ideas so essentially distinct as that of *government,* which is derivative, dependent, and subordinate, with that of the *people,* as an organized political community, which is sovereign, without any other than self-imposed limitations, and such as proceed from the general principles of the personal rights of man.

It has been said in a foregoing chapter that the authors of the Constitution could scarcely have anticipated the idea of such a community as the people of the United States in one mass. Perhaps this expression needs some little qualification, for there is rarely a fallacy, however stupendous, that is wholly original. A careful examination of the records of the convention of 1787 exhibits one or perhaps two instances of such a suggestion—both by the same person—and the result in each case is strikingly significant.

The original proposition made concerning the office of President of the United States contemplated his election by the Congress, or, as it was termed by the proposer, "the national Legislature." On the 17th of July, this proposition being under consideration, Gouverneur Morris moved that the words "national Legislature" be stricken out, and "citizens of the United States" inserted. The proposition was supported by James Wilson—both of these gentlemen being delegates from Pennsylvania, and both among the most earnest advocates of centralism in the convention.

Now, it is not at all certain that Morris had in view an election by the citizens of the United States "in the aggregate," voting as one people. The language of his proposition is entirely consistent with the idea of an election by the citizens of each state, voting separately and independently, though it is ambiguous, and may admit of the other construction. But this is immaterial. The proposition was submitted to a vote, and received the approval of only one state—Pennsylvania, of which Morris and Wilson were both representatives. Nine states voted against it.[1]

Six days afterward (July 23d), in a discussion of the proposed ratification of the Constitution by conventions of the people of each state, Gouverneur Morris—as we learn from Madison—"moved that the reference of the plan [i. e., of the proposed Constitution] be made to one General Convention, chosen and authorized by the people, to consider, amend, and establish the same."[2]

Here the issue seems to have been more distinctly made between the two ideas of people of the states and one people in the aggregate. The fate of the latter is briefly recorded in the two words, "not seconded." Morris was a man of distinguished ability, great personal influence, and undoubted patriotism, but out of all that assemblage—comprising, as it

---

[1] Elliott's *Debates*, Vol. I, p. 239; *Madison Papers*, pp. 1119-1124.
[2] *Madison Papers*, p. 1184.

did, such admitted friends of centralism as Hamilton, King, Wilson, Randolph, Pinckney, and others—there was not one to sustain him in the proposition to incorporate into the Constitution that theory which now predominates, the theory on which was waged the late bloody war, which was called a "war for the Union." It failed for want of a second, and does not even appear in the official journal of the convention. The very fact that such a suggestion was made would be unknown to us but for the record kept by Madison.

The extracts which have been given, in treating of special branches of the subject, from the writings and speeches of the framers of the Constitution and other statesmen of that period, afford ample proof of their entire and almost unanimous accord with the principles which have been established on the authority of the Constitution itself, the acts of ratification by the several states, and other attestations of the highest authority and validity. I am well aware that isolated expressions may be found in the reports of debates on the general and state conventions and other public bodies, indicating the existence of individual opinions seemingly inconsistent with these principles; that loose and confused ideas were sometimes expressed with regard to sovereignty, the relations between governments and people, and kindred subjects; that, while the plan of the Constitution was under discussion, and before it was definitely reduced to its present shape, there were earnest advocates in the convention of a more consolidated system, with a stronger central government. But these expressions of individual opinion only prove the existence of a small minority of dissentients from the principles generally entertained, and which finally prevailed in the formation of the Constitution. None of these ever avowed such extravagances of doctrine as are promulgated in this generation. No statesman of that day would have ventured to risk his reputation by construing an obligation to support the Constitution as an obligation to adhere to the federal government—a construction which would have insured the sweeping away of any plan of union embodying it, by a tempest of popular indignation from every quarter of the country. None of them suggested such an idea as that of the amalgamation of the people of the states into one consolidated mass —unless it was suggested by Gouverneur Morris in the proposition above referred to, in which he stood alone among the delegates of twelve sovereign states assembled in convention.

As to the features of centralism, or nationalism, which they did advocate, all the ability of this little minority of really gifted men failed to secure the incorporation of any one of them into the Constitution, or to obtain their recognition by any of the ratifying states. On the contrary, the very men who had been the leading advocates of such theories, on failing to secure their adoption, loyally accepted the result, and became the ablest and most efficient supporters of the principles which had prevailed. Thus Hamilton, who had favored the plan of a President and Senate both elected to hold office for life (or during good behavior), with a veto power in Congress on the action of the state legislature, became, through the *Federalist,* in conjunction with his associates, Madison and Jay, the most distinguished expounder and advocate of the Constitution, as then proposed and afterward ratified, with all its federal and state-rights features. In the ninth number of that remarkable series of political essays, he quotes, adopts, and applies to the then proposed Constitution, Montesquieu's description of a "confederate republic," a term he (Hamilton) repeatedly employs.

In the eighty-first number of the same series, replying to apprehensions expressed by some that a state might be brought before the federal courts to answer as defendant in suits instituted against her, he repels the idea in these plain and conclusive terms. The italics are my own:

It is inherent in the nature of *sovereignty* not to be amenable to the suit of any individual without its consent. This is the general sense and the general practice of mankind; and the exemption, as one of the *attributes of sovereignty,* is now enjoyed by the government of *every State in the Union.* Unless, therefore, there is a *surrender of this immunity* in the plan of the Convention, *it will remain with the States,* and the danger intimated must be merely ideal. . . . The contracts between *a nation* and individuals are only binding on the conscience of *the sovereign,* and have no pretensions to a compulsive force. They confer no right of action, independent of *the sovereign will.* To what purpose would it be to authorize suits against States for the debts they owe? How could recoveries be enforced? It is evident that it could not be done without *waging war* against the contracting State; and to ascribe to the Federal courts, by mere implication, and in destruction of a preëxisting right of the State governments, a power which would involve such a consequence, would be altogether forced and unwarranted.[3]

This extract is very significant, clearly showing that Hamilton assumed as undisputed propositions, in the first place, that the state was the *"sovereign";* secondly, that this sovereignty could not be alienated, unless by express surrender; thirdly, that no such surrender had been made; fourthly, that the idea of applying coercion to a state, even to enforce the fulfillment of a duty, would be equivalent to waging war against a state—it was "altogether forced and unwarrantable."

In a subsequent number Hamilton, replying to the objection that the

---

[3] *Federalist,* No. LXXXI.

Constitution contains no bill or declaration of rights, argues that it was entirely unnecessary, because in reality the people—that is, of course, the people, respectively, of the several states, who were the only people known to the Constitution or to the country—had surrendered nothing of their inherent sovereignty, but retained it unimpaired. He says: "Here, in strictness, the people *surrender nothing;* and, as they *retain everything,* they have no need of particular reservations." And again: "I go further, and affirm that bills of rights, in the sense and to the extent they are contended for, are not only unnecessary in the proposed Constitution, but would be absolutely dangerous. They would contain various exceptions to *powers not granted,* and on this very account would afford a colorable pretext to claim more than were granted. For why declare that things shall not be done, which there is no power to do?"[4] Could language be more clear or more complete in vindication of the principles laid down in this work? Hamilton declares, in effect, that the grants to the federal government in the Constitution are not surrenders, but delegations of power by the people of the states; that sovereignty remains intact where it was before; that the delegations of power were strictly limited to those expressly granted—in this, merely anticipating the tenth amendment, afterward adopted.

Finally, in the concluding article of the *Federalist,* he bears emphatic testimony to the same principles, in the remark that "every Constitution for the United States must inevitably consist of a great variety of particulars, in which *thirteen independent States* are to be accommodated in their interests or opinions of interest. . . . Hence the necessity of molding and arranging all the particulars, which are to compose the whole, in such a manner as to satisfy *all the parties to the compact.*"[5] There is no intimation here, or anywhere else, of the existence of any such idea as that of the aggregated people of one great consolidated state. It is an incidental enunciation of the same truth soon afterward asserted by Madison in the Virginia convention—that the people who ordained and established the Constitution were "not the people as composing one great body, but the people as composing thirteen sovereignties."

Madison, in the Philadelphia convention, had at first held views of the sort of government which it was desirable to organize, similar to those of Hamilton, though more moderate in extent. He too, however, cordially conformed to the modifications in them made by his colleagues, and

---

[4] *Federalist,* No. LXXXIV.
[5] *Ibid.,* No. LXXXV.

was no less zealous and eminent in defending and expounding the Constitution as finally adopted. His interpretation of its fundamental principles is so fully shown in the extracts which have already been given from his contributions to the *Federalist* and speeches in the Virginia convention, that it would be superfluous to make any additional citation from them.

The evidence of Hamilton and Madison—two of the most eminent of the authors of the Constitution, and the two preëminent contemporary expounders of its meaning—is the most valuable that could be offered for its interpretation. That of all the other statesmen of the period only tends to confirm the same conclusions. The illustrious Washington, who presided over the Philadelphia convention, in his correspondence repeatedly refers to the proposed union as a "Confederacy" of states, or a "confederated Government," and to the several states as "acceding," or signfying their "accession" to it, in ratifying the Constitution. He refers to the Constitution itself as "a compact or treaty," and classifies it among compacts or treaties between "men, bodies of men, or countries." Writing to Count Rochambeau on January 8, 1788, he says that the proposed Constitution "is to be submitted to conventions chosen by *the people in the several States,* and by them approved or rejected"—showing what he understood by "the people of the United States," who were to ordain and establish it. These same people—that is, "the people of the several States"—he says in a letter to Lafayette, April 28, 1788, "retain everything they do not, by express terms, give up." In a letter written to Benjamin Lincoln October 26, 1788, he refers to the expectation that North Carolina will accede to the Union, and adds, "Whoever shall be found to enjoy the confidence of *the States* so far as to be elected Vice-President," etc.—showing that in the "confederated Government," as he termed it, the states were still to act independently, even in the selection of officers of the general government. He wrote to General Knox, June 17, 1788, "I can not but hope that the States which may be disposed to make a secession will think often and seriously on the consequences." June 28, 1788, he wrote to General Pinckney that New Hampshire "had acceded to the new Confederacy," and, in reference to North Carolina, "I should be astonished if that State should withdraw from the Union."

I shall add but two other citations. They are from speeches of John Marshall, afterward the most distinguished Chief Justice of the United States—who has certainly never been regarded as holding high views of state rights—in the Virginia convention of 1788. In the first case, he was speaking of the power of the states over the militia, and is thus reported:

The State governments did not derive their powers from the General Government; but each government derived its powers from the people, and each was to act according to the powers given it. Would any gentleman deny this? . . . Could any man say that this power was not retained by the States, as they had not given it away? For (says he) does not a power remain till it is given away? The State Legislatures had power to command and govern their militia before, and have it still, undeniably, unless there be something in this Constitution that takes it away. . . .

He concluded by observing that the power of governing the militia was not vested in the States by implication, because, being possessed of it antecedently to the adoption of the Government, and not being divested of it by any grant or restriction in the Constitution, they must necessarily be as fully possessed of it as ever they had been, and it could not be said that the States derived any powers from that system, but retained them, though not acknowledged in any part of it.[6]

In the other case, the special subject was the power of the federal judiciary. Marshall said, with regard to this: "I hope that no gentleman will think that a State can be called at the bar of the Federal court. Is there no such case at present? Are there not many cases, in which the Legislature of Virginia is a party, and yet the State is not sued? Is it rational to suppose that the *sovereign power* shall be dragged before a court?"[7]

Authorities to the same effect might be multiplied indefinitely by quotation from nearly all the most eminent statesmen and patriots of that brilliant period. My limits, however, permit me only to refer those in quest of more exhaustive information to the original records, or to the *Republic of Republics,* in which will be found a most valuable collection and condensation of the teaching of the fathers on the subject. There was no dissent, at that period, from the interpretation of the Constitution which I have set forth, as given by its authors, except in the objections made by its adversaries. Those objections were refuted and silenced, until revived long afterward, and presented as the true interpretation, by the school of which Judge Story was the most effective founder.

At an earlier period—but when he had already served for several years in Congress, and had attained the full maturity of his powers—Webster held the views which were presented in a memorial to Congress of citizens of Boston, December 15, 1819, relative to the admission of Missouri, drawn up and signed by a committee of which he was chairman, and which also included among its members Josiah Quincy. He speaks of the states as enjoying *"the exclusive possession of sovereignty"* over their own territory, calls the United States "the American Confederacy," and says, "The only *parties to the Constitution,* contem-

---

[6] Elliott's *Debates,* Vol. III, pp. 389-391.
[7] Elliott's *Debates,* Vol. III, p. 503.

plated by it originally, were the *thirteen confederated States.*" And again: "As between the original States, the representation rests on *compact and plighted faith;* and your memorialists have no wish that that compact should be disturbed, or that plighted faith in the slightest degree violated."

It is satisfactory to know that in the closing year of his life, when looking retrospectively, with judgment undisturbed by any extraneous influence, he uttered views of the government which must stand the test of severest scrutiny and defy the storms of agitation, for they are founded on the rock of truth. In letters written and addresses delivered during the administration of Fillmore, he repeatedly applies to the Constitution the term "compact," which, in 1833, he had so vehemently repudiated. In his speech at Capon Springs, Virginia, in 1851, he says:

If the South were to violate any part of the Constitution intentionally and systematically, and persist in so doing year after year, and no remedy could be had, would the North be any longer bound by the rest of it? And if the North were, deliberately, habitually, and of fixed purpose, to disregard one part of it, would the South be bound any longer to observe its other obligations? . . .

How absurd it is to suppose that, when different parties enter into a compact for certain purposes, either can disregard any one provision, and expect, nevertheless, the other to observe the rest! . . .

I have not hesitated to say, and I repeat, that, if the Northern States refuse, willfully and deliberately, to carry into effect that part of the Constitution which respects the restoration of fugitive slaves, and Congress provide no remedy, the South would no longer be bound to observe the compact. A bargain can not be broken on one side, and still bind the other side.[8]

The principles which have been set forth in the foregoing chapters, although they had come to be considered as peculiarly Southern, were not sectional in their origin. In the beginning and earlier years of our history they were cherished as faithfully and guarded as jealously in Massachusetts and New Hampshire as in Virginia or South Carolina. It was in these principles that I was nurtured. I have frankly proclaimed them during my whole life, always contending in the Senate of the United States against what I believed to be the mistaken construction of the Constitution taught by Webster and his adherents. While I honored the genius of that great man, and held friendly personal relations with him, I considered his doctrines on these points—or rather the doctrines advocated by him during the most conspicuous and influential portions of his public career—to be mischievous, and the more dangerous to the welfare of the country and the liberties of mankind on account of the signal ability and magnificent eloquence with which they were argued.

---

[8]Curtis's *Life of Webster,* Chapt. XXXVII, Vol. II, pp. 518, 519.

CHAPTER XI: *The Right of Secession—The Law of Unlimited Partnerships—The "Perpetual Union" of the Articles of Confederation and the "More Perfect Union" of the Constitution—The Important Powers Conferred Upon the Federal Government and the Fundamental Principles of the Compact the Same in Both Systems—The Right to Resume Grants, When Failing to Fulfill their Purposes, Expressly and Distinctly Asserted in the Adoption of the Constitution.*

THE RIGHT OF SECESSION—that subject which, beyond all others, ignorance, prejudice, and political rancor have combined to cloud with misstatements and misapprehensions — is a question easily to be determined in the light of what has already been established with regard to the history and principles of the Constitution. It is not something standing apart by itself—a factious creation, outside of and antagnostic to the Constitution—as might be imagined by one deriving his ideas from the political literature most current of late years. So far from being against the Constitution or incompatible with it, we contend that, if the right to secede is not prohibited to the states, and no power to prevent it expressly delegated to the United States, it remains as reserved to the states or the people, from whom all the powers of the general government were derived.

The compact between the states which formed the Union was in the nature of a partnership between individuals without limitation of time, and the recognized law of such partnerships is thus stated by an eminent lawyer of Massachusetts in a work intended for popular use:

If the articles between the partners do not contain an agreement that the partnership shall continue for a specified time, it may be dissolved at the pleasure of either partner. But no partner can exercise this power wantonly and injuriously to the other partners, without making himself responsible for the damage he thus causes. If there be a provision that the partnership shall continue a certain time, this is binding.[1]

We have seen that a number of "sovereign, free, and independent" states, during the war of the Revolution, entered into a partnership with one another, which was not only unlimited in duration, but expressly declared to be a "perpetual union." Yet, when that Union failed to accomplish the purposes for which it was formed, the parties withdrew, separately and independently, one after another, without any question

---

[1] Parsons, *Rights of a Citizen,* Chapt. XX, section 3.

made of their right to do so, and formed a new association. One of the declared objects of this new partnership was to form "a more perfect union." This certainly did not mean more perfect in respect of duration; the former union had been declared perpetual, and perpetuity admits of no addition. It did not mean that it was to be more indissoluble; the delegates of the states, in ratifying the former compact of union, had expressed themselves in terms that could scarcely be made more stringent They then said:

And we do further *solemnly plight and engage the faith of our respective constituents,* that they shall abide by the determinations of the United States in Congress assembled, on all questions which, by the said confederation, are submitted to them; and that the articles thereof shall be *involvedly observed* by the States we respectively represent; and that *the Union shall be perpetual.*[2]

The formation of a "more perfect union" was accomplished by the organization of a government more complete in its various branches, legislative, executive, and judicial, and by the delegation to this government of certain additional powers of functions which had previously been exercised by the governments of the respective states—especially in providing the means of operating directly upon individuals for the enforcement of its legitimately delegated authority. There was no abandonment nor modification of the essential principle of a compact between sovereigns, which applied to the one case as fully as to the other. There was not the slightest intimation of so radical a revolution as the surrender of the sovereignty of the contracting parties would have been. The additional powers conferred upon the federal government by the Constitution were merely transfers of some of those possessed by the state governments—not subtractions from the reserved and inalienable sovereignty of the political communities which conferred them. It was merely the institution of a new agent who, however enlarged his powers might be, would still remain subordinate and responsible to the source from which they were derived—that of the sovereign people of each state. It was an amended Union, not a consolidation.

It is a remarkable fact that the very powers of the federal government and prohibitions to the states, which are most relied upon by the advocates of centralism as incompatible with state sovereignty, were in force under the old confederation when the sovereignty of the states was expressly recognized. The general government had then, as now, the exclusive right and power of determining on peace and war, making treaties and alliances, maintaining an army and navy, granting letters of

---

[2]Ratification appended to Articles of Confederation. (See Elliott's *Debates,* Vol. I, p. 113.)

marque and reprisal, regulating coinage, establishing and controlling the postal service—indeed, nearly all the so-called "characteristic powers of sovereignty" exercised by the federal government under the existing Constitution, except the regulation of commerce, and of levying and collecting its revenues directly, instead of through the interposition of the state authorities. The exercise of these first-named powers was prohibited to the states under the old compact, "without the consent of the United States in Congress assembled," but no one has claimed that the confederation had thereby acquired sovereignty.

Entirely in accord with these truths are the arguments of Madison in the *Federalist,* to show that the great principles of the Constitution are substantially the same as those of the Articles of Confederation. He says:

I ask, What are these principles? Do they require that, in the establishment of the Constitution, the States should be regarded as distinct and independent sovereigns? They *are* so regarded by the Constitution proposed. . . . Do these principles, in fine, require that the powers of the General Government should be limited, and that, beyond this limit, the States should be left in possession of their sovereignty and independence? We have seen that, in the new Government as in the old, the general powers are limited; and that the States, in all unenumerated cases, are left in the enjoyment of their sovereign and independent jurisdiction.

The truth is that the great principles of the Constitution proposed by the Convention may be considered *less as absolutely new, than as the expansion of principles which are found in the Articles of Confederation.*[3]

In the papers immediately following, he establishes this position in detail by an analysis of the principle powers delegated to the federal government, showing that the spirit of the original instructions to the convention had been followed in revising "the Federal Constitution" and rendering it "adequate to the exigencies of government and the preservation of the Union."[4]

The present Union owes its very existence to the dissolution, by separate secession of its members, of the former Union, which, as we have thus seen, as to its organic principles, rested upon precisely the same foundation. The right to withdraw from the association results, in either case, from the same principles—principles which, I think, have been established on an impregnable basis of history, reason, law, and precedent.

It is not contended that this right should be resorted to for insufficient cause, or, as the writer already quoted on the law of partnership says,

---

[3] *Federalist,* No. XL.
[4] *Ibid.,* Nos. XLI-XLIV.

"wantonly and injuriously to the other partners," without responsibility of the seceding party for any damage thus done. No association can be dissolved without a likelihood of the occurrence of incidental questions concerning common property and mutual obligations—questions sometimes of a complex and intricate sort. If a wrong be perpetrated, in such case, it is a matter for determination by the means usually employed among independent and sovereign powers—negotiating, arbitration, or, in the failure of these, by war, with which unfortunately, Christianity and civilization have not yet been able entirely to dispense. But the suggestion of possible evils does not at all affect the question of right. There is no great principle in the affairs either of individuals or of nations that is not liable to such difficulties in its practical application.

But, we are told, there is no mention made of secession in the Constitution. Everett says: "The States are not named in it; the word sovereignty does not occur in it; the right of secession is as much ignored in it as the procession of the equinoxes." We have seen how very untenable is the assertion that the states are not named in it, and how much pertinency or significance in the omission of the word "sovereignty." The pertinent question that occurs is, Why was so obvious an attribute of sovereignty not expressly renounced if it was intended to surrender it? It certainly existed; it was not surrendered; therefore it still exists. This would be a more natural and rational conclusion than that it has ceased to exist because it is not mentioned.

The simple truth is that it would have been a very extraordinary thing to incorporate into the Constitution any express provision for the secession of the states and dissolution of the Union. Its founders undoubtedly desired and hoped that it would be perpetual; against the proposition for power to coerce a state, the argument was that it would be a means, not of preserving, but of destroying the Union. It was not for them to make arrangements for its termination—a calamity which there was no occasion to provide for in advance. Sufficient for their day was the evil thereof. It is not usual, either in partnerships between men or in treaties between governments, to make provision for a dissolution of the partnership or a termination of the treaty, unless there be some special reason for a limitation of time. Indeed, in treaties, the usual formula includes a declaration of their perpetuity; but in either case the power of the contracting parties, or of any of them, to dissolve the compact, on terms not damaging to the rights of the other parties, is not the less clearly understood. It was not necessary in the Constitution to affirm the right of secession, because it was an attribute of sovereignty, and the states had reserved all which they had not delegated.

The right of the people of the several states to resume the powers delegated by them to the common agency was not left without positive and ample assertion, even at a period when it had never been denied. The ratification of the Constitution by Virginia has already been quoted, in which the people of that state, through their convention, did expressly "declare and make known that the powers granted under the Constitution, being derived from the people of the United States, may be resumed by them, whensoever the same shall be perverted to their injury or oppression, and that every power not granted thereby remains with them and at their will."[5]

New York and Rhode Island were no less explicit, both declaring that "the powers of government *may be reassumed by the people* whenever it shall become necessary to their happiness."[6]

These expressions are not mere *obiter dicta,* thrown out incidentally, and entitled only to be regarded as an expression of opinion by their authors. Even if only such, they would carry great weight as the deliberately expressed judgment of enlightened contemporaries, but they are more: they are parts of the very acts or ordinances by which these states ratified the Constitution and acceded to the Union, and cannot be detached from them. If they are invalid, the ratification itself was invalid, for they are inseparable. By inserting these declarations in their ordinances, Virginia, New York, and Rhode Island formally, officially, and permanently declared their interpretation of the Constitution as recognizing the right of secession by the resumption of their grants. By accepting the ratifications with this declaration incorporated, the other states as formally accepted the principle which it asserted.

I am well aware that it has been attempted to construe these declarations concerning the right of the people to reassume their delegations of power—especially in the terms employed by Virginia, "people of the United States"—as having reference to the idea of one people, in mass, or "in the aggregate." But it can scarcely be possible that any candid and intelligent reader who has carefully considered the evidence already brought to bear on the subject, can need further argument to disabuse his mind of that political fiction. The "people of the United States," from whom the powers of the federal government were "derived," could have been no other than the people who ordained and ratified the Constitu-

---

[5] See Elliott's *Debates,* Vol. I, p. 360.
[6] *Ibid.,* pp. 361, 369.

tion; this, it has been shown beyond the power of denial, was done by the people of *each state,* severally and independently.   No other *people* were known to the authors of the declarations above quoted.   Madison was a leading member of the Virginia convention, which made that declaration, as well as of the general convention that drew up the Constitution.   We have seen what his idea of "the people of the United States" was—"not the people as composing one great body, but the people as composing thirteen sovereignties."[7]   Lee of Westmoreland ("Light-Horse Harry") in the same convention, answering Henry's objection to the expression, "We, the people," said: "It [the Constitution] is now submitted to *the people of Virginia.* If we do not adopt it, it will be always null and void as to us.   Suppose it was found proper for our adoption, and becoming the government of *the people of Virginia,* by what style should it be done?   Ought we not to make use of the name of the people?   No other style would be proper."[8]   It would certainly be superfluous, after all that has been presented heretofore, to add any further evidence of the meaning that was attached to these expressions by their authors.   "The people of the United States" were in their minds the people of Virginia, the people of Massachusetts, and the people of every other state that should agree to unite.   They could have meant only that the people of their respective states who had delegated certain powers to the federal government, in ratifying the Constitution and acceding to the Union, reserved to themselves the right, in event of the failure of their purposes, to "resume" (or "reassume") those powers by seceding from the same Union.

Finally, the absurdity of the construction attempted to be put upon these expressions will be evident from a very brief analysis.   If the assertion of the right of reassumption of their powers was meant for the protection of the whole people—the people in mass—the people "in the aggregate"—of a consolidated republic—against whom or what was it to protect them?   By whom were the powers granted to be perverted to the injury or oppression of the whole people?   By themselves or by some of the states, all of whom, according to this hypothesis, had been consolidated into one?   As no danger could have been apprehended from either of these, it must have been against the government of the United States that the provision was made; that is to say, the whole people of a republic make this declaration against a government established by themselves and entirely subject to their own control, under a constitution

[7] Elliott's *Debates,* Vol. III, p. 114.
[8] *Ibid.,* p. 71.

which contains provisions for its own amendment by this very same "whole people," whenever they may think proper! Is it not a libel upon the statesmen of that generation to attribute to their grave and solemn declarations a meaning so vapid and absurd?

To those who argue that the grants of the Constitution are fatal to the reservation of sovereignty by the states, the Constitution furnishes a conclusive answer in the amendment which was coeval with the adoption of the instrument, and which declares that all powers not delegated to the government of the Union were reserved to the states or to the people. As sovereignty was not delegated by the states, it was necessarily reserved. It would be superfluous to answer arguments against implied powers of the states; none are claimed by implication, because all not delegated by the states remained with them, and it was only in an abundance of caution that they expressed the right to resume such parts of their unlimited power as was delegated for the purpose enumerated. As these be those who see danger to the perpetuity of the Union in the possession of such power by the states, and insist that our fathers did not intend to bind the states together by a compact no better than "a rope of sand," it may be well to examine their position. From what have dangers to the Union arisen? Have they sprung from too great restriction on the exercise of the granted powers, or from the assumption by the general government of power claimed by implication? The whole record of our Union answers, from the latter only.

Was this tendency to usurpation caused by the presumption of paramount authority in the general government, or by the assertion of the right of a state to resume the powers it had delegated? Reasonably and honestly it cannot be assigned to the latter. Let it be supposed that the "whole people" had recognized the right of a state of the Union, peaceably and independently, to resume the powers which, peaceably and independently, she had delegated to the federal government, would not this have been potent to restrain the general government from exercising its functions to the injury and oppression of such state? To deny that effect would be to suppose that a dominant majority would be willing to drive a state from the Union. Would the admission of the right of a state to resume the grants it had made, have led to the exercise of that right for light and trivial causes? Surely the evidence furnished by the nations, both ancient and modern, refutes the supposition. In the language of the *Declaration of Independence,* "All experience hath shown that mankind are more disposed to suffer, while evils are sufferable, than to right themselves by abolishing the forms to which they are accustomed." Would not real grievances be rendered more tolerable by the consciousness of power to remove them; and would not even imaginary wrongs be embittered by the manifestation of a purpose to make them perpetual? To ask these questions is to answer them.

The wise and brave men who had, at much peril and great sacrifice, secured the independence of the states, were as little disposed to surrender the sovereignty of the states as they were anxious to organize a general government with adequate powers to remedy the defects of the confederation. The Union they formed was not to destroy the states, but to "secure the blessings of liberty to ourselves and our posterity."

CHAPTER XII: *Coercion the Alternative to Secession—Repudiation of it by the Constitution and the Fathers of the Constitutional Era — Difference Between Webster and Hamilton.*

THE alternative to secession is coercion. That is to say, if no such right as that of secession exists—if it is forbidden or precluded by the Constitution—then it is a wrong; by a well settled principle of public law, for every wrong there must be a remedy, which in this case must be the application of force to the state attempting to withdraw from the Union.

Early in the session of the convention which formed the Constitution, it was proposed to confer upon Congress the power "to call forth the force of the Union against any member of the Union failing to fulfill its duty under the articles thereof." When this proposition came to be considered, Madison observed that "a union of the States containing such an ingredient seemed to provide for its own destruction. The use of force against a State would look more like a declaration of war than an infliction of punishment, and would probably be considered by the party attacked as a dissolution of all previous compacts by which it might be bound. He hoped that such a system would be framed as might render this recourse unnecessary, and moved that the clause be postponed." This motion was adopted *nem. con.,* and the proposition was never again revived.[1] Again on a subsequent occasion, speaking of an appeal to force, Madison said: "Was such a remedy eligible? Was it practicable? . . . Any government for the United States, formed on the supposed practicability of using force against the unconstitutional proceedings of the States, would prove as visionary and fallacious as the government of Congress."[2] Every proposition looking in any way to the same or a similar object was promptly rejected by the convention. George Mason of Virginia said of such a proposition: "Will not the citizens of the invaded State assist one another, until they rise as one man and shake off the Union altogether?"[3]

Oliver Ellsworth, in the ratifying convention of Connecticut, said: "This Constitution does not attempt to coerce *sovereign bodies, States,* in their political capacity. No coercion is applicable to such bodies but that of an armed force. If we should attempt to execute the laws of the Union by sending an armed force against a delinquent State, it would in-

---

[1] *Madison Papers,* pp. 732, 761.
[2] *Ibid.,* p. 822.
[3] *Ibid.,* p. 914.

volve the good and bad, the innocent and guilty, in the same calamity."[4]

Hamilton, in the convention of New York, said: "To coerce the States is one of the maddest projects that was ever devised. . . . What picture does this idea present to our view? A complying State at war with a non-complying State: Congress marching the troops of one State into the bosom of another: . . . Here is a nation at war with itself. Can any reasonable man be well disposed toward a government which makes war and carnage the only means of supporting itself—a government that can exist only by the sword? . . . But can we believe that one State will ever suffer itself to be used as an instrument of coercion? The thing is a dream—it is impossible."[5]

Unhappily, our generation has seen that, in the decay of the principles and feelings which animated the hearts of all patriots in that day, this thing, like many others then regarded as impossible dreams, has been only too feasible, and that states have permitted themselves to be used as instruments, not merely for the coercion, but for the destruction of the freedom and independence of their sister states.

Edmund Randolph, governor of Virginia, although the mover of the original proposition to authorize the employment of the forces of the Union against a delinquent member, which had been so signally defeated in the federal convention, afterward, in the Virginia convention, made an eloquent protest against the idea of the employment of force against a state. "What species of military coercion," said he, "could the General Government adopt for the enforcement of obedience to its demands? Either an army sent into the heart of a delinquent State, or blocking up its ports. Have we lived to this, then, that, in order to suppress and exclude tyranny, it is necessary to render the most affectionate friends the most bitter enemies, set the father against the son, and make the brother slay the brother? Is this the happy expedient that is to preserve liberty? Will it not destroy it? If an army be once introduced to force us, if once marched into Virginia, figure to yourselves what the dreadful consequence will be: the most lamentable civil war must ensue."[6]

We have seen already how vehemently the idea of even judicial coercion was repudiated by Hamilton, Marshall, and others. The suggestion of military coercion was uniformly treated, as in the above extracts, with still more abhorrence. No principle was more fully and finally settled on the highest authority than that, under our system, there could be no coercion of a state.

---

[4] Elliott's *Debates*, Vol. II, p. 199.
[5] *Ibid.*, pp. 232, 233.
[6] Elliott's *Debates*, Vol. III, p. 117.

Webster, in his elaborate speech of February 16, 1833, arguing throughout against the sovereignty of the states, and in the course of his argument sadly confounding the ideas of the federal Constitution and the federal government, as he confounds the sovereign people of the states with the state governments, says: "The States *can not* omit to appoint Senators and electors. It is not a matter resting in State discretion or State pleasure. . . . . No member of a State Legislature can refuse to proceed, at the proper time, to elect Senators to Congress, or to provide for the choice of electors of President and Vice-President, any more than the members can refuse, when the appointed day arrives, to meet the members of the other House, to count the votes for those officers and ascertain who are chosen."[7] This was before the invention in 1877 of an electoral commission to relieve Congress of its constitutional duty to count the vote. Hamilton, on the contrary, fresh from the work of forming the Constitution, and familiar with its principles and purposes, said: "It is certainly true that the State Legislatures, by forbearing the appointment of Senators, may destroy the national Government."[8]

It is unnecessary to discuss the particular question on which these two great authorities are thus directly at issue. I do not contend that the state legislatures, of their own will, have a right to forego the performance of any federal duty imposed upon them by the Constitution. But there is a power beyond and above that of either the federal or state governments—the power of the people of the state, who ordained and established the Constitution, as far as it applies to themselves, reserving, as I think has been demonstrated, the right to reassume the grants of power therein made, when they deem it necessary for their safety or welfare to do so. At the behest of this power, it certainly becomes not only the right, but the duty, of their state legislature to refrain from any action implying adherence to the Union, or partnership, from which the sovereign has withdrawn.

---

[7] *Congressional Debates*, Vol. IX, Part I, p. 566.
[8] *Federalist*, No. LIX.

CHAPTER XIII: *Some Objections Considered—The New States —Acquired Territory—Allegiance, False and True—Difference Between Nullification and Secession—Secession a Peaceable Remedy—No Appeal to Arms—Two Conditions Noted.*

IT would be only adding to a superabundance of testimony to quote further from the authors of the Constitution in support of the principle, unquestioned in that generation, that the people who granted—that is to say, of course, the people of the several states—might resume their grants. It will require but few words to dispose of some superficial objections that have been made to the application of this doctrine in a special case.

It is sometimes said that, whatever weight may attach to principles founded on the sovereignty and independence of the original thirteen states, they cannot apply to the states of more recent origin—constituting now a majority of the members of the Union—because these are but the offspring of creatures of the Union, and must of course be subordinate and dependent.

This objection would scarcely occur to any instructed mind, though it may possess a certain degree of specious plausibility for the untaught. It is enough to answer that the entire equality of the states, in every particular, is a vital condition of their union. Every new member that has been admitted into the partnership of states came in, as is expressly declared in the acts for their admission, on a footing of perfect equality in every respect with the original members. This equality is as complete as the equality, before the laws, of the son with the father, immediately on the attainment by the former of his legal majority, without regard to the prior condition of dependence and tutelage. The relations of the original states to one another and to the Union cannot be affected by any subsequent accessions of new members, as the Constitution fixes those relations permanently, and furnishes the normal standard which is applicable to all. The Boston memorial to Congress, referred to in a foregoing chapter, as prepared by a committee with Webster at its head, says that the new states "are universally considered as admitted into the Union upon the same footing as the original States, and as possessing, in respect to the Union, the same rights of *sovereignty, freedom, and independence,* as the other States."

But, with regard to states formed of territory acquired by purchase from France, Spain, and Mexico, it is claimed that, as they were bought

[153]

by the United States, they belong to the same, and have no right to withdraw at will from an association the property which had been purchased by the other parties.

Happy would it have been if the equal rights of the people of all the states to the enjoyment of territory acquired by the common treasure could have been recognized at the proper time! There would then have been no secession and no war.

As for the sordid claim of ownership of states, on account of the money spent for the land which they contain—I can understand the ground of a claim to some interest in the soil, so long as it continues to be public property, but have yet to learn in what way the United States ever became purchaser of the *inhabitants* or of their political rights.

Any question in regard to property has always been admitted to be matter for fair and equitable settlement, in case of the withdrawal of a state.

The treaty by which the Louisiana territory was ceded to the United States expressly provided that the inhabitants thereof should be "admitted, as soon as possible, according to the principles of the Federal Constitution, to the enjoyment of all the rights, advantages, and immunities of citizens of the United States."[1] In all other acquisitions of territory the same stipulation is either expressed or implied. Indeed, the denial of the right would be inconsistent with the character of American political institutions.

Another objection made to the right of secession is based upon obscure, indefinite, and inconsistent ideas with regard to allegiance. It assumes various shapes, and is therefore somewhat difficult to meet, but, as most frequently presented, may be stated thus: that the citizen owes a double allegiance, or a divided allegiance—partly to his state, partly to the United States; that it is not possible for either of these powers to release him from the allegiance due to the other; that the state can no more release him from his obligations to the Union than the United States can absolve him from his duties to his state. This is the most moderate way in which the objection is put. The extreme centralizers go further, and claim that allegiance to the Union, or, as they generally express it, to the government—meaning thereby the federal government—is paramount, and the obligation to the state only subsidiary—if, indeed, it exists at all.

This latter view, if the more monstrous, is at least the more consistent of the two, for it does not involve the difficulty of a divided allegiance,

---

[1] Ray's *Louisiana Digest,* Vol. I, p. 24.

nor the paradoxical position in which the other places the citizen, in case of a conflict between his state and the other members of the Union, of being necessarily a rebel against the general government or a traitor to the state of which he is a citizen.

As to true allegiance, in the light of the principles which have been established, there can be no doubt with regard to it. The primary, paramount allegiance of the citizen is due to the sovereign only. That sovereign, under our system, is the people—the people of the state to which he belongs—the people who constituted the state government which he obeys, and which protects him in the enjoyment of his personal rights— the people who alone (as far as he is concerned) ordained and established the federal Constitution and federal government—the people who have reserved to themselves sovereignty, which involves the power to revoke all agencies created by them. The obligation to support the state or federal Constitution and the obedience due to either state or federal government are alike derived from and dependent on the allegiance due to this sovereign. If the sovereign abolishes the state government and ordains and establishes a new one, the obligation of allegiance requires him to transfer his obedience accordingly. If the sovereign withdraws from association with its confederates in the Union, the allegiance of the citizen requires him to follow the sovereign. Any other course is rebellion or treason—words which, in the cant of the day, have been so grossly misapplied and perverted as to be made worse than unmeaning. His relation to the Union arose from the membership of the state of which he was a citizen, and ceased whenever his state withdrew from it. He cannot owe obedience—much less allegiance—to an association from which his sovereign has separated, and thereby withdrawn him.

Every officer of both federal and state governments is required to take an oath to support the Constitution, a compact the binding force of which is based upon the sovereignty of the states—a sovereignty necessarily carrying with it the principles just stated with regard to allegiance. Every such officer is, therefore, virtually sworn to maintain and support the sovereignty of all the states.

Military and naval officers take, in addition, an oath to obey the lawful orders of their superiors. Such an oath has never been understood to be eternal in its obligations. It is dissolved by the death, dismissal, or resignation of the officer who takes it; such resignation is not a mere optional right, but becomes an imperative duty when continuance in the service comes to be in conflict with the ultimate allegiance due to the sovereignty of the state to which he belongs.

A little consideration of these plain and irrefutable truths would show how utterly unworthy and false are the vulgar taunts which attribute "treason" to those who, in the late secession of the Southern states, were loyal to the only sovereign entitled to their allegiance, and which still more absurdly prate of the violation of oaths to support "the government," an oath which nobody ever could have been legally required to take, and which must have been ignorantly confounded with the prescribed oath to support the Constitution.

Nullification and secession are often erroneously treated as if they were one and the same thing. It is true that both ideas spring from the sovereign right of a state to interpose for the protection of its own people, but they are altogether unlike as to both their extent and the character of the means to be employed. The first was a temporary expedient, intended to restrain action until the question at issue could be submitted to a convention of the states. It was a remedy which its supporters sought to apply within the Union, a means to avoid the last resort—separation. If the application for a convention should fail, or if the state making it should suffer an adverse decision, the advocates of that remedy have not revealed what they proposed as the next step—supposing the infraction of the compact to have been of that character which, according to Webster, dissolved it.

Secession, on the other hand, was the assertion of the inalienable right of a people to change their government, whenever it ceased to fulfill the purpose for which it was ordained and established. Under our form of government, and the cardinal principles upon which it was founded, it should have been a peaceful remedy. The withdrawal of a state from a league has no revolutionary or insurrectionary characteristic. The government of the state remains unchanged as to all internal affairs. It is only its external or confederate relations that are altered. To term this action of a sovereign a "rebellion," is a gross abuse of language. So is the flippant phrase which speaks of it as an appeal to the "arbitrament of the sword." In the late contest, in particular, there was no appeal by the seceding states to the arbitrament of arms. There was on their part no invitation nor provocation to war. They stood in an attitude of self-defense, and were attacked for merely exercising a right guaranteed by the original terms of the compact. They neither tendered nor accepted any challenge to the wager of battle. The man who defends his house against attack cannot with any propriety be said to have submitted the question of his right to it to the arbitrament of arms.

Two moral obligations or restrictions upon a seceding state certainly exist: in the first place, not to break up the partnership without good and sufficient cause; in the second, to make an equitable settlement with former associates, and, as far as may be, to avoid the infliction of loss or damage upon any of them. Neither of these obligations was violated or neglected by the Southern states in their secession.

CHAPTER XIV: *Early Foreshadowings—Opinions of Madison and Rufus King—Safeguards Provided—Their Failure—State Interpositions—The Kentucky and Virginia Resolutions—Their Endorsement by the People in the Presidential Elections of 1800 and Ensuing Terms—South Carolina and Calhoun—The Compromise of 1833—Action of Massachusetts in 1843-'45—Opinions of John Quincy Adams—Necessity for Secession.*

FROM the earliest period, it was foreseen by the wisest of our statesmen that a danger to the perpetuity of the Union would arise from the conflicting interests of different sections, and every effort was made to secure each of these classes of interests against aggression by the other. As a proof of this may be cited the following extract from Madison's report of a speech made by himself in the Philadelphia convention on June 30, 1787:

He admitted that every peculiar interest, whether in any class of citizens or any description of States, ought to be secured as far as possible. Wherever there is danger of attack, there ought to be given a constitutional power of defense. But he contended that the States were divided into different interests, not by their difference of size, but by other circumstances; the most material of which resulted from climate, but principally from the effects of their having or not having slaves. These two causes concurred in forming the great division of interests in the United States. It did not lie between the large and small States; it lay between the Northern and Southern; and, if any defensive power were necessary, it ought to be mutually given to these two interests.[1]

Rufus King, a distinguished member of the convention from Massachusetts, a few days afterward said, to the same effect: "He was fully convinced that the question concerning a difference of interests did not lie where it had hitherto been discussed, between the great and small States, but between the Southern and Eastern. For this reason he had been ready to yield something, in the proportion of representatives, for the security of the Southern. . . . He was not averse to giving them a still greater security, but did not see how it could be done."[2]

The wise men who formed the Constitution were not seeking to bind the states together by the material power of a majority; nor were they so blind to the influences of passion and interest as to believe that paper barriers would suffice to restrain a majority actuated by either or both of these motives. They endeavored, therefore, to prevent the conflicts in-

[1] *Madison Papers,* p. 1006.
[2] *Ibid.,* pp. 1057, 1058.

evitable from the ascendancy of a sectional or party majority, by so distributing the powers of government that each interest might hold a check upon the other. It was believed that the compromises made with regard to representation—securing to each state an equal vote in the Senate, and in the House of Representatives giving the states a weight in proportion to their respective population, estimating the negroes as equivalent to three-fifths of the same number of free whites—would have the effect of giving at an early period a majority in the House of Representatives to the South, while the North would retain the ascendancy in the Senate. Thus it was supposed that the two great sectional interests would be enabled to restrain each other within the limits of purposes and action beneficial to both.

The failure of these expectations need not affect our reverence for the intentions of the fathers, or our respect for the means which they devised to carry them into effect. That they were mistaken, both as to the maintenance of the balance of sectional power and as to the fidelity and integrity with which the Congress was expected to conform to the letter and spirit of its delegated authority, is perhaps to be ascribed less to lack of prophetic foresight, than to that over-sanguine confidence which is the weakness of honest minds, and which was naturally strengthened by the patriotic and fraternal feelings resulting from the great struggle through which they had then but recently passed. They saw, in the sufficiency of the authority delegated to the federal government and in the fullness of the sovereignty retained by the states, a system the strict construction of which was so eminently adapted to indefinite expansion of the confederacy as to embrace every variety of production and consequent diversity of pursuit. Carried out in the spirit in which it was devised, there was in this system no element of disintegration, but every facility for an enlargement of the circle of the family of states (or nations), so that it scarcely seemed unreasonable to look forward to a fulfillment of the aspiration of Hamilton, that it might extend over North America, perhaps over the whole continent.

Not at all incompatible with these views and purposes was the recognition of the right of the states to reassume, if occasion should require it, the powers which they had delegated. On the contrary, the maintenance of this right was the surest guarantee of the perpetuity of the Union, and the denial of it sounded the first serious note of its dissolution. The conservative efficiency of "state interposition" for maintenance of the essential principles of the Union against aggression or decadence, is one of the most conspicuous features in the debates of the various state conventions by which the Constitution was ratified. Perhaps their ideas of the particular form in which this interposition was to be made may have been somewhat indefinite, and left to be reduced to shape by the circumstances when they should arise, but the principle itself was assumed and asserted as fundamental. But for a firm reliance upon it, as a sure resort in case of need, it may safely be said that the Union would never have been formed. It would be unjust to the wisdom and sagacity of the framers of the Constitution to suppose that they entirely relied on paper barriers for the protection of the rights of minorities. Fresh from the defense of violated charters and faithless aggression on inalienable rights, it might, *a priori,* be assumed that they would require something more potent than mere promises to protect them from human depravity and human ambition. That they did so is to be found in the debates both of the general and the state conventions, where state interposition was often declared to be the bulwark against usurpation.

At an early period in the history of the federal government, the states of Kentucky and Virginia found reason to reassert this right of state interposition. In the first of the famous resolutions drawn by Jefferson in 1798, and with some modification adopted by the legislature of Kentucky in November of that year, it is declared that, "whensoever the General Government assumes undelegated powers, its acts are *unauthoritative, void, and of no force;* that to this compact each State acceded as a State, and is an integral party; that this Government, created by this compact, was not made the exclusive or final judge of the extent of the powers delegated to itself; since that would have made its discretion, and not the Constitution, the measure of its powers; but that, as in all other cases of compact among parties having no common judge, *each party has an equal right to judge for itself, as well of infractions as of the mode and measure of redress.*"

In the Virginia resolutions, drawn by Madison, adopted on December 24, 1798, and reaffirmed in 1799, the General Assembly of that state declares that "it views the powers of the Federal Government as resulting from the compact, to which the states are parties, as limited by the plain sense and intention of the instrument constituting that compact, as no further valid than they are authorized by the grants enumerated in that compact; and that, in case of a deliberate, palpable, and dangerous exercise of other powers, not granted by the said compact, the States, who are parties thereto, have the right, and are in duty bound, to interpose, for arresting the progress of the evil, and for maintaining within their respective limits the authorities, rights, and liberties, appertaining to them." Another of the same series of resolutions denounces the indications of a design "to consolidate the States by degrees into one sovereignty."

These, it is true, were only the resolves of two states, and they were dissented from by several other state legislatures—not so much on the ground of opposition to the general principles asserted as on that of their being unnecessary in their application to the alien and sedition laws, which were the immediate occasion of their utterance. Nevertheless, they were the basis of the contest for the presidency in 1800, which resulted in their approval by the people in the triumphant election of Jefferson. They became part of the accepted creed of the Republican, Democratic, State-Rights, or Conservative party, as it has been variously termed at different periods, and as such they were ratified by the people in every presidential election that took place for sixty years, with two exceptions. The last victory obtained under them, and when they were emphasized by adding the construction of them contained in the report of Madison to the Virginia legislature in 1799, was at the election of Buchanan—the last President chosen by vote of a party that could with any propriety be styled "national," in contradistinction to sectional.

At a critical and memorable period, that pure spirit, luminous intellect, and devoted adherent of the Constitution, the great statesman of South Carolina, invoked this remedy of state interposition against the Tariff Act of 1828, which was deemed injurious and oppressive to his state. No purpose was then declared to coerce the state, as such, but measures were taken to break the protective shield of her authority and enforce the laws of Congress upon her citizens, by compelling them to pay outside of her ports the duties on imports, which the state had declared unconstitutional and had forbidden to be collected in her ports.

There remained at that day enough of the spirit in which the Union had been founded—enough of respect for the sovereignty of states and of regard for the limitations of the Constitution—to prevent a conflict of arms. The compromise of 1833 was adopted, which South Carolina agreed to accept, the principle for which she contended being virtually conceded.

Meantime there had been no lack, as we have already seen, of assertions of the sovereign rights of the states from other quarters. The declaration of these rights by the New England states and their representatives, on the acquisition of Louisiana in 1803, on the admission of the state of that name in 1811-'12, and on the question of the annexation of Texas in 1843-'45, have been referred to in another place. Among the resolutions of the Massachusetts legislature, in relation to the proposed annexation of Texas, adopted in February, 1845, were the following:

2. *Resolved,* That there has hitherto been no precedent of the admission of a foreign state or foreign territory into the Union by legislation, granted in the Constitution of the United States to Congress, do not embrace a case of the admission of a foreign state or foreign territory, by legislation, into the Union, such an act of admission *would have no binding force whatever on the people of Massachusetts.*

3. *Resolved,* That the power, *never having been granted by the people of Massachusetts,* to admit into the Union States and Territories not within the same when the Constitution was adopted, *remains with the people, and can only be exercised in such way and manner as the people shall hereafter designate and appoint.*[3]

To these stanch declarations of principles—with regard to which (leaving out of consideration the particular occasion that called them forth) my only doubt would be whether they do not express too decided a doctrine of nullification—may be added the avowal of one of the most distinguished sons of Massachusetts, John Quincy Adams, in his discourse before the New York Historical Society, in 1839:

Nations acknowledge no judge between them upon earth; and their governments, from necessity, must, in their intercourse with each other, decide when the failure of one party to a contract to perform its obligations absolves the other from the reciprocal fulfillment of its own. But this last of earthly powers is not necessary to the freedom or independence of States connected together by the immediate action of the people of whom they consist. To the people alone is there reserved as well the dissolving as the constituent power, and that power can be exercised by them only under the tie of conscience, binding them to the retributive justice of Heaven.

With these qualifications, we may admit the same right as vested in the *people of every State* in the Union, with reference to the General Government, which was exercised by the people of the united colonies with reference to the supreme head of the British Empire, of which they formed a part; and under these limitations have the people of each State in the Union a right to secede from the confederated Union itself.

Thus stands the RIGHT. But the indissoluble link of union between the people of the people of the several States of this confederated nation is, after all, not in the RIGHT, but in the HEART. If the day should ever come (may Heaven avert it!) when the affections of the people of these States shall be alienated from each other, when the fraternal spirit shall give way to cold indifference, or collision of interests shall fester into hatred, the bonds of political association will not long hold together parties no longer attracted by the magnetism of conciliated interests and kindly sympathies; and *far better will it be for the people of the disunited States to part in friendship with each other than to be held together by constraint.* Then will be the time for reverting to the precedents which occurred

---

[3] *Congressional Globe,* Vol. XIV, p. 299.

at the formation and adoption of the Constitution, to form again a *more perfect Union, by dissolving that which could no longer bind,* and to leave the separated parts to be reunited by the law of political gravitation to the center.

Perhaps it is unfortunate that, in earlier and better times, when the prospect of serious difficulties first arose, a convention of the states was not assembled to consider the relations of the various states and the government of the Union. As time rolled on the general government, gathering with both hands a mass of undelegated powers, reached that position which Jefferson had pointed out as an intolerable evil—the claim of a right to judge of the extent of its own authority. Of those then participating in public affairs, it was apparently useless to ask that the question should be submitted for decision to the parties to the compact, under the same conditions as those which controlled the formation and adoption of the Constitution; otherwise, a convention would have been utterly fruitless, for at that period, when aggression for sectional aggrandizement had made such rapid advances, it can scarcely be doubted that more than a fourth, if not a majority of states, would have adhered to that policy which had been manifested for years in the legislation of many states, as well as in that of the federal government. What course would then have remained to the Southern states? Nothing, except either to submit to a continuation of what they believed and felt to be violations of the compact of union, breaches of faith, injurious and oppressive usurpation, or else to assert the sovereign right to reassume the grants they had made, since those grants had been perverted from their original and proper purposes.

Surely the right to resume the powers delegated and to judge of the propriety and sufficiency of the causes for doing so are alike inseparable from the possession of sovereignty. Over sovereigns there is no common judge, and between them can be no umpire, except by their own agreement and consent. The necessity or propriety of exercising the right to withdraw from a confederacy or union must be determined by each member for itself. Once determined in favor of withddrawal, all that remains for consideration is the obligation to see that no wanton damage is done to former associates, and to make such fair settlement of common interest as the equity of the case may require.

CHAPTER XV: *A Bond of Union Necessary after the Declaration of Independence—Articles of Confederation—The Constitution of the United States—The Same Principle for Obtaining Grants of Power in Both—The Constitution an Instrument Enumerating the Powers Delegated—The Power of Amendment Merely a Power to Amend the Delegated Grants—A Smaller Power Required for Amendment than for a Grant—The Power of Amendment Confined to Grants of the Constitution—Limitations on the Power of Amendment.*

IN July, 1776, the Congress of the thirteen united colonies declared that "these united colonies are, and of right ought to be, free and independent States." The denial of this asserted right and the attempted coercion made it manifest that a bond of union was necessary for the common defense.

In November of the next year, 1777, articles of confederation and perpetual union were entered into by the thirteen states under the style of "The United States of America." The government instituted was to be administered by a congress of delegates from the several states, and each state to have an equal voice in legislation. The government so formed was to act through and by the states, and, having no power to enforce its requisition upon the states, embarrassment was early realized in its efforts to provide for the exigencies of war. After the treaty of peace and recognition of the independence of the states, the difficulty of raising revenue and regulating commerce was so great as to lead to repeated efforts to obtain from the states additional grants of power. Under the Articles of Confederation no amendment of them could be made except by the unanimous consent of the states, and this it had not been found possible to obtain for the powers requisite to the efficient discharge of the functions entrusted to the Congress. Hence arose the proceedings for a convention to amend the Articles of Confederation. The result was the formation of a new plan of government, entitled "The Constitution of the United States of America."

This was submitted to the Congress, in order that, if approved by them, it might be referred to the states for adoption or rejection by the several conventions thereof; if adopted by nine of the states, it was to be the compact of union between the states so ratifying the same.

The new form of government differed in many essential particulars from the old one. The delegates, intent on the purpose to give greater efficiency to the government of the Union, proposed greatly to enlarge its powers, so much so that it was not deemed safe to confide them to a single body, and they were consequently distributed between three independent departments of government, which might be a check upon one another. The Constitution did not, like the Articles of Confederation, declare that the states had agreed to a perpetual union, but distinctly indicated the hope of its perpetuity by the expression in the preamble of the purpose to "secure the blessings of liberty to ourselves and our posterity." The circumstances under which the Union of the Constitution was formed justified the hope of its perpetuity, but the brief existence of the confederation may have been a warning against the renewal of the assertion that the compact should be perpetual.

A remedy for the embarrassment which had been realized, under the Articles of Confederation, in obtaining amendments to correct any defects in grants of power, so as to render them effective for the purpose for which they were given, was provided by its fifth article. It is here to be specially noted that new grants of power, as asked for by the convention, were under the Articles of Confederation only to be obtained from the unanimous assent of the states. Therefore it followed that two of the states which did not ratify the Constitution were, so long as they retained that attitude, free from its obligations. Thus it is seen that the same principle in regard to obtaining grants of additional power for the federal government formed the rule for the Union as it had done for the confederation; that is, that the consent of each and every state was a prerequisite. The apprehension which justly existed that several of the states might reject the Constitution, and under the rule of unanimity defeat it, led to the seventh article of the Constitution, which provided that the ratification by the conventions of nine states should be sufficient for the establishment of the Constitution between the states ratifying it, which of course contemplated leaving the others, more or less in number, separate and distinct from the nine states forming a new government. Thus was the Union to be a voluntary compact, and all the powers of its government to be derived from the assent of each of its members.

These powers as proposed by the Constitution were so extensive as to create alarm and opposition by some of the most influential men in many of the states. It is known that the objection of the patriot Samuel Adams was only overcome by an assurance that such an amendment as the tenth would be adopted. Like opposition was by like assurance elsewhere overcome. That article is in these words: "The powers not delegated to the United States by the Constitution, nor prohibited by it to the States, are reserved to the States respectively or to the people."

Amendment, however, of the delegated powers was made more easy than it had been under the confederation. Ratification by three-fourths of the states was sufficient under the Constitution for the adoption of an amendment to it. As this power of amendment threatens to be the Aaron's rod which will swallow up the rest, I propose to give it special examination. What is the Constitution of the United States? The whole body of the instrument, the history of its formation and adoption, as well as the tenth amendment, added in an abundance of caution, clearly show it to be an instrument enumerating the powers delegated by the states to the federal government, their common agent. It is specifically declared that all which was not so delegated was reserved. On this mass of reserved powers, those which the states declined to grant, the federal government was expressly forbidden to intrude. Of what value would this prohibition have been, if three-fourths of the states could, without the assent of a particular state, invade the domain which that state had reserved for its own exclusive use and control?

It has heretofore, I hope, been satisfactorily demonstrated that the states were sovereigns before they formed the Union, and that they have never surrendered their sovereignty, but have only entrusted to their common agent certain functions of sovereignty to be used for their common welfare.

Among the powers delegated was one to amend the Constitution, which, it is submitted, was merely the power to amend the delegated grants, and these were obtained by the separate and independent action of each state acceding to the Union. When we consider how carefully each clause was discussed in the general convention, and how closely each was scrutinized in the conventions of the several states, the conclusion cannot be avoided that all was specified which it was intended to bestow, and not a few of the wisest in that day held that too much power had been conferred.

Aware of the imperfection of everything devised by man, it was foreseen that, in the exercise of the functions entrusted to the general government, experience might reveal the necessity of modification—*i.e.,* amendment—and power was therefore given to amend, in a certain manner, the delegated trusts so as to make them efficient for the purposes designed, or to prevent their misconstruction or abuse to the injury or oppression of any of the people. In support of this view I refer to the historical fact that the first ten amendments of the Constitution, nearly coeval with it, all refer either to the powers delegated, or are directed to the greater security of the rights which were guarded by express limitations.

The distinction in the mind of the framers of the Constitution between amendment and delegation of power seems to me clearly drawn by the fact that the Constitution itself, which was a proposition to the states to grant enumerated powers, was only to have effect between the ratifying states; the fifth article provided that amendments to the Constitution might be adopted by three-fourths of the states, and thereby be valid as part of the Constitution. It thus appears that a smaller power was required for an amendment than for a grant, and the natural if not necessary conclusion is that it was because an amendment must belong to, and grow out of, a grant previously made. If a so-called amendment could have been the means of obtaining a new power, is to be supposed that those watchful guardians of community independence, for which the war of the Revolution had been fought, would have been reconciled to the adoption of the Constitution, by the declaration that the powers not delegated are reserved to the states? Unless the power of amendment be confined to the grants of the Constitution, there can be no security to the reserved rights of a minority less than a fourth of the states. I submit that the word "amendment" necessarily implies an improvement upon something which is possessed, and can have no proper application to that which did not previously exist.

The apprehension that was felt of this power of amendment by the framers of the Constitution is shown by the restrictions placed upon the exercise of several of the delegated powers. For example: power was given to admit new states, but no new state should be erected within the jurisdiction of any other state, nor be formed by the junction of two or more states, or parts of states, without the consent of the legislatures of those states; the power to regulate commerce was limited by the prohibition of an amendment affecting, for a certain time, the migration or importation of persons whom any of the existing states should think proper to admit; by the very important provision for the protection of the smaller states and the preservation of their equality in the Union, the compact in regard to the membership of the two houses of Congress should not be so amended that any "State, without its consent, shall be deprived of its equal suffrage in the Senate." These limitations and prohibitions on the power of amendment all refer to clauses of the Constitution, to things which existed as part of the general government; they were not needed, and therefore not to be found in relation to the reserved powers of the states, on which the general government was forbidden to intrude by the ninth article of the amendments.

In view of the small territory of the New England states, comparatively to that of the Middle and Southern states, and the probability of the creation of new states in the large territory of some of these latter, it might well have been anticipated that in the course of time the New England states would become less than one-fourth of the members of the Union. Nothing is less likely than that the watchful patriots of that region would have consented to a form of government which should give to a majority of three-fourths of the states the power to deprive them of their dearest rights and privileges. Yet to this extremity the new-born theory of the power of amendment would go. Against this insidious assault, this wooden horse which it is threatened to introduce into the citadel of our liberties, I have sought to warn the inheritors of our free institutions, and earnestly do invoke the resistance of all true patriots.

PART III: SECESSION AND CONFEDERATION

CHAPTER I: *Opening of the New Year—The People in Advance of their Representatives—Conciliatory Conduct of Southern Members of Congress—Sensational Fictions—Misstatements of the Count of Paris—Obligations of a Senator—The Southern Forts and Arsenals—Pensacola Bay and Fort Pickens —The Alleged "Caucus" and its Resolutions—Personal Motives and Feelings—The Presidency not a Desirable Office— Letter from the Hon. C. C. Clay.*

WITH the failure of the Senate Committee of Thirteen to come to any agreement, the last reasonable hope of a pacific settlement of difficulties within the Union was extinguished in the minds of those most reluctant to abandon the effort. The year 1861 opened, as we have seen, upon the spectacle of a general belief, among the people of the planting states, in the necessity of an early secession, as the only possible alternative left them.

It has already been shown that the calmness and deliberation, with which the measures requisite for withdrawal were adopted and executed, afford the best refutation of the charge that they were the result of haste, passion, or precipitation. Still more contrary to truth is the assertion, so often recklessly made and reiterated, that the people of the South were led into secession, against their will and their better judgment, by a few ambitious and discontented politicians.

The truth is that the Southern people were in advance of their representatives throughout, and that these latter were not agitators or leaders in the popular movement. They were in harmony with its great principles, but their influence, with very few exceptions, was exerted to restrain rather than to accelerate their application, and to allay rather than to stimulate excitement. As sentinels on the outer wall, the people had a right to look to them for warning of approaching danger; as we have seen, in the last session of the last Congress that preceded the disruption, Southern Senators, of the class generally considered extremists, served on a committee of pacification, and strove earnestly to promote its object. Failing in this, they still exerted themselves to prevent the commission of any act that might result in bloodshed.

Invention has busied itself, to the exhaustion of its resources, in the creation of imaginary "cabals," "conspiracies," and "intrigues," among the Senators and Representatives of the South on duty in Washington at that time. The idle gossip of the public hotels, the sensational rumors of the streets, the *canards* of newspaper correspondents—whatever was floating through the atmosphere of that anxious period—however lightly regarded at the moment by the more intelligent, has since been drawn upon for materials to be used in the construction of what has been widely accepted as authentic history. Nothing would seem to be too absurd for such uses. Thus, it has been gravely stated that a caucus of Southern Senators, held in the early part of January, "resolved to assume to themselves the political power of the South"; that they took entire control of all political and military operations; that they issued instructions for the passage of ordinances of secession, and for the seizure of forts, arsenals, and customhouses; with much more of the like groundless fiction. A foreign prince, who served for a time in the federal army, and has since undertaken to write a history of *The Civil War in America* —a history the incomparable blunders of which are redeemed from suspicion of wilful misstatement only by the writer's ignorance of the subject—speaks of the Southern representatives as having "kept their seats in Congress in order to be able to paralyze its action, forming, at the same time, a center whence they issued directions to their friends in the South to complete the dismemberment of the republic."[1] And again, with reference to the secession of several states, he says that "the word of command issued by *the committee at Washington* was promptly obeyed."[2]

Statements such as these are a travesty upon history. That the representatives of the South held conference with one another and took counsel together, as men having common interests and threatened by common dangers, is true, and is the full extent of the truth. That they communicated to friends at home information of what was passing is to be presumed, and would have been most obligatory if it had not been that the published proceedings rendered such communication needless. But that any such man, or committee of men, should have undertaken to direct the mighty movement then progressing throughout the South, or to control, through the telegraph and the mails, the will and the judgment of conventions of the people, assembled under the full consciousness of the dignity of that sovereignty which they represented, would have been an extraordinary degree of folly and presumption.

The absurdity of the statement is further evident from a consideration of the fact that the movements which culminated in the secession of the several states began before the meeting of Congress. They were

---

[1] *History of the Civil* War, by the Count of Paris; American translation, Vol. I, p. 122.
[2] *Ibid.*, p. 125.

not inaugurated, prosecuted, or controlled by the Senators and Representatives in Congress, but by the governors, legislatures, and finally by the delegates of the people in conventions of the respective states. I believe I may fairly claim to have possessed a full share of the confidence of the people of the state which I in part represented; proof has already been furnished to show how little effect my own influence could have upon their action, even in the negative capacity of a brake upon the wheels, by means of which it was hurried on to consummation.

As for the imputation of holding our seats as a vantage ground in plotting for the dismemberment of the Union—in connection with which the Count of Paris does me the honor to single out my name for special mention—it is a charge so dishonorable, if true, to its object—so disgraceful, if false, to its author—as to be outside of the proper limit of discussion. It is a charge which no accuser ever made in my presence, though I had in public debate more than once challenged its assertion and denounced its falsehood. It is enough to say that I always held, and repeatedly avowed, the principle that a Senator in Congress occupied the position of an ambassador from the state which he represented to the government of the United States, as well as in some sense a member of the government; that, in either capacity, it would be dishonorable to use his powers and privileges for the destruction or for the detriment of the government to which he was accredited. Acting on this principle, as long as I held a seat in the Senate, my best efforts were directed to the maintenance of the Constitution, the Union resulting from it, and to make the general government an effective agent of the states for its prescribed purpose. As soon as the paramount allegiance due to Mississippi forbade a continuance of these efforts, I withdrew from the position. To say that during this period I did nothing secretly, in conflict with what was done or professed openly, would be merely to assert my own integrity, which would be worthless to those who may doubt it, and superfluous to those who believe in it. What has been said on the subject for myself, I believe to be also true of my Southern associates in Congress.

With regard to the forts, arsenals, etc., something more remains to be said. The authorities of the Southern states immediately after, and in some cases a few days before, their actual secession, took possession (in every instance without resistance or bloodshed) of forts, arsenals, customhouses, and other public property within their respective limits. I do not propose at this time to consider the question of their right to do so; that may be more properly done hereafter. But it may not be out of place briefly to refer to the statement, often made, that the absence of troops from the military posts in the South, which enabled the states so quietly to take such possession, was the result of collusion and pre-arrangement between the Southern leaders and the federal Secretary of War, John B. Floyd of Virginia. It is a sufficient answer to this allegation to state the fact that the absence of troops from these posts, instead of being exceptional, was, and still is, their ordinary condition in time of peace. At the very moment when these sentences are being written (1880), although the army of the United States is twice as large as in 1860; although four years of internal war and a yet longer period of subsequent military occupation of the South have habituated the public to the presence of troops in their midst, to an extent that would formerly have been startling if not offensive; although allegations of continued disaffection on the part of the Southern people have been persistently reiterated, for party purposes—yet it is believed that the forts and arsenals in the states of the Gulf are in as defenseless a condition, and as liable to quiet seizure (if any such purpose existed), as in the beginning of the year 1861. Certainly, those within the range of my personal information are occupied, as they were at that time, only by ordnance sergeants or fort keepers.

There were, however, some exceptions to this general rule—especially in the defensive works of the harbor of Charleston, the forts at Key West and the Dry Tortugas, and those protecting the entrance of Pensacola Bay. The events which occurred in Charleston harbor will be more conveniently noticed hereafter. The island forts near the extreme southern point of Florida were too isolated and too remote from population to be disturbed at that time; the situation long maintained at the mouth of Pensacola Bay affords, however, a signal illustration of the forbearance and conciliatory spirit that animated Southern counsels. For a long time Fort Pickens, on the island of Santa Rosa, at the entrance to the harbor, was occupied only by a small body of federal soldiers and marines—less than one hundred, all told. Immediately opposite, and in possession of the other two forts and the adjacent navy yard, was a strong force of volunteer troops of Florida and Alabama (which might, on short notice, have been largely increased), ready and anxious to attack and take possession of Fort Pickens. That they could have done so is unquestionable, and if mere considerations of military advantage had been consulted, it would surely have been done. But the love of peace and the purpose to preserve it, together with a revulsion from the thought of engaging in fraternal strife, were more potent than considerations of probable interest. During the anxious period of uncertainty and apprehension which ensued, the efforts of the Southern Senators in Washington were employed to dissuade (they could not command) from any aggressive movement, however justifiable, that might lead to collision. These efforts were exerted through written and telegraphic communications to the governors of Alabama and Florida, the commander of the Southern troops, and other influential persons near the scene of operations. The records of the telegraphic office, if preserved, will no doubt show this to be a very moderate statement of those efforts. It is believed that by such influence alone a collision was averted; it is certain that its exercise gave great dissatisfaction at the time to some of the ardent advocates of more active measures. It may be that they were right, and that we who counseled delay and forbearance were wrong. Certainly if we could have foreseen the ultimate failure of all efforts for a peaceful settlement, and the perfidy that was afterward to be practiced in connection with them, our advice would have been different.

Certain resolutions, said to have been adopted in a meeting of Senators held on the evening of January 5th,[3] have been magnified, by the representations of artful commentators on the events of the period, into something vastly momentous.

The significance of these resolutions was the admission that we could not longer advise delay, and even that was unimportant under the circumstances, for three of the states concerned had taken final action on the subject before the resolutions could have been communicated to them. As an expression of opinion, they merely stated that of which we had all become convinced by the experience of the previous month —that our long-cherished hopes had proved illusory—that further efforts in Congress would be unavailing, and that nothing remained, except that the states should take the matter into their own hands, as final

[3] Subjoined are the resolutions referred to, adopted by the Senators from Georgia, Florida, Alabama, Mississippi, Louisiana, Texas, and Arkansas. Toombs of Georgia and Sebastian of Arkansas are said to have been absent from the meeting:

"*Resolved,* That, in our opinion, each of the States should, as soon as may be, secede from the Union.

"*Resolved,* That provision should be made for a convention to organize a confederacy of the seceding States: the Convention to meet not later than the 15th of February, at the city of Montgomery, in the State of Alabama.

"*Resolved,* That, in view of the hostile legislation that is threatened against the seceding States, and which may be consummated before the 4th of March, we ask instructions whether the delegations are to remain in Congress until that date, for the purpose of defeating such legislation.

"*Resolved,* That a committee be and are hereby appointed, consisting of Messrs. Davis, Slidell, and Mallory, to carry out the objects of this meeting."

judges of their wrongs and of the measure of redress. They recommended the formation of a confederacy among the seceding states as early as possible after their secession—advice the expediency of which could hardly be questioned, either by friend or foe. As to the "instructions" asked for with regard to the propriety of continuing to hold their seats, I suppose it must have been caused by some diversity of opinion which then and long afterward continued to exist, and the practical value of which must have been confined to Senators of states which did not actually secede. For myself, I can only say that no advice could have prevailed on me to hold a seat in the Senate after receiving notice that Mississippi had withdrawn from the Union. The best evidence that my associates thought likewise is the fact that, although no instructions were given them, they promptly withdrew on the receipt of official information of the withdrawal of the states which they represented.

It will not be amiss here briefly to state what were my position and feelings at the period now under consideration, as they have been the subject of gross and widespread misrepresentation. It is not only untrue, but absurd, to attribute to me motives of personal ambition to be gratified by a dismemberment of the Union. Much of my life had been spent in the military and civil service of the United States. Whatever reputation I had acquired was identified with their history; if future preferment had been the object, it would have led me to cling to the Union as long as a shred of it should remain. If any, judging after the event, should assume that I was allured by the high office subsequently conferred upon me by the people of the Confederate States, the answer to any such conclusion has been made by others, to whom it was well known before the Confederacy was formed, that I had no desire to be its President. When the suggestion was made to me, I expressed a decided objection, and gave reasons of a public and permanent character against being placed in that position.

Furthermore, I then held the office of United States Senator from Mississippi—one which I preferred to all others. The kindness of the people had three times conferred it upon me, and I had no reason to fear that it would not be given again, as often as desired. So far from wishing to change this position for any other, I had specially requested my friends (some of whom had thought of putting me in nomination for the presidency of the United States in 1860) not to permit "my name to be used before the Convention for any nomination whatever."

I had been so near the office for four years, while in the cabinet of Pierce, that I saw it from behind the scenes, and it was to me an office in no wise desirable. The responsibilities were great; the labor, the vexations, the disappointments, were greater. Those who have intimately known the official and personal life of our Presidents cannot fail to remember how few have left the office as happy men as when they entered it, how darkly the shadows gathered around the setting sun, and how eagerly the multitude would turn to gaze upon another orb just rising to take its place in the political firmament.

Worn by incessant fatigue, broken in fortune, debarred by public opinion, prejudice, or tradition, from future employment, the wisest and best who have filled that office have retired to private life, to remember rather the failure of their hopes than the success of their efforts. He must, indeed, be a self-confident man who could hope to fill the chair of Washington with satisfaction to himself, with the assurance of receiving on his retirement the meed awarded by the people to that great man, that he had "lived enough for life and for glory," or even of feeling that the sacrifice of self had been compensated by the service rendered to his country.

The following facts were presented in a letter written several years ago by the Hon. C. C. Clay of Alabama, who was one of my most intimate associates in the Senate, with reference to certain misstatements to which his attention had been called by one of my friends:

The import is, that Mr. Davis, disappointed and chagrined at not receiving the nomination of the Democratic party for President of the United States in 1860, took the lead on the assembling of Congress in December, 1860, in a "conspiracy" of Southern Senators "which planned the secession of the Southern States from the Union," and "on the night of January 5, 1861, . . . framed the scheme of revolution which was implicity and promptly followed at the South." In other words, that Southern Senators (and, chief among them, Jefferson Davis), then and there, instigated and induced the Southern States to secede.

I am quite sure that Mr. Davis neither expected nor desired the nomination for the Presidency of the United States in 1860. He never evinced any such aspiration, by word or sign, to me—with whom he was, I believe, as intimate and confidential as with any person outside of his own family. On the contrary, he requested the delegation from Mississippi not to permit the use of his name before the Convention. And, after the nomination of both Douglas and Breckinridge, he conferred with them, at the instance of leading Democrats, to persuade them to withdraw, that their friends might unite on some second choice—an office he would never have undertaken, had he sought the nomination or believed he was regarded as an aspirant.

Mr. Davis did not take an active part in planning or hastening secession. I think he only *regretfully* consented to it, as a political necessity for the preservation of popular and State rights, which were seriously threatened by the triumph of a sectional party who were pledged to make war on them. I know that some leading men, and even Mississippians, thought him too moderate and backward, and found fault with him for not taking a leading part in secession.

No "plan of secession" or "scheme of revolution" was, to my knowledge, discussed—certainly none matured—at the caucus, 5th of January, 1861, unless, forsooth, the resolutions appended hereto be so held. They comprise the sum and substance of what was said and done. I never heard that the caucus advised the South "to accumulate munitions of war," or "to organize and equip an army of one hundred thousand men," or determined "to hold on as long as possible to the Southern seats." So far from it, a majority of Southern Senators seemed to think there would be no war; that the dominant party in the North desired separation from the South, and would gladly let their "erring sisters go in peace." I could multiply proofs of such a disposition. As to holding on to their seats, no Southern Legislature advised it, no Southern Senator who favored secession did so but one, and none others wished to do so, I believe.

The "plan of secession," if any, and the purpose of secession, unquestionably, originated, not in Washington City, or with the Senators or Representatives of the South, but among the people of the several States, many months before it was attempted. They followed no leaders at Washington or elsewhere, but acted for themselves, with an independence and unanimity unprecedented in any movement of such magnitude. Before the meeting of the caucus of January 5, 1861, South Carolina had seceded, and Alabama, Mississippi, Florida, Louisiana, and Texas had taken the initial step of secession, by calling conventions for its accomplishment. Before the election of Lincoln, all the Southern States, excepting one or two, had pledged themselves to separate from the Union upon the triumph of a sectional party in the Presidential election, by acts or resolutions of their Legislatures, resolves of both Democratic and Whig State Conventions, and of primary assemblies of the people—in every way in which they could commit themselves to any future act. Their purpose was proclaimed to the world through the press and telegraph, and criticised in Congress, in the Northern Legislatures, in press and pulpit, and on the hustings, during many months before Congress met in December, 1860.

Over and above all these facts, the reports of the United States Senate show that, prior to the 5th of January, 1861, Southern Senators united with Northern Democratic Senators in an effort to effect pacification and prevent secession, and that Jefferson Davis was one of a committee appointed by the Senate to consider and report such a measure; that it failed because the Northern Republicans opposed everything that looked to peace; that Senator Douglas arraigned them as trying to precipitate secession, referred to Jefferson Davis as one who sought conciliation, and called upon the Republican Senators to tell what they would do, if anything, to restore harmony and prevent disunion. They did not even deign a response. Thus, by their sullen silence, they made confession (without avoidance) of their stubborn purpose to hold up no hand raised to maintain the Union. . .

CHAPTER II: *Tenure of Public Property Ceded by the States —Sovereignty and Eminent Domain—Principles Asserted by Massachusetts, New York, Virginia, and Other States—The Charleston Forts—South Carolina Sends Commissioners to Washington—Sudden Movement of Major Anderson—Correspondence of the Commissioners with the President—Interviews of the Author with Buchanan—Major Anderson—The "Star of the West"—The President's Special Message—Speech of the Author in the Senate—Further Proceedings and Correspondence Relative to Fort Sumter—Buchanan's Rectitude in Purpose and Vacillation in Action.*

THE sites of forts, arsenals, navy yards, and other public property of the federal government were ceded by the state, within whose limits they were, subject to the condition, either expressed or implied, that they should be used solely and exclusively for the purposes for which they were granted. The ultimate ownership of the soil, or eminent domain, remains with the people of the state in which it lies, by virtue of their sovereignty. Thus, the state of Massachusetts has declared that—

The sovereignty and jurisdiction of the Commonwealth extended to all places within the boundaries thereof, subject only to such rights of *concurrent jurisdiction* as have been or may be granted over any places by the Commonwealth to the United States.[1]

In the acts of cession of the respective states, the terms and conditions on which the grant is made are expressed in various forms, and with differing degrees of precision. The act of New York, granting the use of a site for the Brooklyn Navy Yard, may serve as a specimen. It contains this express condition:

"The United States are to retain such use and jurisdiction, *so long as said tract shall be applied to the defense and safety of the city and port of New York, and no longer.* . . . . But the jurisdiction hereby ceded, and the exemption from taxation herein granted, shall continue in respect to said property, and to each portion thereof, *so long as the same shall remain the property of the United States,* and be used for the purposes aforesaid, *and no longer.*" The cession of the site of the Watervliet Arsenal is made in the same or equivalent terms, except that, instead of "defense and safety of the city and port of New York," etc., the language is, "defense and safety *of the said State,* and no longer."

South Carolina in 1805, by legislative enactment, ceded to the United

<hr/>

[1] *Revised Statutes of Massachusetts,* 1836, p. 56.

States, in Charleston harbor and on Beaufort River, various forts and fortifications, and sites for the erection of forts, on the following conditions, *viz.:*

That, if the United States shall not, within three years from the passing of this act, and notification thereof by the Governor of this State to the Executive of the United States, repair the fortifications now existing thereon or build such other forts or fortifications as may be deemed most expedient by the Executive of the United States on the same, and keep a garrison or garrisons therein; in such case this grant or cession shall be void and of no effect.[2]

It will hardly be contended that the conditions of this grant were fulfilled, and, if it be answered that the state did not demand the restoration of the forts or sites, the answer certainly fails after 1860, when the controversy arose, and the unfounded assertion was made that those forts and sites had been purchased with the money, and were therefore the property, of the United States. The terms of the cession sufficiently manifest that they were free-will offerings of such forts and sites as belonged to the state; public functionaries were bound to know that, by the United States law of March 20, 1794, it was provided "that no purchase shall be made where such are the property of a State."[3]

The stipulations made by Virginia, in ceding the ground for Fortress Monroe and the Rip Raps, on March 1, 1821, are as follows:

AN ACT CEDING TO THE UNITED STATES THE LANDS ON OLD POINT COMFORT, AND THE SHOAL CALLED THE RIP RAPS.

Whereas, It is shown to the present General Assembly that the Government of the United States is solicitous that certain lands at Old Point Comfort, and at the shoal called the Rip Raps, should be, with the right of property and entire jurisdiction thereon, vested in the said United States for the purpose of fortification and other objects of national defense:

1. *Be it enacted by the General Assembly,* That it shall be lawful and proper for the Governor of this Commonwealth, by conveyance or deeds in writing under his hand and the seal of the State, to transfer, assign, and make over unto the said United States the right of property and title, as well as all the jurisdiction which this Commonwealth possesses over the lands and shoal at Old Point Comfort and the Rip Raps: . . .

2. *And be it further enacted,* That, *should the said United States at any time abandon the said lands and shoal, or appropriate them to any other purposes than those indicated in the preamble to this act, that then, and in that case, the same shall revert to and revest in this Commonwealth.*[4]

By accepting such grants, under such conditions, the government of the United States assented to their propriety, and the principle that holds

---

[2] *Statutes at Large of South Carolina,* Vol. V, p. 501.
[3] Act to provide for defense of certain ports and harbors of the United States.
[4] See *Revised Statutes of Virginia.*

good in any one case is of course applicable to all others of the same sort, whether expressly asserted in the act of cession or not. Indeed, no express declaration would be necessary to establish a conclusion resulting so directly from the nature of the case, and the settled principles of sovereignty and eminent domain.

A state withdrawing from the Union would necessarily assume the control theretofore exercised by the general government over all public defenses and other public property within her limits. It would, however, be but fair and proper that adequate compensation should be made to the other members of the partnership, or their common agent, for the value of the works and for any other advantage obtained by the one party, or loss incurred by the other. Such equitable settlement, the seceding states of the South, without exception, as I believe, were desirous to make, and prompt to propose to the federal authorities.

On the secession of South Carolina, the condition of the defenses of Charleston harbor became a subject of anxiety with all parties. Of the three forts in or at the entrance of the harbor, two were unoccupied, but the third (Fort Moultrie) was held by a garrison of but little more than one hundred men—of whom only sixty-three were said to be effectives—under command of Major Robert Anderson of the First Artillery.

About twelve days before the secession of South Carolina, the representatives in Congress from that state had called on the President to assure him, in anticipation of the secession of the state, that no purpose was entertained by South Carolina to attack, or in any way molest, the forts held by the United States in the harbor of Charleston—at least until opportunity could be had for an amicable settlement of all questions that might arise with regard to these forts and other public property—provided that no reënforcements should be sent, and the military status should be permitted to remain unchanged. The South Carolinians understood Buchanan as approving of this suggestion, although declining to make any formal pledge.

It appears, nevertheless, from subsequent developments, that both before and after the secession of South Carolina preparations were secretly made for reënforcing Major Anderson, in case it should be deemed necessary by the government at Washington.[5] On December 11th instructions were communicated to him from the War Department, of which the following is the essential part:

You are carefully to avoid every act which would needlessly tend to provoke

---

[5] *Buchanan's Administration*, Chapt. IX, p. 165, and Chapt. XI, pp. 212-214.

aggression; and for that reason you are not, without evident and imminent necessity, to take up any position which could be construed into the assumption of a hostile attitude, but you are to hold possession of the forts in this harbor, and, if attacked, you are to defend yourself to the last extremity. The smallness of your force will not permit you, perhaps, to occupy more than one of the three forts, but an attack on, or attempt to take possession of either of them, will be regarded as an act of hostility, and you may then put your command into either of them which you may deem most proper to increase its power of resistance. You are also authorized to take similar defensive steps, whenever you have tangible evidence of a design to proceed to a hostile act.[6]

These instructions were afterward modified—as we are informed by Buchanan—so as, instead of requiring him to defend himself "to the last extremity," to direct him to do so as long as any reasonable hope remained of saving the fort.[7]

Immediately after the secession of the state, the convention of South Carolina deputed three distinguished citizens of that state—Robert W. Barnwell, James H. Adams, and James L. Orr—to proceed to Washington, "to treat with the Government of the United States for the delivery of the forts, magazines, lighthouses, and other real estate, with their appurtenances, within the limits of South Carolina, and also for an apportionment of the public debt, and for a division of all other property held by the Government of the United States, as agent of the confederated States, of which South Carolina was recently a member; and generally to negotiate as to all other measures and arrangements proper to be made and adopted in the existing relation of the parties, and for the continuance of peace and amity between this Commonwealth and the Government at Washington."

The commissioners, in the discharge of the duty entrusted to them, arrived in Washington on December 26th. Before they could communicate with the President, however—indeed, on the morning after their arrival—they were startled, and the whole country electrified, by the news that, during the previous night, Major Anderson had "secretly dismantled Fort Moultrie,"[8] spiked his guns, burned his gun carriages, and removed his command to Fort Sumter, which occupied a more commanding position in the harbor. This movement changed the whole aspect of affairs. It was considered by the government and people of South Carolina as a violation of the implied pledge of a maintenance of the *status quo;* the remaining forts and other public property were at once taken possession of by the state; the condition of public feeling

---

[6]*Buchanan's Administration,* Chapt. IX, p. 166.
[7]*Ibid.*
[8]*Ibid.,* Chapt. X, p. 180.

became greatly exacerbated.   An interview between the President and
the commissioners was followed by a sharp correspondence, which was
terminated on January 1, 1861, by the return to the commissioners of
their final communication, with an endorsement stating that it was of
such a character that the President declined to receive it. The negotiations were thus abruptly broken off. This correspondence may be found
in the Appendix.[9]

In the meantime Cass, Secretary of State, had resigned his position
early in December, on the ground of the refusal of the President to send
reënforcements to Charleston.   On the occupation of Fort Sumter by
Major Anderson, Secretary of War Floyd, taking the ground that it was
virtually a violation of a pledge given or implied by the government,
had asked that the garrison should be entirely withdrawn from the harbor of Charleston, and, on the refusal of the President to consent to this,
had tendered his resignation, which was promptly accepted.[10]

This is believed to be a correct outline of the earlier facts with regard
to the Charleston forts, and in giving it I have done so, as far as possible,
without prejudice or any expression of opinion upon the motives of the
actors.

The kind relations, both personal and political, which had long
existed between Buchanan and myself, had led him occasionally, during
his presidency, to send for me to confer with him on subjects that caused
him anxiety, and warranted me in sometimes calling upon him to offer
my opinion on matters of special interest or importance.   Thus it was
that I had communicated with him freely in regard to the threatening
aspect of events in the earlier part of the winter of 1860-'61. When he
told me of the work that had been done, or was doing, at Fort Moultrie
—that is, the elevation of its parapet by crowning it with barrels of
sand—I pointed out to him the impolicy as well as inefficiency of the
measure.   It seemed to me impolitic to make ostensible preparations for
defense, when no attack was threatened; the means adopted were in-
efficient, because any ordinary field piece would knock the barrels off the
parapet, and thus render them hurtful only to the defenders.   He inquired whether the expedient had not been successful at Fort Brown, on
the Rio Grande, in the beginning of the Mexican war, and was answered
that the attack on Fort Brown had been made with small arms, or at
great distance.

After the removal of the garrison to the stronger and safer position

---

[9] See Appendix G.
[10] *Buchanan's Administration*, Chapt. X, pp. 187, 188.

of Fort Sumter, I called upon him again to represent, from my knowledge of the people and the circumstances of the case, how productive the movement would be of discontent, and how likely to lead to collision. One of the vexed questions of the day was by what authority the collector of the port should be appointed, and the rumor was that instructions had been given to the commanding officer at Fort Sumter not to allow vessels to pass, unless under clearance from the United States collector. It was easy to understand that, if a vessel were fired upon under such circumstances, it would be accepted as the beginning of hostilities—a result which both he and I desired to avert, as the greatest calamity that could be foreseen or imagined. My opinion was that the wisest and best course would be to withdraw the garrison altogether from the harbor of Charleston.

The President's objection to this was that it was his bounden duty to preserve and protect the property of the United States. To this I replied, with all the earnestness the occasion demanded, that I would pledge my life that, if an inventory were taken of all the stores and munitions in the fort, and an ordnance sergeant with a few men left in charge of them, they would not be disturbed. As a further guarantee, I offered to obtain from the governor of South Carolina full assurance that, in case any marauders or lawless combination of persons should attempt to seize or disturb the property, he would send from the citadel of Charleston an adequate guard to protect it and to secure its keepers against molestation.

The President promised me to reflect upon this proposition, and to confer with his cabinet upon the propriety of adopting it. All cabinet consultations are secret, which is equivalent to saying that I never knew what occurred in that meeting to which my proposition was submitted. The result was not communicated to me, but the events which followed proved that the suggestion was not accepted.

Major Anderson, who commanded the garrison, had many ties and associations that bound him to the South. He performed his part like the true soldier and man of the finest sense of honor that he was; that it was most painful to him to be charged with the duty of holding the fort as a threat to the people of Charleston is a fact known to many others as well as to myself. We had been cadets together. He was my first acquaintance in that corps, and the friendship then formed was never interrupted. We had served together in the summer and autumn of 1860, in a commission of inquiry into the discipline, course of studies, and general condition of the United States Military Academy. At the close of our labors the commission had adjourned, to meet again in

Washington about the end of the ensuing November, to examine the report and revise it for transmission to Congress. Major Anderson's duties in Charleston harbor hindered him from attending this adjourned meeting of the commission, and he wrote to me, its chairman, to explain the cause of his absence. That letter was lost when my library and private papers were "captured" from my home in Mississippi. If anyone has preserved it as a trophy of war, its publication would show how bright was the honor, how broad the patriotism of Major Anderson, and how fully he sympathized with me as to the evils which then lowered over the country.

In comparing the past and the present among the mighty changes which passion and sectional hostility have wrought, one is profoundly and painfully impressed by the extent to which public opinion has drifted from the landmarks set up by the sages and patriots who formed the constitutional Union, and observed by those who administered its government down to the time when war between the states was inaugurated. Buchanan, the last President of the old school, would as soon have thought of aiding in the establishment of a monarchy among us as of accepting the doctrine of coercing the states into submission to the will of a majority, in mass, of the people of the United States. When discussing the question of withdrawing the troops from the port of Charleston, he yielded a ready assent to the proposition that the cession of a site for a fort, for purposes of public defense, lapses whenever that fort should be employed by the grantee against the state by which the cession was made, on the familiar principle that any grant for a specific purpose expires when it ceases to be used for that purpose. Whether on this or any other ground, if the garrison of Fort Sumter had been withdrawn in accordance with the spirit of the Constitution of the United States, from which the power to apply coercion to a state was deliberately and designedly excluded, and if this had been distinctly assigned as a reason for its withdrawal, the honor of the United States government would have been maintained intact, and nothing could have operated more powerfully to quiet the apprehensions and allay the resentment of the people of South Carolina. The influence which such a measure would have exerted upon the states which had not yet seceded, but were then contemplating the adoption of that extreme remedy, would probably have induced further delay; the mellowing effect of time, with a realization of the dangers to be incurred, might have wrought mutual forbearance—if, indeed, anything could have checked the madness then prevailing among the people of the Northern states in their thirst for power and forgetfulness of the duties of federation.

It would have been easy to concede this point. The little garrison of Fort Sumter served only as a menace; it was utterly incapable of holding the fort if attacked, and the poor attempt soon afterward made to reenforce and provision it, by such a vessel as the *Star of the West,* might by the uncharitable be readily construed as a scheme to provoke hostilities. Yet, from my knowledge of Buchanan, I do not hesitate to say that he had no such wish or purpose. His abiding hope was to avert a collision, or at least to postpone it to a period beyond the close of his official term. The management of the whole affair was what Talleyrand describes as something worse than a crime—a blunder. Whatever treatment the case demanded, should have been prompt; to wait was fatuity.

The ill-advised attempt secretly to throw reënforcements and provisions into Fort Sumter, by means of the steamer *Star of the West,* resulted in the repulsion of that vessel at the mouth of the harbor, by the authorities of South Carolina, on the morning of January 9th. On her refusal to heave-to, she was fired upon, and put back to sea, with her recruits and supplies. A telegraphic account of this event was handed me, a few hours afterward, when stepping into my carriage to go to the Senate chamber. Although I had then, for some time, ceased to visit the President, under the impulse of this renewed note of danger to the country I drove immediately to the executive mansion, and for the last time appealed to him to take such prompt measures as were evidently necessary to avert the impending calamity. The result was even more unsatisfactory than that of former efforts had been.

On the same day the special message of the President on the state of the Union, dated the day previous (January 8), was submitted to Congress. This message was accompanied by the first letter of the South Carolina commissioners to the President, with his answer, but of course not by their rejoinder, which he had declined to receive. Buchanan, in his memoirs, complains that immediately after the reading of his message, this rejoinder (which he terms an "insulting letter") was presented by me to the Senate, and by that body received and entered upon its journal.[11] The simple truth is that, regarding it as essential to a complete understanding of the transaction, and its publication as a mere act of justice to the commissioners, I presented and had it read in the Senate. But its appearance upon the journal as part of the proceedings, instead of being merely a document introduced as part of my remarks, was the

---

[11] *Buchanan's Administration,* Chapt. X, p. 184.

result of a discourteous objection, made by a so-called Republican Senator, to the reading of the document by the clerk of the Senate at my request. This will be made manifest by an examination of the debate and proceedings which ensued.[12] The discourtesy recoiled upon its author and supporters, and gave the letter a vantage ground in respect of prominence which I could not have foreseen or expected.

The next day (January 10) the speech was delivered, the greater part of which may be found in the Appendix[13]—the last that I ever made in the Senate of the United States, except in taking leave, and by the sentiments of which I am content that my career, both before and since, should be judged.

The history of Fort Sumter during the remaining period, until the organization of the Confederate government, may be found in the correspondence given in the Appendix.[14] From this it will be seen that the authorities of South Carolina still continued to refrain from any act of aggression or retaliation, under the provocation of the secret attempt to reënforce the garrison, as they had previously under that of its nocturnal transfer from one fort to another.

Another commissioner (the Hon. I. W. Hayne) was sent to Washington by the governor of South Carolina to effect, if possible, an amicable and peaceful transfer of the fort, and settlement of all questions relating to property. This commissioner remained for nearly a month, endeavoring to accomplish the objects of his mission, but was met only by evasive and unsatisfactory answers, and eventually returned without having effected anything.

There is one passage in the last letter of Colonel Hayne to the President which presents the case of the occupancy of Fort Sumter by the United States troops so clearly and forcibly that it may be proper to quote it. He writes as follows:

You say that the fort was garrisoned for our protection, and is held for the same purposes for which it has been ever held since its construction. Are you not aware, that to hold, in the territory of a foreign power, a fortress against her will, avowedly for the purpose of protecting her citizens, is perhaps the highest insult which one government can offer to another? But Fort Sumter was never garrisoned at all until South Carolina had dissolved her connection with your Government. This garrison entered it in the night, with every circumstance of secrecy, after spiking the guns and burning the gun-carriages and cutting down the flag-staff of an adjacent fort, which was then abandoned. South Carolina had

[12] See *Congressional Globe*, second session, Thirty-fifth Congress, Part I, p. 284 *et seq.*
[13] See Appendix I.
[14] *Ibid.*

not taken Fort Sumter into her own possession, only because of her misplaced confidence in a Government which deceived her.

Thus, during the remainder of Buchanan's administration, matters went rapidly from bad to worse. The old statesman who, with all his defects, had long possessed, and was entitled still to retain, the confidence due to extensive political knowledge and love of his country in all its parts—who had, in his earlier career, looked steadily to the Constitution, as the mariner looks to the compass, for guidance—retired to private life at the expiration of his term of office, having effected nothing to allay the storm which had been steadily gathering during his administration.

Timid vacillation was then succeeded by unscrupulous cunning; for futile efforts, without hostile collision, to impose a claim of authority upon people who repudiated it, were substituted measures which could be sustained only by force.

CHAPTER III: *Secession of Mississippi and Other States—With-drawal of Senators—Address of the Author on Taking Leave of the Senate—Answer to Certain Objections.*

MISSISSIPPI was the second state to withdraw from the Union, her ordinance of secession being adopted on January 9, 1861. She was quickly followed by Florida on the 10th, Alabama on the 11th, and, in the course of the same month, by Georgia on the 18th, and Louisiana on the 26th. The conventions of these states (together with that of South Carolina) agreed in designating Montgomery, Alabama, as the place, and February 4th as the day, for the assembling of a congress of the seceding states, to which each state convention, acting as the direct representative of the sovereignty of the people thereof, appointed delegates.

Telegraphic intelligence of the secession of Mississippi had reached Washington some considerable time before the fact was officially communicated to me. This official knowledge I considered it proper to await before taking formal leave of the Senate. My associates from Alabama and Florida concurred in this view. Accordingly, having received notification of the secession of these three states about the same time, on January 21st Yulee and Mallory of Florida, Fitzpatrick and Clay of Alabama, and myself, announced the withdrawal of the states from which we were respectively accredited, and took leave of the Senate at the same time.

In the action which she then took, Mississippi certainly had no purpose to levy war against the United States, or any of them. As her Senator, I endeavored plainly to state her position in the annexed remarks addressed to the Senate in taking leave of the body:

I rise, Mr. President, for the purpose of announcing to the Senate that I have satisfactory evidence that the State of Mississippi, by a solemn ordinance of her people, in convention assembled, has declared her separation from the United States. Under these circumstances, of course, my functions are terminated here. It has seemed to me proper, however, that I should appear in the Senate to announce that fact to my associates, and I will say but very little more. The occasion does not invite me to go into argument; and my physical condition would not permit me to do so, if it were otherwise; and yet it seems to become me to say something on the part of the State I here represent on an occasion so solemn as this.

It is known to Senators who have served with me here that I have for many years advocated, as an essential attribute of State sovereignty, the right of a State to secede from the Union. Therefore, if I had not believed there was justifiable cause, if I had thought that Mississippi was acting without sufficient provocation, or without an existing necessity, I should still, under my theory of the Government, because of my allegiance to the State of which I am a citizen, have been bound by her action. I however, may be permitted to say that I do think she has justifiable cause, and I approve of her act. I conferred with her people before that act was taken, counseled them then that, if the state of things which they apprehended should exist when their Convention met, they should take the action which they have now adopted.

I hope none who hear me will confound this expression of mine with the advocacy of the right of a State to remain in the Union, and to disregard its constitutional obligations by the nullification of the law. Such is not my theory. Nullification and secession, so often confounded, are, indeed, antagonistic principles. Nullification is a remedy which it is sought to apply within the Union, and against the agent of the States. It is only to be justified when the agent has violated his constitutional obligations, and a State, assuming to judge for itself, denies the right of the agent thus to act, and appeals to the other States of the Union for a decision; but, when the States themselves and when the people of the States have so acted as to convince us that they will not regard our constitutional rights, then, and then for the first time, arises the doctrine of secession in its practical application.

A great man who now reposes with his fathers, and who has often been arraigned for a want of fealty to the Union, advocated the doctrine of nullification because it preserved the Union. It was because of his deep-seated attachment to the Union—his determination to find some remedy for existing ills short of a severance of the ties which bound South Carolina to the other States—that Mr. Calhoun advocated the doctrine of nullification, which he proclaimed to be peaceful, to be within the limits of State power, not to disturb the Union, but only to be a means of bringing the agent before the tribunal of the States for their judgment.

Secession belongs to a different class of remedies. It is to be justified upon the basis that the States are sovereign. There was a time when none denied it. I hope the time may come again when a better comprehension of the theory of our Government, and the inalienable rights of the people of the States, will prevent any one from denying that each State is a sovereign, and thus may reclaim the grants which it has made to any agent whomsoever.

I, therefore, say I concur in the action of the people of Mississippi, believing it to be necessary and proper, and should have been bound by their action if my belief had been otherwise; and this brings me to the important point which I wish, on this last occasion, to present to the Senate. It is by this confounding of nullification and secession that the name of a great man whose ashes now mingle with his mother earth has been evoked to justify coercion against a seceded State. The phrase, "to execute the laws," was an expression which General Jackson applied to the case of a State refusing to obey the laws while yet a member of the Union. That is not the case which is now presented. The laws are to be executed over the United States, and upon the people of the United States. They have no relation to any foreign country. It is a perversion of terms—at least, it is a great misapprehension of the case—which cites that expression for application to a State which has withdrawn from the Union. You may make war on a foreign state. If it be the purpose of gentlemen, they may make war against a State which has withdrawn from the Union; but there are no laws of the United States to be executed within the limits of a seceded State. A State, finding herself in the condition in which Mississippi has judged she is—in which her safety requires that she should provide for the maintenance of her rights out of the Union—surrenders all the benefits (and they are known to be many), deprives herself of the advantages (and they are known to be great), severs all the ties of affection (and they are close and enduring), which have bound her to the Union; and thus divesting herself of every benefit—taking upon herself every burden—she claims to be exempt from any power to execute the laws of the United States within her limits.

I well remember an occasion when Massachusetts was arraigned before the bar of the Senate, and when the doctrine of coercion was rife, and to be applied against her, because of the rescue of a fugitive slave in Boston. My opinion then was the same that it is now. Not in a spirit of egotism, but to show that I am not influenced in my opinions because the case is my own, I refer to that time and that occasion as containing the opinion which I then entertained, and on which my present conduct is based. I then said that if Massachusetts—following her purpose through a stated line of conduct—chose to take the last step, which separates her from the Union, it is her right to go, and I will neither vote one dollar nor one man to coerce her back; but I will say to her, Godspeed, in memory of the kind associations which once existed between her and the other States.

It has been a conviction of pressing necessity—it has been a belief that we are to be deprived in the Union of the rights which our fathers bequeathed to us—which has brought Mississippi to her present decision. She has heard proclaimed the theory that all men are created free and equal, and this made the basis of an attack upon her social institutions; and the sacred Declaration of Independence has been invoked to maintain the position of the equality of the races. That Declaration of Independence is to be construed by the circumstances and purposes for which it was made. The communities were declaring their independence; the people of those communities were asserting that no man was born—to use the language of Mr. Jefferson—booted and spurred, to ride over the rest of mankind; that men were created equal—meaning the men of the political community; that there was no divine right to rule; that no man inherited the right to govern; that there were no classes by which power and place descended to families; but that all stations were equally within the grasp of each member of the body politic. These were the great principles they announced; these were the purposes for which they made their declaration; these were the ends to which their enunciation was directed. They have no reference to the slave; else, how happened it that among the items of arraignment against George III was that he endeavored to do just what the North has been endeavoring of late to do, to stir up insurrection among our slaves? Had the Declaration announced that the negroes were free and equal, how was the prince to be arraigned for raising up insurrection among them? And how was this to be enumerated among the high crimes which caused the colonies to sever their connection with the mother-country? When our Constitution was formed, the same idea was rendered more palpable; for there we find provision made for that very class of persons as property; they were not put upon the footing of equality with white men—not even upon that of paupers and convicts; but, so far as representation was concerned, were discriminated against as a lower caste, only to be represented in the numerical proportion of three fifths. So stands the compact which binds us together.

Then, Senators, we recur to the principles upon which our Government was founded; and when you deny them, and when you deny to us the right to withdraw from a Government which, thus perverted, threatens to be destructive of our rights, we but tread in the path of our fathers when we proclaim our independence and take the hazard. This is done, not in hostility to others, not to injure any section of the country, not even for our own pecuniary benefit, but from the high and solemn motive of defending and protecting the rights we inherited, and which it is our duty to transmit unshorn to our children.

I find in myself perhaps a type of the general feeling of my constituents toward yours. I am sure I feel no hostility toward you, Senators from the North. I am sure there is not one of you, whatever sharp discussion there may have been between us, to whom I can not now say, in the presence of my God, I wish you well; and such, I am sure, is the feeling of the people whom I represent toward those whom you represent. I, therefore, feel that I but express their desire when I say I hope, and they hope, for peaceable relations with you, though we must part. They may be mutually beneficial to us in the future, as they have been in the past, if you so will it. The reverse may bring disaster on every portion of the country, and if you will have it thus, we will invoke the God of our fathers, who delivered them from the power of the lion, to protect us from the ravages of the bear; and thus, putting our trust in God and in our firm hearts and strong arms, we will vindicate the right as best we may.

In the course of my service here, associated at different times with a great variety of Senators, I see now around me some with whom I have served long; there have been points of collision, but, whatever of offense there has been to me, I leave here. I carry with me no hostile remembrance. Whatever offense I have given which has not been redressed, or for which satisfaction has not been demanded, I have, Senators, in this hour of our parting, to offer you my apology for any pain which, in the heat of discussion, I have inflicted. I go hence unencumbered by the remembrance of any injury received, and having discharged the duty of making the only reparation in my power for any injury offered.

Mr. President and Senators, having made the announcement which the occasion seemed to me to require, it only remains for me to bid you a final adieu.

There are some who contend that we should have retained our seats and "fought for our rights in the Union." Could anything be less rational or less consistent than that a Senator, an ambassador from his state, should insist upon representing it in a confederacy from which the state has withdrawn? What was meant by "fighting in the Union" I have never quite understood. If it be to retain a seat in Congress for the purpose of crippling the government and rendering it unable to perform its functions, I can certainly not appreciate the idea of honor that sanctions the suggestion. Among the advantages claimed for this proposition by its supporters was that of thwarting the President in the appointment of his cabinet and other officers necessary for the administration of public affairs. Would this have been to maintain the Union formed by the states? Would such have been the government which Washington recommended as a remedy for the defects of the original confederation, the greatest of which was the paralysis of the action of the general agent by the opposition or indifference of the states? Sad as have been the consequences of the war which followed secession—disastrous in its moral, material, and political relations—still we have good cause to feel proud that the course of the Southern states has left no bolt nor stain upon the honor and chivalry of their people.

And if our children must obey,
They must, but—thinking on our day—
'Twill less debase them to submit.

CHAPTER IV: *Threats of Arrest—Departure from Washington —Indications of Public Anxiety—"Will there be War?"—Organization of the "Army of Mississippi"—Lack of Preparations for Defense in the South—Evidences of the Good Faith and Peaceable Purposes of the Southern People.*

DURING the interval between the announcement by telegraph of the secession of Mississippi and the receipt of the official notification which enabled me to withdraw from the Senate, rumors were in circulation of a purpose, on the part of the United States government, to arrest members of Congress preparing to leave Washington on account of the secession of the states which they represented. This threat received little attention from those most concerned. Indeed, it was thought that it might not be an undesirable mode of testing the question of the right of a state to withdraw from the Union.

No attempt, however, was made to arrest any of the retiring members; after a delay of a few days in necessary preparations, I left Washington for Mississippi, passing through southwestern Virginia, east Tennessee, a small part of Georgia, and north Alabama. A deep interest in the events which had recently occurred was exhibited by the people of these states, and much anxiety was indicated as to the future. Many years of agitation had made them familiar with the idea of separation. Nearly two generations had risen to manhood since it had begun to be discussed as a possible alternative. Few, very few, of the Southern people had ever regarded it as a desirable event, or otherwise than as a last resort for escape from evils more intolerable. It was a calamity which, however threatened, they had still hoped might be averted or indefinitely postponed, and they had regarded with contempt, rather than anger, the ravings of a party in the North which denounced the Constitution and the Union and persistently defamed their brethren of the South.

Now, however, as well in Virginia and Tennessee, neither of which had yet seceded, as in the more Southern states, which had already taken that step, the danger so often prophesied was perceived to be at the door, and eager inquiries were made as to what would happen next—especially as to the probability of war between the states.

The course which events were likely to take was shrouded in the greatest uncertainty. In the minds of many there was the not unreasonable hope (which had been expressed by the commissioner sent from Mississippi to Maryland) that the secession of six Southern states—certainly soon to be followed by that of others—would so arouse the sober thought and better feeling of the Northern people as to compel their representatives to agree to a convention of the states, and that such guarantees would be given as would secure to the South the domestic tranquillity and equality in the Union which were rights assured under the federal compact. There were others, and they the most numerous class, who considered that the separation would be final, but peaceful. For my own part, while believing that secession was a right, and properly a peaceable remedy, I had never believed that it would be permitted to be peaceably exercised. Very few in the South at that time agreed with me, and my answers to queries on the subject were, therefore, as unexpected as they were unwelcome.

On my arrival at Jackson, the capital of Mississippi, I found that the convention of the state had made provision for a state army, and had appointed me to the command, with the rank of a major general. Four brigadier generals, appointed in like manner by the convention, were awaiting my arrival for assignment to duty. After the preparation of the necessary rules and regulations, the division of the state into districts, the apportionment among them of the troops to be raised, and the appointment of officers of the general staff, as authorized by the ordinance of the convention, such measures as were practicable were taken to obtain the necessary arms. The state had few serviceable weapons, and no establishment for their manufacture or repair. This fact (which is true of other Southern states as of Mississippi) is a clear proof of the absence of any desire or expectation of war. If the purpose of the Northern states to make war upon us because of secession had been foreseen, preparation to meet the consequences would have been contemporaneous with the adoption of a resort to that remedy—a remedy the possibility of which had for many years been contemplated. Had the Southern states possessed arsenals, and collected in them the requisite supplies of arms and munitions, such preparation would not only have placed them more nearly on an equality with the North in the beginning of the war, but might, perhaps, have been the best conservator of peace.

Let us, the survivors, however, not fail to do credit to the generous credulity which could not understand how, in violation of the compact of union, a war could be waged against the states, or why they should be invaded because their people had deemed it necessary to withdraw from an association which had failed to fulfill the ends for which they had entered into it, and which, having been broken to their injury by the other parties, had ceased to be binding upon them. It is a satisfaction to know that the calamities which have befallen the Southern states were the result of their credulous reliance on the power of the Constitution, that if it failed to protect their rights, it would at least suffice to prevent an attempt at coercion, if, in the last resort, they peacefully withdrew from the Union.

When, in after times, the passions of the day shall have subsided, and all the evidence shall have been collected and compared, the philosophical inquirer, who asks why the majority of the stronger section invaded the peaceful homes of their late associates, will be answered by history: "The lust of empire impelled them to wage against their weaker neighbors a war of subjugation."

CHAPTER V: *Meeting of the Provisional Congress of the Confederate States—Adoption of a Provisional Constitution—Election of President and Vice-President—Notification to the Author of his Election—His Views with Regard to it—Journey to Montgomery—Interview with Judge Sharkey—False Reports of Speeches on the Way—Inaugural Address—Editor's Note.*

THE congress of delegates from the seceding states convened at Montgomery, Alabama, according to appointment, on February 4, 1861. Their first work was to prepare a provisional constitution for the new confederacy, to be formed of the states which had withdrawn from the Union, for which the style "Confederate States of America" was adopted. The powers conferred upon them were adequate for the performance of this duty, the immediate necessity for which was obvious and urgent. This constitution was adopted on February 8, to continue in force for one year, unless superseded at an earlier date by a permanent organization. It is printed in an appendix, and for convenience of reference the permanent Constitution, adopted several weeks afterward, is exhibited in connection with it, and side by side with the Constitution of the United States, after which it was modeled.[1] The attention of the reader is invited to these documents and to a comparison of them, although a more particular notice of the permanent Constitution will be more appropriate hereafter.

On the next day (February 9) an election was held for the chief executive offices, resulting, as I afterward learned, in my election to the Presidency, with the Hon. Alexander H. Stephens of Georgia as Vice-President. Stephens was a delegate from Georgia to the congress.

While these events were occurring, having completed the most urgent of my duties at the capital of Mississippi, I had gone to my home Brierfield, in Warren County, and had begun, in the homely but expressive language of Clay, "to repair my fences." While thus engaged, notice was received of my election to the presidency of the Confederate States, with an urgent request to proceed immediately to Montgomery for inauguration.

As this had been suggested as a probable event, and what appeared to me adequate precautions had been taken to prevent it, I was surprised, and still more, disappointed. For reasons which it is not now necessary

[1] See Appendix K.

to state, I had not believed myself as well suited to the office as some others. I thought myself better adapted to command in the field; Mississippi had given me the position which I preferred to any other—the highest rank in her army. It was, therefore, that I afterward said in an address delivered in the Capitol before the legislature of the state, with reference to my election to the presidency of the Confederacy, that the duty to which I was thus called was temporary, and that I expected soon to be with the army of Mississippi again.

While on my way to Montgomery, and waiting in Jackson, Mississippi, for the railroad train, I met the Hon. William L. Sharkey, who had filled with great distinction the office of chief justice of the state. He said he was looking for me to make an inquiry. He desired to know if it was true, as he had just learned, that I believed there would be war. My opinion was freely given, that there would be war, long and bloody, and that it behooved everyone to put his house in order. He expressed much surprise, and said that he had not believed the report attributing this opinion to me. He asked how I supposed war could result from the peaceable withdrawal of a sovereign state. The answer was that it was not my opinion that war should be occasioned by the exercise of that right, but that it would be.

Judge Sharkey and I had not belonged to the same political party, he being a Whig, but we fully agreed with regard to the question of the sovereignty of the states. He had been an advocate of nullification—a doctrine to which I had never assented, and which had at one time been the main issue in Mississippi politics. He had presided over the well-remembered Nashville convention in 1849, and had possessed much influence in the state, not only as an eminent jurist, but as a citizen who had grown up with it, and held many offices of honor and trust.

On my way to Montgomery, brief addresses were made at various places, at which there were temporary stoppages of the train, in response to calls from the crowds assembled at such points. Some of these addresses were grossly misrepresented in sensational reports made by irresponsible persons, which were published in Northern newspapers, and were not considered worthy of correction under the pressure of the momentous duties then devolving upon me. These false reports, which represented me as invoking war and threatening devastation of the North, have since been adopted by partisan writers as authentic history. It is a sufficient answer to these accusations to refer to my farewell address to the Senate, already given, as reported for the press at the time, and, in connection therewith, to my inaugural address at Montgomery,

ALEXANDER H. STEPHENS

on assuming the office of President of the Confederate States, on February 18th. These two addresses, delivered at an interval of a month, during which no material change or circumstances had occurred, being one before and the other after the date of the sensational reports referred to, are sufficient to stamp them as utterly untrue. The inaugural was deliberately prepared, and uttered as written, and in connection with the farewell speech to the Senate, presents a clear and authentic statement of the principles and purposes which actuated me on assuming the duties of the high office to which I had been called.

INAUGURAL ADDRESS

Gentlemen of the Congress of the Confederate States of America, Friends, and Fellow-Citizens:

Called to the difficult and responsible station of Chief Magistrate of the Provisional Government which you have instituted, I approach the discharge of the duties assigned to me with humble distrust of my abilities, but with a sustaining confidence in the wisdom of those who are to guide and aid me in the administration of public affairs, and an abiding faith in the virtue and patriotism of the people. Looking forward to the speedy establishment of a permanent government to take the place of this, which by its greater moral and physical power will be better able to combat with many difficulties that arise from the conflicting interests of separate nations, I enter upon the duties of the office to which I have been chosen with the hope that the beginning of our career, as a Confederacy, may not be obstructed by hostile opposition to our enjoyment of the separate existence and independence we have asserted, and which with the blessing of Providence, we intend to maintain.

Our present political position has been achieved in a manner unprecedented in the history of nations. It illustrates the American idea that governments rest on the consent of the governed, and that it is the right of the people to alter or abolish them at will whenever they become destructive of the ends for which they were established. The declared purpose of the compact of the Union from which we have withdrawn was to "establish justice, insure domestic tranquillity, provide for the common defense, promote the general welfare, and secure the blessings of liberty to ourselves and our prosperity"; and when, in the judgment of the sovereign States composing this Confederacy, it has been perverted from the purposes for which it was ordained, and ceased to answer the ends for which it was established, a peaceful appeal to the ballot-box declared that, so far as they are concerned, the Government created by that compact should cease to exist. In this they merely asserted the right which the Declaration of Independence of July 4, 1776, defined to be "inalienable." Of the time and occasion of its exercise they as sovereigns were the final judges, each for itself. The impartial and enlightened verdict of mankind will vindicate the rectitude of our conduct; and He who knows the hearts of men will judge of the sincerity with which we have labored to preserve the Government of our fathers in its spirit.

The right solemnly proclaimed at the birth of the United States, and which has been solemnly affirmed and reaffirmed in the Bills of Rights of the States subsequently admitted into the Union of 1789, undeniably recognizes in the people the power to resume the authority delegated for the purposes of government. Thus the sovereign States here represented have proceeded to form this Confederacy; and it is by abuse of language that their act has been denominated a revolution. They formed a new alliance, but within each State its government has remained; so that the rights of person and property have not been disturbed. The agent through which they communicated with foreign nations is changed, but this does not necessarily interrupt their international relations. Sustained by the consciousness that the transition from the former Union to the present Confederacy has not proceeded from a disregard on our part of just obligations, or any failure to perform every constitutional duty, moved by no interest or passion to invade the rights of others, anxious to cultivate peace and commerce with all nations, if we may not hope to avoid war, we may at least expect that posterity will acquit us of having needlessly engaged in it. Doubly justified by the absence of wrong on our part, and by wanton aggression on the part of others, there can be no cause to doubt that the courage and patriotism of the people of the Confederate States will be found equal to any measures of defense which their honor and security may require.

An agricultural people, whose chief interest is the export of commodities required in every manufacturing country, our true policy is peace, and the freest trade which our necessities will permit. It is alike our interest and that of all those to whom we would sell, and from whom we would buy, that there should be the fewest practicable restrictions upon the interchange of these commodities. There can, however, be but little rivalry between ours and any manufacturing or navigating community, such as the Northeastern States of the American Union. It must follow, therefore, that mutual interest will invite to good-will and kind offices on both parts. If, however, passion or lust of dominion should cloud the judgment or inflame the ambition of those States, we must prepare to meet the emergency and maintain, by the final arbitrament of the sword, the position which we have assumed among the nations of the earth.

We have entered upon the career of independence, and it must be inflexibly pursued. Through many years of controversy with our late associates of the Northern States, we have vainly endeavored to secure tranquillity and obtain respect for the rights to which we were entitled. As a necessity, not a choice, we have resorted to the remedy of separation, and henceforth our energies must be directed to the conduct of our own affairs, and the perpetuity of the Confederacy which we have formed. If a just perception of mutual interest shall permit us peaceably to pursue our separate political career, my most earnest desire will have been fulfilled. But if this be denied to us, and the integrity of our territory and jurisdiction be assailed, it will but remain for us with firm resolve to appeal to arms and invoke the blessings of Providence on a just cause.

As a consequence of our new condition and relations, and with a view to meet anticipated wants, it will be necessary to provide for the speedy and efficient organization of branches of the Executive department having special charge of foreign intercourse, finance, military affairs, and the postal service.

For purposes of defense, the Confederate States may, under ordinary circumstances, rely mainly upon the militia; but it is deemed advisable, in the present condition of affairs, that there should be a well-instructed and disciplined army, more numerous than would usually be required on a peace establishment. I also suggest that for the protection of our harbors and commerce on the high seas, a navy adapted to those objects will be required. But this, as well as other subjects appropriate to our necessities, have doubtless engaged the attention of Congress.

With a Constitution differing only from that of our fathers in so far as it is explanatory of their well-known intent, freed from sectional conflicts, which have interfered with the pursuit of the general welfare, it is not unreasonable to expect that States from which we have recently parted may seek to unite their fortunes to ours under the Government which we have instituted. For this your Constitution makes adequate provision; but beyond this, if I mistake not the judgment and will of the people, a reunion with the States from which we have separated is neither practicable nor desirable. To increase the power, develop the resources, and promote the happiness of the Confederacy, it is requisite that there should be so much of homogeneity that the welfare of every portion shall be the aim of the whole. When this does not exist, antagonisms are engendered which must and should result in separation.

Actuated solely by the desire to preserve our own rights and promote our own welfare, the separation by the Confederate States has been marked by no aggression upon others, and followed by no domestic convulsion. Our industrial pursuits have received no check, the cultivation of our fields has progressed as heretofore, and, even should we be involved in war, there would be no considerable diminution in the production of the staples which have constituted our exports, and in which the commercial world has an interest scarcely less than our own. This common interest of the producer and consumer can only be interrupted by exterior force which would obstruct the transmission of our staples to foreign markets—a course of conduct which would be as unjust, as it would be detrimental, to manufacturing and commercial interests abroad.

Should reason guide the action of the Government from which we have separated, a policy so detrimental to the civilized world, the Northern States included, could not be dictated by even the strongest desire to inflict injury upon us; but, if the contrary should prove true, a terrible responsibility will rest upon it, and the suffering of millions will bear testimony to the folly and wickedness of our aggressors. In the meantime there will remain to us, besides the ordinary means before suggested, the well-known resources for retaliation upon the commerce of an enemy.

Experience in public stations, of subordinate grade to this which your kindness has conferred, has taught me that toil and care and disappointment are the price of official elevation. You will see many errors to forgive, many deficiencies to tolerate; but you shall not find in me either want of zeal or fidelity to the cause that is to me the highest in hope, and of most enduring affection. Your generosity has bestowed upon me an undeserved distinction, one which I neither sought nor desired. Upon the continuance of that sentiment, and upon your wisdom and patriotism, I rely to direct and support me in the performance of the duties required at my hands.

We have changed the constituent parts, but not the system of government. The Constitution framed by our fathers is that of these Confederate States. In their exposition of it, and in the judicial construction it has received, we have a light which reveals its true meaning.

Thus instructed as to the true meaning and just interpretation of that instrument, and ever remembering that all offices are but trusts held for the people, and that powers delegated are to be strictly construed, I will hope by due diligence in the performance of my duties, though I may disappoint your expectations, yet to retain, when retiring, something of the good-will and confidence which welcome my entrance into office.

It is joyous in the midst of perilous times to look around upon a people united in heart, where one purpose of high resolve animates and actuates the whole; where the sacrifices to be made are not weighed in the balance against honor and right and liberty and equality. Obstacles may retard, but they can not long prevent, the progress of a movement sanctified by its justice and sustained by a virtuous people. Reverently let us invoke the God of our Fathers to guide and protect us in our efforts to perpetuate the principles which by his blessing they were able to vindicate, establish, and transmit to their posterity. With the continuance of his favor ever gratefully acknowledged, we may hopefully look forward to success, to peace, and to prosperity.

Statements having been made, seeming to imply that I was a candidate "for the Presidency of the Confederate States; that my election was the result of a misunderstanding, or of accidental complications"; that I held "extreme views," and entertained at that period an inadequate conception of the magnitude of the war probably to be waged, information on the subject has been contributed by several distinguished members of the provisional congress, who still survive. From a number of their letters which have been published, the annexed extracts are given, parts being omitted which refer to matters not of historical interest.

From a communication of the Hon. Alexander M. Clayton of Mississippi, to the Memphis *Appeal* of June 21, 1870:

. . . . I was at the time a member of the Provisional Congress from Mississippi. Believing that Mr. Davis was the choice of the South for the position of President, before repairing to Montgomery I addressed him a letter to ascertain if he would accept it. He replied that it was not the place he desired; that, if he could have his choice, he would greatly prefer to be in active service as commander-in-chief of the army, but that he would give himself to the cause in any capacity whatever. That was the only letter of which I have any knowledge that he wrote on the subject, and that was shown to only a very few persons, and only when I was asked if Mr. Davis would accept the presidency. . . .

There was no electioneering, no management, on the part of any one. Each voter was left to determine for himself in whose hands the destinies of the infant Confederacy should be placed. By a law as fixed as gravitation itself, and as little disturbed by outside influence, the minds of members centered upon Mr. Davis.

After a few days of anxious, intense labor, the Provisional Constitution was framed, and it became necessary to give it vitality by putting some one at the head of the new Government. . . .

Without any effort on the part of the friends of either [Messrs. Davis or Stephens], the election was made without the slightest dissent. Of the accidental complications referred to, I have not the least knowledge, and always thought that the election of Mr. Davis arose from the spontaneous conviction of his peculiar fitness. I have consulted no one on the subject, and have appended my name only to avoid resting an important fact upon anonymous authority. Very respectfully yours,

(Signed)   ALEXANDER M. CLAYTON.

From the Hon. J. A. P. Campbell of Mississippi, now a justice of the Supreme Court of that state:

. . . . If there was a delegate from Mississippi, or any other State, who was opposed to the election of Jefferson Davis as President of the Confederate States, I never heard of the fact. I had the idea that Mr. Davis did not desire to be President, and preferred to be in the military service, but no other man was spoken of for President within my hearing. . . .

It is within my personal knowledge that the statement of the interview, that Mr. Davis did not have a just appreciation of the serious character of the contest between the seceding States and the Union, is wholly untrue. Mr. Davis, more than any man I ever heard talk on the subject, had a correct apprehension of the consequences of secession and of the magnitude of the war to be waged to coerce the seceding States. While at Montgomery, he expressed the belief that heavy fighting must occur, and that Virginia was to be the chief battleground. Years prior to secession, in his address before the Legislature and people of Mississippi, Mr. Davis had earnestly advised extensive preparation for the possible contingency of secession.

After the formation of the Confederate States, he was far in advance of the Constitutional Convention and the Provisional Congress, and, as I believe, of any man in it, in his views of the gravity of the situation and the probable extent and duration of the war, and of the provision which should be made for the defense of the seceding States. Before secession, Mr. Davis thought war would result from it; and, after secession, he expressed the view that the war commenced would be an extensive one. What he may have thought at a later day than the early part of 1862, I do not know; but it is inconceivable that the "interview" can be correct as to that.

The idea that Mr. Davis was so "extreme" in his views is a new one. He was extremely conservative on the subject of secession.

The suggestion that Mississippi would have preferred General Toombs or Mr. Cobb for President has no foundation in fact. My opinion is, that no man could have obtained a single vote in the Mississippi delegation against Mr. Davis, who was then, as he is now, the most eminent and popular of all the citizens of Mississippi. . . . Very respectfully,

(Signed)   J. A. P. CAMPBELL.

From the Hon. Duncan F. Kenner of Louisiana:

. . . . My recollections of what transpired at the time are very vivid and positive. . . .

Who should be President, was the absorbing question of the day. It engaged the attention of all present, and elicited many letters from our respective constituencies. The general inclination was strongly in favor of Mr. Davis. In fact, no other name was so prominently or so generally mentioned. The name of Mr. Rhett, of South Carolina, was probably more frequently mentioned than that of any other person, next to Mr. Davis.

The rule adopted at our election was that each State should have one vote, to be delivered in open session, *viva voce,* by one of the delegates as spokesman for his colleagues. The delegates of the different States met in secret session to select their candidate and spokesman.

Of what occurred in these various meetings I can not speak authoritatively as to other States, as their proceedings were considered secret. I can speak positively, however, of what took place at a meeting of the delegates from Louisiana. We, the Louisiana delegates, without hesitation, and unanimously, after a very short session, decided in favor of Mr. Davis. No other name was mentioned; the claims of no one else were considered, or even alluded to. There was not the slightest opposition to Mr. Davis on the part of any of our delegation; certainly none was expressed; all appeared enthusiastic in his favor, and, I have no reason to doubt, felt so. Nor was the feeling induced by any solicitation on the part of Mr. Davis or his friends. Mr. Davis was not in or near Montgomery at the time. He was never heard from on this subject, so far as I knew. He was never announced as a candidate. We were seeking the best man to fill the position, and the conviction at the time, in the minds of a large majority of the delegates, that Mr. Davis was the best qualified, from both his civil and military knowledge and experience, induced many to look upon Mr. Davis as the best selection that could be made.

This conviction, coupled with his well-recognized conservative views—for in no sense did we consider Mr. Davis extreme, either in his views or purposes —was the deciding consideration which controlled the votes of the Louisiana delegation. Of this I have not the least doubt. I remain, respectfully, very truly yours, etc.

(Signed)   DUNCAN F. KENNER.

From the Hon. James Chesnut of South Carolina:

. . . . Before leaving home I had made up my mind as to who was the fittest man to be President, and who to be Vice-President; Mr. Davis for the first, and Mr. Stephens for the second. And this was known to all my friends as well as to my colleagues.

Mr. Davis, then conspicuous for ability, had long experience in civil service, was reputed a most successful organizer and administrator of the military department of the United States when he was Secretary of War, and came out of the Mexican war with much *éclat* as a soldier. Possessing a combination of these high and needful qualities, he was regarded by nearly the whole South as the fittest man for the position. I certainly so regarded him, and did not change my mind on the way to Montgomery. . . .

Georgia was a great State—great in numbers, comparatively great in wealth, and great in the intellectual gifts and experiences of many of her sons. Conspicuous among them were Stephens, Toombs, and Cobb. In view of these facts, it was thought by all of us expedient—nay, more, positively right and just—that Georgia should have a corresponding weight in the counsels and conduct of the new Government.

Mr. Stephens was also a man of conceded ability, of high character, conservative, devoted to the rights of the States, and known to be a power in his own State; hence all eyes turned to him to fill the second place.

Howell Cobb became President of the Convention, and General Toombs Secretary of State. These two gifted Georgians were called to these respective positions because of their experience, ability, and ardent patriotism. . . .

Mr. Rhett was a very bold and frank man. So was Colonel Keitt; and they, as always, avowed their opinions and acted upon them with energy. Nevertheless, the vote of the delegation was cast for Mr. Davis. . . .

(Signed)   JAMES CHESNUT.

From the Hon. W. Porcher Miles of Virginia, formerly of South Carolina, and a member of the provisional congress of 1861:

OAK RIDGE, January 17, 1880.

. . . . To the best of my recollection there was entire unanimity in the South Carolina delegation at Montgomery on the subject of the choice of a President. I think it very likely that Keitt, from his warm personal friendship for Mr. Toombs, may at first have preferred him. I have no recollections of Chesnut's predilections. I think there was no question that Mr. Davis was the choice of our delegation and of the whole people of South Carolina. . . . I do not think Mr. Rhett ever attempted to influence the course of his colleagues, either in this or in matters generally before the Congress. Nor do I think his personal influence in the delegation was as great as that of some other members of it. If I were to select any one as having a special influence with us, I would consider Mr. Robert Barnwell as the one. His singularly pure and elevated character, entire freedom from all personal ambition or desire for place or position (he declined Mr. Davis's offer of a seat in the Cabinet), as well as his long experience in public life and admirably calm and well-balanced mind, all combined to make his influence with his colleagues very great. But neither could he be said "to lead" the delegation. He had no desire and never made any attempt to do so. I think there was no delegation in the Congress, the individual members of which were more independent in coming to their own conclusions of what was right and expedient to be done. There was always the frankest and freest interchange of opinions among them, but every one determined his own course for himself.

CHAPTER VI: *The Confederate Cabinet—Task of Selection an Agreeable One Due to Unanimity of People—Toombs of Georgia — Mallory of Florida — Benjamin of Louisiana — Reagan of Texas—Memminger of South Carolina—Walker of Alabama.*

AFTER being inaugurated, I proceeded to the formation of my cabinet, that is, the heads of the executive departments authorized by the laws of the provisional congress. The unanimity existing among our people made this a much easier and more agreeable task than where the rivalries in the party of an executive have to be consulted and accommodated, often at the expense of the highest capacity and fitness. Unencumbered by any other consideration than the public welfare, having no friends to reward or enemies to punish, it resulted that not one of those who formed my first cabinet had borne to me the relation of close personal friendship, or had political claims upon me; indeed, with two of them I had no previous acquaintance.

It was my wish that the Hon. Robert W. Barnwell of South Carolina should be Secretary of State. I had known him intimately during a trying period of our joint service in the United States Senate, and he had won alike my esteem and regard. Before making known to him my wish in this connection the delegation of South Carolina, of which he was a member, had resolved to recommend one of their number to be Secretary of the Treasury, and Barnwell, with characteristic delicacy, declined to accept my offer to him.

I had intended to offer the Treasury Department to Toombs of Georgia, whose knowledge on subjects of finance had particularly attracted my notice when we served together in the United States Senate. Barnwell having declined the State Department, and a colleague of his, said to be peculiarly qualified for the Treasury Department, having been recommended for it, Toombs was offered the State Department, for which others believed him to be well qualified.

Mallory of Florida had been chairman of the Committee on Naval Affairs in the United States Senate, was extensively acquainted with the officers of the navy, and for a landsman had much knowledge of nautical affairs; therefore he was selected for Secretary of the Navy.

Benjamin of Louisiana had a very high reputation as a lawyer, and my acquaintance with him in the Senate had impressed me with the

[207]

THE FIRST CONFEDERATE CABINET

lucidity of his intellect, his systematic habits, and capacity for labor. He was therefore invited to the post of Attorney General.

Reagan of Texas, I had known for a sturdy, honest Representative in the United States Congress, and his acquaintance with the territory included in the Confederate States was both extensive and accurate. These, together with his industry and ability to labor, indicated him as peculiarly fit for the office of Postmaster General.

Memminger of South Carolina had a high reputation for knowledge of finance. He bore an unimpeachable character for integrity and close attention to duties, and on the recommendation of the delegation from South Carolina he was appointed Secretary of the Treasury, and proved himself entirely worthy of the trust.

Walker of Alabama was a distinguished member of the bar of north Alabama, and was eminent among the politicians of that section. He was earnestly recommended by gentlemen intimately and favorably known to me, and was therefore selected for the War Department. His was the only name presented from Alabama.

The executive departments having been organized, my attention was first directed to preparation for military defense, for though I, in common with others, desired to have a peaceful separation, and sent commissioners to the United States government to effect, if possible, negotiations to that end, I did not hold the common opinion that we would be allowed to depart in peace, and therefore regarded it as an imperative duty to make all possible preparation for the contingency of war.

CHAPTER VII: *Early Acts of the Confederate Congress— Laws of the United States Continued in Force—Officers of Customs and Revenue Continued in Office—Commission to the United States—Navigation of the Mississippi—Restrictions on the Coasting Trade Removed—Appointment of Commissioners to Washington.*

THE legislation of the Confederate Congress furnishes the best evidence of the temper and spirit which prevailed in the organization of the Confederate government. The very first enactment, made on February 9, 1861—the day after the adoption of the provisional Constitution —was this:

That all the laws of the United States of America in force and in use in the Confederate States of America on the first day of November last, and not inconsistent with the Constitution of the Confederate States, be and the same are hereby continued in force until altered or repealed by the Congress.[1]

The next act, adopted on February 14, was one continuing in office until April 1 next ensuing all officers connected with the collection of customs and the assistant treasurers entrusted with the keeping of the moneys arising therefrom, who were engaged in the performance of such duties within any of the Confederate states, with the same powers and functions which they had been exercising under the government of the United States.[2]

The provisional Constitution itself, in the second section of its sixth article, had ordained as follows:

The Government hereby instituted shall take immediate steps for the settlement of all matters between the States forming it and their other late confederates of the United States, in relation to the public property and public debt at the time of their withdrawal from them; these States hereby declaring it to be their wish and earnest desire to adjust everything pertaining to the common property, common liabilities, and common obligations of that Union, upon the principles of right, justice, equity, and good faith.[3]

In accordance with this requirement of the Constitution, the Congress, on February 15—before my arrival at Montgomery—passed a resolution declaring "that it is the sense of this Congress that a commission of three persons be appointed by the President-elect, as early as may be convenient after his inauguration, and sent to the Government of the United States

---

[1] Statutes at Large, Provisional Government, Confederate States of America, p. 27.
[2] Statutes at Large, Provisional Government, Confederate States of America, pp. 27, 28.
[3] See provisional Constitution, Appendix K, *in loco.*

of America, for the purpose of negotiating friendly relations between that Government and the Confederate States of America, and for the settlement of all questions of disagreement between the two Governments, upon principles of right, justice, equity, and good faith."[4]

Persistent and to a great extent successful efforts were made to inflame the minds of the people of the northwestern states by representing to them that, in consequence of the separation of the states, they would lose the free navigation of the Mississippi River. At that early period in the life of the Confederacy, the intercourse between the North and South had been so little interrupted, that the agitators, whose vocation it was to deceive the masses of the people, could not, or should not, have been ignorant that, as early as February 25, 1861, an act was passed by the Confederate Congress, and approved by the President, "to declare and establish the free navigation of the Mississippi River." That act began with the announcement that "the peaceful navigation of the Mississippi River is hereby declared *free* to the citizens of any of the States upon its borders, or upon the borders of its navigable tributaries," and its provisions secure that freedom for "all ships, boats, or vessels," with their cargoes, "without any duty or hindrance, except light-money, pilotage, and other like charges."[5]

By an act approved on February 26, all laws which forbade the employment in the coasting trade of vessels not enrolled or licensed, and all laws imposing discriminating duties on foreign vessels or goods imported in them, were repealed.[6] These acts and all other indications manifest the well-known wish of the people of the Confederacy to preserve the peace and encourage the most unrestricted commerce with all nations, surely not least with their late associates, the Northern states. Thus far, the hope that peace might be maintained was predominant; perhaps the wish was father to the thought that there would be no war between the states lately united. Indeed, all the laws enacted during the first session of the provisional Congress show how consistent were the purposes and actions of its members with their original avowal of a desire peacefully to separate from those with whom they could not live in tranquillity, albeit the government had been established to promote the common welfare. Under this state of feeling the government of the Confederacy was instituted.

My own views and inclinations, as has already been fully shown, were

---

[4] Statutes at Large, Provisional Government, Confederate States of America, p. 92.
[5] Statutes at Large, Provisional Government, Confederate States of America, pp. 36-38.
[6] *Ibid.*, p. 38.

in entire accord with the disposition manifested by the requirement of the provisional Constitution and the resolution of the Congress above recited, for the appointment of a commission to negotiate friendly relations with the United States and an equitable and peaceable settlement of all questions which would necessarily arise under the new relations of the states toward one another. Next to the organization of a cabinet, that of such a commission was accordingly one of the very first objects of attention. Three discreet, well-informed, and distinguished citizens were selected as said commissioners, and accredited to the President of the Northern states, Lincoln, to the end that by negotiation all questions between the two governments might be so adjusted as to avoid war, and perpetuate the kind relations which had been cemented by the common trials, sacrifices, and glories of the people of all the states. If sectional hostility had been engendered by dissimilarity of institutions, and by a mistaken idea of moral responsibilities, and by irreconcilable creeds—if the family could no longer live and grow harmoniously together—by patriarchal teaching older than Christianity, it might have been learned that it was better to part, to part peaceably, and to continue, from one to another, the good offices of neighbors who by sacred memories were forbidden ever to be foes. The nomination of the members of the commission was made on February 25—within a week after my inauguration—and confirmed by Congress on the same day. The commissioners appointed were A. B. Roman of Louisiana, Martin J. Crawford of Georgia, and John Forsyth of Alabama. Roman was an honored citizen and had been governor of his native state; Crawford had served with distinction in Congress for several years; Forsyth was an influential journalist, and had been minister to Mexico under appointment of Pierce near the close of his term, and continued so under that of Buchanan. These gentlemen, moreover, represented the three great parties which had ineffectually opposed the sectionalism of the so-called Republicans. Ex-Governor Roman had been a Whig in former years, and one of the Constitutional Union, or Bell-and-Everett party in the canvass of 1860; Crawford, as a state-rights Democrat, had supported Breckinridge; Forsyth had been a zealous advocate of the claims of Douglas. The composition of the commission was therefore such as should have conciliated the sympathy and coöperation of every element of conservatism with which they might have occasion to deal. Their commissions authorized and empowered them, "in the name of the Confederate States, to meet and confer with any person or persons duly authorized by the Government of the United States, being furnished with like power and authority, and with him or them to agree, treat, consult, and negotiate" concerning all matters in which the parties were both interested. No secret instructions were given them, for there was nothing to conceal. The objects of their mission were open and avowed, and its inception and conduct throughout were characterized by frankness and good faith. How this effort was received, how the commissioners were kept waiting, and, while fair promises were held to the ear, how military preparations were pushed forward for the unconstitutional, criminal purpose of coercing states, let the shameful record of that transaction attest.

CHAPTER VIII: *The Peace Conference—Demand for "a Little Bloodletting"—Plan Proposed by the Congress—Its Contemptuous Reception and Treatment in the United States Congress —Failure of Last Efforts at Reconciliation and Reunion— Speech of General Lane of Oregon.*

WHILE the events which have just been occupying our attention were occurring, the last conspicuous effort was made within the Union to stay the tide of usurpation which was driving the Southern states into secession. This effort was set on foot by Virginia, the General Assembly of which state, on January 19, 1861, adopted a preamble and resolutions, deprecating disunion and inviting all such states as were willing to unite in an earnest endeavor to avert it by an adjustment of the then existing controversies to appoint commissioners to meet in Washington on February 4 "to consider, and, if practicable, agree upon some suitable adjustment." Ex-President John Tyler, along with William C. Rives, John W. Brockenbrugh, George W. Summers, and James A. Seddon—five of the most distinguished citizens of the state—were appointed to represent Virginia in the proposed conference. If they could agree with the commissioners of other states upon any plan of settlement requiring amendments to the federal Constitution, they were instructed to communicate them to Congress, with a view to their submission to the several states for ratification.

The "border states" in general promptly acceded to this proposition of Virginia, and others followed, so that in the "Peace Congress," or conference, which assembled, according to appointment, on the 4th, and adjourned on the 27th of February, twenty-one states were eventually represented, of which fourteen were Northern, or "non-slaveholding," and seven slaveholding states. The six states which had already seceded were of course not of the number represented; nor were Texas and Arkansas, the secession of which, although not consummated, was obviously inevitable. Three of the Northwestern states—Michigan, Wisconsin, and Minnesota—and the two Pacific states—Oregon and California —also held afoof from the conference. In the case of these last two, distance and lack of time perhaps hindered action. With regard to the other three, their reasons for declining to participate in the movement were not officially assigned, and are therefore only subjects for conjecture. Some remarkable revelations were afterward made, however, with regard to the action of one of them. It appears from correspondence read in the

Senate on February 27, that the two Senators from Michigan had at first opposed the participation of that state in the conference, on the ground that it was, as one of them expressed it, "a step toward obtaining that concession which the imperious slave powers so insolently demand"[1]— that is to say, in plain terms, they objected to it because it might lead to a compromise and pacification. Finding, however, that most of the other Northern states were represented—some of them by men of moderate and conciliatory temper—that writer had subsequently changed his mind, and at a late period of the session of the conference recommended the sending of delegates of "true, unflinching men," who would be "in favor of the Constitution as it is"—that is, who would oppose any amendment proposed in the interests of harmony and pacification.

The other Senator exhibits a similar alarm at the prospect of compromise and a concurrent change of opinion. He urges the sending of "stiff-backed" men, to thwart the threatened success of the friends of peace, and concludes with an expression of the humane and patriotic sentiment that "without a little blood-letting" the Union would not be "worth a rush."[2] With such unworthy levity did these leaders of sectional strife express their exultation in the prospect of the conflict, which was to drench the land with blood and enshroud thousands of homes in mourning!

It is needless to follow the course of the deliberations of the Peace

---

[1] See letter of Hon. S. K. Bingham to Governor Blair of Michigan, in *Congressional Globe,* second session, Thirty-sixth Congress, Part II, p. 1247.

[2] See *Congressional Globe, ut supra.* As this letter, last referred to, is brief and characteristic of the temper of the typical so-called Republicans of the period, it may be inserted entire:

"WASHINGTON, February 11, 1861.

"MY DEAR GOVERNOR: Governor Bingham and myself telegraphed you on Saturday, at the request of Massachusetts and New York, to send delegates to the Peace or Compromise Congress. They admit that we were right, and that they were wrong; that no Republican State should have sent delegates; but they are here, and can not get away; Ohio, Indiana, and Rhode Island are caving in, and there is danger of Illinois; and now they beg us, for God's sake, to come to their rescue, and save the Republican party from rupture. I hope you will send *stiff-backed* men, or none. The whole thing was gotten up against my judgment and advice, and will end in thin smoke. Still, I hope, as a matter of courtesy to some of our erring brethren, that you will send the delegates.

"Truly your friend,
(Signed)   "Z. CHANDLER.

"His Excellency AUSTIN BLAIR."

"P.S.—Some of the manufacturing States think that a fight would be awful. Without *a little bloodletting,* this Union will not, in my estimation, be worth a rush."

The reader should not fall into the mistake of imagining that the "erring brethren," toward whom a concession of courtesy is recommended by the writer of this letter, were the people of the seceding, or even of the border, states. It is evident from the context that he means the people of those so-called Republican states which had fallen into the error of taking part in a plan for peace, which might have averted the bloodletting recommended.

Conference. It included among its members many men of distinction and eminent ability, and some of unquestionable patriotism, from every part of the Union. The venerable John Tyler presided, and took an active and ardent interest in the efforts made to effect a settlement and avert the impending disasters. A plan was finally agreed upon by a majority of the states represented, for certain amendments to the federal Constitution, which it was hoped might be acceptable to all parties and put an end to further contention. In its leading features this plan resembled that of Crittenden, heretofore spoken of, which was still pending in the Senate, though with some variations, which were regarded as less favorable to the South. It was reported immediately to both houses of the United States Congress. In the Senate, Crittenden promptly expressed his willingness to accept it as a substitute for his own proposition, and eloquently urged its adoption. But the arrogance of a sectional majority inflated by recent triumph was too powerful to be allayed by the appeals of patriotism or the counsels of wisdom. The plan of the Peace Conference was treated by the majority with the contemptuous indifference shown to every other movement for conciliation. Its mere consideration was objected to by the extreme radicals, and although they failed in this, it was defeated on a vote, as were the Crittenden propositions.

✦ ✦ ✦ ✦

With the failure of these efforts, which occurred on the eve of the inauguration of Lincoln, and the accession to power of a party founded on a basis of sectional aggression, and now thoroughly committed to its prosecution and perpetuation, expired the last hopes of reconciliation and union.

In the course of the debate in the Senate on these grave propositions, a manly and eloquent speech was made on March 2, 1861, by the Hon. Joseph Lane, a Senator from Oregon, who had been the candidate of the Democratic state-rights party for the vice-presidency of the United States, in the canvass of 1860. Some passages of this speech seem peculiarly appropriate for insertion here. General Lane was replying to a speech of Andrew Johnson of Tennessee, afterward President of the United States:

Mr. President, the Senator from Tennessee complains of my remarks on his speech. He complains of the tone and temper of what I said. He complains that I replied at all, as I was a Northern Senator. Mr. President, I am a citizen of this Union and a Senator of the United States. My residence is in the North, but I have never seen the day, and I never shall, when I will refuse justice as readily to the South as to the North. I know nothing but my country, the whole country, the Constitution, and the equality of the States—the equal right of every man in the common territory of the whole country; and by that I shall stand. The Senator complains that I replied at all, as I was a Northern Senator, and a Democrat whom he had supported at the last election for a high office. Now, I was, as I stated at the time, surprised at the Senator's speech, because I understood it to be for coercion, as I think it was understood by almost everybody else, except, as we are now told, by the Senator himself; and I still think it amounted to a coercion speech, notwithstanding the soft and plausible phrases by which he describes it—a speech for the execution of the laws and the protection of the Federal property. Sir, if there is, as I contend, the right of secession, then, whenever a State exercises that right, this Government has no laws in that State to execute, nor has it any property in any such State that can be protected by the power of this Government. In attempting, however, to substitute the smooth phrases "executing the laws" and "protecting public property" for coercion, for civil war, we have an important concession: that is, that this Government dare not go before the people with a plain avowal of its real purposes and of their consequences. No, sir; the policy is to inveigle the people of the North into civil war, by masking the designs in smooth and ambiguous terms.[3]

---

[3] *Congressional Globe,* second session, Thirty-sixth Congress, p. 1347.

CHAPTER IX: *Northern Protests Against Coercion—The "New York Tribune," Albany "Argus," and "New York Herald"— Great Public Meeting in New York—Speeches of Thayer, ex-Governor Seymour, ex-Chancellor Walworth, and Others— The Press in February, 1861—Lincoln's Inaugural—The Marvelous Change or Suppression of Conservative Sentiment— Historic Precedents.*

IT is a great mistake, or misstatement of fact, to assume that at the period under consideration the Southern states stood alone in the assertion of the principles which have been laid down in this work, with regard to the right of secession and the wrong of coercion. Down to the formation of the Confederate government, the one was distinctly admitted, the other still more distinctly disavowed and repudiated, by many of the leaders of public opinion in the North of both parties—indeed, any purpose of direct coercion was disclaimed by nearly all. If presented at all, it was in the delusive and ambiguous guise of "the execution of the laws" and "protection of the public property."

The *New York Tribune*—the leading organ of the party which triumphed in the election of 1860—had said, soon after the result of that election was ascertained, with reference to secession: "We hold, with Jefferson, to the inalienable right of communities to alter or abolish forms of government that have become oppressive or injurious; and, if the cotton States shall decide that they can do better out of the Union than in it, we insist on letting them go in peace. The right to secede may be a revolutionary right, *but it exists nevertheless;* and we do not see how one party can have *a right to do what another party has a right to prevent.* We must ever resist the asserted right of any State to remain in the Union and nullify or defy the laws thereof: *to withdraw from the Union is quite another matter.* And, whenever a considerable section of our Union shall deliberately resolve to go out, *we shall resist all coercive measures designed to keep her in. We hope never to live in a republic whereof one section is pinned to the residue by bayonets.*[1]

The only liberty taken with this extract has been that of presenting certain parts of it in italics. Nothing that has ever been said by the author of this work, in the foregoing chapters, on the floor of the Senate, or elsewhere, more distinctly asserted the right of secession. Nothing

---

[1] *New York Tribune* of November 9, 1860, quoted in *The American Conflict,* Vol. I, Chapt. XXIII, p. 359.

that has been quoted from Hamilton, or Madison, or Marshall, or John Quincy Adams, more emphatically repudiates the claim of right to restrain or coerce a state in the exercise of its free choice. Nothing that has been said since the war which followed could furnish a more striking condemnation of its origin, prosecution, purposes, and results. A comparison of the sentiments above quoted, with the subsequent career of the party, of which that journal was and long had been the recognized organ, would exhibit a striking incongruity and inconsistency.

The *Tribune* was far from being singular among its Northern contemporaries in the entertainment of such views, as Greeley, its chief editor, has shown by many citations in his book, *The American Conflict*. The Albany *Argus,* about the same time, said in language which Greeley characterizes as "clear and temperate": "We sympathize with and justify the South as far as this: their rights have been invaded to the extreme limit possible within the forms of the Constitution; and, beyond this limit, their feelings have been insulted and their interests and honor assailed by almost every possible form of denunciation and invective; and, if we deemed it certain that the real *animus* of the Republican party could be carried into the administration of the Federal Government, and become the permanent policy of the nation, we should think that all the instincts of self-preservation and of manhood rightfully impelled them to a resort to revolution and a separation from the Union, and we would applaud them and wish them godspeed in the adoption of such a remedy."

Again, the same paper said, a day or two afterward: "If South Carolina or any other State, through a convention of her people, shall formally separate herself from the Union, probably both the present and the next Executive will simply let her alone and *quietly allow all the functions of the Federal Government within her limits to be suspended. Any other course would be madness;* as it would at once enlist all the Southern States in the controversy and plunge the whole country into a civil war. . . . As a matter of policy and wisdom, therefore, independent of the question of right, we should deem resort to force most disastrous."

The *New York Herald*—a journal which claimed to be independent of all party influences—about the same period said: "Each State is organized as a complete government, holding the purse and wielding the sword, possessing the right to break the tie of the confederation as a nation might break a treaty, and to repel coercion as a nation might repel invasion. . . . Coercion, if it were possible, is out of the question."

On January 31, 1861—after six states had already seceded—a great meeting was held in the city of New York, to consider the perilous condition of the country. At this meeting James S. Thayer, "an old-line Whig," made a speech, which was received with great applause. The following extracts from the published report of Thayer's speech will show the character of the views which then commanded the cordial approval of that metropolitan audience:

We can at least, in an authoritative way and a practical manner, arrive at the basis of a *peaceable separation*. [Cheers.] We can at least by discussion enlighten, settle, and concentrate the public sentiment in the State of New York upon this question, and save it from that fearful current, which circuitously but certainly sweeps madly on, through the narrow gorge of "the enforcement of the laws," to the shoreless ocean of civil war! [Cheers.] Against this, under all circumstances, in every place and form, we must now and at all times oppose a resolute and unfaltering resistance. The public mind will bear the avowal, and let us make it—that, if a revolution of force is to begin, *it shall be inaugurated at home*. And if the incoming Administration shall attempt to carry out the line of policy that has been fore-shadowed, we announce that, when the hand of Black Republicanism turns to blood-red, and seeks *from the fragment of the Constitution to construct a scaffolding for coercion—another name for execution*—we will reverse the order of the French Revolution, and save the blood of the people by making those who would inaugurate a reign of terror the first victims of a national guillotine! [Enthusiastic applause.]

And again:

It is announced that the Republican Administration will enforce the laws against and in all the seceding States. A nice discrimination must be exercised in the performance of this duty. You remember the story of William Tell. . . . Let an arrow winged by the Federal bow strike the heart of an American citizen, and who can number the avenging darts that will cloud the heavens in the conflict that will ensue? [Prolonged applause.] What, then, is the duty of the State of New York? What shall we say to our people when we come to meet this state of facts? That the Union must be preserved? But if that can not be, what then? *Peaceable separation*. [Applause.] Painful and humiliating as it is, let us temper it with all we can of love and kindness, so that we may yet be left in a comparatively prosperous condition, in friendly relations with another Confederacy. [Cheers.]

At the same meeting ex-Governor Horatio Seymour asked the question —on which subsequent events have cast their own commentary—whether "successful coercion by the North is less revolutionary than successful secession by the South? Shall we prevent revolution [he added] by being foremost in over-throwing the principles of our Government, and all that makes it valuable to our people and distinguishes it among the nations of the earth?"

The venerable ex-Chancellor Walworth thus expressed himself:

It would be as brutal, in my opinion, to send men to butcher our own brothers of the Southern States as it would be to massacre them in the Northern States. We are told, however, that it is our duty to, and we must, enforce the laws. But why—and what laws are to be enforced? There were laws that were to be enforced in the time of the American Revolution. . . . Did Lord Chatham go for enforcing those laws? No, he gloried in defense of the liberties of America. He made that memorable declaration in the British Parliament, "If I were an American citizen, instead of being, as I am, an Englishman, I never would submit to such laws—never, never, never!" [Prolonged applause.]

Other distinguished speakers expressed themselves in similar terms— varying somewhat in their estimate of the propriety of the secession of the Southern states, but all agreeing in emphatic and unqualified reprobation of the idea of coercion. A series of conciliatory resolutions was adopted, one of which declares that "civil war will not restore the Union, but will defeat for ever its reconstruction."

At a still later period—some time in the month of February—the *Free Press,* a leading paper in Detroit, had the following:

If there shall not be a change in the present seeming purpose to yield to no accommodation of the national difficulties, and if troops shall be raised in the North to march against the people of the South, *a fire in the rear will be opened upon such troops,* which will either stop their march altogether or wonderfully accelerate it.

The *Union,* of Bangor, Maine, spoke no less decidedly to the same effect:

The difficulties between the North and the South must be compromised, or the separation of the States *shall be peaceable.* If the Republican party refuse to go the full length of the Crittenden amendment—*which is the very least the South can or ought to take*—then, here in Maine, not a Democrat will be found who will raise his arm against his brethren of the South. From one end of the State to the other let the cry of the Democracy be, *Compromise or Peaceable Separation!*

That these were not expressions of isolated or exceptional sentiment is evident from the fact that they were copied with approval by other Northern journals.

Lincoln, when delivering his inaugural address on March 4, 1861, had not so far lost all respect for the consecrated traditions of the founders of the Constitution and for the majesty of the principle of state sovereignty as openly to enunciate the claim of coercion. While arguing against the right to secede, and asserting his intention "to hold, occupy, and possess the property and places belonging to the Government, and collect the duties and imposts," he says that, "beyond what may be necessary for these objects, there will be no invasion, no using of force against or among the people anywhere," and appends to this declaration the following pledge:

Where hostility to the United States shall be so great as to prevent competent resident citizens from holding the Federal offices, there will be no attempt to force obnoxious strangers among the people for that object. While the strict legal right may exist of the Government to enforce the exercise of these offices, the attempt to do so would be so irritating, and so nearly impracticable withal, that I deem it better to forego for the time the uses of such offices.

These extracts will serve to show that the people of the South were not without grounds for cherishing the hope, to which they so fondly clung, that the separation would, indeed, be as peaceable in fact as it was, on their part, in purpose; that the conservative and patriotic feeling still existing in the North would control the elements of sectional hatred and bloodthirsty fanaticism; that there would be really "no war."

And here the ingenuous reader may very naturally ask, What became of all this feeling? How was it that, in the course of a few weeks, it had disappeared like a morning mist? Where was the host of men who had declared that an army marching to invade the Southern states should first pass over their dead bodies? No new question had arisen—no change in the attitude occupied by the seceding states—no cause for controversy not already existing when these utterances were made. And yet the sentiments which they expressed were so entirely swept away by the tide of reckless fury which soon afterward impelled an armed invasion of the South, that (with a few praiseworthy but powerless exceptions) scarcely a vestige of them was left. Not only were they obliterated, but seemingly forgotten.

I leave to others to offer, if they can, an explanation of this strange phenomenon. To the student of human nature, however, it may not seem altogether without precedent, when he remembers certain other instances on record of mutations in public sentiment equally sudden and extraordinary. Ten thousand swords that would have leaped from their scabbards—as the English statesman thought—to avenge even a look of insult to a lovely queen, hung idly in their places when she was led to the scaffold in the midst of the vilest taunts and execrations. The case that we have been considering was, perhaps, only an illustration of the general truth that, in times of revolutionary excitement, the higher and better elements are crushed and silenced by the lower and baser—not so much on account of their greater extent, as of their greater violence.

CHAPTER X: *Temper of the Southern People Indicated by the Action of the Confederate Congress—The Permanent Constitution—Modeled after the Federal Constitution—Variations and Special Provisions—Provisions with Regard to Slavery and the Slave Trade—A False Assertion Refuted—Excellence of the Constitution—Admissions of Hostile or Impartial Criticism.*

THE conservative temper of the people of the Confederate States was conspicuously exhibited in the most important product of the early labors of their representatives in Congress assembled. The provisional Constitution, although prepared only for temporary use, and necessarily in some haste, was so well adapted for the purpose which it was intended to serve that many thought it would have been wise to continue it in force indefinitely, or at least until the independency of the Confederacy should be assured. The Congress, however, deeming it best that the system of government should emanate from the people, accordingly, on March 11, prepared the permanent Constitution, which was submitted to and ratified by the people of the respective states.

Of this Constitution—which may be found in an appendix,[1] side by side with the Constitution of the United States—the Hon. Alexander H. Stephens, who was one of its authors, very properly says:

The whole document utterly negatives the idea, which so many have been active in endeavoring to put in the enduring form of history, that the Convention at Montgomery was nothing but a set of "conspirators," whose object was the overthrow of the principles of the Constitution of the United States, and the erection of a great "slavery oligarchy," instead of the free institutions thereby secured and guaranteed. This work of the Montgomery Convention, with that of the Constitution for a Provisional Government, will ever remain, not only as a monument of the wisdom, forecast, and statesmanship of the men who constituted it, but an everlasting refutation of the charges which have been brought against them. These works together show clearly that their only leading object was to sustain, uphold, and perpetuate the fundamental principles of the Constitution of the United States.[2]

The Constitution of the United States was the model followed throughout, with only such changes as experience suggested for better practical working or for greater perspicuity. The preamble to both instruments is the same in substance, and very nearly identical in language.

[1] See Appendix K.
[2] *War between the States*, Vol. II, col. XIX, p. 389.

The words "We, the people of the United States," in one, are replaced by "We, the people of the Confederate States," in the other; the gross perversion which has been made of the former expression is precluded in the latter merely by the addition of the explanatory clause, "each State acting in its sovereign and independent character"—an explanation which, at the time of the formation of the Constitution of the United States, would have been deemed entirely superfluous.

The official term of the President was fixed at six instead of four years, and it was provided that he should not be eligible for reëlection. This was in accordance with the original draft of the Constitution of 1787.[3]

The President was empowered to remove officers of his cabinet, or those engaged in the diplomatic service, at his discretion, but in all other cases removal from office could be made only for cause, and the cause was to be reported to the Senate.[4]

Congress was authorized to provide by law for the admission of "the principal officer in each of the executive departments" (or cabinet officers) to a seat upon the floor of either house, with the privilege of taking part in the discussion of subjects pertaining to his department.[5] This wise and judicious provision, which would have tended to obviate much delay and misunderstanding, was, however, never put into execution by the necessary legislation.

Protective duties for the benefit of special branches of industry, which had been so fruitful a source of trouble under the government of the United States, were altogether prohibited.[6] So, also, were bounties from the treasury,[7] and extra compensation for services rendered by officers, contractors, or employees of any description.[8]

A vote of two-thirds of each house was requisite for the appropriation of money from the treasury, unless asked for by the chief of a department and submitted to Congress by the President, or for payment of the expenses of Congress, or of claims against the Confederacy judicially established and declared.[9] The President was also authorized to approve any one appropriation and disapprove any other in the same bill.[10]

With regard to the impeachment of federal officers, it was entrusted, as formerly, to the discretion of the House of Representatives, with the

---

[3] See Article II, section 1.
[4] *Ibid.*, section 2, par. 3.
[5] Article I, section 6, par. 2.
[6] Article I, section 8, par. 1.
[7] *Ibid.*
[8] *Ibid.*, section 9, par. 10.
[9] *Ibid.*, par. 9.
[10] *Ibid.*, section 7, par. 2.

additional provision, however, that in the case of any judicial or other officer exercising his functions solely within the limits of a particular state, impeachment might be made by the legislature of such state—the trial in all cases to be by the Senate of the Confederate States.[11]

Any two or more states were authorized to enter into compacts with each other for the improvement of the navigation of rivers flowing between or through them.[12] A vote of two-thirds of each house—the Senate voting by states—was required for the admission of a new state.[13]

With regard to amendments of the Constitution, it was made obligatory upon Congress, on the demand of any three states concurring in the proposed amendment or amendments, to summon a convention of all the states to consider and act upon them, voting by states, but restricted in its action to the particular propositions thus submitted. If approved by such convention, the amendments were to be subject to final ratification by two-thirds of the states.[14]

Other changes or modifications, worthy of special notice, related to internal improvements, bankruptcy laws, duties on exports, suits in the federal courts, and the government of the territories.[15]

With regard to slavery and the slave trade, the provisions of this Constitution furnish an effectual answer to the assertion, so often made, that the Confederacy was founded on slavery, that slavery was its "corner stone," etc. Property in slaves, already existing, was recognized and guaranteed, just as it was by the Constitution of the United States; the rights of such property in the common territories were protected against any such hostile discrimination as had been attempted in the Union. But the "extension of slavery," in the only practical sense of that phrase, was more distinctly and effectually precluded by the Confederate than by the Federal Constitution. This will be manifest on a comparison of the provisions of the two relative to the slave trade. These are found at the beginning of the ninth section of the first article of each instrument. The Constitution of the United States has the following:

The migration or importation of such persons as any of the States now existing shall think proper to admit, shall not be prohibited by the Congress prior to the year one thousand eight hundred and eight; but a tax or duty may be imposed on such importations, not exceeding ten dollars for each person.

The Confederate Constitution, on the other hand, ordained as follows:

[11]*Ibid.*, section 2, par. 5.
[12]*Ibid.*, section 10, par. 3.
[13]Article IV, section 3, par. 1.
[14]Article V.
[15]Article I, section 8, paragraphs 1 and 4, section 9, par. 6; Article III, section 2, par. 1; Article IV, section 3, par. 3.

1. The importation of negroes of the African race from any foreign country, other than the slaveholding States or Territories of the United States of America, is hereby forbidden; and Congress is required to pass such laws as shall effectually prevent the same.

2. Congress shall also have the power to prohibit the introduction of slaves from any State not a member of, or Territory not belonging to, this Confederacy.

In the case of the United States, the only prohibition is against any interference by Congress with the slave trade for a term of years, and it was further legitimized by the authority given to impose a duty upon it. The term of years, it is true, had long since expired, but there was still no prohibition of the trade by the Constitution; it was after 1808 entirely within the discretion of Congress either to encourage, tolerate, or prohibit it.

Under the Confederate Constitution, on the contrary, the African slave trade was "hereby forbidden," positively and unconditionally, from the beginning. Neither the Confederate government nor that of any of the states could permit it, and the Congress was expressly "required" to enforce the prohibition. The only discretion in the matter entrusted to the Congress was whether or not to permit the introduction of slaves from any of the United States or their territories.

Lincoln, in his inaugural address, had said: "I have no purpose, directly or indirectly, to interfere with the institution of slavery in the States where it exists. I believe I have no lawful right to do so, and I have no inclination to do so." Now if there was no purpose on the part of the government of the United States to interfere with the institution of slavery within its already existing limits—a proposition which permitted its propagation within those limits by natural increase—and inasmuch as the Confederate Constitution precluded any other than the same natural increase, we may plainly perceive the disingenuousness and absurdity of the pretension by which a factitious sympathy has been obtained in certain quarters for the war upon the South, on the ground that it was a war in behalf of freedom against slavery.[16]

---

[16]As late as April 22, 1861, Seward, United States Secretary of State, in a dispatch to Dayton, minister to France, since made public, expressed the views and purposes of the United States government in the premises as follows. It may be proper to explain that, by what he is pleased to term "the revolution," Seward means the withdrawal of the Southern states; that the words italicized are, perhaps, not so distinguished in the original. He says: "The Territories will remain in all respects the same, whether the revolution shall succeed or shall fail. *The condition of slavery in the several States will remain just the same, whether it succeed or fail.* There is not even a pretext for the complaint that the disaffected States are to be conquered by the United States if the revolution fails; for the rights of the States and *the condition of every being in them* will remain subject to exactly the same laws and forms of administration, whether the revolution shall succeed or whether it shall fail. In

I had no direct part in the preparation of the Confederate Constitution. No consideration of delicacy forbids me, therefore, to say, in closing this brief review of that instrument, that it was a model of wise, temperate, and liberal statesmanship. Intelligent criticism, from hostile as well as friendly sources, has been compelled to admit its excellences, and has sustained the judgment of a popular Northern journal which said, a few days after it was adopted and published:

The new Constitution is the Constitution of the United States with various modifications and some very important and most desirable improvements. We are free to say that the invaluable reforms enumerated should be adopted by the United States, with or without a reunion of the seceded States, and as soon as possible. But why not accept them with the propositions of the Confederate States on slavery as a basis of reunion?[17]

---

the one case, the States would be federally connected with the new Confederacy; in the other, they would, as now, be members of the United States; *but their Constitutions and laws, customs, habits, and institutions in either case, will remain the same."*

[17]*New York Herald,* March 19, 1861.

CHAPTER XI: *The Commission to Washington City—Arrival of Crawford—Buchanan's Alarm—Note of the Commissioners to the New Administration—Mediation of Justices Nelson and Campbell—The Difficulty about Forts Sumter and Pickens—Secretary Seward's Assurances—Duplicity of the Government at Washington—Fox's Visit to Charleston—Secret Preparations for Coercive Measures—Visit of Lamon—Renewed Assurances of Good Faith—Notification to Governor Pickens—Developments of Secret History—Systematic and Complicated Perfidy Exposed.*

THE appointment of commissioners to proceed to Washington, for the purpose of establishing friendly relations with the United States and effecting an equitable settlement of all questions relating to the common property of the states and the public debt, has already been mentioned. No time was lost in carrying this purpose into execution. Crawford—first of the commissioners—left Montgomery on or about February 27, and arrived in Washington two or three days before the expiration of Buchanan's term of office as President of the United States. Besides his official credentials, he bore the following letter to the President, of a personal or semiofficial character, intended to facilitate, if possible, the speedy accomplishment of the objects of his mission:

To the President of the United States.

SIR: Being animated by an earnest desire to unite and bind together our respective countries by friendly ties, I have appointed Martin J. Crawford, one of our most esteemed and trustworthy citizens, as special Commissioner of the Confederate States to the Government of the United States; and I have now the honor to introduce him to you, and to ask for him a reception and treatment corresponding to his station, and to the purposes for which he is sent.

Those purposes he will more particularly explain to you. Hoping that through his agency these may be accomplished, I avail myself of this occasion to offer to you the assurance of my distinguished consideration.

(Signed)   JEFFERSON DAVIS.
MONTGOMERY, February 17, 1861.

It may here be mentioned, in explanation of my desire that the commission, or at least a part of it, should reach Washington before the close of Buchanan's term, that I had received an intimation from him, through a distinguished Senator of one of the border states,[1] that he would be

---
[1] Hunter of Virginia.

happy to receive a commissioner or commissioners from the Confederate States, and would refer to the Senate any communication that might be made through such a commission.

Crawford—now a judge of the Supreme Court of Georgia, and the only surviving member of the commission—in a manuscript account, which he has kindly furnished, of his recollections of events connected with it, says that, on arriving in Washington at the early hour of half-past four o'clock in the morning, he was "surprised to see Pennsylvania Avenue, from the old National to Willard's Hotel, crowded with men hurrying, some toward the former, but most of the faces in the direction of the latter, where the new President [Mr. Lincoln, President-elect], the great political almoner, for the time being, had taken up his lodgings. At this point," continues Judge Crawford, "the crowd swelled to astonishing numbers of expectant and hopeful men, awaiting an opportunity, either to see Mr. Lincoln himself, or to communicate with him through some one who might be so fortunate as to have access to his presence."

Describing his reception in the federal capital, Judge Crawford says:

The feverish and emotional condition of affairs soon made the presence of the special Commissioner at Washington known throughout the city. Congress was still, of course, in session; Senators and members of the House of Representatives, excepting those of the Confederate States, who had withdrawn, were in their seats, and the manifestations of anxious care and gloomy forebodings were plainly to be seen on all sides. This was not confined to sections, but existed among the men of the North and West as well as those of the South. . . .

Mr. Buchanan, the President, was in a state of most thorough alarm, not only for his home at Wheatland, but for his personal safety.[2] In the very few days which had elapsed between the time of his promise to receive a Commissioner from the Confederate States and the actual arrival of the Commissioner, he had become so fearfully panic-stricken, that he declined either to receive him or to send any message to the Senate touching the subject-matter of his mission.

The Commissioner had been for several years in Congress before the Administration of Mr. Buchanan, as well as during his official term, and had always been in close political and social relations with him; yet he was afraid of a public visit from him. He said that he had only three days of official life left, and could incur no further dangers or reproaches than those he had already borne from the press and public speakers of the North.

The intensity of the prevalent feeling increased as the vast crowds, arriving by every train, added fresh material; and hatred and hostility toward our new Government were manifested in almost every conceivable manner.

---

[2] This statement is in accord with a remark which Buchanan made to the author at an earlier period of the same session, with regard to the violence of Northern sentiment then lately indicated, that he thought it not impossible that his homeward route would be lighted by burning effigies of himself, and that on reaching his home he would find it a heap of ashes.

Another of the commissioners (Forsyth) having arrived in Washington on March 12—eight days after the inauguration of Lincoln—the two commissioners then present, Forsyth and Crawford, addressed to Seward, Secretary of State, a note informing him of their presence, stating the friendly and peaceful purposes of their mission, and requesting the appointment of a day, as early as possible, for the presentation to the President of the United States of their credentials and the objects which they had in view. This letter will be found in the Appendix,[3] with other correspondence which ensued, published soon after the events to which it relates. The attention of the reader is specially invited to these documents, but, as additional revelations have been made since they were first published, it will be proper, in order to obtain a full understanding of the transactions to which they refer, to give here a brief statement of the facts.

No written answer to the note of the commissioners was delivered to them for twenty-seven days after it was written. The paper of Seward, in reply, without signature or address, dated March 15,[4] was "filed," as he states, on that day, in the Department of State, but a copy of it was not handed to the commissioners until April 8. But an oral answer had been made to the note of the commissioners at a much earlier date, for the significance of which it will be necessary to bear in mind the condition of affairs at Charleston and Pensacola.

Fort Sumter was still occupied by the garrison under command of Major Anderson, with no material change in the circumstances since the failure of the attempt made in January to reënforce it by means of the *Star of the West.* This standing menace at the gates of the chief harbor of South Carolina had been tolerated by the government and people of that state, and afterward by the Confederate authorities, in the abiding hope that it would be removed without compelling a collision of forces. Fort Pickens, on one side of the entrance to the harbor of Pensacola, was also occupied by a garrison of United States troops, while the two forts (Barrancas and McRee) on the other side were in possession of the Confederates. Communication by sea was not entirely precluded, however, in the case of Fort Pickens; the garrison had been strengthened, and a fleet of federal men-of-war was lying outside of the harbor. The condition of affairs at these forts—especially at Fort Sumter—was a subject of anxiety with the friends of peace, and the hope of settling by negotiation the questions involved in their occupation had been one of the most

---

[3] See Appendix L.
[4] *Ibid.*

urgent motives for the prompt dispatch of the commissioners to Washington.

The letter of the commissioners to Seward was written, as we have seen, on March 12. The oral message above mentioned was obtained and communicated to the commissioners through the agency of two judges of the Supreme Court of the United States—Justices Nelson of New York and Campbell of Alabama. On March 15, according to the statement of Judge Campbell,[5] Justice Nelson visited the Secretaries of State and of the Treasury and the Attorney General (Seward, Chase, and Bates), to dissuade them from undertaking to put in execution any policy of coercion. "During the term of the Supreme Court he had very carefully examined the laws of the United States to enable him to attain his conclusions, and from time to time he had consulted the Chief Justice [Taney] upon the questions which his examination had suggested. His conclusion was that, without very serious violations of Constitution and statutes, coercion could not be successfully effected by the executive department. I had made [continues Judge Campbell] a similar examination, and I concurred in his conclusions and opinions. As he was returning from his visit to the State Department, we casually met, and he informed me of what he had done. He said he had spoken to these officers at large; that he was received with respect and listened to with attention by all, with approbation by the Attorney General, and with great cordiality by the Secretary of State; that the Secretary had expressed gratification to find so many impediments to the disturbance of peace, and only wished there had been more. He stated that the Secretary told him there was a present cause of embarrassment: that the Southern Commissioners had demanded recognition, and a refusal would lead to irritation and excitement in the Southern States, and would cause a counter-irritation and excitement in the Northern States, prejudicial to a peaceful adjustment. Justice Nelson suggested that I might be of service."

The result of the interview between these two distinguished gentlemen, we are informed, was another visit by both of them to the State Department, for the purpose of urging Seward to reply to the commissioners, and assure them of the desire of the United States government for a friendly adjustment. Seward seems to have objected to an immediate recognition of the commissioners, on the ground that the state of public sentiment in the North would not sustain it, in connection with the withdrawal of the troops from Fort Sumter, which had been de-

---

[5] See letter of Judge Campbell to Colonel George W. Munford in "Papers of the Southern Historical Society," appended to *Southern Magazine* for February, 1874.

termined on. "The evacuation of Sumter," he said, "is as much as the Administration can bear."

Judge Campbell adds:

I concurred in the conclusion that the evacuation of Sumter involved responsibility, and stated that there could not be too much caution in the adoption of measures so as not to shock or to irritate the public sentiment, and that the evacuation of Sumter was sufficient for the present in that direction. I stated that I would see the Commissioners, and I would write to Mr. Davis to that effect. I asked him what I should say as to Sumter and as to Pickens. *He authorized me to say that, before that letter could reach him* [Mr. Davis], *he would learn by telegraph that the order for the evacuation of Sumter had been made.* He said the condition of Pickens was satisfactory, and there would be no change made there.

The italics in this extract are my own.

The letter in which this promise was communicated to me has been lost, but it was given in substantially the terms above stated as authorized by Seward—that the order for the evacuation of the fort would be issued before the letter could reach me. The same assurance was given, on the same day, to the commissioners. Judge Campbell tells us that Crawford was slow to consent to refrain from pressing the demand for recognition. "It was only after some discussion and the expression of some objections that he consented" to do so. This consent was clearly one part of a stipulation, of which the other part was the pledge that the fort would be evacuated in the course of a few days. Crawford required the pledge of Seward to be reduced to writing, with Judge Campbell's personal assurance of its genuineness and accuracy.[6] This written statement was exhibited to Judge Nelson, before its delivery, and approved by him. The fact that the pledge had been given in his name and behalf was communicated to Seward the same evening by letter. He was cognizant of, consenting to, and in great part the author of the whole transaction.

It will be observed that not only the commissioners in Washington, but also the Confederate government at Montgomery, were thus assured on the highest authority—that of the Secretary of State of the United States, the official organ of communication of the views and purposes of his government—of the intention of that government to order the evac-

---

[6] "In the course of this conversation I told Judge Crawford that it was fair to tell him that the opinion at Washington was, the secession movements were short-lived; that his Government would wither under sunshine, and that the effect of these measures might be as supposed; that they might have a contrary effect, but that I did not consider the effect. I wanted, above all other things, peace. I was willing to accept whatever peace might bring, whether union or disunion. I did not look beyond peace. He said he was willing to take all the risks of sunshine."—Letter of Judge Campbell to Colonel Munford, as above.

uation of Fort Sumter within a few days from March 15, and not to disturb the existing status at Fort Pickens. Moreover, this was not the mere statement of a fact, but a pledge, given as the consideration of an appeal to the Confederate government and its commissioners to refrain from embarrassing the Federal administration by prosecuting any further claims at the same time. As such a pledge it was accepted, and while its fulfillment was quietly awaited, the commissioners forbore to make any further demand for reply to their note of March 12.

Five days having elapsed in this condition of affairs, the commissioners in Washington telegraphed Brigadier General Beauregard, commander of the Confederate forces at Charleston, inquiring whether the fort had been evacuated, or any action taken by Major Anderson indicating the probability of an evacuation. Answer was made to this dispatch that the fort had not been evacuated, that there were no indications of such a purpose, but that Major Anderson was still working on its defenses. This dispatch was taken to Seward by Judge Campbell. Two interviews occurred in relation to it, at both of which Judge Nelson was also present. Of the result of these interviews, Judge Campbell states:

The last was full and satisfactory. The Secretary was buoyant and sanguine; he spoke of his ability to carry through his policy with confidence. He accounted for the delay as accidental, and *not involving the integrity of his assurance that the evacuation would take place,* and that I should know whenever any change was made in the resolution in reference to Sumter or to Pickens. I repeated this assurance in writing to Judge Crawford, *and informed Governor Seward in writing what I had said.*[7]

It would be incredible, but for the ample proofs which have since been brought to light, that during all this period of reiterated assurances of a purpose to withdraw the garrison from Fort Sumter, and of excuses for delay on account of the difficulties which embarrassed it, the government of the United States was assiduously engaged in devising means for furnishing supplies and reënforcements to the garrison, with the view of retaining possession of the fort!

G. V. Fox, afterward Assistant Secretary of the United States Navy, had proposed a plan for reënforcing and furnishing supplies to the garrison of Fort Sumter in February, during the administration of Buchanan. In a letter published in the newspapers since the war, he gives an account of the manner in which the proposition was renewed to the new administration and its reception by them, as follows:

On the 12th of March I received a telegram from Postmaster-General Blair to come to Washington. I arrived there on the 13th. Mr. Blair having been ac-

---

[7] Letter to Colonel Munford, above quoted. The italics are not in the original.

quainted with the proposition I presented to General Scott, under Mr. Buchanan's Administration, sent for me to tender the same to Mr. Lincoln, informing me that Lieutenant-General Scott had advised the President that the fort could not be relieved, and must be given up. Mr. Blair took me at once to the White House, and I explained the plan to the President. Thence we adjourned to Lieutenant-General Scott's office, where a renewed discussion of the subject took place. The General informed the President that my plan was practicable in February, but that the increased number of batteries erected at the mouth of the harbor since that time rendered it impossible in March.

Finding that there was great opposition to any attempt at relieving Fort Sumter, and that Mr. Blair alone sustained the President in his policy of refusing to yield, I judged that my arguments in favor of the practicability of sending in supplies would be strengthened by a visit to Charleston and the fort. The President readily agreed to my visit, if the Secretary of War and General Scott raised no objection.

Both these gentlemen consenting, I left Washington on the 19th of March, and, passing through Richmond and Wilmington, reached Charleston on the 21st.

Thus we see that at the very moment when Secretary Seward was renewing to the Confederate government, through Judge Campbell, his positive assurance that "the evacuation *would* take place," this emissary was on his way to Charleston to obtain information and devise measures by means of which this promise might be broken.

On his arrival in Charleston, Fox tells us that he sought an interview with Captain Hartstein of the Confederate Navy, and through this officer obtained from Governor Pickens permission to visit Fort Sumter. He fails, in his narrative, to state what we learn from Governor Pickens himself,[8] that this permission was obtained "expressly upon the pledge of 'pacific purposes.' " Notwithstanding this pledge, he employed the opportunity afforded by his visit to mature the details of his plan for furnishing supplies and reënforcements to the garrison. He did not, he says, communicate his plan or purposes to Major Anderson, the commanding officer of the garrison, having discernment enough, perhaps, to divine that the instincts of that brave and honest soldier would have revolted at and rebuked the duplicity and perfidy of the whole transaction. The result of his visit was, however, reported at Washington, his plan was approved by President Lincoln, and he was sent to New York to make arrangements for putting it in execution.

In a very few days after [says Governor Pickens, in the message already quoted above], another confidential agent, Colonel Lamon, was sent by the President [Mr. Lincoln], who informed me that he had come to try and arrange for the removal of the garrison, and, when he returned from the fort, asked if a war-

---

[8] Message to the legislature of South Carolina, November, 1861.

vessel could not be allowed to remove them. I replied that no war-vessel could be allowed to enter the harbor on any terms. He said he believed Major Anderson preferred an ordinary steamer, and I agreed that the garrison might thus be removed. He said he hoped to return in a very few days for that purpose.

This, it will be remembered, occurred while Fox was making active, though secret, preparations for his relief expedition.

Colonel, or Major Lamon, as he is variously styled in the correspondence, did not return to Charleston, as promised. About March 30 (which was Saturday) a telegram from Governor Pickens was received by the commissioners in Washington, making inquiry with regard to Colonel Lamon, and the meaning of the protracted delay to fulfill the promise of evacuation. This was fifteen days after the original assurance of Seward that the garrison would be withdrawn immediately, and ten days after his explanation that the delay was "accidental." The dispatch of Governor Pickens was taken by Judge Campbell to Seward, who appointed the ensuing Monday (April 1) for an interview and answer. At that interview Seward informed Judge Campbell that "the President was concerned about the contents of the telegram—*there was a point of honor involved;* that Lamon had no agency from him, nor title to speak." [9] This late suggestion of the point of *honor* would seem, under the circumstances, to have been made in a spirit of sarcastic pleasantry, like Sir John Falstaff's celebrated discourse on the same subject. The only substantial result of the conversation, however, was the written assurance of Seward, to be communicateed to the commissioners, that "the Government will not undertake to supply Fort Sumter without giving notice to Governor Pickens."

This, it will be observed, was a very material variation from the positive pledge previously given, and reiterated, to the commissioners, to Governor Pickens, and to myself directly, that the fort was to be forthwith evacuated. Judge Campbell in his account of the interview, says: "I asked him [Mr. Seward] whether I was to understand that there had been a change in his former communications. His answer was, 'None.' "[10]

About the close of the same week (the first in April), the patience of the commissioners having now been well-nigh exhausted, and the hostile preparations of the government of the United States, notwithstanding the secrecy with which they were conducted, having become matter of general rumor, a letter was addressed to Seward upon the subject by Judge Campbell, in behalf of the commissioners, again asking whether

---

[9] Letter to Colonel Munford, above cited.
[10] Letter to Munford.

the assurances so often given were well or ill founded. To this the Sec-reetary returned answer in writing: *"Faith as to Sumter fully kept. Wait and see."*

This was on April 7.[11] The very next day (the 8th) the following official notification (without date or signature) was read to Governor Pickens of South Carolina, and General Beauregard, in Charleston, by Chew, an official of the State Department (Seward's) in Washington, who said—as did a Captain or Lieutenant Talbot, who accompanied him —that it was from the President of the United States, and delivered by him to Chew on the 6th—the day before Mr. Seward's assurance of *"faith fully kept."*

I am directed by the President of the United States to notify you to expect an attempt will be made to supply Fort Sumter with provisions only; and that, if such an attempt be not resisted, no effort to throw in men, arms, or ammunition, will be made, without further notice, or in case of an attack upon the fort.[12]

Thus disappeared the last vestige of the plighted faith and pacific pledges of the Federal government.

In order fully to appreciate the significance of this communication, and of the time and circumstances of its delivery, it must be borne in mind that the naval expedition which had been secretly in preparation for some time at New York, under direction of Captain Fox, was now ready to sail, and might reasonably be expected to be at Charleston al-most immediately after the notification was delivered to Governor Pickens, and before preparation could be made to receive it. Owing to cross-purposes or misunderstandings in the Washington cabinet, how-ever, and then to the delay caused by a severe storm at sea, this expecta-tion was disappointed, and the Confederate commander at Charleston had opportunity to communicate with Montgomery and receive instruc-tions for his guidance before the arrival of the fleet, which had been intended to be a surprise.

In publications made since the war by members of Lincoln's cabinet, it has been represented that during the period of the disgraceful trans-actions above detailed, there were dissensions and divisions in the cabi-net—certain members of it urging measures of prompt and decided coercion; the Secretary of State favoring a pacific or at least a dilatory policy; the President vacillating for a time between the two, but eventu-ally adopting the views of the coercionists. In these statements it is rep-

---

[11] Judge Campbell, in his letter to Seward of April 13, 1861 (see Appendix L), written a few days after the transaction, gives this date. In his letter to Colonel Munford, written more than twelve years afterward, he says "Sunday, April 8th."

[12] For this and other documents quoted relative to the transactions of the period, see *The Record of Fort Sumter*, compiled by W. A. Harris, Columbia, South Carolina, 1862.

resented that the assurances and pledges, given by Seward to the Confederate government and its commissioners, were given on his own authority, and without the consent or approval of the President of the United States. The absurdity of any such attempt to dissociate the action of the President from that of his Secretary, and to relieve the former of responsibility for the conduct of the latter, is too evident to require argument or comment. It is impossible to believe that, during this whole period of nearly a month, Lincoln was ignorant of the communications that were passing between the Confederate commissioners and Seward, through the distinguished member of the Supreme Court—still holding his seat as such—who was acting as intermediary. On one occasion, Judge Campbell informs us that the Secretary, in the midst of an important interview, excused himself for the purpose of conferring with the President before giving a final answer, and left his visitor for some time, awaiting his return from that conference, when the answer was given, avowedly and directly proceeding from the President.

If, however, it were possible to suppose that Seward was acting on his own responsibility, and practicing a deception upon his own chief, as well as upon the Confederate authorities, in the pledges which he made to the latter, it is nevertheless certain that the principal facts were brought to light within a few days after the close of the efforts at negotiation. Yet the Secretary of State was not impeached and brought to trial for the grave offense of undertaking to conduct the most momentous and vital transactions that had been or could be brought before the government of the United States, without the knowledge and in opposition to the will of the President, and for having involved the government in dishonor, if not in disaster. He was not even dismissed from office, but continued to be the chief officer of the cabinet and confidential adviser of the President, as he was afterward of the ensuing administration, occupying that station during two consecutive terms. No disavowal of his action, no apology nor explanation, was ever made. Politically and legally, the President is unquestionably responsible in all cases for the action of any member of his cabinet, and in this case it is as preposterous to attempt to dissever from him the moral, as it would be impossible to relieve him of the legal, responsibility that rests upon the government of the United States for the systematic series of frauds perpetrated by its authority.

On the other hand Seward, throughout the whole negotiation, was fully informed of the views of his colleagues in the cabinet and of the President. Whatever his real hopes or purposes may have been in the beginning, it is positively certain that long before the end, and while still reiterating his assurances that the garrison would be withdrawn, he knew that it had been determined, and that active preparations were in progress, to strengthen it.

Gideon Welles, who was Secretary of the Navy in Lincoln's cabinet, gives the following account of one of the transactions of the period:

> One evening in the latter part of the month of March, there was a small gathering at the Executive Mansion, while the Sumter question was still pending. The members of the Cabinet were soon individually and quietly invited to the council-chamber, where, as soon as assembled, the President informed them he had just been advised by General Scott that it was expedient to evacuate Fort Pickens, as well as Fort Sumter, which last was assumed at military headquarters to be a determined fact, in conformity with the views of Secretary Seward and the General-in-Chief. . . .
>
> A brief silence followed the announcement of the amazing recommendation of General Scott, when Mr. Blair, who had been much annoyed by the vacillating course of the General-in-Chief in regard to Sumter, remarked, looking earnestly at Mr. Seward, that it was evident the old General was playing politician in regard to both Sumter and Pickens; for it was not possible, if there was a defense, for the rebels to take Pickens; and the Administration would not be justified if it listened to his advice and evacuated either. Very soon thereafter, I think at the next Cabinet meeting, the President announced his decision *that supplies should be sent to Sumter,* and issued confidential orders to that effect. All were gratified with this decision, except Mr. Seward, who still remonstrated, *but preparations were immediately commenced to fit out an expedition to forward supplies.*[13]

This account is confirmed by a letter of Montgomery Blair.[14] The date of the announcement of the President's final purpose is fixed by Welles, in the next paragraph to that above quoted, as March 28. This was four days before Seward's assurance given Judge Campbell—after conference with the President—that there would be no departure from the pledges previously given (which were that the fort would be evacuated), and ten days before his written renewal of the assurance—*"Faith as to Sumter fully kept. Wait and see!"* This assurance, too, was given at the very moment when a messenger from his own department was on the way to Charleston to notify the governor of South Carolina that faith would *not* be kept in the matter.

It is scarcely necessary to say that the commissioners had, with good reason, ceased to place any confidence in the promises of the United States government, before they ceased to be made. On April 8th they sent the following dispatch to General Beauregard:

WASHINGTON, April 8, 1861.

GENERAL G. T. BEAUREGARD: Accounts uncertain, because of the constant vacillation of this Government. We were reassured yesterday that the status of Sumter would not be changed without previous notice to Governor Pickens, but we have no faith in them. The war policy prevails in the Cabinet at this time.

M. J. CRAWFORD.

On the same day the announcement made to Governor Pickens through Chew was made known. The commissioners immediately applied for a definitive answer to their note of March 12th, which had been permitted to remain in abeyance. The paper of the Secretary of State, dated March 15th, was thereupon delivered to them. This paper, with the final rejoinder of the commissioners and Judge Campbell's letters to the Secretary of April 13th and April 20th, respectively, will be found in the Appendix.

Negotiation was now at an end, and the commissioners withdrew from Washington and returned to their homes. Their last dispatch, before leaving, shows that they were still dependent upon public rumor and the newspapers for information as to the real purposes and preparations of the Federal administration. It was in these words:

WASHINGTON, April 10, 1861.

GENERAL G. T. BEAUREGARD: The "Tribune" of to-day declares the main object of the expedition to be the relief of Sumter, and that a force will be landed which will overcome all opposition.

ROMAN, CRAWFORD, AND FORSYTH.

The annexed extracts from my message to the Confederate Congress at the opening of its special session on April 29, will serve as a recapitulation of the events above narrated, with all of comment that it was then, or is now, considered necessary to add:

EXTRACTS FROM PRESIDENT'S MESSAGE TO THE CONFEDERATE CONGRESS, OF APRIL 29, 1861.

. . . Scarce had you assembled in February last, when, prior even to the inauguration of the Chief Magistrate you had elected, you expressed your desire for the appointment of Commissioners, and for the settlement of all questions of disagreement between the two Governments upon principles of right, justice, equity, and good faith.

It was my pleasure, as well as my duty, to coöperate with you in this work of peace. Indeed, in my address to you, on taking the oath of office, and before receiving from you the communication of this resolution, I had said that, as a necessity, not as a choice, we have resorted to the remedy of separating, and henceforth our energies must be directed to the conduct of our own affairs, and the perpetuity of the Confederacy which we have formed. If a just perception of mutual interest shall permit us to peaceably pursue our separate political career, my most earnest desire will then have been fulfilled.

It was in furtherance of these accordant views of the Congress and the Executive, that I made choice of three discreet, able, and distinguished citizens, who repaired to Washington. Aided by their cordial coöperation and that of the Secretary of State, every effort compatible with self-respect and the dignity of the Confederacy was exhausted, before I allowed myself to yield to the conviction that the Government of the United States was determined to attempt the conquest of this people, and that our cherished hopes of peace were unobtainable.

On the arrival of our Commissioners in Washington on the 5th of March,[15] they postponed, at the suggestion of a friendly intermediator, doing more than giving informal notice of their arrival. This was done with a view to afford time to the President of the United States, who had just been inaugurated, for the discharge of other pressing official duties in the organization of his Administration, before engaging his attention to the object of their mission.

It was not until the 12th of the month that they officially addressed the Secretary of State, informing him of the purpose of their arrival, and stating in the language of their instructions their wish to make to the Government of the United States overtures for the opening of negotiations, assuring the Government of the United States that the President, Congress, and people of the Confederate States desired a peaceful solution of these great questions; that it was neither their interest nor their wish to make any demand which was not founded on the strictest principles of justice, nor to do any act to injure their late confederates.

To this communication, no formal reply was received until the 8th of April. During the interval, the Commissioners had consented to waive all questions of form, with the firm resolve to avoid war, if possible. They went so far even as to hold, during that long period, unofficial intercourse through an intermediary, whose high position and character inspired the hope of success, and through whom constant assurances were received from the Government of the United States of its peaceful intentions—of its determination to evacuate Fort Sumter; and, further, that no measure would be introduced changing the existing status prejudicial to the Confederate States; that, in the event of any change in regard to Fort Pickens, notice would be given to the Commissioners.

The crooked path of diplomacy can scarcely furnish an example so wanting in courtesy, in candor, and directness, as was the course of the United States Government toward our Commissioners in Washington. For proof of this, I refer to the annexed documents marked, [?] taken in connection with further facts, which I now proceed to relate.

Early in April the attention of the whole country was attracted to extraordinary preparations, in New York and other Northern ports, for an extensive military and naval expedition. These preparations were commenced in secrecy for an expedition whose destination was concealed, and only became known when nearly completed; and on the 5th, 6th, and 7th of April, transports and vessels of war, with troops, munitions, and military supplies, sailed from Northern ports, bound southward.

---

[15] Crawford, as we have seen, had arrived some days earlier. The statement in the message refers to the arrival of the full commission, or a majority of it.

Alarmed by so extraordinary a demonstration, the Commissioners requested the delivery of an answer to their official communication of the 12th of March, and the reply, dated on the 15th of the previous month, was obtained, from which it appears that, during the whole interval, while the Commissioners were receiving assurances calculated to inspire hope of the success of their mission, the Secretary of State and the President of the United States had already determined to hold no intercourse with them whatever, to refuse even to listen to any proposals they had to make; and had profited by the delay created by their own assurances, in order to prepare secretly the means for effective hostile operations.

That these assurances were given, has been virtually confessed by the Government of the United States, by its act of sending a messenger to Charleston to give notice of its purpose to use force, if opposed in its intention of supplying Fort Sumter.

No more striking proof of the absence of good faith in the conduct of the Government of the United States toward the Confederacy can be required, than is contained in the circumstances which accompanied this notice.

According to the usual course of navigation, the vessels composing the expedition, and designed for the relief of Fort Sumter, might be looked for in Charleston Harbor on the 9th of April. Yet our Commissioners in Washington were detained under assurances that notice should be given of any military movement. The notice was not addressed to them, but a messenger was sent to Charleston to give notice to the Governor of South Carolina, and the notice was so given at a late hour on the 8th of April, the eve of the very day on which the fleet might be expected to arrive.

That this manœuvre failed in its purpose was not the fault of those who controlled it. A heavy tempest delayed the arrival of the expedition, and gave time to the commander of our forces at Charleston to ask and receive instructions of the Government. . . .

CHAPTER XII: *Protests Against the Conduct of the Government of the United States—Senator Douglas's Proposition to Evacuate the Forts, and Extracts from his Speech in Support of it—General Scott's Advice—Manly Letter of Major Anderson, Protesting Against the Action of the Federal Government—Misstatements of the Count of Paris—Correspondence Relative to Proposed Evacuation of the Fort—A Crisis.*

THE course pursued by the government of the United States with regard to the forts had not passed without earnest remonstrance from the most intelligent and patriotic of its own friends during the period of the events which constitute the subject of the preceding chapter. In the Senate of the United States, which continued in executive session for several weeks after the inauguration of Lincoln, it was the subject of discussion. Douglass of Illinois—who was certainly not suspected of sympathy with secession, or lack of devotion to the Union—on March 15th offered a resolution recommending the withdrawal of the garrisons from all forts within the limits of the states which had seceded, except those at Key West and the Dry Tortugas. In support of this resolution he said:

We certainly can not justify the holding of forts there, much less the recapturing of those which have been taken, unless we intend to reduce those States themselves into subjection. I take it for granted, no man will deny the proposition, that whoever permanently holds Charleston and South Carolina is entitled to the possession of Fort Sumter. Whoever permanently holds Pensacola and Florida is entitled to the possession of Fort Pickens. Whoever holds the States in whose limits those forts are placed is entitled to the forts themselves, unless there is something peculiar in the location of some particular fort that makes it important for us to hold it for the general defense of the whole country, its commerce and interests, instead of being useful only for the defense of a particular city or locality. It is true that Forts Taylor and Jefferson, at Key West and Tortugas, are so situated as to be essentially national, and therefore important to us without reference to our relations with the seceded States. Not so with Moultrie, Johnson, Castle Pinckney, and Sumter, in Charleston Harbor; not so with Pulaski, on the Savannah River; not so with Morgan and other forts in Alabama; not so with those other forts that were intended to guard the entrance of a particular harbor for local defense. . . .

We can not deny that there is a Southern Confederacy, *de facto,* in existence, with its capital at Montgomery. We may regret it. *I* regret it most profoundly; but I can not deny the truth of the fact, painful and mortifying as it is. . . . I proclaim boldly the policy of those with whom I act. We are for peace.

[1] See *The Record of Fort Sumter,* p. 37.

Douglas, in urging the maintenance of peace as a motive for the evacuation of the forts, was no doubt aware of the full force of his words. He knew that their continued occupation was virtually a declaration of war. The general-in-chief of the United States Army, also, it is well known, urgently advised the evacuation of the forts. But the most striking protest against the coercive measures finally adopted was that of Major Anderson himself. The letter in which his views were expressed has been carefully suppressed in the partisan narratives of that period and well-nigh lost sight of, although it does the highest honor to his patriotism and integrity. It was written on the same day on which the announcement was made to Governor Pickens of the purpose of the United States government to send supplies to the fort, and is worthy of reproduction here:[1]

LETTER OF MAJOR ANDERSON, UNITED STATES ARMY, PROTESTING AGAINST
FOX'S PLAN FOR RELIEVING FORT SUMTER.

FORT SUMTER, S. C., April 8, 1861.

To Colonel L. Thomas, Adjutant-General United States Army.

COLONEL: I have the honor to report that the resumption of work yesterday (Sunday) at various points on Morris Island, and the vigorous prosecution of it this morning, apparently strengthening all the batteries which are under the fire of our guns, shows that they either have just received some news from Washington which has put them on the *qui vive*, or that they have received orders from Montgomery to commence operations here. I am preparing, by the side of my barbette guns, protection for our men from the shells which will be almost continually bursting over or in our work.

I had the honor to receive, by yesterday's mail, the letter of the Honorable Secretary of War, dated April 4th, and confess that what he there states surprises me very greatly—following, as it does, and contradicting so positively, the assurance Mr. Crawford telegraphed he was "authorized" to make. I trust that this matter will be at once put in a correct light, as a movement made now, when the South has been erroneously informed that none such would be attempted, would produce most disastrous results throughout our country. It is, of course, now too late for me to give any advice in reference to the proposed scheme of Captain Fox. I fear that its result can not fail to be disastrous to all concerned. Even with his boat at our walls, the loss of life (as I think I mentioned to Mr. Fox) in

---

[2] The Count of Paris libels the memory of Major Anderson, and perverts the truth of history in this, as he has done in other particulars, by saying, with reference to the visit of Captain Fox to the fort, that, "having visited Anderson at Fort Sumter, *a plan had been agreed upon between them for revictualing the garrison.*"—*Civil War in America*, authorized translation, Vol. I, Chapt. IV, p. 137.

Fox himself says, in his published letter, "I made no arrangements with Major Anderson for supplying the fort, nor did I inform him of my plan"; Major Anderson, in the letter above, says the idea had been "merely hinted at" by Captain Fox, and that Colonel Lamon had led him to believe that it had been abandoned.

unloading her will more than pay for the good to be accomplished by the expedition, which keeps us, if I can maintain possession of this work, out of position, surrounded by strong works which must be carried to make this fort of the least value to the United States Government.

We have not oil enough to keep a light in the lantern for one night. The boats will have to, therefore, rely at night entirely upon other marks. I ought to have been informed that this expedition was to come. Colonel Lamon's remark convinced me that the idea, merely hinted at to me by Captain Fox, would not be carried out.[2]

We shall strive to do our duty, thought I frankly say that my heart is not in this war, which I see is to be thus commenced. That God will still avert it, and cause us to resort to pacific means to maintain our rights, is my ardent prayer!

I am, Colonel, very respectfully,

Your obedient servant,

ROBERT ANDERSON,
Major 1st Artillery, commanding.

This frank and manly letter, although written with the reserve necessarily belonging to a communication from an officer to his military superiors, expressing dissatisfaction with orders, fully vindicates Major Anderson from all suspicion of complicity or sympathy with the bad faith of the government which he was serving. It accords entirely with the sentiments expressed in his private letter to me, already mentioned as lost or stolen, and exhibits him in the attitude of faithful performance of a duty inconsistent with his domestic ties and repugnant to his patriotism.

The "relief squadron," as with unconscious irony it was termed, was already under way for Charleston, consisting, according to their own statement, of eight vessels, carrying twenty-six guns and about fourteen hundred men, including the troops sent for reënforcement of the garrison.

These facts became known to the Confederate government, and it was obvious that no time was to be lost in preparing for, and if possible anticipating the impending assault. The character of the instructions given General Beauregard in this emergency may be inferred from the ensuing correspondence, which is here reproduced from contemporary publications:

CHARLESTON, April 8th.

L. P. WALKER, *Secretary of War.*

An authorized messenger from President Lincoln just informed Governor Pickens and myself that provisions will be sent to Fort Sumter peaceably, or otherwise by force.

(Signed)

G. T. BEAUREGARD.

GENERAL G. T. BEAUREGARD

MONTGOMERY, 10th.

General G. T. BEAUREGARD, *Charleston.*

If you have no doubt of the authorized character of the agent who communicated to you the intention of the Washington Government to supply Fort Sumter by force, you will at once demand its evacuation, and, if this is refused, proceed, in such a manner as you may determine, to reduce it. Answer.

(Signed)   L. P. WALKER, *Secretary of War.*

CHARLESTON, April 10.

L. P. WALKER, *Secretary of War.*

The demand will be made to-morrow at twelve o'clock.

(Signed)   G. T. BEAUREGARD.

MONTGOMERY, April 10th.

General BEAUREGARD, *Charleston.*

Unless there are especial reasons connected with your own condition, it is considered proper that you should make the demand at an early hour.

(Signed)   L. P. WALKER, *Secretary of War.*

CHARLESTON, April 10th.

L. P. WALKER, *Secretary of War, Montgomery.*

The reasons are special for twelve o'clock.

(Signed)   G. T. BEAUREGARD.

HEADQUARTERS PROVISIONAL ARMY, C. S. A.
CHARLESTON, S. C., April 11, 1861, 2 P.M.

SIR: The Government of the Confederate States has hitherto forborne from any hostile demonstration against Fort Sumter, in the hope that the Government of the United States, with a view to the amicable adjustment of all questions between the two Governments, and to avert the calamities of war, would voluntarily evacuate it. There was reason at one time to believe that such would be the course pursued by the Government of the United States; and, under that impression, my Government has refrained from making any demand for the surrender of the fort.

But the Confederate States can no longer delay assuming actual possession of a fortification commanding the entrance of one of their harbors, and necessary to its defense and security.

I am ordered by the Government of the Confederate States to demand the evacuation of Fort Sumter. My aides, Colonel Chesnut and Captain Lee, are authorized to make such demand of you. All proper facilities will be afforded for the removal of yourself and command, together with company arms and property, and all private property, to any post in the United States which you may elect. The flag which you have upheld so long and with so much fortitude, under the most trying circumstances, may be saluted by you on taking it down.

Colonel Chesnut and Captain Lee will, for a reasonable time, await your answer.

I am, sir, very respectfully, your obedient servant,

(Signed)   G. T. BEAUREGARD,
                                   Brigadier-General commanding.

Major ROBERT ANDERSON,
   Commanding at Fort Sumter, Charleston Harbor, S. C.

HEADQUARTERS FORT SUMTER, S. C., April 11, 1861.

GENERAL: I have the honor to acknowledge the receipt of your communication demanding the evacuation of this fort; and to say in reply thereto that it is a demand with which I regret that my sense of honor and of my obligations to my Government prevents my compliance.

Thanking you for the fair, manly, and courteous terms proposed, and for the high compliment paid me,

I am, General, very respectfully, your obedient servant,

(Signed)   ROBERT ANDERSON,
                                                Major U. S. Army, commanding.

To Brigadier-General G. T. BEAUREGARD,
Commanding Provisional Army, C. S. A.

MONTGOMERY, April 11th.

General BEAUREGARD, *Charleston.*

We do not desire needlessly to bombard Fort Sumter, if Major Anderson will state the time at which, as indicated by him, he will evacuate, and agree that, in the mean time, he will not use his guns against us, unless ours should be employed against Fort Sumter. You are thus to avoid the effusion of blood. If this or its equivalent be refused, reduce the fort as your judgment decides to be most practicable.

(Signed)   L. P. WALKER, *Secretary of War.*

HEADQUARTERS PROVISIONAL ARMY, C.S.A.,
CHARLESTON, April 11, 1861, 11 P.M.

MAJOR: In consequence of the verbal observations made by you to my aides, Messrs. Chesnut and Lee, in relation to the condition of your supplies, and that you would in a few days be starved out if our guns did not batter you to pieces— or words to that effect—and desiring no useless effusion of blood, I communicated both the verbal observation and your written answer to my Government.

If you will state the time at which you will evacuate Fort Sumter, and agree that in the mean time you will not use your guns against us, unless ours shall be employed against Fort Sumter, we will abstain from opening fire upon you. Colonel Chesnut and Captain Lee are authorized by me to enter into such an agreement with you. You are therefore requested to communicate to them an open answer,

I remain, Major, very respectfully,

Your obedient servant,

(Signed)   G. T. BEAUREGARD,
                                                Brigadier-General commanding.

Major ROBERT ANDERSON,
Commanding at Fort Sumter, Charleston Harbor, S. C.

HEADQUARTERS FORT SUMTER, S. C., 2:30 A.M., April 12, 1861.

GENERAL: I have the honor to acknowledge the receipt of your second communication of the 11th instant, by Colonel Chesnut, and to state, in reply, that, cordially uniting with you in the desire to avoid the useless effusion of blood, I will, if provided with the proper and necessary means of transportation, evacuate Fort Sumter by noon on the 15th instant, should I not receive, prior to that time, controlling instructions from my Government, or additional supplies; and that I will not in the mean time, open my fire upon your forces unless compelled to do so by some hostile act against this fort, or the flag of my Government, by the forces under your command, or by some portion of them, or by the perpetration of some act showing a hostile intention on your part against this fort or the flag it bears.

I have the honor to be, General,

Your obedient servant,

(Signed)   ROBERT ANDERSON,

Major U. S. Army, commanding.

To Brigadier-General G. T. BEAUREGARD,
Commanding Provisional Army, C. S. A.

FORT SUMTER, S. C., April 12, 1861, 3:20 A.M.

SIR: By authority of Brigadier-General Beauregard, commanding the provisional forces of the Confederate States, we have the honor to notify you that he will open the fire of his batteries on Fort Sumter in one hour from this time.

We have the honor to be, very respectfully,

Your obedient servants,

(Signed)   JAMES CHESNUT, JR.,

Aide-de-camp.

(Signed)   STEPHEN D. LEE,

Captain S. C. Army, and Aide-de-camp.

Major ROBERT ANDERSON,
United States Army, commanding Fort Sumter.

It is essential to a right understanding of the last two letters to give more than a superficial attention to that of Major Anderson, bearing in mind certain important facts not referred to in the correspondence. Major Anderson had been requested to state the time at which he would evacuate the fort, if unmolested, agreeing in the meantime not to use his guns against the city and the troops defending it unless Fort Sumter should be first attacked by them. On these conditions General Beauregard offered to refrain from opening fire upon him. In his reply Major Anderson promises to evacuate the fort on April 15th, provided he should not, before that time, receive "controlling instructions" or "additional supplies" from his government. He furthermore offers to pledge himself not to open fire upon the Confederates, unless in the meantime compelled to do so by some hostile act against the fort or the flag of his government.

Inasmuch as it was known to the Confederate commander that the 'controlling instructions" were already issued, and that the "additional supplies" were momentarily expected; inasmuch, also, as any attempt to introduce the supplies would compel the opening of fire upon the vessels bearing them under the flag of the United States—thereby releasing Major Anderson from his pledge—it is evident that his conditions could not be accepted. It would have been merely, after the avowal of a hostile determination by the government of the United States, to await an inevitable conflict with the guns of Fort Sumter and the naval forces of the United States in combination; with no possible hope of averting it, unless in the improbable event of a delay of the expected fleet for nearly four days longer. (In point of fact, it arrived off the harbor on the same day, but was hindered by a gale of wind from entering it.) There was obviously no other course to be pursued than that announced in the answer given by General Beauregard.

It should not be forgotten that during the early occupation of Fort Sumter by a garrison the attitude of which was at least offensive, no restriction had been put upon their privilege of purchasing in Charleston fresh provisions, or any delicacies or comforts not directly tending to the supply of the means needful to hold the fort for an indefinite time.

CHAPTER XIII: *A Pause and a Review—Attitude of the Two Parties—Sophistry Exposed and Shams Torn Away—Forbearance of the Confederate Government—Who was the Aggressor?—Major Anderson's View, and That of a Naval Officer—Horace Greeley on the Fort Sumter Case—The Bombardment and Surrender—Gallant Action of ex-Senator Wigfall—Lincoln's Statement of the Case.*

HERE, in the brief hour immediately before the outburst of the long-gathering storm, although it can hardly be necessary for the reader who has carefully considered what has already been written, we may pause for a moment to contemplate the attitude of the parties to the contest and the grounds on which they respectively stand. I do not now refer to the original causes of controversy—to the comparative claims of statehood and union, or to the question of the right or the wrong of secession —but to the proximate and immediate causes of conflict.

The fact that South Carolina was a state—whatever her relations may have been to the other states—is not and cannot be denied. It is equally undeniable that the ground on which Fort Sumter was built was ceded by South Carolina to the United States in trust for the defense of her own soil and her own chief harbor. This has been shown, by ample evidence, to have been the principle governing all cessions by the states of sites for military purposes, but it applies with special force to the case of Charleston. The streams flowing into that harbor, from source to mouth, lie entirely within the limits of the state of South Carolina. No other state or combination of states could have any distinct interest or concern in the maintenance of a fortress at that point, unless as a means of aggression against South Carolina herself. The practical view of the case was correctly stated by Douglas, when he said: "I take it for granted that whoever permanently holds Charleston and South Carolina is entitled to the possession of Fort Sumter. Whoever permanently holds Pensacola and Florida is entitled to the possession of Fort Pickens. Whoever holds the States in whose limits those forts are placed is entitled to the forts themselves, unless there is something peculiar in the location of some particular fort that makes it important for us to hold it for the general defense of the whole country, its commerce and interests, instead of being useful only for the defense of a particular city or locality."

No such necessity could be alleged with regard to Fort Sumter. The claim to hold it as "public property" of the United States was utterly untenable and unmeaning, apart from a claim of coercive control over the state. If South Carolina was a mere province, in a state of open rebellion, the government of the United States had a right to retain its hold of any fortified place within her limits which happened to be in its possession, and it would have had an equal right to acquire possession of any other. It would have had the same right to send an army to Columbia to batter down the walls of the state Capitol. The subject may at once be stripped of the sophistry which would make a distinction between the two cases. The one was as really an act of war as the other would have been. The right or the wrong of either depended entirely upon the question of the rightful power of the federal government to coerce a state into submission—a power which, as we have seen, was unanimously rejected in the formation of the federal Constitution, and which was still unrecognized by many, perhaps by a majority, even of those who denied the right of a state to secede.

If there existed any hope or desire for a peaceful settlement of the questions at issue between the states, either party had a right to demand that, pending such settlement, there should be no hostile grasp upon its throat. This grip had been held on the throat of South Carolina for almost four months from the period of her secession, and no forcible resistance to it had yet been made. Remonstrances and patient, persistent, and reiterated attempts at negotiation for its removal had been made with two successive administrations of the government of the United States—at first by the state of South Carolina, and by the government of the Confederate States after its formation. These efforts had been met, not by an open avowal of coercive purposes, but by evasion, prevarication, and perfidy. The agreement of one administration to maintain the *status quo* at the time when the question arose, was violated in December by the removal of the garrison from its original position to the occupancy of a stronger. Another attempt was made to violate it, in January, by the introduction of troops concealed below the deck of the steamer *Star of the West*,[1] but this was thwarted by the vigilance of the state service. The protracted course of fraud and prevarication practiced by Lincoln's administration in the months of March and April has been fully exhibited. It was evident that no confidence whatever could be reposed in any pledge or promise of the federal government as then

---

[1] See the report of her commander, Captain McGowan, who says he took on board, in the harbor of New York, four officers and two hundred soldiers. Arriving off Charleston, he says *"The soldiers were now all put below,* and no one allowed on deck except our own crew."

administered. Yet, notwithstanding all this, no resistance, other than that of pacific protest and appeals for an equitable settlement, was made, until after the avowal of a purpose of coercion, and when it was known that a hostile fleet was on the way to support and enforce it. At the very moment when the Confederate commander gave the final notice to Major Anderson of his purpose to open fire upon the fort, that fleet was lying off the mouth of the harbor, and hindered from entering only by a gale of wind.

The forbearance of the Confederate government, under the circumstances, is perhaps unexampled in history. It was carried to the extreme verge, short of a disregard of the safety of the people who had entrusted to that government the duty of their defense against their enemies. The attempt to represent us as the aggressors in the conflict which ensued is as unfounded as the complaint made by the wolf against the lamb in the familiar fable. He who makes the assault is not necessarily he that strikes the first blow or fires the first gun. To have awaited further strengthening of their position by land and naval forces, with hostile purpose now declared, for the sake of having them fire the first gun, would have been as unwise as it would be to hesitate to strike down the arm of the assailant, who levels a deadly weapon at one's breast, until he has actually fired. The disingenuous rant of demagogues about "firing on the flag" might serve to rouse the passions of insensate mobs in times of general excitement, but will be impotent in impartial history to relieve the federal government from the responsibility of the assault made by sending a hostile fleet against the harbor of Charleston, to cooperate with the menacing garrison of Fort Sumter. After the assault was made by the hostile descent of the fleet, the reduction of Fort Sumter was a measure of defense rendered absolutely and immediately necessary.

Such clearly was the idea of the commander of the *Pawnee,* when he declined, as Captain Fox informs us, without orders from a superior, to make any effort to enter the harbor, "there to inaugurate civil war." The straightforward simplicity of the sailor had not been perverted by the shams of political sophistry. Even Horace Greeley, with all his extreme partisan feeling, is obliged to admit that "whether the bombardment and reduction of Fort Sumter shall or shall not be justified by posterity, it is clear that the Confederacy had no alternative but its own dissolution."[2]

According to the notice given by General Beauregard, fire was opened upon Fort Sumter from the various batteries which had been erected

---

[2] *American Conflict,* Vol. I, Chapt. XXIX, p. 449.

around the harbor, at half-past four o'clock on the morning of Friday, April 12, 1861. The fort soon responded. It is not the purpose of this work to give minute details of the military operation, as the events of the bombardment have been often related, and are generally well known, with no material discrepancy in matters of fact among the statements of the various participants. It is enough, therefore, to add that the bombardment continued for about thirty-three or thirty-four hours. The fort was eventually set on fire by shells, after having been partly destroyed by shot, and Major Anderson, after a resolute defense, finally surrendered on the 13th—the same terms being accorded to him which had been offered two days before. It is a remarkable fact—probably without precedent in the annals of war—that notwithstanding the extent and magnitude of the engagement, the number and caliber of the guns, and the amount of damage done to inanimate material on both sides, especially to Fort Sumter, nobody was injured on either side by the bombardment. The only casualty attendant upon the affair was the death of one man and the wounding of several others by the explosion of a gun in the firing of a salute to their flag by the garrison on evacuating the fort the day after the surrender.

A striking incident marked the close of the bombardment. Ex-Senator Louis T. Wigfall of Texas—a man as generous as he was recklessly brave—when he saw the fort on fire, supposing the garrison to be hopelessly struggling for the honor of its flag, voluntarily and without authority, went under fire in an open boat to the fort, and climbing through one of its embrasures asked for Major Anderson, and insisted that he should surrender a fort which it was palpably impossible that he could hold. Major Anderson agreed to surrender on the same terms and conditions that had been offered him before his works were battered in breach, and the agreement between them to that effect was promptly ratified by the Confederate commander. Thus unofficially was inaugurated the surrender and evacuation of the fort.

The President of the United States, in his message of July 4, 1861, to the federal Congress convened in extra session, said:

It is thus seen that the assault upon and reduction of Fort Sumter was in no sense a matter of self-defense on the part of the assailants. They well knew that the garrison in the fort could by no possibility commit aggression upon them. They knew—they were expressly notified—that the giving of bread to the few brave and hungry men of the garrison was all which would on that occasion be attempted, unless themselves, by resisting so much, should provoke more.

Lincoln well knew that, if the brave men of the garrison were hungry, they had only him and his trusted advisers to thank for it. They had been kept for months in a place where they ought not to have been, contrary to the judgment of the general-in-chief of his army, contrary to the counsels of the wisest statesmen in his confidence, and the protests of the commander of the garrison. A word from him would have relieved them at any moment in the manner most acceptable to them and most promotive of peaceful results.

But suppose the Confederate authorities had been disposed to yield, and to consent to the introduction of supplies for the maintenance of the garrison, what assurance would they have had that nothing further would be attempted? What reliance could be placed in any assurances of the government of the United States after the experience of the attempted ruse of the *Star of the West* and the deceptions practiced upon the Confederate commissioners in Washington? He says we were "expressly notified" that nothing more "would *on that occasion* be attempted"—the words in italics themselves constituting a very significant though unobtrusive and innocent-looking limitation. But we had been just as expressly notified, long before, that the garrison would be withdrawn. It would be as easy to violate the one pledge as it had been to break the other.

Moreover, the so-called notification was a mere memorandum, without date, signature, or authentication of any kind, sent to Governor Pickens, not by an accredited agent, but by a subordinate employee of the State Department. Like the oral and written pledges of Seward, given through Judge Campbell, it seemed to be carefully and purposedly divested of every attribute that could make it binding and valid, in case its authors should see fit to repudiate it. It was as empty and worthless as the complaint against the Confederate government based upon it is disingenuous.

PART IV: THE WAR

MEMBERS OF PRESIDENT'S STAFF

CHAPTER I: *Failure of the Peace Congress—Treatment of the Commissioners—Their Withdrawal—Notice of an Armed Expedition—Action of the Confederate Government—Bombardment and Surrender of Fort Sumter—Its Reduction Required by the Exigency of the Case—Disguise Thrown Off—President Lincoln's Call for Seventy-five Thousand Men—His Fiction of "Combinations"—Palpable Violation of the Constitution—Action of Virginia—Of Citizens of Baltimore—The Charge of Precipitation Against South Carolina—Action of the Confederate Government—The Universal Feeling.*

THE Congress, initiated by Virginia for the laudable purpose of endeavoring, by constitutional means, to adjust all the issues which threatened the peace of the country, failed to achieve anything that would cause or justify a reconsideration by the seceded states of their action to reclaim the grants they had made to the general government, and to maintain for themselves a separate and independent existence.

The commissioners sent by the Confederate government, after having been shamefully deceived, as has been heretofore fully set forth, left the United States capital to report the result of their mission to the Confederate government.

The notice received, that an armed expedition had sailed for operations against the state of South Carolina in the harbor of Charleston, induced the Confederate government to meet, as best it might, this assault, in the discharge of its obligation to defend each state of the Confederacy. To this end the bombardment of the formidable work, Fort Sumter, was commenced, in anticipation of the reënforcement which was then moving to unite with its garrison for hostilities against South Carolina.

The bloodless bombardment and surrender of Fort Sumter occurred on April 13, 1861. The garrison was generously permitted to retire with the honors of war. The evacuation of that fort, commanding the entrance to the harbor of Charleston, which, if in hostile hands, was destructive of its commerce, had been claimed as the right of South Carolina. The voluntary withdrawal of the garrison by the United States government had been considered, and those best qualified to judge believed it had been promised. Yet, when instead of the fulfillment of just expectations, instead of the withdrawal of the garrison, a hostile expedition was organized and sent forward, the urgency of the case required its reduction before it should be reënforced. Had there been delay, the more serious conflict between larger forces, land and naval, would scarcely have been bloodless, as the bombardment fortunately was. The event, however, was seized upon to inflame the mind of the Northern people, and the disguise which had been worn in the communications with the Confederate commissioners was now thrown off, and it was cunningly attempted to show that the South, which had been pleading for peace and still stood on the defensive, had by this bombardment inaugurated a war against the United States. But it should be stated that the threats implied in the declarations that the Union could not exist part slave and part free, and that the Union should be preserved, and the denial of the right of a state peaceably to withdraw, were virtually a declaration of war, and the sending of an army and navy to attack was the result to have been anticipated as the consequence of such delaration of war.

On the fifteenth day of the same month, President Lincoln, introducing his farce "of combinations too powerful to be suppressed by the ordinary course of judicial proceedings," called forth the military of the several states to the number of seventy-five thousand, and commanded "the persons composing the combinations" to disperse, etc. It can but surprise anyone in the least degree conversant with the history of the Union, to find states referred to as "persons composing combinations," and that the sovereign creators of the federal government, the states of the Union, should be commanded by their agent to disperse. The levy of so large an army could only mean war; the power to declare war did not, however, reside in the President—it was delegated to the Congress only. If, however, it had been a riotous combination or an insurrection, it must have been, according to the Constitution, against the state; the power of the President to call forth the militia to suppress it was dependent upon an application from the state for that purpose; it could not precede such application, and still less could it be rightfully exercised against the will of a state. The authorities on this subject have been heretofore cited, and need not be referred to again.

Suffice it to say that by section 4, Article IV, of the Constitution, the United States are bound to protect each state against invasion and against domestic violence, whenever application shall have been made by the legislature, or by the executive when the legislature cannot be convened; that to fail to give protection against any invasion whatsoever would be a dereliction of duty. To add that there could be no justification for the invasion of a state by an army of the United States, is but to repeat what has been said, on the absence of any authority in the general government to coerce a state. In any possible view of the case, therefore, the conclusion must be that the calling on some of the states for seventy-five thousand militia to invade other states which were asserted to be still in the Union, was a palpable violation of the Constitution, and the usurpation of undelegated power, or, in other words, of power reserved to the states or to the people.

It might, therefore, have been anticipated that Virginia—one of whose sons wrote the *Declaration of Independence,* another of whose sons led the armies of the United States in the Revolution which achieved their independence, and another of whose sons mainly contributed to the adoption of the Constitution of the Union—would not have been slow, in the face of such events, to reclaim the grants she had made to the general government, and to withdraw from the Union, to the establishment of which she had so largely contributed.

Two days had elapsed between the surrender of Fort Sumter and the proclamation of President Lincoln calling for seventy-five thousand militia as before stated. Two other days elapsed, and Virginia passed her ordinance of secession, and two days thereafter the citizens of Baltimore resisted the passage of troops through that city on their way to make war upon the Southern states. Thus rapidly did the current of events bear us onward from peace to the desolating war which was soon to ensue.

The manly effort of the unorganized, unarmed citizens of Baltimore to resist the progress of armies for the invasion of her Southern sisters, was worthy of the fair fame of Maryland, becoming the descendants of the men who so gallantly fought for the freedom, independence, and sovereignty of the states.

The bold stand, then and thereafter taken, extorted a promise from the executive authorities that no more troops should be sent through the city of Baltimore; this promise, however, was observed only until, by artifice, power had been gained to disregard it.

Virginia, as has been heretofore stated, passed her ordinance of secession on April 17th. It was, however, subject to ratification by the people at an election to be held on the fourth Thursday of May. She was in the meantime, like her Southern sisters, the object of Northern hostilities, and having a common cause with them, properly anticipated the election of May by forming an alliance with the Confederate States, which was ratified by the convention on April 25th.

The convention for that alliance set forth that Virginia, looking to a speedy union with the Confederate States, and for the purpose of meeting pressing exigencies, agreed that "the whole military force and military operations, offensive and defensive, of said Commonwealth, in the impending conflict with the United States, shall be under the chief control and direction of the President of the said Confederate States." The whole was made subject to approval and ratification of the proper authorities of both governments respectively.

To those who criticise South Carolina as having acted precipitately in withdrawing from the Union, it may be answered that intervening occurrences show that her delay could not have changed the result; further, her prompt action had enabled her better to prepare for the contingency which it was found impossible to avert. Thus she was prepared in the first necessities of Virginia to send to her troops organized and equipped.

Before the convention for coöperation with the Confederate States had been adopted by Virginia, that knightly soldier, General Bonham of South Carolina, went with his brigade to Richmond; throughout the Southern states there was a prevailing desire to rush to Virginia, where it was foreseen that the first great battles of the war were to be fought; so that, as early as April 22d, I telegraphed to Governor Letcher that, in addition to the forces heretofore ordered, requisitions had been made for thirteen regiments, eight to rendezvous at Lynchburg, four at Richmond, and one at Harpers Ferry. Referring to an application that had been made to him from Baltimore, I wrote: "Sustain Baltimore if practicable. We will reënforce you." The universal feeling was that of a common cause and common destiny. There was no selfish desire to linger around home, no narrow purpose to separate local interests from the common welfare. The object was to sustain a principle—the broad principle of constitutional liberty, the right of self-government.

The early demonstrations of the enemy showed that Virginia was liable to invasion from the north, from the east, and from the west. Though the larger preparation indicated that the most serious danger to be apprehended was from the line of the Potomac, the first conflicts occurred in the east.

The narrow peninsula between the James and York rivers had topographical features well adapted to defense. It was held by General John B. Magruder, who skillfully improved its natural strength by artificial means; there, on the ground memorable as the field of the last battle of the Revolution, in which General Washington compelled Lord Cornwallis to surrender, Magruder, with a small force, held for a long time the superior forces of the enemy in check.

THE question of supplying arms and munitions of war was the first considered, because it was the want for which it was the most difficult to provide. Of men willing to engage in the defense of their country, there were many more than we could arm.

Though the prevailing sentiment of the Southern people was a cordial attachment to the Union as it was formed by their fathers, their love was for the spirit of the compact, for the liberties it was designed to secure, for the self-government and state sovereignty which had been won by separation from the mother country, and transmitted to them by their Revolutionary sires as a legacy for their posterity forever. The number of those who desired to dissolve the Union, even though the Constitution should be faithfully observed—those who, in the language of the day, were called "secessionists *per se*"—was so small as not to be felt in any popular decision; the number of those who held that the states had surrendered their sovereignty, and had no right to secede from the Union, was so inappreciably small, if indeed any such existed, that I cannot recall the fact of a single Southern advocate of that opinion. The assertion of the right is not to be confounded with a readiness to exercise it. Many who had no doubt as to the right, looked upon its exercise with reluctance amounting to sorrow, and claimed that it should be the last resort, only to be adopted as the alternative to a surrender of the equality in the union of states, free, sovereign, and independent. Of that class, forming a large majority of the people of Mississippi, I may speak with the confidence of one who belonged to it. Thus, after the legislature of

Mississippi had enacted a law for a convention which, representing the sovereignty of the state, should consider the propriety of passing an ordinance to reassume the grants made to the general government, and withdraw from the Union, I, as a United States Senator of Mississippi, retained my position in the Senate, and sought by every practicable mode to obtain such measures as would allay the excitement and afford to the South such security as would prevent the final step, the ordinance of secession from the Union.

When the last hope of preserving the Union of the Constitution was extinguished, and the ordinance of secession was enacted by the convention of Mississippi, which was the highest authority known under our form of government, the question of the expediency of adopting that remedy was no longer open to inquiry by one who acknowledged his allegiance as due to the state of which he was a citizen. To evade the responsibilities resulting from the decree of his sovereign, the people, would be craven; to resist it would be treason. The instincts and affections of the citizens of Mississippi led them with great unanimity to the duty of maintaining and defending their state, without pausing to ask what would be the consequences of refusing obedience to its mandate. A like feeling pervaded all of the seceding states, and it was not only for the military service, but for every service which would strengthen and sustain the Confederacy, that an enthusiasm pervading all classes, sexes, and ages was manifested.

Though our agricultural products had been mainly for export, insomuch that in the planting states the necessary food supplies were to a considerable extent imported from the West, and it would require that the habits of the planters should be changed from the cultivation of staples for export to the production of supplies adequate for home consumption and the support of armies in the field, yet even under the embarrassments of war, this was expected, and for a long time the result justified the expectation, extraordinary as it must appear when viewed by comparison with other people who have been subjected to a like ordeal. Much of our success was due to the much abused institution of African servitude, for it enabled the white men to go into the army, and leave the cultivation of their fields and the care of their flocks, as well as of their wives and children, to those who, in the language of the Constitution, were "held to service or labor." A passing remark may here be appropriate as to the answer thus afforded to the clamor about the "horrors of slavery."

Had these Africans been a cruelly oppressed people, restlessly struggling to be freed from their bonds, would their masters have dared to leave them, as was done, and would they have remained as they did, continuing their usual duties, or could the proclamation of emancipation have been put on the plea of a military necessity, if the fact had been that the negroes were forced to serve, and desired only an opportunity to rise against their masters? It will be remembered that when the proclamation was issued it was confessed by President Lincoln to be a nullity beyond the limit within which it could be enforced by the federal troops.

To direct the production, preservation, collection, and distribution of food for the army required a man of rare capacity and character at the head of the subsistence department. It was our good fortune to have such a one in Colonel L. B. Northrop, who was appointed commissary general at the organization of the bureaus of the executive department of the Confederate government. He had been an officer of the United States army, had served in various parts of the South, had been for some time on duty in the commissariat, and to the special and general knowledge thus acquired added strong practical sense and incorruptible integrity. Of him and the operations of the subsistence department I shall have more to say hereafter, when treating of the bureaus of the Confederacy.

Assured of an army as large as the population of the Confederate States could furnish, and a sufficient supply of subsistence for such an army, at least until the chances of war should interfere with production and transportation, the immediate object of attention was the organization, instruction, and equipment of the army.

As heretofore stated, there was a prevailing belief that there would be no war, or if any, that it would be of very short duration. Therefore the first bill which passed the provisional Congress provided for receiving troops for short periods—as my memory serves, for sixty days. The chairman of the Committee on Military Affairs, the heroic Colonel Bartow, who sealed his devotion to the cause with his life's blood on the field of Manassas, in deference to my earnest remonstrance against such a policy, returned with the bill to the House (the Congress then consisted of but one house), and procured a modification by which the term of service was extended to twelve months unless sooner discharged.

I had urged upon him, in our conference, the adoption of a much longer period, but he assured me that one year was as much as the Congress would agree to. On this, as on other occasions, that Congress showed a generous desire to yield their preconceived opinions to my objections as far as they consistently could, and, there being but one house, it was easier to change the terms of a bill after conference with the Executive than when, under the permanent organization, objections had to be formally communicated in a message to that branch of Congress in which the bill originated, and when the whole proceeding was of record.

This first act to provide for the public defense became a law on February 28, 1861, and its fifth section so clearly indicates the opinions and expectations prevailing when the confederation was formed, that it is inserted here:

That the President be further authorized to receive into the service of this Government such forces now in the service of said States (Confederate States) as may be tendered, or who may volunteer by consent of their State, in such numbers as he may require for any time not less than twelve months unless sooner discharged.

The supremacy of the states is the controlling idea. The President was authorized to receive from the several states the arms and munitions which they might desire to transfer to the Government of the Confederate States, and he was also authorized to receive the forces which the states might tender, or any which should volunteer by the consent of their state, for any time not less than twelve months unless sooner discharged; such forces were to be received with their officers by companies, battalions, or regiments, and the President, by and with the advice and consent of Congress, was to appoint such general officer or officers for said forces as might be necessary for the service.

It will be seen that the arms and munitions within the limits of the several states were regarded as entirely belonging to them, that the forces which were to constitute the provisional army could only be drawn from the several states by their consent, and that these were to be organized under state authority and to be received with their officers so appointed; that the lowest organization was to be that of a company and the highest that of a regiment, and that the appointment of general officers to command these forces was confided to the government of the Confederate States, should the assembling of large bodies of troops require organization above that of a regiment; it will also be observed that provision was made for the discharge of the forces so provided for, before the term of service fixed by the law. No one will fail to perceive how little was anticipated a war of the vast proportions and great duration which ensued, and how tenaciously the sovereignty and self-government of the states were adhered to. At a later period (March 16, 1861) the Congress adopted resolutions recommending to the respective states to "cede the forts, arsenals, navy-yards, dock-yards, and other public establishments within their respective limits to the Confederate States," etc.

The hope which was early entertained of a peaceful solution of the issues pending between the Confederate States and the United States rapidly diminished, so that we find on March 6th that the Congress, in its preamble to an act to provide for the public defense, begins with the declaration that "in order to provide speedily forces to repel invasion," etc., authorized the President to employ the militia, and to ask for and accept the services of any number of volunteers, not exceeding one hundred thousand, and to organize companies into battalions, battalions into regiments, and regiments into brigades and divisions. As in the first law, the President was authorized to appoint the commanding officer of such brigades and divisions, the commissions to endure only while the brigades were in service.

On the same day (March 6, 1861) was enacted the law for the establishment and organization of the army of the Confederate States of America, this being in contradistinction to the provisional army, which was to be composed of troops tendered by the states, as in the first act, and volunteers received, as in the second act, to constitute a provisional army. That the wish and policy of the government was peace is again manifested in this act, which, in providing for the military establishment of the Confederacy, fixed the number of enlisted men of all arms at nine thousand four hundred twenty. Due care was taken to prevent the appointment of incompetent or unworthy persons as officers of the army, and the right to promotion up to and including the grade of colonel was carefully guarded; beyond this the professional character of the army was recognized as follows: "Appointments to the rank of brigadier-general, after the army is organized, shall be made by selection from the army." There being no right of promotion above the grade of colonel in the army of the United States, selection for appointment to the rank of general had no other restriction than the necessity for confirmation by the Senate. The provision just quoted imposed the further restriction of requiring the person nominated by selection to have previously been an officer of the army of the Confederate States.

Regarding the army of the United States as belonging neither to a section of the Union nor to the general government, but to the states conjointly while they remained united, it follows as a corollary of the proposition that, when disintegration occurred, the undivided personnel composing the army would be left free to choose their future place of service. Therefore, provision was made for securing to officers who should leave the army of the United States and join that of the Confederate States, the same relative rank in the latter which they held in the former.

Be it further enacted that all officers who have resigned, or who may within six months tender their resignations, from the Army of the United States, and who have been or may be appointed to original vacancies in the Army of the Confederate States, the commissions issued shall bear one and the same date, so that the relative rank of officers of each grade shall be determined by their former commissions in the United States Army, held anterior to the secession of these Confederate States from the United States.

The provisions hereof are in the view entertained that the army was of the states, not of the government, and was to secure to officers adhering to the Confederate States the same relative rank which they had before those states had withdrawn from the Union. It was clearly the intent of the law to embrace in this provision only those officers who had resigned or who should resign from the United States army to enter the service of the Confederacy, or who, in other words, should thus be transferred from one service to the other. It is also to be noted that, in the eleventh section of the act to which this was amendatory, the right of promotion up to the grade of colonel, in established regiments and corps, was absolutely secured, but that appointments to the higher grade should be by selection, at first without restriction, but after the army had been organized the selection was confined to the army, thus recognizing the profession of arms, and relieving officers from the hazard, beyond the limit of their legal right to promotion, of being superseded by civilians through favoritism or political influence.

How well the government of the Confederacy observed both the letter and the spirit of the law will be seen by reference to its action in the matter of appointments. It is a noteworthy fact that the three highest officers in rank, and whose fame stands unchallenged either for efficiency or zeal, were all so indifferent to any question of personal interest, that they had received their appointment before they were aware it was to be conferred. Each brought from the army of the United States an enviable reputation, such as would have secured to him, had he chosen to remain in it after the war commenced, any position his ambition could have coveted. Therefore, against considerations of self-interest, and impelled by devotion to principle, they severed the ties, professional and personal, which had bound them from their youth up to the time when the Southern states, asserting the consecrated truth that all governments rest on the consent of the governed, decided to withdraw from the union they had voluntarily entered, and the Northern states resolved to coerce them to remain in it against their will. These officers were—first, Samuel

Cooper, a native of New York, a graduate of the United States Military Academy in 1815, and who served continuously in the army until March 7, 1861, with such distinction as secured to him the appointment of adjutant general of the United States army. Second, Albert Sidney Johnston, a native of Kentucky, a graduate of the United States Military Academy in 1826, served conspicuously in the army until 1834, then served in the army of the republic of Texas, and then in the United States Volunteers in the war with Mexico. Subsequently he reëntered the United States army, and for meritorious conduct attained the rank of brevet brigadier general. After the secession of Texas, his adopted state, he resigned his commission in the United States army, May 3, 1861, and traveled by land from California to Richmond to offer his services to the Confederacy. Third, Robert E. Lee, a native of Virginia, a graduate of the United States Military Academy in 1829, when he was appointed in the engineer corps of the United States army, and served continuously and with such distinction as to secure for him in 1847 brevets of three grades above his corps commission. He resigned from the army of the United States April 25, 1861, upon the secession of Virginia, in whose army he served until it was transferred to the Confederate States.

Samuel Cooper was the first of these to offer his services to the Confederacy at Montgomery. Having known him most favorably and intimately as adjutant general of the United States army when I was Secretary of War, the value of his services in the organization of a new army was considered so great that I invited him to take the position of adjutant general of the Confederate army, which he accepted without a question either as to relative rank or anything else. The highest grade then authorized by law was that of brigadier general, and that commission was bestowed upon him.

When General Albert Sidney Johnston reached Richmond he called upon me, and for several days at various intervals we conversed with the freedom and confidence belonging to the close friendship which had existed between us for many years. Consequent to a remark made by me, he asked to what duty I would assign him, and, when answered, to serve in the West, he expressed his pleasure at service in that section, but inquired how he was to raise his command, and for the first time learned that he been nominated and confirmed as a general in the army of the Confederacy.

The third, General Robert E. Lee, had been commissioned by the state of Virginia as major general and commander of her army. When that army was transferred, after the accession of Virginia to the Confederate States, he was nominated to be brigadier general in the Confederate army, but was left for obvious reasons in command of the forces in Virginia. After the seat of government was removed from Montgomery to Richmond, the course of events on the Southern Atlantic coast induced me to direct General Lee to repair thither. Before leaving he said that, while he was serving in Virginia, he had never thought it needful to inquire about his rank; now, when about to go into other states and to meet officers with whom he had not been previously connected, he would like to be informed upon that point. Under recent laws, authorizing appointments to higher grades than that of his first commission, he had been appointed a full general; so wholly had his heart and his mind been consecrated to the public service that he had not remembered, if he ever knew, of his advancement.

In organizing the bureaus it was deemed advisable to select for the chief of each, officers possessing special knowledge of the duties to be performed. The best assurance of that qualification was believed to be service creditably rendered in the several departments of the United States army before resigning from it. Brevet Lieutenant Colonel A. C. Myers, who had held many important trusts in the United States Quartermaster's Department, was appointed quartermaster general of the Confederacy, with the rank of colonel.

Captain L. B. Northrop, a gallant officer of the United States Dragoons who, by reason of a wound disabling him to perform regimental duty, had been employed in the subsistence department, was, after resigning from the United States army, appointed commissary general of the Confederate States Army, with the rank of colonel. I have heretofore alluded to the difficult task thus imposed on him, and the success with which he performed it, and would be pleased here to enter into a fuller recital, but have not the needful information in regard to his administration of that department.

Surgeon L. P. Moore, an officer of recognized merit in the United States Medical Department, from which he had resigned to join the Confederacy, was appointed the surgeon general of the Confederate States army. As in the case of other departments, there was in this a want of the stores requisite, as well for the field as the hospital.

To supply medicines which were declared by the enemy to be contraband of war, our medical department had to seek in the forest for substitutes, and to add surgical instruments and appliances to the small stock on hand as best they could.

It would be quite beyond my power to do justice to the skill and knowledge with which the medical corps performed their arduous task, and regret that I have no report from Surgeon General Moore which would enable me to do justice to the officers of his corps, as well in regard to their humanity as to their professional skill.

In no branch of our service were our needs so great and our means to meet them relatively so small as in the matter of ordnance and ordnance stores. The chief of ordnance, General Gorgas, had been an ordnance officer of the United States army, and resigned to join the Confederacy. He has favored me with a succinct though comprehensive statement, which has enabled me to write somewhat fully of that department; for the better understanding of its operations, the reader is referred to the ordnance report elsewhere.

CHAPTER III: *Commissioners to Purchase Arms and Ammunition—My Letter to Captain Semmes—Resignations of Officers of United States Navy—Our Destitution of Accessories for the Supply of Naval Vessels—Secretary Mallory—Food Supplies —The Commissariat Department—The Quartermaster's Department—The Disappearance of Delusions—The Supply of Powder—Saltpeter—Sulphur—Artificial Niter Beds—Services of General G. W. Rains—Destruction at Harpers Ferry of Machinery — The Master Armorer — Machinery Secured — Want of Skillful Employees — Difficulties Encountered by Every Department of the Executive Branch of the Government.*

ON THE third day after my inauguration at Montgomery, an officer of extensive information and high capacity was sent to the North to make purchases of arms, ammunition, and machinery; soon afterward another officer was sent to Europe to buy in the market as far as possible, and furthermore, to make contracts for arms and munitions to be manufactured. Captain (afterward Admiral) Semmes, the officer who was sent to the North, would have been quite successful but for the intervention of the civil authorities, preventing the delivery of the various articles contracted for. The officer who was sent to Europe, Major Huse, found few serviceable arms upon the market; he succeeded, however, in making contracts for the manufacture of large quantities, being in advance of the agents sent from the Northern government for the same purpose. For further and more detailed information, reference is made to the monograph of the chief of ordnance.

My letter of instructions to Captain Semmes was as follows:

MONTGOMERY, ALABAMA, February 21, 1861.

DEAR SIR: As agent of the Confederate States, you are authorized to proceed, as hereinafter set forth, to make purchases and contracts for machinery and munitions, or for the manufacture of arms and munitions of war.

Of the proprietor of the —— Powder Company, in ——, you will probably be able to obtain cannon- and musket-powder—the former to be of the coarsest grain; and also to engage with him for the establishment of a powder-mill at some point in the limits of our territory.

The quantity of powder to be supplied immediately will exceed his stock on hand, and the arrangement for further supply should, if possible, be by manufacture in our own territory; if this is not practicable, means must be sought for further shipments from any and all sources which are reliable.

At the arsenal at Washington you will find an artisan named ——, who has brought the cap-making machine to its present state of efficiency, and who might furnish a cap-machine, and accompany it to direct its operations. If not in this, I hope you may in some other way be able to obtain a cap-machine with little delay, and have it sent to the Mount Vernon Arsenal, Alabama.

We shall require a manufactory for friction-primers, and you will, if possible, induce some capable person to establish one in our country. The demand of the Confederate States will be the inducement in this as in the case of the powder-mill proposed.

A short time since, the most improved machinery for the manufacture of rifles, intended for the Harpers Ferry Armory, was, it was said, for sale by the manufacturer. If it be so at this time, you will procure it for this Government, and use the needful precaution in relation to its transportation. Mr. —— ——, of the Harpers Ferry Armory, can give you all the information in that connection which you may require. Mr. Ball, the master armorer at Harpers Ferry, is willing to accept service under our Government, and could probably bring with him skilled workmen. If we get the machinery, this will be important.

Machinery for grooving muskets and heavy guns is, I hope, to be purchased ready made. If not, you will contract for its manufacture and delivery. You will endeavor to obtain the most improved shot for rifled cannon, and persons skilled in the preparation of that and other fixed ammunitions. Captain G. W. Smith and Captain Lovell, late of the United States Army, and now of New York City, may aid you in your task; and you will please say to them that we will be happy to have their services in our army.

You will make such inquiries as your varied knowledge will suggest in relation to the supply of guns of different calibers, especially the largest. I suggest the advantage, if to be obtained, of having a few of the fifteen-inch guns, like the one cast at Pittsburg.

I have not sought to prescribe so as to limit your inquiries, either as to object or place, but only to suggest for your reflection and consideration the points which have chanced to come under my observation. You will use your discretion in visiting places where information of persons or things is to be obtained for the furtherance of the object in view. Any contracts made will be sent to the Hon. L. P. Walker, Secretary of War, for his approval; and the contractor need not fear that delay will be encountered in the action of this Government.

Very respectfully yours, etc.,

(Signed)   JEFFERSON DAVIS.

Captain Semmes had also been directed to seek for vessels which would serve for naval purposes, and after his return reported that he could not find any vessels which in his judgment were, or could be made, available for our uses. The Southern officers of the navy who were in command of United States vessels abroad, under an idea more creditable to their sentiment than to their knowledge of the nature of our constitutional Union, brought the vessels they commanded into the ports of the North, and having delivered them to authorities of the United States government, generally tendered their resignations, and repaired to the states from which they had been commissioned in the navy, to serve where they held their allegiance to be due. The theory that they owed allegiance to their respective states was founded on the fact that the federal government was of the states; the sequence was that the navy belonged to the states, not to their agent, the federal government; when the states ceased to be united, the naval vessels and armament should have been divided among the owners. While we honor the sentiment which caused them to surrender their heart-bound associations, and the profession to which they were bred, on which they relied for subsistence, to go, with nothing save their swords and faithful hearts, to fight, to bleed, and to die if need be, in defense of their homes and a righteous cause, we can but remember how much was lost by their view of what their honor and duty demanded. Far, however, be it from their country-men, for that or any other consideration, to wish that their fidelity to the dictates of a conscientious belief should have yielded to any temptation of interest. The course they pursued shows how impossible it was that they should have done so, for what did they not sacrifice to their sense of right! We were doubly bereft by losing our share of the navy we had contributed to build, and by having it all employed to assail us. The application of the appropriations for the navy of the United States had been such that the construction of vessels had been at the North, though much of the timber used and other material employed was transported from the South to Northern shipyards. Therefore, we were without the accessories needful for the rapid supply of naval vessels.

While attempting whatever was practicable at home, we sent a competent, well-deserving officer of the navy to England to obtain there and elsewhere, by purchase or by building, vessels which could be transformed into ships of war. These efforts and their results will be noticed more fully hereafter.

It may not be amiss to remark here that if the anticipations of our people were not realized, it was not from any lack of the zeal and ability of Secretary of the Navy Mallory. As was heretofore stated, his fondness for and aptitude in nautical affairs had led him to know much of vessels, their construction and management, and, as chairman of the Committee on United States Naval Affairs, he had superadded to this a very large acquaintance with officers of the United States navy, which gave him the requisite information for the most useful employment of the instructed officers who joined our service.

At the North many had been deceived by the fictions of preparations at the South for the war of the sections, and among ourselves were few who realized how totally deficient the Southern states were in all which was necessary to the active operations of an army, however gallant the men might be, and however able were the generals who directed and led them. From these causes, operating jointly, resulted undue caution at the North and overweening confidence at the South. The habits of our people in hunting, and protecting their stock in fields from the ravages of ferocious beasts, caused them to be generally supplied with the arms used for such purposes. The facility with which individuals traveled over the country led to very erroneous ideas as to the difficulties of transporting an army. The small amounts of ammunition required in time of peace gave no measure of the amount requisite for warlike operations, and the products of a country which insufficiently supplied food for its inhabitants when peaceful pursuits were uninterrupted, would serve but a short time to furnish the commissariat of a large army. It was, of course, easy to foresee that if war was waged against the seceding states by all of those which remained in the Union, the large supply of provisions which had been annually sent from the Northwest to the South could not, under the altered circumstances, be relied on. That our people did not more immediately turn their attention to the production of food supplies may be attributed to the prevailing delusion that secession would not be followed by war. To the able officer then at the head of the commissariat department, Colonel L. B. Northrop, much credit is due for his well-directed efforts to provide both for immediate and prospective wants. It gives me the greater pleasure to say this because those less informed of all he did, and skillfully tried to do, have been profuse in criticism, and sparing indeed of the meed justly his due. Adequate facilities for transportation might have relieved the local want of supplies, especially in Virginia, where the largest bodies of troops were assembled; unfortunately, the quartermaster's department was scarcely less provided than that of the commissary. Not only were the railroads insufficient in number, but they were poorly furnished with rolling stock, and had been mainly dependent upon Northern foundries and factories for their rails and equipment. Even the skilled operatives of the railroads were generally Northern men, and their desertion followed fast upon every disaster which attended the Confederate arms. In addition to other causes which have been mentioned, the idea that cotton was king, and would produce foreign intervention, as well as a desire of the Northern people for the return of peace and the restoration of trade, exercised a potent influence in preventing our agriculturists from directing at an early period their capital and labor to the production of food supplies rather than that of our staple for export. As one after another the illusions vanished and the material necessities of a great war were recognized by our people, never did patriotic devotion exhibit brighter examples of the sacrifice of self-interest and the abandonment of fixed habits and opinions, or more effective and untiring effort to meet the herculean task which was set before them. Being one of the few who regarded secession and war as inevitably connected, my early attention was given to the organization of military forces and the procurement and preparation of the munitions of war. If our people had not gone to war without counting the cost, they were nevertheless involved in it without means of providing for its necessities. It has been heretofore stated that we had no powder mills. It would be needless to say that the new-born government had no depots of powder, but it may be well to add that, beyond the small supply required for sporting purposes, our local traders had no stock on hand. Having no manufacturing industries which required saltpeter, very little of that was purchasable in our markets. The same would have been the case in regard to sulphur but for the fact that it had been recently employed in the clarification of sugar-cane juice, and thus a considerable amount of it was found in New Orleans. Prompt measures were taken to secure a supply of sulphur, and parties were employed to obtain saltpeter from the caves, as well as from the earth of old tobacco houses and cellars; artificial niter-beds were made to provide for prospective wants. Of soft wood for charcoal there was abundance, and thus materials were procured for the manufacture of gunpowder to meet the demand which would arise when the limited quantity purchased by the Confederate government at the North should be exhausted.

It was our good fortune to secure the services of an able and scientific soldier, General G. W. Rains, who to a military education added experience in a large manufacturing establishment, and to him was confided the construction of a powder mill and the manufacture of powder, both for artillery and small arms. The appalling contemplation of the inauguration of a great war, without powder or a navy to secure its importation from abroad, was soon relieved by the extraordinary efforts of the ordnance department and the well-directed skill of General Rains, to whom it is but a just tribute to say that, beginning without even instructed workmen, he had before the close of the war made what, in the opinion of competent judges, has been pronounced the best powder mill in the world, and in which powder of every variety of grain was manufactured of materials which had been purified from those qualities which cause its deterioration under long exposure to a moist atmosphere.

The avowed purpose and declared obligation of the federal government was to occupy and possess the property belonging to the United States, yet one of the first acts was to set fire to the armory at Harpers Ferry, Virginia, the only establishment of the kind in the Southern states, and the only Southern depository of the rifles which the general government had then on hand.

What conclusion is to be drawn from such action? To avoid attributing a breach of solemn pledges, it must be supposed that Virginia was considered as out of the Union, and a public enemy, in whose borders it was proper to destroy whatever might be useful to her of the common property of the states lately united.

As soon as the United States troops had evacuated the place, the citizens and amorers went to work to save the armory as far as possible from destruction, and to secure valuable material stored in it. The master armorer, Armistead Ball, so bravely and skillfully directed these efforts that a large part of the machinery and materials was saved from the flames. The subduing of the fire was a dangerous and difficult task, and great credit is due to those who, under the orders of Master Armorer Ball, attempted and achieved it. When the fire was extinguished, the work was continued and persevered in until all the valuable machinery and material had been collected, boxed, and shipped to Richmond, about the end of the summer of 1861. The machinery thus secured was divided between the arsenals at Richmond, Virginia, and Fayetteville, North Carolina, and when repaired and put in working condition, supplied to some extent the want which existed in the South of means for the alteration and repair of old or injured arms, and finally contributed to increase the very scanty supply of arms with which our country was furnished when the war began. The practice of the federal government, which had kept the construction and manufacture of the material of war at the North, had consequently left the South without the requisite number of skilled workmen by whose labor machinery could at once be made fully effective if it were obtained; indeed, the want of such employees prevented the small amount of machinery on hand from being worked to its full capacity. The gallant Master Armorer Ball, whose capacity, zeal, and fidelity deserve more than a passing notice, was sent with that part of the machinery assigned to the Fayetteville arsenal. The toil, the anxiety, and responsibility of his perilous position at Harpers Ferry, where he remained long after the protecting force of the Confederate army retired, had probably undermined a constitution so vigorous that, in the face of a great exigency, no labor seemed too great or too long for him to grapple with and endure. So, like a ship which, after having weathered the storm, goes down in the calm, the master armorer, soon after he took his quiet post at Fayetteville, was "found dead in his bed."

The difficulties which on every side met the several departments of the executive branch of the government one must suppose were but little appreciated by many, whose opportunities for exact observation were the best, as one often meets with self-complacent expressions as to modes of achieving readily what prompt, patient, zealous effort proved to be insurmountable. In the progress of this work, it is hoped, will be presented not only the magnitude of the obstacles, but the spirit and capacity with which they were encountered by the unseen and much undervalued labors of the officers of the several departments, on whom devolved provision for the civil service, as well as for the armies in the field. Already has the report of General St. John commissary general of subsistence, of the operations of that department, just before the close of the war, exposed the hollowness of many sensational pictures intended to fix gross neglect or utter incapacity on the Executive.

The hoped-for and expected monograms of other chiefs of bureaus will silence like criticisms on each, so far as they are made by those who are not wilfully blind, or maliciously intent on the circulation of falsehood.

CHAPTER IV: *The Proclamation for Seventy-five Thousand Men by President Lincoln Further Examined—The Reasons Presented by him to Mankind for the Justification of his Conduct Shown to be Mere Fictions, Having no Relation to the Question—What is the Value of Constitutional Liberty, of Bills of Rights, of Limitations of Powers, if They May be Transgressed at Pleasure? — Secession of South Carolina — Proclamation of Blockade—Session of Congress at Montgomery—Extracts from the President's Message—Acts of Congress —Spirit of the People—Secession of Border States—Destruction of United States Property by Order of President Lincoln.*

If any further evidence had been required to show that it was the determination of the Northern people not only to make no concessions to the grievances of the Southern states, but to increase them to the last extremity, it was furnished by the proclamation of President Lincoln, issued on April 15, 1861. This proclamation, which has already been mentioned, requires a further examination, as it was the official declaration, on the part of the government of the United States, of the war which ensued. In it the President called for seventy-five thousand men to suppress "combinations" opposed to the laws, and obstrucing their execution in seven sovereign states which had retired from the Union. Seventy-five thousand men organized and equipped are a powerful army, and when raised to operate against these states, nothing else than war could be intended. The words in which he summoned this force were these: "Whereas the laws of the United States have been for some time past, and now are, opposed, and the execution thereof obstructed, in the States of South Carolina, Georgia, Alabama, Florida, Mississippi, Louisiana, and Texas, by combinations too powerful to be suppressed by the ordinary course of judicial proceedings, or by the powers vested in the marshals by law: Now, therefore, I, Abraham Lincoln, by virtue of the power in me vested by the Constitution and laws," etc.

The power granted in the Constitution is thus expressed: "The Congress shall have power to provide for calling forth the militia to execute the laws of the Union, suppress insurrections, and repel invasions."[1] It was to the Congress, not the Executive, that the power was delegated, and thus early was commenced a long series of usurpations of powers

---

[1] Constitution of the United States, Article I, section 8.

inconsistent with the purposes for which the Union was formed, and destructive of the fraternity it was designed to perpetuate.

On November 6, 1860, the legislature of South Carolina assembled and gave the vote of the state for electors of a President of the United States. On the next day an act was passed calling a state convention to assemble on December 17th, to determine the question of the withdrawal of the state from the United States. Candidates for membership were immediately nominated. All were in favor of secession. The convention assembled on December 17th, and on the 20th passed "an ordinance to dissolve the union between the State of South Carolina and other States united with her under the compact entitled 'The Constitution of the United States of America.' " The ordinance began with these words: "We the people of the State of South Carolina, in convention assembled, do declare and ordain," etc. The state authorities immediately conformed to this action of the convention, and the laws and authority of the United States ceased to be obeyed within the limits of the state. About four months afterward, when the state, in union with others which had joined her, had possessed herself of the forts within her limits, which the United States government had refused to evacuate, President Lincoln issued the above-mentioned proclamation.

The state of South Carolina is designated in the proclamation as a combination too powerful to be suppressed by the ordinary course of judicial proceedings, or by the powers vested in the marshals by law. This designation does not recognize the state, or manifest any consciousness of its existence, whereas South Carolina was one of the colonies that had declared her independence, and after a long and bloody war she had been recognized as a sovereign state by Great Britain, the only power to which she had ever owed allegiance. The fact that she had been one of the colonies in the original Congress, had been a member of the confederation, and subsequently of the Union, strengthens, but surely cannot impair, her claim to be a state. Though President Lincoln designated her as a "combination," it did not make her a combination. Though he refused to recognize her as a state, it did not make her any less a state. By assertion, he attempted to annihilate seven states; the war which followed was to enforce the revolutionary edict, and to establish the supremacy of the general government on the ruins of the blood-bought independence of the states.

By designating the state as a "combination," and considering that under such a name it might be in a condition of insurrection, he assumed to have authority to raise a great military force and attack the state. Yet even if the fact had been as assumed, if an insurrection had existed, the President could not lawfully have derived the power he exercised from such condition of affairs. The provision of the Constitution is as follows: "The United States shall guarantee to every State in this Union a republican form of government, and shall protect each of them against invasion; and, on application of the Legislature, or of the Executive (when the Legislature can not be convened), against domestic violence."[2] So the guarantee availed not at all to justify the act which it was presented to excuse—the fact being that a state, and not an "unlawful combination," as asserted, was the object of assault, and the case one of making war. For a state or union of states to attack with military force another state, is to make war. By the Constitution, the power to make war is given solely to Congress. "Congress shall have power to declare war," says the Constitution.[3] And, again, "to raise and support armies."[4] Thus, under a perverted use of language, the executive at Washington did that which he undeniably had no power to do, under a faithful observance of the Constitution.

To justify himself to Congress and the people, or rather, before the face of mankind, for this evasion of the Constitution of his country, President Lincoln, in his message to Congress of July 4, 1861, resorted to the artifice of saying, "It [meaning the proceedings of the Confederate States] presents to the whole family of man the question whether a constitutional republic or democracy—a government of the people by the same people—can, or can not, maintain its territorial integrity against its own domestic foes?"

The answer to this question is very plain. In the nature of things, no union can be formed except by separate, independent, and distinct parties. Any other combination is not a union; upon the destruction of any of these elements in the parties, the union *ipso facto* ceases. If the government is the result of a union of states, then these states must be separate, sovereign, and distinct, to be able to form a union, which is entirely an act of their own volition. Such a government as ours had no power to maintain its existence any longer than the contracting parties pleased to cohere, because it was founded on the great principle of voluntary federation, and organized "to establish justice and insure domestic tranquillity."[5] Any departure from this principle by the general government not only perverts and destroys its nature, but furnishes a just cause

---

[2] Constitution of the United States, Article IV, section 4.
[3] Article I, section 8.
[4] *Ibid.*
[5] Constitution of the United States, preamble.

to the injured state to withdraw from the union. A new union might subsequently be formed, but the original one could never by coercion be restored. Any effort on the part of the others to force the seceding state to consent to come back is an attempt at subjugation. It is a wrong which no lapse of time or combination of circumstances can ever make right. A forced union is a political absurdity. No less absurd is President Lincoln's effort to dissever the sovereignty of the people from that of the state; as if there could be a state without a people, or a sovereign people without a state.

But the question which Lincoln presents "to the whole family of man" deserves a further notice. The answer which he seems to infer would be given "by the whole family of man" is that such a government as he supposes "can maintain its territorial integrity against its own domestic foes." And therefore he concluded that he was right in the judgment of "the whole family of man" in commencing hostilities against us. He says, "So viewing the issue, no choice was left but to call out the war power of the Government." That is the power to make war against foreign nations, for the government has no other war power. Planting himself on this position, he commenced the devastation and bloodshed which followed to effect our subjugation.

Nothing could be more erroneous than such views. The supposed case which he presents is entirely unlike the real case. The government of the United States is like no other government. It is neither a "constitutional republic or democracy," nor has it ever been thus called. Neither is it a "government of the people by the same people"; it is known and designated as "the Government of the United States." It is an anomaly among governments. Its authority consists solely of certain powers delegated to it, as a common agent, by an association of sovereign and independent states. These powers are to be exercised only for certain specified objects; the purposes, declared in the beginning of the deed or instrument of delegation, were "to form a more perfect union, establish justice, insure domestic tranquillity, provide for the common defense, promote the general welfare, and secure the blessings of liberty to ourselves and our posterity."

The beginning and the end of all the powers of the government of the United States are to be found in that instrument of delegation. All its powers are there expressed, defined, and limited. It was only to that instrument that Lincoln as President should have gone to learn his duties. That was the chart which he had just solemnly pledged himself to the country faithfully to follow. He soon deviated widely from it

—and fatally erroneous was his course. The administration of the affairs of a great people, at a most perilous period, is decided by the answer which it is assumed "the whole family of man" would give to a supposed condition of human affairs which did not exist and which could not exist. This is the ground upon which the rectitude of his cause was placed. He says, "No choice was left but to call out the war power of the Government, and so to resist force employed for its destruction by force for its preservation."

"Here," he says, "no choice was left but to call out the war power of the Government." For what purpose must he call out this war power? He answers by saying, "and so to resist force employed for its destruction by force for its preservation." But this which he asserts is not a fact. There was no "force employed for its destruction." Let the reader turn to the record of the facts in Part III of this work, and peruse the fruitless efforts for peace which were made by us, and which Lincoln did not deign to notice. The assertion is not only incorrect in stating that force was employed by us, but also in declaring that it was for the destruction of the government of the United States. On the contrary, we wished to leave it alone. Our separation did not involve its destruction. To such fiction was Lincoln compelled to resort to give even apparent justice to his cause. He now goes to the Constitution for the exercise of his war power, and here we have another fiction.

On April 19th, four days later, President Lincoln issued another proclamation, announcing a blockade of the ports of seven confedereated states, which was afterward extended to North Carolina and Virginia. It further declared that all persons who should under their authority molest any vessel of the United States, or the persons or cargo on board, should be treated as pirates. In their efforts to subjugate us, the destruction of our commerce was regarded by the authorities at Washington as a most efficient measure. It was early seen that, although acts of Congress established ports of entry where commerce existed, they might be repealed, and the ports nominally closed or declared to be closed; yet such a declaration would be of no avail unless sustained by a naval force, as these ports were located in territory not subject to the United States. An act was subsequently passed authorizing the President of the United States, in his direction, to close our ports, but it was never executed.

The scheme of blockade was resorted to, and a falsehood was asserted on which to base it. Seward writes to Dallas: "You will say (to Lord John Russell) that, by our own laws and the laws of nature and the laws of nations, this Government has a clear right to suppress insurrection.

An exclusion of commerce from national ports which have been seized by insurgents, in the equitable form of blockade, is a proper means to that end."[6] This is the same doctrine of "combinations" fabricated by the authorities at Washington to serve as the basis of a bloody revolution. Under the laws of nations, separate governments when at war blockade each other's ports. This is decided to be justifiable. But the government of the United States could not consent to justify its blockade of our ports on this ground, as it would be an admission that the Confederate States were a separate and distinct sovereignty, and that the war was prosecuted only for subjugation. It therefore assumed that the withdrawal of the Southern states from the Union was an insurrection.

Was it an insurrection? When certain sovereign and independent states form a union with limited powers for some general purposes, and any one or more of them, in the progress of time, suffer unjust and oppressive grievances for which there is no redress but in a withdrawal from the association, is such withdrawal an insurrection? If so, then of what advantage is a compact of union to states? Within the Union are oppressions and grievances; the attempt to go out brings war and subjugation. The ambitious and aggressive states obtain possession of the central authority which, having grown strong in the lapse of time, asserts its entire sovereignty over the states. Whichever of them denies it and seeks to retire is declared to be guilty of insurrection, its citizens are stigmatized as "rebels," as if they had revolted against a master, and a war of subjugation is begun. If this action is once tolerated, where will it end? Where is the value of constitutional liberty? What strength is there in bills of rights—in limitations of power? What new hope for mankind is to be found in written constitutions, what remedy which did not exist under kings or emperors? If the doctrines thus announced by the government of the United States are conceded, then look through either end of the political telescope, and one sees only an empire, and the once famous *Declaration of Independence* trodden in the dust as a "glittering generality," and the compact of union denounced as a "flaunting lie." Those who submit to such consequences without resistance are not worthy of the liberties and the rights to which they were born, and deserve to be made slaves. Such must be the verdict of mankind.

Men do not fight to make a fraternal union, neither do nations. These military preparations of the government of the United States signified nothing less than the subjugation of the Southern states, so that, by one

---

[6] Diplomatic correspondence, May 21, 1861.

devastating blow, the North might grasp forever that supremacy it had so long coveted.

To be prepared for self-defense, I called Congress together at Montgomery on April 29th, and in the message of that date, thus spoke of the proclamation of the President of the United States: "Apparently contradictory as are the terms of this singular document, one point is unmistakably evident. The President of the United States calls for an army of seventy-five thousand men, whose first service is to be the capture of our forts. It is a plain declaration of war, which I am not at liberty to disregard, because of my knowledge that, under the Constitution of the United States, the President is usurping a power granted exclusively to Congress."

I then proceeded to say that I did not feel at liberty to disregard the fact that many of the states seemed quite content to submit to the exercise of the powers assumed by the President of the United States, and were actively engaged in levying troops for the purpose indicated in the proclamation. Meantime, being deprived of the aid of Congress, I had been under the necessity of confining my action to a call on the states for volunteers for the common defense, in accordance with authority previously conferred on me. I stated that there were then in the field, at Charleston, Pensacola, Forts Morgan, Jackson, St. Philip, and Pulaski, nineteen thousand men, and sixteen thousand more were on their way to Virginia; that it was proposed to organize and hold in readiness for instant action, in view of the existing exigencies of the country, an army of one hundred thousand men; that, if a further force should be needed, Congress would be appealed to for authority to call it into the field. Finally, that the intent of the President of the United States, already developed, to invade our soil, capture our forts, blockade our ports, and wage war against us, rendered it necessary to raise means to a much larger amount than had been done, to defray the expenses of maintaining independence and repelling invasion.

A brief summary of the internal affairs of the government followed, and notwithstanding frequent declarations of the peaceful intentions of the withdrawing states had been made in the most solemn manner, it was deemed not to be out of place to repeat them once more; therefore, the message closed with these words: "We protest solemnly, in the face of mankind, that we desire peace at any sacrifice, save that of honor. In independence we seek no conquest, no aggrandizement, no concession of any kind from the States with which we have lately been confederated. All we ask is to be let alone—that those who never held power over us shall not now attempt our subjugation by arms. This we will, we must, resist to the direct extremity. The moment that this pretension is abandoned, the sword will drop from our grasp, and we shall be ready to enter into treaties of amity and commerce that can not but be mutually beneficial. So long as this pretension is maintained, with a firm reliance on that Divine Power which covers with its protection the just cause, we must continue to struggle for our inherent right to freedom, independence, and self-government."

At this session Congress passed acts authorizing the President to use the whole land and naval force to meet the necessities of the war thus commenced; to issue to private armed vessels letters of marque; in addition to the volunteer force authorized to be raised, to accept the services of volunteers, to serve during the war; to receive into the service various companies of the different arms; to make a loan of fifty millions of dollars in bonds and notes; and to hold an election for officers of the permanent government under the new Constitution. An act was also passed to provide revenue from imports; another, relative to prisoners of war; such others as were necessary to complete the internal organization of the government, and establish the administration of public affairs.

In every portion of the country there was exhibited the most patriotic devotion to the common cause. Transportation companies freely tendered the use of their lines for troops and supplies. Requisitions for troops were met with such alacrity that the number offering their services in every instance greatly exceeded the demand and the ability to arm them. Men of the highest official and social position served as volunteers in the ranks. The gravity of age and the zeal of youth rivaled each other in the desire to be foremost in the public defense.

The appearance of the proclamation of the President of the United States, calling out seventy-five thousand men, was followed by the immediate withdrawal of the states of Virginia, North Carolina, Tennessee, and Arkansas, and their union with the Confederate States. The former state, thus placed on the frontier and exposed to invasion, began to prepare for a resolute defense. Volunteers were ordered to be enrolled and held in readiness in every part of the state. Colonel Robert E. Lee, having resigned his commission in the United States cavalry, was on April 22d nominated and confirmed by the state convention of Virginia as "Commander-in-Chief of the military and naval forces of the Commonwealth."

Already the Northern officer in charge had evacuated Harpers Ferry, after having attempted to destroy the public buildings there. His report says: "I gave the order to apply the torch. In three minutes or less, both of the arsenal buildings, containing nearly fifteen thousand stand of arms, together with the carpenter's shop, which was at the upper end of a long and connected series of workshops of the armory proper, were in a blaze. There is every reason for believing the destruction was complete." Simon Cameron, the Secretary of War, on April 22d replied to this report in these words: "I am directed by the President of the United States to communicate to you, and through you to the officers and men under your command at Harpers Ferry Armory, the approbation of the Government of your and their judicious conduct there, and to tender you and them the thanks of the Government for the same." At the same time the shipyard at Norfolk was abandoned after an attempt to destroy it. About midnight of April 20th, a fire was started in the yard, which continued to increase, and before daylight the work of destruction extended to two immense ship houses, one of which contained the entire frame of a seventy-four-gun ship, and to the long ranges of stores and offices on each side of the entrance. The great ship *Pennsylvania* was burned, and the frigates *Merrimac* and *Columbus,* and the *Delaware, Raritan, Plymouth,* and *Germantown* were sunk. A vast amount of machinery, valuable engines, small arms, and chronometers, was broken up and rendered entirely useless. The value of the property destroyed was estimated at several millions of dollars.

This property thus destroyed had been accumulated and constructed with laborious care and skillful ingenuity during a course of years to fulfill one of the objects of the Constitution, which was expressed in these words, "To provide for the common defense" (see preamble of the Constitution). It had belonged to all the states in common, and to each one equally with the others. If the Confederate States were still members of the Union, as the President of the United States asserted, where can he find a justification of these acts?

In explanation of his policy to the commissioners sent to him by the Virginia state convention, he said, referring to his inaugural address, "As I then and therein said, I now repeat, the power confided in me will be used to hold, occupy, and possess property and places belonging to the Government." Yet he tendered the thanks of the government to those who applied the torch to destroy this property belonging, as he regarded it, to the government.

How unreasonable, how blind with rage must have been that administration of affairs which so quickly brought the government to the necessity of destroying its own means of defense in order, as it publicly declared, "to maintain its life"! It would seem that the passions that rule the savage had taken possession of the authorities at the United States capital! In the conflagrations of vast structures, the wanton destruction of public property, and still more in the issue of *lettres de cachet* by the Secretary of State, who boasted of the power of his little bell over the personal liberties of the citizen, the people saw, or might have seen, the rapid strides toward despotism made under the mask of preserving the Union. Yet these and similar measures were tolerated because the sectional hate dominated in the Northern states over the higher motives of constitutional and moral obligation.

CHAPTER V: *Maryland First Approached by Northern Invasion
—Denies to United States Troops the Right of Way Across her
Domain—Mission of Judge Handy—Views of Governor Hicks
—His Proclamation—Arrival of Massachusetts Troops at Baltimore—Passage Through the City Disputed—Activity of the
Police—Burning of Bridges—Letter of President Lincoln to
the Governor—Visited by Citizens—Action of the State Legislature—Occupation of the Relay House—The City Arms Surrendered—City in Possession of United States Troops—Remonstrances of the City to the Passage of Troops Disregarded
—Citizens Arrested; also, Members of the Legislature—Accumulation of Northern Forces at Washington—Invasion of
West Virginia by a Force under McClellan—Attack at Philippi;
at Laurel Hill—Death of General Garnett.*

THE border state of Maryland was an outpost of the South on the
frontier first to be approached by Northern invasion. The first demonstration against state sovereignty was to be made there, and in her fate
were the other slaveholding states of the border to have warning of
what they were to expect. She had chosen to be, for the time at least,
neutral in the impending war, and had denied to the United States troops
the right of way across her domain in their march to invade the Southern
states. The governor (Hicks) avowed a desire, not only that the state
should avoid war, but that she should be a means for pacifying those
more disposed to engage in combat.

Judge Handy, a distinguished citizen of Mississippi who was born in
Maryland, had in December, 1860, been sent as a commissioner from
the state of his adoption to that of his birth, and presented his views and
the object of his mission to Governor Hicks, who in his response (December 19, 1860) declared his purpose to act in full concert with the
other border states, adding, "I do not doubt the people of Maryland are
ready to go with the people of those States for weal or woe."[1] Subsequently, in answer to appeals for and against a proclamation assembling
the legislature, in order to have a call for a state convention, Governor
Hicks issued an address in which, arguing that there was no necessity to
define the position of Maryland, he wrote: "If the action of the Legis-

[1] *Annual Cyclopædia*, Vol. I, p. 443.

lature would be simply to declare that Maryland was with the South in sympathy and feeling; that she demands from the North the repeal of offensive, unconstitutional statutes, and appeals to it for new guarantees; that she will wait a reasonable time for the North to purge her statute-books, to do justice to her Southern brethren; and, if her appeals are vain, will make common cause with her sister border States in resistance to tyranny, if need be, it would only be saying what the whole country well knows," etc.

On April 18, 1861, Governor Hicks issued a proclamation invoking them to preserve the peace, and said, "I assure the people that no troops will be sent from Maryland, unless it may be for the defense of the national capital." On the same day Mayor Brown, of the city of Baltimore, issued a proclamation in which, referring to that of the governor above cited, he said, "I can not withhold my expression of satisfaction at his resolution that no troops shall be sent from Maryland to the soil of any other State." It will be remembered that the capital was on a site which originally belonged to Maryland, and was ceded by her for a special use, so that troops to defend the capital might be considered as not having been sent out of Maryland. It will be remembered that these proclamations were three days after the requisition made by the Secretary of War on the states which had not seceded for their quota of troops to serve in the war about to be inaugurated against the South, and that rumors existed at the time in Baltimore that troops from the Northeast were about to be sent through that city toward the South. On the next day, April 19, 1861, a body of troops arrived at the railroad depot; the citizens assembled in large numbers, and though without arms, disputed the passage through the city. They attacked the troops with the loose stones found in the street, which was undergoing repair, and with such determination and violence, that some of the soldiers were wounded, and they fired upon the multitude, killing a few and wounding many.

The police of Baltimore were very active in their efforts to prevent conflict and preserve the peace; they rescued the baggage and munitions of the troops, which had been seized by the multitude; the rear portion of the troops was, by direction of Governor Hicks, sent back to the borders of the state. The troops who had got through the city took the railroad at the Southern depot and passed on. The militia of the city was called out, and by evening quiet was restored. During the night, on a report that more Northern troops were approaching the city by the railroads, the bridges nearest the city were destroyed, as it was understood, by orders from the authorities of Baltimore.

On April 20th President Lincoln wrote in reply to Governor Hicks and Mayor Brown, saying, "For the future, troops must be brought here, but I make no point of bringing them through Baltimore." On the next day, the 21st, Mayor Brown and other influential citizens, by request of the President, visited him. The interview took place in presence of the cabinet and General Scott, and was reported to the public by the mayor after his return to Baltimore. From that report I make the following extracts. Referring to the President, the mayor uses the following language:

The protection of Washington, he asseverated with great earnestness, was the sole object of concentrating troops there, and he protested that none of the troops brought through Maryland were intended for any purposes hostile to the State, or aggressive as against the Southern States. . . . He called on General Scott for his opinion, which the General gave at great length, to the effect that troops might be brought through Maryland without going through Baltimore, etc. . . . The interview terminated with the distinct assurance, on the part of the President, that no more troops would be sent through Baltimore, unless obstructed in their transit in other directions, and with the understanding that the city authorities should do their best to restrain their own people.

The Mayor and his companions availed themselves of the President's full discussion of the question of the day to urge upon him respectfully, but in the most earnest manner, a course of policy which would give peace to the country, and especially the withdrawal of all orders contemplating the passage of troops through any part of Maryland.

The legislature of the state of Maryland appointed commissioners to the Confederate government to suggest to it the cessation of impending hostilities until the meeting of Congress at Washington in July. Commissioners with like instructions were also sent to Washington. In my reply to the commissioners, dated May 25, 1861, I referred to the uniform expression of desire for peace on the part of the Confederate government, and added:

In deference to the State of Maryland, it again asserts in the most emphatic terms that its sincere and earnest desire is for peace; but that, while the Government would readily entertain any proposition from the Government of the United States tending to a peaceful solution of the present difficulties, the recent attempts of this Government to enter into negotiations with that of the United States were attended with results which forbid any renewal of proposals from it to that Government. . . . Its policy can not but be peace—peace with all nations and people.

On May 5th the Relay House, at the junction of the Washington and Baltimore and Ohio railroads, was occupied by United States troops under General Butler, and, on the 13th of the same month, he moved a portion of the troops to Baltimore, and took position on Federal Hill

—thus was consummated the military occupation of Baltimore. On the next day, reënforcements were received; on the same day, the commanding general issued a proclamation to the citizens, in which he announced to them his purpose and authority to discriminate between citizens, those who agreed with him being denominated "well disposed," and the others described with many offensive epithets. The initiatory step of the policy subsequently developed was found in one sentence: "Therefore, all manufacturers of arms and munitions of war are hereby requested to report to me forthwith, so that the lawfulness of their occupations may be known and understood, and all misconstruction of their doings avoided."

There soon followed a demand for the surrender of the arms stored by the city authorities in a warehouse. The police refused to surrender them without the orders of the police commissioners. The police commissioners, upon representation that the demand of General Butler was by order of the President, decided to surrender the arms under protest, and they were accordingly removed to Fort McHenry.

Baltimore was now disarmed. The army of the United States had control of the city. There was no longer necessity to regard the remonstrance of Baltimore against sending troops through the city, and that more convenient route was henceforth to be employed. George P. Kane, marshal of the police of Baltimore, who had rendered most efficient service for the preservation of peace, as well in the city of Baltimore as at Locust Point, where troops were disembarked to be dispatched to Washington, was arrested at home by a military force, and sent to Fort McHenry, and a provost marshal was appointed by General Banks, who had succeeded to the command. The excuse given for the arrest of Marshal Kane was that he was believed to be cognizant of combinations of men waiting for an opportunity to unite with those in rebellion against the United States government. Whether the suspicion was well or ill founded, it constituted a poor excuse for depriving a citizen of his liberty without legal warrant and without proof. But this was only the beginning of unbridled despotism and a reign of terror. The mayor and police commissioners, Charles Howard, William H. Gatchell, and John W. Davis, held a meeting, and after preparing a protest against the suspension of their functions in the appointment of a provost marshal, resolved that, while they would do nothing to "obstruct the execution of such measures as Major-General Banks may deem proper to take, on his own responsibility, for the preservation of the peace of the city and of public order, they can not, consistently with their views of official duty and of the obligations of their oaths of office, recognize the right of any of the officers and men of the police force, as such, to receive orders or directions from any other authority than from this Board; and that, in the opinion of the Board, the forcible suspension of their functions suspends at the same time the active operations of the police law."[2] The provost marshal, with the plenary powers conferred upon him, commenced a system of search and seizure, in private houses, of arms and munitions of every description.

On July 1st General Banks announced that "in pursuance of orders issued from the headquarters at Washington for the preservation of the public peace in this department, I have arrested, and do detain in custody of the United States, the late members of the Board of Police—Messrs. Charles Howard, William H. Gatchell, Charles D. Hinks, and John W. Davis." If the object had been to preserve order by any proper and legitimate method, the effective means would palpably have been to rely upon men whose influence was known to be great, and whose integrity was certainly unquestionable. The first-named of the commissioners I knew well. He was of an old Maryland family, honored for their public services, and himself adorned by every social virtue. Old, unambitious, hospitable, gentle, loving, he was beloved by the people among whom his long life had been passed. Could such a man be the just object of suspicion if, when laws had been silenced, suspicion could justify arrest and imprisonment? Those who knew him well accept as a just description:

> In action faithful, and in honor clear,
> Who broke no promise, served no private end,
> Who gained no title, and who lost no friend.

Thenceforward, arrests of the most illustrious became the rule. In a land where freedom of speech was held to be an unquestioned right, freedom of thought ceased to exist, and men were incarcerated for opinion's sake.

In the Maryland legislature, the Hon. S. Teacle Wallis, from a committee to whom was referred the memorial of the police commissioners arrested in Baltimore, made a report upon the unconstitutionality of the act, and "appealed in the most earnest manner to the whole people of the country, of all parties, sections, and opinions, to take warnings by the usurpations mentioned, and come to the rescue of the free institutions of the country."[3]

---

[2] *Baltimore American*, June 28, 1861.
[3] New York *World*, August 6, 1861.

For no better reason, so far as the public was informed, than a vote in favor of certain resolutions, General Banks sent his provost marshal to Frederick, where the legislature was in session; a cordon of pickets was placed around the town to prevent anyone from leaving it without a written permission from a member of General Banks's staff; police detectives from Baltimore then went into the town and arrested some twelve or thirteen members and several officers of the legislature, which, thereby left without a quorum, was prevented from organizing, and it performed the only act which it was competent to do, i.e., adjourned. S. Teacle Wallis, the author of the report in defense of the constitutional rights of citizens, was among those arrested. Henry May, a member of Congress, who had introduced a resolution which he hoped would be promotive of peace, was another of those arrested and thrown into prison. Senator Kennedy, of the same state, presented a report of the legislature to the United States Senate, reciting the outrage inflicted upon Maryland in the persons of her municipal officers and citizens, and, after some opposition, merely obtained an order to have it printed. Governor Hicks, whose promises had been so cheering in the beginning of the year, sent his final message to the legislature on December 3, 1861. In that, referring to the action of the Maryland legislature at its several sessions before that when the arrest of its members prevented an organization, he wrote, "This continued until the General Government had ample reason to believe it was about to go through the farce of enacting an ordinance of secession, when the treason was summarily stopped by the dispersion of the traitors. . . ." After referring to the elections of June 13th and November 6th he says the people have "declared, in the most emphatic tones, what I have never doubted, that Maryland has no sympathy with the rebellion, and desires to do her full share in the duty of suppressing it." It would be more easy than gracious to point out the inconsistency between his first statements and this last. The conclusion is inevitable that he kept himself in equipoise, and fell at last, as men without convictions usually do, upon the stronger side.

Henceforth the story of Maryland is sad to the last degree, only relieved by the gallant men who left their homes to fight the battle of state rights when Maryland no longer furnished them a field on which they could maintain the rights their fathers left them. This was a fate doubly sad to the sons of the heroic men who, under the designation of the "Maryland Line," did so much in our Revolutionary struggle to secure the independence of the states; of the men who, at a later day, fought the battle of North Point; of the people of a land which had furnished so many heroes and statesmen, and gave the great Chief Justice Taney to the Supreme Court of the United States.

Though Maryland did not become one of the Confederate States, she was endeared to the people thereof by many most enduring ties. Last in order, but first in cordiality, were the tender ministrations of her noble daughters to the sick and wounded prisoners who were carried through the streets of Baltimore; it is with shame we remember that brutal guards on several occasions inflicted wounds upon gentlewomen who approached these suffering prisoners to offer them the relief of which they so evidently stood in need.

The accumulation of Northern forces at and near Washington City, made it evident that the great effort of the invasion would be from that point, while assaults of more or less vigor might be expected upon all important places which the enemy, by his facilities for transportation, could reach. The concentration of Confederate troops in Virginia was begun, and they were sent forward as rapidly as practicable to the points threatened with attack.

It was soon manifest that, besides the army at Washington, which threatened Virginia, there was a second one at Chambersburg, Pennsylvania, under Major General Patterson, designed to move through Williamsport and Martinsburg, and another forming in Ohio, under the command of Major General McClellan, destined to invade the western counties of Virginia.

This latter force, having landed at Wheeling on May 26th, advanced as far as Grafton on the 29th. At this time Colonel Porterfield, with the small force of seven hundred men sent forward by Governor Letcher of Virginia, was at Philippi. On the night of June 2d he was attacked by General McClellan, with a strong force, and withdrew to Laurel Hill. Reënforcements under General Garnett were sent forward and occupied the hill, while Colonel Pegram, the second in command, held Rich Mountain. On July 11th the latter was attacked by two columns of the enemy, and after a vigorous defense, fell back on the 12th, losing many of his men, who were made prisoners. General Garnett, hearing of this reverse, attempted to fall back, but was pursued by McClellan, and while striving to rally his rear guard, was killed. Five hundred of his men were taken prisoners. This success left the Northern forces in possession of that region.

The difficult character of the country in which the battle was fought, as well from mountain acclivity as dense wood, rendered a minute knowledge of the roads of vast importance. There is reason to believe that competent guides led the enemy, by roads unknown to our army, to the flank and rear of its position, and thus caused the sacrifice of those who had patriotically come to repel the invasion of the very people who furnished the guides to the enemy. It was treachery confounding the counsels of the brave. Thus occurred the disaster of Rich Mountain and Laurel Hill.

General Robert Garnett was a native of Virginia and a graduate of the United States Military Academy. He served in Mexico, on the staff of General Z. Taylor, and was conspicuous for gallantry and good conduct, especially in the battles of Monterey and Buena Vista. Recognizing his allegiance as due to the state of Virginia, from which he was appointed a cadet, and thence won his various promotions in the army, he resigned his commission when the state withdrew from the Union, and earnestly and usefully served as aide-de-camp to General R. E. Lee, the commander in chief of the army of Virginia, until she acceded to the Confederacy.

When Western Virginia was invaded he offered his services to go to her defense, and relying confidently on the sentiment, so strong in his own heart, of devotion to the state by all Virginians, he believed it was only needful for him to have a nucleus around which the people could rally to resist the invasion of their country. How sadly he was disappointed, and how bravely he struggled against adverse fortune, and how gallantly he died in the discharge of his duty, are memories which, though sad, bear with them to his friends the consolation that the manner of his death was worthy of the way in which he lived, and that even his life was an offering he was not unwilling to make for the welfare and honor of Virginia.

He fell while commanding the rear guard, to save his retreating army, thus exemplifying the highest quality of man, self-sacrifice for others, and such devotion and fortitude as made Ney the grandest figure in Bonaparte's retreat from Moscow.

CHAPTER VI: *Removal of the Seat of Government to Richmond —Message to Congress at Richmond—Confederate Forces in Virginia—Forces of the Enemy—Letter to General Johnston —Combat at Bethel Church—Affair at Romney—Movements of McDowell—Battle of Manassas.*

THE provisional Congress, in session at Montgomery, Alabama, on May 21, 1861, resolved "that this Congress will adjourn on Tuesday next, to meet again on the 20th day of July at Richmond, Virginia." The resolution further authorized the President to have the several executive departments, with their archives, removed at such intermediate time as he might determine, and added a proviso that, if any public emergency should "render it impolitic to meet in Richmond," he should call the Congress together at some other place to be selected by him.

The hostile demonstrations of the United States government against Virginia caused the President, at an early day after the adjournment of Congress, to proceed to Richmond and to direct the executive departments, with their archives, to be removed to that place as soon as could be conveniently done.

In the message delivered to the Congress at its meeting in Richmond, according to adjournment, I gave the following explanation of my conduct under the resolution above cited: "Immediately after your adjournment, the aggressive movement of the enemy required prompt, energetic action. The accumulation of his forces on the Potomac sufficiently demonstrated that his efforts were to be directed against Virginia, and from no point could necessary measures for her defense and protection be so effectively decided as from her own capital."

On my arrival in Richmond, General R. E. Lee, as commander of the army of Virginia, was found there, where he had established his headquarters. He possessed my unqualified confidence, both as a soldier and a patriot, and the command he had exercised over the army of Virginia before her accession to the Confederacy, gave him that special knowledge which at the time was most needful. As has been already briefly stated, troops had previously been sent from other states of the Confederacy to the aid of Virginia. The forces there assembled were divided into three armies, at positions the most important and threatened: one, under General J. E. Johnston, at Harpers Ferry, covering the valley of the Shenandoah; another, under General P. G. T. Beauregard, at Manassas, covering the direct approach from Washington to Richmond; the third, under Generals Huger and Magruder, at Norfolk and on the peninsula between the James and York rivers, covering the approach to Richmond from the seaboard.

The first and second of these armies, though separated by the Blue Ridge, had such practicable communication with each other as to render their junction possible when the necessity should be foreseen. They both were confronted by forces greatly superior in numbers to their own, and it was doubtful which would first be the object of attack. Harpers Ferry was an important position, both for military and political considerations, and though unfavorably situated for defense against an enemy which should seek to turn its position by crossing the Potomac above, it was desirable to hold it as long as was consistent with safety. The temporary occupation was especially needful for the removal of the valuable machinery and material in the armory located there, which the enemy had failed to destroy, though he had for that purpose fired the buildings before his evacuation of the post. The demonstrations of General Patterson, commanding the Federal army in that region, caused General Johnston earnestly to insist on being allowed to retire to a position nearer to Winchester. Under these circumstances, an official letter was addressed to him, from which the following extract is made:

ADJUTANT AND INSPECTOR-GENERAL'S OFFICE,
RICHMOND, June 13, 1861.

To General J. E. JOHNSTON, *commanding Harpers Ferry, Virginia.*

SIR: . . . You had been heretofore instructed to exercise your discretion as to retiring from your position at Harpers Ferry, and taking the field to check the advance of the enemy. . . . The ineffective portion of your command, together with the baggage and whatever else would impede your operations in the field, it would be well to send, without delay, to the Manassas road. Should you not be sustained by the population of the Valley, so as to enable you to turn upon the enemy before reaching Winchester, you will continue slowly to retire to the Manassas road, upon some of the passes of which it is hoped you will be able to make an effective stand, even against a very superior force. To this end, it might be well to send your engineer to make a reconnaissance and construct such temporary works as may be useful and proper. . . . For these reasons it has been with reluctance that any attempt was made to give you specific instructions, and you will accept assurances of the readiness with which the freest exercise of discretion on your part will be sustained.

Very respectfully, your obedient servant,
(Signed)   S. COOPER,
Adjutant and Inspector-General.

The earliest combat in this quarter, which, in the inexperience of the time, was regarded as a great battle, may claim a passing notice, as exemplifying the extent to which the individuality, self-reliance, and habitual use of small arms by the people of the South was a substitute for military training, and, on the other hand, how the want of such training made the Northern new levies inferior to the like kind of Southern troops.

A detached work on the right of General Magruder's line was occupied June 11, 1861, by the First Regiment of North Carolina Volunteers and three hundred sixty Virginians under the command of an educated, vigilant, and gallant soldier, then Colonel D. H. Hill, First Regiment North Carolina Volunteers, subsequently a lieutenant general in the Confederate service. He reports that this small force was "engaged for five and a half hours with four and a half regiments of the enemy at Bethel Church, nine miles from Hampton. The enemy made three distinct and well-sustained charges, but were repulsed with heavy loss. Our cavalry pursued them for six miles, when their retreat became a total rout."

On the other side Frederick Townsend, colonel of the Third Regiment of the enemy's forces, after stating with much minuteness the orders and line of march, describes how, "about five or six miles from Hampton, a heavy and well-sustained fire of canister and small-arms was opened upon the regiment," and how it was afterward discovered to be a portion of their own column which had fired upon them. After due care for the wounded and a recognition of their friends, the column proceeded, and the colonel describes his regiment as moving to the attack "in line of battle, as if on parade, in the face of a severe fire of artillery and small-arms." Subsequently, the description proceeds, "a company of my regiment had been separated from the regiment by a thickly-hedged ditch," and marched in the adjoining field in line with the main body. Not being aware of the separation of that company, the colonel states that, therefore, "upon seeing among the breaks in the hedge the glistening of bayonets in the adjoining field, I immediately concluded that the enemy were outflanking, and conceived it to be my duty to immediately retire and repel that advance."[1]

Without knowing anything of the subsequent career of the colonel from whose report these extracts have been made, or of the officers who opened fire upon him while he was marching to the execution of the orders under which they were all acting, it is fair to suppose, after a few months' experience, such scenes as are described could not have

---

[1] See *Rebellion Record*, Vol. II, pp. 164, 165.

occurred, and these citations have been made to show the value of military training.

In further exemplification of the difference between the troops of the Confederate States and those of the United States, before either had been trained in war, I will cite an affair which occurred on the upper Potomac. Colonel A. P. Hill, commanding a brigade at Romney, in western Virginia, having learned that the enemy had a command at the twenty-first bridge on the Baltimore and Ohio Railroad, decided to attack it and to destroy the bridge, so as to interrupt the use of that important line of the enemy's communication. For this purpose he ordered Colonel John C. Vaughn of the Third Tennessee Volunteers to proceed with a detachment of two companies of his regiment and two companies of the Thirteenth Virginia Volunteers to the position where the enemy were reported to be posted.

Colonel Vaughn reports that on June 18, 1861, at 8 P.M., he moved with his command as ordered, marched eighteen miles, and at 5 A.M. the next morning found the enemy on the north bank of the Potomac in some strength of infantry and with two pieces of artillery. He had no picket guards.

After reconnaissance, the order to charge was given. It was necessary, in the execution of the order, to ford the river waist-deep, which Colonel Vaughn reports "was gallantly executed in good order but with great enthusiasm. As we appeared in sight at a distance of four hundred yards, the enemy broke and fled in all directions, firing as they ran only a few random shots. . . . The enemy did not wait to fire their artillery, which we captured, both guns loaded; they were, however, spiked by the enemy before he fled. From the best information, their number was between two and three hundred."

Colonel Vaughn further states that, in pursuance of orders, he fired the bridge and then retired, bringing away the two guns and the enemy's flag, and other articles of little value which had been captured, and arrived at brigade headquarters in the evening with his command in high spirits and good condition.

Colonel A. P. Hill, the energetic brigade commander who directed this expedition, left the United States army when the state, which had given him to the military service of the general government, passed her ordinance of secession. The vigilance and enterprise he manifested on this early occasion in the war of the states gave promise of the brilliant career which gained for him the high rank of a lieutenant general, and which there was nothing for his friends to regret save the honorable death which he met upon the field of battle.

Colonel Vaughn, the commander of the detachment, was new to war. His paths had been those of peace, and his home in the mountains of East Tennessee might reasonably have secured him from any expectation that it would ever be the theatre on which armies were to contend, and that he, in the mutation of human affairs, would become a soldier. He lived until the close of the war, and, on larger fields than that on which he first appeared, proved that, though not educated for a soldier, he had endowments which compensated for that disadvantage.

The activity and vigilance of Stuart, afterward so distinguished as commander of cavalry in the army of Virginia, and the skill and daring of Jackson, soon by greater deeds to become immortal, checked, punished, and embarrassed the enemy in his threatened advances, and his movements became so devoid of a definite purpose that one was at a loss to divine the object of his campaign, unless it was to detain General Johnston with his forces in the valley of the Shenandoah, while General McDowell, profiting by the feint, should make the real attack upon General Beauregard's army at Manassas. However that may be, the evidence finally became conclusive that the enemy under General McDowell was moving to attack the army under General Beauregard. The contingency had therefore arisen for that junction which was necessary to enable us to resist the vastly superior numbers of our assailant; for, though the most strenuous and not wholly unsuccessful exertion had been made to reënforce both the armies of the Shenandoah and of the Potomac, they yet remained far smaller than those of the enemy confronting them, and made a junction of our forces indispensable whenever the real point of attack should be ascertained. For this movement we had the advantage of an interior line, so that, if the enemy should discover it after it commenced, he could not counteract it by adopting the same tactics. The success of this policy, it will readily be perceived, depended upon the time of execution, for though from different causes, failure would equally result if done too soon or too late. The determination as to which army should be reënforced from the other, and the exact time of the transfer, must have been a difficult problem, as both the generals appear to have been unable to solve it (each asking reënforcements from the other).

On July 9th General Johnston wrote an official letter, from which I make the following extracts:

HEADQUARTERS, WINCHESTER, July 9, 1861.

GENERAL: . . . Similar information from other sources gives me the impression that the reënforcements arriving at Martinsburg amount to seven or eight thousand. I have estimated the enemy's force hitherto, you may remember, at eighteen thousand. Additional artillery has also been received. They were greatly superior to us in that arm before.

The object of reënforcing General Patterson must be an advance upon this place. Fighting here against great odds seems to me more prudent than retreat.

I have not asked for reënforcements, because I supposed that the War Department, informed of the state of affairs everywhere, could best judge where the troops at its disposal are most required. . . .

Most respectfully, your obedient servant,

(Signed)   JOSEPH E. JOHNSTON,
                                     Brigadier-General, etc.

If it is proposed to strengthen us against the attack I suggest as soon to be made, it seems to me that General Beauregard might with *great expedition* furnish five or six thousand men for a few days.   J. E. J.

As soon as I became satisfied that Manassas was the objective point of the enemy's movement, I wrote to General Johnston, urging him to make preparations for a junction with General Beauregard, and to his objections, and the difficulties he presented, replied at great length, endeavoring to convince him that the troops he described as embarrassing a hasty march might be withdrawn in advance of the more effective portion of his command. Writing with entire confidence, I kept no copy of my letters, and when subsequent events caused the wish to refer to them, I requested General Johnston to send me copies of them. He replied that his tent had been blown down, and his papers had been scattered. His letters to me, which would show the general purport of mine to him, have shared the fate which during or soon after the close of the war befell most of the correspondence I had preserved, and his retained copies, if still in his possession, do not appear to have been deemed of sufficient importance to be inserted in his published *Narrative.*

On July 17, 1861, the following telegram was sent by the adjutant general:

RICHMOND, July 17, 1861.

To General J. E. JOHNSTON, *Winchester, Virginia.*

General Beauregard is attacked. To strike the enemy a decisive blow, a junction of all your effective force will be needed. If practicable, make the movement, sending your sick and baggage to Culpepper Court-House, either by railroad or by Warrenton. In all the arrangements exercise your discretion.

(Signed)   S. COOPER.
                                     Adjutant and Inspector-General.

The confidence reposed in General Johnston, sufficiently evinced by the important command entrusted to him, was more than equal to the expectation that he would do all that was practicable to execute the order for a junction, as well as to secure his sick and baggage. For the execution of the one great purpose, that he would allow no minor question to interfere with that which was of vital importance, and for which he was informed all his "effective force" would "be needed."

The order referred to was the telegram inserted above, in which the sending the sick to Culpeper Court House might have been after or before the effective force had moved to the execution of the main and only positive part of the order.

All the arrangements were left to the discretion of the general. It seems strange that anyone has construed this expression as meaning that the movement for a junction was left to the discretion of that officer, and that the forming of a junction—the imperious necessity—should have been termed in the order "all the arrangement," instead of referring that word to its proper connection, the route and mode of transportation. The general had no margin on which to institute a comparison as to the importance of his remaining in the Valley, according to his previous assignment, or going where he was ordered by competent authority.

It gives me pleasure to state that, from all the accounts received at the time, the plans of General Johnston for masking his withdrawal to form a junction with General Beauregard were conducted with marked skill, and though all of his troops did not arrive as soon as expected and needed, he has satisfactorily shown that the failure was not due to any defect in his arrangements for their transportation.

The great question of uniting the two armies had been decided at Richmond. The time and place depended on the enemy, and, when it was seen that the real attack was to be against the position at Manassas, the order was sent to General Johnston to move to that point. His letters of the 12th and 15th instant expressed his doubts about his power to retire from before the superior force of General Patterson, therefore the word "practicable" was in this connection the equivalent of possible. That it was, at the time, so understood by General Johnston, is shown by his reply to the telegram.

HEADQUARTERS, WINCHESTER, July 18, 1861.

GENERAL: I have had the honor to receive your telegram of yesterday.

General Patterson, who had been at Bunker Hill since Monday, seems to have moved yesterday to Charlestown, twenty-three miles to the east of Winchester.

Unless he prevents it, we shall move toward General Beauregard to-day. . . .
(Signed)   JOSEPH E. JOHNSTON.
General S. COOPER.

After General Johnston commenced his march to Manassas, he sent to me a telegram, the substance of which, as my memory serves and the reply indicates, was an inquiry as to the relative position he would occupy toward General Beauregard. I returned the following answer:

RICHMOND, July 20, 1861.
General J. E. JOHNSTON, *Manassas Junction, Virginia.*

You are a general in the Confederate Army, possessed of the power attaching to that rank. You will know how to make the exact knowledge of Brigadier-General Beauregard, as well of the grounds as of the troops and preparation, avail for the success of the object in which you coöperate. The zeal of both assures me of harmonious action.
(Signed)   JEFFERSON DAVIS.

General Johnston, by his promotion to the grade of general, as well as his superior rank as a brigadier over Brigadier General Beauregard, gave him precedence; there was no need to ask which of the two would command the whole, when their troops should join and do duty together. Therefore his inquiry, as it was revolved in my mind, created an anxiety, not felt before, lest there should be some unfortunate complication, or misunderstanding, between these officers, when their forces should be united. Regarding the combat of July 18th as the precursor of a battle, I decided, at the earliest moment, to go in person to the army.

As has been heretofore stated, Congress was to assemble on July 20th to hold its first session at the new capital, Richmond, Virginia. My presence on that occasion and the delivery of a message were required by usage and law. After the delivery of the message to Congress on Saturday, July 20th I intended to leave in the afternoon for Manassas, but was detained until the next morning, when I left by rail, accompanied by my aide-de-camp, Colonel J. R. Davis, to confer with the generals on the field. As we approached Manassas railroad junction, a cloud of dust was visible a short distance to the west of the railroad. It resembled one raised by a body of marching troops, and recalled to my remembrance the design of General Beauregard to make the Rappahannock his second line of defense. It was, however, subsequently learned that the dust was raised by a number of wagons which had been sent to the rear for greater security against the contingencies of the battle. The sound of the firing had now become very distinct, so much so as to leave no doubt that a general engagement had commenced. Though that event had been anticipated as being near at hand after the action of the 18th, it was both hoped and desired that it would not occur quite so soon, the more so as it was not known whether the troops from the valley had yet arrived.

On reaching the railroad junction, I found a large number of men, bearing the usual evidence of those who leave the field of battle under a panic. They crowded around the train with fearful stories of a defeat of our army. The railroad conductor announced his decision that the railroad train should proceed no farther. Looking among those who were about us for one whose demeanor gave reason to expect from him a collected answer, I selected one whose gray beard and calm face gave best assurance. He, however, could furnish no encouragement. Our line, he said, was broken, all was confusion, the army routed, and the battle lost. I asked for Generals Johnston and Beauregard; he said they were on the field when he left it. I returned to the conductor and told him that I must go on; that the railroad was the only means by which I could proceed, and that, until I reached the headquarters, I could not get a horse to ride to the field where the battle was raging. He finally consented to detach the locomotive from the train, and, for my accommodation, to run it as far the army headquarters. In this manner Colonel Davis, aide-de-camp, and myself proceeded.

At the headquarters we found Quartermaster General W. L. Cabell and Adjutant General Jordan, of General Beauregard's staff, who courteously agreed to furnish us horses, and also to show us the route. While the horses were being prepared, Colonel Jordan took occasion to advise my aide-de-camp, Colonel Davis, of the hazard of going to the field, and the impropriety of such exposure on my part. The horses were after a time reported ready, and we started to the field. The stragglers soon became numerous, and warnings as to the fate which awaited us if we advanced were not only frequent but evidently sincere.

There were, however, many who turned back, and the wounded generally cheered upon meeting us. I well remember one, a mere stripling who, supported on the shoulders of a man who was bearing him to the rear, took off his cap and waved it with a cheer, that showed within that slender form beat the heart of a hero—breathed a spirit that would dare the labors of Hercules.

As we advanced the storm of that battle was rolling westward, and its fury became more faint. When I met General Johnston, who was upon a hill which commanded a general view of the field of the afternoon's operations, and inquired of him as to the state of affairs, he replied that we had won the battle. I left him there and rode still farther

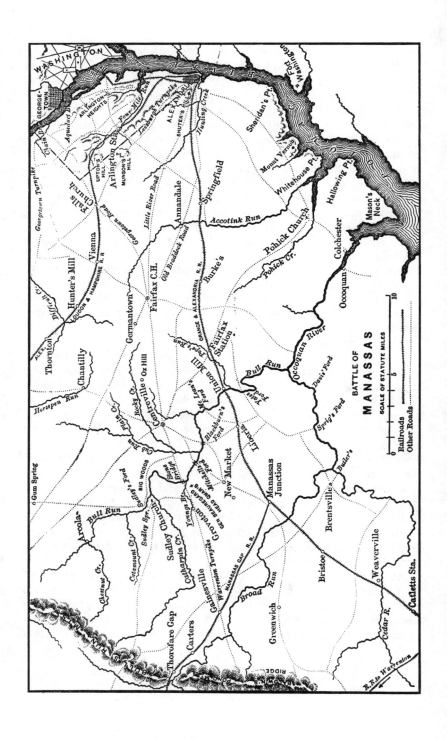

BATTLE OF
MANASSAS

SCALE OF STATUTE MILES

Railroads
Other Roads

to the west. Several of the volunteers on General Beauregard's staff joined me, and a command of cavalry, the gallant leader of which, Captain John F. Lay, insisted that I was too near the enemy to be without an escort. We saw, however, only one column near to us that created a doubt as to which side it belonged; as we were riding toward it, it was suggested that we should halt until it could be examined with a field glass. Colonel Chesnut dismounted so as the better to use his glass, and at that moment the column formed into line, by which the wind struck the flag so as to extend it, and it was plainly revealed to be that of the United States.

Our cavalry, though there was present but the squadron previously mentioned, and from a statement of the commander of which I will make some extracts, dashed boldly forward to charge. The demonstration was followed by the immediate retreat of what was, I believe, the last, thereabout, of the enemy's forces maintaining their organization, and showing a disposition to dispute the possession of the field of battle. In riding over the ground it seemed quite possible to mark the line of a fugitive's flight. Here was a musket, there a cartridge box, there a blanket or overcoat, a haversack, etc., as if the runner had stripped himself, as he went, of all impediments to speed.

As we approached toward the left of our line, the signs of an utter rout of the enemy were unmistakable, and justified the conclusion that the watchword of "On to Richmond!" had been changed to "Off for Washington!"

On the extreme left of our field of operations I found the troops whose opportune arrival had averted impending disaster, and had so materially contributed to our victory. Some of them had, after arriving at the Manassas railroad junction, hastened to our left; their brigadier general, E. K. Smith, was wounded soon after getting into action, and the command of the brigade devolved upon Elzy, by whom it was gallantly and skillfully led to the close of the battle; others, under the command of General (then Colonel) Early, made a rapid march, under the pressing necessity, from the extreme right of our line to and beyond our left, so as to attack the enemy in flank, thus inflicting on him the discomfiture his oblique movement was designed to inflict on us. All these troops and the others near to them had hastened into action without supplies or camp equipage; weary, hungry, and without shelter, night closed around them where they stood, the blood-stained victors on a hard-fought field.

It was reported to me that some of the troops had been so long without food as to be suffering severe hunger, and that no supplies could be got where they were. I made several addresses to them, all to the effect that their position was that best adapted to a pursuit of the enemy, and that they should therefore remain there; I added that I would go to headquarters and direct that supplies be sent to them promptly.

General (then Colonel) Early, commanding a brigade, informed me of some wounded who required attention; one, Colonel Gardner, was, he said, at a house not far from where we were. I rode to see him, and found him in severe pain; from the twitching, visible and frequent, he seemed to be threatened with tetanus. A man sat beside him whose uniform was that of the enemy; he was gentle, however, and appeared to be solicitously attentive. He said that he had no morphine, and did not know where to get any. I found in a short time a surgeon who went with me to Colonel Gardner, having the articles necessary in the case. Before leaving Colonel Gardner, he told me that the man who was attending to him might, without hindrance, have retreated with his comrades, but had kindly remained with him, and he therefore asked my protection for the man. I took the name and the state of the supposed good Samaritan, and at army headquarters directed that he should not be treated as a prisoner. The sequel will be told hereafter.

It was then late, and we rode back in the night, say seven miles, to the army headquarters. I had not seen General Beauregard on the field, and did not find him at his quarters when we returned; the promise made to the troops was therefore communicated to a staff officer, who said he would have the supplies sent out. At a later hour when I met General Beauregard and informed him of what had occurred, he stated that, because of a false alarm which had reached him, he had ordered the troops referred to from the left to the right of our line, so as to be in position to repel the reported movement of the enemy against that flank. That such an alarm should have been credited, and a night march ordered on account of it, shows how little the completeness of the victory was realized.

CHAPTER VII: *Conference with the Generals After the Battle —Order to Pursue the Enemy—Evidences of a Thorough Rout —"Sweet to Die for Such a Cause"—Movements of the Next Day—What More it was Practicable to do—Charge Against the President of Preventing the Capture of Washington—The Failure to Pursue—Reflection on the President—General Beauregard's Report—Endorsement upon it—Strength of the Opposing Forces—Extracts Relating to the Battle, from the Narrative of General Early—Resolutions of Congress—Efforts to Increase the Efficiency of the Army.*

AT A late hour of the night I had a conference with Generals Johnston and Beauregard; the adjutant general of the latter, Colonel Jordan, was present, and sat opposite me at the table.

When, after some preliminary conversation, I asked whether any troops had been sent in pursuit of the enemy, I was answered in the negative. Upon further inquiry as to what troops were in the best position for pursuit, and had been least fatigued during the day, General Bonham's brigade was named. I then suggested that he should be ordered in pursuit; a pause ensued, until Colonel Jordan asked me if I would dictate the order. I at once dictated an order for immediate pursuit. Some conversation followed, the result of which was a modification of the order by myself, so that, instead of immediate pursuit, it should be commenced at early dawn. Colonel Jordan spoke across the table to me, saying, "If you will send the order as you first dictated it, the enemy won't stop till he gets into the Potomac." I believe I remember the words very nearly, and am quite sure that I do remember them substantially. On March 25, 1878, I wrote to General Beauregard as follows:

DEAR SIR: Permit me to ask you to recall the conference held between General Johnston, yourself, and myself, on the night after the close of the battle of Manassas; and to give me, if you can, a copy of the order which I dictated, and which your adjutant-general, T. J. Jordan, wrote at my dictation, directing Brigadier-General Bonham to follow the retreating enemy. If you can not furnish a copy of the order, please give me your recollection of its substance.

Yours respectfully,
(Signed)   JEFFERSON DAVIS.

To this letter General Beauregard courteously replied that his order book was in New York, in the hands of a friend, to whom he would write for a copy of the order desired if it should be in said book, and that he would also write to his adjutant, General Jordan, for his recollection of the order if it had not been inscribed in the order book.

On April 24th General Beauregard forwarded to me the answer to his inquiries in my behalf, as follows:

NEW YORK, 63 BROADWAY, April 18, 1878.

MY DEAR GENERAL: In answer to your note, I hasten to say that properly Mr. Davis is not to be held accountable for our failure to pursue McDowell from the field of Manassas the night of the 21st of July, 1861.

As to the order, to which I presume Mr. Davis refers in his note to you, I recollect the incident very distinctly.

The night of the battle, as I was about to ascend to your quarters over my office, Captain E. P. Alexander, of your staff, informed me that Captain ——, attached to General Johnston's Army of the Shenandoah, reported that he had been as far forward as Centreville, where he had seen the Federal army completely routed and in full flight toward Washington.

This statement I at once repeated to Mr. Davis, General Johnston, and yourself, whom I found seated around your table—Mr. Davis at the moment writing a dispatch to General Cooper.

As soon as I had made my report, Mr. Davis with much animation asserted the necessity for an urgent pursuit that night by Bonham, who, with his own brigade and that of Longstreet, was in close proximity to Centreville at the moment. So I took my seat at the same table with you, and wrote the order for pursuit, substantially at the dictation of Mr. Davis. But, while writing, either I happened to remember, or Captain Alexander himself—as I am inclined to believe—called me aside to remind me that his informant was known among us of the old army as —— ——, because of eccentricities, and in contradistinction with others of the same name. When I repeated this reminder, Mr. Davis recalled the *sobriquet*, as he had a precise personal knowledge of the officers of the old army. He laughed heartily, as did all present.

The question of throwing General Bonham forward that night, upon the unverified report of Captain ——, was now briefly discussed, with a unanimous decision against it; therefore, the order was not dispatched.

It is proper to add in this connection that, so far as I am aware—and I had the opportunity of knowing what occurred—this was the only instance during Mr. Davis's stay at Manassas in which he exercised any voice as to the movement of the troops. Profoundly pleased with the results achieved by the happy juncture of the two Confederate armies upon the very field of battle, his bearing toward the generals who commanded them was eminently proper, as I have testified on a former occasion; and, I repeat, he certainly expressed or manifested no opposition to a forward movement, nor did he display the least disposition to interfere by opinion or authority touching what the Confederate forces should or should not do.

You having at the close of the day surrendered the command, which had been left in your hands, over both Confederate armies during the engagement, General

Johnston was that night in chief command. He was decidedly averse to an immediate offensive, and emphatically discountenanced it as impracticable.

Very truly your friend,

(Signed)   THOMAS JORDAN.

General P. G. T. BEAUREGARD, *New Orleans, Louisiana.*

General Beauregard, in his letter forwarding the above, wrote, "The account given herewith by General Jordan of what occurred there respecting further pursuit that night agrees with my own recollection."

It was a matter of importance, as I regarded it, to follow closely on the retreating enemy, but it was of no consequence then or now as to who issued the order for pursuit, and unless requested, I should not have dictated one, preferring that the generals to whom the operations were confided should issue all orders to the troops. I supposed the order, as modified by myself, had been sent. I have found, however, since the close of the war, that it was not, but that an order to the same effect was sent on the night of July 21st, for a copy of which I am indebted to the kindness of that chivalrous gentleman, soldier, and patriot, General Bonham. It is as follows:

HEADQUARTERS ARMY OF THE POTOMAC,
MANASSAS, July 21, 1861.

(SPECIAL ORDERS, No. 140.)

I. General Bonham will send, as early as practicable in the morning, a command of two of his regiments of infantry, a strong force of cavalry, and one field-battery, to scour the country and roads to his front, toward Centreville. He will carry with him abundant means of transportation for the collection of our wounded, all the arms, ammunition, and abandoned hospital stores, subsistence, and baggage, which will be sent immediately to these headquarters.

General Bonham will advance with caution, throwing out an advanced guard and skirmishers on his right and left, and the utmost caution must be taken to prevent firing into our own men.

Should it appear, while this command is occupied as directed that it is insufficient for the purposes indicated, General Bonham will call on the nearest brigade commander for support.

II. Colonel P. St. George Cocke, commanding, will dispatch at the same time, for similar purposes, a command of the same size and proportions of infantry, artillery, and cavalry on the road via Stone Bridge; and another command of two companies of infantry and one of cavalry on the road by which the enemy retreated toward and *via* Sudley's Mills.

By command of Brigadier-General Beauregard:

(Signed)   THOMAS JORDAN, *A. A. Adjutant-General.*

To Brigadier-General BONHAM.

Impressed with the belief that the enemy was very superior to us, both in numbers and appointments, I had felt apprehensive that, unless pressed, he would recover from the panic under which he fled from the field, rally on his reserves, and renew the contest. Therefore it was that I immediately felt the necessity for a pursuit of the fugitives, and insisted that the troops on the extreme left should retain their position during the night of the 21st, as has been heretofore stated. In conference with the generals that night, this subject was considered, and I dictated an order for a movement on the rear of the enemy at early dawn, which, on account of the late hour at which it was given, differed very little from one for an immediate movement. A rainfall, extraordinary for its violence and duration, occurred on the morning of the succeeding day, so that, over places where during the battle one could scarcely get a drink of water, rolled torrents which, in the afternoon of the 22d, it was difficult to cross.

From these and other causes, the troops were scattered to such an extent that but few commands could have been assembled for immediate service. It was well for us that the enemy, instead of retiring in order, so as to be rallied and again brought to the attack, left hope behind and fled in dismay to seek for safety beyond the Potomac.

Each hour of the day following the battle added to the evidence of a thorough rout of the enemy. Abandoned wagons, stores, guns, caissons, small arms, and ammunition proved his complete demoralization. As far as our cavalry went, no hostile force was met, and all the indications favored the conclusion that the purpose of invasion had for the time been abandoned.

The victory, though decisive and important, both in its moral and physical effect, had been dearly bought by the sacrifice of the lives of many of our bravest and best, who at the first call of their country had rushed to its defense.

When riding to the front, I met an ambulance bearing General Barnard Bee from the field, where he had been mortally wounded, after his patriotism had been illustrated by conspicuous exhibitions of skill, daring, and fortitude. Soon after, I learned that my friend Colonel Bartow had heroically sealed with his life blood his faith in the sanctity of our cause. He had been the chairman of the Committee on Military Affairs in the provisional Congress, and, after the laws were enacted to provide for the public defense, he went to the field to maintain them. It is to such virtuous and devoted citizens that a country is indebted for its prosperity and honor, as well in peace as in war.

Reference has been made to the dispersion of our troops after the battle, and in this connection the following facts are mentioned: in the afternoon of the 22d, with a guide supposed to be cognizant of the positions at which the different commands would be found, I went to visit the wounded, and among them a youth of my family, who, it was reported to me, was rapidly sinking. After driving many miles, and witnessing very painful scenes, but seldom finding the troops in the position where my guide supposed them to be, and always disappointed in not discovering him I particularly sought, I was, at the approach of night, about to abandon the search, when, accidentally meeting an officer of the command to which the youth belonged, I was directed to the temporary hospital to which the wounded of that command had been removed. It was too late; the soul of the young soldier had just left his body; the corpse lay before me. Around him were many gentle boys, suffering in different degrees from the wounds they had received. One bright, refined-looking youth from South Carolina, severely if not fatally wounded, responded to my expression of sympathy by the heroic declaration that it was "sweet to die for such a cause."

Many kindred spirits ascended to the Father from that field of their glory. The roll need not be recorded here; it has a more enduring depository than the pen can make—the traditions of a grateful people.

The victory at Manassas was certainly extraordinary, not only on account of the disparity of numbers and the inferiority of our arms, but also because of many other disadvantages under which we labored. We had no disciplined troops, and though our citizens were generally skilled in the use of small arms, which, with their high pride and courage, might compensate for the want of training while in position, these inadequately substituted military instruction when manœuvres had to be performed under fire, and could not make the old-fashioned musket equal to the long-range, new-model muskets with which the enemy was supplied. The disparity in artillery was still greater, both in the number and kind of guns; thanks to the skill and cool courage of the Reverend Captain W. N. Pendleton, his battery of light, smooth-bore guns, manned principally by the youths whose rector he had been, proved more effective in battle than the long-range rifle-guns of the enemy. The character of the ground brought the forces into close contact, and the ricochet of the round balls carried havoc into the columns of the enemy, while the bolts of their rifle-guns, if they missed their object, penetrated harmlessly into the ground.

The field was very extensive, broken, and wooded. The senior general had so recently arrived that he had no opportunity minutely to learn the ground, and the troops he brought were both unacquainted with the field and with those with whom they had to coöperate. To all this must be added the disturbing fact that the plan of battle, as originally designed, was entirely changed by the movement of the enemy on our extreme left, instead of right and center, as anticipated. The operations, therefore, had to be conducted against the plan of the enemy, instead of on that which our generals had prepared and explained to their subordinate commanders. The promptitude with which the troops moved, and the readiness with which our generals modified their preconceived plans to meet the necessities as they were developed, entitled them to the commendation so liberally bestowed at the time by their countrymen at large.

General Johnston had been previously promoted to the highest grade in our army, and I deemed it but a fitting reward for the services rendered by General Beauregard that he should be promoted to the same grade; therefore I addressed to him the following letter:

MANASSAS, VIRGINIA, July 21, 1861.

SIR: Appreciating your services in the battle of Manassas, and on several other as a commander, your gallantry as a soldier, and your zeal as a patriot, you are promoted to be a general in the army of the Confederate States of America, and, with the consent of the Congress, will be duly commissioned accordingly.

Yours, etc.,

(Signed)   JEFFERSON DAVIS.
General P. G. T. BEAUREGARD, etc.

The 22d, the day after the battle, was spent in following up the line of the retreating foe and collecting the large supplies of arms, of ammunition, and other military stores. The supplies of the army were on a scale of such luxurious extravagance as to excite the surprise of those accustomed only to our rigid economy. The anticipation of an easy victory had caused many to come to the battle as to a joyous feast, and the signs left behind them of the extent to which they had been disappointed in the entertainment, constituted the staple of many laughable stories, which were not without their value because of the lesson they contained as to the uncertainties of war and the mortification that usually follows vain boasting. Among the articles abandoned by the enemy in his flight were some which excited a just indignation, and which indicated the shameless disregard of all the usages of honorable warfare. They were handcuffs, the fit appendage of a policeman, but not of a soldier who came to meet his foeman hilt to hilt. These were reported to have been found in large numbers; some of them were sent to Richmond.

On the night of the 22d I held a second conference with Generals Johnston and Beauregard. All the revelations of the day were of the most satisfactory character as to the completeness of our victory. The large amount gained of fine artillery, small arms, and ammunition, all of which were much needed by us, was not the least gratifying consequence of our success. The generals, like myself, were well content with what had been done.

I propounded to them the inquiry as to what more it was practicable to do. They concurred as to their inability to cross the Potomac, and to the further inquiry as to an advance to the south side of the Potomac, General Beauregard promptly stated that there were strong fortifications there, occupied by garrisons, which had not been in the battle, and were therefore not affected by the panic which had seized the defeated army. He described those fortifications as having wide, deep ditches, with palisades, which would prevent the escalade of the works. Turning to General Johnston, he said, "They have spared no expense." It was further stated in explanation that we had no sappers and miners, nor even the tools requisite to make regular approaches. If we had possessed both, the time required for such operations would have more than sufficed for General Patterson's army and other forces to have been brought to that locality in such numbers as must have rendered the attempt, with our present means, futile.

This view of the matter rests on the supposition that the fortifications and garrisons described did actually exist, of which there seemed then to be no doubt. If the reports which have since reached us be true, that there were at that time neither fortifications nor troops stationed on the south bank of the Potomac; that all the enemy's forces fled to the north side of the river, and even beyond; that the panic of the routed army infected the whole population of Washington city; that no preparation was made, or even contemplated, for the destruction of the bridge across the Potomac—then it may have been, as many have asserted, that our army, following close upon the flying enemy, could have entered and taken possession of the United States capital. These reports, however, present a condition of affairs altogether at variance with the information on which we had to act. Thus it was, and so far as I knew, for the reasons above stated, that an advance to the south bank of the Potomac was not contemplated as the immediate sequence of the victory at Manassas. What discoveries would have been made and what results would have ensued from the establishment of our guns upon the south bank of the river, to open fire upon the capital, are speculative questions upon which it would be useless to enter.

After the conference of the 22d, and because of it, I decided to return to Richmond and employ all the power of my office to increase the strength of the army, so as to better enable it to meet the public need, whether in offensive-defensive or purely defensive operations, as opportunity should offer for the one, or the renewal of invasion require the other.

A short time subsequent to my return, a message was brought to me from the prison, to the effect that a noncommissioned officer, captured at Manassas, claimed to have a promise of protection from me. The name given was Hulburt of Connecticut. I had forgotten the name he gave when I saw him; but, believing that I would recognize the person who had attended to Colonel Gardner, and to whom only such a promise had been given, the officer in charge was directed to send him to me. When he came, I had no doubt of his identity, and explained to him that I had directed that he should not be treated as a prisoner, but that, in the multitude of those wearing the same uniform as his, some neglect or mistake had arisen, for which I was very sorry, and that he should be immediately released and sent down the river to the neighborhood of Fortress Monroe, where he would be among his own people. He then told me that he had a sister residing a few miles in the country, whom he would be very glad to visit. Permission was given him to do so, and a time fixed at which he was to report for transportation; so he left, with manifestations of thankfulness for the kindness with which he had been treated. In due time a newspaper was received, containing an account of his escape, and how he had lingered about the suburbs of Richmond and made drawings of the surrounding fortifications. The treachery was as great as if his drawings had been valuable, which they could not have been, as we had only then commenced the detached works which were designed as a system of defenses for Richmond.

When the smoke of battle had lifted from the field of Manassas, and the rejoicing over the victory had spread over the land and spent its exuberance, some who, like Job's war horse, "sniffed the battle from afar," but in whom the likeness there ceased, censoriously asked why the fruits of the victory had not been gathered by the capture of Washington city. Then some indiscreet friends of the generals commanding in that battle, instead of the easier task of justification, chose the harder one of exculpation for the imputed failure. Their ill-advised zeal, combined perhaps with malice against me, induced the allegation that the President had prevented the generals from making an immediate and vigorous pursuit of the routed enemy.

This, as other stories had been, was left to the correction which time it was hoped would bring, the sooner because it was expected to be refuted by the reports of the commanding generals with whom I had conferred on that subject immediately after the battle.

After considerable time had elapsed, it was reported to me that a member of Congress, who had served on that occasion as a volunteer aide to General Beauregard, had stated in the House of Representatives that I had prevented the pursuit of the enemy after his defeat at Manassas.

This gave to the rumor such official character and dignity as seemed to me to entitle it to notice not theretofore given, wherefore I addressed to General Johnston the following inquiry, which, though restricted in its terms to the allegation, was of such tenor as left it to his option to state all the facts connected with the slander, if he should choose to do me that justice, or should see the public interest involved in the correction, which, as stated in my letter to him, was that which gave it in my estimation its claim to consideration, and had caused me to address him on the subject:

RICHMOND, VIRGINIA, November 3, 1861.

General J. E. JOHNSTON, *commanding Department of the Potomac.*

SIR: Reports have been, and are being, widely circulated to the effect that I prevented General Beauregard from pursuing the enemy after the battle of Manassas, and had subsequently restrained him for advancing upon Washington City. Though such statements may have been made merely for my injury, and in that view might be postponed to a more convenient season, they have acquired importance from the fact that they have served to create distrust, to excite disappointment, and must embarrass the Administration in its further efforts to reenforce the armies of the Potomac, and generally to provide for the public defense. For these public considerations, I call upon you, as the commanding general, and as a party to all the conferences held by me on the 21st and 22d of July, to say whether I obstructed the pursuit of the enemy after the victory of Manassas, or have ever objected to an advance or other active operation which it was feasible for the army to undertake.

Very respectfully, yours, etc.,

(Signed)   JEFFERSON DAVIS.

HEADQUARTERS, CENTREVILLE, November 10, 1861.

To his Excellency the President.

SIR: I have had the honor to receive your letter of the 3d inst., in which you call upon me, as the commanding general, and as a party to all the conferences held by you on the 21st and 22d of July, to say whether you obstructed the pursuit after the victory of Manassas, or have ever objected to an advance or other active operation which it was feasible for the army, to undertake?

To the first question I reply, No. The pursuit was "obstructed" by the enemy's troops at Centreville, as I have stated in my official report. In that report I have also said why no advance was made upon the enemy's capital (for reasons) as follows:

The apparent freshness of the United States troops at Centreville, which checked our pursuit; the strong forces occupying the works near Georgetown, Arlington, and Alexandria; the certainty, too, that General Patterson, if needed, would reach Washington with his army of more than thirty thousand sooner than we could; and the condition and inadequate means of the army in ammunition, provisions, and transportation, prevented any serious thoughts of advancing against the capital.

To the second question I reply that it has never been feasible for the army to advance farther than it has done—to the line of Fairfax Court-House, with its advanced posts at Upton's, Munson's, and Mason's Hills. After a conference at Fairfax Court-House with the three senior general officers, you announced it to be impracticable to give this army the strength which those officers considered necessary to enable it to assume the offensive. Upon which I drew it back to its present position.

Most respectfully, your obedient servant,

(Signed)   J. E. JOHNSTON.

This answer to my inquiry was conclusive as to the charge which had been industriously circulated that I had prevented the immediate pursuit of the enemy, and had obstructed active operations after the battle of Manassas, and thus had caused the failure to reap the proper fruits of the victory.

No specific inquiry was made by me as to the part I took in the conferences of July 21st and 22d, but a general reference was made to them. The entire silence of General Johnston in regard to those conferences is noticeable from the fact that, while his answer was strictly measured by the terms of my inquiry as to pursuit, he added a statement about a conference at Fairfax Court House, which occurred in the autumn, say October, and could have had no relation to the question of pursuit of the enemy after the victory of Manassas, or other active operations therewith connected. The reasons stated in my letter for making an inquiry naturally pointed to the conferences of July 21st and 22d, but surely not to a conference held months subsequent to the battle, and on a question quite different from that of hot pursuit. In regard to the matter of this subsequent conference I shall have more to say hereafter.

I left the field of Manassas proud of the heroism of our troops in battle, and of the conduct of the officers who led them. Anxious to recognize the claim of the army on the gratitude of the country, it was my pleasing duty to bear testimony to their merit in every available form. Those who left the field and did not return to share its glory, it was wished, should only be remembered as exceptions proving a rule.

With all the information possessed at the time by the commanding generals, the propriety of maintaining our position, while seeking objects more easily attained than the capture of the United States capital, seemed to me so demonstrable as to require no other justification than the statements to which I have referred in connection with the conference of July 22d. It would have seemed to me then, as it does now, to be less than was due to the energy and fortitude of our troops, to plead a want of transportation and supplies for a march of about twenty miles through a country which had not then been denuded by the ravages of war.

Under these impressions, and with such feelings, I wrote to General Beauregard as follows:

RICHMOND, VIRGINIA, August 4, 1861.

General BEAUREGARD, *Manassas, Virginia.*

MY DEAR SIR: . . . I think you are unjust to yourself in putting your failure to pursue the enemy to Washington to the account of short supplies of subsistence and transportation. Under the circumstances of our army, in the absence of the knowledge since acquired, if indeed the statements be true, it would have been extremely hazardous to have done more than was performed. You will not fail to remember that, so far from knowing that the enemy was routed, a large part of our forces was moved by you, in the night of the 21st, to repel a supposed attack upon our right, and that the next day's operations did not fully reveal what has since been reported of the enemy's panic. Enough was done for glory, and the measure of duty was full; let us rather show the untaught that their desires are unreasonable, than, by dwelling on possibilities recently developed, give form and substance to the criticisms always easy to those who judge after the event.

With sincere esteem, I am your friend,

(Signed)   JEFFERSON DAVIS.

I had declared myself content and gratified with the conduct of the troops and the officers, and supposed the generals, in recognition of my efforts to aid them by increasing their force and munitions, as well as by my abstinence from all interference with them upon the field, would have neither cause nor motive to reflect upon me in their reports, and it was with equal surprise and regret that in this I found myself mistaken. General Johnston, in his report, represented the order to him to make a junction with General Beauregard as a movement left to his discretion, with the condition that, if made, he should first send his sick and baggage to Culpeper Court House. I felt constrained to put upon his report when it was received the following endorsement:

The telegram referred to by General Johnston in this report as received by him about one o'clock on the morning of the 18th of July is inaccurately reported. The following is a copy:

"RICHMOND, July 17, 1861.

"General J. E. JOHNSTON, *Winchester, Virginia.*

"General Beauregard is attacked. To strike the enemy a decisive blow, a junction of all your effective force will be needed. If practicable, make the movement, sending your sick and baggage to Culpepper Court-House, either by railroad or by Warrenton. In all the arrangements, exercise your discretion.

"S. COOPER, *Adjutant and Inspector-General.*

The word "after" is not found in the dispatch before the words "sending your sick," as is stated in the report; so that the argument based on it requires no comment. The order to move "if practicable" had reference to General Johnston's letters of the 12th and 15th of July, representing the relative strength and positions of the enemy under Patterson and of his own forces to be such as to make it doubtful whether General Johnston had the power to effect the movement.

Upon the receipt of General Beauregard's report of the battle of Manassas, I found that it contained matter which seemed to me out of place, and therefore addressed to him the following letter:

RICHMOND, VIRGINIA, October 30, 1861.

General BEAUREGARD, *Manassas, Virginia.*

SIR: Yesterday my attention was called to various newspaper publications purporting to have been sent from Manassas, and to be a synopsis of your report of the battle of the 21st of July last, and in which it is represented that you have been overruled by me in your plan for a battle with the enemy south of the Potomac for the capture of Baltimore and Washington, and the liberation of Maryland.

I inquired for your long-expected report, and it has been today submitted to my inspection. It appears, by official endorsement, to have been received by the Adjutant-General on the 18th of October, though it is dated August 26, 1861.

With much surprise I found that the newspaper statements were sustained by the text of your report. I was surprised, because, if we did differ in opinion as to the measure and purposes of contemplated campaigns, such fact could have no appropriate place in the report of a battle; further, because it seemed to be an attempt to exalt yourself at my expense; and, especially, because no such plan as that described was submitted to me. It is true that, some time before it was ordered, you expressed a desire for the junction of General Johnston's army with your own. The movement was postponed until the operations of the enemy rendered it necessary, and until it became thereby practicable to make it with safety to the Valley of Virginia. Hence, I believe, was secured the success by which it was attended.

If you have retained a copy of the plan of campaign which you say was submitted to me through Colonel Chesnut, allow me to request that you will furnish me with a duplicate of it.

Very respectfully yours, etc.,

(Signed)   JEFFERSON DAVIS.

As General Beauregard did not think proper to omit that portion of his report to which objection was made, it necessitated, when the entire report was transmitted to Congress, the placing of an endorsement upon it, reviewing that part of the report which I considered objectionable. The Congress, in its discretion, ordered the publication of the report, except that part to which the endorsement referred, thereby judiciously suppressing both the endorsement and the portion of the report to which it related. In this case, and every other official report ever submitted to me, I made neither alteration nor erasure.

That portion of the report which was suppressed by the Congress has, since the war, found its way into the press, but the endorsement which belonged to it has not been published. As part of the history of the time, I will here present both in their proper connection:

General S. COOPER, *Adjutant and Inspector-General, Richmond, Virginia.*

Before entering upon a narration of the general military operations in the presence of the enemy on July 21st, I propose—I hope not unreasonably—first to recite certain events which belong to the strategy of the campaign, and consequently form an essential part of the history of the battle.

Having become satisfied that the advance of the enemy with a decidedly superior force, both as to numbers and war equipage, to attack or turn my position in this quarter was immediately impending, I dispatched, on July 13th, one of my staff, Colonel James Chesnut, of South Carolina, to submit for the consideration of the President a plan of operations substantially as follows:

I proposed that General Johnston should unite, as soon as possible, the bulk of the Army of the Shenandoah with that of the Potomac, then under my command, leaving only sufficient force to garrison his strong works at Winchester, and to guard the five defensive passes of the Blue Ridge, and thus hold Patterson in check. At the same time Brigadier-General Holmes was to march hither with all of his command not essential for the defense of the position of Acquia Creek. These junctions having been effected at Manassas, an immediate, impetuous attack of our combined armies upon General McDowell was to follow, as soon as he approached my advanced position, at and around Fairfax Court-House, with the inevitable result, as I submitted, of his complete defeat, and the destruction or capture of his army. This accomplished, the Army of the Shenandoah, under General Johnston, increased with a part of my forces and rejoined as he returned by the detachment left to hold the mountain-passes, was to march back rapidly into the Valley, fall upon and crush Patterson with a superior force, wheresoever he might be found. This, I confidently estimated, could be achieved within fifteen days after General Johnston should march from Winchester for Manassas.

Meanwhile, I was to occupy the enemy's works on this side of the Potomac, if, as I anticipated, he had been so routed as to enable me to enter them with him or, if not, to retire again for a time within the lines of Bull Run with my main force. Patterson having been virtually destroyed, then General Johnston would reenforce General Garnett sufficiently to make him superior to his opponent (General McClellan) and able to defeat that officer. This done, General Garnett was to form an immediate junction with General Johnston, who was forthwith to cross the Potomac into Maryland with his whole force, arouse the people as he advanced to the recovery of their political rights, and the defense of their homes and families from an offensive invader, and then march to the investment of Washington, in the rear, while I resumed the offensive in front. This plan of operations, you are aware, was not acceptable at the time, from considerations which appeared so weighty as to more than counterbalance its proposed advantages. Informed of these views, and of the decision of the War Department, I then made my preparations for the stoutest practicable defense of the line of Bull Run, the enemy having developed his purpose, by the advance on and occupation of Fairfax Court-House, from which my advance brigade had been withdrawn.

The War Department having been informed by me, by telegraph on July 17th, of the movement of General McDowell, General Johnston was immediately ordered to form a junction of his army corps with mine, should the movement in his judgment be deemed advisable. General Holmes was also directed to push forward with two regiments, a battery, and one company of cavalry.[1]

ENDORSEMENT

The order issued by the War Department to General Johnston was not, as herein reported, to form a junction, "should the movement in his judgment be deemed advisable." The following is an accurate copy of the order:

"General Beauregard is attacked. To strike the enemy a decisive blow, a junction of all your effective force will be needed. If practicable, make the movement, sending your sick and baggage to Culpepper Court-House, either by railroad or by Warrenton. In all the arrangements, exercise your discretion."

The words "if practicable" had reference to letters of General Johnston of the 12th and 15th of July, which made it extremely doubtful if he had the power to make the movement, in view of the relative strength and position of Patterson's forces as compared with his own.

The plan of campaign reported to have been submitted, but not accepted, and to have led to a decision of the War Department, can not be found among its files, nor any reference to any decision made upon it; and it was not known that the army had advanced beyond the line of Bull Run, the position previously selected by General Lee, and which was supposed to have continued to be the defensive line occupied by the main body of our forces. Inquiry has developed the fact that a message, to be verbally delivered, was sent by Hon. Mr. Chesnut. If the conjectures recited in the report were entertained, they rested on the accomplishment of one great condition, namely, that a junction of the forces of Generals Johnston and Holmes should be made with the army of General Beauregard and should gain a victory. The junction was made, the victory was won; but the consequences that were predicted did not result. The reasons why no such consequences could result are given in the closing passages of the reports of both the commanding generals, and the responsibility can not be transferred to the Government at Richmond, which certainly would have united in any feasible plan to accomplish such desirable results.

If the plan of campaign mentioned in the report had been presented in a written communication, and in sufficient detail to permit proper investigation, it must have been pronounced to be impossible at that time, and its proposal could only have been accounted for by the want of information of the forces and positions of the armies in the field. The facts that rendered it impossible are the following:

[1] The foregoing was copied from *The Land we Love,* for February, 1867 (Vol. II, No. 4).

1. It was based, as related from memory by Colonel Chesnut, on the supposition of drawing a force of about twenty-five thousand men from the command of General Johnston. The letters of General Johnston show his effective force to have been only eleven thousand, with an enemy thirty thousand strong in his front, ready to take possession of the Valley of Virginia on his withdrawal.

2. It proposed to continue operations by effecting a junction of a part of the victorious forces with the army of General Garnett in Western Virginia. General Garnett's forces amounted only to three or four thousand men, then known to be in rapid retreat before vastly superior forces under McClellan, and the news that he was himself killed and his army scattered arrived within forty-eight hours of Colonel Chesnut's arrival in Richmond.

3. The plan was based on the improbable and inadmissible supposition that the enemy was to await everywhere, isolated and motionless, until our forces could effect junctions to attack them in detail.

4. It could not be expected that any success obtainable on the battle-field would enable our forces to carry the fortifications on the Potomac, garrisoned, and within supporting distance of fresh troops; nor after the actual battle and victory did the generals on the field propose an advance on the capital, nor does it appear that they have since believed themselves in a condition to attempt such a movement.

It is proper also to observe that there is no communication on file in the War Department, as recited at the close of the report, showing what were the causes which prevented the advance of our forces and prolonged, vigorous pursuit of the enemy to and beyond the Potomac.

(Signed)   JEFFERSON DAVIS.

It has not been my purpose to describe the battles of the war. To the reports of the officers serving on the field, in the armies of both governments, the student of history must turn for knowledge of the details, and it will be the task of the future historian, from comparison of the whole, to deduce the truth.

It is fortunate for the cause of justice that error and misrepresentation have, in their inconsistencies and improbabilities, the elements of self-destruction, while truth is in its nature consistent and therefore self-sustaining. To such general remarks in regard to campaigns, sieges, and battles as may seem to me appropriate to the scope and object of my work, I shall append or insert, from time to time, the evidence of reliable actors in those affairs, as well to elucidate obscurity as to correct error.

From the official reports it appears that the strength of the two armies was: Confederate, 30,167 men of all arms, with 29 guns;[2] Federal, 35,732 men,[3] with a body of cavalry, of which only one company is reported, and a large artillery force not shown in the tabular statement.

---

[2] General Beauregard's report.
[3] General McDowell's return, July 16, 17, 1861.

Of these troops, some on both sides were not engaged in the battle. This, it is believed, was the case to a much larger extent on our side than on that of the enemy. He selected the point of attack, and could concentrate his troops for that purpose, but we were guarding a line of some seven miles front, and therefore widely dispersed.

For the purpose above stated, extracts are herein inserted from a narrative in the "Operations on the Line of Bull Run in June and July, 1861, including the First Battle of Manassas." The name of the author, J. A. Early, will, to all who know him, be a sufficient guarantee for the accuracy of the statements, and for the justice of the conclusions announced. To those who do not know him, it may be proper to state that he was educated as a soldier; after leaving the army he became a lawyer, but when his country was involved in war with Mexico, he volunteered and served in a regiment of his native state, Virginia. After that war terminated, he returned to the practice of his profession, which he was actively pursuing when the controversy between the sections caused the call of a convention to decide whether Virginia should secede from the Union. He was sent by the people of the county in which he resided, to represent them in that convention. There he opposed to the last the adoption of the ordinance for secession; when it was decided, against his opinion, to resort to the remedy of withdrawal from the Union, he, true to his allegiance to the state of which he was a citizen, paused not to cavil or protest, but at once stepped forth to defend her against a threatened invasion. The sword that had rusted in peace gleamed brightly in war. He rose to the high grade of lieutenant general. None have a more stainless record as a soldier, none have shown a higher patriotism or purer fidelity through all the bitter trials to which we have been subjected since open war was ended and nominal peace began.

Extracts from the narrative of General J. A. Early, of events occurring when he was colonel of the Twenty-fourth Regiment of Virginia Infantry and commanding a brigade:

On June 19, 1861, I arrived at Manassas Junction and reported to General P. G. T. Beauregard, the Twenty-fourth Virginia Regiment having been previously sent to him, under the command of Lieutenant-Colonel Hairsten, from Lynchburg, where I had been stationed under the orders of General Robert E. Lee, for the purpose of organizing the Virginia troops which were being mustered into service at that place. . . .

On the morning of July 18th, my brigade was moved, by order of General Beauregard, to the left of Camp Walker, on the railroad, and remained there some time. . . .

On falling back, General Ewell, in pursuance of his instructions, had burned the bridges on the railroad over Pope's Run, from Fairfax Station to Union Mills, and while I was at Camp Walker I saw the smoke ascending from the railroad-bridge over Bull Run, which was burned that morning.

The burning of this bridge had not been included in the previous instructions to Ewell, and I have always been at a loss to know why it was now fired. That bridge certainly was not necessary to the enemy for crossing Bull Run, either with his troops or wagons, as that stream was easily fordable at numerous places, both above and below. The bridge was, moreover, susceptible of easy defense, as there were deep cuts leading to it on both sides. The only possible purpose to be subserved by the burning of that bridge would have been the prevention for a short time of the running of trains over it by the enemy, in the event of our defeat, or evacuation of Manassas without a fight. As it was, we were afterward greatly inconvenienced by its destruction. . . .

The attack made on the 18th is described as directed against our right center, and as having been met and repulsed in a manner quite creditable to our raw troops, of whom he writes:

On the 19th they were occupied in the effort to strengthen their position by throwing up the best defenses they could with the implements at hand, which consisted of a very few picks and spades, some rough bowie-knives, and the bayonets of the muskets. . . . The position was a very weak one, as the banks on the opposite side of Bull Run overlooked and commanded those on the south side, which were but a few feet above the water's edge, and there was an open field in rear of the strip of woods on our side of the stream, for a considerable distance up and down it, which exposed all of our movements on that side to observation from the opposite one, as the strip of woods afforded but a thin veil which could be seen through. . . .

About dusk on the 19th, brigade commanders were summoned to a conference at McLean's house by General Beauregard, and he then informed us of the fact that General Johnston had been ordered, at his instance, from the Valley, and was marching to coöperate with us. He stated that Johnston would march directly across the Blue Ridge toward the enemy's right flank, and would probably attack on that flank at dawn the next morning. Before he had finished his statement of the plans he proposed pursuing in the event of Johnston's attack on the enemy's right flank, a party of horsemen rode up in front of the house, and, dismounting, one of them walked in and reported himself as Brigadier-General T. J. Jackson, who had arrived with the advanced brigade of Johnston's troops by the way of Manassas Gap Railroad, and he stated that his brigade was about twenty-five hundred strong. This information took General Beauregard very much by surprise, and, after ascertaining that General Jackson had taken the cars at Piedmont Station, General Beauregard asked him if General Johnston would not march the rest of his command on the direct road, so as to get on the enemy's right flank. General Jackson replied with some little hesitation, and, as I thought at the time, in rather a stolid manner, that he thought not; that he thought the purpose was to transport the whole force by railroad from Piedmont Station. This was the first time I ever saw General Jackson, and my first impressions of him were not very favorable from the manner in which he gave his information. I subsequently ascertained very well how it was that he seemed to know so little, in the presence of the strangers among whom he found himself, of General Johnston's intended movements, and I presume nothing but the fact of General Beauregard being his superior in rank, and his being ordered to report to him, could have elicited as much information from him, under the circumstances, as was obtained. After General Jackson had given the information above stated, and received instructions where to put his brigade, he retired, and General Beauregard proceeded to develop fully his plans for the next day. The information received from General Jackson was wholly unexpected, but General Beauregard said he thought Jackson was not correctly informed, and was mistaken; that he was satisfied General Johnston was marching with the rest of his troops and would attack the enemy's right flank early next day as he had before stated. Upon this hypothesis, he directed that when General Johnston's attack began and he had become fully engaged, of which we were to judge from the character of the musketry-fire, we should cross Bull Run from our several positions, and move upon the enemy so as to attack him on his left flank and rear. He said that he had no doubt General Johnston's attack would be a complete surprise to the enemy; that the latter would not know what to think of it; that when he turned to meet that attack, and soon found himself assailed on the other side, he would be still more surprised and would not know what to do; that the effect would become a complete rout—a perfect Waterloo; and that, when the enemy took to flight, we would pursue, cross the Potomac, and arouse Maryland. . . .

During the 20th General Johnston arrived at Manassas Junction by the railroad, and that day we received the order from him assuming command of the combined armies of General Beauregard and himself.

Early on the morning of the 21st (Sunday), we heard the enemy's guns open from the heights north of Bull Run, from which they had opened on the 18th, and I soon received orders for the movement of my brigade. . . .

Upon arriving there (McLean's Ford), I found General Jones had returned to the intrenchments with his brigade, and I was informed by him that General Beauregard had directed that I should join him (General Beauregard) with my brigade. . . . He then asked me if I had received an order from General Beauregard to go to him, and, on my replying in the negative, he informed me that he had such an order for me in a note to him. He sent to one of his staff officers for the note, and showed it to me. The note was one directing him to fall back behind Bull Run, and was in pencil. At the foot of it were these words: "Send Early to me." This was all the order that I received to move to the left, and it was shown to me a very little after twelve o'clock. . . . Chisholm, who carried the note to Jones, in which was contained the order I received, passed me at McLean's Ford going on to Jones about, or a little after, eleven o'clock. If I had not received the order until 2 P.M., it would have been impossible for me to get on the field at the time I reached it, about 3:30 P.M. Colonel Chisholm informed me that the order was for all the troops to fall back across Bull Run. . . . I was met by Colonel John S. Preston, one of the General's aides, who informed me that General Beauregard had gone where the fighting was, . . . but that General Johnston was just in front, and his directions were that we should proceed to the left, where there was a heavy fire of musketry. . . . When we reached General Johnston, he expressed great gratification at our arrival, but it was very perceptible that his anticipations were not sanguine. He gave me special instructions as to my movements, directing me to clear our lines completely before going to the front. . . . In some fields on the left of our line we found Colonel Stuart with a body of cavalry and some pieces of artillery, belonging, as I understood, to a battery commanded by Lieutenant Beckham. . . . I found Stuart already in position beyond our extreme left, and, as I understood it, supporting and controlling Beckham's guns, which were firing on the enemy's extreme right flank, thus rendering very efficient service. I feel well assured that Stuart had but *two* companies of cavalry with him, as these were all I saw when he afterward went in pursuit of the enemy. As I approached the left, a young man named Saunders came galloping to me from Stuart with the information that the enemy was about retreating, and a request to hurry on. This was the first word of encouragement we had received since we reached the vicinity of the battle. I told the messenger to inform Stuart that I was then moving as rapidly as my men could move; but he soon returned with another message informing me that the other was a mistake, that the enemy had merely retired behind the ridge in front to form a new flanking column, and cautioning me to be on my guard. This last information proved to be correct. It was the last effort of the enemy to extend his right beyond our left, and was met by the formation of my regiments in his front. . . . The hill on which the enemy's troops were was Chinn's Hill, so often referred to in the accounts of this battle, and the one next year, on the same field. . . . An officer came to me in a gallop, and entreated me not to fire on the troops in front, and I was so much impressed by his earnest manner and confident tone, that I halted my brigade on the side of the hill, and rode to the top of it, when I discovered, about a hundred and fifty yards to my right, a regiment bearing a flag which was drooping around the staff in such a manner as not to be distinguishable from the Confederate flag of that day. I thought that, if the one that had been in front of me was a Virginia regiment, this must also be a Confederate one; but one or two shots from Beckham's guns on the left caused the regiment to face about, when its flag unfurled, and I discovered it to be the United States flag. I forthwith ordered my brigade forward, but it did not reach the top of the hill soon enough to do any damage to the retiring regiment, which retreated precipitately down the hill and across the Warrenton Pike. At that time there was very little distinction between the dress of some of the Federal regiments and some of ours. As soon as the misrepresentation in regard to the character of the troops was corrected, my brigade advanced to the top of the hill that had been occupied by the enemy, and we ascertained that his troops had retired precipitately, and a large body of them was discovered in the fields in rear of Dogan's house, and north of the turnpike. Colonel Cocke, with one of his regiments, now joined us, and our pieces of artillery were advanced and fired upon the enemy's columns with considerable effect, causing them to disperse, and we soon discovered that they were in full retreat. . . . When my column was seen by General Beauregard, he at first thought it was a column of the enemy, having received erroneous information that such a column was on the Manassas Gap Railroad. The enemy took my troops, as they approached his right, for a large body of our troops from the

Valley; and as my men, moving by flank, were stretched out at considerable length, from weariness, they were greatly over-estimated. We scared the enemy worse than we hurt him. . . .

We saw the evidences of the flight all along our march, and unmistakable indications of the overwhelming character of the enemy's defeat in abandoned muskets and equipments. It was impossible for me to pursue the enemy farther, as well because I was utterly unacquainted with the crossings of the Run and the woods in front, as because most of the men belonging to my brigade had been marching the greater part of the day and were very much exhausted. But pursuit with infantry would have been unavailing, as the enemy's troops retreated with such rapidity that they could not have been overtaken by any other than mounted troops. On the next day we found a great many articles that the routed troops had abandoned in their flight, showing that no expense or trouble had been spared by the enemy in equipping his army. . . . In my movement after the retreat of the enemy commenced, I passed the Carter house and beyond our line of battle. The enemy had by this time entirely disappeared, and, having no knowledge of the country whatever, being on the ground for the first time, besides not observing any movement of troops from our line, I halted, with the expectation of receiving further orders. Observing some men near the Carter house, I rode to it, and found some five or six Federal soldiers, who had collected some wounded there of both sides, and among them Colonel Gardner, of the Eighth Georgia Regiment, who was suffering from a very painful wound in the leg, which was fractured just above the ankle. . . . Just after my return from the house where I saw Colonel Gardner, President Davis, in company with several gentlemen, rode to where my command was, and addressed a few stirring remarks to my regiments, in succession, which received him with great enthusiasm.

I briefly informed Mr. Davis of the orders I had received, and the movements of my brigade, and asked him what I should do under the circumstances. He told me that I had better get my men into line, and wait for further orders. I then requested him to inform Generals Johnston and Beauregard of my position, and my desire to receive orders. I also informed him of the condition in which I had found Colonel Gardner, and also of Colonel Jones being in the neighborhood badly wounded, requesting him to have a surgeon sent to their relief, as all of mine were in the rear attending to the wounded of their regiments. While we were talking, we saw a body of troops moving on the opposite side of Bull Run, some distance below us.

Mr. Davis then left me, going to the house where Colonel Gardner was, and I moved my brigade some half a mile farther, and formed it in line across the peninsula formed by a very considerable bend in Bull Run above the stone bridge. I put out a line of pickets in front, and my brigade bivouacked in this position for the night. By the time all these dispositions were made it was night, and I then rode back with Captain Gardner over the route I had moved on, as I knew no other, in order to find General Johnston or General Beauregard, so that I might receive orders, supposing that there would be a forward movement early in the morning. I first went to the Lewis house, which I found to be a hospital filled with wounded men; but was unable to get any information about either of the generals. I then rode toward Manassas, and, after going some distance in that direction, I met an officer who inquired for General Johnston, stating that he was on his staff. I informed him that I was looking for General Johnston also, as well as for General Beauregard, and supposed they were at Manassas; but he said that he was just from Manassas, and neither of the generals was there. . . . At about twelve o'clock at night I lay down in the field in rear of my command, on a couple of bundles of wheat in the straw. My men had no rations with them. I had picked up a haversack on the field, which was filled with hard biscuits, and had been dropped by some Yankee in his flight, and out of its contents I made my own supper, distributing the rest among a number of officers who had nothing.

Very early next morning, I sent Captain Gardner to look out for the generals, and get orders for my command. He went to Manassas, and found General Beauregard, who sent orders to me to remain where I was until further orders, and to send for the camp-equipage, rations, etc., of my command. A number of the men spread over the country in the vicinity of the battlefield, and picked up a great many knapsacks, India-rubber cloths, blankets, overcoats, etc., as well as a good deal of sugar, coffee, and other provisions that had been abandoned by the enemy. . . .

After I had received orders showing that there was no purpose to make a forward movement, I rode over a good deal of the field, north of the Warrenton pike, and to some hospitals in the vicinity, in order to see what care was being taken of the wounded. I found a hospital on the Sudley road, back of the field of battle, at which Colonel Jones, of the Fourth Alabama, had been, which was in charge of a surgeon of a Rhode Island regiment, whose name was Harris, I think. I asked him if he had what he wanted for the men under his care, and he told me he would like to have some morphine, of which his supply was short. I directed a young surgeon of our cavalry, who rode up at the time, to furnish the morphine, which he did, from a pair of medical saddle-pockets which he had. Dr. Harris told me that he knew that their troops had had a great deal of coffee and sugar mixed, ready for boiling, of which a good deal had been left at different points near the field, and asked if there would be any objection to his sending out and gathering some of it for the use of the wounded under his charge, as it would be of much service to them. I gave him the permission to get not only that, but anything else that would tend to the comfort of his patients. There did not come within my observation any instance of harsh or unkind treatment of the enemy's wounded; nor did I see any indication of a spirit to extend such treatment to them. The stories which were afterward told before the Committee on the Conduct of the War (appointed by the Federal Congress), in regard to "rebel atrocities," were very grossly exaggerated, or manufactured from the whole cloth. . . .

On the night following the battle, when I was looking for Generals Beauregard and Johnston, in riding over and to the rear of the battle-field, I discovered that the greater part of the troops that had been engaged in the battle were in a great state of confusion. I saw companies looking for their regiments, and squads looking for their companies, and they were scattered as far as I went toward Manassas. It was very apparent that no considerable body of those troops that had been engaged on the left could have been brought into a condition next day for an advance toward Washington. . . .

The dispute as to who planned the battle, or commanded on the field, General

Johnston or General Beauregard, is a most unprofitable one. The battle which General Beauregard planned was never fought, because the enemy did not move as he expected him to move. The battle which was fought was planned by McDowell, at least so far as the ground on which it was fought was concerned. He made a movement on our left which was wholly unexpected and unprovided for, and we were compelled to fight a defensive battle on that flank, by bringing up reenforcements from other points as rapidly as possible. When Generals Johnston and Beauregard arrived on the field where the battle was actually fought, it had been progressing for some time, with the odds greatly against us. What was required then was to rally the troops already engaged, which had been considerably shattered, and hold the position to which they had been compelled to retire until reënforcements could be brought up. According to the statements of both generals, the command of the troops then on the field was given to General Beauregard, and he continued to exercise it until the close, but in subordination, of course, to General Johnston, as commander-in-chief, while the movements of all the reenforcements as they arrived were unquestionably directed by the latter. According to the statement of both, the movement of Elzey's brigade to the left averted a great danger, and both concur in attributing the turning of the tide of battle to the movement of my brigade against the enemy's extreme right flank (General Beauregard in a letter on the origin of the battle-flag, and General Johnston in his "Narrative" recently published).

General Beauregard unquestionably performed the duty assigned him with great ability, and General Johnston gives him full credit therefor. Where, then, is there any room for a controversy in regard to the actual command, and what profit can there be in it?

General Johnston assumes the responsibility for the failure to advance on Washington, and why, then, should an effort be made to shift it on any one else? He certainly was commander-in-chief, and had the privilege of advancing if he thought proper. The attempt to show that the failure to advance was due to the want of transportation and rations for the army is idle. If the Bull Run bridge had not burned on the 18th, our supplies could have been run to Alexandria, if we could have advanced, as easily as to Manassas, for the enemy had repaired the railroad to Fairfax Station as he moved up, and failed to destroy it when he went back. Moreover, we had abundant transportation at that time for all the purposes of an advance as far as Washington. In my brigade, the two Virginia regiments had about fourteen six-horse wagons each, and that would have furnished enough for the brigade, if the Seventh Louisiana had none. In 1862 we carried into Maryland only enough wagons to convey ammunition, medical supplies, and cooking-utensils, and we started from the battle-field of second Manassas with no rations on hand, being, before we crossed the Potomac, entirely dependent on the country, which, in July, 1861, was teeming with supplies, but in August and September, 1862, was nearly depleted. The pretense, therefore, that the advance in July, 1861, was prevented by the want of transportation and of supplies is wholly untenable.

I will now make the promised extracts from reminiscences of Colonel (then Captain) Lay, which were sent to a friend, and handed to me for my use. The paper bears date February 13, 1878. After some preliminary matter, and stating that his force consisted of three cavalry companies, the narrative proceeds:

I was under orders to be in the saddle at 6.30 A.M., July 21, 1861, and to report immediately to General Beauregard at his headquarters. About 7.30 A.M. I accompanied him and General Johnston to a position near to Mitchell's Ford, where for some hours we remained under an active fire of the long-range guns of the enemy upon the opposite hills. When the unexpected flank movement of the enemy was developed, with the generals named, we rode at rapid speed to the left, when General Beauregard immediately rode to the front, General Johnston taking position near and to the left of the Lewis house. . . . About 3.15 P.M., Captain R. Lindsey Walker, with his battery, took position to the left and in front of the Lewis house and commenced firing. I was near him when the shot from his battery was fired, and watched its effect as it swept through the columns of the enemy, producing perfect confusion and demoralization. . . . I rode to join my brother, Colonel Lay, whom I saw going toward my command from General Johnston. He reported to me that General Johnston said: "Now is your time; push the pursuit." I started at once on a trot, was passing General Johnston, who gave some orders, and I understood him to say, "Salute the President in passing." . . . I saluted, and passed on at a gallop.

I halted at Bull Run to water my horses—then suffering—and to confer a movement or two with my gallant old commander, General Philip St. George Cocke.

I passed on, . . . when to my astonishment I saw the President near me in the orchard. I immediately rode up to him, and said that he was much farther forward than he should be; that the forces of the enemy were not entirely broken, and very few of our troops in front of the Run, and advised him to retire; that I was then about to charge. . . .

We made the charge; a small body of the enemy broke before we reached them, and scattered, and the larger body of troops beyond proved to be of our own troops rapidly advancing upon our left. . . . After parting from the President, I pushed on to Sudley Church, and far beyond. Sent my surgeon, Dr. Randolph Barksdale, to Captains Tillinghast, Ricketts, and other badly wounded United States officers, and was going on until a superior force should stop me, but was recalled by an order and returned over the field to my quarters at Manassas a little before daylight—I and my little gallant squadron—having been actively in the saddle, I think, more than twenty hours. . . .

(Signed)   JOHN F. LAY.
                            Late Colonel of Cavalry, C. S. A.

N. B.—It may be well to add that General R. Lindsey Walker (then Captain Walker, of the battery referred to) is now in my office, and confirms my recollection. . . .   J. F. L.

The quartermaster general of General Beauregard's command, W. L. Cabell, states in a letter written at Dallas, Texas, on August 16, 1880, in regard to the field transportation of General Beauregard's forces before the battle of Manassas, that as nearly as he could remember it was as follows, viz.:

> One four-horse wagon to each company.
> One four-horse wagon for field and staff (regimental).
> One four-horse wagon for ammunition.
> One four-horse wagon for hospital purposes.
> Two four-horse wagons for each battery of artillery.
> Twenty-five wagons in a train for depot purposes.
> One ambulance for each regiment.

Transportation belonging to General Johnston's army did not arrive until the day (or probably two days) after the battle.

If General Johnston, as stated, had nine thousand infantry, the field transportation reported above could surely have been distributed so as to supply this additional force, and have rendered, as General Early states, the pretense wholly untenable that the advance in July, 1861, was prevented by want of transportation.

The deep anxiety which had existed, and was justified by the circumstances, had corresponding gratification among all classes and in all sections of our country. On the day after the victory, the Congress, then sitting in Richmond, upon receiving the dispatch of the President from the field of Manassas, adopted resolutions expressive of their thanks to the most high God, and inviting the people of the Confederate States to offer up their united thanksgiving and praise for the mighty deliverance. The resolutions also deplored the necessity which had caused the soil of our country to be stained with the blood of its sons, and to their families and friends offered the most cordial sympathy; assuring them that in the hearts of our people would be enshrined "the names of the gallant dead as the champions of free and constitutional liberty."

If universal gratulation at our success inspired an overweening confidence, it also begat increased desire to enter the military service; but for our want of arms and munitions, we could have enrolled an army little short of the number of able-bodied men in the Confederate States.

I have given so much space to the battle of Manassas because it was the first great action of the war, exciting intense feeling, and producing important moral results among the people of the Confederacy; further, because it was made the basis of misrepresentation, and unjust reflection upon the chief executive, which certainly had no plausible pretext in the facts, and cannot be referred to a reasonable desire to promote the successful defense of our country.

Impressed with the conviction that time would naturally work to our disadvantage, as training was more necessary to make soldiers of the Northern people than of our own; further, because of their larger population, as well as their greater facility in obtaining recruits from foreign countries, the administration continued assiduously to exert every faculty to increase the efficiency of the army by addition to its numbers, by improving its organization, and by supplying the needful munitions and equipments. Inactivity is the prolific source of evil to an army, especially if composed of new levies who, like ours, had hurried from their homes at their country's call. For these, and other reasons more readily appreciated, it was thought desirable that all our available forces should be employed as actively as might be practicable.

On August 1, 1861, I wrote to General J. E. Johnston, at Manassas, as follows:

We are anxiously looking for the official reports of the battle of Manassas, and have present need to know what supplies and wagons were captured. I wish you would have prepared a statement of your wants in transportation and supplies of all kinds, to put your army on a proper footing for active operations. . . .

I am, as ever, your friend,

(Signed)   JEFFERSON DAVIS.

CHAPTER VIII: *The Kentucky Resolutions of 1798-'99—Their Influence on Political Affairs—Kentucky Declares for Neutrality—Correspondence of Governor Magoffin with the President of the United States and the President of the Confederate States—Occupation of Columbus, Kentucky, by Major General Polk—His Correspondence with the Kentucky Commissioners —President Lincoln's View of Neutrality—Acts of the United States Government—Refugees—Their Motives of Expatriation —Address of ex-Vice-President Breckinridge to the People of the State—The Occupation of Columbus Secured—The Purpose of the United States Government—Battle of Belmont— Albert Sidney Johnston Commands the Department—State of Affairs—Line of Defense—Efforts to Obtain Arms and Troops.*

KENTUCKY, the eldest daughter of Virginia, had moved contemporaneously with her mother in the assertion of the cardinal principles announced in the resolutions of 1798-'99. She then by the properly constituted authority did with due solemnity declare that the government of the United States was the result of a compact between the states to which each acceded as a state; that it possessed only delegated powers, of which it was not the exclusive or final judge; and that, as in all cases of compact among parties having no common judge, "each party has an equal right to judge for itself as well of infractions as of the mode and measure of redress." Thus spoke Kentucky in the first years of her existence as a sovereign. The great truth announced in her series of resolutions was the sign under which the Democracy conquered in 1800, and which constituted the corner stone of the political edifice of which Jefferson was the architect, and which stood unshaken for sixty years from the time its foundation was laid. During this period the growth, prosperity, and happiness of the country seemed unmistakably to confirm the wisdom of the voluntary union of free sovereign states under a written compact confining the action of the general government to the expressly enumerated powers which had been delegated therein. When infractions of the compact had been deliberately and persistently made, when the intent was clearly manifested to pervert the powers of the general government from the purposes for which they had been conferred, and to use them for the injury of a portion of the states, which were the integral parties to the compact, some of them resolved to judge for themselves of the "mode and measure of redress," and to exercise the right, enunciated in the *Declaration of Independence* to be the unalienable endowment of every people, to alter or abolish any form of government, and to institute a new one, "laying its foundation on such principles, and organizing its powers in such form, as to them shall seem most likely to effect their safety and happiness." By no rational mode of construction, in view of the history of the *Declaration of Independence,* or of the resolutions of Kentucky, can it be claimed that the word "people" had any other meaning than that of a distinct community, such as the people of each colony who by their delegates in the Congress declared themselves to be henceforth a state; that none other than the people of each state could, by the resolutions of 1798-'99, have been referred to as the final judge of infractions of their compact, and of the remedy which should be applied.

Kentucky made no decision adverse to this right of a state, but she declared, in the impending conflict between the states seceding from and those adhering to the federal government, that she would hold the position of neutrality. If the question was to be settled by a war of words, that was feasible; if the conflict was to be one of arms, it was utterly impracticable. To maintain neutrality under such circumstances would have required a power greater than that of both the contestants, or a moral influence commanding such respect for her wishes as could hardly have been anticipated from that party which had, in violation of right, inflicted the wrongs which produced the withdrawal of some of the states, and had uttered multiplied threats of coercion if any state attempted to exercise the rights defined in the resolutions of 1798-'99. If, however, any such hope may have been entertained, but few moons had filled and waned before the defiant occupation of her territory and the enrollment of her citizens as soldiers in the army of invasion must have dispelled the illusion.

The following correspondence took place in August between Governor Magoffin of Kentucky and President Lincoln—also between the governor and myself, as President of the Confederate States—relative to the neutrality of the state:

COMMONWEALTH OF KENTUCKY, EXECUTIVE DEPARTMENT.
FRANKFORT, August 19, 1861.
To his Excellency ABRAHAM LINCOLN, *President of the United States.*

SIR: From the commencement of the unhappy hostilities now pending in this country, the people of Kentucky have indicated an earnest desire and purpose, as far as lay in their power, while maintaining their original political status, to do nothing by which to involve themselves in the war. Up to this time they have succeeded in securing to themselves and to the State peace and tranquillity as the fruits of the policy they adopted. My single object now is to promote the continuance of these blessings to this State.

Until within a brief period the people of Kentucky were quiet and tranquil, free from domestic strife, and undisturbed by internal commotion. They have resisted no law, rebelled against no authority, engaged in no revolution, but constantly proclaimed their firm determination to pursue their peaceful avocations, earnestly hoping that their own soil would be spared the presence of armed troops, and that the scene of conflict would be kept removed beyond the border of their State. By thus avoiding all occasions for the introduction of bodies of armed soldiers, and offering no provocation for the presence of military force, the people of Kentucky have sincerely striven to preserve in their State domestic peace and avert the calamities of sanguinary engagements.

Recently a large body of soldiers have been enlisted in the United States army and collected in military camps in the central portion of Kentucky. This movement was preceded by the active organization of companies, regiments, etc., consisting of men sworn into the United States service, under officers holding commissions from yourself. Ordnance, arms, munitions, and supplies of war are being transported into the State, and placed in large quantities in these camps. In a word, an army is now being organized and quartered within the State, supplied with all the appliances of war, without the consent or advice of the authorities of the State, and without consultation with those most prominently known and recognized as loyal citizens. This movement now imperils that peace and tranquility which from the beginning of our pending difficulties have been the paramount desire of this people, and which, up to this time, they have so secured to the State.

Within Kentucky there has been, and is likely to be, no occasion for the presence of military force. The people are quiet and tranquil, feeling no apprehension of any occasion arising to invoke protection from the Federal arm. They have asked that their territory be left free from military occupation, and the present tranquillity of their communication left uninvaded by soldiers. They do not desire that Kentucky shall be required to supply the battle-field for the contending armies, or become the theatre of the war.

Now, therefore, as Governor of the State of Kentucky, and in the name of the people I have the honor to represent, and with the single and earnest desire to avert from their peaceful homes the horrors of war, I urge the removal from the limits of Kentucky of the military force now organized and in camp within the State. If such action as is here urged be promptly taken, I firmly believe the peace of the people of Kentucky will be preserved, and the horrors of a bloody war will be averted from a people now peaceful and tranquil.

I am, very respectfully, your obedient servant,

B. MAGOFFIN.

WASHINGTON, August 24, 1861.

To his Excellency B. MAGOFFIN, *Governor of the State of Kentucky.*

SIR: Your letter of the 19th instant, in which you "urge the removal from the limits of Kentucky of the military force now organized and in camp within that State," is received.

I may not possess full and precisely accurate knowledge upon this subject; but I believe it is true that there is a military force in camp within Kentucky, acting by authority of the United States, which force is not very large, and is not now being augmented.

I also believe that some arms have been furnished to this force by the United States.

I also believe this force consists exclusively of Kentuckians, having their camp in the immediate vicinity of their own homes, and not assailing or menacing any of the good people of Kentucky.

In all I have done in the premises, I have acted upon the urgent solicitation of many Kentuckians, and in accordance with what I believed, and still believe, to be the wish of a majority of all the Union-loving people in Kentucky.

While I have conversed on this subject with many of the eminent men of Kentucky, including a large majority of her members of Congress, I do not remember that any one of them, or any other person except your Excellency and the bearers of your Excellency's letter, has urged me to remove the military force from Kentucky, or to disband it. One very worthy citizen of Kentucky did solicit me to have the augmenting of the force suspended for a time.

Taking all the means within my reach to form a judgment, I do not believe it is the popular wish of Kentucky that this force shall be removed beyond her limits; and, with this impression, I must respectfully decline to so remove it.

I most cordially sympathize with your Excellency in the wish to preserve the peace of my own native State, Kentucky. It is with regret I search for, and can not find, in your not very short letter, any declaration or intimation that you entertain any desire for the preservation of the Federal Union.

Your obedient servant,   A. LINCOLN.

COMMONWEALTH OF KENTUCKY, EXECUTIVE DEPARTMENT,
FRANKFORT, August 24, 1861.

Hon. JEFFERSON DAVIS, *Richmond, Virginia.*

SIR: Since the commencement of the unhappy difficulties pending in the country, the people of Kentucky have indicated a steadfast desire and purpose to maintain a position of strict neutrality between the belligerent parties. They have earnestly striven by their policy to avert from themselves the calamity of war, and protect their own soil from the presence of contending armies. Up to this period they have enjoyed comparative tranquillity and entire domestic peace.

Recently a military force has been enlisted and quartered by the United States authorities within this State. I have on this day addressed a communication and dispatched commissioners to the President of the United States, urging the removal of these troops from the soil of Kentucky, and thus exerting myself to carry out the will of the people in the maintenance of a neutral position. The people of this State desire to be free from the presence of the soldiers of either belligerent, and to that end my efforts are now directed.

Although I have no reason to presume that the Government of the Confederate States contemplate or have ever proposed any violation of the neutral attitude thus assumed by Kentucky, there seems to be some uneasiness felt among the people of some portion of the State, occasioned by the collection of bodies of troops along their southern frontier. In order to quiet this apprehension, and to secure to the people their cherished object of peace, this communication is to present these facts and elicit an authoritative assurance that the Government of the Confederate States will continue to respect and observe the position indicated as assumed by Kentucky.

Very respectfully, your obedient servant,

B. MAGOFFIN.

RICHMOND, August 28, 1861.

To Hon. B. MAGOFFIN, *Governor of Kentucky, etc.*

SIR: I have received your letter informing me that "since the commencement of the unhappy difficulties pending in the country, the people of Kentucky have indicated a steadfast desire to maintain a position of strict neutrality between the belligerent parties." In the same communication you express your desire to elicit "an authoritative assurance that the Government of the Confederate States will continue to respect and observe the neutral position of Kentucky."

In reply to this request, I lose no time in assuring you that the Government of the Confederate States neither desires nor intends to disturb the neutrality of Kentucky. The assemblage of troops in Tennessee, to which you refer, had no other object than to repel the lawless invasion of that State by the forces of the United States, should their Government seek to approach it through Kentucky, without respect for its position of neutrality. That such apprehensions were not groundless has been proved by the course of that Government in the States of Maryland and Missouri, and more recently in Kentucky itself, in which, as you inform me, "a military force has been enlisted and quartered by the United States authorities."

The Government of the Confederate States has not only respected most scrupulously the neutrality of Kentucky, but has continued to maintain the friendly relations of trade and intercourse which it has suspended with the United States generally.

In view of the history of the past, it can scarcely be necessary to assure your Excellency that the Government of the Confederate States will continue to respect the neutrality of Kentucky so long as her people will maintain it themselves.

But neutrality, to be entitled to respect, must be strictly maintained between both parties; or, if the door be opened on the one side for the aggressions of one of the belligerent parties upon the other, it ought not to be shut to the assailed when they seek to enter it for purposes of self-defense.

I do not, however, for a moment believe that your gallant State will suffer its soil to be used for the purpose of giving an advantage to those who violate its neutrality and disregard its rights, over others who respect both.

In conclusion, I tender to your Excellency the assurance of my high consideration and regard, and am, sir, very respectfully,

Yours, etc.,   JEFFERSON DAVIS.

Movements by the Federal forces in southwestern Kentucky revealed such designs as made it absolutely necessary that General Polk, commanding the Confederate forces in that section, should immediately occupy the town of Columbus, Kentucky—a position of much strategic importance on the shore of the Mississippi River.

That position was doubly important because it commanded the opposite shore in Missouri and was the gateway on the border of Tennessee. Two states of the Confederacy were therefore threatened by the anticipated movement of the enemy to get possession of Columbus.

Major General Polk, therefore, crossed the state line, took possession of Hickman on September 3d, and on the 4th secured Columbus. General Grant, who took command at Cairo on September 2d, being thus anticipated, seized Paducah, at the mouth of the Tennessee River, and occupied it in force on the 5th and 6th.

After the occupation, under date of September 4th, I received the following dispatch from Major General Polk: "The enemy having descended the Mississippi River some three or four days since, and seated himself with cannon and intrenched lines opposite the town of Columbus, Kentucky, making such demonstrations as left no doubt upon the minds of any of their intention to seize and forcibly possess said town, I thought proper, under the plenary power delegated to me, to direct a sufficient portion of my command both by the river way and land to concentrate at Columbus, as well to offer to its citizens that protection they unite to a man in accepting, as also to prevent, in time, the occupation by the enemy of a point so necessary to the security of western Tennessee. The demonstration on my part has had the desired effect. The enemy has withdrawn his forces even before I had fortified my position. It is my intention to continue to occupy and hold this place." On the same day I sent the following reply to Major General Polk: "Your telegram received; the necessity must justify the action."

The legislature of Kentucky passed resolutions and appointed a committee to inquire into the action of General Polk, from which the annexed correspondence resulted:

CORRESPONDENCE BETWEEN MAJOR GENERAL POLK AND THE AUTHORITIES
OF KENTUCKY

*Resolutions of the Kentucky Senate relative to the Violation of the Neutrality
of Kentucky.*

Resolved by the Senate, That the special committee of the Senate, raised for the purpose of considering the reported occupation of Hickman and other points in Kentucky by Confederate troops, take into consideration the occupation of Paducah and other places in Kentucky by the Federal authorities, and report thereon when the true state of the case shall have been ascertained. That the Speaker appoint three members of the Senate to visit southern Kentucky, who are directed to obtain all the facts they can in reference to the recent occupation of Kentucky soil by Confederate and Federal forces, and report in writing at as early a day as practicable.

In Senate of Kentucky, Saturday, September 7, A.D. 1861.

Twice read and adopted.

Attest: (Signed)   J. H. JOHNSON, S. S.

In accordance with the foregoing resolution, the Speaker appointed as said committee Messrs. John M. Johnson, William B. Read, and Thornton F. Marshall.

Attest: (Signed)   J. H. JOHNSON, S. S.

Letter of Hon. J. M. Johnson, Chairman of the Committee of the Kentucky Senate, to General Polk.

To Major-General POLK, *commanding forces, etc.*

COLUMBUS, KENTUCKY, September 9, 1861.

SIR: I have the honor to inclose herewith a resolution of the Senate of Kentucky, adopted by that body upon the reception of the intelligence of the military occupation of Hickman, Chalk Bank, and Columbus, by the Confederate troops under your command. I need not say that the people of Kentucky are profoundly astonished that such an act should have been committed by the Confederates, and especially that they should have been the first to do so with an equipped and regularly organized army.

The people of Kentucky, having with great unanimity determined upon a position of neutrality in the unhappy war now being waged, and which they had tried in vain to prevent, had hoped that one place at least in this great nation might remain uninvaded by passion, and through whose good office something might be done to end the war, or at least to mitigate its horrors, or, if this were not possible, that she might be left to choose her destiny without disturbance from any quarter.

In obedience to the thrice-repeated will of the people, as expressed at the polls, and in their name, I ask you to withdraw your forces from the soil of Kentucky.

I will say, in conclusion, that all the people of the State await, in deep suspense, your action in the premises.

I have the honor to be, your obedient servant, etc.,

(Signed)   JOHN M. JOHNSON.
                                 Chairman of Committee.

Letter from General Polk to the Kentucky Commissioners.

COLUMBUS, KENTUCKY, September 9, 1861.

To J. M. JOHNSON, *Chairman of Committee, Senate of Kentucky.*

SIR: I have the honor to acknowledge the receipt of your letter of this date, conveying to me a copy of a resolution of the Senate of Kentucky, under which a committee (of which you are chairman) was raised "for the purpose of considering the reported occupation of Hickman and other points in Kentucky by the Confederate troops, and that they take into consideration the reported occupation of Paducah and other points in Kentucky by the Federal authorities, and report thereon"; also, that they be "directed to obtain all the facts they can in reference to the recent occupation of Kentucky soil by the Confederate and Federal forces, and report, in writing, at as early a day as practicable."

From the terms of the resolution, it appears your office, as committee-men, was restricted merely to collecting the facts in reference to the recent occupation of Kentucky soil by the Confederate and Federal forces, and to report thereon in writing, at as early a day as possible. In answer to these resolutions, I have respectfully to say that, so far as the Confederate forces are concerned, the facts are plain, and shortly stated. The Government which they represent, recognizing as a fundamental principle the right of sovereign States to take such a position as they choose in regard to their relations with other States, was compelled by that principle to concede to Kentucky the right to assume the position of neutrality, which she has chosen in the passing struggle. This it has done on all occasions, and without an exception. The cases alluded to by his Excellency, Governor Magoffin, in his recent message, as "raids," I presume, are the cases of the steamers Cheney and Orr. The former was the unauthorized and unrecognized act of certain citizens of Alabama, and the latter the act of citizens of Tennessee and others, and was an act of reprisal. They can not, therefore, be charged, in any sense, as acts of the Confederate Government.

The first and only instance in which the neutrality of Kentucky has been disregarded is that in which the troops under my command, and by my direction, took possession of the place I now hold, and so much of the territory between it and the Tennessee line as was necessary for me to pass over in order to reach it. This act finds abundant justification in the history of the concessions granted to the Federal Government by Kentucky ever since the war began, notwithstanding the position of neutrality which she had assumed, and the firmness with which she proclaimed her intention to maintain it. That history shows the following among other facts: In January, the House of Representatives of Kentucky passed anti-coercion resolutions—only four dissenting. The Governor, in May, issued his neutrality proclamation. The address of the Union Central Committee, including Mr. James Speed, Mr. Prentice, and other prominent Union men, in April, proclaimed neutrality as the policy of Kentucky, and claimed that an attempt to coerce the South should induce Kentucky to make common cause with her, and take part in the contest on her side, "without counting the cost." The Union speakers and papers, with few exceptions, claimed, up to the last election, that the Union vote was strict neutrality and peace. These facts and events gave assurance of the integrity of the avowed purpose of your State, and we were content with the position she assumed.

Since the election, however, she has allowed the seizure in her port (Paducah) of property of citizens of the Confederate States; she has, by her members in the Congress of the United States, voted supplies of men and money to carry on the war against the Confederate States; she has allowed the Federal Government to cut timber from her forests for the purpose of building armed boats for the invasion of the Southern States; she is permitting to be enlisted in her territory, troops, not only of her own citizens, but of the citizens of other States, for the purpose of being armed and used in offensive warfare against the Confederate States. At Camp Robinson, in the county of Garrard, there are now ten thousand troops, if the newspapers can be relied upon, in which men from Tennessee, Ohio, Indiana, and Illinois are mustered with Kentuckians into the service of the United States, and armed by that Government for the avowed purpose of giving aid to the disaffected in one of the Confederate States, and of carrying out the designs of that Government for their subjugation. Notwithstanding all these and other acts of a similar character, the Confederate States have continued to respect the attitude which Kentucky had assumed as a neutral, and forborne from reprisals, in the hope that Kentucky would yet enforce respect for her position on the part of the Government of the United States.

Our patient expectation has been disappointed, and it was only when we perceived that this continued indifference to our rights and our safety was about to culminate in the seizure of an important part of her territory by the United States forces for offensive operations against the Confederate States, that a regard for self-preservation demanded of us to seize it in advance. We are here, therefore, not by choice, but of necessity, and as I have had the honor to say, in a communication addressed to his Excellency Governor Magoffin, a copy of which is herewith inclosed and submitted as a part of my reply, so I now repeat in answer to your request, that I am prepared to agree to withdraw the Confederate troops from Kentucky, provided she will agree that the troops of the Federal Government be withdrawn simultaneously, with a guarantee (which I will give reciprocally for the Confederate Government) that the Federal troops shall not be allowed to enter nor occupy any part of Kentucky for the future.

In view of the facts thus submitted, I can not but think the world at large will find it difficult to appreciate the "profound astonishment" with which you say the people of Kentucky received the intelligence of the occupation of this place.

I have the honor to be, respectfully,

Your obedient servant, etc.,

LEONIDAS POLK,
Major-General commanding.

Letter from General Polk to Governor Magoffin.

COLUMBUS, KENTUCKY, September 3, 1861.

Governor MAGOFFIN, *Frankfort, Kentucky.*

I should have dispatched to you immediately, as the troops under my command took possession of this position, the very few words I addressed to the people here; but my duties since that time have so preoccupied me, that I have but now the first leisure moment to communicate with you. It will be sufficient for me to inform you (as my short address herewith will do) that I had information, on which I could rely, that the Federal forces intended, and were preparing to seize Columbus. I need not describe to you the danger resulting to western Tennessee from such occupation.

My responsibility could not permit me quietly to lose to the command intrusted to me so important a position. In evidence of the accuracy of the information I possessed, I will state that, as the Confederate forces approached this place, the Federal troops were found in formidable numbers in position upon the opposite bank, with their cannon turned upon Columbus. The citizens of the town had fled with terror, and not a word of assurance of safety or protection had been addressed to them. Since I have taken possession of this place, I have been informed by highly respected citizens of your State that certain representatives of the Federal Government are seeking to take advantage of its own wrong, are setting up complaints against my acts of occupation, and are making it a pretext for seizing other points. Upon this proceeding I have no comments to make. But I am prepared to say that I will agree to withdraw the Confederate troops from Kentucky, provided that she will agree that the troops of the Federal Government be withdrawn simultaneously, with a guarantee (which I will give reciprocally for the Confederate Government) that the Federal troops shall not be allowed to enter or occupy any part of Kentucky in the future.

I have the honor to be, respectfully, your obedient servant,

(Signed)   LEONIDAS POLK,
                                                  Major-General commanding.

However willing the government of Kentucky might have been to accede to the proposition of General Polk, and which from his knowledge of the views of his own government he was fully justified in offering, the state of Kentucky had no power, moral or physical, to prevent the United States government from using her soil as best might suit is purposes in the war it was waging for the subjugation of the seceded states. President Lincoln, in his message of the previous July, had distinctly and reproachfully spoken of the idea of neutrality as existing in some of the border states. He said: "To prevent the Union forces passing one way, or the disunion the other, over their soil, would be disunion completed. . . . At a stroke it would take all the trouble off the hands of secession, except only what proceeds from the external blockade."

The acts of the federal government corresponded with the views announced by its President. Briefly, but conclusively, General Polk showed in his answer that the United States government paid no respect to the neutral position which Kentucky wished to maintain; that it was armed, but not neutral, for the arms and the troops assembled on her soil were for the invasion of the South; that he occupied Columbus to prevent the enemy from taking possession of it. When our troops first entered Columbus they found the inhabitants had been in alarm from demonstrations of the United States forces, but that they felt no dread of the Confederate troops. As far as the truth could be ascertained, a decided majority of the people of Kentucky, especially its southwestern portion, if left to a free choice, would have joined the Confederacy in preference to remaining in the Union. Could they have foreseen what in a short time was revealed, there can be little doubt that mule contracts, and other forms of bribery, would have proved unavailing to make her the passive observer of usurpations destructive of the personal and political rights of which she had always been a most earnest advocate. With the slow and sinuous approach of the serpent, the general government, little by little, gained power over Kentucky, and then, throwing off the mask, proceeded to outrages so regardless of law and the usages of English-speaking people, as could not have been anticipated, and can only be remembered with shame by those who honor the constitutional government created by the states. While artfully urging the maintenance of the Union as a duty of patriotism, the Constitution which gave the Union birth was trampled under foot, and the excesses of the Reign of Terror which followed the French Revolution were reënacted in our land, once the vaunted home of law and liberty. Men who had been most honored by the state, and who had reflected most honor upon it, were seized without warrant, condemned without trial, because they had exercised the privilege of free speech, and for adhering to the principles which were the bed-rock on which our fathers builded our political temple. Members of the legislature vacated their seats and left the state to avoid arrest, the penalty hanging over them for opinion's sake. The venerable Judge Monroe, who had presided over the United States District Court for more than a generation, driven from the land of his birth, the state he had served so long and so well, with feeble step, but upright conscience and indomitable will, sought a resting place among those who did not regard it a crime to adhere to the principles of 1776 and 1787, and the declaratory affirmation of them in the resolutions of 1798-'99. About the same time others of great worth and distinction, impelled by the feeling that "where liberty is there is my country," left the land desecrated by despotic usurpation, to join the Confederacy in its struggle to maintain the personal and political liberties which the men of the Revolution had left as an inheritance to their posterity. Space would not suffice for a complete list of the refugees who became conspicuous in the military events of the Confederacy; let a few answer for the many: J. C. Breckinridge, the late Vice-President of the United States, and whose general and well-deserved popularity might have reasonably led him to expect in the Union the highest honors the states could bestow; William Preston, George W. Johnston, S. B. Buckner, John H. Morgan, and a host of others, alike meritorious and alike gratefully remembered. When the passions of the hour shall have subsided, and the past shall be reviewed with discrimination and justice, the question must arise in every reflecting mind. Why did such men as these expatriate themselves, and surrender all the advantages which they had won by a life of honorable effort in the land of their nativity? To such inquiry the answer must be, the usurpations of the general government foretold to them the wreck of constitutional liberty. The motives which governed them may best be learned from the annexed extracts from the statement made in the address of Breckinridge to the people of Kentucky, whom he had represented in both houses of the United States Congress, with such distinguished ability and zeal for the general welfare as to place him in the front rank of the statesmen of his day:

BOWLING GREEN, KENTUCKY, October 8, 1861.

In obedience, as I supposed, to your wishes, I proceeded to Washington, and at the special session of Congress, in July, spoke and voted against the whole war policy of the President and Congress; demanding, in addition, for Kentucky, the right to refuse, not men only, but money also, to the war, for I would have blushed to meet you with the confession that I had purchased for you exemption from the perils of the battle-field, and the shame of waging war against your Southern brethren, by hiring others to do the work you shrunk from performing. During that memorable session a very small body of Senators and Representatives, even beneath the shadow of a military despotism, resisted the usurpations of the Executive, and, with what degree of dignity and firmness, they willingly submit to the judgment of the world.

Their efforts were unavailing, yet they may prove valuable hereafter, as another added to former examples of manly protest against the progress of tyranny.

On my return to Kentucky, at the close of the late special session of Congress, it was my purpose immediately to resign the office of Senator. The verbal and written remonstrances of many friends in different parts of the State induced me to postpone the execution of my purpose; but the time has arrived to carry it into effect, and accordingly I now hereby return the trust into your hands. . . . In the House of Representatives it was declared that the South should be reduced to "abject submission," or their institutions be overthrown. In the Senate it was said that, if necessary, the South should be depopulated and repeopled from the North; and an eminent Senator expressed a desire that the President should be made dictator. This was superfluous, since they had already clothed him with dictatorial powers. In the midst of these proceedings, no plea for the Constitution is listened to in the North; here and there a few heroic voices are feebly heard protesting against the progress of despotism, but, for the most part, beyond the military lines, mobs and anarchy rule the hour.

The great mass of the Northern people seem anxious to sunder every safeguard of freedom; they eagerly offer to the Government what no European monarch would dare to demand. The President and his generals are unable to pick up the liberties of the people as rapidly as they are thrown at their feet. . . . In every form by which you could give direct expression to your will, you declared for neutrality. A large majority of the people at the May and August elections voted for the neutrality and peace of Kentucky. The press, the public speakers, the candidates—with exceptions in favor of the Government at Washington so rare as not to need mention—planted themselves on this position. You voted for it, and you meant it. You were promised it, and you expected it. . . . Look now at the condition of Kentucky, and see how your expectations have been realized— how these promises have been redeemed. . . . General Anderson, the military dictator of Kentucky, announces in one of his proclamations that he will arrest no one who does not act, write, or speak in opposition to Mr. Lincoln's Government. It would have completed the idea if he had added, or think in opposition to it. Look at the condition of our State under the rule of our new protectors. They have suppressed the freedom of speech and of the press. They seize people by military force upon mere suspicion, and impose on them oaths unknown to the laws. Other citizens they imprison without warrant, and carry them out of the State, so that the writ of *habeas corpus* can not reach them.

Every day foreign armed bands are making seizures among the people. Hundreds of citizens, old and young, venerable magistrates, whose lives have been distinguished by the love of the people, have been compelled to fly from their homes and families to escape imprisonment and exile at the hands of Northern and German soldiers, under the orders of Mr. Lincoln and his military subordinates. While yet holding an important political trust, confided by Kentucky, I was compelled to leave my home and family, or suffer imprisonment and exile. If it is asked why I did not meet the arrest and seek a trial, my answer is, that I would have welcomed an arrest to be followed by a judge and jury; but you well know that I could not have secured these constitutional rights. I would have been transported beyond the State, to languish in some Federal fortress during the pleasure of the oppressor. Witness the fate of Morehead and his Kentucky associates in their distant and gloomy prison.

The case of the gentleman just mentioned is an example of many others, and it meets every element in a definition of despotism. If it should occur in England it would be righted, or it would overturn the British Empire. He is a citizen and native of Kentucky. As a member of the Legislature, Speaker of the House, Representative in Congress from the Ashland district, and Governor of the State, you have known, trusted, and honored him during a public service of a quarter of a century. He is eminent for his ability, his amiable character, and his blameless life. Yet this man, without indictment, without warrant, without accusation, but by the order of President Lincoln, was seized at midnight, in his own house, and in the midst of his own family, and led through the streets of Louisville, as I am informed, with his hands crossed and pinioned before him—was carried out of the State and district, and now lies a prisoner in a fortress in New York Harbor, a thousand miles away. . . .

The Constitution of the United States, which these invaders unconstitutionally swear every citizen whom they unconstitutionally seize to support, has been wholly abolished. It is as much forgotten as if it lay away back in the twilight of history. The facts I have enumerated show that the very rights most carefully reserved by it to the States and to individuals have been most conspicuously violated. . . . Your fellow-citizen,

(Signed)   JOHN C. BRECKINRIDGE.

Such was the "neutrality" suffered by the Confederacy from governments both at home and abroad.

The chivalric people of Kentucky showed their sympathy with the just cause of the people of the Southern states, by leaving the home where they could not serve the cause of right against might, and nobly shared the fortunes of their Southern brethren on many a blood-dyed field. In like manner did the British people see with disapprobation their government, while proclaiming neutrality, make new rules, and give new constructions to old ones, so as to favor our enemy and embarrass us. The Englishman's sense of fair play, and the manly instinct which predisposes him to side with the weak, gave us hosts of friends, but all their good intentions were paralyzed or foiled by their wily Minister for Foreign Affairs, and his coadjutor on this side, the artful, unscrupulous United States Secretary of State.

I have thus presented the case of Kentucky, not because it was the only state where false promises lulled the people into delusive security until, by gradual approaches, usurpation had bound them hand and foot, and where despotic power crushed all the muniments of civil liberty which the Union was formed to secure, but because of the attempt, which has been noticed, to arraign the Confederacy for invasion of the state in disregard of her sovereignty.

The occupation of Columbus by the Confederate forces was only just soon enough to anticipate the predetermined purpose of the federal government, all of which was plainly set forth in the letter of General Polk to the governor of Kentucky, and his subsequent letter to the Kentucky commissioners.

Missouri, like Kentucky, had wished to preserve peaceful relations in the contest which it was foreseen would soon occur between the Northern and the Southern states. When the federal government denied to her the privilege of choosing her own position, which betokened no hostility to the general government, and she was driven to the necessity of deciding whether or not her citizens should be used for the subjugation of the Southern states, her people and their representative, the state government, repelled the arbitrary assumption of authority by military force to control her government and her people.

Among other acts of invasion, the Federal troops had occupied Belmont, a village in Missouri opposite to Columbus, and with artillery threatened that town, inspiring terror in its peaceful inhabitants. After the occupation of Columbus, under these circumstances of full justification, a small Confederate force, Colonel Tappan's Arkansas regiment, and Beltzhoover's battery, were thrown across the Mississippi to occupy and hold the village, in the state of Missouri, then an ally, and soon to become a member, of the Confederacy. On November 6th General Grant left his headquarters at Cairo with a land and naval force, and encamped on the Kentucky shore. This act and a demonstration made by detachments from his force at Paducah were probably intended to induce the belief that he contemplated an attack on Columbus, thus concealing his real purpose to surprise the small garrison at Belmont. General Polk on the morning of the 7th discovered the landing of the Federal forces on the Missouri shore, some seven miles above Columbus, and, divining the real purpose of the enemy, detached General Pillow with four regiments of his division, say two thousand men, to reënforce the garrison at Belmont. Very soon after his arrival the enemy commenced an assault which was sternly resisted, and with varying fortune, for several hours. The enemy's front so far exceeded the length of our line as to enable him to attack on both flanks, and our troops were finally driven back to the bank of the river with the loss of their battery, which had been gallantly and efficiently served until nearly all its horses had been killed, and its ammunition had been expended. The enemy advanced to the bank of the river below the point to which our men had retreated, and opened an artillery fire upon the town of Columbus, to which our guns from the commanding height responded with such effect as to drive him from the river bank. In the meantime General Polk had at intervals sent three regiments to reënforce General Pillow. Upon the arrival of the first of these, General Pillow led it to a favorable position, where it for some time steadily resisted and checked the advance of the enemy. General Pillow, with great energy and gallantry, rallied his repulsed troops and brought them again into action. General Polk now proceeded in person with two other regiments. Whether from this or some other cause, the enemy commenced a retreat. General Pillow, whose activity and daring on the occasion were worthy of all praise, led the first and second detachments, by which he had been reënforced, to attack the enemy in the rear, and General Polk, landing further up the river, moved to cut off the enemy's retreat; some embarrassment and consequent delay which occurred in landing his troops caused him to be too late for the purpose for which he crossed, and to become only a part of the pursuing force.

One would naturally suppose that the question about which there would be the greatest certainty would be the number of troops engaged in a battle, yet there is nothing in regard to which we have such conflicting accounts. It is fairly concluded, from the concurrent reports, that the enemy attacked us on both flanks, and that in the beginning of the action we were outnumbered; the obstinacy with which the conflict was maintained and the successive advances and retreats which occurred in the action indicate, however, that the disparity could not have been very great, and therefore that after the arrival of our reënforcements our troops must have become numerically superior. The dead and wounded left by the enemy upon the field, the arms, ammunition, and military stores abandoned in his flight, so incontestably prove his defeat, that his claim to have achieved a victory is too preposterous for discussion. Though the forces engaged were comparatively small to those in subsequent battles of the war, six hours of incessant combat, with repeated bayonet charges, must place this in the rank of the most stubborn engagements, and the victors must accord to the vanquished the meed of having fought like Americans. One of the results of the battle, which is at least significant, is the fact that General Grant, who had superciliously refused to recognize General Polk as one with whom he could exchange prisoners, did after the battle, send a flag of truce to get such privileges as are recognized between armies acknowledging each other to be "foemen worthy of their steel."

General Polk reported as follows: "We pursued them to their boats, seven miles, and then drove their boats before us. The road was strewed with their dead and wounded, guns, ammunition, and equipments. The number of prisoners taken by the enemy, as shown by their list furnished, was one hundred and six, all of whom have been returned by exchange. After making a liberal allowance to the enemy, a hundred of their prisoners still remain in my hands, one stand of colors, and a fraction over one thousand stand of arms, with knapsacks, ammunition, and other military stores. Our loss in killed, wounded, and missing, was six hundred and forty-one; that of the enemy was probably not less than twelve hundred."

Meanwhile Albert Sidney Johnston, a soldier of great distinction in the United States army, where he had attained the rank of brigadier general by brevet, and was in command of the Department of California, resigned his commission, and came overland from San Francisco to Richmond, to tender his services to the Confederate States. Though he had been bred a soldier, and most of his life had been spent in the army, he had not neglected such study of political affairs as properly belongs to the citizen of a republic, and appreciated the issue made between states claiming the right to resume the powers they had delegated to a general agent and the claims set up by that agent to coerce states, his creators, and for whom he held a trust.

He was a native of Kentucky, but his first military appointment was from Louisiana, and he was a volunteer in the war for independence by Texas, and for a time resided in that state. Much of his military service had been in the West, and he felt most identified with it. On September 10, 1861, he was assigned to command our Department of the West, which included the states of Tennessee, Missouri, Arkansas, the Indian country, and the western part of Mississippi.

General Johnston, on his arrival at Nashville, found that he lacked not only men, but the munitions of war and the means of obtaining them. Men were ready to be enlisted, but the arms and equipments had nearly all been required to fit out the first levies. Immediately on his survey of the situation, he determined to occupy Bowling Green in Kentucky, and ordered Brigadier General S. B. Buckner, with five thousand men, to take possession of the position. This invasion of Kentucky was an act of self-defense rendered necessary by the action of the government of Kentucky, and by the evidences of intended movements of the forces of the United States. It was not possible to withdraw the troops from Columbus in the west, nor from Cumberland Ford in the east, to which General Felix K. Zollicoffer had advanced with four thousand men. A compliance with the demands of Kentucky would have opened the frontiers of Tennessee and the Mississippi River to the enemy; besides, it was essential to the defense of Tennessee.

East of Columbus, Fort Henry, Fort Donelson, and Hopkinsville were garrisoned with small bodies of troops; and the territory between Columbus and Bowling Green was occupied by moving detachments which caused the supposition that a large military force was present and contemplated an advance. A fortified camp was established at Cumberland Gap, as the right of General Johnston's line and an important point for the protection of East Tennessee against invasion. Thus General Johnston located his line of defense, from Columbus on the west to the Cumberland Mountains on the east, with his center at Bowling Green, which was occupied and entrenched. It was a good base for military operations, was a proper depot for supplies, and, if fortified, could be held against largely superior numbers.

On October 28th General Johnston took command at Bowling Green. He states his force to have been twelve thousand men, and that the enemy's force at that time was estimated to be double his own, or twenty-four thousand. He says: "The enemy's force increased more rapidly than our own, so that by the last of November it numbered fifty thousand, and continued to increase until it ran up to between seventy-five and one hundred thousand. My force was kept down by disease, so that it numbered about twenty-two thousand."

The chief anxiety of the commander of the department was to pro-

GENERAL A. S. JOHNSTON

cure arms and men. On the next day after his arrival at Nashville, he wrote to the Governor of Alabama, "I shall beg to rely on your Excellency to furnish us as rapidly as possible, at this point, with every arm it may be in your power to provide—I mean small-arms for infantry and cavalry." The governor replied, "It is out of the power of Alabama to afford you any assistance in the way of arms." The governor of Georgia replied to the same request on September 18th, "It is utterly impossible for me to comply with your request." General Bragg, in command at Pensacola, writes in reply on September 27th: "The mission of Colonel Buckner will not be successful, I fear, as our extreme Southern country has been stripped of both arms and men. We started early in this matter, and have well nigh exhausted our resources." On September 19th General Johnston telegraphed to me: "Thirty thousand stand of arms are a necessity to my command. I beg you to order them, or as many as can be got, to be instantly procured and sent with dispatch." The Secretary of War replied: "The whole number received by us, by that steamer, was eighteen hundred, and we purchased of the owners seventeen hundred and eighty, making in all thirty-five hundred Enfield rifles, of which we have been compelled to allow the governor of Georgia to have one thousand for arming troops to repel an attack now hourly threatened at Brunswick. Of the remaining twenty-five hundred, I have ordered one thousand sent to you, leaving us but fifteen hundred for arming several regiments now encamped here, and who have been awaiting their arms for several months. . . . We have not an engineer to send you. The whole engineer corps comprises only six captains together with three majors, of whom one is on bureau duty. You will be compelled to employ the best material within your reach, by detailing officers from other corps, and by employing civil engineers."

These details are given to serve as an illustration of the deficiencies existing in every department of the military service in the first years of the war. In this respect much relief came from the well-directed efforts of Governor Harris and the legislature of Tennessee. A cap factory, ordnance shops, and workshops were established. The powder mills at Nashville turned out about four hundred pounds a day. Twelve or fourteen batteries were fitted out at Memphis. Laws were passed to impress and pay for the private arms scattered throughout the state, and the utmost efforts were made to collect and adapt them to military uses. The returns make it evident that, during most of the autumn of 1861, fully one half of General Johnston's troops were imperfectly armed, and whole brigades remained without weapons for months.

No less energetic were the measures taken to concentrate and recruit his forces. General Hardee's command was moved from northeastern Arkansas and sent to Bowling Green, which added four thousand men to the troops there. The regiment of Texan rangers was brought from Louisiana, and supplied with horses and sent to the front. Five hundred Kentuckians joined General Buckner on his advance, and five regiments were gradually formed and filled up. A cavalry company under John H. Morgan was also added. At this time (September, 1861), General Johnston, under the authority granted to him by the government, made a requisition for thirty thousand men from Tennessee, ten thousand from Mississippi, and ten thousand from Arkansas. The Arkansas troops were directed to be sent to General McCulloch for the defense of their own frontier. The governor of Mississippi sent four regiments, when this source of supply was closed.

Up to the middle of November only three regiments were mustered in under this call from Tennessee, but by the close of December the number of men who joined was from twelve to fifteen thousand. Two regiments, fifteen hundred strong, had joined General Polk.

In Arkansas five companies and a battalion had been organized, and were ready to join General McCulloch.

A speedy advance of the enemy was now indicated, and an increase of force was so necessary that further delay was impossible. General Johnston, therefore, determined upon a levy *en masse* in his department. He made a requisition on the governors of Tennessee, Alabama, and Mississippi, to call out every able-bodied member of the militia into whose hands arms could be placed, or to provide a volunteer force large enough to use all the arms that could be procured. In his letters to these governors, he plainly presents his view of the posture of affairs on December 24th, points out impending dangers, and shows that to his applications the response had not been such as the emergency demanded. He says:

It was apprehended by me that the enemy would attempt to assail the South, not only by boats and troops moving down the river, to be assembled during the fall and winter, but by columns marching inland, threatening Tennessee, by endeavoring to turn the defenses of Columbus. Further observation confirms me in this opinion; but I think the means employed for the defense of the river will probably render it comparatively secure. The enemy will energetically push toward Nashville the heavy masses. of troops now assembled between Louisville and Bowling Green. The general position of Bowling Green is good and commanding; but the peculiar topography of the place and the length of the line of the Barren River as a line of defense, though strong, require a large force to defend it. There is no position equally defensive as Bowling Green, nor line of defense as good as the Barren River, between the Barren and the Cumberland at Nashville; so that it can not be abandoned without exposing Tennessee, and giving vastly the vantage-ground to the enemy. It is manifest that the Northern generals appreciate this; and, by withdrawing their forces from western Virginia and east Kentucky, they have managed to add them to the new levies from Ohio, Indiana, and Illinois, and to concentrate a force in front of me variously estimated at from sixty to one hundred thousand men, and which I believe will number seventy-five thousand. To maintain my position, I have only about seventeen thousand men in this neighborhood. It is impossible for me to obtain additions to my strength from Columbus; the generals in command in that quarter consider that it would imperil that point to diminish their force, and open Tennessee to the enemy. General Zollicoffer can not join me, as he guards the Cumberland, and prevents the invasion and possible revolt of East Tennessee.

On June 5th General Johnston was reënforced by the brigades of Floyd and Maney from western Virginia. He also sent a messenger to Richmond to ask that a few regiments might be detached from the several armies in the field, and sent to him to be replaced by new levies. He said: "I do not ask that my force shall be made equal to that of the enemy; but, if possible, it should be raised to fifty thousand men." Meantime such an appearance of menace had been maintained as led the enemy to believe that our force was large, and that he might be attacked at any time. Frequent and rapid expeditions through the sparsely settled country gave rise to rumors which kept alive this apprehension.

CHAPTER IX: *The Coercion of Missouri—Answers of the Governors of States to President Lincoln's Requisition for Troops—Restoration of Forts Caswell and Johnson to the United States Government—Condition of Missouri Similar to that of Kentucky—Hostilities, how Initiated in Missouri—Agreement Between Generals Price and Harney—Its Favorable Effects—General Harney Relieved of Command by the United States Government Because of his Pacific Policy—Removal of Public Arms from Missouri—Searches for and Seizure of Arms—Missouri on the Side of Peace—Address of General Price to the People—Proclamation of Governor Jackson—Humiliating Concessions of the Governor to the United States Government, for the Sake of Peace—Demands of the Federal Officers—Revolutionary Principles Attempted to be Enforced by the United States Government—The Action at Booneville—The Patriot Army of Militia—Further Rout of the Enemy—Heroism and Self-sacrifice of the People—Complaints and Embarrassments—Zeal: its Effects—Action of Congress—Battle of Springfield—General Price—Battle at Lexington—Bales of Hemp—Other Combats.*

To preserve the Union in the spirit and for the purposes for which it was established, an equilibrium between the states, as grouped in sections, was essential. When the territory of Missouri constitutionally applied for admission as a state into the Union, the struggle between state rights and that sectional aggrandizement which was seeking to destroy the existing equilibrium gave rise to the contest which shook the Union to its foundation, and sowed the seeds of geographical divisions, which have borne the most noxious weeds that have choked our political vineyard. Again in 1861 Missouri appealed to the Constitution for the vindication of her rights, and again did usurpation and the blind rage of a sectional party disregard the appeal, and assume powers, not only undelegated, but in direct violation of the fourth section of the fourth article of the Constitution, which every federal officer had sworn to maintain, and which secured to every state a republican government, and protection against invasion.

If it be contended that the invasion referred to must have been by other than the troops of the United States, and that their troops were therefore not prohibited from entering a state against its wishes, and for purpose hostile to its policy, the section of the Constitution referred to fortifies the fact, heretofore noticed, of the refusal of the convention, when forming the Constitution, to delegate to the federal government power to coerce a state. By its last clause it was provided that not even to suppress domestic violence could the general government, on its own motion, send troops of the United States into the territory of one of the states. That section reads thus:

The United States shall guarantee to every State in this Union a republican form of government, and shall protect each of them against invasion, and on application of the Legislature, or of the executive (when the Legislature can not be convened), against domestic violence.

Surely, if federal troops could not be sent into a a state without its application, even to protect it against domestic violence, still less could it be done to overrule the will of its people. That, instead of an obligation upon the citizens of other states to respond to a call by the President for troops to invade a particular state, it was in April, 1861, deemed a high crime to so use them: reference is here made to the published answers of the governors of states which had not seceded to the requisition made upon them for troops to be employed against the states which had seceded.

Governor Letcher of Virginia replied to the requisition of the United States Secretary of War as follows:

I am requested to detach from the militia of the State of Virginia the quota designated in a table which you append, to serve as infantry or riflemen, for the period of three months, unless sooner discharged.

In reply to this communication, I have only to say that the militia of Virginia will not be furnished to the powers at Washington for any such use or purpose as they have in view. Your object is to subjugate the Southern States, and a requisition made upon me for such an object—an object, in my judgment, not within the purview of the Constitution, or the Act of 1795—will not be complied with.

Governor Magoffin of Kentucky replied:

Your dispatch is received. In answer, I say emphatically, Kentucky will furnish no troops for the wicked purpose of subduing her sister Southern States.

Governor Harris of Tennessee replied:

Tennessee will not furnish a single man for coercion, but fifty thousand, if necessary, for the defense of our rights, or those of our Southern brothers.

Governor Jackson of Missouri answered:

Requisition is illegal, unconstitutional, revolutionary, inhuman, diabolical, and can not be complied with.

Governor Rector of Arkansas replied:

In answer to your requisition for troops from Arkansas, to subjugate the Southern States, I have to say that none will be furnished. The demand is only adding insult to injury.

Governor Ellis of North Carolina responded to the requisition for troops from that state as follows:

Your dispatch is received, and, if genuine—which its extraordinary character leads me to doubt—I have to say, in reply, that I regard the levy of troops made by the Administration, for the purpose of subjugating the States of the South, as in violation of the Constitution, and a usurpation of power. I can be no party to this wicked violation of the laws of the country, and to this war upon the liberties of a free people. You can get no troops from North Carolina.

Governor Ellis, who had lived long enough to leave behind him an enviable reputation, was a fair representative of the conservatism, gallantry, and tenacity in well-doing, of the state over which he presided. He died too soon for his country's good, and the Confederacy seriously felt the loss of his valuable services. The prompt and spirited answer he gave to the call upon North Carolina to furnish troops for the subjugation of the Southern states was the fitting complement of his earlier action in immediately restoring to the federal government Forts Johnson and Caswell, which had been seized without proper authority. In communicating his action to President Buchanan, he wrote:

My information satisfies me that this popular outbreak was caused by a report, very generally credited, but which, for the sake of humanity, I hope is not true, that it was the purpose of the Administration to coerce the Southern States, and that troops were on their way to garrison the Southern ports, and to begin the work of subjugation. . . . Should I receive assurance that no troops will be sent to this State prior to the 4th of March next, then all will be peace and quiet here, and the property of the United States will be fully protected, as heretofore. If, however, I am unable to get such assurances, I will not undertake to answer for the consequences.

The forts in this State have long been unoccupied, and their being garrisoned at this time will unquestionably be looked upon as a hostile demonstration, and will in my opinion certainly be resisted.

The plea so constantly made by the succeeding administration, as an excuse for its warlike acts, that the duty to protect the public property required such action, is shown by this letter of Governor Ellis to have been a plea created by their usurpations, but for which there might have been peace, as well as safety to property, and, what was of greater worth, the lives, the liberties, and the republican institutions of the country.

There was great similarity in the condition of Missouri to that of Kentucky. They were both border states, and, by their institutions and the origin of a large portion of their citizens, were identified with the South. Both sought to occupy a neutral position in the impending war, and offered guarantees of peace and order throughout their territory if left free to control their own affairs. Both refused to furnish troops to the United States government for the unconstitutional purpose of coercing the Southern states. Both, because of their stronger affinity to the South than to the North, were the objects of suspicion, and consequent military occupation by the troops of the United States government. At the inception of this unwarrantable proceeding, an effort was made by the governor of Missouri to preserve the rights of the state without disturbing its relations to the United States government. If it had been the policy of the government to allow to Missouri the control of her domestic affairs, and an exemption from being a party to the violation of the Constitution in making war against certain of the states, the above-described effort of the governor might and probably would have been successful. The form and purpose of that effort appear in the compact entered into between Major General Price, commanding the militia or "Missouri State Guard," and General Harney, of the United States army, commanding the Department of the West, a geographical division which included the state of Missouri.

During a temporary absence of General Harney, Captain Lyon, commanding United States forces at St. Louis, initiated hostilities against the state of Missouri under the following circumstances:

In obedience to the militia law of the state, an annual encampment was directed by the governor for instruction in tactics. Camp Jackson, near St. Louis, was designated for the encampment of the militia of the county in 1861. Here for some days companies of state militia, amounting to about eight hundred men, under command of Brigadier General D. M. Frost, were being exercised, as is usual upon such occasions. They presented no appearance of a hostile camp. There were no sentinels to guard against surprise; visitors were freely admitted; it was the picnic ground for the ladies of the city, and everything wore the aspect of merrymaking rather than that of grim-visaged war.

Suddenly, Captain (afterward General) Nathaniel Lyon appeared with an overwhelming force of Federal troops, surrounded this holiday encampment, and demanded an unconditional surrender. Resistance was impracticable, and none was attempted; the militia surrendered, and were confined as prisoners; but prisoners of what? There was no war, and no warrant for their arrest as offenders against the law. It is left for the usurpers to frame a vocabulary suited to their act.

After the return of General Harney, Brigadier General D. M. Frost of the Missouri militia appealed to him from his prison, the St. Louis arsenal, on May 11, 1861, representing that "in accordance with the laws of the State of Missouri, which have been existing for some years, and in obedience to the orders of the Governor, on Monday last I entered into an encampment with the militia force of St. Louis County for the purpose of instructing the same in accordance with the laws of the United States and of this State." He further sets forth that every officer and soldier of his command had taken an oath to sustain the Constitution and laws of the United States and of the state of Missouri, and that while in the peaceable performance of their duties the encampment was surrounded by the command of Captain N. Lyon, United States army, and a surrender demanded, to which General Frost replied as follows:

CAMP JACKSON, May 10, 1861.

SIR: I, never for a moment having conceived the idea that so illegal and unconstitutional a demand as I have just received from you would be made by an officer of the United States Army, am wholly unprepared to defend my command from this unwarranted attack, and shall therefore be forced to comply with your demand.

I am sir, very respectfully, your obedient servant,

D. FROST,
Brigadier-General, commanding Camp Jackson, M. M.
Captain N. LYON, *commanding United States troops.*

General Frost's letter to General Harney continues: "My command was, in accordance with the above, deprived of their arms, and surrendered into the hands of Captain Lyon; after which, while thus disarmed and surrounded, a fire was opened on a portion of it by his troops, and a number of my men put to death, together with several innocent lookers-on, men, women, and children." On the occasion of the attack upon Camp Jackson, "a large crowd of citizens, men, women, and children, were gathered around, gazing curiously at these strange proceedings, when a volley was fired into them, killing ten and wounding twenty non-combatants, mostly women and children. A reign of terror was at once established, and the most severe measures were adopted by the Federals to overawe the excitement and the rage of the people."[1]

The massacre at Camp Jackson produced intense excitement throughout the state. The legislature, upon receipt of the news, passed several bills for the enrollment and organization of the militia, and to confer

---

[1] See *Confederate First and Second Missouri Brigades,* Bevier, pp. 24-26.

special powers upon the governor of the state. By virtue of these, general officers were appointed, chief of whom was Sterling Price.

Because of the atrocities at St. Louis, and the violent demonstrations consequent upon them, not only in St. Louis but elsewhere in the state, General Price, well known to be what was termed "a Union man," and not only by his commission as commander in chief of the militia of the state, but also, and even more, because of his influence among the people, was earnestly solicited by influential citizens of St. Louis to unite with General Harney in a joint effort to restore order and preserve peace. With the sanction of Governor Jackson he proceeded to St. Louis, the headquarters of the Department of the West, and, after some preliminary conference, entered into the following agreement, which, being promulgated to the people, was received with general satisfaction, and for a time allayed excitement. The agreement was as follows:

ST. LOUIS, May 21, 1861.

The undersigned, officers of the United States Government and of the government of the State of Missouri, for the purpose of removing misapprehension and of allaying public excitement, deem it proper to declare that they have this day had a personal interview in this city, in which it has been mutually understood, without the semblance of dissent on either part, that each of them has no other than a common object, equally interesting and important to every citizen of Missouri—that of restoring peace and good order to the people of the State in subordination to the laws of the General and State governments.

It being thus understood, there seems no reason why every citizen should not confide in the proper officers of the General and State governments to restore quiet, and, as among the best means of offering no counter-influences, we mutually commend to all persons to respect each other's rights throughout the State, making no attempt to exercise unauthorized powers, as it is the determination of the proper authorities to suppress all unlawful proceedings which can only disturb the public peace. General Price, having by commission full authority over the militia of the State of Missouri, undertakes with the sanction of the Governor of the State, already declared, to direct the whole power of the State officers to maintaining order within the State among the people thereof. General Harney publicly declares that, this object being assured, he can have no occasion, as he has no wish, to make military movements that might otherwise create excitement and jealousy, which he most earnestly desires to avoid.

We, the undersigned, do therefore mutually enjoin upon the people of the State to attend to their civil business, of whatever sort it may be, and it is hoped that the unquiet elements which have threatened so seriously to disturb the public peace may soon subside, and be remembered only to be deplored.

W. S. HARNEY,
Brigadier-General commanding.

STERLING PRICE,
Major-General Missouri State Guard.

The distinct position of General Harney, that the military force of the United States should not be used in Missouri except in case of necessity, together with the emphatic declaration of General Price that he had the power and would use it to preserve peace and order in Missouri, seemed to remove all danger of collision in that state between the federal and local forces. In conformity with this understanding, General Price returned to the capital of the state, and sent to their homes the militia who had been assembled there by the governor for the defense of the capital against an anticipated attack by the troops of the United States.

Those who desired to preserve peace in Missouri had just cause to be gratified at the favorable prospect now presented. Those who desired war had equal ground for dissatisfaction. A few days after the promulgation of the agreement between General Price and General Harney, the latter was removed from command, as many believed, because of his successful efforts to allay excitement and avoid war. Rumors had been in circulation that the Missourians were driving the "Union men" from their homes, and many letters purporting to be written in different parts of the state represented the persecution of Union men. It was suspected that many of them were written in St. Louis, or inspired by the cabal. An incident related in confirmation of the justice of this suspicion is that General Harney received a letter from St. Joseph, stating that ex-Governor Stewart and a number of the most respectable men in St. Joseph had been driven from their homes, and that, unless soldiers were soon sent, the Union men would all have to leave. He called upon the Hon. F. P. Blair, an influential citizen of St. Louis, and asked him if he knew the writer of the letter. The reply was: "Oh, yes, he is perfectly reliable; you can believe anything he says."[2] General Harney said he would write immediately to General Price. Dissatisfaction was then manifested at such delay; two or three days later, a letter from ex-Governor Stewart was published in the *St. Joseph News,* in which was a marked paragraph of the copy sent to General Harney: "Neither I nor any other Union man has been driven out of St. Joe."[3] An attempt has been made to evade the conclusion that General Harney was relieved from command because of his pacific policy. The argument is that the order was dated May 16th, and his agreement with General Price was on the 21st of the same month, an argument more specious than fair, as it appears from the letter of President Lincoln of May 18, 1861, to Hon. F. P. Blair, that the order sent from the War Department to him was to be delivered or

---

[2] See *Life of General Wm. S. Harney,* by L. U. Reavis, p. 373.
[3] See *ibid.,* p. 373.

withheld at his discretion, and that it was not delivered until the 30th of the month, and until after General Harney had not only entered into his agreement with General Price, but had declined to act upon sensational stories of persecution, on which applications were made to send troops into the interior of Missouri. During the days this order was held for his removal, with discretionary power to deliver or withhold it, the above-recited events occurred, and they may fairly be considered as having decided the question of his removal from that command.

The principal United States arsenal at the West was that near to St. Louis. To it had been transferred a large number of the altered muskets sent from Springfield, Massachusetts, so that in 1861 the arms in that arsenal were, perhaps, numerically second only to those of Springfield. These arms, by a conjunction of deceptive and bold measures, were removed from the arsenal in Missouri and transported to Illinois. To whom did those arms belong? Certainly to those whose money had made or purchased them. That is, to the states in common, not to their agent the general government, or to a portion of the states which might be in a condition to appropriate them to their special use, and in disregard of the rights of their partners.

Not satisfied with removing the public arms from the limits of Missouri, the next step was that, in total disrespect of the constitutional right of the citizens to bear arms for their own defense, and to be free from searches and seizures except by warrants duly issued, the officers of the general government proceeded to search the houses of citizens in St. Louis, and to seize arms wherever they were found.

Missouri had refused to engage in war against her sister states of the South; she was therefore first to be disarmed, and then to be made the victim of an invasion characterized by such barbarous atrocities as shame the civilization of the age. The wrongs she suffered, the brave efforts of her unarmed people to defend their hearthstones and their liberties against the desecration and destruction of both, form a melancholy chapter in the history of the United States, which all who would cherish their fair fame must wish could be obliterated.

These acts of usurpation and outrage, as well upon the political as personal rights of the people of Missouri, aroused an intense feeling in that state. It will be remembered that Governor Jackson had responded to the call of Lincoln upon him for troops with the just indignation of one who understood the rights of the state, and the limited powers of the general government. His stern refusal to become a party to the war upon the South made him the object of special persecution. By his side in this critical juncture stood the gallant veteran, General Price. To the latter was confided the conduct of the military affairs of the state, and after exhausting every effort to maintain order by peaceful means, and seeing that the government would recognize no other method than that of force, he energetically applied himself to raise troops and procure arms so as to enable the state to meet force by force. During this and all the subsequent period, the governor and the general were ably seconded by the accomplished, gallant, and indefatigable Lieutenant Governor Reynolds.

The position of Missouri in 1860-'61 was unquestionably that of opposition to the secession of the state. The people generously confided in the disposition of the general government to observe their rights, and continued to hope for a peaceful settlement of the questions then agitating the country. This was evinced by the fact that not a single secessionist was elected to the state convention, and that General Price, an avowed "Union man," was chosen as president of the convention. Hence the general satisfaction with the agreement made between Generals Harney and Price for the preservation of peace and non-intervention by the army of the United States. General Harney, the day before the order for his removal was communicated to him, wrote to the War Department, expressing his confidence in the preservation of peace in Missouri, and used this significant expression: "Interference by unauthorized parties as to the course I shall pursue can alone prevent the realization of these hopes."[4] The "unauthorized parties" here referred to could not have been the people or the government of Missouri. Others than they must have been the parties wishing to use force, provocative of hostilities.

As has been heretofore stated, after his agreement with General Harney at St. Louis, General Price returned to the capital and dismissed to their homes the large body of militia that had been there assembled.

After the removal of General Harney, believed to be in consequence of his determination to avoid the use of military force against the people of Missouri, reports were rife of a purpose on the part of the administration at Washington to disarm the citizens of Missouri who did not sympathize with the views of the federal government, and to put arms into the hands of those who could be relied on to enforce them. On June 4th General Price issued an address to the people of Missouri, and in reference to that report said: "The purpose of such a movement could not be misunderstood; and it would not only be a palpable violation of

---

[4] See *Life of General Wm. S. Harney*, by L. U. Reavis, p. 72.

the agreement referred to, and an equally plain violation of our constitutional rights, but a gross indignity to the citizens of this State, which would be resisted to the last extremity."

The call of President Lincoln for seventy-five thousand volunteers removed any preëxisting doubt as to the intent to coerce the states which should claim to assert their right of sovereignty. Missouri, while avowing her purpose to adhere to the Union, had asserted her right to exercise supreme control over her domestic affairs, and this put her in the category of a state threatened by the proceedings of the United States government. To provide for such contingency as might be anticipated, Governor Jackson on June 13th issued a call for fifty thousand volunteers, and Major General Price took the field in command. In this proclamation Governor Jackson said:

A series of unprovoked and unparalleled outrages has been inflicted on the peace and dignity of this Commonwealth, and upon the rights and liberties of its people, by wicked and unprincipled men professing to act under the authority of the Government of the United States.

In his endeavor to maintain the peace of the state, and to avert, if possible, from its borders a civil war, he caused the aforementioned agreement to be made with the commander of the Northern forces in the state, by which its peace might be preserved. That officer was promptly removed by his government. The governor then, upon the increase of hostile actions, proposed, at an interview with the new officer commanding the forces of the United States government, to disband the state guard, and break up its organization; to disarm all companies that had been armed by the state; to pledge himself not to organize the militia under the military bill; that no arms or munitions of war should be brought into the state; that he would protect the citizens equally in all their rights, regardless of their political opinions; that he would repress all insurrectionary movements within the state; would repel all attempts to invade it, from whatever quarter, and by whomsoever made; and would maintain a strict neutrality and preserve the peace of the state. And further, if necessary, he would invoke the assistance of the United States troops to carry out the pledges. The only conditions to this proposition made by the governor were that the United States government should undertake to disarm the "Home Guard" which it had illegally organized and armed throughout the state, and pledge itself not to occupy with its troops any localities in the state not occupied by them at that time.

The words of a governor of a state who offered such truly generous terms deserve to be inserted: "Nothing but the most earnest desire to avert the horrors of civil war from our beloved State could have tempted me to propose these humiliating terms. They were rejected by the Federal officers."

These demanded not only the disorganization and disarming of the state militia and the nullification of the military bill, but they refused to disarm their own "Home Guard," and insisted that the government of the United States should enjoy an unrestricted right to move and station its troops throughout the state whenever and wherever it might, in the opinion of its officers, be necessary either for the protection of its "loyal subjects" or for the repelling of invasion; and they plainly announced that it was the intention of the administration to take military occupation of the whole state, and to reduce it, as avowed by General Lyon, to the "exact condition of Maryland."

We have already stated that the revolutionary measures which the United States government had undertaken to enforce involved the subjection of every state, either by voluntary submission or subjugation. However much a state might desire peace and neutrality, its own will could not elect. The scheme demanded the absolute sovereignty of the government of the United States, or, in other words, the extinguishment of the independence and sovereignty of the state. Human actions are not only the fruit of the ruling motive, but they are also the evidence of the existence of that motive. Thus, when we see the governor of the state of Missouri offering such generous terms to the government of the United States in order to preserve peace and neutrality, and the latter, rejecting them, avow its intention to do its will with the authorities, the property, and the citizens of the state, and proceed with military force to do it, its actions are both the evidence and the fruit of its theory. These measures were revolutionary in the extreme. They involved the entire subversion of those principles on which the American union was founded, and of the compact or Constitution of that union. The government of the United States, in the hands of those who wielded its authority, was made the bloody instrument to establish these usurpations on the ruins of the crushed hopes of mankind for permanent freedom under constitutional government. For the justness and truthfulness of these allegations I appeal to the impartial and sober judgment of posterity.

The volunteers who were assembled under this proclamation of Governor Jackson, of June 13th, had few arms except their squirrel rifles and shotguns, and could scarcely be said to have any military equipment.

The brigadier generals who were appointed were assigned to geographical divisions, and, with such men as they could collect, reported in obedience to their orders at Booneville and Lexington. On June 20, 1861, General Lyon and Colonel F. P. Blair, with an estimated force of seven thousand well-armed troops, having eight pieces of artillery, ascended the Missouri River, and debarked about five miles below Booneville. To oppose them, the Missourians had there about eight hundred men, poorly armed, without a piece of artillery, and but little ammunition. With courage which must be commended at the expense of their discretion, they resolved to engage the enemy, and after a combat of an hour and a half or more, retired, having inflicted heavy loss upon the enemy, and suffering but little themselves. This first skirmish between the federal troops and the Missouri militia inspired confidence in their fellow citizens, and checked the contemptuous terms in which the militia had been spoken of by the enemy. Governor Jackson, with some two hundred fifty to three hundred of the militia, engaged in the action at Booneville, started toward the southwestern portion of the state. He marched in the direction of a place called Cole Camp and, when within twelve or fifteen miles of it, learned that a force of seven hundred to one thousand of the enemy had been sent to that point by General Lyon and Colonel Blair, with a view to intercepting his retreat. The design, however, was frustrated by an expedition consisting of about three hundred fifty men, commanded by Colonel O'Kane, who had assembled them in a very few hours in the neighborhood south of the enemy's camp. There were no pickets out except in the neighborhood of Jackson's forces, and Colonel O'Kane's surprised the enemy where they were asleep in two large barns. The attack was made at daybreak, the enemy routed after suffering the heavy loss of two hundred six killed and more wounded, and more than a hundred prisoners. Three hundred sixty-two muskets with bayonets were captured. The Missourians lost four killed and fifteen or twenty wounded.

General Price, with a view to drawing his army from the base-line of the enemy, the Missouri River, ordered his troops to the southwestern portion of the state. The column from Lexington marched without transportation, without tents or blankets, and relied for subsistence on the country through which it passed, being in the meantime closely pursued by the enemy. The movement was successfully made, and a junction effected in Cedar County with the forces present with Governor Jackson. The total when assembled was about thirty-six hundred men.

This, then, was the patriot army of Missouri. It was a heterogeneous mass representing every condition of Western life. There were the old and young, the rich and poor, the grave and gay, the planter and laborer, the farmer and clerk, the hunter and boatman, the merchant and woodsman. At least five hundred of these men were entirely unarmed. Many had only the common rifle and shot-gun. None were provided with cartridges or canteens. They had eight pieces of cannon, but no shells, and very few solid shot, or rounds of grape and canister.

Rude and almost incredible devices were made to supply these wants: trace-chains, iron rods, hard pebbles, and smooth stones were substituted for shot; and evidence of the effect of such rough missiles was to be given in the next encounter with the enemy.[5]

Governor Jackson continued his march toward southwestern Missouri. He had received reliable intelligence that he was pursued by General Lyon from the northeast, and by Lane and Sturgis from the northwest, their supposed object being to form a junction in his rear, and he subsequently learned that a column numbering three thousand had been sent out from St. Louis to intercept his retreat, and had arrived at the town of Carthage, immediately in his front. These undisciplined, poorly armed Missourians were, therefore, in a position which would have appalled less heroic men—a large hostile force in their rear, and another, nearly equal in numbers to their own, disputing their passage in front. They cheerfully moved forward, however, attacked the enemy in position, and after a severe engagement routed him, pursued him to a second position, from which he was again driven, falling back to Carthage, where he made his last stand and, upon being driven from which, as was subsequently ascertained, continued his retreat all night. The killed and wounded of the enemy, left along the route of his retreat over a space of ten miles, were estimated at from one hundred fifty to two hundred killed, and from three to four hundred wounded. Several hundred muskets were captured, and the Missourians were better prepared for future conflicts. Our loss was between forty and fifty killed, and from one hundred twenty-five to one hundred fifty wounded.[6]

If any shall ask why I have entered into such details of engagements where the forces were comparatively so small, and the results so little affected the final issue of the war, the reply is that such heroism and self-sacrifice as these undisciplined, partially armed, unequipped men displayed against superior numbers, possessed of all the appliances of war, claim special notice as bearing evidence not only of the virtue of the men, but the sanctity of the cause which could so inspire them. Unsupported save by the consciousness of a just cause, without other sympathy

---

[5] Bevier, pp. 35, 36.
[6] Bevier, pp. 36-38.

than that which the Confederate States fully gave, despising the plea of helplessness, and defying the threats of a powerful government to crush her, Missouri, without arms or other military preparation, took up the gauntlet thrown at her feet, and dared to make war in defense of the laws and liberties of her people.

My motive for promptly removing the seat of government, after authority was given by the provisional Congress, has been heretofore stated, but proximity to the main army of the enemy, and the flanking attacks by which the new capital was threatened, did not diminish the anxiety, which had been felt before removal from Montgomery, in regard to affairs in Missouri, the "far west" of the Confederacy.

The state, which forty years before had been admitted to the Union, against sectional resistance to the right guaranteed by the Constitution, and specifically denominated in the treaty for the acquisition of Louisiana, now, because her governor refused to furnish troops for the unconstitutional purpose of coercing states, became the subject of special hostility and the object of extraordinary efforts for her subjugation.

The little which it would have been possible for the Confederacy to do to promote her military efficiency was diminished by the anomalous condition in which the state troops remained until some time in the second year of the war. A strange misapprehension led to unreasonable complaints, under the supposition that Missouri was generally neglected, and her favorite officer, General Price, was not accorded a commission corresponding to his merit and the wishes of the people. It is due to that gallant soldier and true patriot, that it should here be stated that he was not a party to any such complaints, knew they were unfounded, and realized that his wishes for the defense of Missouri were fully reciprocated by the executive of the Confederacy; all of this was manifested in the correspondence between us, before Missouri had tendered any troops to the Confederate States. It was his statement of the difficulties and embarrassments which surrounded him that caused me to write to the governor of Missouri on December 21, 1861, stating to him my anxiety to have the troops of Missouri tendered and organized into brigades and divisions, so that they might be rendered more effective, and we be better able to provide for them by the appointment of general officers and otherwise.

For a full understanding of the nature and degree of the complaints and embarrassments referred to, I here insert my reply to letters sent to me by the Hon. John B. Clarke, M. C. of Missouri:

RICHMOND, VIRGINIA, January 8, 1862.

Hon. JOHN B. CLARKE, *Richmond, Virginia.*

SIR: I have received the two letters from Governor Jackson sent by you this day. The Governor speaks of delay by the authorities of Richmond, and neglect of the interests of Missouri, and expresses the hope that he has said enough to be well understood by me.

When I remember that he wrote in reply to my call upon him to hasten the tender of Missouri troops, so that they should be put upon the footing of those of other States, and with a knowledge that as militia of the State I had no power to organize or appoint commanders for them, and that it was his duty to attend to their wants, but that I had sent an agent of the Confederate Government as far as practicable to furnish the necessary supplies to the militia of Missouri actually in service, I can only say, I hope he is not understood by me. It is but a short time since, in a conversation of hours, I fully explained to you the case so far as I am connected with it, and there is nothing for me to add to what you then seemed to consider conclusive.

Very respectfully yours,

JEFFERSON DAVIS.

As is usually the case when citizens are called from their ordinary pursuits for the purposes of war, the people of Missouri did not then realize the value of preparation in camp, and were reluctant to enroll themselves for long periods. The state, even less than the Confederate government, could not supply them with the arms, munitions, and equipage necessary for campaigns and battles sieges. Under all these disadvantages, it is a matter of well-grounded surprise that they were able to achieve so much. The Missourians who fought at Vicksburg, and who, after that long, trying, and disastrous siege, asked, when in the camp of paroled prisoners, not if they could get a furlough, not if they might go home when released, but how soon they might hope to be exchanged and resume their places in the line of battle, show of what metal the Missouri troops were made, and of what they were capable when tempered in the fiery furnace of war.

I can recall few scenes during the war which impressed me more deeply than the spirit of those worn prisoners waiting for the exchange that would again permit them to take the hazards of battle for the cause of their country.

This memory leads me to recur with regret to my inability, in the beginning of the war, to convince the governor of Missouri of the necessity for thorough organization and the enrollment of men for long terms, instead of loose combinations of milita for periods always short and sometimes uncertain.

General Price possessed an extraordinary power to secure the personal attachment of his troops, and to inspire them with a confidence which served in no small degree as a substitute for more thorough training. His own enthusiasm and entire devotion to the cause he served were infused throughout his followers and made them all their country's own. To Lord Wellington has been attributed the remark that he did not want zeal in a soldier, and to Napoleon the apothegm that Providence is on the side of the heavy battalions. Zeal was oftentimes our main dependence, and on many a hard-fought field served to drive our small battalions, like a wedge, through the serried works of the enemy.

The Confederate States, yet in their infancy, and themselves engaged in an unequal struggle for existence, by act of their Congress declared that, if Missouri was engaged in repelling a lawless invasion of her territory by armed forces, it was their right and duty to aid the people and government of said state in resisting such invasion, and in securing the means and the opportunity of expressing their will upon all questions affecting their rights and liberties. With small means, compared to their wants, the Confederate Congress on August 6th appropriated one million dollars "to aid the people of the State of Missouri in the effort to maintain, within their own limits, the constitutional liberty which it is the purpose of the Confederate States in the existing war to vindicate," etc.

In the next battle after that of Carthage, which has been noticed, Missourians were no longer to be alone. General McCullough, commanding a brigade of Confederate troops, marched from Arkansas to make a junction with General Price, then threatened with an attack by a large force of the enemy under General Lyon, which was concentrated near Springfield, Missouri. The battle was fiercely contested, but finally won by our troops. In this action General Lyon was killed while gallantly endeavoring to rally his discomfited troops and lead them to the charge. While we cannot forget the cruel wrongs he had inflicted and sought still further to impose upon an unoffending people, we must accord to him the redeeming virtue of courage, and recognize his ability as a soldier. On this occasion General Price exhibited in two instances the magnanimity, self-denial, and humanity which ever characterized him. General McCullough claimed the right to command as an officer of the Confederate States army. General Price, though he ranked him by a grade, replied that "he was not fighting for distinction, but for the defense of the liberties of his countrymen, and that it mattered but little what position he occupied. He said he was ready to surrender not only the command, but his life, as a sacrifice to the cause."[7] He surrendered the command and took a subordinate position, though "he felt assured of victory."

The second instance was an act of humanity to his bitterest enemy. General Lyon's "surgeon came in for his body, under a flag of truce, after the close of the battle, and General Price sent it in his own wagon. But the enemy, in his flight, left the body unshrouded in Springfield. The next morning, August 11th, Lieutenant-Colonel Gustavus Elgin and Colonel R. H. Musser, two members of Brigadier-General Clark's staff, caused the body to be properly prepared for burial."[8]

After the battle of Springfield, General McCullough returned with his brigade to his former position in Arkansas. John C. Fremont had been appointed a general, and assigned to the command made vacant by the death of General Lyon. He signalized his entrance upon the duty by a proclamation, confiscating the estates and slave property of "rebels."

"On the 10th of September, when General Price was about to go into camp, he learned that a detachment of Federal troops was marching from Lexington to Warrensburg, to seize the funds of the bank in that place, and to arrest and plunder the citizens of Johnson County, in accordance with General Fremont's proclamation and instructions."[9] General Price resumed his march and, pressing rapidly forward with his mounted men, arrived about daybreak at Warrensburg, where he learned that the enemy had hastily fled about midnight. He then decided to move with his whole force against Lexington. He found the enemy in strong entrenchments and well supplied with artillery.

The place was stubbornly defended. The siege proper commenced on September 18, 1861, and with varying fortunes. Fierce combats continued through that day and the next. On the morning of the 20th General Price ordered a number of bales of hemp to be transported to the point from which the advance of his troop had been repeatedly repulsed. They were ranged in a line for a breastwork and, when rolled before the men as they advanced, formed a moving rampart which was proof against shot, and only to be overcome by a sortie in force, which the enemy did not dare to make. On came the hempen breastworks, while Price's artillery continued an effective fire. In the afternoon of the 20th the enemy hung out a white flag, upon which General Price ordered a cessation of firing, and sent to ascertain the object of the signal. The

---

[7] Bevier, p. 41.
[8] *Ibid.*, pp. 49, 50.
[9] *Ibid.*, p. 54.

Federal forces surrendered as prisoners of war, to the number of thirty-five hundred; also, seven pieces of artillery, over three thousand stand of muskets, a considerable number of sabres, a valuable supply of ammunition, a number of horses, a large amount of commissary's stores, and other property. Here were also recovered the great seal of the state and the public records, and about nine hundred thousand dollars of which the Bank of Lexington had been robbed. General Price caused the money to be at once returned to the bank.

After the first day of the siege of Lexington, General Price learned that Lane and Montgomery, from Kansas, with about four thousand men, and General Sturgis, with fifteen hundred cavalry, were on the north side of the Missouri River, advancing to reënforce the garrison at Lexington. At the same time, and from the same direction, Colonel Saunders, with about twenty-five hundred Missourians, was coming to the aid of General Price. General D. R. Atchison, who had long been a United States Senator from Missouri, and at the time of his resignation was President *pro tem.* of the Senate, was sent by General Price to meet the command of Colonel Saunders and hasten them forward. He joined them on the north bank of the river, and, after all but about five hundred had been ferried over, General Atchison still remaining with these, they were unexpectedly attacked by the force from Kansas. The ground was densely wooded, and partially covered with water. The Missourians, led and cheered by one they had so long and reservedly honored, met the assault with such determination, and fighting with the skill of woodsmen and hunters, that they put the enemy to rout, pursuing him for a distance of ten miles, and inflicting heavy loss upon him, while that of the Missourians was but five killed and twenty wounded.

The expedient of the bales of hemp was a brilliant conception, not unlike that which made Tarik, the Saracen warrior, immortal, and gave his name to the northern pillar of Hercules.

The victories in Missouri which have been noticed, and which so far exceeded what might have been expected from the small forces by which they were achieved, had caused an augmentation of the enemy's troops to an estimated number of seventy thousand. Against these the army of General Price could not hope successfully to contend; he therefore retired toward the southwestern part of the state.

The want of supplies and transportation compelled him to disband a portion of his troops; with the rest he continued his retreat to Neosho. By proclamation of Governor Jackson, the legislature had assembled at this place, and had passed the ordinance of secession. If other evidence were wanting, the fact that, without governmental aid, without a military chest, without munitions of war, the campaign which has been described had so far been carried on by the voluntary service of the citizens, and the free-will offerings of the people, must be conclusive that the ordinance of secession was the expression of the popular will of Missouri.

The forces of Missouri again formed a junction with the Confederate troops under General McCulloch, and together they moved to Pineville, in McDonald County.

CHAPTER X: *Brigadier General Henry A. Wise Takes Command in Western Virginia—His Movements—Advance of General John B. Floyd—Defeats the Enemy—Attacked by Rosecrans—Controversy Between Wise and Floyd—General R. E. Lee Takes the Command in West Virginia—Movement on Cheat Mountain—Its Failure—Further Operations—Winter Quarters—Lee Sent to South Carolina.*

IN June, 1861, Brigadier General Henry A. Wise, who was well and favorably known to the people of the Kanawha valley, in his enthusiasm for their defense and confidence in his ability to rally them to resist the threatened invasion of that region, offered his services for that purpose. With a small command, which was to serve as a nucleus to the force he hoped to raise, he was sent thither. His success was as great as could have been reasonably expected, and after the small but brilliant affair on Scary Creek, he prepared to give battle to the enemy then advancing up the Kanawha Valley under General Cox; the defeat of our forces at Laurel Hill, which has been already noticed, uncovered his right flank and endangered his rear, which was open to approach by several roads; he therefore fell back to Lewisburg.

Brigadier General John B. Floyd had in the meantime raised a brigade in southwestern Virginia, and advanced to the support of General Wise. Unfortunately, there was a want of concert between these two officers, which prevented their entire coöperation. General Floyd engaged the enemy in several brilliant skirmishes, when he found that his right was threatened by a force which was approaching on that flank, with the apparent purpose of crossing the Gauley River at the Carnifex Ferry so as to strike his line of communication with Lewisburg. He crossed the river with his brigade and a part of Wise's cavalry, leaving that general to check any advance which Cox might make. General Floyd's movement was as successful as it was daring; he met the enemy's forces, defeated and dispersed them, but the want of coöperation between Generals Wise and Floyd prevented a movement against General Cox.

Floyd entrenched himself on the Gauley, in a position of great natural strength, but the small force under his command and the fact that he was separated from that of General Wise probably induced General Rosecrans, commanding the enemy's forces in the Cheat Mountain, to advance and assail the position. Though his numbers were vastly superior, the attack was a failure; after a heavy loss on the part of the enemy, he

GENERAL ROBERT E. LEE

fell back after nightfall. During the night Floyd crossed the river and withdrew to the camp of General Wise, to form a junction of the two forces, and together they fell back toward Sewell's Mountain. The unfortunate controversy between these officers, which had prevented cooperation in the past, grew more bitter, and each complained of the other in terms that left little hope of future harmony; this want of cooperation led to confusion, and threatened further reverses.

General Loring had succeeded General Garnett, and was in command of the remnant of the force defeated at Laurel Hill. His headquarters were at Valley Mountain. General R. E. Lee, on duty at Richmond, aiding the President in the general direction of military affairs, was now ordered to proceed to western Virginia. It was hoped that, by his military skill and deserved influence over men, he would be able to retrieve the disaster we had suffered at Laurel Hill, and by combining all our forces in western Virginia on one plan of operations, give protection to that portion of our country. Such reënforcement as could be furnished had been sent to Valley Mountain, the headquarters of General Loring. Thither General Lee promptly proceeded. The duty to which he was assigned was certainly not attractive by the glory to be gained or the ease to be enjoyed, but Lee made no question as to personal preference, and, whatever were his wishes, they were subordinate to what was believed to be the public interest.

The season had been one of extraordinary rains, rendering the mountain roads, ordinarily difficult, almost impassable. With unfaltering purpose and energy, he crossed the Alleghany Mountains, and, learning that the main encampment of the enemy was in the valley of Tygart River and Elk Run, Randolph County, he directed his march toward that position. The troops under the immediate command of Brigadier General H. R. Jackson, together with those under Brigadier General Loring, were about thirty-five hundred men. The force of the enemy, as far as it could be ascertained, was very much greater. In the detached work at Cheat Mountain Pass, we learned by a provision return found upon the person of a captured staff officer that there were three thousand men, being but a fraction less than our whole force. After a careful reconnaissance, and a full conference with General Loring, Lee decided to attack the main encampment of the enemy by a movement of his troops converging upon the valley from three directions. The colonel of one of his regiments, who had reconnoitered the position of the works at Cheat Mountain Pass, reported that it was feasible to turn it and carry it by assault, and he was assigned to that duty. General Lee ordered other portions of his force to take position on the spurs overlooking the enemy's main encampment, while he led three regiments to the height below and nearest to the position of the enemy. The instructions were that the officer sent to turn the position at Cheat Mountain Pass should approach it at early dawn, and immediately open fire, which was to be the signal for the concerted attack by the rest of the force. It rained heavily during the day, and after a toilsome night march, the force led by General Lee, wet, weary, hungry, and cold, gained their position close to and overlooking the enemy's encampment. In their march they had surprised and captured the picket, without a gun being fired, so that no notice had been given of their approach.

The officer who had been sent to attack the work at Cheat Mountain Pass found on closer examination that he had been mistaken as to the practicability of taking it by assault, and that the heavy abatis which covered it was advanced beyond the range of his rifles. Not having understood that his firing was to be the signal for the general attack, and should therefore be opened, whether it would be effective or not, he withdrew without firing a musket.

The height occupied by General Lee was shrouded in fog, and as morning had dawned without the expected signal, he concluded that some mishap had befallen the force which was to make it. By a tortuous path he went down the side of the mountain low enough to have a distinct view of the camp. He saw the men, unconscious of the near presence of an enemy, engaged in cleaning their arms, cooking, and other morning occupations; then returning to his command, he explained to his senior officers what he had seen, and expressed his belief that, though the plan of attack had failed, the troops there with him could surprise and capture the camp. The officers withdrew, conferred with their men, and reported to the general that the troops were not in condition for the enterprise. As the fog was then lifting, and they would soon be revealed to the enemy below, whose numbers were vastly superior to his own, he withdrew his command by the route they had come, and without observation returned to his camp. Beyond some skirmishes with outposts and reconnoitering parties, our troops had not been engaged, and in these affairs our reported loss was comparatively small.

Colonel John A. Washington, aide-de-camp of General Lee, was killed while making a reconnaissance, by a party in ambuscade. The loss of this valuable and accomplished officer was much regretted by his general and all others who knew him.

The report that Rosecrans and Cox had united their commands and were advancing upon Wise and Floyd caused General Lee to move at once to their support. He found General Floyd at Meadow Bluff and General Wise at Sewell Mountain. The latter position being very favorable for defense, the troops were concentrated there to await the threatened attack by Rosecrans, who advanced and took position in sight of General Lee's entrenched camp, and, having remained there for more than a week, withdrew in the night without attempting the expected attack.

The weak condition of his artillery horses and the bad state of the roads, made worse by the retiring army, prevented General Lee from attempting to pursue; the approach of winter, always rigorous in that mountain region, closed the campaign with a small but brilliant action in which General H. R. Jackson repelled an attack of a greatly superior force, inflicting severe loss on the assailants and losing but six of his own command.

With the close of active operations General Lee returned to Richmond, and though subjected to depreciatory criticism by the carpet knights who make campaigns on assumed hypotheses, he with characteristic self-abnegation made no defense of himself, not even presenting an official report of his night march in the Cheat Mountain, but orally he stated to me the facts which have formed the basis of this sketch. My estimate of General Lee, my confidence in his ability, zeal, and fidelity, rested on a foundation not to be shaken by such criticism as I have noticed. I had no more doubt then, than after his fame had been securely established, that whenever he had the opportunity to prove his worth, he would secure public appreciation. Therefore, as affairs on the coast of South Carolina and Georgia were in an unsatisfactory condition, he was directed to go there and take such measures for the defense, particularly of Savannah and Charleston, as he should find needful. Lest the newspaper attack should have created unjust and unfavorable impressions in regard to him, I thought it desirable to write to Governor Pickens and tell him what manner of man he was who had been sent to South Carolina.

After the withdrawal of the Confederate army from Fairfax Court House and the positions which had been occupied in front of that place, a movement was made by the enemy to cross the Potomac near Leesburg, where we had, under the command of Brigadier General N. S. Evans of South Carolina, four regiments of infantry (*i. e.,* the Thirteenth, Seventeenth, and Eighteenth Mississippi, and the Eighth Virginia), commanded respectively by Colonels Barksdale, Featherston, Burt, and Hunton, a small detachment of cavalry under Lieutenant Colonel Jenifer, and some pieces of artillery.

On October 21st the enemy commenced crossing the river at Edwards's Ferry. A brigade was thrown over and met by the Thirteenth Mississippi, which held them in check at the point of crossing. In the meantime another brigade was thrown over at Ball's Bluff, and as troops continued to cross at that point, where the Eighth Virginia had engaged them, General Evans ordered up the Seventeenth and Eighteenth Mississippi, and the three regiments made such an impetuous attack as to drive back the enemy to the bluff, and their leader, Colonel Baker, having fallen, a panic seemed to seize the command, so that they rushed headlong down the bluff, and crowded into the flat boats, which were their means of transportation, in such numbers that they were sunk and many of the foe were drowned in their attempt to swim the river. The loss of the enemy, prisoners included, exceeded the number of our troops in action. The Confederate loss was reported to be thirty-six killed, one hundred seventeen wounded, and two captured; total, one hundred and fifty-five. Among the killed was the gallant Colonel Burt, a much-respected citizen of Mississippi, where he had held high civil station, and where his death was long deplored.

IT HAS been shown that the Southern states, by their representatives in the two houses of Congress, consistently endeavored, even to the last day when they were by their constituents permitted to remain in the halls of federal legislation, to maintain the Constitution, and preserve the union which the states had by their independent action ordained and established. On the other hand, proof has been adduced to show that the Northern states, by a majority of their representatives in the Congress, had persisted in agitation injurious to the welfare and tranquillity of the Southern states, and at the last moment had refused to make any concessions, or to offer any guarantees to check the current toward secession of the complaining states, whose love for the Union rendered them willing to accept less than justice should have readily accorded. The issue was then presented between submission to empire of the North, or the severance of those ties consecrated by many memories, and strengthened by those habits which render every people reluctant to sever long-existing associations.

The authorities heretofore cited have, I must believe, conclusively shown that the question of changing their government was one that the states had the power to decide by virtue of the unalienable right announced in the *Declaration of Independence,* and which had been proudly denominated the American idea of government. The hope and the wish of the people of the South were that the disagreeable necessity of separation would be peacefully met, and be followed by such commercial regulations as would least disturb the prosperity and future intercourse of the separated states. Every step taken by the Confederate government was directed toward that end. The separation of the states having been decided on, it was sought to effect it in such manner as would be just to the parties concerned, and preserve as far as possible, under separate governments, the fraternal and mutually beneficial relations which had existed between the states when united, and which it was the object of their compact of union to secure. To all the proofs heretofore offered I confidently refer for the establishment of the fact that whatever of bloodshed, of devastation, or shock to republican government has resulted from the war, is to be charged to the Northern states. The invasions of the Southern states, for purposes of coercion, were in violation of the written Constitution, and the attempt to subjugate sovereign states, under the pretext of "preserving the Union," was alike offensive to law, to good morals, and the proper use of language. The Union was the voluntary junction of free and independent states; to subjugate any of them was to destroy constituent parts, and necessarily, therefore, must be the destruction of the Union itself.

That the Southern states were satisfied with a federal government such as their fathers had formed was shown by their adoption of a Constitution so little differing from the instrument of 1787. It was against the violations of that instrument, and usurpations offensive to their pride and injurious to their interests, that they remonstrated, argued, and finally appealed to the inherent, undelegated power of the states to judge of their wrongs, and of the "mode and measure of redress."

After many years of fruitless effort to secure from their Northern associates a faithful observance of the compact of union; after its conditions had been deliberately and persistently broken, and the signs of the times indicated further and more ruthless violations of their rights as equals in the Union, the Southern states, preferring a peaceful separation to continuance in a hostile Union, decided to exercise their sovereign right to withdraw from an association which had failed to answer the ends for which it was formed. It has been shown how they endeavored to effect the change with strict regard to the principles controlling a dissolution of partnership, and how earnestly they desired to remain in friendly relations to the Northern states, and how all their overtures were rejected. When they pleaded for peace, the United States government deceptively delayed to answer, while making ready for war. To the calm judgment of mankind is submitted the question, Who was responsible for the war between the states?

Virginia, whose history, from the beginning of the Revolution of 1776, had been a long course of sacrifices for the benefit of her sister states and for the preservation of the Union she had mainly contributed to establish, clung to it with the devotion of a mother. It has been shown how her efforts to check dissolution were persisted in when the aggrieved were hopeless and the aggressors reckless, and how her mediations were rejected in the "Peace Congress" which on her motion had been assembled. Sorrowing over the failure of this, her blessed though unsuccessful attempt to preserve the Union of the Constitution, she was not permitted to mourn as a neutral, but was required by the United States government to choose between furnishing troops to subjugate her Southern sisters or the reclamation of the grants she had made to the federal government when she became a member of the Union. The first was a violation of the letter and the spirit of the Constitution; the second was a reserved right. The voice of Henry called to her from the ground; the spirits of Washington and Jefferson moved among her people.

There was but one course consistent with her stainless reputation and often-declared tenets, as to the liberties of her people, which she could have adopted. As in 1776, reluctantly she bowed to the necessity of separation from the Crown, so in 1861 the ordinance of secession was adopted. Having exhausted all other means, she took the last resort, and, if for this she was selected as the first object of assault, "methinks the punishment exceedeth the offense."

The large resources and full preparation of the United States government enabled it to girt Virginia as with a wall of fire. It has been shown that she was threatened from the east, from the north, and from the west. The capital of the state and of the Confederacy, Richmond, was the objective point, and on this the march of three columns concentrated. On the east the advance of the enemy was on several occasions feasible, when we consider the number of his forces at and about Fortress Monroe, in comparison with the small means retained for the defense of the capital. On the north the most formidable army of the enemy was assembled; to oppose it we had the comparatively small Army of the Potomac. This being regarded as the line on which the greatest danger was apprehended, our efforts were mostly directed toward giving it the requisite strength. Troops, as rapidly as they could be raised and armed, were sent forward for that purpose. From the beginning to the close of the war, we mainly relied for the defense of the capital on its aged citizens, boys too young for service, and the civil employees of the executive departments. On several occasions these were called out to resist an attack. They answered with alacrity, and always bore themselves gallantly, more than once repelling the enemy in the open field. Had it been practicable to do so, it would surely have been proper to keep a large force in reserve for the defense of the capital, so often and vauntingly proclaimed to be the object of the enemy's campaign. Perhaps the propriety of such provision gave currency and credence to rumors that we had a large force at Richmond. This even led to the application for a detachment from it to reënforce our Army of the Potomac, which caused me to write to General J. E. Johnston at Manassas, Virginia, on September 5, 1861, as follows:

> You have again been deceived as to the forces here. We never have had anything near twenty thousand men, and have now but little over one fourth of that number. . . . Since the date of your glorious victory the enemy have grown weaker in numbers, and far weaker in the character of their troops, so that I had felt it remained with us to decide whether another battle should soon be fought or not. Your remark indicates a different opinion. . . . I wish I could send additional force to occupy Loudon, but my means are short of the wants of each division I am laboring to protect. One ship-load of small-arms would enable me to answer all demands, but vainly have I hoped and waited.

Then, there, and everywhere, our difficulty was the want of arms and munitions of war. Lamentable cries came to us from the West for the supplies which would enable patriotic citizens to defend their homes. The resource upon which the people had so confidently relied, the private arms in the hands of citizens, proved a sad delusion, and elsewhere it has been shown how deficient we were in ammunition, or the means of providing it. The simple fact, was, the country had gone to war without counting the cost.

Undue elation over our victory at Manassas was followed by dissatisfaction at what was termed the failure to reap the fruits of victory; rumors, for which there could be no better excuse than partisan zeal, were circulated that the heroes of the hour were prevented from reaping the fruits of the victory by the interference of the President. Naturally there followed another rumor, that the inaction of the victorious army, to which reënforcements continued to be sent, was due to the policy of the President; he also was held responsible, and with more apparent justice, for the failure to organize the troops of the several states, as the law contemplated, into brigades and divisions composed of the soldiers of each.

Though these unjust criticisms weakened the power of the government to meet its present and provide for its future necessities, I bore them in silence, lest to vindicate myself should injure the public service by turning the public censure to the generals on whom the hopes of the country rested. That motive no longer exists; to justify the faith of those who, without a defense, continued to uphold my hands, I propose to set forth the facts by correspondence and otherwise. So far as, in doing this, blame shall be transferred from me to others, it will be the incident, not the design, as it would be most gratifying to me only to notice for praise each and all who wore the gray.

The fiction of my having prevented the pursuit of the enemy after the victory of Manassas was exploded after it had acquired an authoritative and semiofficial form in the manner and for the reasons heretofore set forth. It only remains, therefore, to notice the other points indicated above:

First, the organization of the army.

Disease and discontent are known to be the attendants of armies lying unemployed in camps, especially, as in our case, when the troops were composed of citizens called from their homes under the idea of a pressing necessity, and with the hope of soon returning to them.

Our citizen soldiers were a powerful political element, and their correspondence, finding its way to the people through the press and to the halls of Congress by direct communication with the members, was felt, by its influence both upon public opinion and general legislation. Members of Congress, and notably the Vice-President, contended that men should be allowed to go home and attend to their private affairs while there were no active operations, and that there was no doubt but that they would return whenever there was to be a battle. The experience of war soon taught our people the absurdity of such ideas, and before its close probably none would have uttered them.

There were very many men out of the army who were anxious to enter it, but for whom we had not arms. This gave rise to the remark, more humorous than profound, that we "stood around the camps with clubs to keep one set in and another set out." Had this been true, it was certainly justifiable to refuse to exchange a trained man for a recruit. All who have seen service know that one old soldier is, in campaign, equal to several who have everything of military life to learn.

A marked characteristic of the Southern people was individuality, and time was needful to teach them that the terrible machine, a disciplined army, must be made of men who had surrendered their freedom of will. The most distinguished of our citizens were not the slowest to learn the lessons, and perhaps no army ever more thoroughly knew it than did that which Lee led into Pennsylvania, and none ever had a leader who in his own conduct better illustrated the lesson.

Our largest army in 1861 was that of the Potomac. It had been formed by the junction of the forces under General J. E. Johnston with those under General P. G. T. Beauregard, with such additions as could be hurriedly sent forward to meet the enemy on the field of Manassas. They were combined into brigades and divisions as pressing exigencies required.

By the act of February 28, 1861, the President was authorized to receive companies, battalions, and regiments to form a part of the provisional army of the Confederate States, and, with the advice and consent of Congress, to appoint general officers for them; by the act of March 6th the President was to apportion the staff and general officers among the respective states from which the volunteers were received. It will thus be seen that the states generously surrendered their right to preserve for those volunteers the character of state troops and to appoint general officers when furnishing a sufficient number of regiments to require such grade for their command; in giving their volunteers to form the provisional army of the Confederacy, it was distinctly suggested that the general officers should be so appointed as to make a just apportionment among the states furnishing the troops.

During the repose which followed the battle of Manassas, it was deemed proper that the regiments of the different states should be assembled in brigades together, and, as far as consistent with the public service, that the spirit of the law should be complied with by the assignment of brigadier generals of the same state from which the troops were drawn. Instructions to that end were therefore given, and again and again repeated, but were for a long time only partially complied with, until the delay formed the basis of the argument that those who had by association become thoroughly acquainted would more advantageously be left united. In the meantime, frequent complaints came to me from the army, of unjust discrimination, the law being executed in regard to the troops of some states but not of others, and of serious discontent arising therefrom.

The duty to obey the law was imperative, and neither the executive nor the officers of the army had any right to question its propriety. I, however, considered the policy of that law wise, and was not surprised when it was stated to me that the persistent obstruction to its execution was repressing the spirit to volunteer in places to which complaints of such supposed favoritism had been transmitted.

About October 1st, at the request of General Johnston, I went to his headquarters, at Fairfax Court House, for the purpose of conference.

At the time of this visit to the army, the attention of the general officers, who then met me in conference, was called to the obligation created by law to organize the troops, when the numbers tendered by any state permitted it, into brigades and divisions composed of the regiments, battalions, or companies of such state, and to assign general and staff officers in the ratio of the troops thus received. After my return to the capital, the importance of the subject weighed so heavily upon me as to lead to correspondence with the generals, which will be best understood by the following extracts from my letters to them which are here appended:

RICHMOND, VIRGINIA, October 10, 1861.

Major-General G. W. SMITH, *Army of Potomac.*

. . . How have you progressed in the solution of the problem I left—the organization of the troops with reference to the States, and term of service? If the volunteers continue their complaints that they are commanded by strangers and do not get justice, and that they are kept in camp to die when reported for hospital by the surgeon, we shall soon feel a reaction in the matter of volunteering. Already I have been much pressed on both subjects, and have answered by promising that the generals would give due attention, and, I hoped, make satisfactory changes. The authority to organize regiments into brigades and the latter into divisions is by law conferred only on the President; and I must be able to assume responsibility of the action taken by whomsoever acts for me in that regard. By reference to the law, you will see that, in surrendering the sole power to appoint general officers, it was nevertheless designed, as far as should be found consistent, to keep up the State relation of troops and generals. Kentucky has a brigadier, but not a brigade; she has, however, a regiment—that regiment and brigadier might be associated together. Louisiana had regiments enough to form a brigade, but no brigadier in either corps; all of the regiments were sent to that corps commanded by a Louisiana general. Georgia has regiments now organized into two brigades; she has on duty with that army two brigadiers, but one of them serves with other troops. Mississippi troops were scattered as if the State were unknown. Brigadier-General Clark was sent to remove a growing dissatisfaction, but, though the State had nine regiments there, he (Clark) was put in command of a post and depot of supplies. These nine regiments should form two brigades. Brigadiers Clark and (as a native of Mississippi) Whiting should be placed in command of them, and the regiments for the war put in the army man's brigade. Both brigades should be put in the division commanded by General Van Dorn, of Mississippi. Thus would the spirit and intent of the law be complied with, disagreeable complaint be spared me, and more of content be assured under the trials to which you look forward. It is needless to specify further. I have been able in writing to you to speak freely, and you have no past associations to disturb the judgment to be passed upon the views presented. I have made and am making inquiries as to the practicability of getting a corps of negroes for laborers to aid in the construction of an intrenched line in rear of your present position.

Your remarks on the want of efficient staff-officers are realized in all their force, and I hope, among the elements which constitute a staff-officer for volunteers, you have duly estimated the qualities of forbearance and urbanity. Many of the privates are men of high social position, of scholarship and fortune. Their pride furnishes the motive for good conduct, and, if wounded, is turned from an instrument of good to one of great power for evil. . . .

RICHMOND, VIRGINIA, October 16, 1861.

General BEAUREGARD, *Manassas, Virginia.*

. . . I have thought often upon the questions of reorganization which were submitted to you, and it has seemed to me that whether in view of disease, or the disappointment and suffering of a winter cantonment on a line of defense, or of a battle to be fought in and near your position, it was desirable to combine the troops, by a new distribution, with as little delay as practicable. They will be stimulated to extraordinary effort when so organized, in that the fame of their State will be in their keeping, and that each will feel that his immediate commander will desire to exalt rather than diminish his services. You pointed me to the fact that you had observed that rule in the case of the Louisiana and Carolina troops, and you will not fail to perceive that others find in the fact a reason for the like disposal of them. In the hour of sickness, and the tedium of waiting for spring, men from the same region will best console and relieve each other. The maintenance of our cause rests on the sentiments of the people. Letters from the camp, complaining of inequality and harshness in the treatment of the men, have already dulled the enthusiasm which filled our ranks with men who by birth, fortune, education, and social position were the equals of any officer in the land. The spirit of our military law is manifested in the fact that the State organization was limited to the regiment. The volunteers come in sufficient numbers to have brigadiers, but have only colonels. It was not then intended (is the necessary conclusion) that those troops should be under the *immediate* command of officers above the grade of colonel. The spirit of the law, then, indicates that brigades should be larger than customary, the general being charged with the care, the direction, the preservation of the men, rather than the internal police.

RICHMOND, VIRGINIA, October 20, 1861.

General BEAUREGARD, *Manassas, Virginia.*

MY DEAR GENERAL . . . Two rules have been applied in the projected reorganization of the Army of the Potomac:

1. As far as practicable, to keep regiments from the same State together; 2. To assign generals to command the troops of their own State. I have not overlooked the objections to each, but the advantages are believed to outweigh the disadvantages of that arrangement. In distributing the regiments of the several States it would, I think, be better to place the regiments for the war in the same brigade of the State, and assign to those brigades the brigadiers whose services could least easily be dispensed with. For this, among other reasons, I will mention but one: the commission of a brigadier expires upon the breaking up of his brigade (see the law for their appointment). Of course, I would not for slight cause change the relations of troops and commanders, especially where it has been long continued and endeared by the trials of battle; but it is to be noted that the regiment was fixed as the unit of organization, and made the connecting link between the soldier and his home. Above that, all was subject to the discretion of the Confederate authorities, save the pregnant intimation in relation to the distribution of generals among the several States. It was generous and con-

fiding to surrender entirely to the Confederacy the appointment of generals, and it is the more incumbent on me to carry out as well as may be the spirit of the volunteer system.

RICHMOND, May 10, 1862.

General J. E. JOHNSTON.

. . . Your attention has been heretofore called to the law in relation to the organization of brigades and divisions—orders were long since given to bring the practice and the law into conformity. Recently reports have been asked for from the commanders of separate armies as to the composition of their respective brigades and divisions. I have been much harassed, and the public interest has certainly suffered, by the delay to place the regiments of some of the States in brigades together, it being deemed that unjust discrimination was made against them, and also by the popular error which has existed as to the number of brigadiers to which appointments could be specially urged on the grounds of residence. While some have expressed surprise at my patience when orders to you were not observed, I have at least hoped that you would recognize the desire to aid and sustain you, and that it would produce the corresponding action on your part. The reasons formerly offered have one after another disappeared, and I hope you will, as you can, proceed to organize your troops as heretofore instructed, and that the returns will relieve us of the uncertainty now felt as to the number and relations of the troops, and the commands of the officers having brigades and divisions. . . . I will not dwell on the lost opportunity afforded along the line of northern Virginia, but must call your attention to the present condition of affairs and probable action of the enemy, if not driven from his purpose to advance on the Fredericksburg route. . . .

Very truly yours,
JEFFERSON DAVIS.

On May 26th General Johnston's attention was again called to the organization of the ten Mississippi regiments into two brigades, and was reminded that the proposition had been made to him in the previous autumn, with an expression of my confidence that the regiments would be more effective in battle if thus associated.

I will now proceed to notice the allegation that I was responsible for inaction by the Army of the Potomac, in the latter part of 1861 and in the early part of 1862. After the explosion of the fallacy that I had prevented the pursuit of the enemy from Manassas in July, 1861, my assailants have sought to cover their exposure by a change of time and place, locating their story at Fairfax Court House, and dating it in the autumn of 1861.

When at that time and place I met General Johnston for conference, he called in the two generals next in rank to himself, Beauregard and G. W. Smith. The question for consideration was, What course should be adopted for the future action of the army? and the preliminary inquiry by me was as to the number of the troops there assembled. To my surprise and disappointment, the effective strength was stated to be but little greater than when it fought the battle of the 21st of the preceding July. The frequent reënforcements which had been sent to that army in no wise prepared me for such an announcement. To my inquiry as to what force would be required for the contemplated advance into Maryland, the lowest estimate made by any of them was about twice the number there present for duty. How little I was prepared for such a condition of things will be realized from the fact that previous suggestions by the generals in regard to a purpose to advance into Maryland had induced me, when I went to that conference, to take with me some drawings made by the veteran soldier and engineer, Colonel Crozet, of the falls of the Potomac, to show the feasibility of crossing the river at that point. Very little knowledge of the condition and military resources of the country must have sufficed to show that I had no power to make such an addition to that army without a total disregard of the safety of other threatened positions. It only remained for me to answer that I had not power to furnish such a number of troops; and, unless the militia bearing their private arms should be relied on, we could not possibly fulfill such a requisition until after the receipt of the small arms which we had early and constantly striven to procure from abroad, and had for some time expected.

After I had written the foregoing, and all the succeeding chapters on kindred subjects, a friend, in October, 1880, furnished me with a copy of a paper relating to the conference at Fairfax Court House, which seems to require notice at my hands.

Therefore I break the chain of events to insert here some remarks in regard to it.

The paper appears to have been written by General G. W. Smith, and to have received the approval of Generals Beauregard and J. E. Johnston, and to bear the date of January 31, 1862.

It does not agree in some respects with my memory of what occurred, and is not consistent with itself. It was not necessary that I should learn in that interview the evil of inactivity. My correspondence of anterior date might have shown that I was fully aware of it, and my suggestions in the interview certainly did not look as if it was necessary to impress me with the advantage of action.

In one part of the paper it is stated that the reënforcements asked for were to be "seasoned soldiers," such as were there present, and who were said to be in the "finest fighting condition." This, if such a proposition had been made, would have exposed its absurdity, as well as the loophole it offered for escape, by subsequently asserting that the troops furnished were not up to the proposed standard.

In another part of the paper it is stated that there were hope and expectation that, before the end of the winter, arms would be introduced into the country, and that then we could successfully invade that of the enemy; but this supply of arms, however abundant, could not furnish "seasoned soldiers," and the two propositions are therefore inconsistent. In one place it is written that "it was felt it might be better to run the risk of almost certain destruction fighting upon the other side of the Potomac, rather than see the gradual dying out and deterioration of this army during a winter," etc.; but, when it was proposed to cross into eastern Maryland on a steamer in our possession for a partial campaign, difficulties arose like the lion in the path of the sluggard, so that the proposition was postponed and never executed. In like manner the other expedition in the Valley of Virginia was achieved by an officer not of this council, General T. J. Jackson.

In one place it is written that the President stated, "At that time no reenforcements could be furnished to the army of the character asked for." In another place he is made to say he could not take any troops from the points named, and, "without arms from abroad, could not reënforce that army." Here, again, it is clear from the answer that the proposition had been for such reënforcements as additional arms would enable him to give. Those arms he expected to receive, barring the dangers of the sea, and of the enemy, which obstacles alone prevented the "positive assurance that they would be received at all."

It was, as stated, with deep regret and bitter disappointment that I found, notwithstanding our diligent efforts to reënforce this army before and after the battle of Manassas, that its strength had but little increased, and that the arms of absentees and discharged men were represented by only twenty-five hundred on hand. I cannot suppose that General Johnston could have noticed the statement that his request for conference had set forth the object of it to be to discuss the question of reenforcement. He would have known that in Richmond, where all the returns were to be found, any consideration of reënforcement, by the withdrawal of troops from existing garrisons, could best be decided. Very little experience or a fair amount of modesty without any experience would serve to prevent one from announcing his conclusion that troops could be withdrawn from a place or places without knowing how many were there, and what was the necessity for their presence.

I was at the conference by request; the confidence felt in those officers is shown by the fact that I met them alone, and did not require any minutes to be made of the meeting. About four months afterward a paper was prepared to make a record of the conversation; the fact was concealed from me, whereas, both for accuracy and frankness, it should have been submitted to me, even if there had been nothing due to our official relations. Twenty years after the event, I learned of this secret report, by one party, without notice having been given to the other, of a conversation said to have lasted two hours.

I have noticed the improbabilities and inconsistencies of the paper, and without remark I submit to honorable men the concealment from me in which it was prepared, whereby they may judge of the chances for such co-intelligence as needs must exist between the executive and the commanders of armies to insure attainable success.

The position at Fairfax Court House, though it would answer very well as a point from which to advance, was quite unfavorable for defense; when I so remarked, the opinion seemed to be that to which the generals had previously arrived. It therefore only remained to consider what change of position should be made in the event of the enemy threatening soon to advance. But in the meantime I hoped that something could be done by detachments from the army to effect objects less difficult than an advance against his main force, and particularly indicated the lower part of Maryland, where a small force was said to be ravaging the country and oppressing our friends. This, I thought, might be feasible by the establishment of a battery near to Aquia Creek, where the channel of the Potomac was said to be so narrow that our guns could prevent the use of the river by the enemy's boats, and, by employing a steamboat lying there, troops enough could be sent over some night to defeat that force, and return before any large body could be concentrated against them. The effect of the battery and of the expedition, it was hoped, would be important in relieving our friends and securing recruits from those who wished to join us. Previously, General Johnston's attention had been called to possibilities in the valley of the Shenandoah, and that these and other like things were not done, was surely due to other causes than "the policy of the Administration," as will appear by the letters hereto annexed:

RICHMOND, VIRGINIA, August 1, 1861.

General J. E. JOHNSTON:

. . . General Lee has gone to western Virginia, and I hope may be able to strike a decisive blow in that quarter, or, failing in that, will be able to organize and post our troops so as to check the enemy, after which he will return to this place.

The movement of Banks will require your attention. It may be a *ruse,* but, if a real movement, when your army has the requisite strength and mobility, you will probably find an opportunity, by a rapid movement through the passes, to strike him in rear or flank, and thus add another to your many claims to your country's gratitude. . . . We must be prompt to avail ourselves of the weakness resulting from the exchange of the new and less reliable forces of the enemy, for those heretofore in service, as well as of the moral effect produced by their late defeat. . . .

> I am, as ever, your friend,
> JEFFERSON DAVIS.

From the correspondence which occurred after the conference at Fairfax Court House, I select a reply made to General Smith, who had written to me in advocacy of the views he had then expressed about large reënforcements to the Army of the Potomac, for an advance into Maryland. Nothing is more common than that a general, realizing the wants of the army with which he is serving, and the ends that might be achieved if those wants were supplied, should overlook the necessities of others, and accept rumors of large forces which do not exist, and assume the absence of danger elsewhere than in his own front.

> RICHMOND, VIRGINIA, October 10, 1861.

Major-General G. W. SMITH, *Army of the Potomac.*

. . . Your remarks about the moral effect of repressing the hope of the volunteers for an advance are in accordance with the painful impression made on me when, in our council, it was revealed to me that the Army of the Potomac had been reduced to about one half the legalized strength, and that the arms to restore the numbers were not in depot. As I there suggested, though you may not be able to advance into Maryland and expel the enemy, it may be possible to keep up the spirits of your troops by expeditions such as that particularly spoken of against Sickles's brigade on the lower Potomac, or Banks's above. By destroying the canal and making other rapid movements wherever opportunity presents, to beat detachments or to destroy lines of communication. . . .

> Very truly, your friend,
> JEFFERSON DAVIS.

> RICHMOND, VIRGINIA, November 18, 1861.

General J. E. JOHNSTON.

. . . If a large force should be landed on the Potomac below General Holmes, with the view to turn or to attack him, the value of the position between Dumfries and Fredericksburg will be so great that I wish you to give to that line your personal inspection. With a sufficient force, the enemy may be prevented from leaving his boats, should he be able to cross the river. To make our force available at either of the points which he may select, it will be necessary to improve the roads connecting the advance posts with the armies of the Potomac and of the Acquia, as well as with each other, and to have the requisite teams to move heavy guns with celerity. . . .   Very respectfully yours,

                                                        JEFFERSON DAVIS.

In November, 1861, reports became current that the enemy were concentrating troops west of the valley of the Shenandoah with a view to a descent upon it. That vigilant, enterprising, and patriotic soldier, General T. J. Jackson, whose steadiness under fire at the first battle of Manassas had procured for him the sobriquet of "Stonewall," was then on duty as district commander of the Shenandoah Valley.

He was a West Virginian; though he had not acquired the fame which subsequently shed such luster upon his name, he possessed a well-deserved confidence among the people of that region. Ever watchful and daring in the discharge of any duty, he was intensely anxious to guard his beloved mountains of Virginia. This, stimulating his devotion to the general welfare of the Confederacy, induced him to desire to march against the enemy, who had captured Romney. On November 20, 1861, he wrote to the War Department, proposing an expedition to Romney, in western Virginia. It was decided to adopt his proposition, endorsed by the commander of the department, and further to insure success, though not recommended in the endorsement, his old brigade (then in the Army of the Potomac) was selected as a part of the command with which he was to make the campaign. General Johnston remonstrated against this transfer and the correspondence is subjoined for a fuller understanding of the matter:

HEADQUARTERS, VALLEY DISTRICT, November 20, 1861.
Hon. J. P. BENJAMIN, *Secretary of War.*

SIR: I hope you will pardon me for requesting that, at once, all the troops under General Loring be ordered to this point. Deeply impressed with the importance of absolute secrecy respecting military operations, I have made it a point to say but little respecting my proposed movements in the event of sufficient reënforcements arriving, but, since conversing with Lieutenant-Colonel J. L. T. Preston upon his return from General Loring, and ascertaining the disposition of the General's forces, I venture to respectfully urge that, after concentrating all his troops here, an attempt should be made to capture the Federal forces at Romney. The attack on Romney would probably induce McClellan to believe that the Army of the Potomac had been so weakened as to justify him in making an advance on Centreville; but, should this not induce him to advance, I do not believe anything will during the present winter. Should the Army of the Potomac be attacked, I would be at once prepared to reënforce it with my present volunteer force, increased by General Loring's. After repulsing the enemy at Manassas, let the troops that marched on Romney return to the Valley and move rapidly westward to the waters of the Monongahela and Little Kanawha. Should General Kelley be defeated, and especially should he be captured, I believe that, by a judicious disposition of the militia, a few cavalry, and a small number of field-pieces, no additional forces would be required for some time in this district. I deem it of very great importance that northwestern Virginia be occupied by Confederate troops this winter. At present, it is to be presumed that the enemy are not expecting an attack there, and the resources of that region necessary for the subsistence of our troops are in greater abundance than in almost any other season of the year. Postpone the occupation of that section until spring, and we may expect to find the enemy prepared for us, and the resources to which I have referred greatly exhausted. I know that what I have proposed will be an arduous undertaking, and can not be accomplished without the sacrifice of much personal comfort, but I feel that the troops will be prepared to make this sacrifice when animated by the prospects of important results to our cause and distinction to themselves. It may be urged, against this plan, that the enemy will advance on Staunton or Huntersville. I am well satisfied that such a step would but make their destruction more certain. Again, it may be said that General Floyd will be cut off. To avoid this, if necessary, the General has only to fall back toward the Virginia and Tennessee Railroad. When northwestern Virginia is occupied in force, the Kanawha Valley, unless it be the lower part of it, must be evacuated by the Federal forces, or otherwise their safety will be endangered by forcing a column across from the Little Kanawha between them and the Ohio River. Admitting that the season is too far advanced, or that from other causes all can not be accomplished that has been named, yet, through the blessing of God, who has thus far so wonderfully prospered our cause, much more may be expected from General Loring's troops, according to this programme, than can be expected from them where they are. If you decide to order them here, I trust that, for the purpose of saving time, all the infantry, cavalry, and artillery will be directed to move immediately upon the reception of the order. The enemy, about five thousand strong, have been for some time slightly fortifying at Romney, and have completed their telegraph from that place to Green Spring Depot. Their forces at and near Williamsport are estimated as high as five thousand, but as yet I have no reliable information of their strength beyond the Potomac. Your most obedient servant,

T. J. JACKSON, *Major-General, P. A. C. S.*

HEADQUARTERS, CENTREVILLE, November 21, 1861.

Respectfully forwarded. I submit that the troops under General Loring might render valuable services by taking the field with General Jackson, instead of going into winter-quarters, as now proposed.

J. E. JOHNSTON, *General.*

HEADQUARTERS, CENTREVILLE, November 22, 1861.

General COOPER, *Adjutant and Inspector-General.*

SIR: I have received Major-General Jackson's plan of operations in his district, for which he asks for reënforcements. It seems to me that he proposes more than can well be accomplished in that high, mountainous country at this season. If the means of driving the enemy from Romney (preventing the reconstruction of the Baltimore and Ohio Railroad, and incursions by marauders into the counties of Jefferson, Berkeley, and Morgan) can be supplied to General Jackson, and with them those objects accomplished, we shall have reason to be satisfied, so far as the Valley district is concerned. The wants of other portions of the frontier—Acquia district, for instance—make it inexpedient, in my opinion, to transfer to the Valley district so large a force as that asked for by Major-General Jackson. It seems to me to be now of especial importance to strengthen Major-General Holmes, near Acquia Creek. The force there is very small, compared with the importance of the position.

Your obedient servant,

[ENDORSEMENT.]   J. E. JOHNSTON, *General.*

Respectfully submitted to the Secretary of War:

S. COOPER, *Adjutant and Inspector-General.*

November 25, 1861.

RICHMOND, VIRGINIA, November 10, 1861.

General J. E. JOHNSTON, *Manassas, Virginia.*

SIR: The Secretary of War has this morning laid before me yours of the 8th instant. I fully sympathize with your anxiety for the Army of the Potomac. If indeed mine be less than yours, it can only be so because the south, the west, and the east, presenting like cause for solicitude, have in the same manner demanded my care. Our correspondence must have assured you that I fully concur in your view of the necessity for unity in command, and I hope by a statement of the case to convince you that there has been no purpose to divide your authority by transferring the troops specified in order No. 206 from the center to the left of your department. The active campaign in the Greenbrier region was considered as closed for the season. There is reason to believe that the enemy is moving a portion of his forces from that mountain-region toward the Valley of Virginia, and that he has sent troops and munitions from the east by the way of the Potomac Canal toward the same point. The failure to destroy his communications by the Baltimore and Ohio Railroad and by the Potomac Canal has left him in possession of great advantages for that operation. General Jackson, for reasons known to you, was selected to command the division of the Valley, but we had only the militia and one mounted regiment within the district assigned to him. The recent activity of the enemy, the capture of Romney, etc., required that he should have for prompt service a body of Confederate troops to coöperate with the militia of that district. You suggest that such force should be drawn from the army at the Greenbrier; this was originally considered, and abandoned, because they could not reach him in time to anticipate the enemy's concentration, and also because General Jackson was a stranger to them, and time was wanting for the growth of that confidence between the commander and his troops, the value of which need not be urged upon you. We could have sent to him from this place an equal number of regiments, being about double the numerical strength of those specified in the order referred to, but they were parts of a brigade now in the Army of the Potomac, or were southern troops, and were ignorant of the country in which they were to serve, and all of them unknown to General Jackson. The troops sent were his old brigade, had served in the Valley, and had acquired a reputation which would give confidence to the people of that region upon whom the General had to rely for his future success. Though the troops sent to you are, as you say, "raw," they have many able officers, and will, I doubt not, be found reliable in the hour of danger. Their greater numbers will to you, I hope, more than compensate for the experience of those transferred; while, in the Valley, the latter, by the moral effect their presence will produce, will more than compensate for the inferiority of their numbers. I have labored to increase the Army of the Potomac, and, so far from proposing a reduction of it, did not intend to rest content with an exchange of equivalents. In addition to the troops recently sent to you, I expected soon to send further reenforcements by withdrawing a part of the army from the Greenbrier Mountains. I have looked hopefully forward to the time when our army could assume the offensive, and select the time and place where battles were to be fought, so that ours should be alternations of activity and repose, theirs the heavy task of constant watching. When I last visited your headquarters, my surprise was expressed at the little increase of your effective force above that of the 21st of July last, notwithstanding the heavy reënforcements which in the mean time, had been sent to you. Since that visit I have frequently heard of the improved health of the troops, of the return of many who had been absent sick; and some increase has been made by reënforcements. You can, then, imagine my disappointment at the information you give, that, on the day before the date of your letter, the army at your position was yet no stronger than on the 21st of July. I can only repeat what has been said to you in our conference at Fairfax Court-House, that we are restricted in our capacity to reënforce by the want of arms. Troops to bear the few arms you have in store have been ordered forward. Your view of the magnitude of the calamity of defeat of the Army of the Potomac is entirely concurred in, and every advantage which is attainable should be seized to increase the power of your present force. I will do what I can to augment its numbers, but you must remember that our wants greatly exceed our resources.

Banks's brigade, we learn, has left the position occupied when I last saw you. Sickles is said to be yet in the lower Potomac, and, when your means will enable you to reach him, I still hope he may be crushed.

I will show this reply to the Secretary of War, and hope there will be no misunderstanding between you in future. The success of the army requires harmonious coöperation.

Very respectfully, etc.,
JEFFERSON DAVIS.

After General Jackson commenced his march, the cold became unexpectedly severe, and as he ascended into the mountainous region, the slopes were covered with ice, which impeded his progress, the more because his horses were smooth-shod; but his tenacity of purpose, fidelity, and daring, too well known to need commendation, triumphed over every obstacle, and he attained his object, drove the enemy from Romney and its surroundings, took possession of the place, and prevented the threatened concentration. Having accomplished this purpose, and being assured that the enemy had abandoned that section of country, he returned with his old brigade to the valley of the Shenandoah, leaving the balance of his command at Romney. General Loring, the senior officer there present, and many others of the command so left, appealed to the War Department to be withdrawn. Their arguments were, as well as I remember, these: that the troops, being from the South, were unaccustomed to, and unprepared for, the rigors of a mountain winter; that they were strangers to the people of that section; that the position had no military strength, and, at the approach of spring, would be accessible to the enemy by roads leading from various quarters.

After some preliminary action, an order was issued from the War Office directing the troops to retire to the valley. As that order has been the subject of no little complaint, both by civil and military functionaries, my letter to the general commanding the department, in explanation of the act of the Secretary of War, is hereto annexed:

RICHMOND, VIRGINIA, February 14, 1862.

General J. E. JOHNSTON, *commanding Department of Northern Virginia, Centreville, Virginia.*

GENERAL: I have received your letter of the 5th instant. While I admit the propriety in all cases of transmitting orders through you to those under your command, it is not surprising that the Secretary of War should, in a case requiring prompt action, have departed from this, the usual method, in view of the fact that he had failed more than once in having his instructions carried out when forwarded to you in the proper manner. You will remember that you were directed, on account of the painful reports received at the War Department in relation to the command at Romney, to repair to that place, and, after the needful examination, to give the orders proper in the case. You sent your adjutant-(inspector?) general, and I am informed that he went no farther than Winchester, to which point the commander of the expedition had withdrawn; leaving the troops, for whom anxiety had been excited, at Romney. Had you given your personal attention to the case, you must be assured that the confidence reposed in you would have prevented the Secretary from taking any action before your report had been received. In the absence of such security, he was further moved by what was deemed reliable information, that a large force of the enemy was concentrating to capture the troops at Romney, and by official report that place had no natural strength and little strategic importance. To insure concert of action in the defense of our Potomac frontier, it was thought best to place all the forces for this object under one command. The reasons which originally induced the adding of the Valley district to your department exist in full force at present, and I can not, therefore, agree to its separation from your command.

I will visit the Army of the Potomac as soon as other engagements will permit, although I can not realize your complimentary assurance that great good to the army will result from it; nor can I anticipate the precise time when it will be practicable to leave my duties here.

Very respectfully and truly yours,

JEFFERSON DAVIS.

To complaints by General Johnston that the discipline of his army was interfered with by irregular action of the Secretary of War, and its numerical strength diminished by furloughs granted directly by the War Department, I replied, after making inquiry at the War Office, by a letter, a copy of which is hereto annexed:

RICHMOND, VIRGINIA, March 4, 1862.

General J. E. JOHNSTON, *Centreville, Virginia.*

DEAR SIR: Yours of the 1st instant received prompt attention, and I am led to the conclusion that some imposition has been practiced upon you. The Secretary of War informs me that he has not granted leaves of absence or furloughs to soldiers of your command for a month past, and then only to divert the current which threatened by legislation to destroy your army by a wholesale system of furloughs. Those which you inform me are daily received must be spurious. The authority to reënlist and change from infantry to artillery, the Secretary informs me, has been given but in four cases—three on the recommendation of General Beauregard, and specially explained to you some time since; the remaining case was that of a company from Wheeling, which was regarded as an exceptional one. I wish, therefore, that you would send to the Adjutant-General the cases of recent date in which the discipline of your troops has been interfered with in the two methods stated, so that an inquiry may be made into the origin of the papers presented. The law in relation to reënlistment provides for reorganization, and was under the policy of electing the officers.

The concession to army opinions was limited to the promotion by seniority after the organization of the companies and regiments had been completed. The reorganization was not to occur before the expiration of the present term. A subsequent law provides for filling up the twelve months' companies by recruits for the war, but the organization ceases with the term of the twelve months' men. Be assured of readiness to protect your proper authority, and I do but justice to the Secretary of War in saying that he can not desire to interfere with the discipline and organization of your troops. He has complained that his orders are not executed, and I regret that he was able to present to me so many instances to justify that complaint, which were in no wise the invasion of your prerogative as a commander in the field.

You can command my attention at all times to any matter connected with your duties, and I hope that full co-intelligence will secure full satisfaction.

Very truly yours,

JEFFERSON DAVIS.

A fortnight after this letter, I received from General Johnston notice that his position was considered unsafe. Many of his letters to me have been lost, and I have thus far not been able to find the one giving the notice referred to, but the reply which is annexed clearly indicates the substance of the letter which was answered:

RICHMOND, VIRGINIA, February 28, 1862.

GENERAL J. E. JOHNSTON: . . . Your opinion that your position may be turned whenever the enemy chooses to advance, and that he will be ready to take the field before yourself, clearly indicates prompt effort to disencumber yourself of everything which would interfere with your rapid movement when necessary, and such thorough examination of the country in your rear as would give you exact knowledge of its roads and general topography, and enable you to select a line of greater natural advantages than that now occupied by your forces.

The heavy guns at Manassas and Evansport, needed elsewhere, and reported to be useless in their present position, would necessarily be abandoned in any hasty retreat. I regret that you find it impossible to move them.

The subsistence stores should, when removed, be placed in positions to answer your future wants. Those can not be determined until you have furnished definite information as to your plans, especially the line to which you would remove in the contingency of retiring. The Commissary-General had previously stopped further shipments to your army, and given satisfactory reasons for the establishment at Thoroughfare.[1] . . .

I need not urge on your consideration the value to our country of arms and munitions of war: you know the difficulty with which we have obtained our small supply; that, to furnish heavy artillery to the advanced posts, we have exhausted the supplies here which were designed for the armament of the city defenses. Whatever can be, should be done to avoid the loss of these guns. . . .

As has been my custom, I have only sought to present general purposes and views. I rely upon your special knowledge and high ability to effect whatever is practicable in this our hour of need. Recent disasters have depressed the weak, and are depriving us of the aid of the wavering. Traitors show the tendencies heretofore concealed, and the selfish grow clamorous for local and personal interests. At such an hour, the wisdom of the trained and the steadiness of the brave possess a double value. The military paradox that impossibilities must be rendered possible, had never better occasion for its application.

The engineers for whom you asked have been ordered to report to you, and further additions will be made to your list of brigadier-generals. Let me hear from you often and fully.

Very truly and respectfully yours,

JEFFERSON DAVIS.

RICHMOND, VIRGINIA, March 6, 1862.

GENERAL J. E. JOHNSTON: . . . Notwithstanding the threatening position of the enemy, I infer from your account of the roads and streams that his active operations must be for some time delayed, and thus I am permitted to hope that you will be able to mobilize your army by the removal of your heavy ordnance and such stores as are not required for active operations, so that, whenever you are required to move, it may be without public loss and without impediment to celerity. I was fully impressed with the difficulties which you presented when discussing the subject of a change of position. To preserve the efficiency of your

---

[1] Thoroughfare Gap was the point at which the commissary general had placed a meat-packing establishment.

army, you will, of course, avoid all needless exposure; and, when your army has been relieved of all useless incumbrance, you can have no occasion to move it while the roads and the weather are such as would involve serious suffering, because the same reasons must restrain the operations of the enemy. . . .

Very respectfully yours,

JEFFERSON DAVIS.

At the conference at Fairfax Court House heretofore referred to, I was sadly disappointed to find that the strength of that army had been little increased, notwithstanding the reënforcements sent to it since July 21st, and that to make an advance the generals required an additional force, which it was utterly impracticable for me to supply. Soon thereafter the army withdrew to Centreville, a better position for defense but not for attack, and thereby suggestive of the abandonment of an intention to advance. The subsequent correspondence with General Johnston during the winter expressed an expectation that the enemy would resume the offensive, and that the position then held was geographically unfavorable. There was a general apprehension at Richmond that the northern frontier of Virginia would be abandoned, and a corresponding earnestness was exhibited to raise the requisite force to enable our army to take the offensive. On March 10th I telegraphed to General Johnston: "Further assurance given to me this day that you shall be promptly and adequately reënforced, so as to enable you to maintain your position, and resume first policy when the roads will permit." The first policy was to carry the war beyond our own border.

Five days thereafter I received notice that our army was in retreat, and replied as follows:

RICHMOND, VIRGINIA, March 15, 1862.

General J. E. JOHNSTON, *Headquarters Army of the Potomac.*

GENERAL: I have received your letter of the 13th instant, giving the first official account I have received of the retrograde movement of your army.

Your letter would lead me to infer that others had been sent to apprise me of your plans and movements. If so, they have not reached me; and, before the receipt of yours of the 13th, I was as much in the dark as to your purposes, condition, and necessities as at the time of our conversation on the subject about a month since.

It is true I have had many and alarming reports of great destruction of ammunition, camp-equipage, and provisions, indicating precipitate retreat; but, having heard of no cause for such a sudden movement, I was at a loss to believe it.

I have not the requisite topographical knowledge for the selection of your new position. I had intended that you should determine that question; and for this purpose a corps of engineers was furnished to make a careful examination of the country to aid you in your decision.

The question of throwing troops into Richmond is contingent upon reverses in the West and Southeast. The immediate necessity for such a movement is not anticipated.

Very respectfully yours,
JEFFERSON DAVIS.

On the same day I sent the following telegram:

RICHMOND, VIRGINIA, March 15, 1862.

General J. E. JOHNSTON, *Culpepper Court-House, Virginia.*

Your letter of the 13th received this day, being the first information of your retrograde movement. I have no report of your reconnaissance, and can suggest nothing as to the position you should take except it should be as far in advance as consistent with your safety.

JEFFERSON DAVIS.

To further inquiry from General Johnston as to where he should take position, I replied that I would go to his headquarters in the field, and found him on the south bank of the river, to which he had retired, in a position possessing great natural advantages. An elevated bank commanded the north side of the river, overlooking the bridge, and an open field beyond it, across which the enemy must pass to reach the bridge, which, if left standing, was an invitation to seek that crossing. Upon inquiring whether the south bank of the river continued to command the other side down to Fredericksburg, General Johnston answered that he did not know; that he had not been at Fredericksburg since he passed there in a stage on his way to West Point, when he was first appointed a cadet. I then proposed that we should go to Fredericksburg, to inform ourselves upon that point. On arriving at Fredericksburg, a reconnaissance soon manifested that the hills on the opposite side commanded the town and adjacent river bank, and therefore Fredericksburg could only be defended by an army occupying the opposite hills, for which our force was inadequate. In returning to the house of Barton, where I was a guest, I found a number of ladies had assembled there to welcome me, and who, with anxiety, inquired as to the result of our reconnaissance. Upon learning that the town was not considered defensible against an enemy occupying the heights on the other side, and that our force was not sufficient to hold those heights against such an attack as might be anticipated, the general answer was, with a self-sacrificing patriotism too much admired to be forgotten, "If the good of our cause requires the defense of the town to be abandoned, let it be done." The purposes of the enemy were then unknown to us. If General Johnston's expectation of a hostile advance in great force should be realized, our course must depend partly upon receiving the reënforcement we had reason to expect from promises previously given and renewed, as was announced to General Johnston in my telegram of March 10, 1862, in these words:

Further assurance given to me this day that you shall be promptly and adequately reënforced, so as to enable you to maintain your position, and resume first policy when the roads will permit.

No immediate decision could therefore be made, and I returned to Richmond to wait the further development of the enemy's plans, and to prepare as best we might to counteract them.

The feeling heretofore noticed as arousing in Virginia a determination to resist the abandonment of her northern frontier, and which caused the assurance of reënforcements, bore fruit in the addition of about thirty thousand men, by a draft made by the governor of the state. These, it is true, were not the disciplined, seasoned troops which were asked for by the generals in the conference at Fairfax Court House, but they were of such men as often during the war won battles for the Confederacy. The development of the enemy's plans, for which we had to wait, proved that instead of advancing in force against our position at Centreville, he had, before the retreat of our army commenced, decided to move down the Potomac for a campaign against Richmond, from the Peninsula as a base. The conflagration at Centreville gave notice of its evacuation, and an advance was made as far as Manassas, but, as appears by General McClellan's report, with no more important design than to attack our rear guard, if it should be encountered. In the report on the conduct of the war by a committee of the United States Congress, evidence is found of much vacillation before the conclusion was finally reached of abandoning the idea of a direct advance upon Richmond for that of concentrating their army at the mouth of the Chesapeake. Whatever doubt or apprehension continued to exist about uncovering the city of Washington by removing their main army from before it, was of course dispelled by the retreat of our army, and the burning of bridges behind it. In this last-mentioned fact, General McClellan says he found the strongest reason to believe that there was no immediate danger of our army returning.

There was an apparent advantage to the enemy in the new base for his operations which was sufficiently illustrated by the events of the last year of the war. Had we possessed an army as large as the enemy supposed, it would have been possible for us at the same time to check his advance from the East and to march against his capital, with fair prospect of capturing it, before the army he had sent against Yorktown could have been brought back for the defense of Washington. On this as on other occasions he greatly magnified the force we possessed, and on this as on other occasions it required the concentration of our troops successfully to resist a detachment of his. Accepting as a necessity the withdrawal of the main portion of our army from northern Virginia to meet the invasion from the seaboard, it was regretted that earlier and more effective means were not employed for the mobilization of the army, a desirable measure in either contingency of advance or retreat, or at the least that the withdrawal was not so deliberate as to secure the removal of our ordnance, subsistence, and quartermasters' stores, which had been collected on the line occupied in 1861 and the early part of 1862.

A distinguished officer of our army, who has since the war made valuable contributions to the history of its operations—especially valuable as well for their accuracy as for their freedom from personal or partisan bias—writes thus of the retreat from Centreville:

A very large amount of stores and provisions had been abandoned for want of transportation, and among the stores was a very large quantity of clothing, blankets, etc., which had been provided by the States south of Virginia for their own troops. The pile of trunks along the railroad was appalling to behold. All these stores, clothing, trunks, etc., were consigned to the flames by a portion of our cavalry left to carry out the work of their destruction. The loss of stores at this point and at White Plains on the Manassas Gap Railroad, where a large amount of meat had been salted and stored, was a very serious one to us, and embarrassed us for the remainder of the war, as it put us at once on a running stock.

The same officer—and the value of his opinion will be recognized by all who know him, wherefore I give his name, General J. A. Early—in a communication subsequent to that from which I have just quoted, writes, in regard to the loss of supplies:

I believe that all might have been carried off from Manassas if the railroads had been energetically operated. The rolling-stock of the Orange and Alexandria, Manassas Gap, and Virginia Central Railroads ought to have been sufficient for the purpose of removing everything in the two weeks allowed, if properly used.

The enemy's plans, the development of which, as has been already stated, was necessary for the determination of our own movements, were soon thereafter found to be the invasion of Virginia from the seaboard, and the principal portion of our army was consequently ordered to the Peninsula, between the York River and the James. Thus the northern frontier of Virginia, which in the first year of the war had been the main field of skirmishes, combats, and battles, of advance and retreat, and the occupation and evacuation of fortified positions, ceased for a time to tremble beneath the tread of contending armies.

To the foregoing narration of events immediately connected with the efforts of the Confederate government to maintain its existence at home, may here be properly added an incident bearing on its foreign relations in the first year of the war.

Our efforts for the recognition of the Confederate States by the European powers, in 1861, served to make us better known abroad, to awaken a kindly feeling in our favor, and cause a respectful regard for the effort we were making to maintain the independence of the states which Great Britain had recognized, and her people knew to be our birthright.

On November 8, 1861, an outrage was perpetrated by an armed vessel of the United States, in the forcible detention, on the high seas, of a British mail steamer, making one of her regular trips from one British port to another, and the seizure, on that unarmed vessel, of our commissioners, Mason and Slidell, who with their secretaries were bound for Europe on diplomatic service. The seizure was made by an armed force against the protest of the captain of the vessel, and of Commander Williams, R. N., the latter speaking as the representative of Her Majesty's government. The commissioners yielded only when force, which they could not resist, was used to remove them from the mail steamer, and convey them to the United States vessel of war.

This outrage was the more marked because the United States had been foremost in resisting the right of "visit and search," and had made it the cause of the War of 1812 with Great Britain.

When intelligence of the event was received in England it excited the greatest indignation among the people; Her Majesty's government, by naval and other preparations, unmistakably exhibited the purpose to redress the wrong.

The commissioners and their secretaries had been transported to the harbor of Boston, and imprisoned in its main fortress.

Diplomatic correspondence resulted from this event. The British government demanded the immediate and unconditional release of the commissioners, "in order that they may again be placed under British protection, and a suitable apology for the aggression which has been committed."

In the meantime Captain Wilkes, commander of the vessel which had made the visit and search of the *Trent*, returned to the United States and was received with general plaudit, both by the people and the government. The House of Representatives passed a vote of thanks, an honor not heretofore bestowed except for some deed deserving well of the country. In the midst of all this exultation at the seizure of our commissioners on board a British merchant ship, came the indignant and stern demand for the restoration of those commissioners to the British protection from which they had been taken, and an apology for the aggression. It was little to be expected, after such explicit commendation of the act, that the United States government would accede to the demand; therefore the War and Navy Departments of the British government made active and extensive provision to enforce it. The haughty temper displayed toward four gentlemen arrested on an unarmed ship subsided in view of a demand to be enforced by the army and navy of Great Britain, and the United States Secretary of State, after a wordy and ingenious reply to the minister of Great Britain at Washington city, wrote: "The four persons in question are now held in military custody at Fort Warren, in the State of Massachusetts. They will be cheerfully liberated. Your lordship will please indicate a time and place for receiving them."

There was a time when the government and the people of the United States would not have sanctioned such aggression on the right of friendly ships to pass unquestioned on the highway of nations, and the right of a neutral flag to protect everything not contraband of war; that was, however, a time when arrogance and duplicity had not led them into false positions, and when the roar of the British lion could not make Americans retract what they had deliberately avowed.

CHAPTER XII: *Supply of Arms at the Beginning of the War; of Powder; of Batteries; of Other Articles—Contents of Arsenals—Other Stores, Mills, etc.—First Efforts to Obtain Powder, Niter, and Sulphur—Construction of Mills Commenced —Efforts to Supply Arms, Machinery, Field Artillery, Ammunition, Equipment, and Saltpeter—Results in 1862—Government Powder Mills; how Organized—Success—Efforts to Obtain Lead—Smelting Works—Troops, how Armed—Winter of 1862—Supplies—Niter and Mining Bureau—Equipment of First Armies—Receipts by Blockade Runners—Arsenal at Richmond—Armories at Richmond and Fayetteville—A Central Laboratory Built at Macon—Statement of General Gorgas —Northern Charge Against General Floyd Answered—Charge of Slowness Against the President Answered—Quantities of Arms Purchased that Could not be Shipped in 1861—Letter of Huse.*

AT THE beginning of the war the arms within the limits of the Confederacy were distributed as follows:

	Rifles	Muskets
At Richmond (State) ....about	4,000	
Fayetteville, North Carolina .... "	2,000	25,000
Charleston, South Carolina .... "	2,000	20.000
Augusta, Georgia .... "	3,000	28,000
Mount Vernon, Alabama .... "	2,000	20,000
Baton Rouge, Louisiana .... "	2,000	27,000
Total	15,000	120,000

There were at Richmond about sixty thousand old flint muskets, and at Baton Rouge about ten thousand old Hall's rifles and carbines. At Little Rock, Arkansas, there were a few thousand stands, and a few at the Texas Arsenal, increasing the aggregate of serviceable arms to about one hundred forty-three thousand. Add to these the arms owned by the several states and by military organizations, and it would make a total of one hundred fifty thousand for the use of the armies of the Confederacy. The rifles were of the caliber .54, known as Mississippi rifles, except those at Richmond taken from Harpers Ferry, which were of the new model caliber .58; the muskets were the old flintlock, caliber .69, altered to percussion. There were a few boxes of sabers at each arsenal, and some short artillery swords. A few hundred holster pistols were scattered about. There were no revolvers.

There was before the war little powder or ammunition of any kind stored in the Southern states, and this was a relic of the war with Mexico. It is doubtful if there were a million of rounds of small-arms cartridges. The chief store of powder was that captured at Norfolk; there was, besides, a small quantity at each of the Southern arsenals, in all sixty thousand pounds, chiefly old cannon powder. The percussion caps did not exceed one quarter of a million, and there was no lead on hand. There were no batteries of serviceable field artillery at the arsenals, but a few old iron guns mounted on Gribeauval carriages fabricated about 1812. The states and the volunteer companies did, however, possess some serviceable batteries. But there were neither harness, saddles, bridles, blankets, nor other artillery or cavalry equipments.

To furnish one hundred fifty thousand men, on both sides of the Mississippi, in May, 1861, there were no infantry accoutrements, no cavalry arms or equipment, no artillery, and above all, no ammunition; nothing save arms, and these almost wholly the old pattern smooth-bore muskets, altered to percussion from flintlocks.

Within the limits of the Confederate States the arsenals had been used only as depots, and no one of them, except that at Fayetteville, North Carolina, had a single machine above the grade of a foot-lathe. Except at the Harpers Ferry armory, all the work of preparation of material had been carried on at the North; not an arm, not a gun, not a gun carriage, and, except during the Mexican War, scarcely a round of ammunition, had for fifty years been prepared in the Confederate States. There were consequently no workmen, or very few, skilled in these arts. Powder, save perhaps for blasting, had not been made at the South. No saltpeter was in store at any Southern point; it was stored wholly at the North. There were no worked mines of lead except in Virginia, and the situation of those made them a precarious dependence. The only cannon foundry existing was at Richmond. Copper, so necessary for field artillery and for percussion caps, was just being obtained in East Tennessee. There was no rolling mill for bar iron south of Richmond, and but few blast furnaces, and these, with trifling exceptions, were in the border states of Virginia and Tennessee.

The first efforts made to obtain powder were by orders sent to the North, which had been early done both by the Confederate government and by some of the states. These were being rapidly filled when the attack was made on Fort Sumter. The shipments then ceased. Niter was contemporaneously sought for in north Alabama and Tennessee. Between four and five hundred tons of sulphur were obtained in New Orleans, at which place it had been imported for use in the manufacture of sugar. Preparations for the construction of a large powder mill were promptly commenced by the government, and two small private mills in East Tennessee were supervised and improved. On June 1, 1861, there was probably two hundred and fifty thousand pounds only, chiefly of cannon powder, and about as much niter, which had been imported by Georgia. There were the two powder mills above mentioned, but we had no experience in making powder, or in extracting niter from natural deposits, or in obtaining it by artificial beds.

For the supply of arms an agent was sent to Europe, who made contracts to the extent of nearly half a million dollars. Some small arms had been obtained from the North, and also important machinery. The machinery at Harpers Ferry armory had been saved from the flames by the heroic conduct of the operatives, headed by Armistead M. Ball, the master armorer. Of the machinery so saved, that for making rifle muskets was transported to Richmond, and that for rifles with sword-bayonets to Fayetteville, North Carolina. In addition to the injuries suffered by the machinery, the lack of skilled workmen caused much embarrassment. In the meantime the manufacture of small arms was undertaken at New Orleans and prosecuted with energy, though with limited success.

In field artillery the manufacture was confined almost entirely to the Tredegar Works in Richmond. Some castings were made in New Orleans, and attention was turned to the manufacture of field and siege artillery at Nashville. A small foundry at Rome, Georgia, was induced to undertake the casting of the three-inch iron rifle, but the progress was very slow. The state of Virginia possessed a number of old four-pounder iron guns which were reamed out to get a good bore, and rifled with three groves, after the manner of Parrott. The army at Harpers Ferry and that at Manassas were supplied with old batteries of six-pounder guns and twelve-pounder howitzers. A few Parrott guns, purchased by the state of Virginia, were with General Magruder at Big Bethel.

For the ammunition and equipment required for the infantry and artillery, a good laboratory and workshop had been established at Richmond. The arsenals were making preparations for furnishing ammunition and knapsacks; generally, however, what little was done in this regard was for local purposes. Such was the general condition of ordnance and ordnance stores in May, 1861.

The progress of development, however, was steady. A refinery of salt-peter was established near Nashville during the summer, which received the niter from its vicinity, and from the caves in East and Middle Tennessee. Some inferior powder was made at two small mills in South Carolina. North Carolina established a mill near Raleigh; a stamping mill was put up near New Orleans, and powder made there before the fall of the city. Small quantities were also received through the blockade. It was estimated that on January 1, 1862, there were fifteen hundred sea-coast guns of various caliber in position from Evansport on the Potomac to Fort Brown on the Rio Grande. If their caliber was averaged at thirty-two pounder, and the charge at five pounds, it would, at forty rounds per gun, require six hundred thousand pounds of powder for them. The field artillery—say three hundred guns, with two hundred rounds to the piece—would require one hundred twenty-five thousand pounds; the small-arm cartridges—say ten million—would consume one hundred twenty-five thousand pounds more, making in all eight hundred fifty thousand pounds. Deducting two hundred fifty thousand pounds, supposed to be on hand in various shapes, the increment is six hundred thousand pounds for the year 1861. Of this, perhaps two hundred thousand pounds had been made at the Tennessee and other mills, leaving four hundred thousand pounds to be supplied through the blockade, or before the beginning of hostilities.

The liability of powder to deteriorate in damp atmospheres results from the impurity of the niter used in its manufacture, and this it is not possible to detect by any of the usual tests. Security, therefore, in the purchase, depends on the reliability of the maker. To us, who had to rely on foreign products and the open market, this was equivalent to no security at all. It was, therefore, as well for this reason as because of the precariousness of thus obtaining the requisite supply, necessary that we should establish a government powder mill. It was our good fortune to have a valuable man whose military education and scientific knowledge had been supplemented by practical experience in a large manufactory of machinery. He, General G. W. Rains, was at the time resident in the state of New York; when his native state, North Carolina, seceded from the Union and joined the Confederacy, true to the highest instincts of patriotism, he returned to the land of his birth, and only asked where he could be most useful. The expectations which his reputation justified caused him to be assigned to the task of making a great powder mill, which should alike furnish an adequate supply and give assurance of its possessing all the requisite qualities. This problem, which, under the existing circumstances seemed barely possible, was fully solved. Not only was powder made of every variety of grain and exact uniformity in each, but the niter was so absolutely purified that there was no danger of its deterioration in service. Had Admiral Semmes been supplied with such powder it is demonstrated, by the facts which have since been established, that the engagement between the *Alabama* and the *Kearsarge* would have resulted in a victory for the former.

These government powder mills were located at Augusta, Georgia, and satisfactory progress was made in the construction during the year. All the machinery, including the very heavy rollers, was made in the Confederate States. Contracts were made abroad for the delivery of niter through the blockade; for obtaining it immediately, we resorted to caves, tobacco houses, cellars, etc. The amount delivered from Tennessee was the largest item in the year's supply, but the whole was quite inadequate to existing and prospective needs.

The consumption of lead was mainly met by the Virginia lead mines at Wytheville, the yield from which was from sixty to eighty thousand pounds per month. Lead was also collected by agents in considerable quantities throughout the country, and the battlefield of Manassas was closely gleaned, from which much lead was collected. A laboratory for the smelting of other ores was constructed at Petersburg, Virginia, and was in operation before midsummer of 1862.

By the close of 1861, eight arsenals and four depots had been supplied with materials and machinery, so as to be efficient in producing the various munitions and equipments, the want of which had caused early embarrassment. Thus a good deal had been done to produce the needed material of war, and to refute the croakers who found in our poverty application for the maxim, *Ex nihilo nihil fit.*

The troops were, however, still very poorly armed and equipped. The old smooth-bore musket was the principal weapon of the infantry; the artillery had mostly the six-pounder gun and the twelve-pounder howitzer; the cavalry were armed with such various weapons as they could get—sabers, horse pistols, revolvers, Sharp's carbines, musketoons, short Enfield rifles, Holt's carbines, muskets cut off, etc. Equipments were in many cases made of stout cotton domestic, stitched in triple folds and covered with paint or rubber varnish. But poor as were the arms, enough of them, such as they were, could not be obtained to arm the troops pressing forward to defend their homes and their political rights.

In December, 1861, arms purchased abroad began to come in, and a good many Enfield rifles were in the hands of the troops at the battle of Shiloh. The winter of 1862 was the period when our ordnance deficiencies were most keenly felt. Powder was called for on every hand; the equipments most needed were those we were least able to supply. The abandonment of the line of the Potomac and the upper Mississippi from Columbus to Memphis did somewhat, however, reduce the pressure for heavy artillery; after the fall of 1862, when the powder mills at Augusta had got into full operation, there was no further inability to meet all requisitions for ammunition. To provide the iron needed for cannon and projectiles, it had been necessary to stimulate by contracts the mining and smelting of its ores.

But it was obviously beyond the power of even the great administrative capacity of the chief of ordnance, General J. Gorgas, to whose monograph I am indebted for these details, to add, to his already burdensome labors, the numerous and increasing cares of obtaining the material from which ammunition, arms, and equipments were to be manufactured. On his recommendation a niter and mining bureau was organized, and Colonel St. John, who had been hitherto assigned to duty in connection with procuring supplies of niter and iron, was appointed chief of this bureau. A large, difficult, and most important field of operations was thus assigned to him, and well did he fulfill its requirements. To his recent experience was added scientific knowledge, and to both, untiring, systematic industry, and his heart's thorough devotion to the cause he served. The tree is known by its fruit, and he may confidently point to results as the evidence on which he is willing to stand for judgment. Briefly, they will be noticed.

Niter was to be obtained from caves and other like sources, and by the formation of niter beds, some of which had previously been begun at Richmond. These beds were located at Columbia (South Carolina), Charleston, Savannah, Augusta, Mobile, Selma, and various other points. At the close of 1864 there were two million eight hundred thousand feet of earth collected, and in various stages of nitrification, of which a large proportion was presumed to yield one and a half pound of niter per foot of earth. The whole country was laid off into districts, each of which was under the charge of an officer, who obtained details of workmen from the army, and made his monthly reports. Thus the niter production, in the course of a year, was brought up to something like half of the total consumption. The district from which the most constant yield could be relied on had its chief office at Greensboro, North Carolina, a region which had no niter caves in it. The niter was obtained from lixiviation of nitrous earth found under old houses, barns, etc. The supervision of the production of iron, lead, copper, and all the minerals which needed development, as well as the manufacture of sulphuric and nitric acids (the latter required for the supply of the fulminate of mercury for percussion caps), without which the firearms of our day would have been useless, was added to the niter bureau. Such was the progress that in a short time the bureau was aiding or managing some twenty to thirty furnaces with an annual yield of fifty thousand tons or more of pig iron. The lead-and copper-smelting works erected were sufficient for all wants, and the smelting of zinc of good quality had been achieved. The chemical works were placed at Charlotte, North Carolina, to serve as a reserve when the supply from abroad might be cut off.

In equipping the armies first sent into the field, the supply of accessories was embarrassingly scant. There were arms, such as they were, for over one hundred thousand men, but no accoutrements nor equipments, and a meager supply of ammunition. In time the knapsacks were supplanted by haversacks, which the women could make. But soldiers' shoes and cartridge boxes must be had; leather was also needed for artillery harness and for cavalry saddles; as the amount of leather which the country could furnish was quite insufficient for all these purposes, it was perforce apportioned among them. Soldiers' shoes were the prime necessity. Therefore, a scale was established, by which first shoes and then cartridge boxes had the preference; after these, artillery harness, and then saddles and bridles. To economize leather, the waist and cartridge-box belts were made of prepared cotton cloth stitched in three or four thicknesses. Bridle reins were likewise so made, and then cartridge boxes were thus covered, except the flap. Saddle skirts, too, were made of heavy cotton cloth strongly stitched. To get leather, each department procured its quota of hides, made contracts with the tanners, obtained hands for them by exemptions from the army, got transportation over the railroads for the hides and for supplies. To the varied functions of this bureau was finally added that of assisting the tanners to procure the necessary supplies for the tanneries. A fishery, even, was established on Cape Fear River to get oil for mechanical purposes, and at the same time food for the workmen. In cavalry equipments the main thing was to get a good saddle which would not hurt the back of the horse. For this purpose various patterns were tried, and reasonable success was obtained. One of the most difficult wants to supply in this branch of the service was the horseshoe for cavalry and artillery. The want of iron and of skilled labor was strongly felt. Every wayside blacksmith shop accessible, especially those in and near the theatre of operations, was employed. These, again, had to be supplied with material, and the employees exempted from service.

It early became manifest that great reliance must be placed on the introduction of articles of prime necessity through the blockaded ports. A vessel capable of stowing six hundred fifty bales of cotton was purchased by the agent in England, and kept running between Bermuda and Wilmington. Some fifteen to eighteen successive trips were made before she was captured. Another was added, which was equally successful. These vessels were long, low, rather narrow, and built for speed. They were mostly of pale sky color, and, with their lights out and with fuel that made little smoke, they ran to and from Wilmington with considerable regularity. Several others were added, and devoted to bringing in ordnance, and finally general supplies. Depots of stores were likewise made at Nassau and Havana, Another organization was also necessary, that the vessels coming in through the blockade might have their return cargoes promptly on their arrival. These resources were also supplemented by contracts for supplies brought through Texas from Mexico.

The arsenal in Richmond soon grew into very large dimensions, and produced all the ordnance stores that the army required, except cannon and small arms, in quantities sufficient to supply the forces in the field. The arsenal at Augusta was very serviceable to the armies serving in the south and west, and turned out a good deal of field artillery complete. The government powder mills were entirely successful. The arsenal and workshops at Charleston were enlarged, steam introduced, and good work done in various departments. The arsenal at Mount Vernon, Alabama, was moved to Selma, in that state, where it grew into a large and well-ordered establishment of the first class. Mount Vernon arsenal was dismantled, and served to furnish lumber and timber for use elsewhere. At Montgomery, shops were kept up for the repair of small arms and the manufacture of articles of leather. There were many other small establishments and depots.

The chief armories were at Richmond and at Fayetteville, North Carolina. The former turned out about fifteen hundred stands per month, and the latter only four hundred per month, for want of operatives. To meet the want of cavalry arms, a contract was made for the construction in Richmond of a factory for Sharp's carbines; this being built, it was then converted into a manufactory of rifle carbines, caliber .58. Smaller establishments grew up at Asheville, North Carolina, and at Tallahassee, Alabama. A great part of the work of the armories consisted in the repair of arms. In this manner the gleanings of the battlefields were utilized. Nearly ten thousand stands were saved from the field of Manassas, and from those about Richmond in 1862 about twenty-five thousand excellent arms. All the stock of inferior arms disappeared from the armories during the first two years of the war, and were replaced by a better class of arms, rifled and percussioned. Placing the good arms lost previous to July, 1863, at one hundred thousand, there must have been received from various sources four hundred thousand stands of infantry arms in the first two years of the war.

Among the obvious requirements of a well-regulated service was one central laboratory of sufficient capacity to prepare all ammunition, and thus to secure the vital advantage of absolute uniformity. Authority was therefore granted to concentrate this species of work at Macon, Georgia. Plans of the buildings and of the machinery required were submitted and approved, and the work was begun with energy. The pile of buildings had a façade of six hundred feet, was designed with taste, and comprehended every possible appliance for good and well-organized work. The buildings were nearly ready for occupation at the close of the war, and some of the machinery had arrived at Bermuda. This project preceded that of a general armory for the Confederacy, and was much nearer completion. These, with the admirable powder mills at Augusta, would have been completed, and with them the government would have been in a condition to supply arms and ammunition to three hundred thousand men. To these would have been added a foundry for heavy guns at Selma or Brierfield, Alabama, where the strongest cast iron in the country had been made.

Thus has been briefly sketched the development of the resources from which our large armies were supplied with arms and ammunition, while our country was invaded on land and water by armies much larger than our own. It will be seen under what disadvantages our people successfully prosecuted the (to them) new pursuits of mining and manufacturing. The chief of ordnance was General J. Gorgas, a man remarkable for his scientific attainment, for the highest administrative capacity and moral purity, all crowned by zeal and fidelity to his trust, in which he achieved results greatly disproportioned to the means at his command. He closes his excellent monograph in the following words:

We began in April, 1861, without an arsenal, laboratory, or powder-mill of any capacity, and with no foundry or rolling-mill, except in Richmond, and, before the close of 1863, or within a little over two years, we supplied them. During the harassments of war, while holding our own in the field defiantly and successfully against a powerful enemy; crippled by a depreciated currency;

throttled with a blockade that deprived us of nearly all the means of getting material or workmen; obliged to send almost every able-bodied man to the field; unable to use the slave-labor, with which we were abundantly supplied, except in the most unskilled departments of production; hampered by want of transportation even of the commonest supplies of food; with no stock on hand even of articles such as steel, copper, leather, iron, which we must have to build up our establishments—against all these obstacles, in spite of all these deficiencies, we persevered at home, as determinedly as did our troops in the field, against a more tangible opposition; and in that short period created, almost literally out of the ground, foundries and rolling-mills at Selma, Richmond, Atlanta, and Macon; smelting-works at Petersburg, chemical works at Charlotte, North Carolina; a powder-mill far superior to any in the United States and unsurpassed by any across the ocean; and a chain of arsenals, armories, and laboratories equal in their capacity and their improved appointments to the best of those in the United States, stretching link by link from Virginia to Alabama.

The same officer writes:

It was a charge often repeated at the North against General Floyd, that, as Secretary of War, he had with traitorous intent abused his office by sending arms to the South just before the secession of the States. The transactions which gave rise to this accusation were in the ordinary course of an economical administration of the War Department. After it had been determined to change the old flint-lock muskets which the United States possessed to percussion, it was deemed cheaper to bring all the flintlock arms in store at Southern arsenals to the Northern arsenals and armories for alteration, rather than to send the necessary machinery and workmen to the South. Consequently, the Southern arsenals were stripped of their deposits, which were sent to Springfield, Watervliet, Pittsburg, St. Louis, and other points. After the conversion had been effected, the denuded Southern arsenals were again supplied with about the same number, perhaps slightly augmented, that had formerly been stored there. The quota deposited at the Charleston Arsenal, where I was stationed in 1860, arrived there full a year before the opening of the war.

The charge was made early in the war that I was slow in procuring arms and munitions of war from Europe. We were not only in advance of the government of the United States in the markets of Europe, but the facts presented in the following extracts from a letter of our agent, Caleb Huse, dated December 30, 1861, and addressed to Major C. C. Anderson, will serve to place the matter in its proper light:

LONDON, December 30, 1861.

DEAR MAJOR: We are all waiting with almost breathless anxiety for the arrival of the answer from the United States to the unqualified demand of England for the captured commissioners. Will Mr. Lincoln disregard the international writ of *habeas corpus* served by Great Britain? We shall soon know. If the prisoners are given up, the affair will result in great inconvenience to us in the way of shipping goods.

I have now more than enough to load three "Bermudas," and can not ship a package, though I have a steamer off the wharf, all ready to receive her cargo. We are literally fighting two governments here. Government watchmen guard the wharf where our goods are stowed and others in the neighborhood, night and day—and the wharfinger has orders not to ship or deliver, by land or water, any goods marked W. D., without first acquainting the honorable Board of Customs. I have applied myself to ship to Bermuda, offering to give bonds to double the amount of value of the goods, that they should be held in Bermuda, subject to the direction of her Majesty's representative in Bermuda. I . . . has applied for permission to ship to Cardenas, agreeing to hold the goods subject to the order of the Spanish authorities—but all without avail, and our army must suffer for the want of blankets, overcoats, shoes, socks, field forges, arms, and ammunition, which have been collected to an amount more than double that I have yet received.

It is miserable to have to look at the immense pile of packages in the warehouse at St. Andrews Wharf, and not be able to send anything—only read the following: twenty-five thousand rifles; two thousand barrels of powder; five hundred thousand caps; ten thousand friction-tubes; five hundred thousand cartridges; thirteen thousand accoutrements; thirteen thousand knapsacks; thirteen thousand gun-slings; forty-four thousand three hundred and twenty-eight pairs of socks; sixteen thousand four hundred and eighty-four blankets; two hundred and twenty-six saddles; saddlers' tools; artillery-harness; leather, etc.

Very truly yours,
CALEB HUSE.

CHAPTER XIII: *Extracts from my Inaugural—Our Financial System—Receipts and Expenditures of the First Year—Resources, Loans, and Taxes — Loans Authorized — Notes and Bonds—Funding Notes—Treasury Notes Guaranteed by the States— Measure to Reduce the Currency—Operation of the General System — Currency Fundable — Taxation — Popular Aversion—Compulsory Reduction of the Currency—Tax Law —Successful Result—Financial Condition of the Government at its Close—Sources Whence Revenue was Derived—Total Public Debt—System of Direct Taxes and Revenue—The Tariff—War Tax of Fifty Cents on a Hundred Dollars—Property Subject to it—Every Resource of the Country to be Reached —Tax Paid by the States Mostly—Obstacle to the Taking of the Census—The Foreign Debt—Terms of the Contract—Premium —False Charge Against me of Repudiation—Facts Stated.*

IN my inaugural address in 1862 I said:

The first year of our history has been the most eventful in the annals of this continent. A new Government has been established, and its machinery put in operation over an area exceeding seven hundred thousand square miles. The great principles upon which we have been willing to hazard everything that is dear to man, have made conquests for us which could never have been achieved by the sword. Our Confederacy has grown from six to thirteen States; and Maryland, already united to us by hallowed memories and material interests, will, I believe, when enabled to speak with unstifled voice, connect her destiny with the South. Our people have rallied with unexampled unanimity to the support of the great principles of constitutional government, with firm resolve to perpetuate by arms the rights which they could not peacefully secure. A million of men, it is estimated, are now standing in hostile array and waging war along a frontier of thousands of miles. Battles have been fought, sieges have been conducted, and, although the contest is not ended, and the tide for the moment is against us, the final result in our favor is not doubtful. . . . Fellow-citizens, after the struggles of ages had consecrated the right of the Englishman to constitutional representative government, our colonial ancestors were forced to vindicate that birthright by an appeal to arms. Success crowned their efforts, and they provided for their posterity a peaceful remedy against future aggression.

The tyranyy of an unbridled majority, the most odious and the least responsible form of despotism, has denied us both the right and the remedy. Therefore, we are in arms to renew such sacrifices as our forefathers made to the holy cause of constitutional liberty.

The financial system which had been adopted from necessity proved adequate at this early period to supply all the wants of the government and of the people. An unexpected and very large increase of expenditures had resulted from the great enlargement of the necessary means of defense. Yet the government enterd on its second year without a floating debt and with its credit unimpaired. The total expenditures of the first year, ending February 1, 1862, amounted to one hundred seventy million dollars. A statement of the Secretary of the Treasury, comprising the period from the organization of the government to August 1, 1862, presents the following results:

Expenditures: War Department	$298,376,549.41
Navy "	14,605,777.86
Civil and miscellaneous	15,766,503.43
Total	$328,748,830.70
Outstanding requisitions	18,524,128.15
Total expenditures	347,272,958.85
Total receipts	302,482,096.60
Deficient Treasury notes authorized	16,755,165.00
" " " to be provided	28,035,697.25
	$44,790,862.25

The receipts were derived as follows:

Customs	$ 1,437,399.96	
War tax	10,539,910.70	
Miscellaneous	1,974,760.33	$ 13,952,079.99
Loans, bonds, February, 1861	15,000,000.00	
Bonds, August, 1861	22,613,346.61	
Call certificates, December, 1861	37,515,200.00	
Treasury notes, April, 1861	22,799,900.00	
Demand notes, August, 1861	187,130,670.00	
One and two dollar notes	846,900.00	
Due banks	2,645,000.00	$288,551,016.61
Total receipts		$302,503,096.60

Such was the result presented by the treasury of a government that had been in existence only eighteen months. It commenced that existence without a treasury, and, without the sinews and the munitions of war, was in less than two months invaded on every side by an implacable foe. Its ways and means consisted in loans and taxes, and to these it resorted. On February 28th I was authorized by Congress to borrow, at any time within twelve months, fifteen million dollars, or less, as might be needed. It was to be applied to the payment of appropriations for the support of the government, and for the public defense. Certificates of stock or bonds, payable in ten years at eight per cent interest, were issued. For the payment of the interest and principal of this loan a tax or duty of one-eighth of one per cent per pound was laid on all cotton exported. On March 9th an issue of one million dollars in treasury notes of fifty dollars and upward was authorized, payable in one year from date, at 3.65 per cent interest, and receivable for all public debts except the export duty on cotton. A reissue was authorized for a year. On May 16th a loan of fifty million dollars in bonds, payable after twenty years at eight per cent interest, was authorized. The bonds were "to be sold for specie, military stores, or for the proceeds of sales of raw produce or manufactured articles, to be paid in the form of specie or with foreign bills of exchange." The bonds could not be issued in fractional parts of a hundred dollars, or be exchanged for treasury notes or the notes of any bank, corporation, or individual. In lieu of any amount of these bonds, not exceeding twenty million dollars, an equal amount of treasury notes, without interest, in denominations of five dollars and upward, was authorized to be issued. These notes were payable in two years in specie, and were receivable for all debts or taxes except the export duty on cotton. They were also convertible into bonds payable in ten years at eight per cent interest. On August 19th another issue of treasury notes, amounting with those then issued to one hundred million dollars, was authorized. They were of the denominations of five dollars and upward. They were receivable for the war tax and all other public dues except the export duty on cotton. These notes were convertible into twenty-year bonds, bearing eight per cent interest, of which the issue was limited to one hundred million dollars. Thirty millions were to be a substitute for the same amount, authorized by the act of May 16, 1861. These bonds could be exchanged for specie, military and naval stores, or for the proceeds of raw produce and manufactured articles. On December 19th ten million dollars in Treasury notes were issued to pay the advance of the banks. On December 24th an additional issue of fifty millions of treasury notes like those of the act of August 19th was authorized. An additional issue of thirty millions of bonds was also authorized. On April 12, 1862, an issue of treasury notes, certificates of stock and bonds, as the public necessities might require, to the amount of two hundred and fifteen millions, was authorized. Of these, fifty millions in treasury notes were issued without reserve, ten millions in treasury notes retained as a reserve fund to pay any sudden or unexpected call for deposits, and one hundred and sixty-five millions certificates of stock or bonds. Bonds to the amount of fifty million dollars, payable in ten years at six per cent interest were authorized and made exchangeable for any of the above treasury notes. All these notes and bonds were subject to the same conditions as those of the acts of August 19 and December 24, 1861. On April 17th five millions of treasury notes were authorized to be issued in denominations of one and two dollars, which were receivable for all public dues except the cotton duty. An amount of treasury notes bearing interest at two cents per day on each hundred dollars, as a substitute for as much of the one hundred and sixty-five millions of bonds authorized, was also authorized to be issued. On September 19, 1862, three million five hundred thousand dollars in bonds was authorized to be issued to meet a contract for six ironclad vessels of war. On September 23, 1862, the amount of treasury notes under the denomination of five dollars was increased from five million to ten million dollars, and a further issue of bonds or certificates of stock, to the amount of fifty million dollars, was authorized.

On March 23, 1863, an effort was made to remove from circulation some of the issues of treasury notes by funding them. For this purpose it was provided that all treasury notes not bearing interest, issued prior to December, 1862, should be fundable in eight per cent bonds or stock during the ensuing thirty days, and during the succeeding three months in seven per cent bonds or stock, after which they ceased to be fundable. All treasury notes not bearing interest, and issued after December 1, 1862, until ten days after the passage of the act, were made fundable in seven per cent bonds or stock during the ensuing four months, and afterward only in four per cent thirty-year bonds. Call certificates were made fundable in thirty-year bonds at eight per cent, and all outstanding on the ensuing July 1st were deemed bonds at six per cent, payable in thirty years. A monthly issue of treasury notes, without interest, to the amount of fifty million dollars, was also authorized. These were made fundable during the first year of their issue in six per cent thirty-year bonds, and after the expiration of the year in four per cent thirty-year bonds. The further issue of call certificates was suspended; but treasury notes fundable in the six per cent bonds might be converted, at the pleasure of the holder, into such certificates at five per cent interest, which were reconvertible into like notes within six months, or afterward exchanged for thirty-year six per cent bonds. Treasury notes fundable in four per cent bonds were convertible in like manner at four per cent. All disposable means in the treasury were to be applied to the purchase of treasury notes, bearing no interest, until the amount in circulation did not exceed one hundred seventy-five millions. The issue of five million dollars, in notes of two dollars, one dollar, and fifty cents, was also authorized. It was further provided in this act that six per cent bonds, as above mentioned, might be sold to any of the states for treasury notes, and, being guaranteed by any of the states, they might be used to purchase treasury notes. The whole amount of such bonds could not exceed two hundred million dollars. Treasury notes so purchased were not to be reissued. The issue of six per cent coupon bonds to the amount of one hundred million dollars, which were to be applied only to the absorption of treasury notes, was also authorized. The coupons were payable either in the currency in which interest on other bonds was paid, or in cotton certificates pledging the government to pay the same in cotton of New Orleans middling quality, delivered at the rate of eight pence sterling per pound.

An important measure was adopted on February 17, 1864, the object of which was to reduce the currency and to authorize a new issue of notes and bonds. All treasury notes above the denomination of five dollars, and not bearing interest, were, if offered within a short period, made fundable in registered twenty-year bonds at four per cent. At the same time a new issue of treasury notes was authorized, and made receivable for all public dues, except customs duties, at the rate of two dollars for three of the old. The issue of other treasury notes, after the first of the ensuing April, was prohibited.

To pay the expenses of the government an issue of five hundred million dollars in six per cent bonds was authorized. For the payment of interest the receipts of the export and import duties, payable in specie, were pledged.

A review of this statement of the legislation of Congress will clearly present the financial system of the government. The first action of the provisional Congress was confined to the adoption of a tariff law, and an act for a loan of fifteen million dollars, with a pledge of a small export duty on cotton, to provide for the redemption of the debt. At the next session, after the commencement of the war, provision was made for the issue of twenty million dollars in treasury notes, and for borrowing thirty million dollars in bonds. At the same time the tariff was revised, and preparatory measures taken for the levy of internal taxes. After the purpose of subjugation became manifest by the action of the Congress of the United States, early in July, 1861, and the certainty of a long war was demonstrated, there arose the necessity that a financial system should be devised on a basis sufficiently large for the vast proportions of the approaching contest. The plan then adopted was founded on the theory of issuing treasury notes, convertible at the pleasure of the holder into eight per cent bonds, with the interest payable in coin. It was assumed that any tendency to depreciation, which might arise from the overissue of the currency, would be checked by the constant exercise of the holder's right to fund the notes at a liberal interest, payable in specie. The success of this system depended on the ability of the government constantly to pay the interest in specie. The measures, therefore, adopted to secure that payment consisted in the levy of an internal tax, termed a war tax, and the appropriation of the revenue from imports.

The first operation of this plan was quite successful. The interest was paid from the reserve of coin existing in the country, and experience sustained the expectations of those who devised the system.

Wheat, in the beginning of the year 1862, was selling at one dollar and thirty cents per bushel, thus but little exceeding its average price in time of peace. The other agricultural products of the country were at similarly moderate rates, thus indicating that there was no excess of circulation. At the same time the premium on coin had reached about twenty per cent. But it had become apparent that the commerce of our country was threatened with permanent suspension by reason of the conduct of neutral nations, who virtually gave aid to the United States government by sanctioning its declaration of a blockade. Those neutral nations treated our invasion by our former limited and special agent as though it were the attempt of a sovereign to suppress a rebellion against lawful authority. This exceptional cause heightened the premium on specie, because it indicated the exhaustion of our reserve, without the possibility of renewing the supply.

At the inauguration of the permanent government, in February, 1862, a popular aversion to internal taxation had been so strongly manifested as to indicate its partial failure. This will be further explained presently in our statement of the system of taxation.

Under all these circumstances the effort was made to avoid the increase in the volume of notes in circulation, by offering inducements to voluntary funding. The measures adopted for that purpose were but partially successful. Meanwhile the intervening exigencies from the fortunes of war permitted no delay. The issues of treasury notes were increased until, in December, 1863, the currency in circulation amounted to more than six hundred million dollars, or more than threefold the amount required by the business of the country. The evil effects of this financial condition were but too apparent. In addition to the difficulty presented to the necessary operations of the government, and the efficient conduct of the war, the most deplorable of all its results was, undoubtedly, its corrupting influence on the morals of the people. The possession of large amounts of treasury notes led to a desire for investment; with a constantly increasing volume of currency, there was an equally constant increase of price in all objects of investment. This effect stimulated purchase by the apparent certainty of profit, and a spirit of speculation was thus fostered, which had so debasing an influence and such ruinous consequences that it became our highest duty to remove the cause by prompt and stringent measures.

I therefore recommended to Congress in December, 1863, the compulsory reduction of the currency to the amount required by the business of the country, accompanied by a pledge that, under no stress of circumstances, would the amount be increased. I stated that, if the currency was not greatly and promptly reduced, the existing scale of inflated prices would not only continue, but by the very fact of the large amounts thus made requisite in the conduct of the war, these prices would reach rates still more extravagant, and the whole system would fall under its own weight, rendering the redemption of the debt impossible, and destroying its value in the hands of the holder. If, on the contrary, a funded debt, with interest secured by adequate taxation, could be substituted for the outstanding currency, its entire amount would be made available to the holder, and the government would be in a condition, beyond the reach of any probable contingency, to prosecute the war to a successful issue.

This recommendation was followed by the passage of the act of February 17, 1864, above mentioned. One of its features is the tax levied on the circulation. Regarding the government when contracting a debt as the agent of the people, its debt is their debt. As the currency was held exclusively by ourselves, it was obvious that, if each person held treasury notes in exact proportion to the valuation of his whole estate, each would in fact owe himself the amount of the notes held by him; were it possible to distribute the currency among the people in this exact proportion, a tax levied on the currency alone, to an amount sufficient to reduce it to its proper limits, would afford the best of all remedies. Under such circumstances, the notes remaining in the hands of each holder after the payment of his tax would be worth quite as much as the whole sum previously held, for it would have an equal purchasing capacity.

After this law had been in operation for one year, it was manifest that it had the desired effect of withdrawing from circulation the large excess of treasury notes which had been issued. On July 1, 1864, the outstanding amount was estimated at two hundred thirty million dollars. The estimate of the amount funded under this act, about this time, was three hundred million dollars, while new notes were authorized to be issued to the extent of two-thirds of the sum received under its provisions. The chief difficulty apprehended in connection with our finances, up to the close of the war, resulted from the depreciation of our treasury notes, which was to be attributed to the increasing redundancy in amount and the diminishing confidence in their ultimate redemption.

The financial condition of the government, near its close, is very correctly represented in the report of the Treasury Department. The total receipts of the treasury for the two quarters ending September 30, 1864, amounted to $415,191,550, which sum, added to the balance, $308,282,722, that remained in the treasury on April 1, 1864, formed a total of $723,474,272. Of this total, not far from half—that is to say, $342,560,327—were applied to the extinction of the public debt; while the total expenditures were $272,378,505, leaving a balance in the treasury on October 1, 1864, of $108,435,440. The sources from which this revenue was derived were as follows:

Four per cent registered bonds, act of February 17, 1864	$ 13,363,500
Six per cent bonds, $500,000,000 loan, act of February 17, 1864	14,481,050
Four per cent call certificates, act of February 17, 1864	20,978,100
Tax on old issue of certificates redeemed	14,440,566
Repayments by disbursing officers	20,115,830
Treasury notes, act of February 17, 1864	277,576,950
War tax	42,294,314
Sequestrations	1,338,732
Customs	50,004
Export duty	4,320
Coin seized by the Secretary of War	1,653,200
Premium on loans	4,822,249
Soldiers' tax	908,622

The total amount of the public debt on October 1, 1864, on the books of the register of the treasury, was $1,147,970,208, of which $530,340,090 was funded debt, bearing interest, and $283,880,150 was treasury notes of the new issue, and the remainder consisted of the former issue of treasury notes which were converted into other forms of debt, and ceased to exist on December 31st. In consequence, however, of the absence of certain returns from distant officers, the true amount of the debt was less by $21,500,000 than appeared on the books of the register; so that the total public debt, on October 1st, might have been fairly considered to have been $1,126,381,095. Of this amount $541,-340,090 consisted of funded debt, and the balance unfunded debt, or treasury notes. The foreign debt is omitted in these statements. It amounted to £2,200,000, and was provided for by about two hundred and fifty thousand bales of cotton collected by the government.[1]

The aggregate appropriations called for by the different departments of the government for the six months ending on June 30, 1865, amounted to $438,416,504. It was estimated that the remains of former appropriations would, on January 1, 1865, amount to a balance of $467,416,504. No additional appropriations were therefore required for the ensuing six months.

A system of measures by which to obtain a revenue from direct taxes and duties was commenced at the first session of Congress under the provisional government. The officers who, at the time of the adoption of the provisional Constitution, held any officer connected with the collection of the customs, duties, and imposts in the several states of the Confederacy, or as assistant treasurers entrusted with the keeping of moneys arising therefrom, were continued in office with the same powers and subject to the same duties. The tariff laws of the United States were continued in force until they might be altered. The free list was enlarged so as to embrace many articles of necessity; additional ports and places of entry were established; restrictive laws were repealed, and foreign vessels were admitted to the coasting trade. A lighthouse bureau was organized; a lower rate of duties was imposed on a number of enumerated articles, and an export duty of one-eighth of one cent per pound was imposed on all cotton exported in the raw state. At the second session, in May, a complete tariff law was enacted, with a lower scale of duties than had previously existed. On August 19, 1861, a war tax of fifty cents on each hundred dollars of certain classes of property was levied for the special purpose of paying the principal and interest of the public debt, and of supporting the government. The different classes of property on which the tax was levied were as follows: real estate of all kinds; slaves; merchandise; bank stocks; railroad and other corporation stocks; money at interest, or invested by individuals in the

---

[1] These bales were the security for the foreign cotton bonds, and were seized by the United States government. Was it not liable to the bondholders?

purchase of bills, notes, and other securities for money, except the bonds of the Confederate States, and cash on hand, or on deposit; cattle, horses, and mules; gold watches, gold and silver plate, pianos, and pleasure carriages. There were some exemptions, such as the property of educational, charitable, and religious institutions, and of a head of a family having property worth less than five hundred dollars. An act was passed for the sequestration of the property of alien enemies, as a retaliatory measure, to offset the confiscation act of the United States.

On April 24, 1863, a new act was passed relative to internal or direct taxes. It was designed to reach, as far as practicable, every resource of the country except the capital invested in real estate and slaves, and, by means of an income tax and a tax in kind on the produce of the soil, as well by licenses on business occupations and professions, to command resources sufficient for the wants of the country. On February 17, 1864, an amendment to this last-mentioned act was passed. It levied additional taxes on all business of individuals, of copartnerships and corporations, also on trades, sales, liquor dealers, hotel keepers, distillers, and a tax in kind on agriculturists. On June 10, 1864, an act was passed which levied a tax equal to one-fifth of the amount of the existing tax upon all subjects of taxation for the year.

Within six months after the passage of the war tax of August 19, 1861, the popular aversion to internal taxation by the general government had so influenced the legislation of the several states that only in South Carolina, Mississippi, and Texas were the taxes actually collected from the people. The quotas of the remaining states had been raised by the issue of bonds and state treasury notes. The public debt of the country was thus actually increased instead of being diminished by the taxation imposed by Congress.

At the first and second sessions of Congress in 1862 no means were provided by taxation for maintaining the government. The legislation was confined to authorizing further sales of bonds and issues of treasury notes. An obstacle had arisen against successful taxation. About two-thirds of the entire taxable property of the Confederate States consisted in land and slaves. Under the provisional Constitution, which ceased to be in force on February 22, 1862, the power of Congress to levy taxes was not restricted by any other condition than that "all duties, imposts, and excises should be uniform throughout the States of the Confederacy." But in the permanent Constitution, which took effect on the same day (February 22d), it was specially provided that "representatives and direct taxes shall be apportioned among the several States according to their respective numbers, which shall be determined by adding to the whole number of free persons—including those bound to service for a term of years, and excluding Indians not taxed—three fifths of all slaves." According to the received construction of the Constitution of the United States, which had been acquiesced in for sixty years, taxes on lands and slaves were direct taxes. In repeating, without modification, in our Constitution this language of the United States Constitution, our convention necessarily seems to have intended to attach to it the meaning which had been sanctioned by long and uninterrupted acquiescence—thus deciding that taxes on lands and slaves were direct taxes. Our Constitution further ordered that a census should be made within three years after the first meeting of Congress, and that "no capitation or other direct tax shall be laid, unless in proportion to the census or enumeration hereinbefore directed to be taken."

So long as there seemed to be a probability of being able to carry out these provisions of the Constitution fully, and in conformity with the intentions of its authors, there was an obvious difficulty in framing any system of taxation. A law which should exempt from the burden two-thirds of the property of the country would be as unfair to the owners of the remaining third as it would be inadequate to meet the requirements of the public service. The urgency of the need, however, was such that, after great embarrassment, the law of April 24, 1863, above mentioned, was framed. Still, a very large proportion of these resources was unavailable for some time, and, the intervening exigencies permitting of no delay, a resort to further issues of treasury notes became unavoidable.

The foreign debt of the Confederate States at the close of the war was twenty-two hundred thousand pounds. The earliest proposals on which this debt was contracted were issued in London and Paris in March, 1863. The bonds bore interest at seven per cent per annum, in sterling, payable half-yearly. They were exchangeable for cotton on application, at the option of the holder, or redeemable at par in sterling, in twenty years, by half-yearly drawings, commencing March 1, 1864. The special security of these bonds was the engagement of the government to deliver cotton to the holders. Each bond, at the option of the holder, was convertible at its nominal amount into cotton at the rate of sixpence sterling for each pound of cotton—say four thousand pounds of cotton for each bond of a hundred pounds, or twenty-five hundred francs; this could be done at any time not later than six months after the ratification of a treaty of peace between the belligerents. Sixty days after the notice, the cotton was to be delivered, if in a state of peace, at the ports of Charleston, Savannah, Mobile, or New Orleans; if at war, at points in the interior of the country, within ten miles of a railroad, or a stream navigable to the ocean. The delivery was to be made free of all charges, except the export duty of one-eighth of one cent per pound. The quality of the cotton was to be the standard of New Orleans middling. An annual sinking fund of five per cent was provided for, whereby two and a half per cent of the bonds unredeemed by cotton should be drawn by lot half-yearly, so as finally to extinguish the loan in twenty years from the first drawing. The bonds were issued at ninety per cent, payable in installments. The loan soon stood in the London market at five per cent premium. The amount asked for was three million pounds. The amount of applications in London and Paris exceeded fifteen million pounds.

Great efforts had previously been made by agents of the United States government to reflect upon the credit of the Confederate States, by resuscitating an almost forgotten accusation of repudiation against the state of Mississippi, and especially by an emissary sent to Great Britain, than whom no one knew better how false were the attempts to implicate my name in that charge. The slanderous tongues of Northern hatred even went so far as to style me "the father of repudiation." How unjust all such assertions were, will be manifest by a simple statement of the case.[2]

We should not omit to refer once more to the most prolific source of sectional strife and alienation, which is believed to have been the question of the tariff, or duties upon imports. Its influence extended to and affected subjects with which it was not visibly connected, and finally assumed a form surely not contemplated in the original formation of the Union. In the Articles of Confederation, the first Constitution of the United States, the theory was that of direct taxation, and the manner was to impose upon the states an amount which each was to furnish to the common treasury to defray expenses for the common defense and general welfare.

During the period of our colonial existence, the policy of the British government had been to suppress the growth of manufacturing industry.

---

[2]The facts with regard to the Mississippi "Union Bank" bonds may be briefly stated as follows:

The constitution of Mississippi required that no law should ever be passed "to raise a loan of money on the credit of the State, or to pledge the faith of the State for the payment or redemption of any loan or debt," unless such law should be proposed and adopted by the legislature, then published for three months previous to the next regular election, and finally reënacted by the succeeding legislature. The object was to enable the people of the state to consider the question intelligently, and to indicate and exercise their will upon it by the election of representatives to the ensuing legislature, whose views upon the subject would be known, and with such instructions, express or implied, as they might think proper to give.

In 1837 a law was passed by the legislature for incorporating the "Union Bank of Mississippi," with a capital of fifteen million five hundred thousand dollars, "to be raised by means of a loan to be obtained by the directors of the institution." In order to secure this loan, the stockholders were required to give mortgages on productive and unencumbered property, to be in all cases of value greater, by a fixed ratio, than the amount of their stock. When the stock had been thus secured, as a further guarantee for the redemption of the loan, the governor was directed to issue bonds, in the name and behalf of the state, equal in amount to the stock secured by mortgage on private property. No bonds as thus directed were ever issued.

This act was duly promulgated to the people, and duly reënacted by the succeeding legislature on February 5, 1838, in strict accordance with the constitution.

Ten days afterwards, however, viz., on February 15th, the legislature passed an act supplemental to the act chartering the Union Bank, which materially changed or abolished the essential conditions for the pledge of the credit of the state. By this supplemental act the governor was instructed, as soon as the books of subscription should be opened, to "subscribe for, in behalf of the State, fifty thousand shares of the stock of the original capital of said bank, to be paid for out of the proceeds of the State bonds to be executed by the said bank, as already provided for in the said charter." This act was passed in the ordinary mode of legislation, and was not referred, published, nor reënacted, as prescribed by the constitution. As soon as the directory was organized and the books of subscription were opened, and before the mortgages required by the charter were executed, the governor, in behalf of the state, subscribed for fifty thousand shares of the stock, and issued the bonds of the state for five million dollars, payable to the order of the bank.

These bonds were sold to Nicholas Biddle, President of the United States Bank of Pennsylvania, and by him sent to Great Britain as collateral security for a loan previously made. None of the money received for them went into the treasury of the state of Mississippi, nor was any of it used for a public improvement. All the consideration ever received by the state was its stock in the Union Bank. The bank soon failed, and the stock became utterly worthless.

Before the bonds became due, the governor of the state had declared them to be null and void, among other causes, in consequence of the failure to sell them at par, as required by the "supplemental act," under which they were issued.

It is not necessary here to discuss the question of the validity or nullity of the bonds. The object is merely to state the principal facts.

While these events were occurring, and until a period several years subsequent to their consummation, I, who had just resigned my commission in the army, was a private citizen, had never held any civil office, and took no part in political affairs. Indeed, I have never at any time before, during, or since those events held any civil office under the state government, and neither had nor could have had any part in shaping the policy of the state. When brought out as a candidate for office, my nomination was opposed by that section of my party which advocated "repudiation," on account of my opinions in favor of the payment of the bonds.

As a private citizen, it may be stated that I held that the question of the validity of the bonds should be decided by the courts. The constitution of Mississippi authorized suit to be brought against the state in such cases in her own courts, and this I regarded as the proper course to be pursued by the bondholders, holding that the state would be bound by the judicial decision, if it should sustain the validity of the claim. This course, however, was not adopted until long afterward, when the question had become complicated with political issues, which rendered the effort to obtain a settlement entirely nugatory.

When I was a member of the Senate of the United States, my official influence was exerted to promote the objects of a citizen of Mississippi, who, with quasi-credentials from the United States Secretary of State, Buchanan, went to London to propose to the bondholders an arrangement by which the claim, or the greater portion of it, might be paid by private subscription, on consideration of the cancellation of the bonds. This effort failed, from a mistaken estimate on the part of some of the principal bondholders, to whom the proposition was made, of the extent to which state pride would induce our citizens to contribute, and to the belief in a power to coerce payment. The gentleman who bore the proposal, indignant of the offensive manner of its rejection, and conscious of the disinterestedness of his motives, abandoned the negotiation in disgust, and the opportunity was lost.

It was forcibly expressed by Lord North in the declaration that "not a hobnail should be made in the American colonies." The consequence was that in the War of the Revolution our armies and people suffered so much from the want of the most necessary supplies that General Washington, after we had achieved our independence, expressed the opinion that the government should, by bounties, encourage the manufacture of such materials as were necessary in time of war.

In the convention which framed the Constitution for a "more perfect union," one of the greatest difficulties in agreeing upon its terms was found in the different interests of the states, but among the compromises which were made, there prominently appears the purpose of a strict equality in the burdens to be borne, as well as the blessings to be enjoyed, by the people of the several states. For a long time after the formation of the "more perfect Union," but little capital was invested in manufacturing establishments; though in the early part of the present century the amount had considerably increased, the products were yet quite insufficient for the necessary supplies of our armies in the War of 1812. Government contracts, high prices, and to some extent, no doubt, patriotic impulses, led to the investment of capital in the articles required for the prosecution of the war. With the restoration of peace and the renewal of commerce, prices naturally declined, and it was represented that the investments made in manufacturing establishments were so unprofitable as to involve the ruin of those who had made them. The Congress of the United States, in 1816, from motives at least to be commended for their generosity, enacted a law to protect from the threatened ruin those of their countrymen who had employed their capital for purposes demanded by the general welfare and common defense. These good intentions, if it be conceded that the danger was real which it was designed to avert, were most unfortunate as the beginning of a policy the end of which was fraught with the greatest evils that have ever befallen the Union. By the Constitution of 1789 power was conferred upon Congress—

To lay and collect taxes, duties, imposts, and excises, to pay the debts and provide for the common defense and general welfare of the United States; but all duties, imposts, and excises shall be uniform throughout the United States.

In the exercise of this delegated trust, tariff laws were enacted, and had been in operation to the satisfaction of all parts of the Union, from the organization of the government down to 1816; throughout that period all of those laws were based upon the principle of duties for revenue. It was true, and of course it was known, that such duties would give incidental protection to any industry producing an article on which the duty was levied; while the money was collected for the purposes enumerated, and the rate kept down to the lowest revenue standard, the consumer had no cause to complain of the indirect benefit received by the manufacturer, and the history of the time shows that it produced no discontent. Not so with the tariff law of 1816: though sustained by men from all sections of the Union, and notably by so strict a constructionist as Calhoun, there were not wanting those who saw in it a departure from the limitation of the Constitution, and sternly opposed it as the usurpation of a power to legislate for the benefit of a class. The law derived much of its support from the assurance that it was only a temporary measure, and intended to shield those whose patriotism had exposed them to danger, thus presenting the not uncommon occurrence of a good case making a bad precedent. For the first time a tariff law had protection for its object, and for the first time it produced discontent. In the law there was nothing which necessarily gave to it or in its terms violated the obligation that duties should be uniform throughout the United States. The fact that it affected the sections differently was due to physical causes—that is, geographical differences. The streams of the Southern Atlantic states ran over wide plains into the sea; their last falls were remote from ocean navigation; their people, almost exclusively agricultural, resided principally on this plain, and as near to the seaboard as circumstances would permit. In the Northern Atlantic states the highlands approached more nearly to the sea, and the rivers made their last leap near to harbors of commerce. Water power being relied on before the steam engine had been made, and ships the medium of commerce before railroads and locomotives were introduced, it followed that the staples of the Southern plains were economically sent to the water power of the North to be manufactured. This remark, of course, applies to such articles as were not exported to foreign countries, and is intended to explain how the North became the seat of manufactures, and the South remained agricultural. From this it followed that legislation for the benefit of manufacturers became a Northern policy. It was not, as has been erroneously stated, because of the agricultural character of the Southern people, that they were opposed to the policy inaugurated by the tariff act of 1816. This is shown by the fact that anterior to that time they had been the friends of manufacturing industry, without reference to its location. As long as duties were imposed for revenue, so that the object was to supply the common treasury, it had been cheerfully borne, and the agriculture of one section and the manufacturing of another were properly regarded as handmaids, and not infrequently referred to as the means of strengthening and perpetuating the bonds by which the states were united. When duties were imposed, not for revenue, but as a bounty to a particular industry, it was regarded both as unjust and without warrant, expressed or implied, in the Constitution.

Then arose the controversy, quadrennially renewed and with increasing provocation, in 1820, in 1824, and in 1828—each stage intensifying the discontent, arising more from the injustice than the weight of the burden borne. It was not the twenty-shilling ship-money tax, but the violation of Magna Charta, which Hampden and his associates resisted. It was not the stamp duty nor the tea tax, but the principle involved in taxation without representation, against which our colonial fathers took up arms. So the tariff act in 1828, known at the time as "the bill of abominations," was resisted by Southern representatives because it was the invasion of private rights in violation of the compact by which the states were united. In the last stage of the proceeding, after the friends of the bill. had advocated it as a measure for protecting capital invested in manufactures, Drayton of South Carolina moved to amend the title so that it should read, "An act to increase the duties upon certain imports, for the purpose of increasing the profits of certain manufacturers," and stated his purpose for desiring to amend the title to be that, upon some case which would arise under the execution of the law, an appeal might be made to the Supreme Court of the United States to test its constitutionality. Those who had passed the bill refused to allow the opportunity to test the validity of a tax imposed for the protection of a particular industry. Though the debates showed clearly enough the purpose to be to impose duties for protection, the phraseology of the law presented it as enacted to raise revenue, and therefore the victims of the discrimination were deprived of an appeal to the tribunal instituted to hear and decide on the constitutionality of a law.

South Carolina, oppressed by onerous duties and stung by the injustice of a refusal to allow her the ordinary remedy against unconstitutional legislation, asserted the right, as a sovereign state, to nullify the law. This conflict between the authority of the United States and one of the states threatened for a time such disastrous consequences as to excite intense feeling in all who loved the Union as the fraternal federation of equal states. Before an actual collision of arms occurred, Congress wisely adopted the compromise act of 1833. By that the fact of protection remained, but the principle of duties for revenue was recognized by a sliding scale of reduction, and it was hoped the question had been placed upon a basis that promised a permanent peace. The party of protective duties, however, came into power about the close of the period when the compromise measure had reached the result it proposed, and the contest was renewed with little faith on the part of the then dominant party and with more than all of its former bitterness. The cause of the departure from a sound principle of a tariff for revenue, which had prevailed during the first quarter of a century, and the adoption in 1816 of the rule imposing duties for protection, was stated by McDuffie to be that politicians and capitalists had seized upon the subject and used it for their own purposes—the former for political advancement, the latter for their own pecuniary profit—and that the question had become one of partisan politics and sectional enrichment. Contemporaneously with this theory of protective duties arose the policy of making appropriations from the common treasury for local improvements. As the Southern representatives were mainly those who denied the constitutional power to make such expenditures, it naturally resulted that the mass of those appropriations were made for Northern works. Now that direct taxes had in practice been so wholly abandoned as to be almost an obsolete idea, and now that the treasury was supplied by the collection of duties upon imports, two golden streams flowed steadily to enrich the Northern and manufacturing region by the impoverishment of the Southern and agricultural section. In the train of wealth and demand for labor followed immigration and the more rapid increase of population in the Northern than in the Southern states. I do not deny the existence of other causes, such as the fertile region of the Northwest, the better harbors, the greater amount of shipping of the Northeastern states, and the prejudice of Europeans against contact with the negro race; the causes I have first stated were, I think, the chief, and those only which are referable to the action of the general government. It was not found that the possession of power mitigated the injustice of its use by the North, and discontent therefore was steadily accumulating, and, as stated in the beginning of this chapter, I think was due to class legislation in the form of protective duties and its consequences more than to any or all other causes combined. Turning from the consideration of this question in its sectional aspect, I now invite attention to its general effect upon the character of our institutions. If the common treasury of the states had, as under the Confederation, been supplied by direct taxation, who can doubt that a rigid economy would have been the rule of the government; that representatives would have returned to their tax-paying constituents to justify appropriations for which they had voted by showing that they were required for the general welfare, and were authorized by the Constitution under which they were acting? When the money was obtained by indirect taxation, so that but few could see the source from which it was derived, it readily followed that a constituency would ask, not why the representative had voted for the expenditure of money, but how much he had got for his own district, and perhaps he might have to explain why he did not get more. Is it doubtful that this would lead to extravagance, if not to corruption? Nothing could be more fatal to the independence of the people and the liberties of the states than dependence for support upon the public treasury, whether it be in the form of subsidies, of bounties, or restrictions on trade for the benefit of special interests. In the decline of the Roman Empire, the epoch in which the hopelessness of renovation was made manifest was that in which the people accepted corn from the public granaries: it preceded but a little the time when the post of emperor became a matter of purchase. How far would it differ from this if constituencies should choose their representatives, not for their integrity, not for their capacity, not for their past services, but because of their ability to get money from the public treasury for the benefit of their local interests; how far would it differ from a purchase of the office if a President were chosen because of the favor he would show to certain moneyed interests?

Now that fanaticism can no longer inflame the prejudices of the uninformed, it may be hoped that our statesmen will review the past, and give to our country a future in accordance with its early history, and promotive of true liberty.

CHAPTER XIV: *Military Laws and Measures — Agricultural Products Diminished—Manufactures Flourishing—The Call for Volunteers—The Term of Three Years—Improved Discipline—The Law Assailed—Important Constitutional Question Raised—Its Discussion at Length—Power of the Government Over Its Own Armies and the Militia—Object of Confederations—The War Powers Granted—Two Modes of Raising Armies in the Confederate States—Is the Law Necessary and Proper?—Congress is the Judge Under the Grant of Specific Power—What is Meant by Militia—Whole Military Strength Divided into Two Classes—Powers of Congress—Objections Answered—Good Effects of the Law—The Limitations Enlarged—Results of the Operations of These Laws—Act for the Employment of Slaves — Message to Congress — "Died of a Theory"—Act to Use Slaves as Soldiers Passed—Not Time to Put it in Operation.*

THE agricultural products were diminished every year during the war. Its demands diminished the number of cultivators, and their labors were more extensively devoted to grain crops. The amount of the cotton crop was greatly reduced, and numbers of bales were destroyed when in danger of falling into the hands of the enemy.

The manufacturing industry became more extensive than ever before, and in many branches more highly developed. The results in the ordnance department of the government, stated elsewhere in these pages, serve as an illustration of the achievements in many branches of industry.

During the first year of the war the authority granted to the President to call for volunteers in the army for a short period was sufficient to secure all the military force which we could fit out and use advantageously. As it became evident that the contest would be long and severe, better measures of preparation were enacted. I was authorized to call out and place in the military service for three years, unless the war should sooner end, all white men residents of the Confederate States between the ages of eighteen and thirty-five years, and to continue those already in the field until three years from the date of their enlistment. But those under eighteen years and over thirty-five were required to remain ninety days. The existing organization of companies, regiments, etc. was preserved, but the former were filled up to the number of one hundred twenty-five men. This was the first step toward placing the army in a permanent and efficient condition. The term of service being lengthened, the changes by discharges and by receiving recruits were diminished, so that, while additions were made to the forces already in the field, the discipline was greatly improved. At the same time, on March 13, 1862, General Robert E. Lee was "charged with the conduct of the military operations of the armies of the Confederacy" under my direction. Nevertheless, the law upon which our success so greatly depended was assailed with unexpected criticism in various quarters. A constitutional question of high importance was raised, which tended to involve the harmony of coöperation, so essential in this crisis, between the general and the state governments. It was advanced principally by the governor of Georgia, Hon. Joseph E. Brown, and the following extracts are taken from my reply to him, dated

EXECUTIVE DEPARTMENT, RICHMOND, May 29, 1862.

I propose, from my high respect for yourself and for other eminent citizens who entertain opinions similar to yours, to set forth somewhat at length my own views on the power of the Confederate Government over its own armies and the militia, and will endeavor not to leave without answer any of the positions maintained in your letters.

The main, if not the only, purpose for which independent states form unions, or confederations, is to combine the power of the several members in such manner as to form one united force in all relations with foreign powers, whether in peace or in war. Each state, amply competent to administer and control its own domestic government, yet too feeble successfully to resist powerful nations, seeks safety by uniting with other states in like condition, and by delegating to some common agent the use of the combined strength of all, in order to secure advantageous commercial relations in peace, and to carry on hostilities with effect in war.

Now, the powers delegated by the several States to the Confederate Government, which is their common agent, are enumerated in the eighth section of the Constitution; each power being distinct, specific, and enumerated in paragraphs separately numbered. The only exception is the eighteenth paragraph, which by its own terms is made dependent on those previously enumerated, as follows: "18. To make all laws which shall be necessary and proper for carrying into execution the foregoing powers," etc.

Now the *war-powers* granted to the Congress are conferred in the following paragraphs: No. 1 "gives authority to raise revenue necessary to pay the debts, provide for *the common defense,* and carry on the Government," etc. No. 11, "To declare war, grant letters of marque and reprisal, and make rules concerning captures on land and water." No. 12, "To raise and support armies, but no appropriations of money to that use shall be for a longer term than two years."

No. 13, "To provide and maintain a navy." No. 14, "To make rules for the government and regulation of *the land and naval forces."*

It is impossible to imagine a more broad, ample, and unqualified delegation of the whole war power of each State than is here contained, with the solitary limitations of the appropriations to two years. The States not only gave power to raise money for the common defense, to declare war, to raise and support armies (in the plural), to provide and maintain a navy, to govern and regulate both land and naval forces, but they went further, and covenanted, by the third paragraph of the tenth section, not "to engage in war, unless actually invaded, or in such imminent danger as will not admit of delay."

I know of but two modes of raising armies within the Confederate States, *viz.,* voluntary enlistment and draft, or conscription. I perceive, in the delegation of power, to raise armies, no restriction as to the mode of procuring troops. I see nothing which confines Congress to one class of men, nor any greater power to receive volunteers than conscripts into its service. I see no limitation by which enlistments are to be received of individuals only, but not of companies, or battalions, or squadrons, or regiments. I find no limitation of time or service, but only of duration of appropriation. I discover nothing to confine Congress to waging war within the limits of the Confederacy, nor to prohibit offensive war. In a word, when Congress desires to raise an army, and passes a law for that purpose, the solitary question is under the eighteenth paragraph, *viz.,* "Is the law one that is necessary and proper to execute the power to raise armies?"

On this point you say: "But did the necessity exist in this case? The conscription act can not aid the Government in increasing its supply of *arms* or *provisions,* but can only enable it to call a larger number of men into the field. The difficulty has never been to get *men.* The States have already furnished the Government more than it can arm," etc.

I would have very little difficulty in establishing to your entire satisfaction that the passage of the law was not only necessary, but that it was absolutely indispensable; that numerous regiments of twelve months' men were on the eve of being disbanded, whose places could not be supplied by raw levies in the face of superior numbers of the foe, without entailing the most disastrous results; that the position of our armies was so critical as to fill the bosom of every patriot with the liveliest apprehension; and that the provisions of this law were effective in warding off a pressing danger. But I prefer to answer your objection on other and broader grounds.

I hold that, when a specific power is granted by the Constitution, like that now in question, "to raise armies," Congress is the judge whether the law passed for the purpose of executing that power is "necessary and proper." It is not enough to say that armies might be raised in other ways, and that, therefore, this particular way is not "necessary." The same argument might be used against *every* mode of raising armies. To each successive mode suggested, the objection would be that other modes were practicable, and that, therefore, the particular mode used was not "necessary." The true and only test is to inquire whether the law is intended and calculated to carry out the object; whether it devises and creates an instrumentality for executing the specific power granted; and, if the answer be in the affirmative, the law is constitutional. None can doubt that the conscription law is calculated and intended to "raise armies"; it is, therefore, "necessary and proper" for the execution of that power, and is constitutional, unless it comes in conflict with some other provision of our Confederate compact.

You express the opinion that this conflict exists, and support your argument by the citation of those clauses which refer to the militia. There are certain provisions not cited by you, which are not without influence on my judgment, and to which I call your attention. They will aid in defining what is meant by "militia," and in determining the respective powers of the States and the Confederacy over them.

The several States agree "not to keep troops or ships of war in time of peace."[1] They further stipulate that, "a well-regulated militia being necessary for the security of a free State, the right of the people to keep and bear arms shall not be infringed."[2]

"That no person shall be held to answer for a capital or otherwise infamous crime, unless on a presentment or indictment of a grand jury, except in cases arising in the *land* or *naval forces*, or in *the militia* when in actual service in times of war or public danger."[3]

What, then, are militia? They can only be created by law. The arms-bearing inhabitants of a State are liable to become its militia, if the law so order; but, in the absence of a law to that effect, the men of a State capable of bearing arms are no more militia than they are seamen.

The Constitution also tells us that militia are not *troops*, nor are they any part of the *land* or *naval forces*; for militia exist in time of peace, and the Constitution forbids the States to keep troops in time of peace, and they are expressly distinguished and placed in a separate category from land or naval forces in the sixteenth paragraph above quoted; and the words *land* and *naval forces* are shown by paragraphs 12, 13, and 14, to mean the Army and Navy of the Confederate States.

Now, if militia are not the citizens taken singly, but a body created by law; if they are not troops; if they are no part of the Army and Navy of the Confederacy, we are led directly to the definition, quoted by the Attorney-General, that militia are "a body of soldiers in a State enrolled for discipline." In other words, the term "militia" is a collective term meaning a body of men organized, and can not be applied to the separate individuals who compose the organization.

The Constitution divides the whole military strength of the States into only two classes of organized bodies: one, the armies of the Confederacy; the other, the militia of the States.

In the delegation of power to the Confederacy, after exhausting the subject of declaring war, raising and supporting armies, and providing a navy, in relation to all which the grant of authority to Congress is *exclusive*, the Constitution proceeds to deal with the other organized body, the militia; and, instead of delegating power to Congress alone, or reserving it to the States alone, the power is divided as follows, *viz.:* Congress is to have power "to provide for calling forth the

[1] Article I, Section 10, paragraph 3.
[2] *Ibid.*, Section 9, Part XIII.
[3] *Ibid.*, Section 9, paragraph 16.

militia to execute the laws of the *Confederate* States, suppress insurrections, and *repel invasions.*"[4]

"To provide for organizing, arming, and disciplining the militia, and for governing such part of them as may be employed in the service of the Confederate States; *reserving* to *the States respectively the appointment of the officers,* and the *authority of training the militia,* according to the discipline prescribed by Congress."[5]

Congress, then, has the power to provide for *organizing* the arms-bearing people of the State into militia. Each *State* has the power to officer and *train* them when organized.

Congress may call forth the militia to execute Confederate laws; the *State* has not surrendered the power to call them forth to execute State laws.

Congress may call them forth to repel invasion; so may the State, for the power is impliedly reserved of governing all the militia, except the part in actual service of the Confederacy.

I confess myself at a loss to perceive in what manner these careful and well-defined provisions of the Constitution, regulating the organization and government of the militia, can be understood as applying in the remotest degree to the armies of the Confederacy, nor can I conceive how the grant of *exclusive* power to declare and carry on war by armies raised and supported by the Confederacy is to be restricted or diminished by the clauses which grant a *divided* power over the militia. On the contrary, the delegation of authority over the militia, so far as granted, appears to me to be plainly an *additional* enumerated power intended to strengthen the hands of the Confederate Government in the discharge of its paramount duty, the common defense of the States.

You state, after quoting the twelfth, fifteenth, and sixteenth grants of power to Congress, that "these grants of power all relate to the same subject-matter, and are all contained in the same section of the Constitution, and, by a well-known rule of construction, must be taken as a whole and construed together."

This argument appears to me unsound. *All* the powers of Congress are enumerated in one section, and the three paragraphs quoted can no more control each other by reason of their location in the same section than they can control any of the other paragraphs preceding, intervening, or succeeding. So far as the subject-matter is concerned, I have already endeavored to show that the armies mentioned in the twelfth paragraph are a subject-matter as distinct from the militia mentioned in the fifteenth and sixteenth as they are from the navy mentioned in the thirteenth. Nothing can so mislead as to construe together, and as a whole, the carefully separated clauses which define the different powers ·to be exercised over distinct subjects by the Congress.

But you add that, "by the grant of power to Congress to raise and support armies without qualification, the framers of the Constitution intended the regular armies of the Confederacy, and not armies composed of the whole militia of all the States."

I must confess myself somewhat at a loss to understand this position. If I am right that the militia is a body of enrolled State soldiers, it is not possible in

[4] Section 8, paragraph 15.
[5] *Ibid.*, paragraph 16.

the nature of things that armies raised by the Confederacy can "be composed of the whole militia of all the States." The militia may be called forth in whole or in part into the Confederate service, but do not thereby become part of the "armies raised" by Congress. They remain militia, and go home when the emergency which provoked their call has ceased. Armies raised by Congress are of course raised out of the *same population* as the militia organized by the States, and to deny to Congress the power to draft a citizen into the army, or to receive his voluntary offer of services, because he is a member of the State militia, is to deny the power to raise an army at all; for, practically, all men fit for service in the army may be embraced in the militia organization of the several States. You seem, however, to suggest, rather than directly to assert, that the conscript law may be unconstitutional, because it comprehends all arms-bearing men between eighteen and thirty-five years; at least, this is an inference which I draw from your expression, "armies composed of the *whole* militia of *all* the States." But it is obvious that, if Congress have power to draft into the armies raised by it any citizens at all (without regard to the fact whether they are, or not, members of militia organizations), the power must be coextensive with the exigencies of the occasion, or it becomes illusory; and the extent of the exigency must be determined by Congress; for the Constitution has left the power without any other check or restriction than the Executive veto. Under ordinary circumstances, the power thus delegated to Congress is scarcely felt by the States. At the present moment, when our very existence is threatened by armies vastly superior in numbers to ours, the necessity for defense has induced a call, not for "the whole militia of all the States," not for any militia, but for men to compose *armies* for the Confederate States.

Surely there is no mystery in this subject. During our whole past history, as well as during our recent one year's experience as a new Confederacy, the militia "have been called forth to repel invasion" in numerous instances, and they never came otherwise than as bodies organized by the States with their company, field, and *general officers;* and, when the emergency had passed, they went home again. I can not perceive how any one can interpret the conscription law as taking away from the States the power to appoint officers to their militia. You observe on this point in your letter that, unless your construction is adopted, "the very object of the States in reserving the power of appointing the officers is defeated, and that portion of the Constitution is not only a nullity, but the whole military power of the States, and the entire control of the militia, with the appointment of the officers, is vested in the Confederate government, whenever it chooses to call its own action 'raising an army,' and not 'calling forth the militia.' "

I can only say, in reply to this, that the power of Congress depends on the real nature of the act it proposes to perform, not on the name given to it; and I have endeavored to show that its action is really that of "raising an army," and bears no semblance to "calling forth the militia." I think I may safely venture the assertion that there is not one man out of a thousand of those who will do service under the conscription act that will describe himself while in the Confederate service as being a militiaman; and, if I am right in this assumption, the popular understanding concurs entirely with my own deductions from the Constitution as to the meaning of the word "militia."

My answer has grown to such a length, that I must confine myself to one more quotation from your letter. You proceed: "Congress shall have power to *raise armies*. How shall it be done? The answer is clear. In conformity to the provisions of the Constitution, which expressly provides that, when the militia of the States are called forth to *repel invasion,* and employed in the service of the Confederate States, which is now the case, the State shall appoint the officers."

I beg you to observe that the answer which you say is clear is not an answer to the question put. The question is, How are armies to be raised? The answer given is, that, when militia are called upon to repel invasion, the State shall appoint the officers.

There seems to me to be a conclusive test on this whole subject. By our Constitution, Congress may declare war, *offensive* as well as *defensive*. It may acquire territory. Now, suppose that, for good cause and to right unprovoked injuries, Congress should declare war against Mexico and invade Sonora. The militia could not be called forth in such a case, the right to call it being limited "to repel invasions." Is it not plain that the law now under discussion, if passed under such circumstances, could by no possibility be aught else than a law to "raise an army"? Can one and the same law be construed into a "calling forth the militia," if the war be defensive, and a "raising of armies," if the war be offensive?

At some future day, after our independence shall have been established, it is no improbable supposition that our present enemy may be tempted to abuse his naval power by depredations on our commerce, and that we may be compelled to assert our rights by offensive war. How is it to be carried on? Of what is the army to be composed? If this Government can not call on its arms-bearing population otherwise than as militia, and if the militia can only be called forth to repel invasion, we should be utterly helpless to vindicate our honor or protect our rights. War has been well styled "the terrible litigation of nations." Have we so formed our Government that in this litigation we must never be plaintiffs? Surely this can not have been the intention of the framers of our compact.

In no respect in which I can view this law can I find just reason to distrust the propriety of my action in approving and signing it; and the question presented involves consequences, both immediate and remote, too momentous to permit me to leave your objections unanswered.

JEFFERSON DAVIS.

The operation of this law was suspended in the states of Kentucky, Missouri, and Maryland, because of their occupation by the armies of the federal government. The opposition to it, where its execution was continued, soon became limited, and before June 1st its good effects were seen in the increased strength and efficiency of our armies. At the same time I was authorized to commission officers to form bands of "Partisan Rangers," either of infantry or cavalry, which were subsequently confined to cavalry alone. On September 27, 1862, all white men between the ages of thirty-five and forty-five were placed in the military service for three years. All persons subject to enrollment might be enrolled wherever found, and were made subject to the provisions of the law. Authority was also given for the reception of volunteers from the states in which the law was suspended. On February 11, 1864, it was enacted by Congress that all white men between the ages of seventeen and fifty should be in the military service for the war; also, that all then in the service between the ages of eighteen and forty-five should be retained during the war. An enrollment was also ordered of all persons between the ages of seventeen and eighteen and between forty-five and fifty years, who should constitute a reserve for state defense and detail duty. On February 17th all male free negroes between the ages of eighteen and fifty years were made liable to perform duties with the army, or in connection with the military defenses of the country in the way of work upon the fortifications, or in government works for the production or preparation of materials of war, or in military hospitals. The Secretary of War was also authorized to employ for the same duties any number of negro slaves not exceeding twenty thousand.

In the operation of the military laws we found the exemption from military duty accorded by the law to all persons engaged in certain specified pursuits or professions to be unwise. Indeed, it seems to be indefensible in theory. The defense of home, family, and country is universally recognized as the paramount political duty of every member of society; in a form of government where each citizen enjoys an equality of rights and privileges, nothing can be more invidious than an unequal distribution of duties or obligations. No pursuit nor position should relieve anyone who is able to do active duty from enrollment in the army, unless his functions or services are more useful to the defense of his country in another sphere. But the exemption from service of entire classes should be wholly abandoned.

The act of February 17, 1864 (above mentioned), which authorized the employment of slaves, produced less results than had been anticipated. It brought forward, however, the question of the employment of the negroes as soldiers in the army, which was warmly advocated by some and as ardently opposed by others. My own views upon it were expressed freely and frequently in intercourse with members of Congress, and emphatically in my message of November 7, 1864, when, urging upon Congress the consideration of the propriety of a radical modification of the theory of the law, I said:

Viewed merely as property, and therefore as the subject of impressment, the service or labor of the slave has been frequently claimed for short periods in the construction of defensive works. The slave, however, bears another relation to the state—that of a person. The law of last February contemplates only the relation of the slave to the master, and limits the impressment to a certain term of service.

But, for the purposes enumerated in the act, instruction in the manner of camping, marching, and packing trains is needful, so that even in this limited employment length of service adds greatly to the value of the negro's labor. Hazard is also encountered in all the positions to which negroes can be assigned for service with the army, and the duties required of them demand loyalty and zeal.

In this aspect the relation of person predominates so far as to render it doubtful whether the private right of property can consistently and beneficially be continued, and it would seem proper to acquire for the public service the entire property in the labor of the slave, and to pay therefor due compensation, rather than to impress his labor for short terms; and this the more especially as the effect of the present law would vest this entire property in all cases where the slave might be recaptured after compensation for his loss had been paid to the private owner. Whenever the entire property in the service of a slave is thus acquired by the Government, the question is presented by what tenure he should be held. Should he be retained in servitude, or should his emancipation be held out to him as a reward for faithful service, or should it be granted at once on the promise of such service; and if emancipated what action should be taken to secure for the freed man the permission of the State from which he was drawn to reside within its limits after the close of his public service? The permission would doubtless be more readily accorded as a reward for past faithful service, and a double motive for zealous discharge of duty would thus be offered to those employed by the Government—their freedom and the gratification of the local attachment which is so marked a characteristic of the negro and forms so powerful an incentive to his action. The policy of engaging to liberate the negro on his discharge after service faithfully rendered seems to me preferable to that of granting immediate manumission, or that of retaining him in servitude. If this policy should commend itself to the judgment of Congress, it is suggested that, in addition to the duties heretofore performed by the slave, he might be advantageously employed as a pioneer and engineer laborer, and, in that event, that the number should be augmented to forty thousand.

Beyond this limit and these employments it does not seem to me desirable under existing circumstances to go.

A broad, moral distinction exists between the use of slaves as soldiers in defense of their homes and the incitement of the same persons to insurrection against their masters. The one is justifiable, if necessary, the other is iniquitous and unworthy of civilized people; and such is the judgment of all writers on public law, as well as that expressed and insisted on by our enemies in all wars prior to that now waged against us. By none have the practices of which they are now guilty been denounced with greater severity than by themselves in the two wars with Great Britain, in the last and in the present century, and in the Declaration of Independence in 1776, when an enumeration was made of the wrongs which justified the revolt from Great Britain. The climax of atrocity was deemed to be reached only when the English monarch was denounced as having "excited domestic insurrection among us."

The subject is to be viewed by us, therefore, solely in the light of policy and our social economy. When so regarded, I must dissent from those who advise a general levy and arming of the slaves for the duty of soldiers. Until our white population shall prove insufficient for the armies we require and can afford to keep in the field, to employ as a soldier the negro, who has merely been trained to labor, and, as a laborer, the white man accustomed from his youth to the use of arms, would scarcely be deemed wise or advantageous by any; and this is the question now before us. But should the alternative ever be presented of subjugation, or of the employment of the slave as a soldier, there seems no reason to doubt what should then be our decision. Whether our view embraces what would, in so extreme a case, be the sum of misery entailed by the dominion of the enemy, or be restricted solely to the effect upon the welfare and happiness of the negro population themselves, the result would be the same. The appalling demoralization, suffering, disease, and death, which have been caused by partially substituting the invaders' system of police for the kind relation previously subsisting between the master and slave, have been a sufficient demonstration that external interference with our institution of domestic slavery is productive of evil only. If the subject involved no other consideration than the mere right of property, the sacrifices heretofore made by our people have been such as to permit no doubt of their readiness to surrender every possession in order to secure independence. But the social and political question which is exclusively under the control of the several States has a far wider and more enduring importance than that of pecuniary interest. In its manifold phases it embraces the stability of our republican institutions, resting on the actual political equality of all its citizens, and includes the fulfillment of the task which has been so happily begun—that of Christianizing and improving the condition of the Africans who have by the will of Providence been placed in our charge. Comparing the results of our own experience with those of the experiments of others who have borne similar relations to the African race, the people of the several States of the Confederacy have abundant reason to be satisfied with the past, and to use the greatest circumspection in determining their course. These considerations, however, are rather applicable to the improbable contingency of our need of resorting to this element of assistance than to our present condition. If the recommendation above, made for the training of forty thousand negroes for the service indicated, shall meet your approval, it is certain that even this limited number, by their preparatory training in intermediate duties, would form a more valuable reserve force in case of urgency than threefold their number suddenly called from field-labor, while a fresh levy could to a certain extent supply their places in the special service for which they are now employed.

Subsequent events advanced my views from a prospective to a present need for the enrollment of negroes to take their place in the ranks. Strenuously I argued the question with members of Congress who called to confer with me. To a member of the Senate (the house in which we most needed a vote) I stated, as I had done to many others, the fact of having led negroes against a lawless body of armed white men, and the assurance which the experiment gave me that they might, under proper conditions, be relied on in battle, and finally used to him the expression which I believe I can repeat exactly: "If the Confederacy falls, there should be written on its tombstone, 'Died of a theory.' " General Lee was brought before a committee to state his opinion as to the probable efficiency of negroes as soldiers, and disappointed the probable expectation by his unqualified advocacy of the proposed measure.

After much discussion in Congress, a bill authorizing the President to ask for and accept from their owners such a number of able-bodied negro men as he might deem expedient subsequently passed the House, but was lost in the Senate by one vote. The Senators of Virginia opposed the measure so strongly that only legislative instruction could secure their support of it. Their legislature did so instruct them, and they voted for it. Finally the bill passed, with an amendment providing that not more than twenty-five per cent of the male slaves between the ages of eighteen and forty-five should be called out. But the passage of the act had been so long delayed that the opportunity was lost. There did not remain time enough to obtain any result from its provisions.

APPENDIXES

APPENDIX B

THE OREGON QUESTION

EXTRACTS from speech of Jefferson Davis of Mississippi in the House of Representatives, February 6, 1846, on the resolution to terminate the joint occupation of the Oregon Territory.

Mr. Chairman: In negotiations between governments, in attempts to modify existing policies, the circumstances of the time most frequently decide between success and failure.

How far the introduction of this question may affect our foreign intercourse, the future only can determine; but I invite attention to the present posture of affairs. Amicable relations, after a serious interruption, have been but recently restored between the United States and Mexico. The most delicate and difficult of questions, the adjustment of a boundary between us, remains unsettled; and many eyes are fixed upon our minister at Mexico, with the hope that he may negotiate a treaty which will remove all causes of dispute, and give to us territorial limits, the ultimate advantages of which it would be difficult to over-estimate.

If, sir, hereafter we shall find that, by this excited discussion, portentous of a war with England, unreasonable demands upon the part of Mexico should be encouraged, the acquisition of California be defeated, that key to Asiatic commerce be passed from our hands for ever—what will we have gained to compensate so great a loss? We know the influence which Great Britain exercises over Mexico; we should not expect her to be passive, nor doubt that the prospect of a war between England and the United States would serve to revive the former hopes and to renew the recent enmity of Mexico.

Sir, I have another hope, for the fulfillment of which the signs of the times seem most propitious. An unusually long exemption from a general war has permitted the bonds of commerce to extend themselves around the civilized world, and nations from remote quarters of the globe have been drawn into that close and mutual dependence which foretold unshackled trade and a lasting peace. In the East, there appeared a rainbow which promised that the waters of national jealousy and proscription were about to recede from the earth for ever, and the spirit of free trade to move over the face thereof.

In perspective, we saw the ports of California united to the ports and forests of Oregon, and our countrymen commanding the trade of the Pacific. The day seemed at hand when the overcharged granaries of the West should be emptied to the starving millions of Europe and Asia; when the canvas-winged doves of our commerce should freely fly forth from the ark, and return across every sea with the olive of every land. Shall objects like these be endangered by the impatience of petty ambition, the promptings of sectional interest, or the goadings of fanatic hate? Shall the good of the whole be surrendered to the voracious demands of the few? Shall class interests control the great policy of our country, and the voice of reason be drowned in the clamor of causeless excitement? If so, not otherwise, we may agree with him who would reconcile us to the evils of war by the promise of "emancipation from the manufacturers of Manchester and Birmingham"; or leave unanswered the heresy boldly announced, though by history condemned, that war is the purifier, blood is the aliment, of free institutions. Sir it is true that republics have often been cradled in war, but more often they have met with a grave in that cradle. Peace is the interest, the policy, the nature of a popular government. War may bring benefits to a few, but privation and loss are the lot of the many. An appeal to arms should be the last resort, and only by national rights or national honor can it be justified.

To those who have treated this as a case involving the national honor, I reply that, whenever that question shall justly be raised, I trust an American Congress will not delay for weeks to discuss the chances, or estimate the sacrifices, which its maintenance may cost. But, sir, instead of rights invaded or honor violated, the question before us is, the expediency of terminating an ancient treaty, which, if it be unwise, it can not be dishonorable, to continue. Yet, throughout this long discussion, the recesses and vaulted dome of this hall have reëchoed to inflammatory appeals and violent declamations on the sanctity of national honor; and then, as if to justify them, followed reflections most discreditable to the conduct of our Government. The charge made elsewhere has been repeated here, that we have trodden upon Mexico, but cowered under England.

Sir, it has been my pride to believe that our history was unstained by an act of injustice or of perfidy; that we stood recorded before the world as a people haughty to the strong, generous to the weak; and nowhere has this character been more exemplified than in our intercourse with Mexico. We have been referred to the treaty of peace that closed our last war with Great Britain, and told that our injuries were unredressed, because the question of impressment was not decided. There are other decisions than those made by commissioners, and sometimes they outlast the letter of a treaty. On sea and land we settled the question of impressment before negotiations were commenced at Ghent. Further, it should be remembered that there was involved within that question a cardinal principle of each Government. The power of expatriation, and its sequence, naturalization, were denied by Great Britain; and hence a right asserted to impress native-born Britons, though naturalized as citizens of the United States. This violated a principle which lies at the foundation of our institutions, and could never be permitted; but, not being propagandists, we could afford to leave the political opinion unnoticed, after having taught a lesson which would probably prevent any future attempt to exercise it to our injury. Let the wisdom of that policy be judged by subsequent events. . . .

Davis then proceeded to state and argue at length the historical questions involved, making copious citations from original authorities. He continued:

Waiving the consideration of any sinister motive or sectional hate which may have brought allies to the support of the resolution now before us, I will treat it as simply aiming at the object which in common we desire—to secure the whole of Oregon to the United States.

Thus considered, the dissolution of the Oregon convention becomes a mere question of time. As a friend to the extension of our Union, and therefore prone to insist upon its territorial claims, I have thought this movement premature; that we should have put ourselves in the strongest attitude for the enforcement of our claims before we fixed a day on which negotiations should be terminated. That nation negotiates to most advantage which is best prepared for war. Gentlemen have treated the idea of preparation for war as synonymous with the raising of an army. It is not so; indeed, that is the last measure, and should only be resorted to when war has become inevitable; and then a very short time will always be, I trust, sufficient. But, sir, there are preparations which require years, and can only be made in a state of peace. Such are the fortifications of the salient points and main entrances of our coast. For twenty-odd years Southern men have urged the occupation of the Tortugas. Are those who have so long opposed appropriations for that purpose ready to grant them now in such profusion that the labor of three years may be done in one? No, sir; the occasion, by increasing the demand for money elsewhere, must increase the opposition. That rock, which Nature placed like a sentinel to guard the entrance into the Mediterranean of our continent, and which should be Argus-eyed to watch it, will stand without an embrasure to look through.

How is the case in Oregon? Our settlements there must be protected, and under present circumstances an army of operations in that country must draw its food from this; but we have not a sufficient navy to keep open a line of communication by sea around Cape Horn; and the rugged route and the great distance forbid the idea of supplying it by transportation across the mountains. Now, let us see what time and the measures more pointedly recommended by the President would effect. Our jurisdiction extended into Oregon, the route guarded by stockades and troops, a new impulse would be given to immigration: and in two or three years the settlement on the Willamette might grow into a colony, whose flocks and herds and granaries would sustain an army, whenever one should be required.

By agencies among the Indian tribes, that effective ally of Great Britain, which formerly she has not scrupled to employ, would be rendered friendly to our people. In the mean time, roads could be constructed for the transportation of munitions of war. Then we should be prepared to assert, and effectively maintain, our claims to their ultimate limits.

I could not depreciate my countrymen; I would not vaunt the prowess of an enemy; but, sir, I tell those gentlemen who, in this debate, have found it so easy to drive British troops out of Oregon, that, between England and the United States, if hostilities occur in that remote territory, the party must succeed which has bread within the country. . . .

Mr. Chairman, unfortunately, the opinion has gone forth that no politician dares to be the advocate of peace when the question of war is mooted. That will be an evil hour—the sand of our republic will be nearly run—when it shall be in the power of any demagogue, or fanatic, to raise a war-clamor, and control the legislation of the country. The evils of war must fall upon the people, and with them the war-feeling should originate. We, their representatives, are but a mirror to reflect the light, and never should become a torch to fire the pile. But, sir, though gentlemen go, torch in hand, among combustible materials, they still declare there is no danger of a fire. War-speeches and measures threatening war are mingled with profuse assurances of peace. Sir, we can not expect, we should not require, our adversary to submit to more than we would bear; and I ask, after the notice has been given and the twelve months have expired, who would allow

Great Britain to exercise exclusive jurisdiction over Oregon? If we would resist such act by force of arms, before ourselves performing it we should prepare for war.

Some advocates of this immediate notice have urged their policy by reference to a resolution of the Democratic Baltimore Convention, and contended that the question was thereby closed to members of the Democratic party. That resolution does not recommend immediate notice, but recommends "the reannexation of Texas" and the "reoccupation of Oregon" at "the earliest practicable period." The claim is strongly made to the "whole of Oregon"; and the resolution seems directed more pointedly to space than time. Texas and Oregon were united in the resolution; and, had there been a third question involving our territorial extension, I doubt not it would have been united with the other two. The addition of territory to our Union is part of the Democratic faith, and properly was placed in the declaration of our policy at that time. To determine whether that practicable period has arrived is now the question; and those who cordially agree upon the principle of territorial enlargement have differed, and may continue still to differ, on that question. Sir, though it is demonstrable that haste may diminish but can not increase our chances to secure the whole of Oregon, yet, because Southern men have urged the wisdom of delay, we have had injurious comparisons instituted between our conduct on Texas annexation and Oregon occupation. Is there such equality between the cases that the same policy must apply to each? Texas was peopled, the time was present when it must be acquired, or the influences active to defeat our annexation purpose would probably succeed, and the country be lost to us for ever. Oregon is, with a small exception, still a wilderness; our claim to ultimate sovereignty can not be weakened during the continuance of the Oregon convention. That ill-starred partnership has robbed us of the advantages which an early occupation would have given to our people in the fur-trade of the country, and we are now rapidly advancing to a position from which we can command the entire Territory. In Texas annexation we were prompted by other and higher considerations than mere interest. Texas had been a member of our family: in her infancy had been driven from the paternal roof, surrendered to the government of harsh, inquisitorial Spain; but, true to her lineage, preserved the faith of opposition to monarchial oppression. She now returned, and asked to be admitted to the hearth of the homestead. She pointed to the band of noble sons who stood around her and said: "Here is the remnant of my family; the rest I gave a sacrifice at the altar of our fathers' God—the God of Liberty." One, two, three, of the elder sisters strove hard to close the door upon her; but the generous sympathy, the justice of the family, threw it wide open, and welcomed her return. Such was the case of Texas; is there a parallel in Oregon?

But who are those that arraign the South, imputing to us motives of sectional aggrandizement? Generally, the same who resisted Texas annexation, and now most eagerly press on the immediate occupation of the whole of Oregon. The source is worthy the suspicion. These were the men whose constitutional scruples resisted the admission of a country gratuitously offered to us, but who now look forward to gaining Canada by conquest. These, the same who claim a weight to balance Texas, while they attack others as governed by sectional considerations.

Sir, this doctrine of a political balance between different sections of our Union is not of Southern growth. We advocated the annexation of Texas as a "great national measure"; we saw in it the extension of the principles intrusted to our care; and, if in the progress of the question it assumed a sectional hue, the coloring came from the opposition that it met—an opposition based, not upon a showing of the injury it would bring to them, but upon the supposition that benefits would be obtained by us.

Why is it that Texas is referred to, and treated as a Southern measure merely, though its northern latitude is 42°? And why has the West so often been reminded of its services upon Texas annexation? Is it to divide the South and West? If so, let those who seek this object cease from their travail, for their end can never be obtained. A common agricultural interest unites us in a common policy, and the hand that sows seeds of dissension between us will find, if they spring from the ground, that the foot of fraternal intercourse will tread them back to earth.

The streams that rise in the West flow on and are accumulated into the rivers of the South; they bear the products of one to the other, and bind the interests of the whole indissolubly together. The wishes of the one wake the sympathies of the other. On Texas annexation the voice of Mississippi found an echo in the West, and Mississippi reëchoes the call of the West on the question of Oregon. Though this Government has done nothing adequate to the defense of Mississippi, though by war she has much to lose and nothing to gain, yet she is willing to encounter it, if necessary to maintain our rights in Oregon. Her Legislature has recently so resolved, and her Governor, in a late message, says, "If war comes, to us it will bring blight and desolation, yet we are ready for the crisis." Sir, could there be a higher obligation on the representative of such a people than to restrain excitement—than to oppose a policy that threatens an unnecessary war? . . .

Mr. Chairman, why have such repeated calls been made upon the South to rally to the rescue? When, where, or how, has she been laggard or deserter?

In 1776 the rights of man were violated in the outrages upon the Northern colonies, and the South united in a war for their defense. In 1812 the flag of our Union was insulted, our sailors' rights invaded; and, though the interests infringed were mainly Northern, war was declared, and the opposition to its vigorous prosecution came not from the South. We entered it for the common cause, and for the common cause we freely met its sacrifices. If, sir, we have not been the "war party in peace," neither have we been the "peace party in war," and I will leave the past to answer for the future.

If we have not sought the acquisition of provinces by conquest, neither have we desired to exclude from our Union such as, drawn by the magnet of free institutions, have peacefully sought for admission. From sire to son has descended our federative creed, opposed to the idea of sectional conflict for private advantage, and favoring the wider expanse of our Union. If envy and jealousy and sectional strife are eating like rust into the bonds our fathers expected to bind us, they come from causes which our Southern atmosphere has never furnished. As we have shared in the toils, so we have gloried in the triumphs, of our country. In our hearts, as in our history, are mingled the names of Concord, and Camden, and Saratoga, and Lexington, and Plattsburg, and Chippewa, and Erie, and Moultrie, and New Orleans, and Yorktown, and Bunker Hill. Grouped together, they form a record of the triumphs of our cause, a monument of the common glory of our Union. What Southern man would wish it less by one of the Northern names of which it is composed? Or where is he who, gazing on the obelisk that rises from the ground made sacred by the blood of Warren, would feel his patriot's pride suppressed by local jealousy? Type of the men, the event, the purpose, it commemorates, that column rises, stern, even severe in its simplicity; neither niche nor molding for parasite or creeping thing to rest on; composed of material that defies the waves of time, and pointing like a finger to the source of noblest thought. Beacon of freedom, it guides the present generation to retrace the fountain of our years and stand beside its source; to contemplate the scene where Massachusetts and Virginia, as stronger brothers of the family, stood foremost to defend our common rights; and remembrance of the petty jarrings of to-day are buried in the nobler friendship of an earlier time.

Yes, sir, and when ignorance, led by fanatic hate, and armed by all uncharitableness, assails a domestic institution of the South, I try to forgive, for the sake of the righteous among the wicked—our natural allies, the Democracy of the North. Thus, sir, I leave to silent contempt the malign predictions of the member from Ohio, who spoke in the early stage of this discussion, while it pleases me to remember the manly and patriotic sentiments of the gentleman who sits near me [Mr. McDowell], and who represents another portion of that State. In him I recognize the feelings of our Western brethren; his were the sentiments that accord with their acts in the past, and which, with a few ignoble exceptions, I doubt not they will emulate, if again the necessity should exist. Yes, sir, if ever they hear that the invader's foot has been pressed upon our soil, they will descend to the plain like an avalanche, rushing to bury the foe.

In conclusion, I will say that, free from any forebodings of evil, above the influence of taunts, beyond the reach of treasonable threats, and confiding securely in the wisdom and patriotism of the Executive, I shrink from the assertion of no right, and will consent to no restrictions on the discretion of the treaty-making power of our Government.

APPENDIX C

SPEECHES, AND EXTRACTS FROM SPEECHES, OF THE AUTHOR IN THE
SENATE OF THE UNITED STATES DURING THE FIRST SESSION OF THE
THIRTY-FIRST CONGRESS, 1849-1850.

SPEECH of Davis of Mississippi in the Senate of the United States, on the resolutions of compromise proposed by Clay, January 29, 1850:

I do not rise to continue the discussion, but, as it has been made an historical question as to what the position of the Senate was twelve years ago, and, as with great regret I see this, the conservative branch of the Government, tending toward that fanaticism which seems to prevail with the majority in the United States, I wish to read from the journals of that date the resolutions then adopted, and to show that they went further than the honorable Senator from Kentucky has stated. I take it for granted, from the date to which the honorable Senator has alluded, he means the resolutions introduced by the honorable Senator from South Carolina [Mr. Calhoun], not now in his seat, and to which the Senator from Kentucky proposed certain amendments. Of the resolutions introduced by the Senator from South Carolina, I will read the fifth in the series, that to which the honorable Senator from Kentucky must have alluded. It is in these words:

"*Resolved*, That the intermeddling of any State or States, or their citizens, to abolish slavery in the District, or any of the Territories, on the ground, or under the pretext, that it is immoral or sinful, or the passage of any act or measure of Congress with that view, would be a direct and dangerous attack on the institutions of all the slaveholding States."

Such is the general form of the proposition. It was variously modified, but never, in my opinion, improved. On the 27th, the fifth resolution being again under consideration, Mr. Clay, of Kentucky, moved to amend the amendment by striking out all after the word "resolved," and insert:

"That the interference, by the citizens of any of the States, with a view to the abolition of slavery in this District, is endangering the rights and security of the people of the District; and that any act or measure of Congress designed to abolish slavery in this District would be a violation of the faith implied in the cessions by the States of Virginia and Maryland; a just cause of alarm to the people of the slaveholding States, and have a direct and inevitable tendency to disturb and endanger the Union.

"*And, resolved,* That it would be highly inexpedient to abolish slavery within any district of country set apart for the Indian tribes, where it now exists, or in Florida, the only Territory of the United States in which it now exists, because of the serious alarm and just apprehensions which would be thereby excited in the States sustaining that domestic institution; because the people of that Territory have not asked it to be done, and, when admitted into the Union, will be exclusively entitled to decide that question for themselves; because it would be in violation of the stipulations of the treaty between the United States and Spain of the 22d of February, 1819; and, also, because it would be in violation of a solemn compromise, made at a memorable and critical period in the history of this country, by which, while slavery was prohibited north, it was admitted south, of the line of thirty-six degrees and thirty minutes north latitude."

But this resolution was not finally adopted. Upon the motion of Mr. Buchanan to amend said amendment, by striking out the second clause thereof, commencing with the word "resolved," it was determined in the affirmative, and finally the resolution which here follows was substituted in place of the second clause:

"That the interference by the citizens of any of the States, with a view to the abolition of slavery in this District, is endangering the rights and security of the people of the District; and that any act or measure of Congress designed to abolish slavery in this district, would be a violation of the faith implied in the cessions by the States of Virginia and Maryland; a just cause of alarm to the people of the slaveholding States, and have a direct and inevitable tendency to disturb and endanger the Union."

This was the form in which the resolution was finally adopted, passing by a vote of thirty-six to eight. Here, then, was fully and broadly asserted the danger resulting from the interference in the question of slavery in the District of Columbia, as trenching upon the rights of the slaveholding States. Twelve years only have elapsed, yet this brief period has swept away even the remembrance of principles then deemed sacred and necessary to secure the safety of the Union. Now, an honorable and distinguished Senator, to whom the country has been induced to look for something that would heal the existing dissensions, instead of raising new barriers against encroachment, dashes down those heretofore erected and augments the existing danger. A representative from one of the slaveholding States raises his voice for the first time in disregard of this admitted right. Nor, Mr. President, did he stop here. The boundary of a State, with which we have no more right to interfere than with the boundary of the State of Kentucky, is encroached upon. The United States, sir, as the agent for Texas, had a right to settle the question of boundary between Texas and Mexico. Texas was not annexed as a Territory, but was admitted as a State, and, at the period of her admission, her boundaries were established by her Congress. She, by the terms of annexation, gave to the United States the right to define her boundary by treaty with Mexico; but the United States, in the treaty made with Mexico subsequent to the war with that country, received from Mexico not merely a cession of the territory that was claimed by Texas, but much that lay beyond the asserted limits. Shall we, then, acting simply as the agent of Texas in the settlement of this question of boundary, take from the principal for whom we act that territory which belongs to her, to which we asserted her title against Mexico, and appropriate it to ourselves? Why, sir, it would be a violation of justice, and of a principle of law which is so plain that it does not require one to have been bred to the profession of law to understand it. The principle I refer to is, that an agent can not take for his own benefit anything resulting from the matter in controversy, after having acquired it as belonging to the principal for whom he acts. The agent can not appropriate to himself rights acquired for his client. The right of Texas, therefore, to that boundary was made complete by the treaty of peace, which silenced the only rival claim to the territory. It was distinctly defined by the acts of her Congress, before the time of annexation; and I have only to refer to those acts to show that the boundary of Texas was the Rio Bravo del Norte, from its mouth to its source. What justice, or even decent regard for fairness, can there be, now that Texas has acceded to annexation upon certain terms, to propose a change of boundary, in violation of those terms, and by the power we hold over her as a part of the Union? Can this power extend so far as to take from her a portion of her territory, or to assert that there is a portion to which she is not entitled?

These constitute with me two great objections to the propositions of the honorable Senator from Kentucky; but, without stating all the objections that I have, and they are very many, I will merely point out a few of the prominent points to which I object in the argument of the Senator. He assumes as facts things which are mere matters of opinion, and, I think, of erroneous and injurious opinion. But, deferring the discussion to another occasion, I desire at present merely to notice the assertion of the honorable Senator, that slavery would never under any circumstances be established in California. This, though stated as a fact, is but a mere opinion—an opinion with which I do not accord. It was to work the gold-mines on this continent that the Spaniards first brought Africans to the country. The European races now engaged in working the mines of California sink under the burning heat and sudden changes of the climate to which the African race are altogether better adapted. The production of rice, sugar, and cotton, is no better adapted to slave-labor than the digging, washing, and quarrying of the gold-mines.

We, sir, have not asked that slavery should be established in California. We have only asked that there should be no restriction; that climate and soil should be left free to establish the institution or not, as experience should determine. Sir, after the agitation of the subject within these halls and elsewhere has prevented the introduction of slavery—by preventing the emigration of slaveholders with their property—are we now to be told that the question is settled? More than that: when we have acquired territory over which the Constitution of the United States is thereby extended, and which the citizens of the United States have a right to occupy, and to establish therein what laws they please, in accordance with the principles of the Constitution—in which they have a right to establish what institutions they please—it is now claimed that the municipal regulations which previously existed shall still govern the people, and that a portion of the citizens of the United States shall thus be precluded from going there with their property. This rule has, however, in discussion here, only been applied to the property of slaveholders; as though slaves were the only property under the laws of Mexico prohibited from entering California. It is to be remembered that the late Secretary of the Treasury, in a report to Congress, stated that the Mexican law prohibited the entrance of some sixty articles of commerce; this was prohibition by law of Congress, and slavery has never been so prohibited. It never has been prohibited by the Mexican Congress in California; and the only prohibition ever issued was that contained in the edict of a usurper, under the specious pretext that it was necessary, in order to oppose the invasion of the country by Spain. This decree was recognized by a subsequent Congress, so far as to pass a law authorizing payment for slaves so liberated. It was the emancipation of all the slaves in Mexico; an act, if you please, of abolition, not of prohibition; not, whatever construction may be placed upon it, done in the forms of law and requirements of their Constitution. But we have not proposed to inquire into the legality of the abolition, neither has any Southern man asked that that decree should be repealed, or that those liberated under its provisions should be returned to slavery. We only claim that there shall be an equality of immunities and privileges among citizens of all parts of the United States; that Mexican law shall not be applied so as to create inequality between citizens, by preventing the immigration of any.

But, sir, we are called on to receive this as a measure of compromise! Is a measure in which we of the minority are to receive nothing a compromise? I look upon it as but a modest mode of taking that, the claim to which has been more boldly asserted by others; and, that I may be understood upon this question, and that my position may go forth to the country in the same columns that convey the sentiments of the Senator from Kentucky, I here assert that never will I take less than the Missouri compromise line extended to the Pacific Ocean, with the specific recognition of the right to hold slaves in the territory below that line; and that, before such Territories are admitted into the Union as States, slaves may be taken there from any of the United States at the option of their owners. I can never consent to give additional power to a majority to commit further aggressions upon the minority in this Union; and will never consent to any proposition which will have such a tendency, without a full guarantee or counteracting measure is connected with it. I forbear commenting at any further length upon the propositions embraced in the resolutions at this time.

Remarks of Davis of Mississippi in the Senate of the United States, on the question of the reception of a memorial from inhabitants of Pennsylvania and Delaware, presented by Hale of New Hampshire, praying that Congress would adopt measures for an immediate and peaceful dissolution of the Union. February 8, 1850.

Mr. President: I rise merely to make a few remarks upon the right of petition, and to notice the error which I think has pervaded the comparisons that have been instituted between certain resolutions which were presented by the Senator from North Carolina and the petition which it is now proposed shall be received. The resolutions which were presented from North Carolina were published in yesterday's paper, and, after reading them, I think they refer to a state of case which the people of North Carolina might properly present as their grievance. They were resolutions for preserving the Union, calling upon Congress to take all measures in its power for that purpose. This was all legitimate. They had a right to petition Congress for a redress of grievances; and, if it were in our power to redress those grievances, if it were within the legitimate functions of our legislation, we were bound to receive the petition and respectfully consider it. This case is exactly the reverse. Here is no grievance, unless the Union is a grievance to those who petition. And they call upon Congress to do that which every one must admit Congress has no power to do—to dissolve peaceably the union of the States. Then, sir, in the first place, there is no grievance; in the next place, there is no power; and, beyond all that, it is offensive to the Senate. It is offensive to recommend legislation for the dissolution of the Union—offensive to the Senate and to the whole country. If this Union is ever to be dissolved, it must be by the action of the States and their people. Whatever power Congress holds, it holds under the Constitution, and that power is but a part of the Union. Congress has no power to legislate upon that which will be the destruction of the whole foundation upon which its authority rests.

I recollect, a good many years ago, that the Senator from Massachusetts [Mr. John Davis], who addressed the Senate this morning, very pointedly described the right of petition as a very humble right—as the mere right to beg. This is my own view. The right peaceably to assemble, I hold as the right which it was intended to grant to the people; that was the only right which had ever been denied in our colonial condition. The right of petition had never been denied by Parliament. It was intended only to secure to the people, I say, the right peaceably to assemble, whenever they choose to do so, with intent to petition for a redress of grievances.

But, sir, the right of petition, though but a poor right—the mere right to beg—may yet be carried to such an extent that we are bound to abate it as a nuisance. If the avenues to the Capitol were to be obstructed, so that members would find themselves unable to reach the halls of legislation, because hordes of beggars presented themselves in the way calling for relief, it would be a nuisance that would require to be abated, and Congress, in self-defense, would be compelled to remove them. But such a collection of beggars would not be half so great an evil as the petitions presented here on the subject of slavery. They disturb the peace of the country; they impede and pervert legislation by the excitement they create; they do more to prevent rational investigation and proper action in this body than any, if not all, other causes. Good, if ever designed, has never resulted, and it would be difficult to suppose that good is expected ever to flow from them. Why, then, should we be bound to receive such petitions to the detriment of the public business; or, rather, why are they presented? I am not of those who believe we should be turned from the path of duty by out-of-door clamor, or that the evil can be removed by partial concession. To receive is to give cause for further demands, and our direct and safe course is rejection.

Yes, sir, their reception would serve only to embarrass Congress, to disturb the tranquillity of the country, and to peril the Union of the States. By every obligation, therefore, that rests upon us under the Constitution, upon every great principle upon which the Constitution is founded, we are bound to abate this as a great and growing evil. This petition, sir, was well described by the Senator from Pennsylvania as being spurious; and I have been assured of the fact, from other sources of information, that petitions are sent round in reference to other subjects —of temperance, generally—and, after a long list of names has been obtained, the caption is cut off, and the list of signatures attached to an abolition caption and sent here to excite one section of the Union against the other, to disturb the country, and distract the legislation of Congress, to execute which we have our seats in this Chamber. For the reasons first stated, I voted to receive the resolutions that were presented by the Senator from North Carolina, and for the reasons I have just given shall vote to reject this petition.

Conclusion of speech of Jefferson Davis of Mississippi in the Senate of the United States, on the resolutions of Clay, relative to slavery in the territories, etc., February 13 and 14, 1850.

. . . Sir, it has been asked on several occasions during the present session, What ground of complaint has the South? Is this agitation in the two halls of

Congress, in relation to the domestic institutions of the South, no subject for complaint? Is the denunciation heaped upon us by the press of the North, and the attempts to degrade us in the eyes of Christendom—to arraign the character of our people and the character of our fathers, from whom our institutions are derived—no subject for complaint? Is this sectional organization, for the purpose of hostility to our portion of the Union, no subject for complaint? Would it not, between foreign nations—nations not bound together and restrained as we are by compact—would it not, I say, be just cause for war? What difference is there between organizations for circulating incendiary documents and promoting the escape of fugitives from a neighboring State and the organization of an armed force for the purpose of invasion? Sir, a State relying securely on its own strength would rather court the open invasion than the insidious attack. And for what end, sir, is all this aggression? They see that the slaves in their present condition in the South are comfortable and happy; they see them advancing in intelligence; they see the kindest relations existing between them and their masters; they see them provided for in age and sickness, in infancy and in disability; they see them in useful employment, restrained from the vicious indulgences to which their inferior nature inclines them; they see our penitentiaries never filled, and our poor-houses usually empty. Let them turn to the other hand, and they see the same race in a state of freedom at the North; but, instead of the comfort and kindness they receive at the South, instead of being happy and useful, they are, with few exceptions, miserable, degraded, filling the penitentiaries and poor-houses, objects of scorn, excluded in some places from the schools, and deprived of many other privileges and benefits which attach to the white men among whom they live. And yet, they insist that elsewhere an institution which has proved beneficial to this race shall be abolished, that it may be substituted by a state of things which is fraught with so many evils to the race which they claim to be the object of their solicitude! Do they find in the history of St. Domingo, and in the present condition of Jamaica, under the recent experiments which have been made upon the institution of slavery in the liberation of the blacks, before God, in his wisdom, designed it should be done—do they there find anything to stimulate them to future exertion in the cause of abolition? Or should they not find there satisfactory evidence that their past course was founded in error? And is it not the part of integrity and wisdom, as soon as they can, to retrace their steps? Should they not immediately cease from a course mischievous in every stage, and finally tending to the greatest catastrophe? We may dispute about measures, but, as long as parties have nationality, as long as it is a difference of opinion between individuals passing into every section of the country, it threatens no danger to the Union. If the conflicts of party were the only cause of apprehension, this Government might last for ever—the last page of human history might contain a discussion in the American Congress upon the meaning of some phrase, the extent of the power conferred by some grant of the Constitution. It is, sir, these sectional divisions which weaken the bonds of union and threaten their final rupture. It is not differences of opinion—it is geographical lines, rivers and mountains—which divide State from State, and make different nations of mankind.

Are these no subjects of complaint for us? And do they furnish no cause for repentence to you? Have we not a right to appeal to you as brethren of this

Union? Have we not a right to appeal to you, as brethren bound by the compact of our fathers, that you should, with due regard to your own rights and interests and constitutional obligations, do all that is necessary to preserve our peace and promote our prosperity?

If, sir, the seeds of disunion have been sown broadcast over this land, I ask by whose hand they have been scattered? If, sir, we are now reduced to a condition when the powers of this Government are held subservient to faction; if we can not and dare not legislate for the organization of territorial governments—I ask, sir, who is responsible for it? And I can with proud reliance say, it is not the South—it is not the South! Sir, every charge of disunion which is made on that part of the South which I in part represent, and whose sentiments I well understand, I here pronounce to be grossly calumnious. The conduct of the State of Mississippi in calling a convention has already been introduced before the Senate; and on that occasion I stated, and now repeat, that it was the result of patriotism, and a high resolve to preserve, if possible, our constitutional Union; that all its proceedings were conducted with deliberation, and it was composed of the first men of the State.

The Chief-Justice—a man well known for his high integrity, for his powerful intellect, for his great legal attainments, and his ability in questions of constitutional law—presided over that Convention. After calm and mature deliberation, resolutions were adopted, not in the spirit of disunion, but announcing, in the first resolution of the series, their attachment to the Union. They call on their brethren of the South to unite with them in their holy purpose of preserving the Constitution, which is its only bond and reliable hope. This was their object; and for this and for no other purpose do they propose to meet in general convention at Nashville. As I stated on a former occasion, this was not a party movement in Mississippi. The presiding officer belongs to the political minority in the State; the two parties in the State were equally represented in the numbers of the Convention, and its deliberations assumed no partisan or political character whatever. It was the result of primary meetings in the counties; an assemblage of men known throughout the State, having first met and intimated to those counties a time when the State Convention should, if deemed proper, be held. Every movement was taken into deliberation, and every movement then taken was wholly independent of the action of anybody else; unless it be intended, by the remarks made here, to refer its action to the great principles of those who have gone before us, and who have left us the rich legacy of the free institutions under which we live. If it be attempted to assign the movement to the nullification tenets of South Carolina, as my friend near me seemed to understand, then I say you must go further back, and impute it to the State rights and strict-construction doctrines of Madison and Jefferson. You must refer these in their turn to the principles in which originated the Revolution and separation of these then colonies from England. You must not stop there, but go back still further, to the bold spirit of the ancient barons of England. That spirit has come down to us, and in that spirit has all the action since been taken. We will not permit aggressions. We will defend our rights; and, if it be necessary, we will claim from this Government, as the barons of England claimed from John, the grant of another *Magna Charta* for our protection.

Sir, I can but consider it as a tribute of respect to the character for candor and sincerity which the South maintains, that every movement which occurs in the Southern States is closely scrutinized, and the assertion of a determination to maintain their constitutional rights is denounced as a movement of disunion; while violent denunciations against the Union are now made, and for years have been made, at the North by associations, by presses and conventions, yet are allowed to pass unnoticed as the idle wind—I suppose for the simple reason that nobody believed there was any danger in them. It is, then, I say, a tribute paid to the sincerity of the South, that every movement of hers is watched with such jealousy; but what shall we think of the love for the Union of those in whom this brings us corresponding change of conduct, who continue the wanton aggravations which have produced and justify the action they deprecate? Is it well, is it wise, is it safe, to disregard these manifestations of public displeasure, though it be the displeasure of a minority? Is it proper, or prudent, or respectful, when a representative, in accordance with the known will of his constituents, addresses you the language of solmen warning, in conformity to his duty to the Constitution, the Union, and to his own conscience, that his course should be arraigned as the declaration of ultra and dangerous opinions? If these warnings were received in the spirit in which they are given, it would augur better for the country. It would give hopes which are now denied us, if the press of the country, that great lever of public opinion, would enforce these warnings, and bear them to every cottage, instead of heaping abuse upon those whose love of ease would prompt them to silence—whose speech, therefore, is evidence of sincerity. Lightly and loosely, representatives of Southern people have been denounced as disunionists by that portion of the Northern press which most disturbs the harmony and endangers the perpetuity of the Union. Such, even, has been my own case, though the man does not breathe at whose door the charge of disunion might not as well be laid as at mine. The son of a Revolutionary soldier, attachment to this Union was among the first lessons of my childhood; bred to the service of my country, from boyhood to mature age, I wore its uniform. Through the brightest portion of my life I was accustomed to see our flag, historic emblem of the Union, rise with the rising and fall with the setting sun. I look upon it now with the affection of early love, and seek to preserve it by a strict adherence to the Constitution, from which it had its birth, and by the nurture of which its stars have come so much to outnumber its original stripes. Shall that flag, which has gathered fresh glory in every war, and become more radiant still by the conquest of peace—shall that flag now be torn by domestic faction, and trodden in the dust by sectional rivalry? Shall we of the South, who have shared equally with you all your toils, all your dangers, all your adversities, and who equally rejoice in your prosperity and your fame— shall we be denied those benefits guaranteed by our compact, or gathered as the common fruits of a common country? If so, self-respect requires that we should assert them; and, as best we may, maintain that which we could not surrender without losing your respect as well as our own.

If, sir, this spirit of sectional aggrandizement—or, if gentlemen prefer, this love they bear the African race—shall cause the disunion of these States, the last chapter of our history will be a sad commentary upon the justice and the wisdom of our people. That this Union, replete with blessings to its own citizens, and diffusive of hope to the rest of mankind, should fall a victim to a selfish aggrandizement and a pseudo-philanthropy, prompting one portion of the Union to war upon the domestic rights and peace of another, would be a deep reflection on the good sense and patriotism of our day and generation. But, sir, if this last chapter in our history shall ever be written, the reflective reader will ask, Whence proceeded this hostility of the North against the South? He will find it there recorded that the South, in opposition to her own immediate interests, engaged with the North in the unequal struggle of the Revolution. He will find again, that, when Northern seamen were impressed, their brethren of the South considered it cause for war, and entered warmly into the contest with the haughty power then claiming to be mistress of the seas. He will find that the South, afar off, unseen and unheard, toiling in the pursuits of agriculture, had filled the shipping and supplied the staple for manufactures, which enriched the North. He will find that she was the great consumer of Northern fabrics—that she not only paid for these their fair value in the markets of the world, but that she also paid their increased value, derived from the imposition of revenue duties. And, if, still further, he seeks for the cause of this hostility, it at last is to be found in the fact that the South held the African race in bondage, being the descendants of those who were mainly purchased from the people of the North. And this was the great cause. For this the North claimed that the South should be restricted from future growth—that around her should be drawn, as it were, a sanitary cordon to prevent the extension of a "moral leprosy"; and, if for that it shall be written that the South resisted, it would be but in keeping with every page she has added to the history of our country.

It depends on those in the majority to say whether this last chapter in our history shall be written or not. It depends on them now to decide whether the strife between the different sections shall be arrested before it has become impossible, or whether it shall proceed to a final catastrophe. I, sir—and I only speak for myself—am willing to meet any fair proposition—to settle upon anything which promises security for the future; anything which assures me of permanent peace, and I am willing to make whatever sacrifice I may properly be called on to render for that purpose. Nor, sir, is it a light responsibility. If I strictly measured my conduct by the late message of the Governor, and the recent expressions of opinion in my State, I should have no power to accept any terms save the unqualified admission of the equal rights of the citizens of the South to go into any of the Territories of the United States with any and every species of property held among us. I am willing, however, to take my share of the responsibility which the crisis of our country demands. I am willing to rely on the known love of the people I represent for the whole country, and the abiding respect which I know they entertain for the Union of these States. If, sir, I distrusted their attachment to our Government, and if I believed that they had that restless spirit of disunion which has been ascribed to the South, I should know full well that I had no such foundation as this to rely upon—no such great reserve in the heart of the people to fall back upon in the hour of accountability.

Mr. President, is there any such incompatibility of interest between the two sections of this country that they can not profitably live together? Does the agriculture of the South injure the manufactures of the North? On the other hand, are they not their life-blood? And think you, if one portion of the Union, however great it might be in commerce and manufactures, was separated from all the agricultural districts, that it would long maintain its supremacy? If any one so believes, let him turn to the written history of commercial states: let him look upon the moldering palaces of Venice; let him ask for the faded purple of Tyre, and visit the ruins of Carthage; there he will see written the fate of every country which rests its prosperity on commerce and manufactures alone. United we have grown to our present dignity and power—united we may go on to a destiny which the human mind can not measure. Separated, I feel that it requires no prophetic eye to see that the portion of the country which is now scattering the seeds of disunion to which I have referred will be that which will suffer most. Grass will grow on the pavements now worn by the constant tread of the human throng which waits on commerce, and the shipping will abandon your ports for those which now furnish the staples of trade. And we who produce the great staples upon which your commerce and manufactures rest, we will produce those staples still; shipping will fill our harbors; and why may we not found the Tyre of modern commerce within our own limits? Why may we not bring the manufacturers to the side of agriculture, and commerce, too, the ready servant of both?

But, sir, I have no disposition to follow this subject. I certainly can derive no pleasure from the contemplation of anything which can impair the prosperity of any portion of this Union; and I only refer to it that those who suppose we are tied by interest or fear should look the question in the face and understand that it is mainly a feeling of attachment to the Union which has long bound, and now binds, the South. But, Mr. President, I ask Senators to consider how long affection can be proof against such trial, and injury, and provocation, as the South is continually receiving.

The case in which this discrimination against the South is attempted, the circumstances under which it was introduced, render it especially offensive. It will not be difficult to imagine the feeling with which a Southern soldier during the Mexican war received the announcement that the House of Representatives had passed that odious measure, the Wilmot Proviso; and that he, although then periling his life, abandoning all the comforts of home, and sacrificing his interests, was, by the Legislature of his country, marked as coming from a portion of the Union which was not entitled to the equal benefits of whatever might result from the service to which he was contributing whatever power he possessed. Nor will it be difficult to conceive, of the many sons of the South whose blood has stained those battle-fields, whose ashes now mingle with Mexican earth, that some when they last looked on the flag of their country, may have felt their dying moments embittered by the recollection that that flag cast not an equal shadow of protection over the land of their birth, the graves of their parents, and the homes of their children, so soon to be orphans. Sir, I ask Northern Senators to make the case their own—to carry to their own firesides the idea of such intrusion and offensive discrimination as is offered to us—realize these irritations, so galling to the humble, so intolerable to the haughty, and wake, before it is too late, from the dream that the South will tamely submit. Measure the consequences to us of your assumption, and ask yourselves whether, as a free, honorable, and brave people, you would submit to it?

It is essentially the characteristic of the chivalrous that they never speculate upon the fears of any man, and I trust that no such speculations will be made upon the idea that may be entertained in any quarter that the South, from fear of her slaves, is necessarily opposed to a dissolution of the Union. She has no such fear; her slaves would be to her now, as they were in the Revolution, an element of military strength. I trust that no speculations will be made upon either the condition or the supposed weakness of the South. They will bring sad disappointments to those who indulge them. Rely upon her devotion to the Union, rely upon the feeling of fraternity she inherited and has never failed to manifest; rely upon the nationality and freedom from sedition which have in all ages characterized an agricultural people; give her justice, sheer justice, and the reliance will never fail you.

Then, Mr. President, I ask that some substantial proposition may be made by the majority in regard to this question. It is for those who have the power to pass it to propose one. It is for those who are threatening us with the loss of that which we are entitled to enjoy, to state, if there be any compromise, what that compromise is. We are unable to pass any measure, if we propose it; therefore I have none to suggest. We are unable to bend you to any terms which we may offer; we are under the ban of your purpose; therefore from you, if from anywhere, the proposition must come. I trust that we shall meet it, and bear the responsibility as becomes us; that we shall not seek to escape from it; that we shall not seek to transfer to other places, or other times, or other persons, that responsibility which devolves upon us; and I hope the earnestness which the occasion justifies will not be mistaken for the ebullition of passion, nor the language of warning be construed as a threat. We can not, without the most humiliating confession of the supremacy of faction, evade our constitutional obligations, and our obligations under the treaty with Mexico to organize governments in the Territories of California and New Mexico. I trust that we will not seek to escape from the responsibility, and leave the country unprovided for, unless by an irregular admission of new States; that we will act upon the good example of Washington in the case of Tennessee, and of Jefferson in the case of Louisiana; that we will not, if we abandon those high standards, do more than come down to modern examples; that we will not go further than to permit those who have the forms of government, under the Constitution, to assume sovereignty over territory of the United States; that we may at least, I say, assert the right to know who they are, how many they are—where they voted, how they voted—and whose certificate is presented to us of the fact, before it is conceded to them to determine the fundamental law of the country, and to prescribe the conditions on which other citizens of the United States may enter it. To reach all this knowledge, we must go through the intermediate stage of territorial government.

How will you determine what is the seal, and who are the officers, of a community unknown as an organized body to the Congress of the United States? Can the right be admitted in that community to usurp the sovereignty over territory which belongs to the States of the Union? All these questions must be answered before I can consent to any such irregular proceeding as that which is now presented in the case of California.

Mr. President, thanking the Senate for the patience they have shown toward me, I again express the hope that those who have the power to settle this distracting question—those who have the ability to restore peace, concord, and lasting harmony to the United States—will give us some substantial proposition, such as magnanimity can offer, and such as we can honorably accept. I, being one of the minority in the Senate and the Union, have nothing to offer, except an assurance of coöperation in anything which my principles will allow me to adopt, and which promises permanent, substantial security.

APPENDIX D

SPEECH of Davis of Mississippi in the Senate of the United States (chiefly in answer to Fessenden of Maine, on the message of the President of the United States transmitting to Congress the "Lecompton Constitution" of Kansas), February 8, 1858:

I wish to express not only my concurrence with the message of the President, but my hearty approbation of the high motive which actuated him when he wrote it. In that paper breathes the sentiment of a patriot, and it stands out in bold contrast with the miserable slang by which he was pursued this morning. It may serve the purposes of a man who little regards the Union to perpetrate a joke on the hazard of its dissolution. It may serve the purpose of a man who never looks to his own heart to find there any impulses of honor, to arraign everybody, the President and the Supreme Court, and to have them impeached and vilified on his mere suspicion. It ill becomes such a man to point to Southern institutions as to him a moral leprosy, which he is to pursue to the end of extermination, and, perverting everything, ancient and modern, to bring it tributary to his own malignant purposes. Not even could that clause of the Constitution which refers to the importation or migration of persons be held up to public consideration by the Senator [Mr. Fessenden] in a studied argument, save as a permission for the slave-trade. Then, everything that is most prominent in relation to the protection of property in that instrument he holds to have been swept away by a statute which prohibited the further importation of Africans. The language of that clause of the Constitution is far broader than the importation of Africans. It is not confined or limited at all to that subject. It says:

"The migration or importation of such persons as any of the States now existing shall think proper to admit shall not be prohibited by the Congress prior to the year 1808, but a tax or duty may be imposed on such importation, not exceeding ten dollars for each person."

That was a power given to Congress far broader than the slave-trade; and yet the Senator gravely argues that, when that prohibition against the further importation of Africans took place by act of Congress, thenceforward the constitutional shield, which had been thrown over slave property, fell. Sir, it is the only private property in the United States which is specifically recognized in the Constitution and protected by it.

There was a time when there was a higher and holier sentiment among the men who represented the people of this country. As far back as the time of the Confederation, when no narrow, miserable prejudice between Northern and Southern men governed those who ruled the States, a committee of three, two of whom were Northern men, reporting upon what they considered the bad faith of Spain in Florida, in relation to fugitive slaves, proposed that negotiations should be instituted to require Spain to surrender, as the States did then surrender, all fugitives escaped into their limits. Hamilton and Sedgwick from the North, and Madison from the South, made that report—men, the loftiness of whose purpose and genius might put to shame the puny efforts now made to disturb that which lies at the very foundation of the Government under which we live.

A man not knowing into what presence he was introduced, coming into this

Chamber, might, for a large part of this session, have supposed that here stood the representatives of belligerent States, and that, instead of men assembled here to confer together for the common welfare, for the general good, he saw here ministers from States preparing to make war upon each other; and then he would have felt that vain, indeed, was the vaunting of the prowess of one to destroy another. Or if, sir, he had known more—if he had recognized the representatives of the States of the Union—still he would have traced through this same eternal, petty agitation about sectional success, that limit which can not fail, however the Senator from New York (Mr. Seward) may regret it, to bring about a result which every man should, from his own sense of honor, feel, when he takes his seat in this Chamber, that he is morally bound to avoid as long as he retains possession of his seat.

To express myself more distinctly: I hold that a Senator, while he sits here as the representative of a State in the Federal Government, is in the relation of a minister to a friendly court, and that the moment he sees this Government in hostility to his own, the day he resolves to make war on this Government, his honor and the honor of his State compel him to vacate the seat he holds.

It is a poor evasion for any man to say: "I make war on the rights of one whole section; I make war on the principles of the Constitution; and yet, I uphold the Union, and I desire to see it protected." Undermine the foundation, and still pretend that he desires the fabric to stand! Common sense rejects it. No one will believe the man who makes the assertion, unless he believes him under the charitable supposition that he knows not what he is doing.

Sir, we are arraigned, day after day, as the aggressive power. What Southern Senator, during this whole session, has attacked any portion, or any interest, of the North? In what have we now, or ever, back to the earliest period of our history, sought to deprive the North of any advantage it possessed? The whole charge is, and has been, that we seek to extend our own institutions into the common territory of the United States. Well and wisely has the President of the United States pointed to that common territory as the joint possession of the country. Jointly we held it, jointly we enjoyed it in the earlier period of our country; but when, in the progress of years, it became apparent that it could not longer be enjoyed in peace, the men of that day took upon themselves, wisely or unwisely, a power which the Constitution did not confer, and, by a geographical line, determined to divide the Territories, so that the common field, which brothers could not cultivate in peace, should be held severally for the benefit of each. Wisely or unwisely, that law was denied extension to the Pacific Ocean.

I was struck, in the course of these debates, to which I have not been in the habit of replying, to hear the Senator from New Hampshire [Mr. Hale], who so very ardently opposed the extension of that line to the Pacific Ocean, who held it to be a political stain upon the history of our country, and who would not even allow the southern boundary of Utah to be the parallel of 36° 30', because of the political implication which was contained in it (the historical character of the line), plead, as he did a few days ago, for the constitutionality and legality and for the sacred character of that so-called Missouri Compromise.

I, for one, never believed Congress had the power to pass that law; yet, as one who was willing to lay down much then, as I am now, to the peace, the harmony, and the welfare of our common country, I desired to see that line extended to the Pacific Ocean, and that strife which now agitates the country never renewed; but with a distinct declaration: "Go ye to the right, and we will go to the left; and we go in peace and good-will toward each other." Those who refused then to allow the extension of that line, those who declared then that it was a violation of principle, and insisted on what they termed non-intervention, must have stood with very poor grace in the same Chamber when, at a subsequent period, the Senator from Illinois [Mr. Douglas], bound by his honor on account of his previous course, moved the repeal of that line to throw open Kansas; they must have stood with very bad grace, in this presence, to argue that that line was now sacred, and must be kept for ever.

The Senator from Illinois stood foremost as one who was willing, at an early period, to sacrifice his own prejudices and his own interests (if, indeed, his interests be girt and bounded by the limits of a State) by proposing to extend that line of pacification to the Pacific Ocean; and, failing in that, then become foremost in the advocacy of the doctrine of non-intervention; and upon that I say, he was in honor bound to wipe out that line and throw Kansas open, like any other Territory. But, sir, was it then understood by the Senator from Illinois, or anybody else, that throwing open the Territory of Kansas to free emigration was to be the signal for the marching of cohorts from one section or another to fight on that battlefield for mastery? Or, did he not rather think that emigration was to be allowed to take its course, and soil and climate be permitted to decide the great question? We were willing to abide by it. We were willing to leave natural causes to decide the question. Though I differed from the Senator from New York [Mr. Seward], though I did not believe that natural causes, if permitted to flow in their own channel, would have produced any other result than the introduction of slave property into the Territory of Kansas, I am free to admit that I have not yet reached the conclusion that that property would have permanently remained there. That is a question which interest decides. Vermont would not keep African slaves, because they were not valuable to her; neither will any population, whose density is so great as to trade rapidly on the supply of bread, be willing to keep and maintain an improvident population, to feed them in infancy, to care for them in sickness, to protect them in age. And thus it will be found in the history of nations, that, whenever population has reached that density in the temperate zones, serfdom, villenage, or slavery, whatever it has been called, has disappeared.

Ours presents a new problem, one not stated by those who wrote on it in the earlier period of our history. It is the problem of a semi-tropical climate, the problem of malarial districts, of staple products. This produces a result different from that which would be found in the farming districts and cooler climates. A race suited to our labor exists there. Why should we care whether they go into other Territories or not? Simply because of the war which is made against our institutions; simply because of the want of security which results from the action of our opponents in the Northern States. Had you made no political war upon us, had you observed the principles of our confederacy as States, that the people of each State were to take care of their domestic affairs, or, in the language of the Kansas bill, to be left perfectly free to form and regulate their institutions in their own way, then, I say, within the limits of each State the population there would have gone on to attend to their own affairs, and would have had little regard to whether this species of property, or any other, was held in any other portion of the Union. You have made it a political war. We are on the defensive. How far are you to push us?

The Senator from Alabama [Mr. Clay] has been compelled to notice the resolutions of his State; nor does that State stand alone. To what issue are you now pressing us? To the conclusion that, because within the limits of a Territory slaves are held as property, a State is to be excluded from the Union. I am not in the habit of paying lip-service to the Union. The Union is strong enough to confer favors; it is strong enough to command service. Under these circumstances, the man deserves but little credit who sings pæans to its glory. If, through a life, now not a short one, a large portion of which has been spent in the public service, I have given no better proof of my affection for this Union than by declarations, I have lived to little purpose, indeed. I think I have given evidence, in every form in which patriotism is ever subjected to a test, and I trust, whatever evil may be in store for us by those who wage war on the Constitution and our rights under it, that I shall be able to turn at least to the past and say, "Up to that period when I was declining into the grave, I served a Government I loved and served it with my whole heart." Nor will I stop to compare services with those gentlemen who have fair phrases, while they undermine the very foundation of the temple our fathers built. If, however, there be those here who do really love the Union, and the Constitution, which is the life-blood of the Union, the time has come when we should look calmly, though steadily, the danger which besets us in the face.

Violent speeches, denunciatory of people in any particular section of the Union, the arraignment of institutions which they inherited and intend to transmit, as leprous spots on the body-politic, are not the means by which fraternity is to be preserved, or this Union rendered perpetual. These were not the arguments which our fathers made when, through the struggles of the Revolutionary War, they laid the foundation of the Union. These are not the principles on which our Constitution, a bundle of compromises, was made. Then the navigating and the agricultural States did not war to see which could most injure the other; but each conceded something from that which it believed to be its own interest to promote the welfare of the other. Those debates, while they brought up all that struggle which belongs to opposite interests and opposite localities, show none of that bitterness which, so unfortunately, characterizes every debate in which this body is involved.

The meanest thing—I do not mean otherwise than the smallest thing—which can arise among us, incidentally, runs into this sectional agitation, as though it were an epidemic and gave its type to every disease. Not even could the committees of this body, when we first assembled, before any one had the excuse of excitement to plead, be organized without sectional agitation springing up. Forcibly, I suppose gravely and sincerely, it was contended here that a great wrong was done because New York, the great commercial State, and the emporium of commerce within her limits, was not represented upon the Committee of Commerce. This will go forth to remote corners, and descend, perhaps, to after-times, as an instance in which the Democratic party of the Senate behaved with unfairness toward its opponents; for with it will not descend the fact that the Democratic party only arranged for itself its own portion of the committees, taking the control of them, and left blanks on the committees to be filled by the Opposition; that the Opposition did fill the blanks; that the Opposition had both the Senators from New York, but did not choose to put either of them on that committee, though it afterward formed the basis and staple of their complaint.

Mr. President, I concur with my friend from Virginia [Mr. Hunter], and when I rose I did not intend to consume anything like so much time as I have occupied. I think there are points, which have been sprung upon the Senate to-day and heretofore, that require to be answered and to be met. Like my friend from Virginia, I shall feel that it devolves on me, as a representative in part of that constituency which is peculiarly assailed, on another occasion to meet, and, if I am able, to answer, the allegations and accusations which have been heaped, as well on the section in which I live as upon every man who has performed his duty by extending over them the protection for which our Constitution and Government were formed.

APPENDIX E

IN the summer of 1858, Davis being in Portland, Maine, a vast concourse of its citizens assembled in front of his hotel to offer him a welcome to their city, whereupon he made to them an address, from which the following extracts are given:

Fellow-Citizens: Accept my sincere thanks for this manifestation of your kindness. Vanity does not lead me so far to misconceive your purpose as to appropriate the demonstration to myself; but it is not the less gratifying to me to be made the medium through which Maine tenders an expression of regard to her sister, Mississippi. It is, moreover, with feelings of profound gratification that I witness this indication of that national sentiment and fraternity which made us, and which alone can keep us, one people. At a period but as yesterday, when compared with the life of nations, these States were separate, and in some respects opposing colonies; their only relation to each other was that of a common allegiance to the Government of Great Britain. So separate, indeed almost hostile, was their attitude, that when General Stark, of Bennington memory, was captured by savages on the head-waters of the Kennebec, he was subsequently taken by them to Albany, where they went to sell furs, and again led away a captive, without interference on the part of the inhabitants of that neighboring colony to demand or obtain his release. United as we now are, were a citizen of the United States, as an act of hostility to our country, imprisoned or slain in any quarter of the world, whether on land or sea, the people of each and every State of the Union, with one heart and with one voice, would demand redress, and woe be to him against whom a brother's blood cried to us from the ground! Such is the fruit of the wisdom and the justice with which our fathers bound contending colonies into confederation, and blended different habits and rival interests into an harmonious whole, so that, shoulder to shoulder, they entered on the trial of the Revolution, and step with step trod its thorny paths until they reached the height of national independence, and founded the constitutional representative liberty which is our birthright. . . .

By such men, thus trained and ennobled, our Constitution was framed. It stands a monument of principle, of forecast, and, above all, of that liberality which made each willing to sacrifice local interest, individual prejudice, or temporary good to the general welfare and the perpetuity of the republican institutions which they had passed through fire and blood to secure. The grants were as broad as were necessary for the functions of the general agent, and the mutual concessions were twice blessed, blessing him who gave and him who received. Whatever was necessary for domestic government—requisite in the social organization of each community—was retained by the States and the people thereof; and these it was made the duty of all to defend and maintain. Such, in very general terms, is the rich political legacy our fathers bequeathed to us. Shall we preserve and transmit it to posterity? Yes, yes, the heart responds; and the judgment answers, the task is easily performed. It but requires that each should attend to that which most concerns him, and on which alone he has rightful power to decide and to act; that each should adhere to the terms of a written compact, and that all should co-operate for that which interest, duty, and honor demand.

For the general affairs of our country, both foreign and domestic, we have a national Executive and a national Legislature. Representatives and Senators are chosen by districts and by States, but their acts affect the whole country, and their obligations are to the whole people. He, who, holding either seat, would confine his investigations to the mere interests of his immediate constituents, would be derelict to his plain duty; and he who would legislate in hostility to any section would be morally unfit for the station, and surely an unsafe depositary, if not a treacherous guardian, of the inheritance with which we are blessed. No one more than myself recognizes the binding force of the allegiance which the citizen owes to the State of his citizenship, but, that State being a party to our compact, a member of the Union, fealty to the Federal Constitution is not in opposition to, but flows from the allegiance due to, one of the United States. Washington was not less a Virginian when he commanded at Boston, nor did Gates or Greene weaken the bonds which bound them to their several States by their campaigns in the South. In proportion as a citizen loves his own State will he strive to honor her by preserving her name and her fame, free from the tarnish of having failed to observe her obligations and to fulfill her duties to her sister States. Each page of our history is illustrated by the names and deeds of those who have well understood and discharged the obligation. Have we so degenerated that we can no longer emulate their virtues? Have the purposes for which our Union was formed lost their value? Has patriotism ceased to be a virtue, and is narrow sectionalism no longer to be counted a crime? Shall the North not rejoice that the progress of agriculture in the South has given to her great staple the controlling influence of the commerce of the world, and put manufacturing nations under bond to keep the peace with the United States? Shall the South not exult in the fact that the industry and persevering intelligence of the North have placed her mechanical skill in the front ranks of the civilized world; that our mother-country, whose haughty minister, some eighty-odd years ago, declared that not a hobnail should be made in the colonies which are now the United States, was brought, some four years ago, to recognize our preëminence by sending a commission to examine our workshops and our machinery, to perfect their own manufacture of the arms requisite for their defense? Do not our whole people, interior and seaboard, North, South, East, and West, alike feel proud of the hardihood, the enterprise, the skill, and the courage of the Yankee sailor, who has borne our flag far as the ocean bears its foam, and caused the name and character of the United States to be known and respected wherever there is wealth enough to woo commerce, and intelligence to honor merit? So long as we preserve and appreciate the achievements of Jefferson and Adams, of Franklin and Madison, of Hamilton, of Hancock, and of Rutledge, men who labored for the whole country, and lived for mankind, we can not sink to the petty strife which would sap the foundations and destroy the political fabric our fathers erected and bequeathed as an inheritance to our posterity for ever.

Since the formation of the Constitution, a vast extension of territory and the varied relations arising therefrom have presented problems which could not have been foreseen. It is just cause for admiration, even wonder, that the provisions of the fundamental law should have been so fully adequate to all the wants of a government, new in its organization, and new in many of the principles on which it was founded. Whatever fears may have once existed as to the consequences of territorial expansion must give way before the evidence which the past affords. The General Government, strictly confined to its delegated functions, and the State left in the undisturbed exercise of all else, we have a theory and practice which fit our Government for immeasurable domain, and might, under a millennium of nations, embrace mankind.

From the slope of the Atlantic our population, with ceaseless tide, has poured into the wide and fertile valley of the Mississippi, with eddying whirl has passed to the coast of the Pacific; from the West and the East the tides are rushing toward each other, and the mind is carried to the day when all the cultivable land will be inhabited, and the American people will sigh for more wilderness to conquer. But there is here a physico-political problem presented for our solution. Were it purely physical, your past triumphs would leave but little doubt of your capacity to solve it. A community which, when less than twenty thousand, conceived the grand project of crossing the White Mountains, and unaided, save by the stimulus which jeers and prophecies of failure gave, successfully executed the herculean work, might well be impatient if it were suggested that a physical problem was before us too difficult for mastery. The history of man teaches that high mountains and wide deserts have resisted the permanent extension of empire, and have formed the immutable boundaries of states. From time to time, under some able leader, have the hordes of the upper plains of Asia swept over the adjacent country, and rolled their conquering columns over Southern Europe. Yet, after the lapse of a few generations, the physical law to which I have referred has asserted its supremacy, and the boundaries of those states differ little now from those which were obtained three thousand years ago.

Rome flew her conquering eagles over the then known world, and has now subsided into the little territory on which the great city was originally built. The Alps and the Pyrenees have been unable to restrain imperial France; but her expansion was a feverish action, her advance and her retreat were tracked with blood, and those mountain-ridges are the reëstablished limits of her empire. Shall the Rocky Mountains prove a dividing barrier to us? Were ours a central, consolidated Government, instead of a Union of sovereign States, our fate might be learned from the history of other nations. Thanks to the wisdom and independent spirit of our forefathers, this is not the case. Each State having sole charge of its local interests and domestic affairs, the problem, which to others has been insoluble, to us is made easy. Rapid, safe, and easy communication between the Atlantic and the Pacific will give cointelligence, unity of interest, and coöperation among all parts of our continent-wide republic. The network of railroads which bind the North and the South, the slope of the Atlantic and the valley of the Mississippi, together, testifies that our people have the power to perform, in that regard, whatever it is their will to achieve.

We require a railroad to the States of the Pacific for present uses; the time no doubt will come when we shall have need of two or three, it may be more. Because of the desert character of the interior country, the work will be difficult and expensive. It will require the efforts of a united people. The bickerings of little politicians, the jealousies of sections, must give way to dignity of purpose and zeal for the common good. If the object be obstructed by contention and division as to whether the route shall be Northern, Southern, or central, the handwriting is on the wall, and it requires little skill to see that failure is the interpretation of the inscription. You are practical people, and may ask, How is that contest to be avoided? By taking the question out of the hands of politicians altogether. Let the Government give such aid as it is proper for it to render to the company which shall propose the most feasible plan; then leave to capitalists, with judgments sharpened by interest, the selection of the route, and the difficulties will diminish, as did those which you overcame when you connected your harbor with the Canadian provinces.

It would be to trespass on your kindness, and to violate the proprieties of the occasion, were I to detain the vast concourse which stands before me, by entering on the discussion of controverted topics, or by further indulging in the expression of such reflections as circumstances suggest. I came to your city in quest of health and repose. From the moment I entered it you have showered upon me kindness and hospitality. Though my experience has taught me to anticipate good rather than evil from my fellow-man, it had not prepared me to expect such unremitting attentions as have here been bestowed. I have been jocularly asked in relation to my coming here, whether I had secured a guarantee for my safety, and lo! I have found it. I stand in the midst of thousands of my fellow-citizens. But, my friends, I came neither distrusting nor apprehensive. . . .

In the autumn of 1858 Davis visited Boston, and was invited to address a public meeting at Faneuil Hall. He was introduced by the Hon. Caleb Cushing, with whom he had been four years associated in the cabinet of President Pierce. Cushing's speech, on account of its great merit, is inserted here, except some complimentary portions of it.

Mr. President—Fellow-Citizens: I present myself before you at the instance of your chairman, not so much in order to occupy your time with observations of my own, as to prepare you for that higher gratification which you are to receive from the remarks of the eminent man here present to address you in the course of the evening. I will briefly and only suggest to you such reflections as are appropriate to that duty.

We are assembled here, my friends, at the call of the Democratic ward and county committee of Suffolk, for the purpose of ratifying the nominations made at the late Democratic State Convention—the nomination of our distinguished and honored fellow-citizen [Hon. Erasmus D. Beach] who has already addressed to you the words of wisdom and of patriotism; as also the nomination of others of our fellow-citizens, whom—if we may—we ought, whom the welfare and the honor of our Commonwealth demand of us, to place in power in the stead of the existing authorities of the Commonwealth. I would to God it were in our power to say with confidence that shall be done! ["It can be done."] We do say that it shall not depend upon us that it shall not be done. We do say that in so far as depends upon us it shall be done; and whatsoever devoted love of our country and our Commonwealth; whatsoever of our noble and holy principles; whatsoever desire to vindicate our Commonwealth from the stain that has so long rested upon the name may prompt us to do, that we will do, leaving the result to the good providence of God.

I say we are invited here by the ward and county committee to ratify these nominations, and we do ratify them with our whole heart. And we pledge our most earnest efforts at the polls to give success to these nominations. That call is comprehensive; it is addressed not only to Democrats, but to all national men, and so it should be. We know full well that there are multitudes of men in this Commonwealth who oppose the Democratic party, but who are yet impelled toward us by sympathy for the principles we profess, and by the repulsion they have toward the opinions and purposes of the leaders of the Republican party. They sympathize with our principles, and we invite them to coöperate with us in the maintenance of the principles of the Constitution and in the vindication of the Commonwealth—all national men, whatsoever may have been their past party affinities. But, while we do so, we declare that it is our belief that the Democratic party is now recognized as that only existing national party in the United States—the only constitutional party—the only party which by its present principles is competent to govern these United States, whose principles are based upon the Constitution—the only party with a platform coextensive with this great Union—this is the great Democratic party. I have heard again and again, remonstrances have been addressed to me more than once, because of the condemnation which Democratic speakers so continually utter about the unnationality as well as the unconstitutionality of the Republican party.

Let us reflect a moment; let us recall to mind that the honor of the existing organization of this Federal Administration was by the votes of the people of these United States sustained when James Buchanan was nominated for the Presidency, and that he is a worthy representative of the Democratic party. Let us reflect also that John C. Fremont was nominated as the candidate of the Republican party. I pray you, gentlemen, to reflect upon the different methods by which these nominations were presented to the people of the United States. On the one hand, there assembled at the Democratic Convention, at Cincinnati, the delegates of every one of the States in the Union. That Convention was national in its constitution, national in its character, national in its purpose, and cordially presented to the suffrages of the people of the United States a national candidate, a candidate of the whole United States; and that candidate was elected not by the votes of one section of the Union alone, or another section of the Union alone, but by the concurrent votes of the South and the North.

How was it on the other side? On the other side there assembled a convention which, by the very tenor of its call, was confined to sixteen of the thirty-one States of the Union, which, by the very tenor of its call, excluded from its councils fifteen of the thirty-one States of the Union, a convention in which appeared the representatives of only sixteen of the States of the Union—nay, I mistake—as to the remaining fifteen States of the Union, in their name, pretendedly in their name and their behalf, there appeared one man—one man only—and he a self-appointed delegate by pretension from the State of Maryland. That was the Convention which presented John C. Fremont to the people of the United States. I say that was a sectional Convention, a sectional nomination, a sectional party; and no reasoning, no remonstrances, no protestations, can discharge the Republican party from the ineffaceable stigma of that sectional Convention, that sectional nomination, and that sectional candidate for the suffrages of the United States.

That party itself has placed upon its back that shirt of Nessus which clings to it and stings it to death. I repeat, then, and I say it in confidence and vindication, in so far as regards my own belief, I say it in all good spirit toward multitudes of men in this Commonwealth of the Whig and American parties in their heretofore organization; I say it to multitudes of men who have been betrayed by the passions of the hour into joining the sectional combinations of the Republican party; I say that in the Democratic party and in that alone is the tower of strength for the liberties, the position, and the honor of the United States. But why need I indulge in these reflections in proof of my proposition? Gentlemen, we have here this evening the living proof, the visible, tangible, audible, incontestable, immortal proof, that the position of the Democratic party, in the existing organization of parties, is the national, constitutional party of the United States. Gentlemen, I ask you to challenge your memories, and look upon the history of the past four years of the United States, and can you point me to a Republican assembly here, in the city of Boston, or anywhere else; can you point me in the last four years of our history to any occasion on which Faneuil Hall has been crowded to its utmost capability with a Republican assembly in which appeared any one of those preëminent statesmen of the Southern States to honor not merely their States, but these United States? When, sir, did that ever happen? When, sir, was that a possible fact, morally speaking, that any eminent Southern statesman appeared in a Republican assembly in any one of the States of this Union? There never was a Republican assembly—an assembly of the Republican party in fifteen of these States—and I again ask, when, in the remaining sixteen States, was there ever convened an assembly of the Republican party which, by reason of bigotry, proscriptive bigotry, of unnational hatred of the South, and of determined insult of all Southern statesmen, did not render it an impossible fact that any Southern statesman should thus make his appearance as a member in such Republican Convention? You know it is so, gentlemen; and yet, have we not a common country? Did those thirteen colonies which, commencing with that combat at Concord, and following it with that battle at Bunker's Hill, and pursuing it in every battlefield of this continent, did those thirteen colonies form one country or thirteen countries? Nay, did they form two countries, or one country? I would imagine when I listen to a Republican speech here in the State of Massachusetts, when I read a Republican address in Massachusetts, I would imagine fifteen States of this Union—our fellow-citizens or fellow-sufferers, our fellow-heroes of the Revolution—I would imagine not that they are our countrymen endeared to us by ties of consanguinity, but that they are from some foreign country, that they belong to some French or British or Mexican enemies. There never was a day in which the forces of war were marshaled against the most flagrant abuses toward these United States; there never was a war in which these United States have been engaged, never even in the death-struggle of the Revolution, never in our war for maritime independence, never in our war with France and Mexico, never was there a time when any party in these United States expressed, avowed, proclaimed, ostentatiously proclaimed more intense hostility to the British, French, Mexican enemy, than I have heard uttered or proclaimed concerning our fellow-citizens—brothers in the fifteen States of this Union. It is the glory of the Democratic party that we can assume the burden of our nationality for the Union; that we can make all due sacrifices in order to show our reprobation of sectionalism, that we of the North can sacrifice to the South, from dear attachment to our fellow-citizens of the South, and they in the South in like manner meet with us upon that ground, in order to show their love for the Federal Union, and at the risk of encountering local prejudices. In the Democratic party alone, as parties are now organized, is this catholic, generous, universal spirit to be found. I say, then, the Democratic party has such a character of constitutionality and of nationality.

And now, gentlemen, I have allowed myself unthinkingly to be carried beyond my original purpose. I return to it to remind you that here among us is a citizen of one of the Southern States, eloquent among the most eloquent in debate, wise among the wisest in council, and brave among the bravest in the battle-field. A citizen of a Southern State who knows that he can associate with you, the representatives of the Democracy and the nationality of Massachusetts, that he can associate with you on equal footing with the fellow-citizens and common members of these United States.

My friends, there are those here present, and in fact there is no one here present of whom it can not be said that, in memory and admiration at least, and if not in the actual fact, yet in proud and bounding memory, they have been able to tread the glorious tracks of the victorious achievements of Jefferson Davis on the fields of Monterey and Buena Vista, and all have heard or have read the accents of eloquence addressed by him to the Senate of the United States; and there is one at least who, from his own personal observation, can bear witness to the fact of the surpassing wisdom of Jefferson Davis in the administration of the Government of the United States. Such a man, fellow-citizens, you are this evening to hear, and to hear as a beautiful illustration of the working of our republican institutions of these United States; of the republican institutions which in our own country, our own republic, as in the old republics of Athens and of Rome, exhibit the same combinations of the highest military and civic qualities in the same person. It must naturally be so, for in a republic every citizen is a soldier, and every soldier a citizen. Not in these United States on the occurrence of foreign war is that spectacle exhibited which we have so recently seen in our mother-country, of the administration of the country going abroad begging and stealing soldiers throughout Europe and America. No! And while I ask you, my friends, to ponder this fact in relation to that disastrous struggle of giants which so recently occurred in our day—the Crimean War—I ask you whether any English gentleman, any member of the British House of Commons, any member of the British House of Peers, abandoned the ease of home, abandoned his easy hours at home, and went into the country among his friends, tenants, and fellow-countrymen, volunteering there to raise troops for the service of England in that hour of her peril; did any such fact occur? No! But here in these United States we had examples, and illustrious ones, of the fact that men, eminent in their place in Congress, abandoned their stations and their honors to go among fellow-citizens of their own States, and there raise troops with which to vindicate the honor and the flag of their country. Of such men was Jefferson Davis.

There is now living one military man of prominent distinction in the public eye of England and the United States—I mean Sir Colin Campbell, now Lord Clyde of Clydesdale. He deserves the distinction he enjoys, for he has redeemed the British flag on the ensanguined, burning plains of India. He has restored the glory of the British name in Asia. I honor him. Scotland, England, Wales, and Ireland are open, for their counties, as well as their countries, and their poets, orators, and statesmen, and their generals, belong to our history as well as theirs. I will never disavow Henry V on the plains of Agincourt; never Oliver Cromwell on the fields of Marston Moor and Naseby; never Sarsfield on the banks of the Boyne. The glories and honors of Sir Campbell are the glories of the British race, and the races of Great Britain and Ireland, from whom we are descended.

But what gained Sir Colin Campbell the opportunity to achieve those glorious results in India? Remember that, and let us see what it was. On one of those bloody battles fought by the British before the fortress of Sebastopol, in the midst of the perils, the most perilous of all the battle-fields England ever encountered in Europe, in one of the bloody charges of the Russian cavalry, there was an officer—a man who felt and who possessed sufficient confidence in the troops he commanded, and in the authority of his own voice and example—received that charge not in the ordinary, commonplace, and accustomed manner, by forming his troops into a hollow square, and thus arresting the charge, but by forming into two diverging lines, and thus receiving upon the rifles of his Highlandmen the charge of the Russian cavalry and repelling it. How all England rang with the glory of that achievement! How the general voice of England placed upon the brows of Sir Colin Campbell the laurels of the future mastership of victory for the arms of England! And well they might do so. But who originated that movement; who set the example of that gallant operation—who but Colonel Jefferson Davis, of the First Mississippi Regiment, on the field of Buena Vista? He was justly entitled to the applause of the restorer of victory to the arms of the Union. Gentlemen, in our country, in this day, such a man, such a master of the art of war, so daring in the field, such a man may not only aspire to the highest places in the executive government of the Union, but such a man may acquire what nowhere else, since the days of Cimon and Miltiades, of the Cincinnati and the Cornelii of Athens and of Rome, has been done by the human race, the combination of eminent powers, of intellectual cultivation, and of eloquence with the practical qualities of a statesman and general.

But, gentlemen, I am again betrayed beyond my purpose. Sir [addressing General Davis], we welcome you to the Commonwealth of Massachusetts. You may not find here the ardent skies of your own sunny South, but you will find as ardent hearts, as warm and generous hands to welcome you to our Commonwealth. We welcome you to the city of Boston, and you have already experienced how open-hearted, how generous, how free from all possible taint of sectional thought are the hospitality and cordiality of the city of Boston. We welcome you to Faneuil Hall. Many an eloquent voice has in all times resounded from the walls of Faneuil Hall. It is said that no voice is uttered by man in this air we breathe but enters into that air. It continues there immortal as the portion of the universe into which it has passed. If it be so, how instinct is Faneuil Hall with the voice of the great, good, and glorious of past generations, and of our own, whose voices have echoed through its wall, whose eloquent words have thrilled the hearts of hearers, as if a pointed sword were passing them through and through. Here Adams aroused his countrymen in the War of Independence, and Webster invoked them almost with the dying breath of his body—invoked with that voice of majesty and power which he alone possessed—invoked them to a union between the North and South. Ay, sir, and who, if he were here present, who from those blest abodes on high from which he looks down upon us would congratulate us for this scene. First, and above all, because his large heart would have appreciated the spectacle of a statesman eminent among the most eminent of the Southern States here addressing an assembly of the people in the city of Boston. Because, in the second place, he would have remembered that, though divided from you by party relations, in one of the critical hours of his fame and his honor, your voice was not wanting for his vindication in the Congress of the United States. Sir, again, I say we welcome you to Faneuil Hall.

And now, my fellow-citizens, I will withdraw myself and present to you the Hon. Jefferson Davis.

Address of Jefferson Davis at Faneuil Hall, Boston, October 12, 1858.

Countrymen, Brethren, Democrats: Most happy am I to meet you, and to have received here renewed assurance—of that which I have so long believed—that the pulsation of the Democratic heart is the same in every parallel of latitude, on every meridian of longitude, throughout the United States. It required not this to confirm me in a belief I have so long and so happily enjoyed. Your own great statesman [the Hon. Caleb Cushing], who has introduced me to this assembly, has been too long associated with me, too nearly connected, we have labored too many hours, until one day ran into another, in the cause of our country, for me to fail to understand that a Massachusetts Democrat has a heart as wide as the Union, and that its pulsations always beat for the liberty and happiness of his country. Neither could I be unaware that such was the sentiment of the Democracy of New England. For it was my fortune lately to serve under a President drawn from the neighboring State of New Hampshire, and I know that he spoke the language of his heart, for I learned it in four years of intimate relations with him, when he said he knew "no North, no South, no East, no West, but sacred maintenance of the common bond and true devotion to the common brotherhood." Never, sir, in the past history of our country, never, I add, in its future destiny, however bright it may be, did or will a man of higher and purer patriotism, a man more devoted to the common weal of his country, hold the helm of our great ship of state, than Franklin Pierce.

I have heard the resolutions read and approved by this meeting; I have heard the address of your candidate for Governor; and these, added to the address of my old and intimate friend, General Cushing, bear to me fresh testimony, which I shall be happy to carry away with me, that the Democracy, in the language of your own glorious Webster, "still lives"; lives, not as his great spirit did, when it hung 'twixt life and death, like a star upon the horizon's verge, but lives like the germ that is shooting upward; like the sapling that is growing to a mighty tree, and I trust it may redeem Massachusetts to her glorious place in the Union, when she led the van of the defenders of State rights.

When I see Faneuil Hall thus thronged it reminds me of another meeting, when it was found too small to contain the assembly that met here, on the call of the people, to know what should be done in relation to the tea-tax, and when, Faneuil Hall being too small, they went to the old South Church, which still stands a monument of your early day. I hope the time will soon come when many Democratic meetings in Boston will be too large for Faneuil Hall. I am welcomed to this hall, so venerable for all the associations of our early history; to this hall of which you are so justly proud, and the memories of which are part of the inheritance of every American citizen; and I felt, as I looked upon it, and remembered how many voices of patriotic fervor have filled it—how here the first movement originated from which the Revolution sprang; how here began the system of town meetings and free discussion—that, though my theme was more humble than theirs, as befitted my humbler powers, I had enough to warn me that I was assuming much to speak in this sacred chamber. But, when I heard your distinguished orator say that words uttered here could never die, that they lived and became a part of the circumambient air, I feel a hesitation which increases upon me with the remembrance of his expressions. But, if those voices which breathed the first impulse into the colonies—now the United States—to proclaim independence, and to unite for resistance against the power of the mother-country —if those voices live here still, how must they fare who come here to preach treason to the Constitution and to assail the union of these States? It would seem that their criminal hearts would fear that those voices, so long slumbering, would break silence, that those forms which hang upon these walls behind me might come forth, and that the sabers so long sheathed would leap from their scabbards to drive from this sacred temple those who desecrate it as did the money-changers who sold doves in the temple of the living God.

Here you have, to remind you, and to remind all who enter this hall, the portraits of those men who are dear to every lover of liberty, and part and parcel of the memory of every American citizen; and highest among them all I see you have placed Samuel Adams and John Hancock. You have placed them the highest, and properly; for they were two, the only two, excepted from the proclamation of mercy, when Governor Gage issued his anathema against them and against their fellow-patriots. These men, thus excepted from the saving grace of the crown, now occupy the highest places in Faneuil Hall, and thus seem to be the highest in the reverence of the people of Boston. This is one of the instances in which we find tradition so much more reliable than history; for tradition has borne the name of Samuel Adams to the remotest of the colonies, and the new States formed out of what was territory of the old colonies; and there it is a name as sacred among us as it is among you.

We all remember how early he saw the necessity of *community independence*. How, through the dim mists of the future, and in advance of his day, he looked forward to the proclamation of the independence of Massachusetts; how he steadily strove, through good report and evil report, with a great, unwavering heart, whether in the midst of his fellow-citizens, cheered by their voices, or communing with his own heart, when driven from his home, his eyes were still fixed upon his first, last hope, the community independence of Massachusetts! Always a commanding figure, we see him, at a later period, the leader in the correspondence which waked the feelings of the other colonies to united fraternal association—the people of Massachusetts with the people of the other colonies —there we see his letters acknowledging the receipt of rice of South Carolina, and the money of New York and Pennsylvania—all these poured in to relieve

Boston of the sufferings inflicted upon her when the port was closed by the despotism of the British crown—we see the beginning of that which insured the coöperation of the colonies throughout the desperate struggle of the Revolution. And we there see that which, if the present generation be true to the memory of their sires, to the memory of the noble men from whom they descended, will perpetuate for them that spirit of fraternity in which the Union began. But it is not here alone, nor in reminiscences connected with the objects which present themselves within this hall, that the people of Boston have much to excite their patriotism and carry them back to the great principles of the Revolutionary struggle. Where will you go and not meet some monument to inspire such sentiments? Go to Lexington and Concord, where sixty brave countrymen came with their fowling-pieces to oppose six hundred veterans—where they forced those veterans back, pursuing them on the road, fighting from every barn, and bush, and stock, and stone, till they drove them, retreating, to the ships from which they went forth! And there stand those monuments of your early patriotism, Breed's and Bunker's Hills, whose soil drank the martyr-blood of men who lived for their country and died for mankind! Can it be that any of you should tread that soil and forget the great purposes for which those men died? While, on the other side, rise the heights of Dorchester, where once stood the encampment of the Virginian, the man who came here, and did not ask, Is this a town of Virginia? but, Is this a town of my brethren? The steady courage and cautious wisdom of Washington availed to drive the British troops out from the city which they had so confidently held. Here, too, you find where once the old Liberty Tree, connected with so many of your memories, grew. You ask your legend, and learn that it was cut down for firewood by British soldiers, as some of your meeting-houses were destroyed; they burned the old tree, and it warmed the soldiers long enough to leave town, and, had they burned it a little longer, its light would have shown Washington and his followers where their enemies were.

But they are gone, and never again shall a hostile foot set its imprint upon your soil. Your harbor is being fortified, to prevent an unexpected attack on your city by a hostile fleet. But woe to the enemy whose fleet shall bear him to your shores to set his footprint upon your soil; he goes to a prison or to a grave! American fortifications are not built from any fear of invasion, they are intended to guard points where marine attacks can be made; and, for the rest, the hearts of Americans are our ramparts.

But, my friends, it is not merely in these associations, so connected with the honorable pride of Massachusetts, that one who visits Boston finds much for gratification, hope, and instruction. If I were selecting a place where the advocate of strict construction, the extreme expounder of democratic State-rights doctrine should go for his texts, I would send him into the collections of your historical associations. Instead of going to Boston as a place where only consolidation would be found, he would find written, in letters of living light, that sacred creed of State rights which has been miscalled the ultra opinions of the South; he could find among your early records that this Faneuil Hall, the property of the town at the time when Massachusetts was under a colonial government, administered by a man appointed by the British crown, guarded by British soldiers, was refused to a British Governor in which to hold a British festival, because he was going to bring with him the agents for collecting, and naval officers sent here to enforce, an oppressive tax upon your Commonwealth. Such was the proud spirit of independence manifested even in your colonial history. Such is the great foundation-stone on which may be erected an eternal monument of State rights. And so, in an early period of our country, you find Massachusetts leading the movements, prominent of all the States, in the assertion of that doctrine which has been recently so much belied. Having achieved your independence, having passed through the Confederation, you assented to the formation of our present constitutional Union. You did not surrender your sovereignty. Your fathers had sacrificed too much to claim, as a reward of their toil, merely that they should have a change of masters; and a change of masters it would have been had Massachusetts surrendered her State sovereignty to the central Government, and consented that that central Government should have the power to coerce a State. But, if this power does not exist, if this sovereignty has not been surrendered, then, who can deny the words of soberness and truth spoken by your candidate this evening, when he has pleaded to you the cause of State independence, and the right of every community to be judge of its own domestic affairs? This is all we have ever asked—we of the South, I mean—for I stand before you as one of those who have always been called the ultra men of the South, and I speak, therefore, for that class; and I tell you that your candidate for Governor has uttered to-night everything which we have claimed as a principle for our protection. And I have found the same condition of things in the neighboring State of Maine. I have found that the Democrats there asserted the same broad constitutional principle for which we have been contending, by which we are willing to live, for which we are willing to die!

In this state of the case, my friends, why is the country agitated? The old controversies have passed away, or they have subsided, and have been covered up by one dark pall of somber hue, which increases with every passing year. Why is it, then, I say, that you are thus agitated in relation to the domestic affairs of other communities? Why is it that the peace of the country is disturbed in order that one people may judge of what another people may do? Is there any political power to authorize such interference? If so, where is it? You did not surrender your sovereignty. You gave to the Federal Government certain functions. It was your agent, created for specified purposes. It can do nothing save that which you have given it power to perform. Where is the grant? Has it a right to determine what shall be property? Surely not; that belongs to every community to decide for itself; you judge in your case—every other State must judge in its case. The Federal Government has no power to destroy property. Do you pay taxes, then, to an agent, that he may destroy your property? Do you support him for that purpose? It is an absurdity on the face of it. To ask the question is to answer it. The Government is instituted to protect, not to destroy, property. And, in abundance of caution, your fathers provided that the Federal Government should not take private property for its own use unless by making due compensation therefor. It is prohibited from attempting to destroy property. One of its great purposes was protection to the States. Whenever that power is made a source of danger, we destroy the purpose for which the Government was formed.

Why, then, have you agitators? With Pharisaical pretension it is sometimes said it is a moral obligation to agitate, and I suppose they are going through a sort of vicarious repentance for other men's sins. With all due allowance for their zeal, we ask, how do they decide that it is a sin? By what standard do they measure it? Not the Constitution; the Constitution recognizes the property in slaves in many forms, and imposes obligations in connection with that recognition. Not the Bible; that justifies it. Not the good of society; for, if they go where it exists, they find that society recognizes it as good. What, then, is their standard? The good of mankind? Is that seen in the diminished resources of the country? Is that seen in the diminished comfort of the world? Or is not the reverse exhibited? Is there, in the cause of Christianity, a motive for the prohibition of the system which is the only agency through which Christianity has reached that inferior race, the only means by which they have been civilized and elevated? Or is their piety manifested in denunciation of their brethren, who are deterred from answering their denunciation only by the contempt which they feel for a mere brawler, who intends to end his brawling only in empty words?

What, my friends, must be the consequences? Good or evil? They have been evil, and evil they must be only to the end. Not one particle of good has been done to any man, of any color, by this agitation. It has been insidiously working the purpose of sedition, for the destruction of that Union on which our hopes of future greatness depend.

On the one side, then, you see agitation tending slowly and steadily to that separation of States, which, if you have any hope connected with the liberty of mankind; if you have any national pride connected with making your country the greatest on the face of the earth; if you have any sacred regard for the obligations which the deeds and the blood of your fathers entailed upon you, that hope should prompt you to reject anything that would tend to destroy the result of that experiment which they left it to you to conclude and perpetuate. On the other hand, if each community, in accordance with the principles of our Government, should regard its domestic interests as a part of the common whole, and struggle for the benefit of all, this would steadily lead us to fraternity, to unity, to coöperation, to the increase of our happiness and the extension of the benefits of our useful example over mankind. The flag of the Union, whose stars have already more than doubled their original number, with its ample folds may wave, the recognized flag of every State or the recognized protector of every State upon the Continent of America.

In connection with the view which I have presented of the early idea of community independence, I will add the very striking fact that one of the colonies, about the time they had resolved to unite for the purpose of achieving their independence, addressed the Colonial Congress to know in what condition it would be in the interval between its separation from the Government of Great Britain and the establishment of a government on this continent. The answer of the Colonial Congress was exactly what might have been expected—exactly what State-rights Democracy would answer to-day to such an inquiry—that they "had nothing to do with it." If such sentiment had continued, if it had governed in every State, if representatives had been chosen upon it, then your halls of Federal legislation would not have been disturbed about the question of the domestic institutions of the different States. The peace of the country would not have been hazarded by the arraignment of the family relations of people over whom the Government has no control. If in harmony working together, with co-intelligence for the conservation of the interests of the country—if protection to the States and the other great ends for which the Government was established, had been the aim and united effort of all—what effects would not have been produced? As our Government increases in expansion it would increase in its beneficent effect upon the people; we should, as we grow in power and prosperity, also grow in fraternity, and it would be no longer a wonder to see a man coming from a Southern State to address a Democratic audience in Boston.

But I have referred to the fact that Massachusetts stood preëminently forward among those who asserted community independence: and this reminds me of another incident. President Washington visited Boston when John Hancock was Governor, and Hancock refused to call upon the President, because he contended that any man who came within the limits of Massachusetts must yield rank and precedence to the Governor of the State. He eventually only surrendered the point on account of his personal regard and respect for the character of George Washington. I honor him for this, and value it as one of the early testimonies in favor of State rights. I wish all our Governors had the same regard for the dignity of the State as had the great and glorious John Hancock.

In the beginning the founders of this Government were true democratic State-rights men. Democracy was State rights, and State rights was democracy, and it is to-day. Your resolutions breathe it. The Declaration of Independence embodied the sentiments which had lived in the hearts of the country for many years before its formal assertion. Our fathers asserted the great principle—the right of the people to choose their own government—and that government rested upon the consent of the governed. In every form of expression it uttered the same idea, community independence and the dependence of the Union upon the communities of which it consisted. It was an American declaration of the unalienable right of man; it was a general truth, and I wish it were accepted by all men. But I have said that this State sovereignty—this community independence—has never been surrendered, and that there is no power in the Federal Government to coerce a State. Will any one ask me, then, how a State is to be held to the fulfillment of its obligations? My answer is, by its honor. The obligation is the more sacred to observe every feature of the compact, because there is no power to enforce it. The great error of the Confederation was, that it attempted to act upon the States. It was found impracticable, and our present form of government was adopted, which acts upon individuals, and is not designed to act upon States. The question of State coercion was raised in the Convention which framed the Constitution, and, after discussion, the proposition to give power to the General Government to enforce against any State obedience to the laws was rejected. It is upon the ground that a State can not be coerced that observance of the compact is a sacred obligation. It was upon this principle that our fathers depended for the perpetuity of a fraternal Union, and for the security of the rights that the Constitution was designed to preserve. The fugitive slave compact in the Constitution of the United States implied that the States should fulfill it voluntarily. They expected the States to legislate so as to secure the rendition of fugitives; and in 1778 it was a matter of complaint that the Spanish colony of Florida did not restore fugitive negroes from the United States who escaped into that colony, and a committee, composed of Hamilton, of New York, Sedgwick, of Massachusetts, and Mason, of Virginia, reported resolutions in the Congress, instructing the Secretary of Foreign Affairs to address the chargé d'affaires at Madrid to apply to his Majesty of Spain to issue orders to his governor to compel them to secure the rendition of fugitive negroes. This was the sentiment of the committee, and they added, also, that the States would return any slaves from Florida who might escape into their limits.

When the constitutional obligation was imposed, who could have doubted that every State, faithful to its obligations, would comply with the requirements of the Constitution, and waive all questions as to whether the institution should or should not exist in another community over which they had no control? Congress was at last forced to legislate on the subject, and they have continued, up to a recent period, to legislate, and this has been one of the causes by which you have been disturbed. You have been called upon to make war against a law which need never to have been enacted, if each State had done the duty which she was called upon by the Constitution to perform.

Gentlemen, this presents one phase of agitation—negro agitation: there is another and graver question, it is in relation to the prohibition by Congress of the introduction of slave property into the Territories. What power does Congress possess in this connection? Has it the right to say what shall be property anywhere? If it has, from what clause of the Constitution does it derive that power? Have other States the power to prescribe the condition upon which a citizen of another State shall enter upon and enjoy territory—common property of all? Clearly not. Shall the inhabitants who first go into the Territory deprive any citizen of the United States of those rights which belong to him as an equal owner of the soil? Certainly not. Sovereign jurisdiction can only pass to these inhabitants when the States, the owners of that Territory shall recognize their right to become an equal member of the Union. Until then, the Constitution and the laws of the Union must be the rule governing within the limits of a Territory.

The Constitution recognizes all property, and gives equal privileges to every citizen of the States; and it would be a violation of its fundamental principles to attempt any discrimination.

There is nothing of truth or justice with which to sustain this agitation, or ground for it, unless it be that it is a very good bridge over which to pass into office; a little stock of trade in politics built up to aid men who are missionaries staying at home; reformers of things which they do not go to learn; preachers without a congregation; overseers without laborers and without wages; war-horses who snuff the battle afar off and cry: "Aha! aha! I am afar off."

Thus it is that the peace of the Union is disturbed; thus it is that brother is arrayed against brother; thus it is that the people come to consider not how they can promote each other's interest, but how they may successfully war upon them. And among the things most odious to my mind is to find a man who enters upon a public office, under the sanction of the Constitution, and taking an oath to support the Constitution—the compact between the States binding each for the common defense and general welfare of the other—and retaining to himself a mental reservation that he will war upon the institutions and the property of any of the States of the Union. It is a crime too low to characterize as it deserves before this assembly. It is one which would disgrace a gentleman—one which a man with self-respect would never commit. To swear that he will support the Constitution, to take an office which belongs in many of its relations to all the States, and to use it as a means of injuring a portion of the States of whom he is thus an agent, is treason to everything that is honorable in man. It is the base and cowardly attack of him who gains the confidence of another in order that he may wound him. But I have often heard it argued, and I have seen it published: I have seen a petition that was circulated for signers, announcing that there was an incompatibility between the different sections of the Union; that it had been tried long enough, and that they must get rid of those sections in which the curse of slavery existed. Ah! those sages, so much wiser than our fathers, have found out that there is incompatibility in that which existed when the Union was formed. They have found an incompatibility inconsistent with union, in that which existed when South Carolina sent her rice to Boston, and Maryland and Pennsylvania and New York brought in their funds for her relief. The fact is that, from that day to this, the difference between the people of the colonies has been steadily diminishing, and the possible advantages of union in no small degree augmented. The variety of product of soil and of climate has been multiplied, both by the expansion of our country and by the introduction of new tropical products not cultivated at that time; so that every motive to union which your fathers had, in a diversity which should give prosperity to the country, exists in a higher degree to-day than when this Union was formed, and this diversity is fundamental to the prosperity of the people of the several sections of the country.

It is, however, to-day, in sentiment and interest, less than on the day when the Declaration of Independence was made. Diversity there is—diversity of character—but it is not of that extreme kind which proves incompatibility; for your Massachusetts man, when he comes into Mississippi, adopts our opinions and our institutions, and frequently becomes the most extreme man among us. As our country has extended, as new products have been introduced into it, this Union and the free trade that belongs to it have been of increasing value. And I say, moreover, that it is not an unfortunate circumstance that this diversity of pursuit and character still remains. Originally it sprang in no small degree from natural causes. Massachusetts became a manufacturing and commercial State because of her fine harbors—because of her water-power, making its last leap into the sea, so that the ship of commerce brought the staple to the manufacturing power. This made you a commercial and a manufacturing people. In the Southern States great plains interpose between the last leaps of the streams and the sea. Those plains were cultivated in staple crops, and the sea brought their products to your streams to be manufactured. This was the first beginning of the differences.

Then your longer and more severe winters, your soil not so favorable for agriculture, in a degree kept you a manufacturing and a commercial people. Even after the cause had passed away—after railroads had been built—after the steam-engine had become a motive power for a large part of manufacturing machinery, the natural causes from which your people obtained a manufacturing ascendancy and ours became chiefly agriculturists continued to act in a considerable measure to preserve that relation. Your interest is to remain a manufacturing, and ours to remain an agricultural people. Your prosperity, then, is to receive our staple and to manufacture it, and ours to sell it to you and buy the manufactured goods. This is an interweaving of interests which makes us all the richer and happier.

But this accursed agitation, this intermeddling with the affairs of other people, is that alone which will promote a desire in the mind of any one to separate these great and glorious States. The seeds of dissension may be sown by invidious reflections. Men may be goaded by the constant attempts to infringe upon rights and to disturb tranquillity, and in the resentment which follows it is not possible to tell how far the way may rush. I therefore plead to you now to arrest a fanaticism which has been evil in the beginning and must be evil in the end. You may not have the numerical power requisite; and those at a distance may not understand how many of you there are desirous to put a stop to the course of this agitation. For me, I have learned since I have been in New England the vast mass of true State-rights Democrats to be found within its limits—though not represented in the halls of Congress. And if it comes to the worst—if, availing themselves of a majority in the two Houses of Congress, they should attempt to trample upon the Constitution; if they should attempt to violate the rights of the States; if they should attempt to infringe upon our equality in the Union—I believe that even in Massachusetts, though it has not had a representative in Congress for many a day, the State-rights Democracy, in whose breast beats the spirit of the Revolution, can and will whip the black Republicans. I trust we shall never be thus purified, as it were, by fire; but that the peaceful, progressive revolution of the ballot-box will answer all the glorious purposes of the Constitution and the Union. And I marked that the distinguished orator and statesman who preceded me, in addressing you, used the words "national" and "constitutional" in such relation to each other as to show that in his mind the one was a synonym of the other. I say so: we become national by the Constitution, the bond for uniting the States, and national and constitutional are convertible terms.

Your candidate for the high office of Governor—whom I have been once or twice on the point of calling Governor, and whom I hope I may be able soon to call so—in his remarks to you has presented the same idea in another form. And well may Massachusetts orators, without even perceiving what they are saying, utter sentiments which lie at the foundation of your colonial as well as your subsequent political history, which existed in Massachusetts before the Revolution, and have existed ever since, whenever the true spirit which comes down from the Revolutionary sires has swelled and found utterance within her limits.

It has been not only, my friends, in this increasing and mutual dependence of interest that we have found new ties to you. Those bonds are both material and mental. Every improvement or invention, every construction of a railroad, has formed a new reason for our being one. Every new achievement, whether it has been in arts or science, in war or in manufactures, has constituted for us a new bond and a new sentiment holding us together.

Why, then, I would ask, do we see these lengthened shadows which follow in the course of our political history? Is it because our sun is declining to the horizon? Are they the shadows of evening, or are they, as I hopefully believe, but the mists which are exhaled by the sun as it rises, but which are to be dispersed by its meridian glory? Are they but the little evanishing clouds that flit between the people and the great objects for which the Constitution was established? I hopefully look toward the reaction which will establish the fact that our sun is still in the ascendant—that that cloud which has so long covered our political horizon is to be dispersed—that we are not again to be divided on parallels of latitude and about the domestic institutions of States—a sectional attack on the prosperity and tranquillity of a nation—but only by differences in opinion upon measures of expediency, upon questions of relative interest, by discussions as to the powers of the States and the rights of the States, and the powers of the Federal Government—such discussion as is commemorated in this picture of your own great and glorious Webster, when he specially addressed our best, most tried, and greatest man, the pure and incorruptible Calhoun, represented as intently listening to catch the accents of eloquence that fell from his lips. Those giants strove each for his conviction, not against a section—not against each other; they stood to each other in the relation of personal affection and esteem, and never did I see Mr. Webster so agitated, never did I hear his voice falter, as when he delivered the eulogy on John C. Calhoun.

But allusion was made to my own connection with your great and favorite departed statesman. Of that I will only say, on this occasion, that very early in my Congressional life Mr. Webster was arraigned for an offense which affected him most deeply. He was no accountant, and all knew that. He was arraigned on a pecuniary charge—the misapplication of what is known as the secret-service fund—and I was one of the committee that had to investigate the charge. I endeavored to do justice. I endeavored to examine the evidence with a view to ascertain the truth. It is true I remembered that he was an eminent American statesman. It is true that as an American I hoped he would come out without a stain upon his garments. But I entered upon the investigation to find the truth and to do justice. The result was, he was acquitted of every charge that was made against him, and it was equally my pride and my pleasure to vindicate him in every form which lay within my power. No one that knew Daniel Webster could have believed that he would ever ask whether a charge was made against a Massachusetts man or a Mississippian. No! It belonged to a lower, to a later, and I trust a shorter-lived race of statesmen, who measure all facts by considerations of latitude and longitude.

I honor that sentiment which makes us oftentimes too confident, and to despise too much the danger of that agitation which disturbs the peace of the country. I respect that feeling which regards the Union as too strong to be broken. But, at the same time, in sober judgment, it will not do to treat too lightly the danger which has existed and still exists. I have heard our Constitution and Union compared to the granite shores which face the sea, and, dashing back the foam of the waves, stand unmoved by their fury. Now I accept the simile: and I have stood upon the shore, and I have seen the waves of the sea dash upon the granite of your own shores which frowns over the ocean, have seen the spray thrown back from the cliffs. But, when the tide had ebbed, I saw that the rock was seamed and worn; and, when the tide was low, the pieces that had been riven from the granite rock were lying at its base.

And thus the waves of sectional agitation are dashing themselves against the granite patriotism of the land. But even that must show the seams and scars of the conflict. Sectional hostility will follow. The danger lies at your door, and it is time to arrest it. Too long have we allowed this influence to progress. It is time that men should go back to the first foundation of our institutions. They should drink the waters of the fountain at the source of our colonial and early history.

You, men of Boston, go to the street where the massacre occurred in 1770. There you should learn how your fathers strove for community rights. And near the same spot you should learn how proudly the delegation of democracy came to demand the removal of the troops from Boston, and how the venerable Samuel Adams stood asserting the rights of democracy, dauntless as Hampden, clear and eloquent as Sidney; and how they drove out the myrmidons who had trampled on the rights of the people.

All over our country, these monuments, instructive to the present generation, of what our fathers did, are to be found. In the library of your association for the collection of your early history, I found a letter descriptive of the reading of the church service to his army by General Washington, during one of those winters when the army was ill-clad and without shoes, when he built a little log-cabin for a meeting-house, and there, reading the service to them his sight failed him, he put on his glasses and, with emotion which manifested the reality of his feelings, said, "I have grown gray in serving my country, and now I am growing blind."

By the aid of your records you may call before you the day when the delegation of the army of the democracy of Boston demanded compliance with its requirements for the removal of the troops, A painfully thrilling case will be found in the heroic conduct of your father's friends, the patriots in Charleston, South Carolina. The prisoners were put upon the hulks, where the small-pox existed, and where they were brought on shore to stay the progress of the infection, and were offered, if they would enlist in his Majesty's service, release from all their sufferings, present and prospective; while, if they would not, the rations would be taken from their families, and they would be sent back to the hulks and again exposed to the infection. Emaciated as they were, with the prospect of being returned to confinement, and their families turned out into the streets, the spirit of independence, the devotion to liberty, was so supreme in their breasts, that they gave one loud huzza for General Washington, and went to meet death in their loathsome prison. From these glorious recollections, from the emotions which they create, when the sacrifices of those who gave you the heritage of liberty are read in your early history, the eye is directed to our present condition. Mark the prosperity, the growth, the honorable career of your country under the voluntary union of independent States. I do not envy the heart of that American whose pulse does not beat quicker, and who does not feel within him a high exultation and pride, in the past glory and future prospects of his country. With these prospects are associated—if we are only wise, true, and faithful, if we shun sectional dissension—all that man can conceive of the progression of the American people. And the only danger which threatens those high prospects is that miserable spirit which, disregarding the obligations of honor, makes war upon the Constitution; which induces men to assume powers they do not possess, trampling as well upon the great principles which lie at the foundation of the Declaration of Independence, and the Constitution of the Union, as upon the honorable obligations which were fixed upon them by their fathers. They with internecine strife would sacrifice themselves and their brethren to a spirit which is a disgrace to our common country. With these views, it will not be surprising, to those who most differ from me, that I feel an ardent desire for the success of this State-rights Democracy; that, convinced as I am of the ill consequences of the described heresies unless they be corrected; of the evils upon which they would precipitate the country unless they are restrained—I say, none need be surprised if, prompted by such aspirations, and impressed by such forebodings as now open themselves before me, I have spoken freely, yielding to motives I would suppress and can not avoid. I have often, elsewhere than in the State of which I am a citizen, spoken in favor of that party which alone is national, in which alone lies the hope of preserving the Constitution and the perpetuation of the Government and of the blessings which it was ordained and established to secure.

My friends, my brethren, my countrymen, I thank you for the patient attention you have given me. It is the first time it has ever befallen me to address an audience here. It will probably be the last. Residing in a remote section of the country, with private as well as public duties to occupy the whole of my time, it would only be for a very hurried visit, or under some such necessity for a restoration to health as brought me here this season, that I could ever expect to remain long among you, or in any other portion of the Union than the State of which I am a citizen.

I have staid long enough to feel that generous hospitality which evinces itself to-night, which has evinced itself in Boston since I have been here, and showed itself in every town and village of New England where I have gone. I have staid here, too, long enough to learn that, though not represented in Congress, there is a large mass of as true Democrats as are to be found in any portion of the Union within the limits of New England. Their purposes, their construction of the Constitution, their hopes for the future, their respect for the past, is the same as that which exists among my beloved brethren in Mississippi. . . .

In the hour of apprehension I shall turn back to my observations here, in this consecrated hall, where men so early devoted themselves to liberty and community independence; and I shall endeavor to impress upon others, who know you only as you are represented in the two Houses of Congress, how true and how many are the hearts that beat for constitutional liberty, and faithfully respect every clause and guarantee which the Constitution contains for any and every portion of the Union.

APPENDIX F

SPEECH of Davis of Mississippi in the Senate of the United States, on the resolutions offered by him relative to the relations of the states, the federal government, and the territories, May 7, 1860.

Mr. President: Among the many blessings for which we are indebted to our ancestry is that of transmitting to us a written Constitution; a fixed standard to which, in the progress of events, every case may be referred, and by which it may be measured. But for this, the wise men who formed our Government dared not have hoped for its perpetuity; for they saw, floating down the tide of time, wreck after wreck, marking the short life of every republic which had preceded them. With this, however, to check, to restrain, and to direct their posterity, they might reasonably hope the Government they founded should last for ever; that it should secure the great purposes for which it was ordained and established; that it would be the shield of their posterity equally in every part of the country, and equally in all time to come. It was this which mainly distinguished the formation of our Government from those confederacies or republics which had preceded it; and this is the best foundation for our hope to-day. The resolutions which have been read, and which I had the honor to present to the Senate, are little more than the announcement of what I hold to be the clearly-expressed declarations of the Constitution itself. To that fixed standard it is sought, at this time, when we are drifting far from the initial point, and when clouds and darkness hover over us, to bring back the Government, and to test our condition to-day by the rules which our fathers laid down for us in the beginning.

The differences which exist between different portions of the country, the rivalries and the jealousies of to-day, though differing in degree, are exactly of the nature of those which preceded the formation of the Constitution. Our fathers were aware of the different interests of the navigating and planting States, as they were then regarded. They sought to compose those difficulties, and, by compensating advantages given by one to the other, to form a Government equal and just in its operation, and which, like the gentle showers of heaven, should fall twice blessed, blessing him that gives and him that receives. This beneficial action and reaction between the different interests of the country constituted the bond of union and the motive of its formation. They constitute it to-day, if we are sufficiently wise to appreciate our interests, and sufficiently faithful to observe our trust. Indeed, with the extension of territory, with the multiplication of interests, with the varieties, increasing from time to time, of the products of this great country, the bonds which bind the Union together should have increased. Rationally considered, they have increased, because the free trade which was established in the beginning has now become more valuable to the people of the United States than their trade with all the rest of the world.

I do not propose to argue questions of natural rights and inherent powers. I plant my reliance upon the Constitution; that Constitution which you have all sworn to support; that Constitution which you have solemnly pledged yourself to maintain while you hold the seat you now occupy in the Senate; to which you are bound in its spirit and in its letter not grudgingly, but willingly, to render your obedience and support as long as you hold office under the Federal Government.

When the tempter entered the garden of Eden and induced our common mother to offend against the law which God had given to her through Adam, he was the first teacher of that "higher law" which sets the will of the individual above the solemn rule which he is bound, as a part of every community, to observe. From the effect of the introduction of that higher law in the garden of Eden, and the fall consequent upon it, came sin into the world; and from sin came death and banishment and subjugation, as the punishment of sin; the loss of life, unfettered liberty, and perfect happiness followed from that first great law which was given by God to fallen man.

Why, then, shall we talk about natural rights? Who is to define them? Where is the judge who is to sit over the court to try natural rights? What is the era at which you will fix the date by which you will determine the breadth, the length, and the depth of those called the rights of nature? Shall it be after the fall, when the earth was covered with thorns, and man had to earn his bread in the sweat of his brow? Or shall it be when there was equality between the sexes, when he lived in the garden, when all his wants were supplied, and when thorns and thistles were unknown on the face of the earth? Shall it be then? Shall it be after the flood, when, for the first sin committed after the waters retired from the face of the earth, the doom of slavery was fixed upon the mongrel descendants of Ham? If after the flood, and after that decree, how idle is all this prating about natural rights as standing above the obligations of civil government! The Constitution is the law supreme to every American. It is the plighted faith of our fathers; it is the hope of our posterity. I say, then, I come not to argue questions outside of or above the Constitution, but to plead the cause of right, of law and order, under the Constitution, and to plead it to those who have sworn to abide by that obligation.

One of the fruitful sources, as I hold it, of the errors which prevail in our country, is the theory that this is a Government of one people; that the Government of the United States was formed by a mass. The Government of the United States is a compact between the sovereign members who formed it; and, if there be one feature common to all the colonies planted upon the shores of America, it is desire for community independence. It was for this the Puritan, the Huguenot, the Catholic, the Quaker, the Protestant, left the land of their nativity, and, guided by the shadows thrown by the fires of European persecution, they sought and found the American refuge of civil and religious freedom. While they existed as separate and distinct colonies they were not forebearing toward each other. They oppressed opposite religions. They did not come here with the enlarged idea of no established religion. The Puritans drove out the Quakers; the Church-of-England men drove out the Catholics. Persecution reigned through the colonies, except, perhaps, that of the Catholic colony of Maryland; but the rule was—persecution. Therefore, I say the common idea, and the only common idea, was community independence—the right of each independent people to do as they pleased in their domestic affairs.

The Declaration of Independence was made by the colonies, each for itself. The recognition of their independence was not for the colonies united, but for each of the colonies which had maintained its independence; and so, when the

Constitution was formed, the delegates were not elected by the people *en masse,* but they came from each one of the States; and when the Constitution was formed it was referred, not to the people *en masse,* but to the States severally, and severally by them ratified and approved. But, if there be anything which enforces this idea more than another, it is the unequal dates at which it received this approval. From first to last, nearly two years and a half elapsed; and the Government went into operation something like a year—I believe more than a year—before the last ratification was made. Is it then contended that, by this ratification and adoption of the Constitution, the States surrendered that sovereignty which they had previously gained? Can it be that men who braved the perils of the ocean, the privations of the wilderness, who fought the war of the Revolution, in the hour of their success, when all was sunshine and peace around them, came voluntarily forward to lay down that community independence for which they had suffered so much and so long? Reason forbids it; but, if reason did not furnish a sufficient answer, the action of the States themselves forbids it. The great State of New York—great, relatively, then, as she is now—manifested her wisdom in not receiving merely that implication which belongs to the occasion, which was accepted by the other States, but she required the positive assertion of that retention of her sovereignty and power over all her affairs as the condition on which she ratified the Constitution itself. I read from Elliott's *Debates* (page 327). Among her resolutions of ratification is the following:

"That the powers of government may be reassumed by the people whensoever it shall become necessary to their happiness; that every power, jurisdiction, and right which is not by the said Constitution clearly delegated to the Congress of the United States, or the departments of the Government thereof, remain to the people of the several States, or to their respective State governments to which they may have granted the same."

North Carolina, with the Scotch caution which subsequent events have so well justified, in 1788 passed this resolution:

"*Resolved,* That a declaration of rights, asserting and securing from encroachments the great principles of civil and religious liberty, and the unalienable rights of the people, together with amendments to the most ambiguous and exceptionable parts of the said Constitution of Government, ought to be laid before Congress and the convention of the States that shall or may be called for the purpose of amending the said Constitution, for their consideration, previous to the ratification of the Constitution aforesaid, on the part of the State of North Carolina."

And in keeping with this North Carolina withheld her ratification; she allowed the Government to be formed with the number of States which was required to put it in operation, and still she remained out of the Union, asserting and recognized in the independence which she had maintained against Great Britain, and which she had no idea of surrendering to any other power; and the last State which ratified the Constitution long after it had in fact gone into effect, Rhode Island, in the third of her resolutions, says:

"III. That the powers of government may be reassumed by the people whensoever it shall become necessary to their happiness. That the rights of the States respectively to nominate and appoint all State officers, and every other power, jurisdiction, and right, which is not by the said Constitution clearly delegated to the Congress of the United States, or the departments of Government thereof, remain to the people of the several States, or their respective State governments to whom they may have granted the same."

Here the use of the phrase "State governments" shows how utterly unwarrantable the construction has been, to say that the reference here was to the whole people of the States—to the people of all the States—and not to the people of each of the States severally.

I spoke, however, Mr. President, but a moment ago, of the difference of politics, products, population, constituting the great motive for the Union. It was, indeed, its necessity. Had all the people been alike—had their institutions all been the same—there would have been no interest to bring them together; there would have been no cause or necessity for any restraint being imposed upon them. It was the fact that they differed which rendered it necessary to have some law governing their intercourse. It was the fact that their products were opposite—that their pursuits were various—that rendered it the great interest of the people that they should have free trade existing among each other; that free trade which Franklin characterized as being between the States such as existed between the counties of England.

Since that era, however, a fiber then unknown in the United States, and the production of which is dependent upon the domestic institution of African slavery, has come to be cultivated in such amounts, to enter so into the wearing apparel of the world, so greatly to add to the comfort of the poor, that it may be said to-day that that little fiber, cotton, wraps the commercial world and binds it to the United States in bonds to keep the peace with us which no Government dare break. It has built up the Northern States. It is their great manufacturing interest to-day. It supports their shipping abroad. It enables them to purchase in the markets of China, when the high premium to be paid on the milled dollar would otherwise exclude them from that market. These are a part of the blessings resulting from that increase and variety of product which could not have existed if we had all been alike; which would have been lost to-day unless free trade between the United States was still preserved.

And here it strikes me as somewhat strange that a book recently issued has received the commendation of a large number of the representatives of the manufacturing and commercial States, though, apart from its falsification of statistics and low abuse of Southern States, institutions, and interests, the great feature which stands prominently out from it is the arraignment of the South for using their surplus money in buying the manufactures of the North. How a manufacturing and commercial people can be truly represented by those who would inculcate such doctrines as these, is to me passing strange. Is it vain boasting which renders you anxious to proclaim to the world that we buy our buckets, our rakes, and our shovels from you? No, there is too much good sense in the people for that; and, therefore, I am left at a loss to understand the motive, unless it be that deep-rooted hate which makes you blind to your own interest when that interest is weighed in the balance with the denunciation and detraction of your brethren of the South.

The great principle which lay at the foundation of this fixed standard, the Constitution of the United States, was the equality of rights between the States. This was essential; it was necessary; it was a step which had to be taken first, before any progress could be made. It was the essential requisite of the very idea of sovereignty in the State; of a compact voluntarily entered into between sovereigns; and it is that equality of right under the Constitution on which we now insist. But more: when the States united they transferred their forts, their armament, their ships, and their right to maintain armies and navies, to the Federal Government. It was the disarmament of the States, under the operation of a league which made the warlike operations, the powers of defense, common to them all. Then, with this equality of the States, with this disarmament of the States, if there had been nothing in the Constitution to express it, I say the protection of every constitutional right would follow as a necessary incident, and could not be denied by any one who could understand and would admit the true theory of such a Government.

We claim protection, first, because it is our right; secondly, because it is the duty of the General Government; and, thirdly, because we have entered into a compact together, which deprives each State of the power of using all the means which it might employ for its own defense. This is the general theory of the right of protection. What is the exception to it? Is there an exception? If so, who made it? Does the Constitution discriminate between different kinds of property? Did the Constitution attempt to assimilate the institutions of the different States confederated together? Was there a single State in this Union that would have been so unfaithful to the principles which had prompted them in their colonial position, and which had prompted them, at a still earlier period, to seek and try the temptations of the wilderness; is there one which would have consented to allow the Federal Government to control or to discriminate between her institutions and those of her confederate States?

But, if it be contended that this is argument, and that you need authority, I will draw it from the fountain; from the spring before it had been polluted; from the debates in the formation of the Constitution; from the views of those who at least it will be admitted understood what they were doing.

Mr. Randolph, it will be recollected, introduced a *projet* for a Government, consisting of a series of resolutions. Among them was one which proposed to give Congress the power "to call forth the force of the Union against any member of the Union failing to fulfill its duty under the articles thereof." That was, to give Congress the power to coerce the States; to bring the States into subjection to the Federal Government. Now, sir, let us see how that was treated; and first I will refer to one whose wisdom, as we take a retrospective view, seems to me marvelous. Not conspicuous in debate, at least not among the names which first occur when we think of that bright galaxy of patriots and statesmen, he was the man who, above all others, it seems to me, laid his finger upon every danger, and indicated the course which that danger was to take. I refer to Mr. Mason.

"Mr. Mason observed, not only that the present Confederation was deficient in not providing for coercion and punishment against delinquent States, but argued very cogently that punishment could not, in the nature of things, be executed on the States collectively; and, therefore, that such a Government was necessary as could directly operate on individuals, and would punish those only whose guilt required it."[1]

---

[1] Elliott's *Debates*, Vol. V, p. 133.

Mr. Madison, who has been called sometimes the father of the Constitution, upon the same question, said:

"A union of the States containing such an ingredient seemed to provide for its own destruction. The use of force against a State would look more like a declaration of war than an infliction of punishment, and would probably be considered by the party attacked as a dissolution of all previous compacts by which it might be bound."

Mr. Hamilton, who, if I were to express a judgment by way of comparison, I would say was the master intellect of the age in which he lived, whose mind seemed to penetrate profoundly every question with which he grappled, and who seldom failed to exhaust the subject which he treated—Mr. Hamilton, in speaking of the various powers necessary to maintain a Government, came to clause four:

"4. Force, by which may be understood a *coercion of laws, or coercion of arms.* Congress have not the former, except in few cases. In particular States, this coercion is nearly sufficient; though he held it, in most cases not entirely so. A certain portion of military force is absolutely necessary in large communities. Massachusetts is now feeling this necessity, and making provision for it. But how can this force be exerted on the States collectively? It is impossible. It amounts to a war between the parties. Foreign powers, also, will not be idle spectators. They will interpose; the confusion will increase; and a dissolution of the Union will ensue."

The consequence was, the proposition was lost. In support of this same idea of community independence, which I have suggested, the argument upon the proposition least likely to have exhibited it, that to give power to restrain the slave-trade, shows the Northern and Southern men all arguing and presenting different views, yet concurred in this, that there could be no power to restrain a State from importing what she pleased. As the Senator from Vermont [Mr. Collamer] looks somewhat surprised at my statement, I will refer to the authority. Mr. Rutledge said:

"Religion and humanity had nothing to do with this question. Interest alone is the governing principle with nations. The true question at present is, whether the Southern States shall or shall not be parties to the Union. If the Northern States consult their interest, they will not oppose the increase of slaves, which will increase the commodities of which they will become the carriers."[2]

Mr. Pinckney: "South Carolina can never receive the plan if it prohibits the slave-trade. In every proposed extension of the powers of Congress, that State has expressly and watchfully excepted that of meddling with the importation of negroes. If the States be all left at liberty on this subject, South Carolina may, perhaps, by degrees, do of herself what is wished, as Virginia and Maryland already have done."[3]

"Mr. Sherman was for leaving the clause as it stands. He disapproved of the slave-trade; yet, as the States were now possessed of the right to import slaves, as the public good did not require it to be taken from them, and as it was expedient

[2]*Ibid.*, p. 457.
[3]Elliott's *Debates*, Vol. V, p. 457.

to have as few objections as possible to the proposed scheme of government, he thought it best to leave the matter as we find it."[4]

"Mr. Baldwin had conceived national objects alone to be before the Convention: not such as, like the present, were of a local nature. Georgia was decided on this point. That State has always hitherto supposed a General Government to be the pursuit of the central States, who wished to have a vortex for everything; that her distance would preclude her from equal advantage; and that she could not prudently purchase it by yielding national powers. From this, it might be understood in what light she would view an attempt to abridge one of her favorite prerogatives.

"If left to herself, she may probably put a stop to the evil. As one ground for this conjecture, he took notice of the sect of ————, which, he said was a respectable class of people who carried their ethics beyond the mere *equality of men,* extending their humanity to the claims of the whole animal creation."[5]

"Mr. Gerry thought we had nothing to do with the conduct of the States as to slaves, but ought to be careful not to give any sanction to it."[6]

"Mr. King thought the subject should be considered in a political light only. If two States will not agree to the Constitution, as stated on one side, he could affirm with equal belief, on the other, that great and equal opposition would be experienced from the other States. He remarked on the exemption of slaves from duty, while every other import was subjected to it, as an inequality that could not fail to strike the commercial sagacity of the Northern and Middle States."[7]

Here, as will be observed, everywhere was recognized and admitted the doctrine of community independence and State equality—no interference with the institutions of a State—no interference even prospectively save and except with their consent; and thus it followed that at one time it was proposed to except, from the power to prohibit the further introduction of Africans, those States which insisted upon retaining the power; and finally it was agreed that a date should be fixed beyond which, probably, none of them desired to retain it. These were States acting in their sovereign capacity; they possessed power to do as they pleased; and that was the view which they took of it. I ask, then, how are we, their descendants, those holding under their authority, to assume a power which they refused to admit, upon principles eternal and lying at the foundation of the Constitution itself?

If, then, there be no such distinction or discrimination; if protection be the duty (and who will deny it?) with which this Government is charged, and for which the States pay taxes, because of which they surrendered their armies and their navies; if general protection be the general duty, I ask, in the name of reason and constitutional right—I ask you to point me to authority by which a discrimination is made between slave-property and any other. Yet this is the question now fraught with evil to our country. It is this which has raised the hurricane threatening to sweep our political institutions before it. This is the dark spot which some already begin to fear may blot out the constellation of the Union from the political firmament of mankind. Does it not become us, then, calmly to consider it, justly to

[4] *Ibid.*
[5] *Ibid.,* p. 459.
[6] *Ibid.*
[7] *Ibid.,* p. 460.

weigh it; to hold it in balances from which the dust has been blown, in order that we may see where truth, right, and the obligations of the Constitution require us to go?

It may be pardoned to one who, from his earliest youth up, has been connected with a particular party, who has always believed that the welfare and the safety of the country most securely rested with that party, who has seen in the triumph of Democracy the triumph of the Union, and who has believed for years past that the downfall of Democracy would be its destruction—it may be pardoned, I say, under such circumstances as these, to such a person as that, to refer even in this connection to that feature of the particular point which I am discussing, which has been brought forward by the recent action of that party. States met together to consult as brethren, to see whether they could agree as well upon the candidate as upon the creed, and it was apparent that division had entered into our ranks. After days of discussion, we saw that party convention broken. We saw the enemies of Democracy waiting to be invited to its funeral, and jestingly looking into the blank faces of those of us to whom the telegraph brought the sad intelligence. I hope this is, however, but the mist of the morning. I have faith in the Democracy, and that it still lives. I have faith in the patriotism and in the good sense of the Democracy, that they will assert the truth, boldly pronounce it, meet the issue, and I trust in the good sense and patriotism of the people for their success.

In this connection, it may be permissible to review our present party condition. For a long time two parties divided the people of the United States. The controversy was mainly upon questions of expediency; sometimes of constitutionality. They divided men in all of the States. The contest was sometimes won by one, and sometimes by the other. The Whig party lives now but in history, yet it has a history of which any of its members may be proud. It bore the high but not successful part of stemming the tide of popular impulse, and thus failed to attain the highest power. Differing from them upon the points at issue, I offer the homage of my respect to those who, adhering to what they believed to be true, go down sooner than find success in the abandonment of principle. With the disappearance of that party—and perhaps for the very reasons that caused its disappearance— up rose radical organizations who strode so far beyond progressive Democracy that Democracy took the place now left vacant by the old Whig party, and became the reservoir into which all conservatism was poured. Therefore it is that so many of those men, eminent in their day, eminent for their services, eminent in their history, have approved of the Democratic party in the present condition of the country as the only conservative element which remains in our politics. In the midst of this radicalism, of this revolutionary tendency, it becomes not the regret of a partisan merely; it is the sadness of an American citizen, that the party on which the conservative hopes of the country hang has been threatened with division, and possibly may not hereafter be united. Thanks to a sanguine temperament, thanks to an abiding faith, thanks to a confidence in the Providence which has so long ruled for good the destiny of my country, I believe it will reunite, and reunite upon sound and acceptable principles. At least, I hope so.

From the postulates which I have laid down result the fourth and fifth resolutions. They are the two which I expect to be opposed. They contain the assertion of the equality of rights of all the people of the United States in the Territories, and they declare the obligation of the Congress to see these rights protected. I admit that the United States may acquire eminent domain. I admit that the United States may have sovereignty over territory; otherwise the sovereign jurisdiction which we obtained by conquest or treaty would not pass to us. I deny that their agent, the Federal Government, under the existing Constitution, can have eminent domain; I deny that it can have sovereignty. I consider it as the mere agent of the States—an agent of limited power; and that it can do nothing save that which the Constitution empowers it to perform; and that, though the treaty or the deed of cession may direct or control, it can not enlarge or expand the powers of the Congress; that it is not sovereign in any essential particular. It has functions to perform, and those functions I propose now to consider.

The power of Congress over the Territories—a subject not well defined in the Constitution of the United States—has been drawn from various sources by different advocates of that power. One has found it in the grant of power to dispose of the Territory and other public property. That is to say, because the agent was authorized to sell a particular thing, or to dispose of it by grant or barter, therefore he has sovereign power over that and all else which the principal, constituting him an agent, may hereafter acquire! The property, besides the land, consisted of forts, of ships, of armaments, and other things which had belonged to the States in their separate capacity, and were turned over to the Government of the Confederation, and transferred to the Government of the United States, and of this, together with the land so transferred, the Federal Government had the power to dispose; and of territory thereafter acquired, of arms thereafter made or purchased, of forts thereafter constructed, or custom-houses, or docks, or lights, or buoys; of all these, of course, it had power to dispose. It had the power to create them; it must, of necessity, have had the power to dispose of them. It was only necessary to confer the power to dispose of those things which the Federal Government did not create, of those things which came to it from the States, and over which they might signify their will for its control.

I look upon it as the mere power to dispose of, for considerations and objects defined in the trust, the land held in the United States, none of which then was within the limits of the States, and the other public property which the United States received from the States after the formation of the Union. I do not agree with those who say the Government has no power to establish a temporary and civil government within a Territory. I stand half-way between the extremes of squatter sovereignty and of Congressional sovereignty. I hold that the Congress has power to establish a civil government; that it derives it from the grants of the Constitution—not the one which is referred to; and I hold that that power is limited and restrained, first, by the Constitution itself, and then by every rule of popular liberty and sound discretion, to the narrowest limits which the necessities of the case require. The Congress has power to defend the territory, to repel invasions, to suppress insurrection; the Congress has power to see the laws executed. For this it may have a civil magistracy—territorial courts. It has the power to establish a Federal judiciary. To that Federal judiciary, from these local courts, may come up to be decided questions with regard to the laws of the United States and the Constitution of the United States. These, combined, give power to establish a temporary government, sufficient, perhaps, for the simple wants of the inhabitants of a Territory, until they shall acquire the population, until they shall have the resources and the interests which justify them in becoming a State. I am sustained in this view of the case by an opinion of the Supreme Court of the United States in 1845, in the case of Pollard's Lessee *vs.* P. Hagan (3 Howard, 222, 223), in which the court say:

"Taking the legislative acts of the United States, and the States of Virginia and Georgia, and their deeds of cession to the United States, and giving to each separately, and to all jointly, a fair interpretation, we must come to the conclusion that it was the intention of the parties to invest the United States with the eminent domain of the country ceded, both national and municipal, for the purposes of temporary government; and to hold it in trust for the performance of the stipulations and conditions expressed in the deeds of cession and the legislative acts connected with them."

This was a question of land. It was land lying between high and low water, over which the United States claimed to have and to exercise authority, because of the terms on which Alabama had been admitted into the Union. In that connection the Court say, in the same case:

"When Alabama was admitted into the Union, on an equal footing with the original States, she succeeded to all the rights of sovereignty, jurisdiction, and eminent domain which Georgia possessed at the date of the cession, except so far as this right was diminished by the public lands remaining in the possession and under the control of the United States for the temporary purpose provided for in the deeds of cession and the legislative acts connected with it. Nothing remained in the United States, according to the terms of the agreement, but the public lands; and if an express stipulation had been inserted in the agreement, granting the municipal right of sovereignty and eminent domain to the United States, such stipulation would have been void and inoperative; because the United States has no constitutional capacity to exercise municipal jurisdiction, sovereignty, or eminent domain within the limits of a State or elsewhere, except in the cases in which it is expressly granted."

Another case arose not long afterward, in which not land, but religion, was involved, where suit was brought against the municipality of New Orleans because they would not allow a dead body to be exposed at a place where, according to the religious rites of those interested, it was deemed they had a right thus to expose it. On that the Supreme Court say, speaking of the ordinance for the government of Louisiana:

"So far as they conferred political rights and secured civil and religious liberties (which are political rights) the laws of Congress were all suspended by the State Constitution; nor is any part of them in force, unless they were adopted by the Constitution of Louisiana, as laws of the State."[8]

Thus we find the Supreme Court sustaining the proposition that the Federal Government has power to establish a temporary civil government within the limits of a Territory, but that it can enact no law which will endure beyond the temporary purposes for which such government was established. In other cases the decisions of the Court run in the same line; and in 1855 the then Attorney-General, most learned in his profession—and in what else is he not learned, for he may be said to be a man of universal acquirements?—Attorney-General Cushing

---

[8] *Permoli vs. First Municipality,* 3 Howard, 610.

then foretold what must have been the decision of the Supreme Court on the Missouri Compromise, anticipating the decision subsequently made in the case of Dred Scott; that decision for which the venerable justices have been so often and so violently arraigned. He foretold it as the necessary consequence from the line of precedents descending from 1842, affirmed and reaffirmed in different cases, and now bearing on a case similar in principle, and only different in the mere reference to the subject involved from those which had gone before. As connected with the decision which had agitated the peace of the country; as the anticipation of that decision before it was made, viewing it as the necessary consequence of the decision the court had made before; if it be the pleasure of the Senate, I ask my friend from South Carolina [Mr. Chesnut] to read for me a letter of the Attorney-General, being an official answer made by him in relation to the military reservation which was involved in the question before him.

Mr. Chesnut read from the "Opinions of the Attorneys-General," vol. vii, page 575:

"The Supreme Court has determined that the United States never held any municipal sovereignty, jurisdiction, or right of soil in the territory of which any of the new States have been formed, except for temporary purposes, and to execute the trusts created by the deeds of cession. . . .

"By the force of the same principle, and in the same line of adjudications, the Supreme Court would have had to decide that the provision of the act of March 6, 1820, which undertakes to determine in advance the municipal law of all that portion of the original province of Louisiana which lies north of the parallel 36° 30' north latitude, was null and void *ab incepto*, if it had not been repealed by a recent act of Congress. (Compare iv, Statutes at Large, p. 848, and x, Statutes at Large, p. 289.) For an act of Congress which pretends of right, and without consent of compact, to impose on the municipal power of any new State or States limitations and restrictions not imposed on all, is contrary to the fundamental condition of the Confederation, according to which there is to be equality of right between the old and new States 'in all respects whatsoever.' "

Mr. Davis: It was not long after this official opinion of the Attorney-General before the case arose on which the decision was made which has so agitated the country. Fortunate indeed was it for the public peace that land and religion had been decided—those questions on which men might reason had been the foundation of judicial decision—before that which drives all reason, it seems, from the mind of man, came to be presented the question whether Cuffee should be kept in his normal condition or not; the question whether the Congress of the United States could decide what might or might not be property in a Territory— the case being that of an officer of the army sent into a Territory to perform his public duty, having taken with him his negro slave. The court, however, in giving their decision in this case—or their opinion, if it suits gentlemen better—have gone into the question with such clearness, such precision, and such amplitude, that it will relieve me from the necessity of arguing it any further than to make a reference to some sentences contained in that opinion. And here let me say, I can not see how those who agreed on a former occasion that the constitutional right of the slaveholder to take his property into the Territory—the constitutional power of the Congress and the constitutional power of the Territory to legislate upon that subject—should be a judicial question, can now attempt to escape the operation of an opinion which covers the exact political question which, it was known beforehand, the Court would be called upon to decide. Decided in strictness of technical language, it was known it could not be. Hundreds, thousands, a vast variety of cases may arise, and centuries elapse, and leave that Court if our Union still exists, deciding questions in relation to that character of property in the Territories; but the great and fundamental idea was that, after thirty years of angry controversy, dividing the people and paralyzing the arm of the Federal Government, some umpire should be sought which would compose the difficulty and set it upon a footing to leave us in future to proceed in peace; and that umpire was selected which the Constitution had provided to decide questions of law. I ask my friend to read some extracts from the decision.

Mr. Chesnut read as follows, from the case of Dred Scott *vs.* Sandford, pp. 55-57:

"The Territory being a part of the United States, the Government and the citizen both entered it under the authority of the Constitution, with their respective rights defined and marked out; and the Federal Government can exercise no power over his person or property beyond what that instrument confers, nor lawfully deny any right which it has reserved. . . .

"The powers over person and property, of which we speak, are not only not granted to Congress, but are in express terms denied, and they are forbidden to exercise them. And this prohibition is not confined to the States, but the words are general, and extend to the whole territory over which the Constitution gives it power to legislate, including those portions of it remaining under territorial government, as well as that covered by States. It is a total absence of power everywhere within the dominion of the United States, and places the citizens of a Territory, so far as these rights are concerned, on the same footing with citizens of the States, and guards them as firmly and plainly against any inroads which the General Government might attempt under the plea of implied or incidental powers. And if Congress itself can not do this—if it is beyond the powers conferred on the Federal Government—it will be admitted, we presume, that it could not authorize a territorial government to exercise them. It could confer no power on any local government, established by its authority, to violate the provisions of the Constitution. . . .

"And if the Constitution recognizes the right of property of the master in the slave, and makes no distinction between that description of property and other property owned by a citizen, no tribunal, acting under the authority of the United States, whether it be legislative, executive, or judicial, has a right to draw such a distinction, or deny to it the benefit of the provisions and guarantees which have been provided for the protection of private property against the encroachments of the Government. . . .

"This is done in plain words—too plain to be misunderstood. And no word can be found in the Constitution which gives Congress a greater power over slave-property, or which entitles property of that kind to less protection than property of any other description. The only power conferred is the power coupled with the duty of guarding and protecting the owner in his rights.

"Upon these considerations, it is the opinion of the Court that the act of Congress which prohibited a citizen from holding and owning property of this kind, in the territory of the United States north of the line therein mentioned, is not warranted by the Constitution, and is therefore void; and that neither Dred Scott himself, nor any of his family, were made free by being carried into this territory, even if they had been carried there by the owner, with the intention of becoming a permanent resident."

Mr. Davis: Here, then, Mr. President, I say the umpire selected as the referee in the controversy has decided that neither the Congress nor its agent, the territorial government, has the power to invade or impair the right of property within the limits of a Territory. I will not inquire whether it be technically a decision or not. It was obligatory on those who selected the umpire and agreed to abide by the award.

It is well known to those who have been associated with me in the two Houses of Congress that, from the commencement of the question, I have been the determined opponent of what is called squatter sovereignty. I never gave it countenance, and I am now least of all disposed to give it quarter. In 1848 it made its appearance for good purposes. It was ushered in by a great and good man. He brought it forward because of that distrust which he had in the capacity of the Government to bear the rude shock to which it was exposed. His apprehension, no doubt, to some extent sharpened and directed his patriotism, and his reflection led him to a conclusion to which, I doubt not, to-day he adheres as tenaciously as ever; but from which it was my fortune, good or ill, to dissent when his letter was read to me in manuscript—I being, together with some other persons, asked, though not by the writer, whether or not it should be sent. At the first blush I believed it to be a fallacy—a fallacy fraught with mischief; that it escaped an issue which was upon us which it was our duty to meet; that it escaped it by a side path, which led to a greater danger. I thought it a fallacy which would surely be exploded. I doubted then, and still more for some time afterward, when held to a dread responsibility for the position which I occupied. I doubted whether I should live to see that fallacy exploded. It has been more speedily, and, to the country, more injuriously than I anticipated. In the mean time, what has been its operations? Let Kansas speak—the first great field on which the trial was made. What was then the consequence? The Federal Government withdrawing control, leaving the contending sections, excited to the highest point upon this question, each to send forth its army, Kansas became the battle-field, and Kansas the cry, which well nigh led to civil war. This was the first fruit. More deadly than the fatal upas, its effect was not limited to the mere spot of ground on which the dew fell from its leaves, but it spread throughout the United States; it kindled all which had been collected for years of inflammable material. It was owing to the strength of our Government and the good sense of the quiet masses of the people that it did not wrap our country in one widespread conflagration.

What right had Congress then, or what right has it now, to abdicate any power conferred upon it as trustee of the States? What right had Congress then, or has it now, to shrink from the performance of a duty because the mere counters spread on the table may be swept off, when they have not answered the purpose for which they were placed? What is it to you, or me, or any one, when we weight our own continuation in place against the great interests of which we are conservators; against the welfare of the country, and the liberty of our posterity to the remotest ages? What is it, I say, which can be counted in the balance on our side against the performance of that duty which is imposed upon us? If any one believes

Congress has not the constitutional power, he acts conscientiously in insisting upon Congress not usurping it. If any one believes that the squatters upon the lands of the United States within a Territory are invested with sovereignty, having won it by some of these processes unknown to history, without grant, or without revolution, without money and without price, he, adhering to the theory, may pursue it to its conclusion. To the first class, who claim sovereign power over the Territories for Congress, I say, lay your hand upon the Constitution, and find there the warrant of your authority. Of the second, those of whom I have last spoken, I ask, in the Constitution, reason, right, or justice, what is there to sustain your theory?

The phraseology which has been employed on this question seems to me to betray a strange confusion of ideas—to speak of a sovereignty, a plenary legislative power deriving its power from an agent; a sovereignty held subject to articles with the formation of which that sovereignty had nothing to do; a compact to which it was not a party! You say to a sovereign: "A and B have agreed on certain terms between themselves, and you must govern your conduct according to them; yet I do not deny your sovereignty!" That is, the power to do as they please, provided it conforms to the rule which others chose to lay down! Can this be a definition of sovereignty?

But again, sir, nothing seems to me more illogical than the argument that this power is acquired by a grant from the Congress, connected with the other argument that Congress have not got the power to do the act themselves; that is to say, that the recipient takes more than the giver possessed; that a Territorial Legislature can do anything which a State Legislature can do, and that "subject to the Constitution" means merely the restraints imposed upon both. This is confounding the whole theory and the history of our Government. The States were the grantors; they made the compact; they gave the Federal agent its powers; they inhibited themselves from doing certain things, and all else they retained to themselves. This Federal agent got just so much as the States chose to give— no more. It could do nothing save by warrant of the authority of the grant made by the States. Therefore its powers are not comparable to the powers of the State Legislature, because one is the creature of grant, and the other the exponent of sovereign power. The Supreme Court have covered the whole ground of the relation of the Congress to the Territorial Legislatures—the agent of the States and the agent of the Congress—and the restrictions put upon the one are those put upon the other, in language so clear as to render it needless further to labor the subject.

In 1850, following the promulgation of this notion of squatter sovereignty, we had the idea of non-intervention introduced into the Senate of the United States, and it is strange to me how that idea has expanded. It seems to have been more malleable than gold; to have been hammered out to an extent that covers boundless regions undiscovered by those who proclaimed the doctrine. Non-intervention then meant, as the debates show, that Congress should neither prohibit nor establish slavery in the Territories. That I hold to now. Will any one suppose that Congress then meant by non-intervention that Congress should legislate in no regard in respect to property in slaves? Why, sir, the very acts which they passed at the time refute it. There is the fugitive slave law, and that abomination of laws which assumed to confiscate the property of a citizen who should attempt to bring it into this District with intent to remove it to sell it at some other time and at some other place. Congress acted then upon the subject —acted beyond the limit of its authority, as I believed, confidently believed; and, if ever that act comes before the Supreme Court, I feel satisfied they will declare it null and void. Are we to understand that those men, thus acting at the very moment, intended by non-intervention to deny and repudiate the laws they were then creating? The man who stood most prominently the advocate of the measures of that year, who, great in many periods of our history, perhaps shone then with the brightest light his genius ever emitted—I refer to Henry Clay—has given his own view on this subject; and I suppose he may be considered as the highest authority. On June 18, 1850, I had introduced an amendment to the compromise bill, providing:

"And that all laws, or parts of laws, usages, or customs, preëxisting in the Territories acquired by the United States from Mexico, and which in said Territories restrict, abridge, or obstruct, the full enjoyment of any right of person or property of a citizen of the United States, as recognized or guaranteed by the Constitution or laws of the United States, are hereby declared and shall be held as repealed."

Upon that, Mr. Clay said:

"*Mr. President:* I thought that upon this subject there had been a clear understanding in the Senate that the Senate would not decide itself upon the *lex loci* as it respects slavery; that the Senate would not allow the Territorial Legislature to pass any law upon that question. In other words, that it would leave the operation of the local law, or of the Constitution of the United States upon that local law, to be decided by the proper and competent tribunal—the Supreme Court of the United States."[9]

That was the position taken by Mr. Clay, the leader. A mere sentence will show with what view I regarded the dogma of non-intervention when that amendment was offered. I said:

"But what is non-intervention seems to vary as often as the light and shade of every fleeting cloud. It has different meanings in every State, in every county, in every town. If non-intervention means that we shall not have protection for our property in slaves, then I always was, and always shall be, opposed to it. If it means that we shall not have the protection of the law because it would favor slaveholders, that Congress shall not legislate so as to secure to us the benefits of the Constitution, then I am opposed to non-intervention, and shall always be opposed to it."[10]

Mr. Downs, one of the Committee of Thirteen, and an advocate of the measures, said:

"What I understand by non-intervention is, an interposition of Congress prohibiting, or establishing, or interfering with slavery."[11]

By what species of legerdemain this doctrine of non-intervention has come to extend to a paralysis of the Government on the whole subject, to exclude the Congress from any kind of legislation whatever, I am at a loss to conceive. Certain it is, it was not the theory of that period, and it was not contended for in all

[9] *Appendix to Congressional Globe,* Thirty-first Congress, First Session, p. 916.
[10] *Appendix to Congressional Globe,* Thirty-first Congress, First Session, p. 919.
[11] *Appendix to Congressional Globe,* Thirty-first Congress, First Session, p. 99

the controversies we had then. I had no faith in it then; I considered it an evasion; I held that the duty of Congress ought to be performed; that the issue was before us, and ought to be met, the sooner the better; that truth would prevail if presented to the people; borne down to-day, it would rise up to-morrow; and I stood then on the same general plea which I am making now. The Senator from Illinois [Mr. Douglas] and myself differed at that time, as I presume we do now. We differed radically then. He opposed every proposition which I made, voting against propositions to give power to a Territorial Legislature to protect slave-property which should be taken there; to remove the obstructions of the Mexican laws; voting for a proposition to exclude the conclusion that slavery might be taken there; voting for the proposition expressly to prohibit its introduction; voting for the proposition to keep in force the laws of Mexico which prohibit it. Some of these votes, it is but just to him I should say, I think he gave perforce of his instructions; but others of them, I think it is equally fair to suppose, were outside of the limits of any instructions which could have been given before the fact.

In 1854, advancing in this same general line of thought, the Congress, in enacting territorial bills, left out a provision which had before been usually contained in them, requiring the Legislature of the Territory to submit its laws to the Congress of the United States. It has been sometimes assumed that this was the recognition of the power of the Territorial Legislature to exercise plenary legislation, as might that of a State. It will be remembered that, when our present form of government was instituted, there were those who believed the Federal Government should have the power of revision over the laws of a State. It was long and ably contended for in the Convention which formed the Constitution; and one of the compromises which was made was an appellate power—to lodge power in the Supreme Court to decide all questions of constitutional law.

But did this omission of the obligation to send here the laws of the Territories work this grant of power to the Territorial Legislature? Certainly not; it could not; and that it did not is evinced by the fact that, at a subsequent period, the organic act was revised because the legislation of the Territory of Kansas was offensive to the Congress of the United States. Congress could not abdicate its authority; it could not abandon its trust; and, when it omitted the requirement that the laws should be sent back, it created a *casus* which required it to act without the official records being laid before it, as they would have been if the obligation had existed. That was all the difference. It was not enforcing upon the agent the obligation to send the information. It left Congress, as to its power, just where it was. I find myself physically unable to go as fully into the subject as I intended, and therefore, omitting a reference to those acts, suffice it to say that here was the recognition of the obligation of Congress to interpose against a Territorial Legislature for the protection of personal right. That is what we ask of Congress now. I am not disposed to ask this Congress to go into speculative legislation. I am not one of those who would willingly see this Congress enact a code to be applied to all Territories and for all time to come. I only ask that cases, as they arise, may be met according to the exigency. I ask that when personal and property rights in the Territories are not protected, then the Congress, by existing laws and governmental machinery, shall intervene and provide such means as will secure in each case, as far as may be, an adequate remedy.

I ask no slave code, nor horse code, nor machine code. I ask that the Territorial Legislature be made to understand beforehand that the Congress of the United States does not concede to them the power to interfere with the rights of person or property guaranteed by the Constitution, and that it will apply the remedy, if the Territorial Legislature should so far forget its duty, so far transcend its power, as to commit that violation of right. That is the announcement of the fifth resolution.

These are the general views which I entertain of our right of protection and the duty of the Government. They are those which are entertained by the constituency I have the honor to represent, whose delegation has recently announced those principles at Charleston. I honor them, and I approve their conduct. I think their bearing was worthy of the mother-State which sent them there; and I doubt not she will receive them with joy and gratitude. They have asserted and vindicated her equality of right. By that asserted equality of right I doubt not she will stand. For weal or for woe, for prosperity or adversity, for the preservation of the great blessings which we enjoy, or the trial of a new and separate condition, I trust Mississippi never will surrender the smallest atom of the sovereignty, independence, and equality, to which she was born, to avoid any danger or any sacrifice to which she may hereby be exposed.

The sixth resolution of the series declares at what time a State may form a Constitution and decide upon her domestic institutions. I deny this right to the territorial condition, because the Territory belongs in common to the States. Every citizen of the United States, as a joint owner of that Territory, has a right to go into it with any property which he may possess. These territorial inhabitants require municipal law, police, and government. They should have them, but they should be restricted to their own necessities. They have no right within their municipal power to attempt to decide the rights of the people of the States. They have no right to exclude any citizen of the United States from owning and equally enjoying this common possession; it is for the purpose of preserving order, and giving protection to rights of person and property, that a municipal territorial government should be instituted.

The last resolution refers to a law founded on a provision of the Constitution, which contains an obligation of faith to every State of the Union; and that obligation of faith has been violated by thirteen States of the Confederacy—as many as originally fought the battles of the Revolution and established the Confederation. Is it to be expected that a compact thus broken in part, violated in its important features, will be regarded as binding in all else? Is the free trade which the North sought in the formation of the Union, and for which the States generally agreed to give Congress the power to regulate commerce, to be trampled under foot by laws of obstruction, not giving to the citizens of the South that free transit across the territory of the Northern States which we might claim from any friendly state under Christendom; and is Congress to stand powerless by, on the doctrine of non-intervention? We have a right to claim abstinence from interference with our rights from any Government on the earth. Shall we claim no more from that which we have constituted for our own purposes, and which we support by draining our own means for its support?

We have had agitation, changing in its form, and gathering intensity, for the last forty years. It was first for political power, and directed against new States;

now it has assumed a social form, is all-prevailing, and has reached the point of revolution and civil war. For it was only last fall that an overt act was committed by men who were sustained by arms and money, raised by extensive combination among the non-slaveholding States, to carry treasonable war against the State of Virginia, because now, as before the Revolution, and ever since, she held the African in bondage. This is part of the history and marks the necessity of the times. It warns us to stop and reflect, to go back to the original standard, to measure our acts by the obligation of our fathers, by the pledges they made one to the other, to see whether we are conforming to our plighted faith, and to ask seriously, solemnly, looking each other inquiringly in the face, what we should do to save our country.

This agitation being at first one of sectional pride for political power, has at last degenerated or grown up to (as you please) a trade. There are men who habitually set aside a portion of money which they are annually to apply to what are called "charitable purposes"—that is to say, so far as I understand it, to support some vagrant lecturer, whose purpose is agitation and mischief wherever he goes. This constitutes, therefore, a trade; a class of people are thus employed —employed for mischief, for incendiary purposes, perhaps not always understood by those who furnish the money; but such is the effect; such is the result of their action; and in this state of the case I call upon the Senate to affirm the great principles on which our institutions rest. In no spirit of crimination have I stated the reasons why I present it. For these reasons I call upon them now to restrain the growth of evil passion, and to bring back the public sense as far as in them lies, by earnest and united effort, if it may be, to crown our country with peace, and start it once more in its primal channel on a career of progressive prosperity and justice.

The majority section can not be struggling for additional power in order to preserve their rights. If any of them ever believed in what is called Southern aggression, they know now they have the majority in the representative districts and in the electoral college. They can not, therefore, fear an invasion of their rights. They need no additional political power to protect them from that. The argument, then, or the reason on which this agitation commenced, has passed away; and yet we are asked, if a party hostile to our institutions shall gain possession of the Government, that we shall stand quietly by, and wait for an overt act. Overt act! Is not a declaration of war an overt act? What would be thought of a country that, after a declaration of war, and while the enemy's fleets were upon the sea, should wait until a city had been sacked before it would say that war existed, or resistance should be made? The power of resistance consists, in no small degree, in meeting the evil at the outer gate. I can speak for myself—and I have no right to speak for others—when I say that, if I belonged to a party organized on the basis of making war on any section or interest in the United States, if I know myself, I would instantly quit it. We have made no war against you. We have asked no discrimination in our favor. We claim to have but the Constitution fairly and equally administered. To consent to less than this would be to sink in the scale of manhood; would be to make our posterity so degraded that they would curse this generation for robbing them of the rights their Revolutionary fathers bequeathed them. . . .

Among the great purposes declared in the preamble of the Constitution is one to provide for the general welfare. Provision for the general welfare implies general fraternity. This Union was not expected to be held together by coercion; the power of force as a means was denied. They sought, however, to bind it perpetually together with that which was stronger than triple bars of brass and steel—the ceaseless current of kind offices, renewing and renewed in an eternal flow, and gathering volume and velocity as it rolled. It was a function intended not for the injury of any. It declared its purpose to be the benefit of all. Concessions which were made between the different States in the Convention prove the motive. Each gave to the other what was necessary to it; what each could afford to spare. Young as a nation, our triumphs under this system have had no parallel in human history. We have tamed a wilderness; we have spanned a continent. We have built up a granary that secures the commercial world against the fear of famine. Higher than all this, we have achieved a moral triumph. We have received, by hundreds of thousands, a constant tide of immigrants—energetic, if not well educated, fleeing, some from want, some from oppression, some from the penalties of violated law—received them into our society; and by the gentle suasion of a Government which exhibits no force, by removing want and giving employment, they have subsided into peaceful citizens, and have increased the wealth and power of our country.

If, then, this temple so blessed, and to the roof of which we were about to look to see it extended over the continent, giving a protecting arm to infant republics that need it—if this temple is tottering on its pillars, what, I ask, can be a higher or nobler duty for the Senate to perform than to rush to its pillars and uphold them, or be crushed in the attempt? We have tampered with a question which has grown in magnitude by each year's delay. It requires to be plainly met—the truth to be told. The patriotism and the sound sense of the people, whenever the Federal Government from its high places of authority shall proclaim the truth in unequivocal language, will, in my firm belief, receive and approve it. But so long as we deal, like the Delphic oracle, in words of double meaning, so long as we attempt to escape from responsibility, and exhibit our fear to declare the truth by the fact that we do not act upon it, we must expect speculative theory to occupy the mind of the public, and error to increase as time rolls on. But, if the sad fate should be ours, for this most minute cause, to destroy our Government, the historian who shall attempt philosophically to examine the question will, after he has put on his microscopic glasses and discovered it, be compelled to cry out, "Veritably so the unseen insect in the course of time destroys the mighty oak!" Now, I believe—may I not say I believe? if not, then I hope—there is yet time, by the full, explicit declaration of the truth, to disabuse the popular mind, to arouse the popular heart, to expose the danger from lurking treason and ill-concealed hostility; to rally a virtuous people to their country's rescue, who, circling closer and deeper as the storm gathers fury, around the ark of their fathers' covenant, will place it in security, there happily to remain a sign of fraternity, justice, and equality, to our remotest posterity.

APPENDIX G

CORRESPONDENCE between the commissioners of South Carolina and the President of the United States (Buchanan) relative to the forts in the harbor of Charleston.

LETTER OF THE COMMISSIONERS TO THE PRESIDENT

Washington, December 28, 1860.

Sir: We have the honor to transmit to you a copy of the full powers from the Convention of the People of South Carolina, under which we are "authorized and empowered to treat with the Government of the United States for the delivery of the forts, magazines, lighthouses, and other real estate, with their appurtenances, within the limits of South Carolina, and also for an apportionment of the public debt, and for a division of all other property held by the Government of the United States as agent of the confederated States of which South Carolina was recently a member; and generally to negotiate as to all other measures and arrangements proper to be made and adopted in the existing relation of the parties, and for the continuance of peace and amity between this Commonwealth and the Government at Washington."

In the execution of this trust, it is our duty to furnish you, as we now do, with an official copy of the ordinance of secession, by which the State of South Carolina has resumed the powers she delegated to the Government of the United States, and has declared her perfect sovereignty and independence.

It would also have been our duty to have informed you that we were ready to negotiate with you upon all such questions as are necessarily raised by the adoption of this ordinance, and that we were prepared to enter upon this negotiation with the earnest desire to avoid all unnecessary and hostile collision, and so to inaugurate our new relations as to secure mutual respect, general advantage, and a future of good-will and harmony beneficial to all the parties concerned.

But the events of the last twenty-four hours render such an assurance impossible. We came here the representatives of an authority which could, at any time within the past sixty days, have taken possession of the forts in Charleston Harbor, but which, upon pledges given in a manner that, we can not doubt, determined to trust to your honor rather than to its own power. Since our arrival here an officer of the United States, acting, as we are assured, not only without but against your orders, has dismantled one fort and occupied another, thus altering, to a most important extent, the condition of affairs under which we came.

Until these circumstances are explained in a manner which relieves us of all doubt as to the spirit in which these negotiations shall be conducted, we are forced to suspend all discussion as to any arrangements by which our mutual interests might be amicably adjusted.

And, in conclusion, we would urge upon you the immediate withdrawal of the troops from the harbor of Charleston. Under present circumstances, they are a standing menace which renders negotiation impossible, and, as our recent experience shows, threatens speedily to bring to a bloody issue questions which ought to be settled with temperance and judgment.

We have the honor, sir, to be, very respectfully, your obedient servants,

R. W. BARNWELL,
J. H. ADAMS, } *Commissioners.*
JAMES L. ORR,

To the President of the United States.

REPLY OF THE PRESIDENT TO THE COMMISSIONERS

Washington City, December 30, 1860.

Gentlemen: I have the honor to receive your communication of 28th inst., together with a copy of your "full powers from the Convention of the People of South Carolina," authorizing you to treat with the Government of the United States on various important subjects therein mentioned, and also a copy of the ordinance bearing date on the 20th inst., declaring that "the union now subsisting between South Carolina and other States, under the name of 'The United States of America,' is hereby dissolved."

In answer to this communication, I have to say that my position as President of the United States was clearly defined in the message to Congress of the 3d instant. In that I stated that, "apart from the execution of the laws, so far as this may be practicable, the Executive has no authority to decide what shall be the relations between the Federal Government and South Carolina. He has been invested with no such discretion. He possesses no power to change the relations heretofore existing between them, much less to acknowledge the independence of that State. This would be to invest a mere executive officer with the power of recognizing the dissolution of the confederacy among our thirty-three sovereign States. It bears no resemblance to the recognition of a foreign *de facto* government—involving no such responsibility. Any attempt to do this would, on his part, be a naked act of usurpation. It is, therefore, my duty to submit to Congress the whole question, in all its bearings."

Such is my opinion still. I could, therefore, meet you only as private gentlemen of the highest character, and was entirely willing to communicate to Congress any proposition you might have to make to that body upon the subject. Of this you were well aware. It was my earnest desire that such a disposition might be made of the whole subject by Congress, who alone possess the power, as to prevent the inauguration of a civil war between the parties in regard to the possession of the Federal forts in the harbor of Charleston; and I therefore deeply regret that, in your opinion, "the events of the last twenty-four hours render this impossible." In conclusion, you urge upon me "the immediate withdrawal of the troops from the harbor of Charleston," stating that, "under present circumstances, they are a standing menace, which renders negotiation impossible, and, as our present experience shows, threatens speedily to bring to a bloody issue questions which ought to be settled with temperance and judgment."

The reason for this change in your position is that, since your arrival in Washington, "an officer of the United States, acting as we (you) are assured, not only without your (my) orders, has dismantled one fort and occupied another, thus altering, to a most important extent, the condition of affairs under which we (you) came." You also allege that you came here "the representatives of an authority which could at any time within the past sixty days have taken possession of the forts in Charleston Harbor, but which, upon pledges given in a manner that we (you) can not doubt, determined to trust to your (my) honor rather than to its own power."

This brings me to a consideration of the nature of those alleged pledges, and in what manner they have been observed. In my message of the 3d of December last, I stated, in regard to the property of the United States in South Carolina, that it "has been purchased for a fair equivalent 'by the consent of the Legislature of the State, for the erection of forts, magazines, arsenals,' etc., and over these the authority 'to exercise exclusive legislation' has been expressly granted by the Constitution to Congress. It is not believed that any attempt will be made to expel the United States from this property by force; but, if in this I should prove to be mistaken, the officer in command of the forts has received orders to act strictly on the defensive. In such a contingency, the responsibility for consequences would rightfully rest upon the heads of the assailants." This being the condition of the parties on Saturday, 8th December, four of the representatives from South Carolina called upon me and requested an interview. We had an earnest conversation on the subject of these forts, and the best means of preventing a collision between the parties, for the purpose of sparing the effusion of blood. I suggested, for prudential reasons, that it would be best to put in writing what they said to me verbally. They did so accordingly, and on Monday morning, the 10th instant, three of them presented to me a paper signed by all the representatives from South Carolina, with a single exception, of which the following is a copy:

"To his Excellency James Buchanan, President of the United States:

"In compliance with our statement to you yesterday, we now express to you our strong convictions that neither the constituted authorities, nor any body of the people of the State of South Carolina, will either attack or molest the United States forts in the harbor of Charleston, previously to the action of the Convention, and, we hope and believe, not until an offer has been made, through an accredited representative, to negotiate for an amicable arrangement of all matters between the State and Federal Government, provided that no reënforcements shall be sent into those forts, and their relative military *status* shall remain as at present.

> "JOHN MCQUEEN,
> "WILLIAM PORCHER MILES,
> "M. L. BONHAM,
> "W. W. BOYCE,
> "LAWRENCE M. KEITT.

"Washington, December 9, 1860."

And here I must, in justice to myself, remark that, at the time the paper was presented to me, I objected to the word "provided," as it might be construed into an agreement, on my part, which I never would make. They said that nothing was further from their intention; they did not so understand it, and I should not so consider it. It is evident they could enter into no reciprocal agreement with me on the subject. They did not profess to have authority to do this, and were acting in their individual character. I considered it as nothing more, in effect, than the promise of highly honorable gentlemen to exert their influence for the purpose expressed. The event has proved that they have faithfully kept this promise, although I have never since received a line from any one of them, or from any member of the Convention on the subject. It is well known that it was my determination, and this I freely expressed, not to reënforce the forts in the harbor, and thus produce a collision, until they had been actually attacked, or until I had certain evidence that they were about to be attacked. This paper I received most cordially, and considered it as a happy omen that peace might still be preserved, and that time might thus be gained for reflection. This is the whole foundation for the alleged pledge.

But I acted in the same manner I would have done had I entered into a positive and formal agreement with parties capable of contracting, although such an agreement would have been, on my part, from the nature of my official duties, impossible.

The world knows that I have never sent any reënforcements to the forts in Charleston Harbor, and I have certainly never authorized any change to be made "in their relative military *status.*"

Bearing upon this subject, I refer you to an order issued by the Secretary of War, on the 11th instant, to Major Anderson, but not brought to my notice until the 21st instant. It is as follows:

"Memorandum of verbal instructions to Major Anderson, First Artillery, com-
manding Fort Moultrie, South Carolina:

"You are aware of the great anxiety of the Secretary of War that a collision of the troops with the people of this State shall be avoided, and of his studied determination to pursue a course, with reference to the military force and forts in this harbor, which shall guard against such a collision. He has, therefore, carefully abstained from increasing the force at this point, or taking any measures which might add to the present excited state of the public mind, or which would throw any doubt on the confidence he feels that South Carolina will not attempt by violence to obtain possession of the public works, or to interfere with their occupancy. But, as the counsel of rash and impulsive persons may possibly disappoint these expectations of the Government, he deems it proper that you should be prepared with instructions to meet so unhappy a contingency. He has, therefore, directed me, verbally, to give you such instructions.

"You are carefully to avoid every act which would needlessly tend to provoke aggression; and, for that reason, you are not, without evident and imminent necessity, to take up any position which could be construed into the assumption of a hostile attitude; but you are to hold possession of the forts in this harbor, and, if attacked, you are to defend yourself to the last extremity. The smallness of your force will not permit you, perhaps, to occupy more than one of the three forts; but an attack on or attempt to take possession of either of them will be regarded as an act of hostility, and you may then put your command into either of them which you may deem most proper, to increase its power of resistance. You are also authorized to take similar defensive steps whenever you have tangible evidence of a design to proceed to a hostile act.

D. P. BUTLER, *Assistant Adjutant-General.*

Fort Moultrie, South Carolina, December 11, 1860.

"This is in conformity to my instructions to Major Buel.

"JOHN B. FLOYD, *Secretary of War.*"

These were the last instructions transmitted to Major Anderson before his removal to Fort Sumter, with a single exception in regard to a particular which does not, in any degree, affect the present question. Under these circumstances it is clear that Major Anderson acted upon his own responsibility, and without authority, unless, indeed, he had "tangible evidence of a design to proceed to a hostile act" on the part of the authorities of South Carolina, which has not yet been alleged. Still he is a brave and honorable officer, and justice requires that he should not be condemned without a fair hearing.

Be this as it may, when I learned that Major Anderson had left Fort Moultrie, and proceeded to Fort Sumter, my first promptings were to command him to return to his former position, and there to await the contingencies presented in his instructions. This could only have been done, with any degree of safety to the command, by the concurrence of the South Carolina authorities. But, before any steps could possibly have been taken in this direction, we received information, dated on the 28th instant, that "the Palmetto flag floated out to the breeze at Castle Pinckney, and a large military force went over last night (the 27th) to Fort Moultrie." Thus the authorities of South Carolina, without waiting or asking for any explanation, and doubtless believing, as you have expressed it, that the officer had acted not only without, but against my orders, on the very next day after the night when the removal was made, seized, by a military force, two of the three Federal forts in the harbor of Charleston, and have covered them under their own flag, instead of that of the United States. At this gloomy period of our history, startling events succeed each other rapidly. On the very day (the 27th instant) that possession of these two forts was taken, the Palmetto flag was raised over the Federal Custom-House and Post-Office in Charleston; and on the same day every officer of the customs—collector, naval officers, surveyors, and appraisers—resigned their offices. And this, although it was well known, from the language of my message, that as an executive officer I felt myself bound to collect the revenue at the port of Charleston under the existing laws. In the harbor of Charleston we now find three forts confronting each other, over all of which the Federal flag floated only four days ago; but now over two of them this flag has been supplanted, and the Palmetto flag has been substituted in its stead. It is under all these circumstances that I am urged immediately to withdraw the troops from the harbor of Charleston, and am informed that, without this, negotiation is impossible. This I can not do; this I will not do. Such an idea was never thought of by me in any possible contingency. No allusion to it had ever been made in any communication between myself and any human being. But the inference is, that I am bound to withdraw the troops from the only fort remaining in the possession of the United States in the harbor of Charleston, because the officer then in command of all the forts thought proper, without instructions, to change his position from one of them to another. I can not admit the justice of any such inference.

At this point of writing I have received information, by telegram, from Captain Humphreys, in command of the arsenal at Charleston, that "it has to-day

(Sunday, the 30th) been taken by force of arms." It is estimated that the munitions of war belonging to the United States in this arsenal are worth half a million of dollars.

Comment is needless. After this information, I have only to add that, while it is my duty to defend Fort Sumter, as a portion of the public property of the United States, against hostile attacks from whatever quarter they may come, by such means as I may possess for this purpose, I do not perceive how such a defense can be construed into a menace against the city of Charleston.

With great personal regard, I remain

Yours, very respectfully,

JAMES BUCHANAN.

To Honorable Robert W. Barnwell, James H. Adams, James L. Orr.

REPLY OF THE COMMISSIONERS TO THE PRESIDENT

Washington, D. C., January 1, 1861.

Sir: We have the honor to acknowledge the receipt of your letter of the 30th December, in reply to a note addressed by us to you on the 28th of the same month, as commissioners from South Carolina.

In reference to the declaration with which your reply commences, that "your position as President of the United States was clearly defined in the message to Congress of the 3d instant," that you possess "no power to change the relations heretofore existing" between South Carolina and the United States, "much less to acknowledge the independence of that State"; and that, consequently, you could meet us only as private gentlemen of the highest character, with an entire willingness to communicate to Congress any proposition we might have to make, we deem it only necessary to say that, the State of South Carolina having, in the exercise of that great right of self-government which underlies all our political organizations, declared herself sovereign and independent, we, as her representatives, felt no special solicitude as to the character in which you might recognize us. Satisfied that the State had simply exercised her unquestionable right, we were prepared, in order to reach substantial good, to waive formal considerations which your constitutional scruples might have prevented you from extending. We came here, therefore, expecting to be received as you did receive us, and perfectly content with that entire willingness of which you assured us, to submit any proposition to Congress which we might have to make upon the subject of independence of the State. The willingness was ample recognition of the condition of public affairs which rendered our presence necessary. In this position, however, it is our duty, both to the State which we represent and to ourselves, to correct several important misconceptions of our letter into which you have fallen.

You say, "It was my earnest desire that such a disposition might be made of the whole subject by Congress, who alone possesses the power to prevent the inauguration of a civil war between the parties in regard to the possession of the Federal forts in the harbor of Charleston; and I, therefore, deeply regret that, in your opinion, 'the events of the last twenty-four hours render this impossible.' " We expressed no such opinion, and the language which you quote as ours is altered in its sense by the omission of a most important part of the sentence.

What we did say was, "But the events of the last twenty-four hours render *such an assurance* impossible." Place that "assurance," as contained in our letter, in the sentence, and we are prepared to repeat it.

Again, professing to quote our language, you say: "Thus the authorities of South Carolina, without waiting or asking for any explanation, and doubtless believing, as you have expressed it, that the officer had acted not only without, but against my orders," etc. We expressed no such opinion in reference to the belief of the people of South Carolina. The language which you have quoted was applied solely and entirely to *our assurance*, obtained here, and based, as you well know, upon your own declaration—a declaration which, at that time, it was impossible for the authorities of South Carolina to have known. But without following this letter into all its details, we propose only to meet the chief points of the argument.

Some weeks ago, the State of South Carolina declared her intention, in the existing condition of public affairs, to secede from the United States. She called a convention of her people to put her declarations in force. The Convention met and passed the ordinance of secession. All this you anticipated, and your course of action was thoroughly considered. In your annual message you declared that you had no right, and would not attempt, to coerce a seceding State, but that you were bound by your constitutional oath, and would defend the property of the United States within the borders of South Carolina, if an attempt was made to take it by force. Seeing very early that this question of property was a difficult and delicate one, you manifested a desire to settle it without collision. You did not reënforce the garrisons in the harbor of Charleston. You removed a distinguished and veteran officer from the command of Fort Moultrie, because he attempted to increase his supply of ammunition. You refused to send additional troops to the same garrison when applied for by the officer appointed to succeed him. You accepted the resignation of the oldest and most eminent member of your Cabinet, rather than allow these garrisons to be strengthened. You compelled an officer stationed at Fort Sumter to return immediately to the arsenal forty muskets which he had taken to arm his men. You expressed, not to one, but to many, of the most distinguished of our public characters, whose testimony will be placed upon the record whenever it is necessary, your anxiety for a peaceful termination of this controversy, and your willingness not to disturb the military *status* of the forts, if commissioners should be sent to the Government, whose communications you promised to submit to Congress. You received and acted on assurances from the highest official authorities of South Carolina, that no attempt would be made to disturb your possession of the forts and property of the United States, if you would not disturb their existing condition until commissioners had been sent, and the attempt to negotiate had failed. You took from the members of the House of Representatives a written memorandum that no such attempt should be made, "provided that no reënforcements shall be sent into those forts, and their relative military *status* shall remain as at present." And, although you attach no force to the acceptance of such a paper, although you "considered it as nothing more in effect than the promise of highly honorable gentlemen," as an obligation on one side without corresponding obligation on the other, it must be remembered (if we are rightly informed) that you were pledged, if you ever did send reënforcements, to return it to those from whom you had received it before you executed your resolution. You sent orders to your officers, commanding them strictly to follow a line of conduct in conformity with such an understanding.

Besides all this, you had received formal and official notice, from the Governor of South Carolina, that we had been appointed commissioners and were on our way to Washington. You knew the implied condition under which we came; our arrival was notified to you, and an hour appointed for an interview. We arrived in Washington on Wednesday, at three o'clock, and you appointed an interview with us at one the next day. Early on that day, Thursday, the news was received here of the movement of Major Anderson. That news was communicated to you immediately, and you postponed our meeting until half-past two o'clock on Friday, in order that you might consult your Cabinet. On Friday we saw you, and we called upon you then to redeem your pledge. You could not deny it. With the facts we have stated, and in the face of the crowning and conclusive fact that your Secretary of War had resigned his seat in the Cabinet, upon the publicly avowed ground that the action of Major Anderson had violated the pledged faith of the Government, and that unless the pledge was instantly redeemed he was dishonored, denial was impossible; you did not deny it. You do not deny it now, but you seek to escape from its obligations on two grounds: 1. That *we* terminated all negotiation by demanding, as a preliminary, the withdrawal of the United States troops from the harbor of Charleston; and, 2. That the authorities of South Carolina, instead of asking explanation and giving you the opportunity to vindicate yourself, took possession of other property of the United States. We will examine both.

In the first place, we deny positively that we have ever, in any way, made any such demand. Our letter is in your possession; it will stand by this on the record. In it we inform you of the objects of our mission. We say that it would have been our duty to assure you of our readiness to commence negotiations with the most earnest and anxious desire to settle all questions between us amicably, and to our mutual advantage, but that events had rendered that assurance impossible. We stated the events, and we said that, until some satisfactory explanation of these events was given us, we could not proceed; and then, having made this request for explanation, we added: "And, in conclusion, we would urge upon you the immediate withdrawal of the troops from the harbor of Charleston. Under present circumstances they are a standing menace, which renders negotiation impossible," etc. "Under present circumstances"! What circumstances? Why, clearly the occupation of Fort Sumter, and the dismantling of Fort Moultrie by Major Anderson, in the face of your pledges, and without explanation or practical disavowal. And there is nothing in the letter which would or could have prevented you from declining to withdraw the troops, and offering the restoration of the *status* to which you were pledged, if such had been your desire. It would have been wiser and better, in our opinion, to have withdrawn the troops, and this opinion we urged upon you, but we *demanded* nothing but such an explanation of the events of the last twenty-four hours as would restore our confidence in the spirit with which the negotiation should be conducted. In relation to this withdrawal of the troops from the harbor, we are compelled, however, to notice one passage of your letter. Refering to it, you say: "This I can not do; this I will not do. Such an idea was never thought of by me in any possible contingency. No allusion to it had ever been made in any communication between myself and any human being."

In reply to this statement, we are compelled to say that your conversation with us left upon our minds the distinct impression that you did seriously contemplate the withdrawal of the troops from Charleston Harbor. And, in support of this impression, we would add that we have the positive assurance of gentlemen of the highest possible public reputation and the most unsullied integrity—men whose name and fame, secured by long service and patriotic achievement, place their testimony beyond cavil—that such suggestions had been made to and urged upon you by them, and had formed the subject of more than one earnest discussion with you. And it was this knowledge that induced us to urge upon you a policy which had to recommend it its own wisdom and the weight of such authority. As to the second point, that the authorities of South Carolina, instead of asking explanations, and giving you the opportunity to vindicate yourself, took possession of other property of the United States, we would observe, first, that, even if this were so, it does not avail you for defense, for the opportunity for decision was afforded you before these facts occurred. We arrived in Washington on Wednesday. The news from Major Anderson reached here early on Thursday, and was immediately communicated to you. All that day, men of the highest consideration—men who had striven successfully to lift you to your great office —who had been your tried and true friends through the troubles of your Administration—sought you and entreated you to act—to act at once. They told you that every hour complicated your position. They only asked you to give the assurance that, if the facts were so—if the commander had acted without and against your orders, and in violation of your pledges—you would restore the *status* you had pledged your honor to maintain.

You refused to decide. Your Secretary of War—your immediate and proper adviser in this whole matter—waited anxiously for your decision, until he felt that delay was becoming dishonor. More than twelve hours passed, and two Cabinet meetings had adjourned before you knew what the authorities of South Carolina had done, and your prompt decision at any moment of that time would have avoided the subsequent complications. But, if you had known the acts of the authorities of South Carolina, should that have prevented your keeping your faith? What was the condition of things? For the last sixty days, you have had in Charleston Harbor not force enough to hold the forts against an equal enemy. Two of them were empty; one of those two, the most important in the harbor. It could have been taken at any time. You ought to know, better than any man, that it would have been taken, but for the efforts of those who put their trust in your honor. Believing that they were threatened by Fort Sumter especially, the people were, with difficulty, restrained from securing, with blood, the possession of this important fortress. After many and reiterated assurances given on your behalf, which we can not believe unauthorized, they determined to forbear, and in good faith sent on their commissioners to negotiate with you. They meant you no harm, wished you no ill. They thought of you kindly, believed you true, and were willing, as far as it was consistent with duty, to spare you unnecessary and hostile collision. Scarcely had their commissioners left, than Major Anderson waged war. No other words will describe his action. It was not a peaceful change from one fort to another; it was a hostile act in the highest sense—one only justified in the presence of a superior enemy and in imminent peril. He abandoned his position, spiked his guns, burned his gun-carriages, made preparations for the destruction of his post, and withdrew under cover of the night to a safer position. This was war. No man could have believed (without your assurance) that any officer could have taken such a step, "not only without orders, but against orders." What the State did was in simple self-defense; for this act, with all its attending circumstances, was as much war as firing a volley; and, war being thus begun, until those commencing it explained their action, and disavowed their intention, there was no room for delay; and, even at this moment, while we are writing, it is more than probable, from the tenor of your letter, that reënforcements are hurrying on to the conflict, so that, when the first gun shall be fired, there will have been, on your part, one continuous consistent series of actions commencing in a demonstration essentially warlike, supported by regular reënforcement, and terminating in defeat or victory. And all this without the slightest provocation; for, among the many things which you have said, there is one thing you can not say—you have waited anxiously for news from the seat of war, in hopes that delay would furnish some excuse for this precipitation. But this "tangible evidence of a design to proceed to a hostile act, on the part of the authorities of South Carolina" (which is the only justification of Major Anderson), you are forced to admit "has not *yet* been alleged." But you have decided. You have resolved to hold by force what you have obtained through our misplaced confidence, and, by refusing to disavow the action of Major Anderson, have converted his violation of orders into a legitimate act of your Executive authority. Be the issue what it may, of this we are assured, that, if Fort Moultrie has been recorded in history as a memorial of Carolina gallantry, Fort Sumter will live upon the succeeding page as an imperishable testimony of Carolina faith.

By your course you have probably rendered civil war inevitable. Be it so. If you choose to force this issue upon us, the State of South Carolina will accept it, and, relying upon Him who is the God of justice as well as the God of hosts, will endeavor to perform the great duty which lies before her, hopefully, bravely, and thoroughly.

Our mission being one for negotiation and peace, and your note leaving us without hope of a withdrawal of the troops from Fort Sumter, or of the restoration of the *status quo* existing at the time of our arrival, and intimating, as we think, your determination to reënforce the garrison in the harbor of Charleston, we respectfully inform you that we propose returning to Charleston on to-morrow afternoon.

We have the honor to be, sir, very respectfully, your obedient servants,

R. W. BARNWELL,
J. H. ADAMS,   } *Commissioners.*
JAMES L. ORR,

To his Excellency the President of the United States.

The last communication is endorsed as follows:

Executive Mansion, 3½ o'clock, Wednesday.

This paper, just presented to the President, is of such a character that he declines to receive it.

APPENDIX H

SPEECH on the state of the country, by Davis of Mississippi, in the Senate of the United States, January 10, 1861—a motion to print the special message of the President of the United States, of January 9th, being under consideration.

Mr. Davis: Mr. President, when I took the floor yesterday, I intended to engage somewhat in the argument which has heretofore prevailed in the Senate upon the great questions of constitutional right, which have divided the country from the beginning of the Government. I intended to adduce some evidences, which I thought were conclusive, in favor of the opinions which I entertain; but events, with a current hurrying on as it progresses, have borne me past the point where it would be useful for me to argue, by the citing of authorities, the question of rights. To-day, therefore, it is my purpose to deal with events. Abstract argument has become among the things that are past. We have to deal now with facts; and, in order that we may meet those facts and apply them to our present condition, it is well to inquire what is the state of the country. The Constitution provides that the President shall, from time to time, communicate information on the state of the Union. The message which is now under consideration gives us very little, indeed, beyond that which the world—less, indeed, than reading men generally—knew before it was communicated.

What, Senators, to-day is the condition of the country? From every corner of it comes the wailing cry of patriotism, pleading for the preservation of the great inheritance we derived from our fathers. Is there a Senator who does not daily receive letters appealing to him to use even the small power which one man here possesses to save the rich inheritance our fathers gave us? Tears are trickling down the stern faces of men who have bled for the flag of their country, and are willing now to die for it; but patriotism stands powerless before the plea that the party about to come into power laid down a platform and that come what will, though ruin stare us in the face, consistency must be adhered to, even though the Government be lost.

In this state of the case, then, we turn and ask, What is the character of the Administration? What is the Executive department doing? What assurance have we there for the safety of the country? But we come back from that inquiry with a mournful conviction that feeble hands now hold the reins of state; that drivelers are taken in as counselors, not provided by the Constitution; that vacillation is the law; and the policy of this great Government is changed with every changing rumor of the day; nay, more, it is changing with every new phase of causeless fear. In this state of the case, after complications have been introduced into the question, after we were brought to the verge of war, after we were hourly expecting by telegraph to learn that the conflict had commenced, after nothing had been done to insure the peace of the land, we are told in this last hour that the question is thrown at the door of Congress, and here rests the responsibility.

Had the garrison at Charleston, representing the claim of the Government to hold the property in a fort there, been called away thirty days, nay, ten days ago, peace would have spread its pinions over this land, and calm negotiation would have been the order of the day. Why was it not recalled? No reason yet has been offered, save that the Government is bound to preserve its property; and yet look from North to South, from East to West, wherever we have constructed forts to defend States against a foreign foe, and everywhere you find them without a garrison, except at a few points where troops are kept for special purposes; not to coerce or to threaten a State, but stationed in seacoast fortifications, there merely for the purposes of discipline and instruction as artillerists You find all the other forts in the hands of fort-keepers and ordnance-sergeants, and, before a moral and patriotic people, standing safely there as the property of the country.

I asked in this Senate, weeks ago: "What causes the peril that is now imminent at Fort Moultrie; is it the weakness of the garrison?" and then I answered, "No, it is its presence, not its weakness." Had an ordnance-sergeant there represented the Federal Government, had there been no troops, no physical power to protect it, I would have pledged my life upon the issue that no question ever would have been made as to its seizure. Now, not only there, but elsewhere, we find movements of troops further to complicate this question, and probably to precipitate us upon the issue of civil war; and, worse than all, this Government, reposing on the consent of the governed; this Government, strong in the affections of the people; this Government (I describe it as our fathers made it) is now furtively sending troops to occupy positions lest "the mob" should seize them. When before in the history of our land was it that a mob could resist the sound public opinion of the country? When before was it that an unarmed magistrate had not the power, by crying, "I command the peace," to quell a mob in any portion of the land? Yet now we find, under cover of night, troops detached from one position to occupy another. Fort Washington, standing in its lonely grandeur, and overlooking the home of the Father of his Country, near by the place where the ashes of Washington repose, built there to prevent a foreign foe from coming up the Potomac with armed ships to take the capital—Fort Washington is garrisoned by marines sent secretly away from the navy-yard at Washington. And Fort McHenry, memorable in our history as the place where, under bombardment, the star-spangled banner floated through the darkness of night, the point which was consecrated by our national song—Fort McHenry, too, has been garrisoned by a detachment of marines, sent from this place in an extra train, and sent under cover of the night, so that even the mob should not know it.

Senators, the responsibility is thrown at the door of Congress. Let us take it. It is our duty in this last hour to seize the pillars of our Government and uphold them, though we be crushed in the fall. Then what is our policy? Are we to drift into war? Are we to stand idly by, and allow war to be precipitated upon the country? Allow an officer of the army to make war? Allow an unconfirmed head of a department to make war? Allow a general of the army to make war? Allow a President to make war? No, sir. Our fathers gave to Congress the power to declare war, and even to Congress they gave no power to make war upon a State of the Union. It could not have been given, except as a power to dissolve the Union. When, then, we see, as is evident to the whole country, that we are drifting into a war between the United States and an individual State, does it become the Senate to sit listlessly by and discuss abstract questions, and read patchwork from the opinions of men now mingled with the dust? Are we not bound to meet events as they come before us, manfully and patriotically to struggle with the difficulties which now oppress the country?

In the message yesterday, we were even told that the District of Columbia was in danger. In danger of what? From whom comes the danger? Is there a man here who dreads that the deliberations of this body are to be interrupted by an armed force? Is there one who would not prefer to fall with dignity at his station, the representative of a great and peaceful Government, rather than to be protected by armed bands? And yet the rumor is—and rumors seem now to be so authentic that we credit them rather than other means of information—that companies of artillery are to be quartered in this city to preserve peace, where the laws have heretofore been supreme, and that this District is to become a camp by calling out every able-bodied man within its limits to bear arms under the militia law. Are we invaded? Is there an insurrection? Are there two Senators here who would not be willing to go forth as a file, and put down any resistance which showed itself in this District against the Government of the United States? Is the reproach meant against these, my friends from the South, who advocate Southern rights and State rights? If so, it is a base slander. We claim our rights under the Constitution; we claim our rights reserved to the States; and we seek by no brute force to gain any advantage which the law and the Constitution do not give us. We have never appealed to mobs. We have never asked for the army and the navy to protect us. On the soil of Mississippi, not the foot of a Federal soldier has been impressed since 1819, when, flying from the yellow fever, they sought refuge within the limits of our State; and on the soil of Mississippi there breathes not a man who asks for any other protection than that which our Constitution gives us, that which our strong arms afford, and the brave hearts of our people will insure in every *contingency*.

Senators, we are rapidly drifting into a position in which this is to become a government of the army and navy; in which the authority of the United States is to be maintained, not by law, not by constitutional agreement between the States, but by physical force; and will you stand still and see this policy consummated? Will you fold your arms, the degenerate descendants of those men who proclaimed the eternal principle that government rests on the consent of the governed; and that every people have a right to change, modify, or abolish a government when it ceases to answer the ends for which it was established, and permit this Government imperceptibly to slide from the moorings where it was originally anchored, and become a military despotism? It was well said by the senator from New York [Mr. Seward], whom I do not now see in his seat—well said in a speech wherein I found but little to commend—that this Union could not be maintained by force, and that a Union of force was a despotism. It was a great truth, come from what quarter it may. That was not the Government instituted by our fathers; and against it, so long as I live, with heart and hand, I will rebel.

This brings me to a passage in the message which says:

"I certainly had no right to make aggressive war upon any State; and I am perfectly satisfied that the Constitution has wisely withheld that power even from Congress"—very good—"but the right and the duty to use military force defensively against those who resist the Federal officers in the exercise of their legal functions, and against those who assail the power of the Federal Government, are clear and undeniable."

Is it so? Where does he get it? Our fathers were so jealous of a standing army, that they scarcely would permit the organization and maintenance of any army! Where does he get the "clear and undeniable" power to use the force of the United States in the manner he there proposes? To execute a process, troops may be summoned in a *posse comitatus;* and here, in the history of our Government, it is not to be forgotten that in the earlier and, as it is frequently said, the better days of the republic—and painfully we feel that they were better indeed—a President of the United States did not recur to the army; he went to the people of the United States. Vaguely and confusedly, indeed, did the Senator from Tennessee [Mr. Johnson] bring forward the case of the great man, Washington, as one in which he had used a means which, he argued, was equivalent to the coercion of a State; for he said that Washington used the military power against a portion of a people of the State; and why might he not as well have used it against the whole State? Let me tell that Senator that the case of General Washington has no such application as he supposes. It was a case of insurrection in the State of Pennsylvania; and the very message from which he read communicated the fact that Governor Mifflin thought it was necessary to call the militia of the adjoining States to aid him. President Washington coöperated with Governor Mifflin; he called the militia of adjoining States to coöperate with those of Pennsylvania. He used the militia, not as a standing army. It was by the consent of the Governor; it was by his advice. It was not the invasion of the State; it was not the coercion of the State; but it was aiding the State to put down insurrection, and in the very manner provided for in the Constitution itself.

But, I ask again, what power has the President to use the army and navy except to execute process? Are we to have drum-head courts substituted for those which the Constitution and laws provide? Are we to have sergeants sent over the land instead of civil magistrates? Not so thought the elder Adams; and here, in passing, I will pay him a tribute he deserves, as the one to whom, more than any other man among the early founders of this Government, credit is due for the military principles which prevail in its organization. Associated with Mr. Jefferson originally, in preparing the rules and articles of war, Mr. Adams reverted through the long pages of history back to the empire of Rome, and drew from that foundation the very rules and articles of war which govern in our country to-day, and drew them thence because he said they had brought two nations to the pinnacle of glory—referring to the Romans and the Britons, whose military law was borrowed from them. Mr. Adams, however, when an insurrection occurred in the same State of Pennsylvania, not only relied upon the militia, but his orders, through Secretary McHenry, required that the militia of the vicinage should be employed; and, though he did order troops from Philadelphia, he required the militia of the northern counties to be employed as long as they were able to execute the laws; and the orders given to Colonel McPherson, then in New Jersey, were, that Federal troops should not go across the Jersey line except in the last resort. I say, then, when we trace our history to its early foundation, under the first two Presidents of the United States, we find that this idea of using the army and the navy to execute the laws at the discretion of the President was one not even entertained, still less acted upon, in any case.

Then, Senators, we are brought to consider passing events. A little garrison in the harbor of Charleston now occupies a post which, I am sorry to say, it gained by the perfidious breach of an understanding between the parties concerned;

and here, that I may do justice to one who had not the power, on this floor at least, to right himself—who has no friend here to represent him—let me say that remark does not apply to Major Anderson; for I hold that, though his orders were not so designed, as I am assured, they did empower him to go from one post to another, and to take his choice of the posts in the harbor of Charleston; but in so doing he committed an act of hostility. When he dismantled Fort Moultrie, when he burned the carriages and spiked the guns bearing upon Fort Sumter, he put Carolina in the attitude of an enemy of the United States; and yet he has not shown that there was any just cause for apprehension. Vague rumors had reached him—and causeless fear seems now to be the impelling motive of every public act —vague rumors of an intention to take Fort Moultrie. But, sir, a soldier should be confronted by an overpowering force before he spikes his guns and burns his carriages. A soldier should be confronted by a public enemy before he destroys the property of the United States lest it should fall into the hands of such an enemy. Was that fort built to make war upon Carolina? Was an armament put into it for such a purpose? Or was it built for the protection of Charleston Harbor; and was it armed to make that protection effective? If so, what right had any soldier to destroy that armament lest it should fall into the hands of Carolina?

Some time since I presented to the Senate resolutions which embodied my views upon this subject, drawing from the Constitution itself the data on which I based those resolutions. I then invoked the attention of the Senate in that form to the question as to whether garrisons should be kept within a State against the consent of that State. Clear was I then, as I am now, in my conclusion. No garrison should be kept within a State, during a time of peace, if the State believes the presence of that garrison to be either offensive or dangerous. Our army is maintained for common defense; our forts are built out of the common Treasury, to which every State contributes; and they are perverted from the purpose for which they were erected whenever they are garrisond with a view to threaten, to intimidate, or to control a State in any respect.

Yet, we are told this is no purpose to coerce a State; we are told that the power does not exist to coerce a State; but the Senator from Tennessee [Mr. Johnson] says it is only a power to coerce individuals; and the Senator from Ohio [Mr. Wade] seems to look upon this latter power as a very harmless power in the hands of the President, though the results of such coercion might be to destroy the State. What is a State? Is it land and houses? Is it taxable property? Is it the organization of the local government? Or is it all these combined with the people who possess them? Destroy the people, and yet not make war upon the State! To state the proposition is to answer it, by reason of its very absurdity. It is like making desolation, and calling it peace. There being, as it is admitted on every hand, no power to coerce a State, I ask what is the use of a garrison within a State where it needs no defense? The answer from every candid mind must be, there is none. The answer from every patriotic breast must be, peace requires under all such circumstances that the garrison should be withdrawn. Let the Senate to-day, as the responsibility is thrown at our door, pass those resolutions, or others which better express the idea contained in them, and you have taken one long step toward peace, one long stride toward the preservation of the Government of our fathers.

The President's message of December, however, has all the characteristics of a diplomatic paper, for diplomacy is said to abhor certainty as Nature abhors a vacuum; and it was not within the power of man to reach any fixed conclusion from that message. When the country was agitated, when opinions were being formed, when we were drifting beyond the power ever to return, this was not what we had a right to expect from the Chief Magistrate. One policy or the other he ought to have taken. If believing this to be a government of force, if believing it to be a consolidated mass, and not a confederation of States, he should have said: "No State has a right to secede; every State is subordinate to the Federal Government, and the Federal Government must empower me with physical means to reduce to subjugation the State asserting such a right." If not, if a State-rights man and a Democrat—as for many years it has been my pride to acknowledge our venerable Chief Magistrate to be—then another line of policy should have been taken. The Constitution gave no power to the Federal Government to coerce a State; the Constitution gave an army for the purposes of common defense, and to preserve domestic tranquillity; but the Constitution never contemplated using that army against a State. A State exercising the sovereign function of secession is beyond the reach of the Federal Government, unless we woo her with the voice of fraternity, and bring her back to the enticements of affection. One policy or the other should have been taken; and it is not for me to say which, though my opinion is well known; but one policy or the other should have been pursued. He should have brought his opinion to one conclusion or another, and to-day our country would have been safer than it is.

What is the message before us? Does it benefit the case? Is there a solution offered here? We are informed in it of propositions made by commissioners from South Carolina. We are not informed even as to how they terminated. No countervailing proposition is presented; no suggestion is made. We are left drifting loosely, without chart or compass.

There is in our recent history, however, an event which might have suggested a policy to be pursued. When foreigners having no citizenship within the United States declared war against it and made war upon it; when the inhabitants of a Territory, disgraced by institutions offensive to the laws of every State of the Union, held this attitude of rebellion; when the Executive there had power to use troops, he first sent commissioners of peace to win them back to their duty. When South Carolina, a sovereign State, resumes the grants she had delegated; when South Carolina stands in an attitude which threatens within a short period to involve the country in a civil war unless the policy of the Government be changed, no suggestion is made to us that this Government might send commissioners to her; no suggestion is made to us that better information should be sought; there is no policy of peace, but we are told the army and navy are in the hands of the President of the United States, to be used against those who assail the power of the Federal Government.

Then, my friends, are we to allow events to drift onward to this fatal consummation? Are we to do nothing to restore peace? Shall we not, in addition to the proposition I have already made, to withdraw the force which complicates the question, send commissioners there in order that we may learn what this community desire, what this community will do, and put the two Governments upon friendly relations?

I will not weary the Senate by going over the argument of coercion. My friend from Ohio [Mr. Pugh], I may say, has exhausted the subject. I thank him, because it came appropriately from one not identified by his position with South Carolina. It came more effectively from him than it would have done from me, had I (as I have not) a power to present it as forcibly as he has done. Sirs, let me say, among the painful reflections which have crowded upon me by day and by night, none have weighed more heavily upon my heart than the reflection that our separation severs the ties which have so long bound us to our Northern friends, of whom we are glad to recognize the Senator as a type.

Now let us return a moment to consider what would have been the state of the case if the garrison at Charleston had been withdrawn. The fort would have stood there, not dismantled, but unoccupied. It would have stood there in the hands of an ordnance-sergeant. Commissioners would have come to treat of all questions with the Federal Government, of these forts as well as others. They would have remained there to answer the ends for which they were constructed—the ends of defense. If South Carolina was an independent State, then she might hold to us such a relation as Rhode Island held after the dissolution of the Confederation and before the formation of the Union, when Rhode Island appealed to the sympathies existing between the States connected in the struggles of the Revolution, and asked that a commercial war should not be waged upon her. These forts would have stood there then to cover the harbor of a friendly State; and, if the feeling which once existed among the people of the States had subsisted still, and that fort had been attacked, brave men from every section would have rushed to the rescue, and there imperiled their lives in the defense of a State identified with their early history, and still associated in their breasts with affectionate memories; the first act of this kind would have been one appealing to every generous motive of those people, again to reconsider the question of how we could live together, and through that bloody ordeal to have brought us into the position in which our fathers left us. There need have been no collision, as there could have been no question of property which that State was not ready to meet. If it was a question of dollars and cents, they came here to adjust it. If it was a question of covering an interior State, their interests were identical. In whatever way the question could have been presented, the consequence would have been to relieve the Government of the charge of maintaining the fort, and to throw it upon the State which had resolved to be independent.

Thus we see that no evil could have resulted. We have yet to learn what evil the opposite policy may bring. Telegraphic intelligence, by the man who occupied the seat on the right of me in the old Chamber, was never relied on. He was the wisest statesman I ever knew—a man whose prophetic vision foretold all the trials through which we are now passing; whose clear intellect, elaborating everything, borrowing nothing from anybody, seemed to dive into the future, and to unveil those things which are hidden to other eyes. Need I say I mean Calhoun? No other man than he would have answered this description. I say, then, not relying upon telegraphic dispatches, we still have information enough to notify us that we are on the verge of civil war; that civil war is in the hands of men irresponsible, as it seems to us; their acts unknown to us; their discretion not covered by any existing law or usage; and we now have the responsibility thrown upon us, which justifies us in demanding information to meet an emergency in which the country is involved.

Is there any point of pride which prevents us from withdrawing that garrison? I have heard it said by a gallant gentleman, to whom I make no special reference, that the great objection was an unwillingness to lower the flag. To lower the flag! Under what circumstances? Does any man's courage impel him to stand boldly forth to take the life of his brethren? Does any man insist upon going upon the open field with deadly weapons to fight his brother on a question of courage? There is no point of pride. These are your brethren; and they have shed as much glory upon that flag as any equal number of men in the Union. They are the men, and that is the locality, where the first Union flag was unfurled, and where was fought a gallant battle before our independence was declared—not the flag with thirteen stripes and thirty-three stars, but a flag with a cross of St. George, and the long stripes running through it. When the gallant Moultrie took the British Fort Johnson and carried it, for the first time, I believe, did the Union flag fly in the air; and that was in October, 1775. When he took the position and threw up a temporary battery with palmetto-logs and sand, upon the site called Fort Moultrie, that fort was assailed by the British fleet, and bombarded until the old logs, clinging with stern tenacity, were filled with balls, but the flag still floated there, and, though many bled, the garrison conquered. Those old logs are gone; the eroding current is even taking away the site where Fort Moultrie stood; the gallant men who held it now mingle with the earth; but their memories live in the hearts of a brave people, and their sons yet live, and they, like their fathers, are ready to bleed and die for the cause in which their fathers triumphed. Glorious are the memories clinging around that old fort which now, for the first time, has been abandoned—abandoned not even in the presence of a foe, but under the maginings that a foe might come; and guns spiked and carriages burned where the band of Moultrie bled, and, with an insufficient armament, repelled the common foe of all the colonies. Her ancient history compares proudly with the present.

Can there, then, be a point of pride upon so sacred a soil as this, where the blood of the fathers cries to heaven against civil war? Can there be a point of pride against laying upon that sacred soil to-day the flag for which our fathers died? My pride, Senators, is different. My pride is that that flag shall not set between contending brothers; and that, when it shall no longer be the common flag of the country, it shall be folded up and laid away like a vesture no longer used; that it shall be kept as a sacred memento of the past, to which each of us can make a pilgrimage and remember the glorious days in which we were born.

In the answer of the commissioners which I caused to be read yesterday, I observed that they referred to Fort Sumter as remaining a memento of Carolina faith. It is an instance of the accuracy of the opinion which I have expressed. It stood without a garrison. It commanded the harbor, and the fort was known to have the armament in it capable of defense. Did the Carolinians attack it? Did they propose to seize it? It stood there safe as public property; and there it might have stood to the end of the negotiations without a question, if a garrison had not been sent into it. It was the faith on which they relied, that the Federal Government would take no position of hostility to them, that constituted its safety, and by which they lost the advantage they would have had in seizing it when unoccupied.

I think that something is due to faith as well as fraternity; and I think one of the increasing and accumulative obligations upon us to withdraw the garrison from that fort is from the manner in which it was taken—taken, as we heard by the reading of the paper yesterday, while Carolina remained under the assurance that the *status* would not be violated; while I was under that assurance, and half a dozen other Senators now within the sound of my voice felt secure under the same pledge, that nothing would be done until negotiations had terminated, unless it was to withdraw the garrison. Then we, the Federal Government, broke the faith; we committed the first act of hostility; and from this first act of hostility arose all those acts to which reference is made in the message as unprovoked aggressions—the seizing of forts elsewhere. Why were they seized? Self-preservation is the first law of nature; and when they no longer had confidence that this Federal Government would not seize the forts constructed for their defense, and use them for their destruction, they only obeyed the dictates of self-preservation when they seized the forts to prevent the enemy from taking possession of them as a means of coercion, for they then were compelled to believe this Federal Government had become an enemy.

Now, what is the remedy? To assure them that you do not intend to use physical force against them is your first remedy; to assure them that you intend to consider calmly all the propositions which they make, and to recognize the rights which the Union was established to secure; that you intend to settle with them upon a basis in accordance with the Declaration of Independence and the Constitution of the United States. When you do that, peace will prevail over the land, and force become a thing that no man will consider necessary.

I am here confronted with a question which I will not argue. The position which I have taken necessarily brings me to its consideration. Without arguing it, I will merely state it. It is the right of a State to withdraw from the Union. The President says it is not a constitutional right. The Senator from Ohio [Mr. Wade], and his ally, the Senator from Tennessee [Mr. Johnson], argued it as no right at all. Well, let us see. What is meant by a constitutional right? Is it meant to be a right derived from the Constitution—a grant made in the Constitution? If that is what is meant, of course we all see at once that we do not derive it in that way. Is it intended that it is not a constitutional right, because it is not granted in the Constitution? That shows, indeed, but a poor appreciation of the nature of our Government. All that is not granted in the Constitution belongs to the States; and nothing but what is granted in the Constitution belongs to the Federal Government; and, keeping this distinction in view, it requires but little argument to see the conclusion at which we necessarily arrive. Did the States surrender their sovereignty to the Federal Government? Did the States agree that they never could withdraw from the Federal Union?

I know it has been argued here that the Confederation said the Articles of Confederation were to be a perpetual bond of union, and that the Constitution was made to form a more perfect union; that is to say, a Government beyond perpetuity, or one day, or two or three days, after doomsday. But that has no foundation in the Constitution itself; it has no basis in the nature of our Government. The Constitution was a compact between independent States; it was not a national Government; and hence Mr. Madison answered with such effectiveness to Patrick Henry, in the Convention of Virginia, which ratified the Constitution, denying his proposition that it was to form a nation, and stating to him the conclusive fact that "we sit here as a convention of the State to ratify or reject that Constitution; and how, then, can you say that it forms a nation, and is adopted by the mass of the people?" It was not adopted by the mass of the people, as we all know historically; it was adopted by each State; each State, voluntarily ratifying it, entered the Union; and that Union was formed whenever nine States should enter it; and, in abundance of caution, it was stated, in the resolutions of ratification of three of the States, that they still possessed the power to withdraw the grants which they had delegated, whenever they should be used to their injury or oppression. I know it is said that this meant the people of all the States; but that is such an absurdity that I suppose it hardly necessary to answer it—for to speak of an elective Government rendering itself injurious and oppressive to the whole body of the people by whom it is elected is such an absurdity that no man can believe it; and to suppose that a State convention, speaking for a State and having no authority to speak for anybody else, would say that it was declaring what the people of the other States would do, would be an assumption altogether derogatory to the sound sense and well-known sentiments of the men who formed the Constitution and ratified it.

But in abundance of caution not only was this done, but the tenth amendment of the Constitution declared that all which had not been delegated was reserved to the States or to the people. Now, I ask, where among the delegated grants to the Federal Government do you find any power to coerce a State; where among the provisions of the Constitution do you find any prohibition on the part of a State to withdraw; and, if you find neither one nor the other, must not this power be in that great depository, the reserved rights of the States? How was it ever taken out of that source of all power to be given to the Federal Government? It was not delegated to the Federal Government; it was not prohibited to the States; it necessarily remains, then, among the reserved powers of the States.

This question has been so forcibly argued by the Senator from Louisiana [Mr. Benjamin] that I think it unnecessary to pursue it. Three times the proposition was made to give power to coerce the States, in the Convention, and as often refused—opposed as a proposition to make war on a State, and refused on the ground that the Federal Government could not make war upon a State. The Constitution was to form a Government for such States as should unite; it had no application beyond those who should voluntarily adopt it. Among the delegated powers there is none which interferes with the exercise of the right of secession by a State. As a right of sovereignty it remained to the States under the Confederation; and, if it did not, you arraign the faith of the men who framed the Constitution to which you appeal, for they provided that nine States should secede from thirteen. Eleven did secede from the thirteen, and put themselves in the very position which, by a great abuse of language, is to-day called treason, against the two States of North Carolina and Rhode Island; they still claiming to adhere to the perpetual Articles of Confederation, these eleven States absolving themselves from the obligations which arose under them.

The Senator from Tennessee, to whom I must refer again—and I do because he is a Southern Senator—taking the most hostile ground against us, refers to the State of Tennessee, and points to the time when that State may do those things which he has declared it an absurdity for any State to perform. I will read a single paragraph from his speech, showing what his language is, in order that I may not, by any possibility, produce an impression upon others which his language does not justify. Here are the expressions to which I refer. I call the Senator's attention to them:

"If there are grievances, why can not we all go together, and write them down and point them out to our Northern friends after we have agreed on what those grievances were, and say: 'Here is what we demand; here our wrongs are enumerated; upon these terms we have agreed; and now, after we have given you a reasonable time to consider these additional guarantees in order to protect ourselves against these wrongs, if you refuse them, then, having made an honorable effort, having exhausted all other means, we may declare the association to be broken up, and we may go into an act of revolution.' We can then say to them, 'You have refused to give us guarantees that we think are needed for the protection of our institutions and for the protection of our interests.' When they do this, I will go as far as he who goes the farthest."

Now, it does appear that he will go that far; and he goes a little further than anybody, I believe, who has spoken in vindication of the right, for he says:

"We do not intend that you shall drive us out of this House that was reared by the hands of our fathers. It is our House. It is the constitutional House. We have a right here; and because you come forward and violate the ordinances of this House, I do not intend to go out; and, if you persist in the violation of the ordinances of the House, we intend to eject you from the building and retain the possession ourselves."

I wonder if this is what caused the artillery companies to be ordered here, and the militia of this city to be organized? I think it was a mere figure of speech. I do not believe the Senator from Tennessee intended to kick you out of the House; and, if he did, let me say to you, in all sincerity, we who claim the constitutional right of a State to withdraw from the Union do not intend to help him. He says, however, and this softens it a little:

"We do not think, though, that we have just cause for going out of the Union now. We have just cause of complaint; but we are for remaining in the Union, and fighting the battle like men."

What does that mean? In the name of common sense, I ask how are we to fight in the Union? We take an oath of office to maintain the Constitution of the United States. The Constitution of the United States was formed for domestic tranquillity; and how, then, are we to fight in the Union? I have heard the proposition from others; but I have not understood it. I understand how men fight when they assume attitudes of hostility; but I do not understand how men, remaining connected together in a bond as brethren, sworn to mutual aid and protection, still propose to fight each other. I do not understand what the Senator means. If he chooses to answer my question, I am willing to hear him, for I do not understand how we are to fight in the Union.

Mr. Johnson, of Tennessee: When my speech is taken altogether, I think my meaning can be very easily understood. What I mean by fighting the battle in the Union is, I think, very distinctly and clearly set forth in my speech; and, if the Senator will take it from beginning to end, I apprehend that he will have no difficulty in ascertaining what I meant. But, for his gratification upon this particular point, I will repeat, in substance, what I then said as to fighting the battle in the Union. I meant that we should remain here under the Constitution of the

United States and contend for all its guarantees; and by preserving the Constitution and all its guarantees we would preserve the Union. Our true place, to maintain these guarantees and to preserve the Constitution, is in the Union, there to fight our battle. How? By argument; by appeals to the patriotism, to the good sense, and to the judgment of the whole country; by showing the people that the Constitution had been violated; that all its guarantees were not complied with; and I have entertained the hope that, when they were possessed of that fact, there would be found patriotism and honesty enough in the great mass of the people, North and South, to come forward and do what was just and right between the contending sections of the country. I meant that the true way to fight the battle was for us to remain here and occupy the places assigned to us by the Constitution of the country. Why did I make that statement? It was because on the 4th day of March next we shall have six majority in this body; and if, as some apprehended, the incoming Administration shall show any disposition to make encroachments upon the institution of slavery, encroachments upon the rights of the States, or any other violation of the Constitution, we, by remaining in the Union, and standing at our places, will have the power to resist all these encroachments. How? We have the power even to reject the appointment of the Cabinet officers of the incoming President. Then, should we not be fighting the battles in the Union, by resisting even the organization of the Administration in a constitutional mode, and thus, at the very start, disable an Administration which was likely to encroach on our rights and to violate the Constitution of the country? So far as appointing even a Minister abroad is concerned, the incoming Administration will have no power without our consent, if we remain here. It comes into office handcuffed, powerless to do harm. We, standing here, hold the balance of power in our hands; we can resist it at the very threshold effectually; and do it inside of the Union, and in our House. The incoming Administration has not even the power to appoint a postmaster whose salary exceeds one thousand dollars a year, without consultation with and the acquiescense of the Senate of the United States. The President has not even the power to draw his salary—his twenty-five thousand dollars per annum—unless we appropriate it. I contend, then, that the true place to fight the battle is in the Union, and within the provisions of the Constitution. The army and navy cannot be sustained without appropriations by Congress; and, if we were apprehensive that encroachments would be made on the Southern States and on their institutions, in violation of the Constitution, we could prevent him from having a dollar even to feed his army or his navy.

Mr. Davis: I receive the answer from the Senator, and I think I comprehend now that he is not going to use any force, but it is a sort of fighting that is to be done by votes and words; and I think, therefore, the President need not bring artillery and order out the militia to suppress them. I think, altogether, we are not in danger of much bloodshed in the mode proposed by the Senator from Tennessee.

Mr. Johnson: I had not quite done; but if the Senator is satisfied—

Mr. Davis: Quite satisfied. I am entirely satisfied that the answer the Senator shows me he did not intend to fight at all; that it was a mere figure of speech, and does not justify converting the Federal capital into a military camp. But it is a sort of revolution which he proposes; it is a revolution under the forms of the

Government. Now, I have to say, once for all, that, as long as I am a Senator here, I will not use the powers I possess to destroy the very Government to which I am accredited. I will not attempt, in the language of the Senator, to handcuff the President. I will not attempt to destroy the Administration by refusing any officers to administer its functions. I should vote, as I have done in Administrations to which I stood in nearest relation, against a bad nomination; but I never would agree, under the forms of the Constitution, and with the powers I bear as a Senator of the United States, to turn those powers to the destruction of the Government I was sent to support. I leave that to gentlemen who take the oath with a mental reservation. It is not my policy. If I must have revolution, I say let it be a revolution such as our fathers made when they were denied their natural rights.

So much for that. It has quieted apprehension; and I hope that the artillery will not be brought here; that the militia will not be called out; and that the female schools will continue their sessions as heretofore. [Laughter.] The authority of Mr. Madison, however, was relied on by the Senator from Tennessee; and he read fairly an extract from Mr. Madison's letter to Mr. Webster, and I give him credit for reading what it seems to me destroys his whole argument. It is this clause:

"The powers of the Government being exercised, as in other elective and responsible governments, under the control of its constituents, the people, and the Legislatures of the States, and subject to the revolutionary rights of the people in extreme cases."

Now, sir, we are confusing language very much. Men speak of revolution; and when they say revolution they mean blood. Our fathers meant nothing of the sort. When they spoke of revolution they meant an unalienable right. When they declared as an unalienable right the power of the people to abrogate and modify their form of government whenever it did not answer the ends for which it was established, they did not mean that they were to sustain that by brute force. They meant that it was a right; and force could only be invoked when that right was wrongfully denied. Great Britain denied the right in the case of the colonies, and therefore our revolution for independence was bloody. If Great Britain had admitted the great American doctrine, there would have been no blood shed; and does it become the descendants of those who proclaimed this as the great principle on which they took their place among the nations of the earth, now to proclaim, if that is a right, it is one which you can only get as the subjects of the Emperor of Austria may get their rights, by force overcoming force? Are we, in this age of civilization and political progress, when political philosophy had advanced to the point which seemed to render it possible that the millennium should now be seen by prophetic eyes—are we now to roll back the whole current of human thought, and again to return to the mere brute force which prevails between beasts of prey, as the only method of settling questions between men?

If the Declaration of Independence be true (and who here gainsays it?), every community may dissolve its connection with any other community previously made, and have no other obligation than that which results from the breach of an alliance between States. Is it to be supposed; could any man, reasoning *a priori,* come to the conclusion that the men who fought the battles of the Revolution for community independence—that the men who struggled against the then greatest military power on the face of the globe in order that they might possess those unalienable rights which they had declared—terminated their great efforts by transmitting posterity to a condition in which they could only gain those rights by force? If so, the blood of the Revolution was shed in vain; no great principles were established; for force was the law of nature before the battles of the Revolution were fought.

I see, then—if gentlemen insist on using the word "revolution" in the sense of a resort to force—a very great difference between their opinion and that of Mr. Madison. Mr. Madison put the rights of the people over and above everything else, and he said this was the Government *de jure* and *de facto*. Call it by what name you will, he understood ours to be a Government of the people. The people never have separated themselves from those rights which our fathers had declared to be unalienable. They did not delegate to the Federal Government the powers which the British Crown exercised over the colonies; they did not achieve their independence for any purpose so low as that. They left us to the inheritance of freemen, living in independent communities, the States united for the purposes which they thought would bless posterity. It is in the exercise of this reserved right as defined by Mr. Madison, as one to which all the powers of Government are subject, that the people of a State in convention have claimed to resume the functions which in like manner they had made to the Federal Government. . . .

The question which now presents itself to the country is, What shall we do with events as they stand? Shall we allow this separation to be total? Shall we render it peaceful, with a view to the chance that, when hunger shall brighten the intellects of men, and the teachings of hard experience shall have tamed them, they may come back, in the spirit of our fathers, to the task of reconstruction? Or will they have that separation partial; will they give to each State all its military power; will they give to each State its revenue power; will they still preserve the common agent, and will they thus carry on a Government different from that which now exists, yet not separating the States so entirely as to make the work of reconstruction equal to a new creation; not separating them so as to render it utterly impossible to administer any functions of the Government in security and peace?

I waive the question of duality, considering that a dual Executive would be the institution of a King Log. I consider a dual legislative department would be to bring into antagonism the representatives of two different countries, to war perpetually, and thus to continue, not union, but the irrepressible conflict. There is no duality possible (unless there be two confederacies) which seems to me consistent with the interests of either or of both. It might be that two confederacies could be so organized as to answer jointly many of the ends of our present Union; it might be that States, agreeing with each other in their internal policy—having a similarity of interests and an identity of purpose—might associate together, and that these two confederacies might have relations to each other so close as to give them a united power in time of war against any foreign nation. These things are possibilities; these things it becomes us to contemplate; these things it devolves on the majority section to consider now; for with every motion of that clock is passing away your opportunity. It was greater when we met on the first Monday in December than it is now; it is greater now than it will be on the first day of next week. We have waited long; we have come to the conclusion that you mean to do nothing. In the Committee of Thirteen, where the resolutions of the Senator from Kentucky [Mr. Crittenden] were considered, various attempts were made, but no prospect of any agreement on which it was possible for us to stand, in security for the future, could be matured. I offered a proposition, which was but the declaration of that which the Constitution announces; but that which the Supreme Court had, from time to time, and from an early period asserted; but that which was necessary for equality in the Union. Not one single vote of the Republican portion of that committee was given for the proposition.

Looking, then, upon separation as inevitable, not knowing how that separation is to occur, or at least what States it is to embrace, there remains to us, I believe, as the consideration which is most useful, the inquiry, How can this separation be effected so as to leave to us the power, whenever we shall have the will, to reconstruct? It can only be done by adopting a policy of peace. It can only be done by denying to the Federal Government all power to coerce. It can only be done by returning to the point from which we started, and saying, "This is a Government of fraternity, a Government of consent, and it shall not be administered in a departure from those principles."

I do not regard the failure of our constitutional Union, as very many do, to be the failure of self-government—to be conclusive in all future time of the unfitness of man to govern himself. Our State governments have charge of nearly all the relations of person and property. This Federal Government was instituted mainly as a common agent for foreign purposes, for free trade among the States, and for common defense. Representative liberty will remain in the States after they are separated. Liberty was not crushed by the separation of the colonies from the mother-country, then the most constitutional monarchy and the freest Government known. Still less will liberty be destroyed by the separation of these States, to prevent the destruction of the spirit of the Constitution by the mal-administration of it. There will be injury—injury to all; differing in degree, differing in manner. The injury to the manufacturing and navigating States will be to their internal prosperity. The injury to the Southern States will be mainly to their foreign commerce. All will feel the deprivation of that high pride and power which belong to the flag now representing the greatest republic, if not the greatest Government, upon the face of the globe. I would that it still remained to consider what we might calmly have considered on the first Monday in December—how this could be avoided; but events have rolled past that point. You would not make propositions when they would have been effective. I presume you will not make them now; and I know not what effect they would have if you did. Your propositions would have been most welcome if they had been made before any question of coercion, and before any vain boasting of power; for pride and passion do not often take counsel of pecuniary interest, at least among those whom I represent. But you have chosen to take the policy of clinging to words [the Chicago platform], in disregard of passing events, and have hastened them onward. It is true, as shown by the history of all revolutions, that they are most precipitated and intensified by obstinacy and vacillation. The want of a policy, the obstinate adherence to unimportant things, have brought us to a condition where I close my eyes, because I can not see anything that encourages me to hope.

In the long period which elapsed after the downfall of the great republics of the East, when despotism seemed to brood over the civilized world, and only here and there constitutional monarchy even was able to rear its head—when all the great principles of republican and representative government had sunk deep, fathomless, into the sea of human events—it was then that the storm of our Revolution moved the waters. The earth, the air, and the sea became brilliant; and from the foam of ages rose the constellation which was set in the political firmament, as a sign of unity and confederation and community independence, coexistent with confederate strength. That constellation has served to bless our people. Nay, more; its light has been thrown on foreign lands, and its regenerative power will outlive, perhaps, the Government as a sign for which its was set. It may be pardoned to me, sir, who, in my boyhood, was given to the military service, and who have followed, under tropical suns and over northern snows, the flag of the Union, if I here express the deep sorrow which always overwhelms me when I think of taking a last leave of that object of early affection and proud association; feeling that henceforth it is not to be the banner which, by day and by night, I was ready to follow; to hail with the rising and bless with the setting sun. But God, who knows the hearts of men, will judge between you and us, at whose door lies the responsibility. Men will see the efforts made, here and elsewhere; that we have been silent when words would not avail, and have curbed an impatient temper, and hoped that conciliatory counsels might do that which could not be effected by harsh means. And yet, the only response which has come from the other side has been a stolid indifference, as though it mattered not: "Let the temple fall, we do not care!" Sirs, remember that such conduct is offensive, and that men may become indifferent even to the objects of their early attachments.

If our Government should fail, it will not be from the defect of the system, though each planet was set to revolve in an orbit of its own, each moving by its own impulse, yet being all attracted by the affections and interests which countervailed each other; there was no inherent tendency to disruption. It has been the perversion of the Constitution; it has been the substitution of theories of morals for principles of government; it has been forcing crude opinions upon the domestic institutions of others, which has disturbed these planets in their orbit; it is this which threatens to destroy the constellation which, in its power and its glory, had been gathering stars one after another, until, from thirteen, it had risen to thirty-three.

If we accept the argument of to-day in favor of coercion as the theory of our Government, its only effect will be to precipitate men who have pride and self-reliance into the assertion of the freedom and independence to which they were born. Our fathers would never have entered into a confederate Government which had within itself the power of coercion. I would not agree to remain one day in such a Government after I had the power to get out of it. To argue that the man who follows the mandate of his State, resuming her sovereign jurisdiction and power, is disloyal to his allegiance to the United States, which allegiance he only owed through his State, is such a confusion of ideas as does not belong to an ordinary comprehension of our Government. It is treason to the principle of community independence. It is to recur to that doctrine of passive obedience which, in England, cost one monarch his head and drove another into exile; a doctrine which, since the Revolution of 1688, has obtained nowhere where men speak the English tongue. Yet all this it is needful to admit, before we accept this doctrine of coercion, which is to send an army and a navy to do that which there are no courts to perform; to execute the law without a judicial decision, and without an officer to serve process. This, I say, would degrade us to the basest despotism under which man could live—the despotism of a many-headed monster, without the sensibility or regardful consideration which might belong to an hereditary king.[1]

✦ ✦ ✦

There is a strange similarity in the position of affairs at the present day to that which the colonies occupied. Lord North asserted the right to collect the revenue, and insisted on collecting it by force. He sent troops to Boston Harbor and to Charlestown, and he quartered troops in those towns. The result was, collision; and out of that collision came the separation of the colonies from the mother-country. The same thing is being attempted to-day. Not the law, not the civil magistrate, but troops, are relied upon now to execute the laws. To gather taxes in the Southern ports, the army and navy must be sent to perform the functions of magistrates. It is the old case over again. Senators of the North, you are reënacting the blunders which statesmen in Great Britain committed; but among you there are some who, like Chatham and Burke, though not of our section, yet are vindicating our rights.

I have heard, with some surprise, for it seemed to me idle, the repetition of the assertion heretofore made, that the cause of the separation was the election of Mr. Lincoln. It may be a source of gratification to some gentlemen that their friend is elected; but no individual had the power to produce the existing state of things. It was the purpose, the end, it was the declaration by himself and his friends, which constitute the necessity of providing new safeguards for ourselves. The man was nothing, save as he was the representative of opinions, of a policy, of purposes, of power, to inflict upon us those wrongs to which freemen never tamely submit.

Senators, I have spoken longer than I desired. I had supposed it was possible, avoiding argument and not citing authority, to have made to you a brief address. It was thought useless to argue a question which now belongs to the past. The time is near at hand when the places which have known us as colleagues laboring together can know us in that relation no more for ever. I have striven to avert the catastrophe which now impends over the country, unsuccessfully; and I regret it. For the few days which I may remain, I am willing to labor in order that that catastrophe shall be as little as possible destructive to public peace and prosperity. If you desire at this last moment to avert civil war, so be it; it is better so. If you will but allow us to separate from you peaceably, since we can not live peace-ably together, to leave with the rights we had before we were united, since we can not enjoy them in the Union, then there are many relations which may still subsist between us, drawn from the associations of our struggles from the Revo-lutionary era to the present day, which may be beneficial to you as well as to us.

If you will not have it thus—if in the pride of power, if in contempt of reason, and reliance upon force, you say we shall not go, but shall remain as subjects to you—then, gentlemen of the North, a war is to be inaugurated the like of which men have not seen. Sufficiently numerous on both sides, in close contact, with only imaginary lines of division, and with many means of approach, each sus-

---

[1] Here occurred a colloquy with another Senator, followed by some paragraphs not essential to the completeness of the subject.

tained by productive sections, the people of which will give freely both of money and of store, the conflicts must be multiplied indefinitely, and masses of men, sacrificed to the demon of civil war, will furnish hecatombs, such as the recent campaign in Italy did not offer. At the end of all this what will you have effected? Destruction upon both sides; subjugation upon neither; a treaty of peace leaving both torn and bleeding; the wail of the widow and the cry of the orphan substituted for those peaceful notes of domestic happiness that now prevail throughout the land; and then you will agree that each is to pursue his separate course as best he may. This is to be the end of war. Through a long series of years you may waste your strength, distress your people, and yet at last must come to the position which you might have had at first, had justice and reason, instead of selfishness and passion, folly and crime, dictated your course.

Is there wisdom, is there patriotism in the land? If so, easy must be the solution of this question. If not, then Mississippi's gallant sons will stand like a wall of fire around their State; and I go hence, not in hostility to you, but in love and allegiance to her, to take my place among her sons, be it for good or for evil.

I shall probably never again attempt to utter here the language either of warning or of argument. I leave the case in your hands. If you solve it not before I go, you will have still to decide it. Toward you individually, as well as to those whom you represent, I would that I had the power now to say there shall be peace between us for ever. I would that I had the power now to say the intercourse and the commerce between the States, if they can not live in one Union, shall still be uninterrupted; that all the social relations shall remain undisturbed; that the son in Mississippi shall visit freely his father in Maine, and the reverse; and that each shall be welcomed when he goes to the other, not by himself alone, but also by his neighbors; and that all that kindly intercourse which has subsisted between the different sections of the Union shall continue to exist. This is not only for the interest of all, but it is my profoundest wish, my sincerest desire, that such remnant of that which is passing away may grace the memory of a glorious though too brief existence.

Day by day you have become more and more exasperated. False reports have led you to suppose there was in our section hostility to you with manifestations which did not exist. In one case, I well remember when the Senator from Vermont [Mr. Collamer] was serving with me on a special committee, it was reported that a gentleman who had gone from a commercial house in New York had been inhumanly treated at Vicksburg, and this embarrassed a question which we then had pending. I wrote to Vicksburg for information, and my friends could not learn that such a man had ever been there; but, if he had been there, no violence certainly had been offered to him. Falsehood and suspicion have thus led you on step by step in the career of crimination, and perhaps has induced to some part of your aggression. Such evil effects we have heretofore suffered, and the consequences now have their fatal culmination. On the verge of war, distrust and passion increase the danger. To-day it is in the power of two bad men, at the opposite ends of the telegraphic line between Washington and Charleston, to precipitate the State of South Carolina and the United States into a conflict of arms without other cause to have produced it. And still will you hesitate; still will you do nothing? Will you sit with sublime indifference and allow events to shape themselves? No longer can you say the responsibility is upon the Executive.

He has thrown it upon you. He has notified you that he can do nothing; and you therefore know he will do nothing. He has told you the responsibility now rests with Congress; and I close as I began, by invoking you to meet that responsibility, bravely to act the patriot's part. If you will, the angel of peace may spread her wings, though it be over divided States; and the sons of the sires of the Revolution may still go on in friendly intercourse with each other, ever renewing the memories of a common origin; the sections, by the diversity of their products and habits, acting and reacting beneficially, the commerce of each may swell the prosperity of both, and the happiness of all be still interwoven together. Thus may it be; and thus it is in your power to make it.

538 RISE AND FALL OF THE CONFEDERATE GOVERNMENT

APPENDIX I

CORRESPONDENCE and extracts from correspondence relative to Fort Sumter, from the affair of the *Star of the West*, January 9, 1861, to the withdrawal of the envoy of South Carolina from Washington, February 8, 1861.

MAJOR ANDERSON TO THE GOVERNOR OF SOUTH CAROLINA

To his Excellency the Governor of South Carolina.

SIR: Two of your batteries fired this morning upon an unarmed vessel bearing the flag of my Government. As I have not been notified that war has been declared by South Carolina against the Government of the United States, I can not but think that this hostile act was committed without your sanction or authority. Under that hope, and that alone, did I refrain from opening fire upon your batteries.

I have the honor, therefore, respectfully to ask whether the above mentioned act—one I believe without a parallel in the history of our country, or of any other civilized Government—was committed in obedience to your instructions, and to notify you, if it be not disclaimed, that I must regard it as an act of war, and that I shall not, after a reasonable time for the return of my messenger, permit any vessels to pass within range of the guns of my fort.

In order to save as far as in my power the shedding of blood, I beg that you will have due notification of this my decision given to all concerned.

Hoping, however, that your answer may be such as will justify a further continuance of forbearance on my part, I have the honor to be,

Very respectfully, your obedient servant,

ROBERT ANDERSON,
Major First Artillery U. S. A., commanding.

Fort Sumter, South Carolina, January 9, 1861.

EXTRACTS FROM REPLY OF THE GOVERNOR TO MAJOR ANDERSON

State of South Carolina, Executive Office, Headquarters,
Charleston, January 9, 1861.

SIR: Your letter has been received. In it you make certain statements which very plainly show that you have not been fully informed by your Government of the precise relations which now exist between it and the State of South Carolina. Official information has been communicated to the Government of the United States that the political connection heretofore existing between the State of South Carolina and the States which were known as the United States had ceased, and that the State of South Carolina had resumed all the power it had delegated to the United States under the compact known as the Constitution of the United States. The right which the State of South Carolina possessed to change the political relations it held with other States, under the Constitution of the United States, has been solemnly asserted by the people of this State, in convention, and now does not admit of discussion.

* * * * *

The attempt to reënforce the troops now at Fort Sumter, or to retake and resume possession of the forts within the waters of this State, which you have abandoned, after spiking the guns placed there, and doing otherwise much damage, can not be regarded by the authorities of this State as indicative of any other purpose than the coercion of this State by the armed force of the Government. To repel such an attempt is too plainly its duty to allow it to be discussed. But, while defending its waters, the authorities of the State have been careful so to conduct the affairs of the State that no act, however necessary for its defense, should lead to a useless waste of life. Special agents, therefore, have been off the bar, to warn all approaching vessels, if armed, or unarmed and having troops to reënforce the forts on board, not to enter the harbor of Charleston; and special orders have been given to the commanders of all the forts and batteries not to fire at such vessels until a shot fired across their bows would warn them of the prohibition of the State.

Under these circumstances, the Star of the West, it is understood, this morning attempted to enter this harbor, with troops on board; and, having been notified that she could not enter, was fired into. The act is perfectly justified by me.

In regard to your threat in relation to vessels in the harbor, it is only necessary to say, that you must judge of your responsibilities. Your position in this harbor has been tolerated by the authorities of the State. And, while the act of which you complain is in perfect consistency with the rights and duties of the State, it is not perceived how far the conduct which you propose to adopt can find a parallel in the history of any country, or be reconciled with any other purpose of your Government than that of imposing upon this State the condition of a conquered province.

F. W. PICKENS.

To Major Robert Anderson, commanding Fort Sumter.

MAJOR ANDERSON TO THE GOVERNOR

Headquarters, Fort Sumter, South Carolina, January 9, 1861.

To his Excellency F. W. Pickens,
Governor of the State of South Carolina.

SIR: I have the honor to acknowledge the receipt of your communication of to-day, and to say that, under the circumstances, I have deemed it proper to refer the whole matter to my Government; and that I intend deferring the course indicated in my note of this morning until the arrival from Washington of the instructions I may receive. I have the honor also to express a hope that no obstructions will be placed in the way of, and that you will do me the favor to afford every facility to, the departure and return of the bearer, Lieutenant T. Talbot, U. S. Army, who has been directed to make the journey.

I have the honor to be, very respectfully,

ROBERT ANDERSON,
Major U. S. Army, commanding.

THE GOVERNOR TO THE PRESIDENT OF THE UNITED STATES

State of South Carolina, Executive Office,
Headquarters, Charleston, January 11, 1861.

SIR: At the time of the separation of the State of South Carolina from the United States, Fort Sumter was, and still is, in the possession of troops of the

United States, under the command of Major Anderson. I regard that possession as not consistent with the dignity or safety of the State of South Carolina; and I have this day addressed to Major Anderson a communication to obtain from him the possession of that fort, by the authorities of this State. The reply of Major Anderson informs me that he has no authority to do what I required, but he desires a reference of the demand to the President of the United States.

Under the circumstances now existing, and which need no comment by me, I have determined to send to you the Hon. I. W. Hayne, the Attorney-General of the State of South Carolina, and have instructed him to demand the delivery of Fort Sumter, in the harbor of Charleston, to the constituted authorities of the State of South Carolina.

The demand I have made of Major Anderson, and which I now make of you, is suggested because of my earnest desire to avoid bloodshed which a persistence in your attempt to retain the possession of that fort will cause, and which will be unavailing to secure you that possession, but induce a calamity most deeply to be deplored.

If consequences so unhappy shall ensue, I will secure for this State, in the demand which I now make, the satisfaction of having exhausted every attempt to avoid it.

In relation to the public property of the United States within Fort Sumter, the Hon. I. W. Hayne, who will hand you this communication, is authorized to give you the pledge of the State that the valuation of such property will be accounted for, by this State, upon the adjustment of its relations with the United States, of which it was a part.

F. W. PICKENS.

To the President of the United States.

EXTRACTS FROM INSTRUCTIONS OF THE STATE DEPARTMENT OF SOUTH CAROLINA TO HON. I. W. HAYNE

State of South Carolina, Executive Office,
State Department, Charleston, January 12, 1861.

SIR: The Governor has considered it proper, in view of the grave questions which now affect the State of South Carolina and the United States, to make a demand upon the President of the United States for the delivery to the State of South Carolina of Fort Sumter, now within the territorial limits of this State and occupied by troops of the United States.

*   *   *   *   *

You are now instructed to proceed to Washington, and there, in the name of the government of the State of South Carolina, inquire of the President of the United States whether it was by his order that troops of the United States were sent into the harbor of Charleston to reënforce Fort Sumter; if he avows that order, you will then inquire whether he asserts a right to introduce troops of the United States within the limits of this State, to occupy Fort Sumter; and you will, in case of his avowal, inform him that neither will be permitted, and either will be regarded as his declaration of war against the State of South Carolina.

The Governor, to save life, and determined to omit no course of proceeding usual among civilized nations, previous to that condition of general hostilities which belongs to war, and not knowing under what order, or by what authority, Fort Sumter is now held, demanded from Major Robert Anderson, now in command of that fort, its delivery to the State. That officer, in his reply, has referred the Governor to the Government of the United States at Washington. You will, therefore, demand from the President of the United States the withdrawal of the troops of the United States from that fort, and its delivery to the State of South Carolina.

You are instructed not to allow any question of property claimed by the United States to embarrass the assertion of the political right of the State of South Carolina to the possession of Fort Sumter. The possession of that fort by the State is alone consistent with the dignity and safety of the State of South Carolina; but such possession is not inconsistent with a right to compensation in money in another Government, if it has against the State of South Carolina any just claim connected with that fort. But the possession of the fort can not, in regard to the State of South Carolina, be compensated by any consideration of any kind from the Government of the United States, when the possession of it by the Government is invasive of the dignity and affects the safety of the State. That possession can not become now a matter of discussion or negotiation. You will, therefore, require from the President of the United States a positive and distinct answer to your demand for the delivery of the fort. And you are further authorized to give the pledge of the State to adjust all matters which may be, and are in their nature, susceptible of valuation in money, in the manner most usual, and upon the principles of equity and justice always recognized by independent nations, for the ascertainment of their relative rights and obligations in such matters. . . .

Respectfully, your obedient servant, A. G. MAGRATH.

To Hon. W. Hayne, special envoy from the State of South Carolina to the President of the United States.

LETTERS OF SENATORS OF SECEDING STATES TO HON. I. W. HAYNE

Washington City, January 15, 1861.

Hon. Isaac W. Hayne.

SIR: We are apprised that you visit Washington, as an envoy from the State of South Carolina, bearing a communication from the Governor of your State to the President of the United States, in relation to Fort Sumter. Without knowing its contents, we venture to request you to defer its delivery to the President for a few days, or until you and he have considered the suggestions which we beg leave to submit.

We know that the possession of Fort Sumter by troops of the United States, coupled with the circumstances under which it was taken, is the chief, if not only, source of difficulty between the government of South Carolina and that of the United States. We would add that we, too, think it a just cause of irritation and of apprehension on the part of your State. But we have also assurances, notwithstanding the circumstances under which Major Anderson left Fort Moultrie and entered Fort Sumter with the forces under his command, that it was not taken, and is not held, with any hostile or unfriendly purpose toward your State, but merely as property of the United States, which the President deems it his duty to protect and preserve.

We will not discuss the question of right or duty on the part of either Government touching that property, or the late acts of either in relation thereto; but we think that, without any compromise of right or breach of duty on either side, an amicable adjustment of the matter of differences may and should be adopted. We desire to see such an adjustment, and to prevent war or the shedding of blood. We represent States which have already seceded from the United States, or will have done so before the 1st of February next, and which will meet your State in convention on or before the 15th of that month. Our people feel that they have a common destiny with your people, and expect to form with them, in that Convention, a new Confederation and Provisional Government. We must and will share your fortunes, suffering with you the evils of war if it can not be avoided; and enjoying with you the blessings of peace, if it can be preserved. We, therefore, think it especially due from South Carolina to our States—to say nothing of other slaveholding States—that she should, as far as she can, consistently with her honor, avoid initiating hostilities between her and the United States or any other power. We have the public declaration of the President that he has not the constitutional power or the will to make war on South Carolina, and that the public peace shall not be disturbed by any act of hostility toward your State.

We, therefore, see no reason why there may not be a settlement of existing difficulties, if time be given for calm and deliberate counsel with those States which are equally involved with South Carolina. We, therefore, trust that an arrangement will be agreed on between you and the President, at least till the 15th of February next; by which time your and our States may, in convention, devise a wise, just, and peaceable solution of existing difficulties.

In the mean time, we think your State should suffer Major Anderson to obtain necessary supplies of food, fuel, or water, and enjoy free communication, by post or special messenger, with the President; upon the understanding that the President will not send him reënforcements during the same period. We propose to submit this proposition and your answer to the President.

If not clothed with power to make such arrangement, then we trust that you will submit our suggestions to the Governor of your State for his instructions. Until you have received and communicated his response to the President, of course your State will not attack Fort Sumter, and the President will not offer to reënforce it.

We most respectfully submit these propositions, in the earnest hope that you, or the proper authority of your State may accede to them.

We have the honor to be, with profound esteem,

Your obedient servants,

LOUIS T. WIGFALL,
JOHN HEMPHILL,
D. L. YULEE,
S. R. MALLORY,
JEFFERSON DAVIS,
C. C. CLAY, JR.,
BENJAMIN FITZPATRICK,
A. IVERSON,
JOHN SLIDELL,
J. P. BENJAMIN.

LETTER OF HON. I. W. HAYNE IN REPLY TO SENATORS
FROM SECEDING STATES

Washington, January, 1861.

Gentlemen: I have just received your communication, dated the 15th instant. You represent, you say, States which have already seceded from the United States, or *will have* done so before the 1st of February next, and which will meet South Carolina in convention, on or before the 15th of that month; that your people feel they have a common destiny with our people, and expect to form with them in that Convention a new Confederacy and Provisional Government; that you must and *will* share our fortunes, suffering with us the evils of war, if it can not be avoided, and enjoying with us the blessings of peace, if it *can* be preserved.

I feel, gentlemen, the force of this appeal, and, so far as my authority extends, most cheerfully comply with your request.

I am *not* clothed with power to make the arrangements you suggest, but provided you can get assurances, with which you are entirely satisfied, that *no* reënforcements will be sent to Fort Sumter in the interval, and that public peace shall *not* be disturbed by any act of hostility toward South Carolina, I will refer your communication to the authorities of South Carolina, and, withholding their communication, with which I am at present charged, will wait for their instructions.

Major Anderson and his command, let me assure you, *do* now obtain all necessary supplies of food (including fresh meat and vegetables), and, I believe, fuel and water; and *do* now enjoy free communication, by post and special messengers, with the President, and will continue to do so, certainly, until the door of negotiation shall be closed.

If your proposition is acceded to, you may assure the President that *no* attack will be made on Fort Sumter until a response from the Governor of South Carolina has been received by me, and communicated to him.

With great consideration and profound esteem,

Your obedient servant,

ISAAC W. HAYNE,
Envoy from the Governor and Council of South Carolina.

LETTER OF SENATORS OF SECEDING STATES TO THE PRESIDENT

Senate-Chamber, January 19, 1861.

Sir: We have been requested to present to you copies of a correspondence between certain Senators of the United States and Colonel Isaac W. Hayne, now in this city, in behalf of the government of South Carolina, and to ask that you will take into consideration the subject of said correspondence.

Very respectfully, your obedient servants,

BENJAMIN FITZPATRICK,
S. R. MALLORY,
JOHN SLIDELL.

To his Excellency James Buchanan, President United States.

To the letter above, an evasive reply was returned on the 22d by the Hon. Joseph Holt, Secretary of War *ad interim,* on behalf of the President, the material points of which are contained in the following paragraph:

In regard to the proposition of Colonel Hayne, that "no reënforcements will be sent to Fort Sumter in the interval, and that the public peace will not be disturbed by any act of hostility toward South Carolina," it is impossible for me to give you any such assurances. The President has no authority to enter into such an agreement or understanding. As an executive officer, he is simply bound to protect the public property, so far as this may be practicable; and it would be a manifest violation of his duty to place himself under engagements that he would not perform this duty either for an indefinite or limited period. At the present moment it is not deemed necessary to reënforce Major Anderson, because he makes no such request, and feels quite secure in his position. Should his safety, however, require reënforcements, every effort will be made to supply them.

Holt concludes his letter by saying:

Major Anderson is not menacing Charleston; and I am convinced that the happiest result which can be attained is, that both he and the authorities of South Carolina shall remain on their present amicable footing, neither party being bound by any obligations whatever, except the high Christian and moral duty to keep the peace, and to avoid all causes of mutual irritation.

Very respectfully, your obedient servant,

J. HOLT, *Secretary of War ad interim.*

LETTER OF SENATORS OF SECEDING STATES TO HON. I. W. HAYNE

Hon. Isaac W. Hayne.   Washington, January 23, 1861.

Sir: In answer to your letter of the 17th inst. we have now to inform you that, after communicating with the President, we have received a letter signed by the Secretary of War, and addressed to Messrs. Fitzpatrick, Mallory, and Slidell, on the subject of our proposition, which letter we now inclose to you. Although its terms are not as satisfactory as we could have desired, in relation to the ulterior purposes of the Executive, we have no hesitation in expressing our entire confidence that no reënforcements will be sent to Fort Sumter, nor will the public peace be disturbed within the period requisite for full communication between yourself and your government; and we trust, therefore, that you will feel justified in applying for further instructions before delivering to the President any message with which you may have been charged.

We take this occasion to renew the expression of an earnest hope that South Carolina will not deem it incompatible with her safety, dignity, or honor to refrain from initiating any hostilities against any power whatsoever, or from taking any steps tending to produce collision, until our States, which are to share her fortunes, shall have an opportunity of joining their counsels with hers.

We are, with great respect, your obedient servants,

LOUIS T. WIGFALL,	JOHN HEMPHILL,
D. L. YULEE,	JOHN SLIDELL,
J. P. BENJAMIN,	C. C. CLAY, JR.
A. IVERSON,	

P. S.—Some of the signatures to the former letter addressed to you are not affixed to the foregoing communication, in consequence of the departure of several Senators, now on their way to their respective States.

LETTER OF HON. I. W. HAYNE TO SENATORS OF SECEDING STATES

To the Honorable Louis T. Wigfall, D. L. Yulee, J. P. Benjamin, A. Iverson, John Hemphill, John Slidell, and C. C. Clay, Jr.

Gentlemen: I have received your letter of the 23d inst., inclosing a communication dated the 22d inst., addressed to Messrs. Fitzpatrick, Mallory, and Slidell, from the Secretary of War *ad interim*. This communication from the Secretary is far from being satisfactory to me. But, inasmuch as you state that "we (you) have no hesitation in expressing an entire confidence that no reënforcements will be sent to Fort Sumter, nor will the public peace be disturbed within the period requisite for full communication between yourself (myself) and your (my) Government," in compliance with our previous understanding, I withhold the communication with which I am at present charged, and refer the whole matter to the authorities of South Carolina, and will await their reply.

Mr. Gourdin, of South Carolina, now in this city, will leave here by the evening's train, and will lay before the Governor of South Carolina and his Council the whole correspondence between yourselves and myself, and between you and the Government of the United States, with a communication from me, asking further instructions.

I can not, in closing, but express my deep regret that the President should deem it necessary to keep a garrison of troops at Fort Sumter for the protection of the *"property"* of the United States. South Carolina scorns the idea of appropriating to herself the *property* of another, whether of a government or an individual, without accounting, to the last dollar, for everything which, for the protection of her citizens and in vindication of her own honor and dignity, she may deem it necessary to take into her own possession. As *property,* Fort Sumter is in far greater jeopardy occupied by a garrison of United States troops than it would be if delivered over to the State authorities, with the pledge that, in regard to that and all other property claimed by the United States within the jurisdiction of South Carolina, they would fully account, upon a fair adjustment.

Upon the other point of the preservation of the peace, and the avoidance of bloodshed—is it supposed that the occupation of a fort in the midst of a harbor, with guns bearing upon every position of it, by a Government no longer acknowledged, can be other than the occasion of constant irritation, excitement, and indignation? It creates a condition of things which I fear is but little calculated to advance the observance of the "high Christian and moral duty to keep the peace, and to avoid all causes of mutual irritation," recommended by the Secretary of War in his communication.

In my judgment, to continue to hold Fort Sumter, by United States troops, is the worst possible means of protecting it as property, and the worst possible means of effecting a peaceful solution of present difficulties.

I beg leave, in conclusion, to say that it is in deference to the unanimous opinion expressed by the Senators present in Washington, "representing States which have already seceded from the United States, or will have done so before the 1st of February next," that I comply with your suggestions. And I feel assured that suggestions from such a quarter will be considered with profound respect by the authorities of South Carolina, and will have great weight in determining their action.

With high consideration, I have the honor to be, very respectfully, your obedient servant,

ISAAC W. HAYNE,

Envoy from the Governor and Council of South Carolina.

MR. HAYNE TO THE PRESIDENT OF THE UNITED STATES

Washington, January 31, 1861.

To his Excellency James Buchanan, President.

Sir: I had the honor to hold a short interview with you on the 14th inst., informal and unofficial. Having previously been informed that you desired that whatever was official should be, on both sides, conducted by written communications, I did not at that time present my credentials, but verbally informed you that I bore a letter from the Governor of South Carolina in regard to the occupation of Fort Sumter, which I would deliver the next day under cover of a written communication from myself. The next day, before such communication could be made, I was waited upon by a Senator from Alabama, who stated that he came on the part of all the Senators then in Washington from the States which had already seceded from the United States, or would certainly have done so before the 1st day of February next. The Senator from Alabama urged that he and they were interested in the subject of my mission in almost an equal degree with the authorities of South Carolina. He said that hostilities commenced between South Carolina and your Government would necessarily involve the States represented by themselves in civil strife, and, fearing that the action of South Carolina might complicate the relations of your Government to the seceded and seceding States, and thereby interfere with a peaceful solution of existing difficulties, these Senators requested that I would withhold my message to yourself until a consultation among themselves could be had. To this I agreed, and the result of the consultation was the letter of these Senators addressed to me, dated 15th January, a copy of which is in your possession. To this letter I replied on the 17th, and a copy of that reply is likewise in your possession. This correspondence, as I am informed, was made the subject of a communication from Senators Fitzpatrick, Mallory, and Slidell, addressed to you, and your attention called to the contents. These gentlemen received on the 22d day of January a reply to their application, conveyed in a letter addressed to them, dated the 22d, signed by the Hon. J. Holt, Secretary of War *ad interim.* Of this letter you of course have a copy. This letter from Mr. Holt was communicated to me under the cover of a letter from all the Senators of the seceded and seceding States, who still remained in Washington; and of this letter, too, I am informed you have been furnished with a copy.

This reply of yours through the Secretary of War *ad interim* to the application made by the Senators, was entirely unsatisfactory to me. It appeared to me to be not only a rejection in advance of the main proposition made by these Senators, to wit, that "an arrangement should be agreed on between the authorities of South Carolina and your Government, at least until the 15th of February next, by which time South Carolina and the States represented by the Senators might, in convention, devise a wise, just, and peaceable solution of existing difficulties"; "in the mean time," they say, "we think" (that is, these Senators) "that your State" (South Carolina) "should suffer Major Anderson to obtain necessary supplies of food, fuel, or water, and enjoy free communication, by post or special messenger, with the President, upon the understanding that the President will not send him reënforcements during the same period"; but, besides this rejection of the main proposition, there was in Mr. Holt's letter a distinct refusal to make any stipulation on the subject of reënforcement, even for the short time that might be required to communicate with my government.

This reply to the Senators was, as I have stated, altogether unsatisfactory to me, and I felt sure that it would be so to the authorities whom I represented. It was not, however, addressed to me, or to the authorities of South Carolina; and, as South Carolina had addressed nothing to your Government, and had asked nothing at your hands, I looked not to Mr. Holt's letter but to the note addressed to me by the Senators of the seceded and seceding States. I had consented to withhold my message at *their* instance, provided they could get assurances *satisfactory to them* that no reënforcements would be sent to Fort Sumter in the interval, and that the peace should not be disturbed by any act of hostility. The Senators expressed, in their note to me of the 23d instant, their "entire confidence that no reënforcements will be sent to Fort Sumter, nor will the public peace be disturbed within the period requisite for full communication between you (myself) and your (my) Government"; and renewed their request that I would withhold the communication with which I stood charged, and await further instructions. This I have done. The further instructions arrived on the 30th instant and bear date the 26th. I now have the honor to make to you my first communication as special envoy from the government of South Carolina. You will find inclosed the original communication to the President of the United States from the Governor of South Carolina, with which I was charged in Charleston on the 12th day of January, instant, the day on which it bears date. I am now instructed by the Governor of South Carolina to say that "his opinion as to the propriety of the demand which is contained in this letter has not only been confirmed by the circumstances which your (my) mission has developed, but is now increased to a conviction of its necessity. The safety of the State requires that the position of the President should be distinctly understood. The safety of all seceding States requires it as much as the safety of South Carolina. If it be so, that Fort Sumter is held as *property,* then as property, the rights, whatever they may be, of the United States can be ascertained, and for the satisfaction of these rights the pledge of the State of South Carolina you are" (I am) "authorized to give. If Fort Sumter is not held as property, it is held," say my instructions, "as a military post, and such a post within the limits of South Carolina, can not be tolerated."

You will perceive that it is upon the presumption that it is solely as property that you continue to hold Fort Sumter that I have been selected for the performance of the duty upon which I have entered. I do not come as a military man to demand the surrender of a fortress, but as the legal officer of the State, its Attorney-General, to claim for the State the exercise of its undoubted right of eminent domain, and to pledge the State to make good all injury to the rights of property which may arise from the exercise of the claim.

South Carolina, as a separate, independent sovereignty, assumes the right to take into her possession everything within her limits essential to maintain her honor or her safety, irrespective of the question of property, subject only to the moral duty requiring that compensation should be made to the owner. This right she can not permit to be drawn into discussion. As to compensation for any property, whether of an individual or a Government, which she may deem it necessary for her honor or safety to take into her possession, her past history gives ample guarantee that it will be made, upon a fair accounting, to the last dollar. The proposition now is, that her law officer should, under authority of the Governor and his Council, distinctly pledge the faith of South Carolina to make such compensation in regard to Fort Sumter, and its appurtenances and contents, to the full extent of the money value of the property of the United States delivered over to the authorities of South Carolina by your command.

I will not suppose that a pledge like this can be considered insufficient security. Is not the money value of the property of the United States in this fort, situated where it can not be made available to the United States for any one purpose for which it was originally constructed, worth more to the United States than the property itself? Why, then, *as property,* insist on holding it by an armed garrison? Yet such has been the ground upon which you have invariably placed your occupancy of this fort by troops; beginning, prospectively, with your annual message of the 4th December; again in your special message of the 9th [8th] January, and still more emphatically in your message of the 28th January. The same position is set forth in your reply to the Senators, through the Secretary of War *ad interim.* It is there virtually conceded that Fort Sumter "is held merely as property of the United States, which you deem it your duty to protect and preserve."

Again, it is submitted that the continuance of an armed possession actually jeopards the property you desire to protect. It is impossible but that such a possession, if continued long enough, must lead to collision. No people, not completely abject and pusillanimous, could submit, indefinitely, to the armed occupation of a fortress in the midst of the harbor of its principal city, and commanding the ingress and egress of every ship that enters the port, the daily ferryboats that ply upon the waters moving but at the sufferance of aliens. An attack upon this fort would scarcely improve it as property, whatever the result; and, if captured, it would no longer be the subject of account.

To protect Fort Sumter merely as property, it is submitted that an armed occupancy is not only unnecessary, but that it is manifestly the worst possible means which can be resorted to for such an object.

Your reply to the Senators, through Mr. Holt, declares it to be your sole object "to act strictly on the defensive, and to authorize no movement against South Carolina unless justified by a hostile movement on their part," yet, in reply to the proposition of the Senators that no reënforcements should be sent to Fort Sumter, provided South Carolina agrees that during the same period no attack should be made, you say: "It is impossible for me (your Secretary) to give you (the Senators) any such assurance," that it "would be a manifest violation of his (your) duty to place himself (yourself) under engagements that he (you) would not perform the duty either for an indefinite or a limited period."

In your message of the 28th inst., in expressing yourself in regard to a similar proposition, you say: "However, strong may be my desire to enter into such an agreement, I am convinced that I do not possess the power. Congress, and Congress alone, under the war-making power, can exercise the discretion of agreeing to abstain 'from any and all acts calculated to produce a collision of arms' between this and other governments. It would, therefore, be a usurpation for the Executive to attempt to restrain their hands by an agreement in regard to matters over which he has no constitutional control. If he were thus to act, they might pass laws which he should be bound to obey, though in conflict with his agreement." The proposition, it is suggested, was addressed to you under the laws as they now are, and was not intended to refer to a new condition of things arising under new legislation. It was addressed to the Executive discretion, acting under existing laws. If Congress should, under the war-making power, or in any other way, legislate in a manner to affect the peace of South Carolina, her interests or her rights, it would not be accomplished in secret. South Carolina would have timely notice, and she would, I trust, endeavor to meet the emergency.

It is added in the letter of Mr. Holt that "at the present moment it is not deemed necessary to reënforce Major Anderson, because he makes no such request, and feels quite secure in his position. But, should his safety require it, every effort will be made to supply reënforcements." This would seem to ignore the other branch of the proposition made by the Senator, viz., that no attack was to be made on Fort Sumter during the period suggested, and that Major Anderson should enjoy the facilities of communication, etc.

I advert to this point, however, for the purpose of saying that to send reenforcements to Fort Sumter could not serve as a means of *protecting* and *preserving* property, for, as must be known to your Government, it would inevitably lead to immediate hostilities, in which property on all sides would necessarily suffer.

South Carolina has every disposition to preserve the public peace, and feels, I am sure, in full force, those high "Christian and moral duties" referred to by your Secretary; and it is submitted that on her part there is scarcely any consideration of mere property, apart from honor and safety, which could induce her to do aught to jeopard that peace, still less to inaugurate a protracted and bloody civil war. She rests her position on something higher than mere property. It is a consideration of her own dignity as a sovereign, and the safety of her people, which prompts her to demand that this property should not longer be used as a military post by a Government she no longer acknowledges. She feels this to be an imperative duty. It has, in fact, become an absolute necessity of her condition.

Repudiating, as you do, the idea of coercion, avowing peaceful intentions, and expressing a patriot's horror for civil war and bloody strife among those who once were brethren, it is hoped that on further consideration you will not, on a mere question of property, refuse the reasonable demand of South Carolina, which honor and necessity alike compel her to vindicate. Should you disappoint this hope, the responsibility for the result surely does not rest with her. If the evils of war are to be encountered, especially the calamities of civil war, an elevated statesmanship would seem to require that it should be accepted as the unavoidable alternative of something still more disastrous, such as national dishonor or measures materially affecting the safety or permanent interests of a people —that it should be a choice deliberately made, and entered upon as war, and of set purpose. But that war should be the incident or accident, attendant on a policy professedly peaceful, and not required to effect the object which is avowed as the only end intended, can only be excused when there has been no warning given as to the consequences.

I am further instructed to say that South Carolina can not, by her silence, appear to acquiesce in the imputation that she was guilty of an act of unprovoked aggression in firing on the Star of the West. Though an unarmed vessel, she was filled with armed men entering her territory against her will, with the purpose of reënforcing a garrison held, within her limits, against her protest. She forbears to recriminate by discussing the question of the propriety of attempting such a reenforcement at all, as well as of the disguised and secret manner in which it was intended to be effected. And on this occasion she will say nothing as to the manner in which Fort Sumter was taken into the possession of its present occupants.

The interposition of the Senators who have addressed you was a circumstance unexpected by my government, and unsolicited certainly by me. The Governor, while he appreciates the high and generous motives by which they were prompted, and while he fully approves the delay which, in deference to them, has taken place in the presentation of this demand, feels that it can not longer be withheld.

I conclude with an extract from the instructions just received by me from the government of South Carolina:

"The letter of the President, through Mr. Holt, may be received as the reply to the question you were instructed to ask, as to his assertion of his right to send reenforcements to Fort Sumter. You were instructed to say to him, if he asserted that right, that the State of South Carolina regarded such a right when asserted, or with an attempt at its exercise, as a declaration of war.

"If the President intends it shall not be so understood, it is proper, to avoid any misconception hereafter, that he should be informed of the manner in which the Governor will feel bound to regard it.

"If the President, when you have stated the reasons which prompt the Governor in making the demand for the delivery of Sumter, shall refuse to deliver the fort upon the pledge you have been authorized to make, you will communicate that refusal without delay to the Governor. If the President shall not be prepared to give you an immediate answer, you will communicate to him that his answer may be transmitted within a reasonable time to the Governor at this place (Charleston, South Carolina).

"The Governor does not consider it necessary that you (I) should remain longer in Washington than is necessary to execute this, the closing duty of your (my) mission, in the manner now indicated to you (me). As soon as the Governor shall receive from you information that you have closed your mission, and the reply, whatever it may be, of the President, he will consider the conduct which may be necessary on his part."

Allow me to request that you would, as soon as possible, inform me whether, under these instructions, I need await your answer in Washington; and, if not, I would be pleased to convey from you, to my government, information as to the time when an answer may be expected in Charleston.

With high consideration.

I am, very respectfully,

ISAAC W. HAYNE, *Special Envoy.*

Some further correspondence ensued, but without the presentation of any new feature necessary to a full understanding of the case. The result was to leave it as much unsettled in the end as it had been in the beginning, and the efforts at negotiation were terminated by the retirement from Washington of Colonel Hayne on February 8, 1861.

APPENDIX K

THE CONSTITUTIONS

THE provisional Constitution of the Confederate States, adopted on February 8, 1861, is here presented, followed by the Constitution of the United States, with all its amendments to the period of the secession of the Southern states, and the permanent Constitution of the Confederate States (adopted on March 11, 1861), in parallel columns. The variations from the Constitution of the United States, in the permanent Constitution of the Confederate States, are indicated by italics; the parts omitted by periods.

CONSTITUTION FOR THE PROVISIONAL GOVERNMENT OF THE CONFEDERATE STATES OF AMERICA

We, the deputies of the sovereign and independent States of South Carolina, Georgia, Florida, Alabama, Mississippi, and Louisiana, invoking the favor of Almighty God, do hereby, in behalf of these States, ordain and establish this Constitution for the provisional Government of the same: to continue one year from the inauguration of the President, or until a permanent Constitution or Confederation between the said States shall be put in operation, whichsoever shall first occur.

ARTICLE I.

SECTION 1.—All legislative powers herein delegated shall be vested in this Congress now assembled until otherwise ordained.

SECTION 2.—When vacancies happen in the representation from any State, the same shall be filled in such manner as the proper authorities of the State shall direct.

SECTION 3.—1. The Congress shall be the judge of the elections, returns, and qualifications of its members; any number of deputies from a majority of the States being present, shall constitute a quorum to do business; but a smaller number may adjourn from day to day, and may be authorized to compel the attendance of absent members; upon all questions before the Congress each State shall be entitled to one vote, and shall be represented by any one or more of its deputies who may be present.

2. The Congress may determine the rules of its proceedings, punish its members for disorderly behavior, and, with the concurrence of two thirds, expel a member.

3. The Congress shall keep a journal of its proceedings, and from time to time publish the same, excepting such parts as may in their judgment require secrecy; and the yeas and nays of the members on any question shall, at the desire of one fifth of those present, or at the instance of any one State, be entered on the journal.

SECTION 4.—The members of Congress shall receive a compensation for their services, to be ascertained by law, and paid out of the Treasury of the Confederacy. They shall in all cases, except treason, felony, and breach of the peace, be privileged from arrest during their attendance at the session of the Congress, and in going to and returning from the same; and for any speech or debate they shall not be questioned in any other place.

SECTION 5.—1. Every bill which shall have passed the Congress shall, before it becomes a law, be presented to the President of the Confederacy; if he approve, he shall sign it; but, if not, he shall return it with his objections to the Congress, who shall enter the objections at large on their journal, and proceed to reconsider it. If, after such reconsideration, two thirds of the Congress shall be determined by yeas and nays; and the names of the persons voting for and against the bill shall be entered on the journal. If any bill shall not be returned by the President within ten days (Sundays excepted) after it shall have been presented to him, the same shall be a law, in like manner as if he had signed it, unless the Congress by their adjournment, prevent its return, in which case it shall not be a law. The President may veto any appropriation or appropriations, and approve any other appropriation or appropriations, in the same bill.

2. Every order, resolution, or vote intended to have the force and effect of a law, shall be presented to the President, and, before the same shall take effect, shall be approved by him, or, being disapproved by him, shall be repassed by two thirds of the Congress, according to the rules and limitations prescribed in the case of a bill.

3. Until the inauguration of the President, all bills, orders, resolutions, and votes adopted by the Congress shall be of full force without approval by him.

SECTION 6.—1. The Congress shall have power to lay and collect taxes, duties, imposts, and excises, for the revenue necessary to pay the debts and carry on the Government of the Confederacy; and all duties, imposts, and excises shall be uniform throughout the States of the Confederacy.

2. To borrow money on the credit of the Confederacy.

3. To regulate commerce with foreign nations, and among the several States, and with the Indian tribes.

4. To establish a uniform rule of naturalization and uniform laws on the subject of bankruptcies throughout the Confederacy.

5. To coin money, regulate the value thereof and of foreign coin, and fix the standard of weights and measures.

6. To provide for the punishment of counterfeiting the securities and current coin of the Confederacy.

7. To establish post-offices and post-roads.

8. To promote the progress of science and useful arts by securing for limited times to authors and inventors the exclusive right to their respective writings and discoveries.

9. To constitute tribunals inferior to the Supreme Court.

10. To define and punish piracies and felonies committed on the high seas, and offenses against the law of nations.

11. To declare war, grant letters of marque and reprisal, and make rules concerning captures on land and water.

12. To raise and support armies; but no appropriation of money to that use shall be for a longer term than two years.

13. To provide and maintain a navy.

14. To make rules for the government and regulation of the land and naval forces.

15. To provide for calling forth the militia to execute the laws of the Confederacy, suppress insurrections, and repel invasion.

16. To provide for organizing, arming, and disciplining the militia, and for governing such part of them as may be employed in the service of the Confederacy, reserving to the States respectively the appointment of the officers, and the authority of training the militia according to the discipline prescribed by Congress.

17. To make all laws that shall be necessary and proper for carrying into execution the foregoing powers and all other powers expressly delegated by this Constitution to this provisional Government.

18. The Congress shall have power to admit other States.

19. This Congress shall also exercise executive powers until the President is inaugurated.

SECTION 7.—1. The importation of African negroes from any foreign country, other than the slaveholding States of the United States, is hereby forbidden; and Congress are required to pass such laws as shall effectually prevent the same.

2. The Congress shall also have power to prohibit the introduction of slaves from any State not a member of this Confederacy.

3. The privilege of the writ of *habeas corpus* shall not be suspended unless, when in case of rebellion or invasion, the public safety may require it.

4. No bill of attainder or *ex post facto* law shall be passed.

5. No preference shall be given, by any regulation of commerce or revenue, to the ports of one State over those of another; nor shall vessels bound to or from one State be obliged to enter, clear, or pay duties in another.

6. No money shall be drawn from the Treasury, but in consequence of appropriations made by law; and a regular statement and account of the receipts and expenditures of all public money shall be published from time to time.

7. Congress shall appropriate no money from the Treasury unless it be asked and estimated for by the President or some one of the heads of departments, except for the purpose of paying its own expenses and contingencies.

8. No title of nobility shall be granted by the Confederacy; and no person holding any office of profit or trust under it shall, without the consent of the Congress, accept of any present, emolument, office, or title of any kind whatever from any king, prince, or foreign state.

9. Congress shall make no law respecting an establishment of religion or prohibiting the free exercise thereof; or abridging the freedom of speech, or of the press; or the right of the people peaceably to assemble and to petition the Government for a redress of such grievances as the delegated powers of this Government may warrant it to consider and redress.

10. A well-regulated militia being necessary to the security of a free state, the right of the people to keep and bear arms shall not be infringed.

11. No soldier shall, in time of peace, be quartered in any house without the consent of the owner; nor in time of war, but in a manner to be prescribed by law.

12. The right of the people to be secure in their persons, houses, papers, and effects against unreasonable searches and seizures shall not be violated; and no warrants shall issue but upon probable cause, supported by oath or affirmation,

and particularly describing the place to be searched, and the persons or things to be seized.

13. No person shall be held to answer for a capital or otherwise infamous crime, unless on a presentment or indictment of a grand jury, except in cases arising in the land or naval forces or in the militia, when in actual service in time of war or public danger; nor shall any person be subject for the same offense to be twice put in jeopardy of life or limb; nor shall be compelled in any criminal case to be a witness against himself; nor be deprived of life, liberty, or property without due process of law; nor shall private property be taken for public use without just compensation.

14. In all criminal prosecutions, the accused shall enjoy the right to a speedy and public trial by an impartial jury of the State and district wherein the crime shall have been committed, which district shall have been previously ascertained by law, and to be informed of the nature and cause of the accusation; to be confronted with the witness against him; to have compulsory process for obtaining witnesses in his favor; and to have the assistance of counsel for his defense.

15. In suits at common law, where the value in controversy shall exceed twenty dollars, the right of trial by jury shall be preserved; and no fact tried by a jury shall be otherwise reëxamined in any court of the Confederacy than according to the rules of the common law.

16. Excessive bail shall not be required, nor excessive fines imposed, nor cruel and unusual punishment inflicted.

17. The enumeration, in the Constitution, of certain rights shall not be construed to deny or disparage others retained by the people.

18. The powers not delegated to the Confederacy by the Constitution, nor prohibited by it to the States, are reserved to the States respectively, or to the people.

19. The judicial power of the Confederacy shall not be construed to extend to any suit in law or equity, commenced or prosecuted against one of the States of the Confederacy, by citizens of another State, or by citizens or subjects of any foreign state.

SECTION 8.—1. No State shall enter into any treaty, alliance, or confederation; grant letters of marque and reprisal; coin money; emit bills of credit; make anything but gold and silver coin a tender in payment of debts; pass any bill of attainder, *ex post facto* law, or law impairing the obligation of contracts; or grant any title of nobility.

2. No State shall, without the consent of the Congress, lay any imports or duties on imports or exports, except what may be absolutely necessary for executing its inspection laws; and the net produce of all duties and imposts, laid by any State on imports or exports, shall be for the use of the Treasury of the Confederacy, and all such laws shall be subject to the revision and control of the Congress. No State shall, without the consent of Congress, lay any duty on tonnage, enter into any agreement or compact with another State, or with a foreign power, or engage in war unless actually invaded, or in such imminent danger as will not admit of delay.

ARTICLE II.

SECTION 1.—1. The Executive power shall be vested in a President of the Confederate States of America. He, together with the Vice-President, shall hold his office for one year, or until this Provisional Government shall be superseded by a permanent Government, whichsoever shall first occur.

2. The President and Vice-President shall be elected by ballot by the States represented in this Congress, each State casting one vote, and a majority of the whole being requisite to elect.

3. No person except a natural-born citizen, or a citizen of one of the States of this Confederacy at the time of the adoption of this Constitution, shall be eligible to the office of President; neither shall any person be eligible to that office who shall not have attained the age of thirty-five years, and been fourteen years a resident of one of the States of this Confederacy.

4. In case of the removal of the President from office, or of his death, resignation, or inability to discharge the powers and duties of the said office (which inability shall be determined by a vote of two thirds of the Congress), the same shall devolve on the Vice-President; and the Congress may by law provide for the case of removal, death, resignation, or inability both of the President and Vice-President, declaring what officer shall then act as President; and such officer shall act accordingly, until the disability be removed or a President shall be elected.

5. The President shall, at stated times, receive for his services during the period of the Provisional Government a compensation at the rate of twenty-five thousand dollars per annum; and he shall not receive during that period any other emolument from this Confederacy, or any of the States thereof.

6. Before he enters on the execution of his office, he shall take the following oath or affirmation:

I do solemnly swear (or affirm) that I will faithfully execute the office of President of the Confederate States of America, and will, to the best of my ability, preserve, protect, and defend the Constitution thereof.

SECTION 2.—1. The President shall be Commander-in-Chief of the Army and Navy of the Confederacy, and of the militia of the several States, when called into the actual service of the Confederacy; he may require the opinion in writing of the principal officer in each of the executive departments, upon subjects relating to the duties of their respective offices; and he shall have power to grant reprieves and pardons for offenses against the Confederacy, except in cases of impeachment.

2. He shall have power, by and with the advice and consent of the Congress, to make treaties, provided two thirds of the Congress concur; and he shall nominate and, by and with the advice and consent of the Congress, shall appoint ambassadors, other public ministers, and consuls, judges of the courts, and all other officers of the Confederacy whose appointments are herein otherwise provided for, and which shall be established by law. But the Congress may, by law, vest the appointment of such inferior officers as they think proper in the President alone, in the courts of law, or in the heads of departments.

3. The President shall have power to fill up all vacancies that may happen during the recess of the Congress, by granting commissions which shall expire at the end of their next session.

SECTION 3.—1. He shall from time to time give to the Congress information of the state of the Confederacy, and recommend to their consideration such measures as he shall judge necessary and expedient; he may, on extraordinary occasions, convene the Congress at such times as he shall think proper; he shall receive amabassadors and other public ministers; he shall take care that the laws be faithfully executed; and shall commission all the officers of the Confederacy.

2. The President, Vice-President, and all civil officers of the Confederacy shall be removed from office on conviction by the Congress of treason, bribery, or other high crimes and misdemeanors; a vote of two thirds shall be necessary for such conviction.

ARTICLE III.

SECTION 1.—1. The judicial power of the Confederacy shall be vested in one Supreme Court, and in such inferior courts as are herein directed, or as the Congress may from time to time ordain and establish.

2. Each State shall constitute a district in which there shall be a court called a District Court, which, until otherwise provided by the Congress, shall have the jurisdiction vested by the laws of the United States, as far as applicable, in both the District and Circuit Courts of the United States, for that State; the judge whereof shall be appointed by the President by and with the advice and consent of the Congress, and shall, until otherwise provided by the Congress, exercise the power and authority vested by the laws of the United States in the judges of the District and Circuit Courts of the United States for that State, and shall appoint the times and places at which the courts shall be held. Appeals may be taken directly from the District Courts to the Supreme Court, under similar regulations to those which are provided in cases of appeal to the Supreme Court of the United States, or under such regulations as may be provided by the Congress. The commissions of all the judges shall expire with this provisional Government.

3. The Supreme Court shall be constituted of all the district judges, a majority of whom shall be a quorum, and shall sit at such times and places as the Congress shall appoint.

4. The Congress shall have power to make laws for the transfer of any causes which were pending in the courts of the United States to the courts of the Confederacy, and for the execution of the orders, decrees, and judgments heretofore rendered by the said courts of the United States; and also all laws which may be requisite to protect the parties to all such units, orders, judgments, or decrees, their heirs, personal representatives, or assignees.

SECTION 2.—1. The judicial power shall extend to all cases of law and equity arising under this Constitution, the laws of the United States and of this Confederacy, and treaties made, or which shall be made, under its authority; to all cases affecting ambassadors, other public ministers and consuls; to all cases of admiralty and maritime jurisdiction; to controversies to which the Confederacy shall be a party; controversies between two or more States; between citizens of different States; between citizens of the same State claiming lands under grants of different States.

2. In all cases affecting ambassadors, other public ministers and consuls, and those in which a State shall be a party, the Supreme Court shall have original jurisdiction. In all the other cases before mentioned, the Supreme Court shall have appellate jurisdiction both as to law and fact, with such exceptions and under such regulations as the Congress shall make.

3. The trial of all crimes, except in cases of impeachment, shall be by jury, and such trial shall be held in the State where the said crimes shall have been com-

mitted; but, when not committed within any State, the trial shall be at such place or places as the Congress may by law have directed.

SECTION 3.—1. Treason against this Confederacy shall consist only in levying war against it, or in adhering to its enemies, giving them aid and comfort. No person shall be convicted of treason unless on the testimony of two witnesses to the same overt act, or on confession in open court.

2. The Congress shall have power to declare the punishment of treason; but no attainder of treason shall work corruption of blood, or forfeiture, except during the life of the person attained.

ARTICLE IV.

SECTION 1.—1. Full faith and credit shall be given in each State to the public acts, records, and judicial proceedings of every other State. And the Congress may by general laws prescribe the manner in which such acts, records, and proceedings shall be proved, and the effect of such proof.

SECTION 2.—1. The citizens of each State shall be entitled to all privileges and immunities of citizens in the several States.

2. A person charged in any State with treason, felony, or other crime, who shall flee from justice, and be found in another State, shall, on demand of the Executive authority of the State from which he fled, be delivered up to be removed to the State having jurisdiction of the crime.

3. A slave in one State escaping to another shall be delivered up, on claim of the party to whom said slave may belong, by the Executive authority of the State in which such slave shall be found, and, in case of any abduction or forcible rescue, full compensation, including the value of the slave and all costs and expenses, shall be made to the party by the State in which such abduction or rescue shall take place.

SECTION 3.—1. The Confederacy shall guarantee to every State in this Union a republican form of government, and shall protect each of them against invasion; and on application of the Legislature, or of the Executive (when the Legislature can not be convened), against domestic violence.

ARTICLE V.

1. The Congress, by a vote of two thirds, may at any time alter or amend this Constitution.

ARTICLE VI.

1. This Constitution, and the laws of the Confederacy which shall be made in pursuance thereof, and all treaties made, or which shall be made, under the authority of the Confederacy, shall be the supreme law of the land; and the judges in every State shall be bound thereby, anything in the Constitution or laws of any State to the contrary notwithstanding.

2. The Government hereby instituted shall take immediate steps for the settlement of all matters between the States forming it, and their other late confederates of the United States, in relation to the public property and public debt at the time of their withdrawal from them; these States hereby declaring it to be their wish and earnest desire to adjust everything pertaining to the common property, common liability, and common obligations of that Union upon the principles of right, justice, equity, and good faith.

3. Until otherwise provided by the Congress, the city of Montgomery, in the State of Alabama, shall be the seat of government.

4. The members of the Congress and all executive and judicial officers of the Confederacy shall be bound by oath or affirmation to support this Constitution; but no religious test shall be required as a qualification to any office or public trust under this Confederacy.

CONSTITUTION OF THE UNITED STATES OF AMERICA.[1]

WE the People of the United States, in order to form a more perfect Union, establish Justice, insure domestic Tranquillity, provide for the common defence, promote the general Welfare, and secure the Blessings of Liberty to ourselves and our Posterity, do ordain and establish this CONSTITUTION for the United States of America.

CONSTITUTION OF THE CONFEDERATE STATES OF AMERICA.

WE, the People of the *Confederate* States, *each State acting in its sovereign and independent character, in order to form a permanent Federal Government,* establish justice, insure domestic tranquillity, and secure the blessings of liberty to ourselves and our posterity—*invoking the favor and guidance of Almighty God*—do ordain and establish this Constitution for the *Confederate* States of America.

ARTICLE I.

SECTION 1. All legislative Powers herein granted shall be vested in a Congress of the United States, which shall consist of a Senate and House of Representatives.

SECTION 2. The House of Representatives shall be composed of Members chosen every second Year by the People of the several States, and the Electors in each State shall have the Qualifications requisite for Electors of the most numerous Branch of the State Legislature.

ARTICLE I.

SECTION 1. All legislative powers herein *delegated* shall be vested in a Congress of the *Confederate* States, which shall consist of a Senate and House of Representatives.

SECTION 2. The House of Representatives shall be composed of members chosen every second year by the people of the several States; and the electors in each State shall *be citizens of the Confederate States, and* have the qualifications requisite for electors of the most numerous branch of the State Legislature; *but no person of foreign birth, not a citizen of the Confederate States, shall be allowed to vote for any officer, civil or political, State or Federal.*

No Person shall be a Representative who shall not have attained to the Age of twenty-five Years, and been seven Years a Citizen of the United States, and who shall not, when elected, be

No person shall be a Representative who shall not have attained the age of twenty-five years, and *be a citizen of the Confederate* States, and who shall not, when elected, be an inhabitant of

---

[1] This is an exact copy of the original in punctuation, spelling, capitals, etc.

an Inhabitant of that State in which he shall be chosen.

Representatives and direct Taxes shall be apportioned among the several States which may be included within this Union, according to their respective Numbers,[2] which shall be determined by adding to the whole Number of free Persons, including those bound to Service for a Term of Years, and excluding Indians not taxed, three-fifths of all other Persons.[3] The actual Enumeration shall be made within three Years after the first meeting of the Congress of the United States, and within every subsequent Term of ten Years, in such Manner as they shall by Law direct. The Number of Representatives shall not exceed one for every thirty Thousand, but each State shall have at Least one Representative; and until such enumeration shall be made, the State of New Hampshire shall be entitled to chuse three, Massachusetts eight, Rhode-Island and Providence Plantations one, Connecticut five, New York six, New Jersey four, Pennsylvania eight, Delaware one, Maryland six, Virginia ten, North Carolina five, South Carolina five, and Georgia three.

When vacancies happen in the Representation from any State, the Executive Authority thereof shall issue Writs of Election to fill such Vacancies.

The House of Representatives shall chuse their Speaker and other officers;[4] and shall have the sole Power of Impeachment.

SECTION 3. The Senate of the United States shall be composed of two Sena-

that State in which he shall be chosen.

Representatives and direct taxes shall be apportioned among the several States, which may be included within this *Confederacy,* according to their respective numbers, which shall be determined by adding to the whole number of free persons, including those bound to service for a term of years, and excluding Indians not taxed, three fifths of all *slaves.* The actual enumeration shall be made within three years after the first meeting of the Congress of the *Confederate* States, and within every subsequent term of ten years, in such manner as they shall by law direct. The number of Representatives shall not exceed one for every *fifty* thousand, but each State shall have at least one Representative; and until such enumeration shall be made, the State of *South Carolina* shall be entitled to choose *six, the State of Georgia ten, the State of Alabama nine, the State of Florida two, the State of Mississippi seven, the State of Louisiana six, and the State of Texas six.*

When vacancies happen in the representation from any State, the Executive authority thereof shall issue writs of election to fill such vacancies.

The House of Representatives shall choose their Speaker and other officers; and shall have the sole power of impeachment, *except that any judicial or other Federal officer, resident and acting solely within the limits of any State, may be impeached by a vote of two thirds of both branches of the Legislature thereof.*

SECTION 3. The Senate of the *Confederate* States shall be composed of

---

[2] Under the census of 1860 one representative is allowed for every 127,381 persons.

[3] "Other persons" refers to slaves. See Amendments, Art. XIV, Sections 1 and 2.

[4] The principal of these are the clerk, sergeant-at-arms, doorkeeper, and postmaster.

tors from each State, chosen by the Legislature thereof, for six Years; and each Senator shall have one Vote.

Immediately after they shall be assembled in Consequence of the first Election, they shall be divided as equally as may be into three Classes. The Seats of the Senators of the first Class shall be vacated at the Expiration of the second Year, of the second Class at the Expiration of the fourth Year, and of the third class at the Expiration of the sixth Year, so that one-third may be chosen every second year; and if Vacancies happen by Resignation, or otherwise, during the Recess of the Legislature of any State, the Executive thereof may make temporary Appointments until the next Meeting of the Legislature, which shall then fill such Vacancies.

No person shall be a Senator who shall not have attained to the Age of thirty Years, and been nine Years a Citizen of the United States, and who shall not, when elected, be an Inhabitant of that State for which he shall be chosen.

The Vice President of the United States shall be President of the Senate, but shall have no Vote, unless they be equally divided.

The Senate shall chuse their other Officers, and also a President pro tempore, in the absence of the Vice President, or when he shall exercise the Office of President of the United States.

The Senate shall have the sole Power to try all Impeachments. When sitting for that Purpose, they shall be on Oath or Affirmation. When the President of the United States is tried, the Chief Justice shall preside: And no Person shall be convicted without the Concur-

two Senators from each State, chosen for six years by the Legislature thereof, *at the regular session next immediately preceding the commencement of the term of service;* and each Senator shall have one vote.

Immediately after they shall be assembled, in consequence of the first election, they shall be divided as equally as may be into three classes. The Seats of the Senators of the first class shall be vacated at the expiration of the second year; of the second class at the expiration of the fourth year; and of the third class at the expiration of the sixth year; so that one third may be chosen every second year; and if vacancies happen by resignation or otherwise, during the recess of the Legislature of any State, the Executive thereof may make temporary appointments until the next meeting of the Legislature, which shall than fill such vacancies.

No person shall be a Senator who shall not have attained the age of thirty years, and *be a citizen of the Confederate States;* and who shall not, when elected, be an inhabitant of *the* State for which he shall be chosen.

The Vice-President of the *Confederate* States shall be President of the Senate, but shall have no vote unless they be equally divided.

The Senate shall choose their other officers; and also a President *pro tempore* in the absence of the Vice-President, or when he shall exercise the office of President of the *Confederate* States.

The Senate shall have the sole power to try all impeachments. When sitting for that purpose, they shall be on oath or affirmation. When the President of the *Confederate* States is tried, the Chief-Justice shall preside; and no person be convicted without the con-rence of two-thirds of the Members present.

Judgment in Cases of Impeachment shall not extend further than to removal from Office, and Disqualification to hold and enjoy any Office of Honour, Trust or Profit under the United States: but the Party convicted shall nevertheless be liable and subject to Indictment, Trial, Judgment and Punishment, according to Law.

SECTION 4. The Times, Places and Manner of holding Elections for Senators and Representatives, shall be prescribed in each State by the Legislature thereof: but the Congress may at any time by Law make or alter such Regulations, except as to the places of chusing Senators.

The Congress shall assemble at least once in every Year, and such Meeting shall be on the first Monday in December, unless they shall by Law appoint a different Day.

SECTION 5. Each House shall be the Judge of the Elections, Returns and Qualifications of its own Members, and a Majority of each shall constitute a Quorum to do Business; but a smaller Number may adjourn from day to day, and may be authorized to compel the Attendance of absent Members, in such Manner, and under such Penalties as each House may provide.

Each House may determine the Rules of its Proceedings, punish its Members for disorderly Behaviour, and, with the Concurrence of two-thirds, expel a Member.

Each House shall keep a Journal of its Proceedings, and from time to time publish the same, excepting such Parts as may in their Judgment require Secrecy; and the Yeas and Nays of the Members of either House on any question shall, at the Desire of one-fifth of those Present, be entered on the Journal.

currence of two thirds of the members present.

Judgment in cases of impeachment shall not extend further than to removal from office, and disqualification to hold and enjoy any office of honor, trust, or profit, under the *Confederate* States; but the party convicted shall, nevertheless, be liable and subject to indictment, trial, judgment, and punishment according to law.

SECTION 4. The times, place, and manner of holding elections for Senators and Representatives, shall be prescribed in each State by the Legislature thereof, *subject to the provisions of this Constitution;* but the Congress may, at any time, by law, make or alter such regulations, except as to the *times and* places of choosing Senators.

The Congress shall assemble at least once in every year; and such meeting shall be on the first Monday in December, unless they shall, by law appoint a different day.

SECTION 5. Each House shall be the judge of the elections, returns, and qualifications of its own members, and a majority of each shall constitute a quorum to do business; but a smaller number may adjourn from day to day, and may be authorized to compel the attendance of absent members, in such manner and under such penalties as each House may provide.

Each House may determine the rules of its proceedings, punish its members for disorderly behavior, and, with the concurrence of two thirds of the whole number, expel a member.

Each House shall keep a journal of its proceedings, and from time to time publish the same, excepting such parts as may in their judgment require secrecy; and the yeas and nays of the members of either House, on any question, shall, at the desire of one fifth of those present, be entered on the journal.

Neither House, during the Session of Congress, shall, without the Consent of the other, adjourn for more than three days, nor to any other Place than that in which the two Houses shall be sitting.

SECTION 6. The Senators and Representatives shall receive a Compensation for their Services, to be ascertained by law, and paid out of the Treasury of the United States. They shall in all Cases, except Treason, Felony and Breach of the Peace, be privileged from Arrest during their Attendance at the Session of their respective Houses, and in going to and returning from the same; and for any Speech or Debate in either House, they shall not be questioned in any other Place.

No Senator or Representative shall, during the time for which he was elected, be appointed to any civil Office under the Authority of the United States, which shall have been created, or the Emoluments whereof shall have increased during such time; and no Person holding any Office under the United States, shall be a Member of either House during his Continuance in Office.

SECTION 7. All Bills for raising Revenue shall originate in the House of Representatives; but the Senate may propose or concur with Amendments as on other Bills.

Every Bill which shall have passed the House of Representatives and the Senate, shall, before it become a Law, be presented to the President of the United States; If he approve he shall sign it, but if not he shall return it, with his Objections to that House in which it shall have originated, who

Neither House, during the session of Congress, shall, without the consent of the other, adjourn for more than three days, nor to any other place than that in which the two Houses shall be sitting.

SECTION 6. The Senators and Representatives shall receive a compensation for their services, to be ascertained by law, and paid out of the Treasury of the *Confederate* States. They shall, in all cases, except treason, felony and breach of the peace, be privileged from arrest during their attendance at the session of their respective Houses, and in going to and returning from the same; and, for any speech or debate in either House, they shall not be questioned in any other place.

No Senator or Representative shall, during the time for which he was elected, be appointed to any civil office under the authority of the *Confederate* States, which shall have been created, or the emoluments whereof shall have been increased during such time; and no person holding any office under the *Confederate* States shall be a member of either House during his continuance in office. *But Congress may, by law, grant to the principal officer in each of the executive departments a seat upon the floor of either House, with the privilege of discussing any measures appertaining to his department.*

SECTION 7. All bills for raising *the* revenue shall originate in the House of Representatives; but the Senate may propose or concur with amendments, as on other bills.

Every bill which shall have passed *both Houses,* shall, before it becomes a law, be presented to the President of the *Confederate* States; if he approve, he shall sign it; but if not, he shall return it, with his objections, to that House in which it shall have originated, who shall enter the objections at large

shall enter the Objections at large on their Journal, and proceed to reconsider it. If after such Reconsideration two-thirds of that House shall agree to pass the Bill, it shall be sent, together with the Objections, to the other House, by which it shall likewise be reconsidered, and if approved by two-thirds of that House, it shall become a Law. But in all such Cases the Votes of Both Houses shall be determined by Yeas and Nays, and the Names of the Persons voting for and against the Bill shall be entered on the Journal of each House respectively. If any Bill shall not be returned by the President within ten Days (Sundays excepted) after it shall have been presented to him, the Same shall be a law, in like Manner as if he had signed it, unless the Congress by their Adjournment prevent its Return, in which Case it shall not be a Law.

on their journal, and proceed to reconsider it. If, after such reconsideration, two thirds of that House shall agree to pass the bill, it shall be sent, together with the objections, to the other House, by which it shall likewise be reconsidered, and, if approved by two thirds of that House, it shall become a law. But, in all such cases, the votes of both Houses shall be determined by yeas and nays, and the names of the persons voting for and against the bill shall be entered on the journal of each House, respectively. If any bill shall not be returned by the President within ten days (Sundays excepted) after it shall have been presented to him, the same shall be a law, in like manner as if he had signed it, unless the Congress, by their adjournment, prevent its return; in which case it shall not be a law. *The President may approve any appropriation and disapprove any other appropriation in the same bill. In such case he shall, in signing the bill, designate the appropriations disapproved; and shall return a copy of such appropriations, with his objections, to the House in which the bill shall have originated; and the same proceedings shall then be had as in case of other bills disapproved by the President.*

Every Order, Resolution, or Vote to which the Concurrence of the Senate and House of Representatives may be necessary (except on a question of Adjournment) shall be presented to the President of the United States; and before the Same shall take Effect, shall be approved by him, or being disapproved by him, shall be repassed by two-thirds of the Senate and House of Representatives, according to the Rules and Limitations prescribed in the Case of a Bill.

Every order, resolution, or vote, to which the concurrence of *both Houses* may be necessary (except on a question of adjournment), shall be presented to the President of the *Confederate* States; and, before the same shall take effect, shall be approved by him; or, being disapproved, shall be repassed by two thirds of *both Houses,* according to the rules and limitations prescribed in case of a bill.

SECTION 8. The Congress shall have Power

To lay and collect Taxes, Duties,

SECTION 8. The Congress shall have power—

To lay and collect taxes, duties, im-

Imposts and Excises, to pay the Debts and provide for the common Defense and general Welfare of the United States; but all Duties, Imposts and Excises shall be uniform throughout the United States;

To borrow Money on the credit of the United States;

To regulate Commerce with foreign Nations, and among the several States, and with the Indian Tribes;

To establish an uniform Rule of Naturalization, and uniform Laws on the subject of Bankruptcies throughout the United States;

To coin Money, regulate the Value thereof, and of foreign Coin, and fix the Standard of Weights and Measures;

To provide for the Punishment of counterfeiting the Securities and current Coin of the United States;

To establish Post Offices and post Roads;

posts, and excises, *for revenue necessary* to pay the debts, provide for the common defense, *and carry on the Government of the Confederate* States; *but no bounties shall be granted from the Treasury; nor shall any duties or taxes on importations from foreign nations be laid to promote or foster any branch of industry; and all duties, imposts, and excises shall be uniform throughout the Confederate States:*

To borrow money on the credit of the *Confederate* States:

To regulate commerce with foreign nations, and among the several States, and with the Indian tribes; *but neither this, nor any other clause contained in the Constitution, shall ever be construed to delegate the power to Congress to appropriate money for any internal improvement intended to facilitate commerce; except for the purpose of furnishing lights, beacons, and buoys, and other aid to navigation upon the coasts, and the improvement of harbors and the removing of obstructions in river navigation, in all which cases, such duties shall be laid on the navigation facilitated thereby, as may be necessary to pay the costs and expenses thereof:*

To establish uniform *laws* of naturalization, and uniform laws on the subject of bankruptcies, throughout the *Confederate* States; *but no law of Congress shall discharge any debt contracted before the passage of the same:*

To coin money, regulate the value thereof, and of foreign coin, and fix the standard of weights and measures:

To provide for the punishment of counterfeiting the securities and current coin of the *Confederate* States:

To establish post-offices and post *routes; but the expenses of the Post-Office Department, after the first day of March, in the year of our Lord,*

To promote the progress of science and useful Arts, by securing for limited Times to Authors and Inventors the exclusive Right to their respective Writings and Discoveries;

To constitute Tribunals inferior to the supreme Court;

To define and punish Piracies and Felonies committed on the high Seas, and Offences against the Law of Nations;

To declare War, grant Letters of Marque and Reprisal, and make Rules concerning Captures on Land and Water;

To raise and support Armies, but no Appropriation of Money to that Use shall be for a longer Term than two Years;

To provide and maintain a Navy;

To make Rules for the Government and Regulation of the land and naval Forces;

To provide for calling forth the Militia to execute the Laws of the Union, suppress Insurrections and repel Invasions;

To provide for organizing, arming, and disciplining, the Militia, and for governing such Part of them as may be employed in the Service of the United States, reserving to the States respectively, the Appointment of the Officers, and the Authority of training the Militia according to the Discipline prescribed by Congress;

To exercise exclusive Legislation in all Cases whatsoever, over such District (not exceeding ten Miles square) as may, by Cession of particular States, and the Acceptance of Congress, become the Seat of the Government of the United States, and to exercise like Authority over all Places purchased by the Consent of the Legislature of the State in which the Same shall be, for the

eighteen hundred and sixty-three, shall be paid out of its own revenue:

To promote the progress of science and useful arts, by securing for limited times to authors and inventors the exclusive right to their respective writings and discoveries:

To constitute tribunals inferior to the Supreme Court:

To define and punish piracies and felonies committed on the high-seas, and offenses against the law of nations:

To declare war, grant letters of marque and reprisal, and make rules concerning captures on land and on water:

To raise and support armies, but no appropriation of money to that use shall be for a longer term than two years:

To provide and maintain a navy;

To make rules for the government and regulation of the land and naval forces:

To provide for calling forth the militia to execute the laws of the *Confederate* States, suppress insurrections, and repel invasions:

To provide for organizing, arming, and disciplining the militia, and for governing such part of them as may be employed in the service of the *Confederate* States, reserving to the States, respectively, the appointment of the officers, and the authority of training the militia according to the discipline prescribed by Congress:

To exercise exclusive legislation in all cases whatsoever, over such district (not exceeding ten miles square) as may, by cession of *one or more* States, and the acceptance of Congress, become the seat of the Government of the *Confederate* States, and to exercise like authority over all places purchased by the consent of the Legislature of the State in which the same shall be, for the

Erection of Forts, Magazines, Arsenals, Dock-Yards, and other needful Buildings;—And

To make all Laws which shall be necessary and proper for carrying into Execution the foregoing Powers, and all other Powers vested by this Constitution in the Government of the United States, or in any Department or Officer thereof.

SECTION 9. The Migration or Importation of such Persons as any of the States now existing shall think proper to admit, shall not be prohibited by the Congress prior to the Year one thousand eight hundred and eight, but a Tax or Duty may be imposed on such Importation, not exceeding ten dollars for each Person.

The Privilege of the Writ of Habeas Corpus shall not be suspended, unless when in Cases of Rebellion or Invasion the public Safety may require it.

No Bill of Attainder or ex post facto Law shall be passed.

No Capitation, or other direct, Tax shall be laid, unless in Proportion to the Census or Enumeration herein before directed to be taken.

No Tax or Duty shall be laid on Articles exported from any State.

No Preference shall be given by any Regulation of Commerce or Revenue to the Ports of one State over those of another: nor shall Vessels bound to, or from, one State, be obliged to enter, clear, or pay Duties in another.

No Money shall be drawn from the Treasury, but in Consequence of Appropriations made by Law; and a regular Statement and Account of the Receipts and Expenditures of all public

erection of forts, magazines, arsenals, dock-yards, and other needful buildings; and

To make all laws which shall be necessary and proper for carrying into execution the foregoing powers, and all other powers vested by this Constitution in the Government of the *Confederate* States, or in any department or officer thereof.

SECTION 9. The importation of *negroes of the African race, from any foreign country other than the slaveholding States or Territories of the United States of America, is hereby forbidden; and Congress is required to pass such laws as shall effectually prevent the same.*

Congress shall also have power to prohibit the introduction of slaves from any State not a member of, or Territory not belonging to, this Confederacy.

The privilege of the writ of *habeas corpus* shall not be suspended, unless when, in case of rebellion or invasion, the public safety may require it.

No bill of attainder, *ex post facto* law, *or law denying or impairing the right of property in negro slaves shall be passed.*

No capitation or other direct tax shall be laid, unless in proportion to the census or enumeration hereinbefore directed to be taken.

No tax or duty shall be laid on articles exported from any State *except by a vote of two thirds of both Houses.*

No preference shall be given by any regulation of commerce or revenue to the ports of one State over those of another.

No money shall be drawn from the Treasury, but in consequence of appropriations made by law; and a regular statement and account of the receipts and expenditures of all public money

Money shall be published from time to time.

shall be published from time to time.

Congress shall appropriate no money from the Treasury, except by a vote of two thirds of both Houses, taken by yeas and nays, unless it be asked and estimated for by some one of the heads of departments, and submitted to Congress by the President; or for the purpose of paying its own expenses and contingencies; or for the payment of claims against the Confederate States, the justice of which shall have been judicially declared by a tribunal for the investigation of claims against the Government, which it is hereby made the duty of Congress to establish.

All bills appropriating money shall specify, in Federal currency, the exact amount of each appropriation, and the purposes for which it is made; and Congress shall grant no extra compensation to any public contractor, officer, agent, or servant, after such contract shall have been made or such service rendered.

No Title of Nobility shall be granted by the United States: And no Person holding any Office of Profit or Trust under them, shall, without the Consent of the Congress, accept of any present, Emolument, Office, or Title, of any kind whatever, from any King, Prince, or foreign State.

No title of nobility shall be granted by the *Confederate* States; and no person holding any office of profit or trust under them shall, without the consent of the Congress, accept of any present, emolument, office, or title of any kind whatever, from any king, prince, or foreign state.

Congress shall make no law respecting an establishment of religion, or prohibiting the free exercise thereof; or abridging the freedom of speech, or of the press; or the right of the people peaceably to assemble and petition the Government for a redress of grievances.

A well-regulated militia being necessary to the security of a free state, the right of the people to keep and bear arms shall not be infringed.

No soldier shall, in time of peace, be quartered in any house without the consent of the owner; nor in time of war, but in a manner to be prescribed by law.

The right of the people to be secure in their persons, houses, papers, and effects, against unreasonable searches and seizures, shall not be violated; and no warrants shall issue but upon probable cause, supported by oath or affirmation, and particularly describing the place to be searched, and the persons or things to be seized.

No person shall be held to answer for a capital or otherwise infamous crime, unless on a presentment or indictment of a grand jury, except in cases arising in the land or naval forces, or in the militia, when in actual service in time of war or public danger; nor shall any person be subject, for the same offense, to be twice put in jeopardy of life or limb; nor be compelled, in any criminal case, to be a witness against himself; nor be deprived of life, liberty, or property, without due process of law; nor shall private property be taken for public use without just compensation.

In all criminal prosecutions, the accused shall enjoy the right to a speedy and public trial, by an impartial jury of the State and district wherein the crime shall have been committed, which district shall have been previously ascertained by law, and to be informed of the nature and cause of the accusation; to be confronted with the witnesses against him; to have compulsory process for obtaining witnesses in his favor; and to have the assistance of counsel for his defense.

In suits at common law, where the value in controversy shall exceed twenty dollars, the right of trial by jury shall be preserved; and no fact *so* tried by a jury shall be otherwise reëxamined in any court of the *Confederacy,* than according to the rules of the common law.

Excessive bail shall not be required, nor excessive fines imposed, nor cruel and unusual punishment inflicted.

Every law, or resolution having the force of law, shall relate to but one subject, and that shall be expressed in the title.

SECTION 10. No State shall enter into any Treaty, Alliance, or Confederation; grant Letters of Marque and Reprisal; coin Money; emit Bills of Credit; make any Thing but gold and silver Coin a Tender in Payment of Debts; pass any Bill of Attainder, ex post facto Law, or Law impairing the Obligation of Contracts, or grant any Title of Nobility.

No State shall, without the consent of the Congress, lay any Imposts or Duties on Imports or Exports, except what may be absolutely necessary for executing its inspection Laws: and the net Produce of all Duties and Imposts, laid by any State on Imports or Exports, shall be for the Use of the Treasury of the United States; and all such Laws shall be subject to the Revision and Control of the Congress.

No State shall, without the Consent of Congress, lay any Duty of Tonnage, keep Troops, or Ships of War in time of Peace, enter into any Agreement or Compact with another State, or with a foreign Power, or engage in War, unless actually invaded, or in such imminent Danger as will not admit of Delay.

SECTION 10. No State shall enter into any treaty, alliance, or confederation; grant letters of marque and reprisal; coin money; make anything but gold and silver coin a tender in payment of debts; pass any bill of attainder, or *ex post facto* law, or law impairing the obligation of contracts, or grant any title of nobility.

No State shall, without the consent of the Congress, lay any imposts or duties on imports or exports, except what may be absolutely necessary for executing its inspection laws; and the net produce of all duties and imposts, laid by any State on imports or exports, shall be for the use of the Treasury of the *Confederate* States; and all such laws shall be subject to the revision and control of Congress.

No State shall, without the consent of Congress, lay any duty *on* tonnage, *except on sea-going vessels for the improvement of its rivers and harbors navigated by the said vessels; but such duties shall not conflict with any treaties of the Confederate States with foreign nations. And any surplus revenue thus derived shall, after making such improvement, be paid into the common Treasury;* nor shall any State keep troops or ships of war in time of peace, enter into any agreement or compact with another State, or with a foreign power, or engage in war unless actually invaded, or in such imminent danger as will not admit of delay. *But when any river divides or flows through two or more States, they may enter into compacts with each other to improve the navigation thereof.*

ARTICLE II.

SECTION 1. The executive Power shall be vested in a President of the United States of America. He shall hold his Office during the Term of four Years, and, together with the Vice President, chosen for the same Term, be elected, as follows:

Each State shall appoint, in such Manner as the Legislature thereof may direct, a Number of Electors, equal to the whole Number of Senators and Representatives to which the State may be entitled in the Congress: but no Senator or Representative, or Person holding an Office of Trust or Profit under the United States, shall be appointed an Elector.

[5]The Electors shall meet in their respective States, and vote by Ballot for two Persons, of whom one at least shall not be an Inhabitant of the same State with themselves. And they shall make a List of all the Persons voted for, and of the Number of Votes for each; which List they shall sign and certify, and transmit sealed to the Seat of the Government of the United States, directed to the President of the Senate. The President of the Senate shall, in the Presence of the Senate and House of Representatives, open all the Certificates, and the Votes shall then be counted. The Person having the greatest Number of Votes shall be the President, if such Number be a Majority of the whole Number of Electors appointed; and if there be more than one who have such Majority and have an equal Number of Votes, then the House of Representatives shall immediately chuse by Ballot one of them for President;

ARTICLE II.

SECTION 1. The Executive power shall be vested in a President of the *Confederate* States of America. *He and the Vice-President shall hold their offices for* the term of *six* years; *but the President shall not be reëligible. The President and the Vice-President shall* be elected as follows:

Each State shall appoint, in such manner as the Legislature thereof may direct, a number of electors, equal to the whole number of Senators and Representatives to which the State may be entitled in the Congress; but no Senator or Representative, or person holding an office of trust or profit under the *Confederate* States, shall be appointed an elector.

The electors shall meet in their respective States and vote by ballot for President and Vice-President, one of whom, at least, shall not be an inhabitant of the same State with themselves; they shall name in their ballots the person voted for as President, and in distinct ballots the person voted for as Vice-President, and they shall make distinct lists of all persons voted for as President, and of all persons voted for as Vice-President, and of the number of votes for each, which list they shall sign and certify, and transmit sealed to the seat of the Government of the *Confederate* States, directed to the President of the Senate. The President of the Senate shall, in the presence of the Senate and House of Representatives, open all the certificates and the votes shall then be counted. The person having the greatest number of votes for President shall be the President, if such number be a majority of the whole

---

[5] Superseded by the twelfth amendment.

and if no Person have a Majority, then from the five highest on the List the said House shall in like Manner chuse the President. But in chusing the President, the Votes shall be taken by States, the Representation from each State having one Vote; a Quorum for this Purpose shall consist of a Member or Members from two-thirds of the States, and a Majority of all the States shall be necessary to a Choice. In every Case, after the Choice of the President, the Person having the greatest Number of Votes of the Electors shall be the Vice President. But if there should remain two or more who have equal Votes, the Senate shall chuse from them by Ballot the Vice President.

The Congress may determine the Time of chusing the Electors, and the Day on which they shall give their Votes; which Day shall be the same throughout the United States.

No Person except a natural born Citizen or a Citizen of the United States, at the time of the Adoption of this Constitution, shall be eligible to the Office of President; neither shall any

number of electors appointed; and if no person have such majority; then from the persons having the highest numbers not exceeding three on the list of those voted for as President, the House of Representatives shall choose immediately, by ballot, the President. But in choosing the President, the votes shall be taken by States, the representation from each State having one vote; a quorum for this purpose shall consist of a member or members from two thirds of the States, and a majority of all the States shall be necessary to a choice And if the House of Representatives shall not choose a President whenever the right of choice shall devolve upon them, before the fourth day of March next following, then the Vice-President shall act as President, as in the case of the death or other constitutional disability of the President.

The person having the greatest number of votes as Vice-President, shall be the Vice-President, if such number be a majority of the whole number of electors appointed; and if no person have a majority, then from the two highest numbers on the list the Senate shall choose the Vice-President. A quorum for the purpose shall consist of two thirds of the whole number of Senators, and a majority of the whole number shall be necessary to a choice.

But no person constitutionally ineligible to the office of President shall be eligible to that of Vice-President of the *Confederate* States.

The Congress may determine the time of choosing the electors, and the day on which they shall give their votes; which day shall be the same throughout the *Confederate* States.

No person except a natural born citizen of the *Confederate* States, or a citizen thereof at the time of the adoption of this Constitution, *or a citizen thereof born in the United States prior*

Person be eligible to that Office who shall not have attained to the Age of thirty-five Years, and been fourteen Years a Resident within the United States.

In Case of the Removal of the President from Office, or of his Death, Resignaton, or Inability to discharge the Powers and Duties of the said office, the same shall devolve on the Vice President, and the Congress may by Law provide for the Case of Removal, Death, Resignation, or Inability, both of the President and Vice President, declaring what Officer shall then act as President, and such Officer shall act accordingly, until the Disability be removed, or a President shall be elected.

The President shall, at stated Times, receive for his Services, a Compensation, which shall neither be encreased nor diminished during the Period for which he shall have been elected, and he shall not receive within that Period any other Emolument from the United States, or any of them.

Before he enter on the Execution of his Office, he shall take the following Oath or Affirmation:

"I do solemnly swear (or affirm) "that I will faithfully execute the Of- "fice of President of the United States, "and will to the best of my Ability, "preserve, protect and defend the "Constitution of the United States."

SECTION 2. The President shall be Commander in Chief of the Army and Navy of the United States, and of the Militia of the several States, when called into the actual Service of the United States; he may require the Opinion, in writing, of the principal Officer in each of the executive Departments, upon any Subject relating to the Duties of their respective Of-

to the 20th of December, 1860, shall be eligible to the office of President; neither shall any person be eligible to that office who shall not have attained the age of thirty-five years, and been fourteen years a resident within the *limits of the Confederate* States, *as they may exist at the time of his election.*

In case of the removal of the President from office, or of his death, resignation, or inability to discharge the powers and dutes of the said office, the same shall devolve on the Vice-President; and the Congress may, by law, provide for the case of removal, death, resignation, or inability, both of the President and Vice-President, declaring what officer shall then act as President; and such officer shall act accordingly, until the disability be removed or a President shall be elected.

The President shall, at stated times, receive for his services a compensation, which shall neither be increased nor diminished during the period for which he shall have been elected; and he shall not receive within that period any other emolument from the *Confederate* States, or any of them.

Before he enters on the execution of his office, he shall take the following oath or affirmation:

"I do solemnly swear (or affirm) that I will faithfully execute the office of President of the *Confederate* States *of America,* and will to the best of my ability, preserve, protect, and defend the Constitution *thereof."*

SECTION 2. The President shall be Commander-in-Chief of the Army and Navy of the *Confederate* States, and of the militia of the several States, when called into the actual service of the *Confederate* States; he may require the opinion, in writing, of the principal officer in each of the executive departments, upon any subject relating to the duties of their respective offices, and

fices, and he shall have Power to grant Reprieves and Pardons for Offences against the United States, except in Cases of Impeachment.

He shall have Power, by and with the Advice and Consent of the Senate, to make Treaties, provided two-thirds of the Senators present concur; and he shall nominate, and by and with the Advice and Consent of the Senate, shall appoint Ambassadors, other public Ministers and Consuls, Judges of the supreme Court, and all other Officers of the United States, whose Appointments are not herein otherwise provided for, and which shall be established by Law: but the Congress may by law vest the Appointment of such inferior Officers, as they think proper, in the President alone, in the Courts of Law, or in the Heads of Departments.

The President shall have Power to fill up all Vacancies that may happen during the Recess of the Senate, by granting Commissions which shall expire at the End of their next Session.

SECTION 3. He shall from time to time give to the Congress Information of the State of the Union, and recommend to their Consideration such Measures as he shall judge necessary

he shall have power to grant reprieves and pardons for offenses against the *Confederacy*, except in cases of impeachment.

He shall have power, by and with the advice and consent of the Senate, to make treaties, provided two thirds of the Senators present concur; and he shall nominate, and by and with the advice and consent of the Senate shall appoint ambassadors, other public ministers and consuls, Judges of the Supreme Court and all other officers of the *Confederate* States, whose appointments are not herein otherwise provided for, and which shall be established by law; but the Congress may by law vest the appointment of such inferior officers, as they think proper, in the President alone, in the courts of law, or in the heads of departments.

The principal officer in each of the executive departments, and all persons connected with the diplomatic service, may be removed from office at the pleasure of the President. All other civil officers of the executive department may be removed at any time by the President, or other appointing power, when their services are unnecessary, or for dishonesty, incapacity, inefficiency, misconduct, or neglect of duty; and, when so removed, the removal shall be reported to the Senate, together with the reasons therefor.

The President shall have power to fill up all vacancies that may happen during the recess of the Senate, by granting commissions which shall expire at the end of their next session. *But no person rejected by the Senate shall be reappointed to the same office during their ensuing recess.*

SECTION 3. *The President* shall from time to time give to the Congress information of the state of the *Confederacy*, and recommend to their consideration such measures as he shall

and expedient; he may, on extraordinary Occasions, convene both Houses, or either of them, and in Case of Disagreement between them, with Respect to the time of Adjournment, he may adjourn them to such Time as he shall think proper; he shall receive Ambassadors and other public Ministers; he shall take Care that the Laws be faithfully executed, and shall Commission all the officers of the United States.

SECTION 4. The President, Vice President and all civil Officers of the United States, shall be removed from Office on Impeachment for, and Conviction of, Treason, Bribery, or other high Crimes and Misdemeanors.

ARTICLE III.

SECTION 1. The Judicial Power of the United States, shall be vested in one supreme Court, and in such inferior Courts as the Congress may from time to time ordain and establish. The Judges, both of the supreme and inferior Courts, shall hold their offices during good Behavior, and shall, at stated times, receive for their Services, a Compensation which shall not be diminished during their Continuance in Office.

SECTION 2. The judicial Power shall extend to all Cases, in Law and Equity, arising under this Constitution, the Laws of the United States, and Treaties made, or which shall be made, under their Authority;—to all Cases affecting Ambassadors, other public Ministers and Consuls;—to all Cases of admiralty and maritime Jurisdiction;—to Controversies to which the United States shall be a Party;—to Controversies between two or more States;—between a State and Citizens of another State;—between Citizens of different States;—between Citizens of the same State claiming Lands under Grants of dif-

judge necessary and expedient: he may on extraordinary occasions convene both Houses, or either of them; and in case of disagreement between them, with respect to the time of adjournment, he may adjourn them to such time as he shall think proper; he shall receive ambassadors and other public ministers; he shall take care that the laws be faithfully executed, and shall commission all the officers of the *Confederate* States.

SECTION 4. The President, Vice-President, and all civil officers of the *Confederate* States, shall be removed from office on impeachment for and conviction of, treason, bribery, or other high crimes and misdemeanors.

ARTICLE III.

SECTION 1. The judicial power of the *Confederate* States shall be vested in one Supreme Court, and in such inferior Courts, as the Congress may from time to time ordain and establish. The Judges, both of the Supreme and inferior Courts, shall hold their offices during good behavior, and shall, at stated times, receive for their services a compensation, which shall not be diminished during their continuance in office.

SECTION 2. The judicial power shall extend to all cases arising under this Constitution, the laws of the *Confederate* States, and treaties made, or which shall be made, under their authority; to all cases affecting ambassadors, other public ministers, and consuls; to all cases of admiralty and maritime jurisdiction; to controversies to which the *Confederate* States shall be a party; to controversies between two or more States; between a State and citizens of another State, *where the State is plaintiff;* between citizens claiming lands under grants of different States, and between a State or the citizens thereof,

ferent States, and between a State, or the Citizens thereof, and foreign States, Citizens or Subjects.

In all Cases affecting Ambassadors, other public Ministers and Consuls, and those in which a State shall be Party, the supreme Court shall have original Jurisdiction. In all the other Cases before mentioned, the supreme Court shall have appellate Jurisdiction, both as to Law and Fact, with such Exceptions, and under such Regulations as the Congress shall make.

The trial of all Crimes, except in Cases of Impeachment, shall be by Jury; and such Trial shall be held in the State where the said Crimes shall have been committed; but when not committed within any State, the Trial shall be at such Place or Places as the Congress may by Law have directed.

SECTION 3. Treason against the United States, shall consist only in levying War against them, or in adhering to their Enemies, giving them Aid and Comfort. No Person shall be convicted of Treason unless on the Testimony of two Witnesses to the same overt Act, or on Confession in open Court.

The Congress shall have Power to declare the Punishment of Treason, but no Attainder of Treason shall work Corruption of Blood, or Forfeiture except during the Life of the Person attainted.

ARTICLE IV.

SECTION 1. Full Faith and Credit shall be given in each State to the public Acts, Records, and judicial Proceedings of every other State. And the Congress may by general Laws prescribe the Manner in which such Acts, Records and Proceedings shall be proved, and the Effect thereof.

SECTION 2. The Citizens of each State shall be entitled to all Privileges

and foreign states, citizens, or subjects. *But no State shall be sued by a citizen or subject of any foreign state.*

In all cases affecting ambassadors, other public ministers and consuls, and those in which a State shall be party, the Supreme Court shall have original jurisdiction. In all the other cases before mentioned, the Supreme Court shall have appellate jurisdiction, both as to law and fact, with such exceptions and under such regulations as the Congress shall make.

The trial of all crimes, except in cases of impeachment, shall be by jury, and such trial shall be held in the State where the said crimes shall have been committed; but when not committed within any State the trial shall be at such place or places as the Congress may by law have directed.

SECTION 3. Treason aganst the *Confederate* States shall consist only in levying war against them, or in adhering to their enemies, giving them aid and comfort. No person shall be convicted of treason unless on the testimony of two witnesses to the same overt act, or on confession in open court.

The Congress shall have power to declare the punishment of treason; but no attainder of treason shall work corruption of blood, or forfeiture, except during the life of the person attainted.

ARTICLE IV.

SECTION 1. Full faith and credit shall be given in each State to the public acts, records, and judicial proceedings of every other State. And the Congress may, by general laws, prescribe the manner in which such acts, records, and proceedings shall be proved, and the effect thereof.

SECTION 2. The citizens of each State shall be entitled to all the privi-

and Immunities of Citizens in the several States.

A Person charged in any State with Treason, Felony, or other Crime, who shall flee from Justice, and be found in another State, shall on Demand of the executive Authority of the State from which he fled, be delivered up, to be removed to the State having Jurisdiction of the Crime.

No Person held to Service or Labour in one State, under the Laws thereof, escaping into another, shall, in Consequence of any Law or Regulation therein, be discharged from such Service or Labour, but shall be delivered up on Claim of the Party to whom such Service or Labour may be done.

SECTION 3. New States may be admitted by the Congress into this Union; but no new State shall be formed or erected within the Jurisdiction of any other State; nor any State be formed by the Junction of two or more States, or Parts of States, without the Consent of the Legislatures of the States concerned as well as of the Congress.

The Congress shall have power to dispose of and make all needful Rules and Regulations respecting the Territory or other Property belonging to the United States; and nothing in this Constitution shall be so construed as to Prejudice any Claims of the United States, or of any particular State.

leges and immunities of citizens in the several States, *and shall have the right of transit and sojourn in any State of this Confederacy, with their slaves and other property; and the right of property in said slaves shall not be thereby impaired.*

A person charged in any State with treason, felony, or other crime *against the laws of such State,* who shall flee from justice, and be found in another State, shall on demand of the Executive authority of the State from which he fled, be delivered up, to be removed to the State having jurisdiction of the crime.

No slave or other person held to service or labor *in any State or Territory of the Confederate States,* under the laws thereof, escaping *or lawfully carried* into another, shall, in consequence of any law or regulation therein, be discharged from such service or labor; but shall be delivered up on claim of the party *to whom such slave belongs, or* to whom such service or labor may be due.

SECTION 3. *Other States may be admitted into this Confederacy by a vote of two thirds of the whole House of Representatives and two thirds of the Senate, the Senate voting by States;* but no new State shall be formed or erected within the jurisdiction of any other State; nor any State be formed by the junction of two or more States, or parts of States, without the consent of the Legislatures of the States concerned, as well as of the Congress.

The Congress shall have power to dispose of and make all needful rules and regulations *concerning* the *property of the Confederate* States, *including the lands thereof.*

The Confederate States may acquire

new territory; and Congress shall have power to legislate and provide governments for the inhabitants of all territory belonging to the Confederate States, lying without the limits of the several States; and may permit them, at such times and in such manner as it may by law provide, to form States to be admitted into the Confederacy. In all such territory, the institution of negro slavery, as it now exists in the Confederate States, shall be recognized and protected by Congress and by the territorial government; and the inhabitants of the several Confederate States and Territories shall have the right to take to such Territory any slaves lawfully held by them in any of the States or Territories of the Confederate States.

SECTION 4. The United States shall guarantee to every State in this Union a Republican Form of Government, and shall protect each of them against Invasion, and on Application of the Legislature, or of the Executive (when the Legislature cannot be convened) against domestic Violence.

The *Confederate* States shall guarantee to every State *that now is, or hereafter may become, a member of this Confederacy,* a republican form of government; and shall protect each of them against invasion; and on application of the Legislature (or of the Executive when the Legislature *is not in session*), against domestic violence.

ARTICLE V.

The Congress, whenever two-thirds of both Houses shall deem it necessary, shall propose Amendments to this Constitution, or, on the Application of the Legislatures of two-thirds of the several States, shall call a Convention for proposing Amendments, which, in either Case, shall be valid to all Intents and Purposes, as Part of this Constitution, when ratified by the Legislatures of three-fourths of the several States, or by Conventions in three-fourths thereof, as the one or the other Mode of Ratification may be proposed by the Congress: Provided that no Amendment which may be made prior to the Year one thousand eight hundred and eight shall in any Manner affect the first

ARTICLE V.

SECTION 1. *Upon the demand of any three States, legally assembled in their several conventions, the Congress shall summon a Convention of all the States, to take into consideration such amendments to the Constitution as the said States shall concur in suggesting at the time when the said demand is made; and should any of the proposed amendments to the Constitution be agreed on by the said Convention—voting by States—and the same be ratified by the Legislatures of two thirds of the several States, or by conventions in two-thirds thereof—as the one or the other mode of ratification may be proposed by the general Convention—they shall thenceforward form a part of this Con-*

and fourth Clauses in the Ninth Section of the first Article; and that no State, without its Consent, shall be deprived of its equal Suffrage in the Senate.

ARTICLE VI.

All Debts contracted and Engagements entered into, before the Adoption of this Constitution, shall be as valid against the United States under this Constitution, as under the Confederation.

This Constitution, and the Laws of the United States which shall be made in Pursuance thereof; and all Treaties made, or which shall be made, under the authority of the United States, shall the supreme law of the land; and the Judges in every State shall be bound thereby, anything in the Constitution or laws of any State to the contrary notwithstanding.

The Senators and Representatives before mentioned, and the Members of the several State Legislatures, and all executives and judicial Officers, both of the United States and of the several States, shall be bound by Oath or Affirmation, to support this Constitution; but no religious Test shall ever be required as a Qualification to any Office or public Trust under the United States.

stitution. But no State shall, without its consent, be deprived of its equal *representation* in the Senate.

ARTICLE VI.

The Government established by this Constitution is the successor of the Provisional Government of the Confederate States of America, and all the laws passed by the latter shall continue in force until the same shall be repealed or modified; and all the officers appointed by the same shall remain in office until their successors are appointed and qualified, or the offices abolished.

All debts contracted and engagements entered into before the adoption of this Constitution shall be as valid against the *Confederate* States under this Constitution as under the *Provisional Government.*

This Consttution, and the laws of the *Confederate* States made in pursuance thereof, and all treaties made or which shall be made under the authority of the *Confederate* States, shall be the supreme Law of the Land; and the Judges in every State shall be bound thereby, anything in the Constitution or Laws of any State to the Contrary notwithstanding.

The Senators and Representatives before mentioned, and the members of the several State Legislatures, and all executive and judicial officers, both of the *Confederate* States and of the several States, shall be bound by oath or affirmation to support this Constitution; but no religious test shall ever be required as a qualification to any office or public trust under the *Confederate* States.

The enumeration, in the Constitution, of certain rights, shall not be construed to deny or disparage others retained by the people *of the several States.*

The powers not delegated to the *Confederate* States by the Constitution, nor prohibited by it to the States, are reserved to the States, respectively, or to the people *thereof*.

ARTICLE VII.

The Ratification of the Conventions of nine States, shall be sufficient for the Establishment of this Constitution between the States so ratifying the Same.

ARTICLE VII.

The ratification of the Conventions of *five* States shall be sufficient for the establishment of this Constitution between the States so ratifying the same.

When five States shall have ratified this Constitution, in the manner before specified, the Congress under the Provisional Constitution shall prescribe the time for holding the election of President and Vice-President, and for the meeting of the electoral college, and for counting the votes, and inaugurating the President. They shall also prescribe the time for holding the first election of members of Congress under this Constitution, and the time for assembling the same. Until the assembling of such Congress, the Congress under the Provisional Constitution shall continue to exercise the legislative powers granted them; not extending beyond the time limited by the Constitution of the Provisional Government.

ARTICLES IN ADDITION TO, AND AMENDMENT OF, THE CONSTITUTION OF THE UNITED STATES OF AMERICA. PROPOSED BY CONGRESS, AND RATIFIED BY THE LEGISLATURES OF THE SEVERAL STATES, PURSUANT TO THE FIFTH ARTICLE OF THE ORIGINAL CONSTITUTION.

ARTICLE I.

Congress shall make no law respecting an establishment of religion, or prohibiting the free exercise thereof; or abridging the freedom of speech, or of the press; or the right of the people peaceably to assemble, and to petition the Government for a redress of grievances.

ARTICLE II.

A well regulated Militia, being necessary to the security of a free State, the right of the people to keep and bear Arms, shall not be infringed.

ARTICLE III.

No Soldier shall, in time of peace be quartered in any house, without the consent of the Owner, nor in time of war, but in a manner to be prescribed by law.

ARTICLE IV.

The right of the people to be secure in their persons, houses, papers, and effects, against unreasonable searches and seizures, shall not be violated, and no Warrants shall issue, but upon probable cause, supported by Oath or affirmation, and particularly describing the place to be searched, and the persons or things to be seized.

ARTICLE V.

No person shall be held to answer for a capital, or otherwise infamous crime, unless on a presentment or indictment of a Grand Jury, except in cases arising in the land or naval forces, or in the Militia, when in actual service in time of War or public danger; nor shall any person be subject for the same offence to be twice put in jeopardy of life or limb; nor shall be compelled in any Criminal Case to be a witness against himself, nor be deprived of life, liberty, or property, without due process of law; nor shall private property be taken for public use, without just compensation.

ARTICLE VI.

In all criminal prosecutions, the accused shall enjoy the right to a speedy and public trial, by an impartial jury of the State and district wherein the crime shall have been committed, which district shall have been previously ascertained by law, and to be informed of the nature and cause of the accusation; to be confronted with the witnesses against him; to have Compulsory process for obtaining Witnesses in his favour, and to have the Assistance of Counsel for his defence.

ARTICLE VII.

In Suits at common law, where the value in controversy shall exceed twenty dollars, the rght of trial by jury shall be preserved, and no fact tried by a jury shall be otherwise reëxamined in any Court of the United States, than according to the rules of the common law.

ARTICLE VIII.

Excessive bail shall not be required, nor excessive fines imposed, nor cruel and unusual punishments inflicted.

ARTICLE XII.[6]

The Electors shall meet in their respective states, and vote by ballot for President and Vice President, one of whom, at least, shall not be an inhabitant of the same state with themselves; they shall name in their ballots the person voted for as President, and in distinct ballots the person voted for as Vice President, and they shall make distinct lists of all persons voted for as President, and of all persons voted for as Vice President, and of the number of votes for each, which lists they shall sign and certify, and transmit sealed to the seat of the government of the United States, directed to the President of the Senate;—The President of the Senate shall, in presence of the Senate and House of Representatives, open all the certificates and the votes shall then be counted;—The person having the greatest number of votes for President, shall be the President, if such number be a majority of the whole number of Electors appointed; and if no person have such

---

[6]This article is substituted for Clause 3, Sec. I, Art. II, page 662, and annuls it. It was declared adopted in 1804.

majority, then from the persons having the highest numbers not exceeding three on the list of those voted for as President, the House of Representatives shall choose immediately, by ballot, the President. But in choosing the President, the votes shall be taken by states, the representation from each state having one vote; a quorum for this purpose shall consist of a member or members from two-thirds of the states, and a majority of all the states shall be necessary to a choice. And if the House of Representatives shall not choose a President whenever the right of choice shall devolve upon them, before the fourth day of March next following, then the Vice President shall act as President, as in the case of the death or other constitutional disability of the President.—The person having the greatest number of votes as Vice President, shall be the Vice President, if such number be a majority of the whole number of Electors appointed, and if no person have a majority, then from the two highest numbers on the list, the Senate shall choose the Vice President; a quorum for the purpose shall consist of two-thirds of the whole number of Senators, and a majority of the whole number shall be necessary to a choice. But no person constitutionally ineligible to the office of President shall be eligible to that of Vice President of the United States.

APPENDIX L

CORRESPONDENCE BETWEEN THE CONFEDERATE COMMISSIONERS,
SECRETARY SEWARD AND JUDGE CAMPBELL.
THE COMMISSIONERS TO SEWARD

Washington City, March 12, 1861.

Hon. William H. Seward, Secretary of State of the United States.

Sir: The undersigned have been duly accredited by the Government of the Confederate States of America as commissioners to the Government of the United States, and, in pursuance of their instructions, have now the honor to acquaint you with the fact, and to make known, through you to the President of the United States, the objects of their presence in this capital.

Seven States of the late Federal Union, having in the exercise of the inherent right of every free people to change or reform their political institutions, and through conventions of their people, withdrawn from the United States and reassumed the attributes of sovereign power delegated to it, have formed a government of their own. The Confederate States constitute an independent nation, *de facto* and *de jure,* and possess a government perfect in all parts, and endowed with all the means of self-support.

With a view to a speedy adjustment of all questions growing out of this political separation, upon such terms of amity and good-will as the respective interests, geographical contiguity, and future welfare of the two nations may render necessary, the undersigned are instructed to make to the Government of the United States overtures for the opening of negotiations, assuring the Government of the United States, that the President, Congress, and people of the Confederate States earnestly desire a peaceful solution of these great questions; that it is neither their interest nor their wish to make any demand which is not founded in strictest justice, nor do any act to injure their late confederates.

The undersigned have now the honor, in obedience to the instructions of their Government, to request you to appoint as early a day as possible, in order that they may present to the President of the United States the credentials which they bear and the objects of the mission with which they are charged.

We are, very respectfully, your obedient servants,

(Signed)   JOHN FORSYTH.
(Signed)   MARTIN J. CRAWFORD.

MEMORANDUM

Department of State, Washington, March 15, 1861.

Mr. John Forsyth, of the State of Alabama, and Mr. Martin J. Crawford, of the State of Georgia, on the 11th inst., through the kind offices of a distinguished Senator, submitted to the Secretary of State their desire for an unofficial interview. This request was, on the 12th inst., upon exclusively public considerations, respectfully declined.

On the 13th inst., while the Secretary was preoccupied, Mr. A. D. Banks, of

Virginia, called at this department, and was received by the Assistant Secretary, to whom he delivered a sealed communication, which he had been charged by Messrs. Forsyth and Crawford to present to the Secretary in person.

In that communication Messrs. Forsyth and Crawford inform the Secretary of State that they have been duly accredited by the Government of the Confederate States of America as commissioners to the Government of the United States, and they set forth the objects of their attendance at Washington. They observe that seven States of the American Union, in the exercise of a right inherent in every free people, have withdrawn, through conventions of their people, from the United States, reassumed the attributes of sovereign power, and formed a government of their own, and that those Confederate States now constitute an independent nation, *de facto* and *de jure,* and possess a government perfect in all its parts, and fully endowed with all the means of self-support.

Messrs. Forsyth and Crawford, in their aforesaid communication, thereupon proceeded to inform the Secretary that, with a view to a speedy adjustment of all questions growing out of the political separation thus assumed, upon such terms of amity and good-will as the respective interests, geographical contiguity, and the future welfare of the supposed two nations might render necessary, they are instructed to make to the Government of the United States overtures for the opening of negotiations, assuring this Government that the President, Congress, and the people of the Confederate States earnestly desire a peaceful solution of these great questions, and that it is neither their interest nor their wish to make any demand which is not founded in the strictest justice, nor do any act to injure their late confederates.

After making these statements, Messrs. Forsyth and Crawford close their communication, as they say, in obedience to the instructions of their Government, by requesting the Secretary of State to appoint as early a day as possible, in order that they may present to the President of the United States the credentials which they bear and the objects of the mission with which they are charged.

The Secretary of State frankly confesses that he understands the events which have recently occurred, and the condition of political affairs which actually exists in the part of the Union to which his attention has thus been directed, very differently from the aspect in whch they are presented by Messrs. Forsyth and Crawford. He sees in them, not a rightful and accomplished revolution and an independent nation, with an established Government, but rather a perversion of a temporary and partisan excitement to the inconsiderate purposes of an unjustifiable and unconstitutional aggression upon the rights and the authority vested in the Federal Government, and hitherto benignly exercised, as from their very nature they always must so be exercised, for the maintenance of the Union, the preservation of liberty, and the security, peace, welfare, happiness, and aggrandizement of the American people. The Secretary of State, therefore, avows to Messrs. Forsyth and Crawford that he looks patiently, but confidently, for the cure of evils which have resulted from proceedings so unnecessary, so unwise, so unusual, and so unnatural, not to irregular negotiations, having in view new and untried relations with agencies unknown to and acting in derogation of the Constitution and laws, but to regular and considerate action of the people of those States, in coöperation with their brethren in the other States, through the Congress of the United States, and such extraordinary conventions, if there shall be need thereof, as the Federal Constitution contemplates and authorizes to be assembled.

It is, however, the purpose of the Secretary of State, on this occasion, not to invite or engage in any discussion of these subjects, but simply to set forth his reasons for declining to comply with the request of Messrs. Forsyth and Crawford.

On the 4th of March instant, the then newly elected President of the United States, in view of all the facts bearing on the present question, assumed the Executive Administration of the Government, first delivering, in accordance with an early, honored custom, an inaugural address to the people of the United States. The Secretary of State respectfully submits a copy of this address to Messrs. Forsyth and Crawford.

A simple reference to it will be sufficient to satisfy these gentlemen that the Secretary of State, guided by the principles therein announced, is prevented altogether from admitting or assuming that the States referred to by them have, in law or in fact, withdrawn from the Federal Union, or that they could do so in the manner described by Messrs. Forsyth and Crawford, or in any other manner than with the consent and concert of the people of the United States, to be given through a National Convention, to be assembled in conformity with the provisions of the Constitution of the United States. Of course, the Secretary of State can not act upon the assumption, or in any way admit that the so-called Confederate States constitute a foreign power, with whom diplomatic relations ought to be established.

Under these circumstances, the Secretary of State, whose official duties are confined, subject to the direction of the President, to the conducting of the foreign relations of the country, and do not at all embrace domestic questions, or questions arising between the several States and the Federal Government, is unable to comply with the request of Messrs. Forsyth and Crawford, to appoint a day on which they may present the evidence of their authority and the objects of their visit to the President of the United States. On the contrary, he is obliged to state to Messrs. Forsyth and Crawford that he has no authority, nor is he at liberty, to recognize them as diplomatic agents, or hold correspondence or other communication with them.

Finally, the Secretary of State would observe that, although he has supposed that he might safely and with propriety have adopted these conclusions, without making any reference of the subject to the Executive, yet, so strong has been his desire to practice entire directness, and to act in a spirit of perfect respect and candor toward Messrs. Forsyth and Crawford, and that portion of the people of the Union in whose name they present themselves before him, that he has cheerfully submitted this paper to the President, who coincides generally in the views it expresses, and sanctions the Secretary's decision declining official intercourse with Messrs. Forsyth and Crawford.

April 8, 1861.

The foregoing memorandum was filed in this department on the 15th of March last. A delivery of the same to Messrs. Forsyth and Crawford was delayed, as was understood, with their consent. They have now, through their secretary, communicated their desire for a definite disposition of the subject. The Secretary of State therefore directs that a duly verified copy of the paper be now delivered.

THE COMMISSIONERS IN REPLY TO SEWARD

Washington, April 9, 1861.

Hon. William H. Seward,

Secretary of State for the United States, Washington:

The "memorandum" dated Department of State, Washington, March 15, 1861, with postscript under date of 8th instant, has been received through the hands of Mr. J. T. Pickett, secretary of this commission, who, by the instructions of the undersigned, called for it on yesterday at the department.

In that memorandum you correctly state the purport of the official note addressed to you by the undersigned on the 12th ultimo. Without repeating the contents of that note in full, it is enough to say here that its object was to invite the Government of the United States to a friendly consideration of the relations between the United States and the seven States lately the Federal Union, but now separated from it by the sovereign will of their people, growing out of the pregnant and undeniable fact that those people have rejected the authority of the United States, and established a government of their own. Those relations had to be friendly or hostile. The people of the old and new Governments, occupying contiguous territories, had to stand to each other in the relation of good neighbors, each seeking their happiness and pursuing their national destinies in their own way, without interference with the other; or they had to be rival and hostile nations. The Government of the Confederate States had no hesitation in electing its choice in this alternative. Frankly and unreservedly, seeking the good of the people who had intrusted them with power, in the spirit of humanity, of the Christian civilization of the age, and of that Americanism which regards the true welfare and happiness of the people, the Government of the Confederate States, among its first acts, commissioned the undersigned to approach the Government of the United States with the olive-branch of peace, and to offer to adjust the great questions pending between them in the only way to be justified by the consciences and common sense of good men who had nothing but the welfare of the people of the two confederacies at heart.

Your Government has not chosen to meet the undersigned in the conciliatory and peaceful spirit in which they are commissioned. Persistently wedded to those fatal theories of construction of the Federal Constitution always rejected by the statesmen of the South, and adhered to by those of the Administration school, until they have produced their natural and often predicted result of the destruction of the Union, under which we might have continued to live happily and gloriously together, had the spirit of the ancestry who framed the common Constitution animated the hearts of all their sons, you now, with a persistence untaught and uncured by the ruin which has been wrought, refuse to recognize the great fact presented to you of a completed and successful revolution; you close your eyes to the existence of the Government founded upon it, and ignore the high duties of moderation and humanity which attach to you in dealing with this great fact. Had you met these issues with the frankness and manliness with which the undersigned were instructed to present them to you and treat them, the undersigned had not now the melancholy duty to return home and tell their Government and their countrymen that their earnest and ceaseless efforts in behalf of peace had been futile, and that the Government of the United States meant to subjugate them by force of arms. Whatever may be the result, impartial history will record the innocence of the Government of the Confederate States, and place the responsibility of the blood and mourning that may ensue upon those who have denied the great fundamental doctrine of American liberty, that "governments derive their just powers from the consent of the governed," and who have set naval and land armaments in motion to subject the people of one portion of this land to the will of another portion. That that can never be done, while a freeman survives in the Confederate States to wield a weapon, the undersigned appeal to past history to prove. These military demonstrations against the people of the seceded States are certainly far from being in keeping and consistency with the theory of the Secretary of State, maintained in his memorandum, that these States are still component parts of the late American Union, as the undersigned are not aware of any constitutional power in the President of the United States to levy war, without the consent of Congress, upon a foreign people, much less upon any portion of the people of the United States.

The undersigned, like the Secretary of State, have no purpose to "invite or engage in discussion" of the subject on which their two Governments are so irreconcilably at variance. It is this variance that has broken up the old Union, the disintegration of which has only begun. It is proper, however, to advise you that it were well to dismiss the hopes you seem to entertain that, by any of the modes indicated, the people of the Confederate States will ever be brought to submit to the authority of the Government of the United States. You are dealing with delusions, too, when you seek to separate our people from our Government, and to characterize the deliberate sovereign act of that people as a "perversion of a temporary and partisan excitement." If you cherish these dreams, you will be awakened from them and find them as unreal and unsubstantial as others in which you have recently indulged. The undersigned would omit the performance of an obvious duty, were they to fail to make known to the Government of the United States that the people of the Confederate States have declared their independence with a full knowledge of all the responsibilities of that act, and with as firm a determination to maintain it by all the means with which nature has endowed them as that which sustained their fathers when they threw off the authority of the British Crown.

The undersigned clearly understand that you have declined to appoint a day to enable them to lay the objects of the mission with which they are charged before the President of the United States, because so to do would be to recognize the independence and separate nationality of the Confederate States. This is the vein of thought that pervades the memorandum before us. The truth of history requires that it should distinctly appear upon the record that the undersigned did not ask the Government of the United States to recognize the independence of the Confederate States. They onlly asked audience to adjust, in a spirit of amity and peace, the new relations springing from a manifest and accomplished revolution in the Government of the late Federal Union. Your refusal to entertain these overtures for a peaceful solution, the active naval and military preparations of this Government, and a formal notice to the commanding General of the Confederate forces in the harbor of Charleston that the President intends to provision Fort Sumter by forcible means, if necessary, are viewed by the undersigned, and can only be received by the world, as a declaration of war against the Confederate States; for the President of the United States knows that Fort Sumter can not be provisioned without the effusion of blood. The undersigned, in behalf of their Government and people, accept the gage of battle thus thrown down to them; and, appealing to God and the judgment of mankind for the righteousness of their cause, the people of the Confederate States will defend their liberties to the last, against this flagrant and open attempt at their subjugation to sectional power.

This communication can not be properly closed without adverting to the date of your memorandum. The official note of the undersigned, of the 12th of March, was delivered to the Assistant Secretary of State on the 13th of that month, the gentleman who delivered it informing him that the secretary of this commission would call at twelve o'clock, noon, on the next day, for an answer. At the appointed hour Mr. Pickett did call, and was informed by the Assistant Secretary of State that the engagements of the Secretary of State had prevented him from giving the note his attention. The Assistant Secretary of State then asked for the address of Messrs. Crawford and Forsyth, the members of the commission then present in this city, took note of the address on a card, and engaged to send whatever reply might be made to their lodgings. Why this was not done, it is proper should be here explained. The memorandum is dated March 15th, and was not delivered until April 8th. Why was it withheld during the intervening twenty-three days? In the postscript to your memorandum you say it "was delayed, as was understood, with their (Messrs. Forsyth and Crawford's) consent." This is true; but it is also true that, on the 15th of March, Messrs. Forsyth and Crawford were assured by a person occupying a high official position in the Government, and who, as they believed, was speaking by authority, that Fort Sumter would be evacuated in a very few days, and that no measure changing the existing *status* prejudicially to the Confederate States, as respects Fort Pickens, was then contemplated, and these assurances were subsequently repeated, with the addition that any contemplated change as respects Pickens would be notified to us. On the 1st of April we were again informed that there might be an attempt to supply Fort Sumter with provisions, but that Governor Pickens should have previous notice of this attempt. There was no suggestion of any reënforcement. The undersigned did not hesitate to believe that these assurances expressed the intentions of the Administration at the time, or at all events of prominent members of that Administration. This delay was assented to for the express purpose of attaining the great end of the mission of the undersigned, to wit, a pacific solution of existing complications. The inference deducible from the date of your memorandum, that the undersigned had, of their own volition and without cause, consented to this long *hiatus* in the grave duties with which they were charged, is therefore not consistent with a just exposition of the facts of the case. The intervening twenty-three days were employed in active unofficial efforts, the object of which was to smooth the path to a pacific solution, the distinguished personage alluded to co-operating with the undersigned; and every step of that effort is recorded in writing and now in the possession of the undersigned and of their Government. It was only when all those anxious efforts for peace had been exhausted, and it became clear that Mr. Lincoln had determined to appeal to the sword to reduce the people of the Confederate States to the will of the section or party whose President he is, that the undersigned resumed the official negotiation temporarily suspended, and sent their secretary for a reply to their official note of March 12th.

It is proper to add that, during these twenty-three days, two gentlemen, of official distinction as high as that of the personage hitherto alluded to, aided the undersigned as intermediaries in these unofficial negotiations for peace.

The undersigned, commissioners of the Confederate States of America, having thus made answer to all they deem material in the memorandum filed in the department on the 15th of March last, have the honor to be

JOHN FORSYTH,
MARTIN J. CRAWFORD,
A. B. ROMAN.

SEWARD IN REPLY TO THE COMMISSIONERS

Department of State, Washington, April 10, 1861.

Messrs. Forsyth, Crawford, and Roman, having been apprised by a memorandum, which has been delivered to them, that the Secretary of State is not at liberty to hold official intercourse with them, will, it is presumed, expect no notice from him of the new communication which they have addressed to him under date of the 9th inst., beyond the simple acknowledgment of the receipt thereof, which he hereby very cheerfully gives.

JUDGE CAMPBELL TO SEWARD

Washington City, Saturday, April 13, 1861.

Sir: On the 15th of March, ultimo, I left with Judge Crawford, one of the commissioners of the Confederate States, a note in writing, to the effect following:

"I feel entire confidence that Fort Sumter will be evacuated in the next ten days. And this measure is felt as imposing great responsibility on the Administration.

"I feel entire confidence that no measure changing the existing *status* prejudicially to the Southern Confederate States is at present contemplated.

"I feel an entire confidence that an immediate demand for an answer to the communication of the commissioners will be productive of evil and not of good. I do not believe that it ought, at this time, to be pressed."

The substance of this statement I communicated to you the same evening by letter. Five days elapsed, and I called with a telegram from General Beauregard, to the effect that Sumter was not evacuated, but that Major Anderson was at work making repairs.

The next day, after conversing with you, I communicated to Judge Crawford in writing that the failure to evacuate Sumter was not the result of bad faith, but was attributable to causes consistent with the intention to fullfill the engagement, and that, as regarded Pickens, I should have notice of any design to alter the existing *status* there. Mr. Justice Nelson was present at these conversations, three in number, and I submitted to him each of my written communications to Judge Crawford, and informed Judge Crawford that they had his (Judge Nelson's) sanction. I gave you, on the 22d of March, a substantial copy of the statement I had made on the 15th.

The 30th of March arrived, and at that time a telegram came from Governor

Pickens, inquiring concerning Colonel Lamon, whose visit to Charleston he supposed had a connection with the proposed evacuation of Fort Sumter. I left that with you, and was to have an answer the following Monday (1st of April). On the 1st of April I received from you the statement in writing, "I am satisfied the Government will not undertake to supply Fort Sumter without giving notice to Governor P." The words "I am satisfied" were for me to use as expressive of confidence in the remainder of the declaration.

The proposition, as originally prepared, was, "The President *may desire* to supply Sumter, but will not do so," etc., and your verbal explanation was, that you did not believe any such attempt would be made, and that there was no design to reënforce Sumter.

There was a departure here from the pledges of the previous month, but, with the verbal explanation, I did not consider it a matter then to complain of. I simply stated to you that I had that assurance previously.

On the 7th of April I addressed you a letter on the subject of the alarm that the preparations by the Government had created, and asked you if the assurances I had given were well or ill-founded. In respect to Sumter, your reply was, "Faith as to Sumter fully kept—wait and see." In the morning's paper I read, "An authorized messenger from President Lincoln informed Governor Pickens and General Beauregard that provisions will be sent to Fort Sumter—peaceably, or *otherwise by force.*" This was the 8th of April, at Charleston, the day following your last assurance, and is the last evidence of the full faith I was invited to *wait for* and *see*. In the same paper I read that intercepted dispatches disclosed the fact that Mr. Fox, who had been allowed to visit Major Anderson, on the pledge that his purpose was pacific, employed his opportunity to devise a plan for supplying the fort by force, and that this plan had been adopted by the Washington Government, and was in process of execution. My recollection of the date of Mr. Fox's visit carries it to a day in March. I learn he is a near connection of a member of the Cabinet. My connection with the commissioners and yourself was superinduced by a conversation with Justice Nelson. He informed me of your strong disposition in favor of peace, and that you were oppressed with a demand of the commissioners of the Confederate States for a reply to their first letter, and that you desired to avoid it, if possible, at that time.

I told him I might perhaps be of some service in arranging the difficulty. I came to your office entirely at his request, and without the knowledge of either of the commissioners. Your depression was obvious to both Judge Nelson and myself. I was gratified at the character of the counsels you were desirous of pursuing, and much impressed with your observation that a civil war might be prevented by the success of my mediation. You read a letter of Mr. Weed, to show how irksome and responsible the withdrawal of troops from Sumter was. A portion of my communication to Judge Crawford, on the 15th of March, was founded upon these remarks, and the pledge to evacuate Sumter is less forcible than the words you employed. These words were, "Before this letter reaches you [a proposed letter by me to President Davis], Sumter will have been evacuated."

The commissioners who received those communications conclude they have been abused and overreached. The Montgomery Government hold the same opinion. The commissioners have supposed that my communications were with you, and upon the [that] hypothesis were prepared to arraign you before the country, in connection with the President. I placed a peremptory prohibition upon this, as being contrary to the terms of my communications with them. I pledged myself to them to communicate information, upon what I considered as the best authority, and they were to confide in the ability of myself, aided by Judge Nelson, to determine upon the credibility of my informant.

I think no candid man, who will read over what I have written, and consider for a moment what is going on at Sumter, but will agree that the equivocating conduct of the Administration, as measured and interpreted in connection with these promises, is the proximate cause of the great calamity.

I have a profound conviction that the telegrams of the 8th of April, of General Beauregard, and of the 10th of April, of General Walker, the Secretary of War, can be referred to nothing else than their belief that there has been systematic duplicity practiced on them through me. It is under an impressive sense of the weight of this responsibility that I submit to you these things for your explanation.

Very respectfully,

(Signed)   JOHN A. CAMPBELL,
Associate Justice of the Supreme Court, United States.

JUDGE CAMPBELL TO SECRETARY SEWARD

Washington, April 20, 1861.

SIR: I inclose you a letter, corresponding very nearly with one I addressed to you one week ago (April 13th), to which I have not had any reply. The letter is simply one of inquiry in reference to facts concerning which, I think, I am entitled to an explanation. I have not adopted any opinion in reference to them which may not be modified by explanation; nor have I affirmed in that letter, nor do I in this, any conclusion of my own unfavorable to your integrity in the whole transaction. All that I have said and mean to say is, that an explanation is due from you to myself. I will not say what I shall do in case this request is not complied with, but I am justified in saying that I shall feel at liberty to place these letters before any person who is entitled to ask an explanation of myself.

Very respectfully,

JOHN A. CAMPBELL,
Associate Justice of the Supreme Court, United States.

Hon. William H. Seward, Secretary of State.

No reply has been made to this letter, April 24, 1861.

INDEX